BARRIE PENROSE and SIMON FREEMAN

Conspiracy of Silence

The Secret Life of Anthony Blunt

GRAFTON BOOKS

A Division of the Collins Publishing Group

LONDON GLASGOW
TORONTO SYDNEY AUCKLAND

Grafton Books
A Division of the Collins Publishing Group
8 Grafton Street, London W1X 3LA

Revised edition published by Grafton Books 1987

First published in Great Britain by
Grafton Books 1986

ISBN 0-586-06017-0

Printed and bound in Great Britain by
Collins, Glasgow

Set in Times

CONTENTS

LIST OF ILLUSTRATIONS

Blunt's paternal grandparents. *BFA**
Blunt's maternal grandparents. *BFA*
The Reverend Stanley Blunt. *BFA*
Bournemouth, *c*. 1909. *BFA*
The three Blunt brothers. *BFA*
Blunt at St Peter's preparatory school. *BFA*
Blunt with his parents in Paris, 1921. *BFA*
Anthony Blunt, Louis MacNeice and John Hilton.
    Courtesy of John Hilton
Anthony Blunt, Donald Lucas, Julian Bell and Jean
    Stewart, 1929 or 1930. *Courtesy of John Lehmann*
Guy Burgess. *Sir Steven Runciman*
Kim Philby, Cambridge 1934
Andrew Gow. *Sketch by Sir Thomas Monnington, PRA*
Michael Straight at Cambridge, 1936. *Michael Straight*
Victor Rothschild, at Trinity College, Cambridge, *c*. 1932.
    *Photograph by Ramsey and Muspratt © Peter Lofts
    Studio, Cambridge*
Anthony Blunt, Francis Warre-Cornish, Dickon Steele,
    George 'Dadie' Rylands and Eddie Playfair,
    photographed by Lytton Strachey. *Courtesy of Mrs
    Francis Partridge*
The Apostles. *Photograph by Ramsey & Muspratt © Peter
    Lofts*

* BFA: Blunt Family Archives

Anthony Blunt as royal art adviser, 1959. *Topham*
Anthony Blunt with his brother Christopher in 1958. *BFA*
Eliezer and Rebecca at the Well by Poussin. *Fitzwilliam Museum, Cambridge*
Goronwy Rees, the Welsh academic. *Goronwy Rees*
A. J. P. Taylor. *Courtesy of A. J. P. Taylor*
Sir Dennis Proctor. *Observer*
Captain Peter Montgomery. *Courtesy of BBC Publicity, Northern Ireland*
John Cairncross in Rome, December 1979. © *Barrie Penrose*
Alister Watson. *Sunday Times*
Leo Long. *Topham*
Peter Wright. *Popperfoto*
Brian Sewell. *Topham*
Anthony Blunt faces the press: November 1979. *Camera Press*

PREFACE

On Thursday 15 November 1979 the Conservative Prime Minister, Margaret Thatcher, told the House of Commons that Sir Anthony Blunt, the distinguished art historian who was a former Surveyor of the Queen's Pictures, was a self-confessed Soviet spy. Blunt, she said, had admitted this *fifteen years earlier*, in April 1964. But there was more, and worse, to come. MPs listened, incredulous, disbelieving, outraged, as the Prime Minister explained that Blunt had only confessed after being promised that he would never be prosecuted. Blunt had been 'a talent-spotter' for Soviet Intelligence during the 1930s, when he was a don at Cambridge University. He had worked for the Security Service, better known as MI5, from 1940 until 1945, and in that time had 'passed information regularly to the Russians'. MI5 had first 'become suspicious' of Blunt after two friends, Guy Burgess and Donald Maclean, defected to Moscow in 1951. Twelve years later Kim Philby, too, defected to Moscow but that 'produced nothing which implicated Blunt'. MI5's spy-catchers had done their best. Blunt had been interviewed eleven times but he had never broken. There had been no choice; he had to be offered immunity from prosecution.

After leaving MI5, Blunt, she continued, no longer had any secrets to give to the Soviets, although he had helped Burgess and Maclean leave the country in 1951. Thatcher anticipated the obvious objections. Why had a traitor been offered this immoral deal – because there was no other way to persuade him to tell the truth and because, apart from his own, damning testimony, there had never been any firm evidence against him. Why had he been allowed to continue as a servant of the Royal Family – because there was no risk to national security and because MI5 did not want to 'put at risk his cooperation' by having him dismissed. Had the Queen been told – well, her private secretary had been informed so, MPs rightly deduced, Her Majesty must have known. Had MI5 briefed successive British governments, Labour as well as Conservative, about Blunt – yes, successive Attorney Generals had been shown the relevant files.

The story was front-page news in Britain and around the world. This was not surprising. Espionage, the world of treachery, bluff and counter-bluff, double and triple agents, has a fascination which transcends national boundaries. It is one of fiction's favourite themes, for serious, as well as for popular, writers. Newspapers know that the public always enjoys a rollicking good spy scandal, though real life, alas, rarely delivers the sort of twists that are obligatory in any self-respecting espionage novel. The Blunt affair, however, promised to be as good as any le Carré; it might even turn out to be more entertaining because le Carré would not have dared put a Soviet spy into Buckingham Palace. That would have been stretching the readers' credulity too far.

Thatcher's statement had been provoked by a book called *The Climate of Treason*, written by Andrew Boyle, a former BBC journalist. Boyle had not risked naming Blunt but the similarities – in family and educational backgrounds, careers and sexual preferences – between him and a Soviet spy whom Boyle called 'Maurice' were unmistakable. Until the publication of Boyle's book it had been assumed that there were probably no more significant revelations to be wrung from the story of Messrs Burgess, Maclean and Philby, otherwise known as the Cambridge spies because they had become communists when they were students there. Millions of words had been written about the triumvirate by journalists; there had been documentaries, which purported to be factual, and novels, plays and films, which had no such pretensions but which tried to examine the deeper issues raised by the drama. But any further studies would only be, or so we thought, reinterpretations of the familiar material. Boyle's book proved us wrong.

Thatcher's statement, laudably frank though it was, had done no more than whet the appetite; inevitably, she had posed many more questions than she had answered. The exposure of Blunt meant that every accepted fact, indeed the entire chronology of events of the Cambridge spy saga, had to be reassessed. And then there was Blunt himself. What sort of man was he? Why had he done it? What damage had he caused? There was another, intriguing thought. If Blunt had escaped then perhaps there were others; respectable men (or women) who had become spies for the Soviet Union in the 1930s because they believed communism offered the hope of a better world.

Every newspaper launched investigations in the wake of Thatcher's statement. We were both recent recruits to the *Sunday Times* but that did not matter; any ideas were welcome, especially since no one was sure how to take the story further after Blunt had held his press conference in November 1979. At first we worked independently. Barrie Penrose travelled to Rome and was the first journalist to interview a former civil servant, John Cairncross, about his relationship with Burgess and Blunt. In November 1981 Simon Freeman sat in Leo Long's living room in north London and listened to Long describe, again for the first time, how he had passed secret information to Blunt when he worked for military intelligence during the War. We collaborated on many other stories which emerged as a result of Blunt's exposure. We wrote about the dozens of men and women who had been questioned by MI5 during the 1960s and 1970s; about their links with the communist movement in the 1930s; and we described the battles and feuds within British Intelligence which followed the defections of Burgess, Maclean and Philby.

Spies were Big News and newspapers and television programmes competed for exclusives. Understandably many people, friends of the Cambridge spies or ex-student radicals from the 1930s, felt threatened. Would they, too, be accused of treachery by the media? The extent of this unease was well illustrated when a London solicitor contacted us and said that he represented a man who had been a member of the Communist Party of Great Britain at Cambridge and who had worked in Washington during the War. His client, the solicitor told us, feared that we intended to 'expose him' in the *Sunday Times*. In fact, we had never heard of this man and had no intention of 'exposing' him. In retrospect, perhaps it did appear as if newspapers were indulging in a McCarthyite witchhunt of ex-student communists. Yet, we have to say, we always tried to emphasize, as far as possible in the limited space of a newspaper article, the conditions in the 1930s which persuaded thousands of young intellectuals, many of them from wealthy or middle-class backgrounds, to become communists and, in a handful of cases, spies for the Soviet Union.

At the beginning of 1983 Grafton Books, then called Granada Publishing, asked us if we would write a book about Blunt and his fellow-conspirators. We said that we would not rush into print, though we were aware that Grafton wanted the book as fast as possible, before the Blunt story had faded from the public's memory. We knew that we faced a difficult task. There were a number of excellent books on the Cambridge spies, notably *The Climate of Treason*; *Philby: the Spy who Betrayed a Generation*, by three former *Sunday Times* journalists, Bruce Page, David Leitch and Phillip Knightley; and *Philby: the Long Road to Moscow*, by Patrick Seale and Maureen McConville. How, we asked ourselves, could we improve on these and other books? One problem lay in the nature of the subject. There was little documentary evidence available. It was true that there were files which had been released in Washington under the Freedom of Information Act and which dealt with the activities in the United States of Burgess and Maclean, and to a lesser extent, Philby. But these files had been gutted by earlier authors and there was little new to be gleaned from them. We hoped that the British government's decision to identify Blunt might mean that previously classified American files would now be released. We were disappointed. We tried again early in 1987, after the hardback edition of this book had been published. We were sent a thick bundle of documents from Washington but many pages were blank, apart from a scribbled sentence on each saying that they had been withheld for security reasons. Even those pages which had survived the censors in Washington turned out to be worthless; most names and over two thirds of the text had been deleted. But at least there were *some* American documents. In Britain there were no official records of the activities of the Cambridge spies, apart from a few titbits which had slipped past the officials in Whitehall who spend their days ensuring that the records of 'sensitive' matters are never published.

We also needed to persuade the friends and families of the *dramatis personae* to talk to us. This, we feared, would not be easy, especially since many of them had already had more than enough of journalists. We needed, too, the cooperation of retired officers from MI5 and MI6, who had worked alongside and then investigated men such as Blunt. A few of these former intelligence officers had quietly leaked material to journalists in the past but they had done so in order to advance their own theories. It did not mean that they would talk to us on our terms. We knew that we could not hope to establish the unequivocal 'truth' about the Cambridge spies. After all, we were dealing with espionage, in which, as bestselling spy authors constantly remind us, nothing is ever quite as it appears. But we could aim to describe, as accurately as possible, without intrusive moralizing, what happened and why.

We did not have much success at first and considered abandoning the project. Then, in March 1983, Blunt died. His family, friends, former students and colleagues from the art world, who had felt that it would be disloyal to say anything while Anthony was alive, were now willing to talk to us. We were helped, too, by the fact that many retired MI5 and MI6 officers, trained never to discuss their work, were extraordinarily helpful. Some spoke to us because they wanted to reopen the debate about Soviet penetration of Whitehall and the British intelligence services. Others agreed to be interviewed because, while they did not care for journalists, they saw no harm in correcting some of the more extravagant nonsense that had been written about their old services. Like most journalists, we are convinced that official secrecy on the scale that is traditionally practised here is both inefficient and dangerous. We believe, in common with a growing number of civil servants and politicians, that the intelligence services should be more open to scrutiny by Parliament (and the public) – for the good of everyone, including the intelligence services. But we must stress that we are not suggesting that any of the officers who were kind enough to help us did so because they supported the campaign for freedom of information. Indeed, many of them insisted that they still believed, as firmly as they had when they were employed by MI5 or MI6, in the need to protect the two services from American-style accountability.

Originally we had intended to write a general book about the Cambridge spies, giving equal space to each of the four main characters, but it soon became apparent that Blunt and Burgess would be our central figures. Blunt was emerging as a far more complex individual than anyone who had seen television reports of his press conference late in 1979 could have imagined; then, he had seemed self-contained, unemotional, a desiccated old academic remarkable only because he had once handed a few secrets to Soviet Intelligence. There were many contradictions and paradoxes. He was the Soviet spy who had always been proud of his links, first through his family and then as a professional art historian, with the Royal Family. He had never been that interested in politics and yet he had risked everything for communism. He had once visited the Soviet Union and had no wish ever to return there, yet he went on to become an agent of Soviet Intelligence. Many friends conceded that he was an intellectual snob who had no time for ordinary, working people. Yet, as a homosexual, he was attracted to labourers, painters and the like. We wondered, after Barrie Penrose interviewed an elderly, aristocratic lady whom Blunt had once tentatively courted, whether as a young man he had tried to fight against his homosexuality and fall in love with a woman. Blunt had always placed loyalty to friends above loyalty to his country and yet he had, coolly and calculatingly, deceived close friends who had trusted him. He was often kind and considerate yet he could also be spiteful and unforgiving. He taught his students at the Courtauld Institute of Art that they had to dedicate themselves to the Truth and yet his own life was based on lies. Finally, there was the tragedy of this eminent academic ending his days as a disgraced and lonely old man, frightened to pick up the telephone in case it was a reporter and forever fearful that he would be photographed by newspapers if he ventured outside his flat.

Blunt began work on his autobiography after Thatcher's statement but he gave up after writing just 30,000 words, saying that he was unable to go on because he had not kept his diaries. After his death his brother, Wilfrid, was allowed to read it in the office of Blunt's solicitor, Michael Rubinstein. Although Wilfrid said that there was 'little meat' in it, John Gaskin, Anthony's companion for over thirty years, decided that he did not want anyone else to have the chance to judge for themselves. Gaskin presented the manuscript, which had been valued for probate at the absurdly high figure of £120,000, to the British Museum, on condition that it would not be released for 30 years. Naturally, we were disappointed by Gaskin's decision but we do not believe that our views on Blunt would have changed significantly if we had been given access to the book. Wilfrid, a charming, witty man and a writer of considerable talent, assured us that we really had not missed much. Frankly, Wilfrid said, he had been bored by Anthony's book. Certainly, there was nothing, he added, which explained *why* Anthony had acted as he had done.

Burgess proved just as many-sided as Blunt. He had always been portrayed as a brilliant eccentric, a sometimes lovable, sometimes infuriating rogue, who had been no more than an entertaining supporting player in the Cambridge spy drama. But this was not the man who was described to us by people who had known him well. From what they told us, it seemed that Burgess had been misunderstood and underestimated. They talked about the power of Burgess's personality and the range of his intellect. They stressed the strength of the bond between him and Blunt and insisted that, in many ways, Burgess was the dominant personality in the relationship. As we researched we realized that we would not be able to speculate sensibly about either Blunt or Burgess unless we first tried to understand the homosexual world they inhabited.

We wanted to explain why so many young intellectuals became communists in the 1930s. We have, therefore, written at length about Cambridge in that period and about the reactions of undergraduates there to mass unemployment at home and the threat of fascism in Britain and Europe. We were helped greatly by the honesty and courtesy of students from those days. They convinced us that many previous accounts, with breathless descriptions of sinister communist cells and conspiratorial meetings with Soviet spies, were over-excitable distortions of the truth. Some of these interviewees had been communists at Cambridge; a few had remained party members throughout their lives. But they still spoke to us about those heady days in the 1930s when they thought that Utopia might be attainable. We were fortunate that so many ex-student communists were now willing to talk. Earlier authors had to be more circumspect. In the 1969 paperback edition of *Philby: the Spy who Betrayed a Generation* there is a passage, clearly written with the expert assistance of a libel lawyer, which describes how the student magazines of the 1930s at Cambridge were 'riddled with references to the leftist sympathies of men who are now diplomats, millionaires, bulwarks of the Church, the establishment and the established'. The book went on: 'They include people like Victor (now Lord) Rothschild and Anthony Blunt (now Keeper of the Queen's Pictures). F. E. Hovell-Thurlow-Cumming-Bruce, now a distinguished diplomat, was said to sing the Red Flag in his bath. None of these people were communists even then . . .' Yet when Simon Freeman telephoned this splendidly named diplomat, living in retirement as plain Lord Thurlow, he described, quite happily and very amusingly, how he had been a member of a so-called communist cell at Cambridge. There were many others like Lord Thurlow who no longer worried that they would be accused of anything dreadful if they admitted their youthful idealism. They talked about their fears then of a British sell-out to Hitler, the failure of capitalism, and their hopes that a better society was being built in the Soviet Union. They described the drudge of having to plod through the works of Marx and Lenin and their disillusion at the Nazi–Soviet pact of 1939. We trust that none of these men and women regret having spoken so openly to us.

We have written at length, too, about MI5 and MI6 because it is impossible to understand the story of the Cambridge spies without some idea of the ethos of the two services. The dearth of official documentation is a grave handicap to any author but we hope that we have at least shown that, despite the newspaper headlines and the spy novels, most British Intelligence officers are sane, sensible and normal people. That does not mean, we must add, that we believe that the services handled the investigation into the Cambridge spies well or efficiently.

We always tried to cross-check information but sometimes this was impossible and we had to rely on the recollections of an individual. We tried to interview key sources together in an effort to avoid misunderstandings over what had been said, though pressure of time often forced us to conduct important interviews separately. We were aware that in a book such as this, which necessarily leans heavily on oral testimony, we might be criticized for putting too much trust on hearsay or gossip. We tried, therefore, to be sceptical about the more controversial claims. We have added a postscript to this edition to take account of developments since the publication of the hardback edition in November 1986, notably the revelations which emerged during the British government's attempt in the Australian courts to prevent Peter Wright, the retired MI5 spy-catcher who interrogated Blunt, publishing his memoirs. The writing of the first draft of this book was divided between the authors, but to ensure that, whatever its faults, it did at least have a uniform style, Simon Freeman wrote this, the final manuscript.

We do not pretend that this will be the definitive work on Anthony Blunt and the other Cambridge spies. Other authors may well shock us with new twists; perhaps this book contains the clues which will help them do that. We have tried to present the evidence, to avoid easy allegations or glib conclusions, and to offer possible reasons for the phenomenon of the Cambridge spies. But there is a central theme, and it is secrecy. Foolish, indefensible official secrecy allowed the Cambridge spies to prosper. Official secrecy protected them. And now official secrecy prevents historians from examining the records which would help us better understand the story of the Cambridge spies. There was, too, the secrecy of friends of Blunt, Burgess, Philby and Maclean, who, through loyalty or cowardice, stayed silent for so long. In 1984 Lord Rothschild published a short essay describing how he felt when he learnt that his friend, Sir Anthony Blunt, was a Soviet spy. He entitled the essay, 'The File Is Never Closed'. Rothschild was right. The file on Blunt will remain open for as long as people are interested in the story of the man who betrayed both his country and his friends.

Simon Freeman
Barrie Penrose
London, February 1987

ACKNOWLEDGEMENTS

We owe a great debt to the many people who helped us in the research of this book. We do not have the space here to thank everyone by name, although we have listed the key sources in our reference section.

After the hardback edition of this book was published in November 1986 a number of people took the trouble to write to us, pointing out factual mistakes, expanding what they had originally told us and, in a few cases, taking issue with our interpretation of events or characters. We have corrected the factual errors and, where we agreed with criticisms, redrafted other passages. We are grateful, therefore, to the following for making this book more accurate: the late Wilfrid Blunt, Christopher Blunt, Brian Sewell, George Zarnecki, Lord Annan, Professor M. R. D. Foot, Christopher Andrew, Nigel West and John Hilton. We hope that there are no further mistakes but, if there are, then they are our responsibility alone. If readers spot errors then we ask that they let us know so that they can be corrected in later editions. Our conclusions are, of course, entirely our own.

We would like to thank:

Our fellow-authors, Nigel West, Andrew Boyle and Paul Levy, who behaved as colleagues not rivals. E. G. H. Kempson gave us invaluable briefings on Marlborough. Charles Madge, Margot Heinemann and Brian Simon provided fresh insights into the Cambridge of the 1930s. Lady Mary Dunn talked to us about her friendship with the young Anthony Blunt. George Carey-Foster supplied us with a useful description of the events which led to the defections of Burgess and Maclean. John Hilton offered us new perspectives on Blunt. Robert Harbinson gave us a great deal of material, of which we were only able to use a fraction. Brian Sewell was always ready with advice. Rosamond Lehmann, Lillian Gurry, Lady Proctor, Malcolm and Kitty Muggeridge, John Gaskin and Michael Rubinstein filled in vital gaps. Michael Straight, John Cairncross and Leo Long agreed to help despite the fact that we had written newspaper articles about them which we know they found hurtful. We hope that we have given them a fair hearing. Jack Hewit shared his memories of Blunt and Burgess and without him this book would have been far duller. Many former officers of MI5 and MI6 were helpful. We hope that they do not regret this despite the government's displeasure that they had dared to talk to us. Finally, we have to mention the late Wilfrid Blunt and his brother, Christopher. They could not have been more courteous and patient. We are delighted that they felt that we did not abuse their trust.

We would like to thank Andrew Neil, editor of the *Sunday Times*, for allowing us the time to write this book, and Anthony Bambridge and Tony Rennell, also of the *Sunday Times*, for making sure that we were not disturbed during our leave. Our agent, Gordon Fielden, of the Anglo-German Literary Agency, was always supportive and Richard Johnson, our editor at Grafton Books, remained confident in the project through many difficulties. We must thank, too, Jonathan Lloyd and John Boothe, of Grafton Books, for keeping their nerve when under pressure. Janet Law, our copy editor, suggested many improvements. Chris Bates helped us solve endless problems with our word processors. The staff of the *Sunday Times* library, notably Ray Smith, were always ready to help. The London Library and the Kent Library Service found us books which were not available elsewhere. Rachel Priestman of the Courtauld Institute library dug out important art catalogues and books.

Finally we would like to thank the publishers of all the books which we either quoted or used as background. In particular we must thank the following for permission to quote from books: Faber and Faber (*The Strings are False*, by Louis MacNeice); Chatto and Windus (*A Chapter of Accidents*, by Goronwy Rees); Collins (*After Long Silence*, by Michael Straight); Michael Russell (*Married to a Single Life* and *Slow on the Feather*, both by Wilfrid Blunt); Weidenfeld and Nicolson (*Guy Burgess: A Portrait with a Background*, by Tom Driberg); Panther/Granada (*My Silent War*, by Kim Philby).

Simon Freeman writes: I must thank the many friends who put up with me during the research and writing of this book. I would like to mention a few, very special friends for their good humour, common sense and constant encouragement: Felicity Hawkins, Patrick Bishop, Mark Webster and Kim Fletcher. I would also like to thank Joan McArdle, without whom I would never have started writing, and Sara Wittekind, for helping me through the final stages. I am grateful to John Cooper of the City University for helping me find a word processor and then telling me how to use it. Finally, I must thank my mother for her understanding and encouragement.

Barrie Penrose writes: I owe a special debt to Nicole le Breton, who has helped make the path easier in many ways. Without her help and encouragement the going would have been much tougher. I am grateful to my mother for reading the first draft and making helpful suggestions. I would also like to thank my children, Edward, Isabelle and Amelie, for their patience and, I hope, understanding of why the task was worthwhile, and Dr Robin Moffat and his wife, Beryl, for their kind support. Equal encouragement came from Lionel Levy and Karen Busse.

CHAPTER 1
Royal Ties

Anthony Frederick Blunt was born on 26 September 1907, in Bournemouth on the south coast of England, the third and last child of the Reverend Arthur Stanley Vaughan Blunt and Hilda Violet Master.

The youngest of three boys, he was tall, slim and frail. His mother fussed constantly over him, which puzzled his two brothers, Wilfrid and Christopher, who thought that Anthony was just as robust as they were. Christopher later recalled: 'My mother was very close to Anthony, who was her youngest. He was slightly delicate as a child but my mother exaggerated this and would give him tonics all the time.'[1]

Anthony had hazel eyes, a fair complexion, light brown hair and very thin lips. He grew into a gangling, physically awkward boy, like his brothers and his father; from his mother he had inherited his shyness and the prominent teeth which added to the impression of clumsiness. He was extremely close to her; partly because he was her last child; partly, too, because he was six years younger than Wilfrid and three years younger than Christopher. This intimacy deepened as it became clear that Anthony was indisputably the brightest of the three.

Stanley Blunt had married Hilda Master, who was ten years his junior, in 1900. At thirty, Stanley (no one ever called him Arthur) was vicar of the parish of Ham in

Surrey, an attractive village on the then rural outskirts of London. He had a hearty manner which many people, including his sons, found irritating. His small salary was supplemented by Hilda's dowry. At first the couple lived in a comfortable, late Regency house in Ham. There was a maid and a gardener and a nurse to help Hilda look after Wilfrid and Christopher, both of whom had been born there. They might not have been wealthy, but Hilda's sisters had married into the landed gentry and Arthur's position as a clergyman conferred a respectability that money could not buy. Bishops sat in the House of Lords and humble parsons were honoured members of fashionable foxhunts which turned away the *nouveaux riches*. The son of a vicar who had become Suffragan Bishop of Hull, Stanley was, therefore, secure in the Edwardian order. The Blunts had another weapon in their social armoury: their links with the Royal Family, described by Anthony's eldest brother as his family's 'cult of royalty'. After all, not every parish priest could claim blood ties with the aristocracy. Wilfrid Blunt, who took a keen interest in the family genealogy, argued that if it could be:

> definitely established that my great[×7]-grandfather, John Blunt of Lindfield in Sussex (*temp*. James I), was the son of a certain William Blunt, the descent would be unbroken from Rudolf le Blond or Blount, 3rd Count of Guisnes in Normandy, through their son Robert, 1st Baron of Ixworth. In that case, Elizabeth Blunt, mistress of Henry VIII, would be my great[×11]-aunt.[2]

In fact, Anthony, Wilfrid and Christopher claimed half a century later that they were distant relatives of Queen Elizabeth II and third cousins of Queen Elizabeth, the Queen Mother because they shared a great-great-great grandfather – George Smith, MP for Midhurst and Wendover and brother of the first Lord Carrington – with the Queen Mother. Yet their mother boasted far closer ties with the Royal Family. When Anthony's maternal grand-parents settled at Montrose House in Petersham, not far from Richmond Park and Ham, they became neighbours and friends of the Duke and Duchess (Princess Mary Adelaide) of Teck and their daughter, Princess May, later Queen Mary, the wife of King George V. The Tecks lived at White Lodge in Richmond Park, a former royal hunting lodge which Queen Victoria had provided for her cousin, Princess Mary Adelaide.

Hilda was the youngest child. Her parents, John and Gertrude Master, had lived in India, where John had worked as a magistrate in Madras, before returning to England in 1877. They survived on private money and John's pension of £1000 a year. Hilda's parents made sure their daughter realized very early that they had royal neighbours. One of Anthony Blunt's friends said:

> Oh, the Blunts loved their friendship with royalty. Even Anthony, who became such a communist was a terrific snob when it came to the royals. When Pa Blunt died Queen Mary wrote a very, very nice personal letter to his wife. They were very, very close. They were so close they were let into royal secrets. Now parsons and lawyers in any family scandal – they know all about it![3]

John Master taught the future Queen Mary how to skate on the Penn Ponds in Richmond Park and even taught Hilda, then aged seven, to curtsey on skates in case they bumped into their royal neighbour on the ice. Princess Mary called Hilda's father 'Dear Jack' and seemed genu-inely fond of him and his wife. The two women had similar interests; according to Wilfrid Blunt, they 'shared exactly the same brand of evangelical piety'. Both shared, too, a passion for performing noble acts of charity. There was the Surrey Needlework Guild, which provided clothing for the poor, the Royal Cambridge Asylum, an old people's home, and the Ivy House for Friendless Girls. The two women sat on the same charitable committees and reminded their own children of their duties towards those less fortunate than themselves.

The two girls, Hilda and May, also enjoyed each other's company. They regularly hunted for blackberries in Richmond Park, though Hilda had to leave the low ones for her royal friend who was too short and stout to reach for the higher branches.

The Blunt boys were fond of their grandfather, John, who sported a magnificent, flowing beard, turned white, so family legend suggested, when he had been mauled by a bear in India. When his grandsons visited Montrose House he used to take them on exciting boat trips down the Thames. But his wife Gertrude was a much tougher proposition. Her humour did not improve with age, especially after she had injured her leg in a fall (caused by someone stepping on the train of her dress). She bought a large invalid carriage which sported two brass oil-lamps and a black canopy which covered her like a baby in a pram. She was often seen wearing cast-offs from White Lodge, reasoning that there was no disgrace in taking clothes which had been worn by royalty. Wilfrid wrote in his autobiography:

To Aunt Mabel, as well as to my mother [Hilda] and my other aunts, the Queen used to pass on dresses, hats and parasols that she felt obliged to discard after wearing them or carrying them a few times on public occasions. This was a *dead secret*, and we were told never to divulge it . . . The time came, however, when Aunt Mabel, who was only five years younger than the Queen and very like her in gait and figure, made so few modifications in the toques and dresses that in the street she was often greeted by passers-by with a bow or a curtsey. This, I am sure, gave her intense pleasure; for – and let me now come clean – Aunt Mabel was a royalty snob.[4]

Anthony was brought up on a rich diet of stories about his family's links with royalty. One in particular appealed to his parents because it emphasized that the Blunts were really just as good as the royals. The story, told again and again, involved Grandmother Gertrude, who had always demanded an immediate reply to any letters that she sent to White Lodge. On one occasion, when a letter was not answered by return, she had sent a servant with a pencil and writing paper. Princess Mary Adelaide apologized: 'You dear practical soul! I am writing with your pencil . . .' Anthony's father, too, was proud of his friendship with the Queen. 'My father got on very well with Queen Mary,' said Wilfrid Blunt. 'She liked having her leg pulled and he was very good at that.'[5] Years later, Aunt Mabel laboriously collected the hundreds of letters written by the family and Queen Mary and Princess Mary Adelaide and had them bound in leather. But Hilda, less obsessed with royalty, refused to buy a copy from Aunt Mabel.

Stanley Blunt accepted that his wife's royal links placed him, socially at least, one step behind her. On the other hand, he told friends, his father was related to the celebrated Victorian poet, Wilfrid Scawen Blunt. Stanley called himself 'Broad Evangelical' and at Ham Church, an uninspiring Gothic Revival building, he avoided sermons, hymns or ceremony which might be thought remotely Roman Catholic, or 'Popish' as his congregation put it. He was called Stanley, after his godfather Dean Stanley. His other godfather, Dean Vaughan, had been headmaster of Harrow, until he had been forced to resign after seducing one of his pupils. The incident was, naturally enough, never mentioned by the family. Stanley Blunt was an uncomplicated, simple man who, said Wilfrid, 'knew that right was right and wrong was wrong and that the twain never met'. He was balding by the time he was thirty and wore old-fashioned, dark frock-coats and high, starched wing collars on formal occasions. He enjoyed golf, walking his Samoyed sledge-dog, Ivan, and puffing on a pipe, though his wife rationed his smoking.

In 1906, the year before Anthony was born, the family moved to the seaside town of Bournemouth, exactly 100 miles from London. Bournemouth thought itself far more genteel than other south coast resorts such as Margate or Ramsgate. It had far fewer pubs than Brighton or South-end, which Hilda, a teetotaller, thought made it an admirable place in which to bring up children. The Blunts wanted a sedate life and they found it in Bournemouth. Stanley's church, Holy Trinity, was larger than Ham and its vicarage gave the Blunts much-needed extra space. Its gardens were well stocked with yellow azaleas and delphiniums, to which Hilda, a keen gardener, added a rose garden. Donkey-rides and Punch-and-Judy shows were available on the beach during the week but never on the sabbath. Indeed, the town even banned Sunday trains until the beginning of the First World War. Wilfrid recalled:

The Bournemouth of 1906, the year we went to live there, was still a place where in the summer one could pitch one's own little tent on the almost deserted beach, leave it there all night, and find it intact the next morning. It was already a town of sinuous roads, pines, chines, retired colonels, invalids and Bath chairs . . . But we were moving with the times, for the Winter Gardens provided excellent concerts, to one of which I was taken, and Beale's Fancy Fair – a real emporium – made us feel quite in the swing.[6]

Bournemouth was the only south coast resort with its own full orchestra, which Sir Dan Godfrey regularly conducted at the Winter Garden, and Stanley, who enjoyed classical music, especially the English composer, Edward Elgar, fitted in as many concerts as possible between services and his many duties. He could always count on the support of his wife; she might have been puritanical but she was intensely loyal to her husband. Wilfrid said:

She worshipped my father and supported him in everything, did the work of two unpaid curates and towards the end of his life waited on him hand and foot. Her Scottish shrewdness and sound common sense were invaluable to him, for all Blunts are emotional, sentimental, gullible. My father was what I would call hearty. He was a popularizer, like me.[7]

Stanley knew that he was no great scholar and did not pretend to be one. But his parishioners felt at ease with him. His sermons were direct and simple and he was not afraid to introduce a light-hearted element into them. It was astonishing, Wilfrid thought later, that this bluff, hearty man, one of life's well-intentioned amateurs, had a son like Anthony, who became a serious student almost as soon as he was able to read and write. Stanley did, in fact, once try to prove that he was capable of sustained intellectual effort when he wrote a biography of his father, the Suffragan Bishop of Hull. Sir Frederick Macmillan, a friend of the family, published this in 1913, more out of kindness than any hope that it would sell.

However, the powerful Christian, puritanical views of his family seem to have left Anthony unmoved. It was ironic – and it would have horrified his parents – that he chose the atheism of Marxism as the main guiding force of his adult life. Anthony grew up in the confident atmosphere of a genteel English, Edwardian family. His mother held family prayers daily and insisted that they attended church as often as possible. Yet this kind of secure, comfortable, God-fearing existence, mirrored in countless middle-class homes around the country, was slowly being threatened by new social forces. Fewer people, even in Bournemouth, worshipped in church. 'Our forefathers were content with a Heaven after death; we demand a Heaven down here,' said the cynics. While the Church thundered against gambling and drinking, millions read in popular newspapers of the antics of self-made 'Champagne Charlie millionaires' who enjoyed flaunting their wealth. By 1908 the Church of England was short of 5000 clergymen. The majority in England claimed to be Christian but the dull Victorian sabbath had been turned into a day for cycling or playing tennis or golf. The motor car meant that more people could travel further; people knew more, saw more and had more. But that did not satisfy them; it merely made them more envious. Ordinary working people wondered why they had to slog out a miserable living while the rest of the country dedicated itself to the pursuit of pleasure. There were demands for reforms, encouraged by prominent politicians such as Keir Hardie, Lloyd George and Winston Churchill. While Edward VII and his clique of millionaires could shoot game at weekend country-house parties, or enjoy the gambling at Monte Carlo, many of his subjects lived in poverty. Casual labourers in London's East End had to survive on twenty-one shillings a week, assuming that they were lucky enough to find work in the first place. Women elementary schoolteachers lived on an average of £75 a year. In contrast, families could live comfortably on £1000 a year. Labour was so cheap that servants were plentiful.

Amid the clatter of Edwardian progress Stanley Blunt quietly followed his parish vocation, blissfully oblivious to social unrest. He certainly did not preach social revolution or justice for the poor; nor did he attack gambling or horse-racing, possibly because the King attended meetings at Ascot and Epsom each year where his stable's colours – purple, scarlet and gold – were the most familiar on the course. Edward VII was also, Stanley hardly needed to remind himself, the Head of the Church of England.

It was Stanley's friend, the Bishop of Winchester, a regular guest for tea at the vicarage, who encouraged him to send his sons to Marlborough College, which offered fee-saving scholarships to the sons of Anglican clergymen. Grandmother Gertrude and her husband, who felt that Eton would have been more appropriate for their grandsons, were also regular visitors, arriving in their impressive but extremely noisy Darracq car. Wilfrid was always impressed by his father's kindness to the destitute but his mother could be less sympathetic to ordinary people, betraying, her eldest son later felt, the most unattractive side of her personality. This inability to cope with people less educated and less fortunate than herself became, too, a characteristic of the adult Anthony and was as unappealing in him as it was in her.

In May 1910 – the month of Edward VII's death – Anthony and his brothers caught whooping cough. In panic, Hilda moved them to lodgings above the police station in the nearby seaside resort of Swanage. Hilda hoped that the Swanage air, though not noticeably different from Bournemouth's, would help them recover more quickly. Outside the police station a wanted poster was headlined: 'DR CRIPPEN WANTED FOR MURDER', which left Wilfrid worrying that Crippen would pounce on him.

But the year was not just memorable because the Blunt

boys caught – and survived – an unpleasant illness. Stanley's father died. The family's long-standing friend, Princess May, became Queen Mary when her husband became King. In late June the following year the Blunts travelled to London for Coronation Day and, from a balcony in the Haymarket, loyally waved at George V and Queen Mary and at the passing procession of foreign royalty and troops. Behind the gold-painted, cumbrous Coronation coach were members of the Royal Family whom the Blunts already knew and would meet again, including Queen Mary's brother Prince Alge (Lord Athlone), to whom Aunt Mabel had taught the 'Eton Boating Song'.

Less than a year after the Coronation, Stanley Blunt decided that he needed a new challenge and in mid-April 1912 he was appointed Chaplain to the British Embassy Church in Paris. Whether royal patronage played a role in securing the job is uncertain, but the family's association with Queen Mary could hardly have been a drawback.

In Paris the Blunts lived first in a small furnished house close to the Bois de Boulogne. Wilfrid remained in England, boarding at Wychwood Preparatory School, which he did not much like. (Anthony later went to a prep school on the Sussex coast.) Anthony was given a governess in Paris while Christopher was sent to a day-school, l'école Villiers (which Anthony joined just after the outbreak of the First World War). Christopher said later: 'It was a typical Parisian school of the day. We used to learn rhymes and read La Fontaine's fables. I was probably the only foreigner when I was there. It was like an English dame school although it probably went a little higher than that.'[8]

By Easter 1913, the Blunts had moved to a larger house in the rue Jouffroy in the 17th *arrondissement* of Paris. Not far from the house was the Parc Monceau where Anthony was often taken by his French governess. It was, said

Wilfrid, a 'pretty and excessively French little public garden with mock ruins, vivid green but forbidden grass . . . and quantities of those slightly absurd monuments where yearning marble maidens clutch pedestals crowned with top-heavy busts of French immortals'.

When war broke out, Stanley, now forty-four, and Hilda volunteered to sit on committees set up to aid the first victims of the conflict.

The Blunts remained in Paris when the German guns came dangerously close in September and the French government withdrew south to Bordeaux. In the chaotic atmosphere of wartime France, Hilda heard from a friend that there were 8000 wounded in Limoges and only six nurses. Wilfrid recalled:

This information she passed on to my grandmother, who immediately told the Queen. But at some stage in the transmission the word 'Limoges' had been lost sight of; therefore not a little consternation was caused when, almost by return of post, the royal gift of 150 Red Cross nurses and thirty surgeons arrived unheralded at the Hotel Astoria in Paris, where they lingered for days in exquisite boredom.[9]

For the Blunt children the war was just a game which they enacted daily on a smaller scale by placing French and English flags on a map of Europe. When generals dropped in for tea the boys would ask, or take, army buttons as souvenirs for their 'museum'. Fearing that on-leave soldiers might be tempted by the many delights of Parisian nightlife, Stanley and a popular actress named Decima Moore, later Lady Guggisberg, opened a Leave Club for them, producing 35,000 meals a month. Wilfrid said: 'One gala day at the Club my parents were naïve enough to dress my brother Christopher as a nurse and let him loose as a dancing partner among the soldiers. Christopher was then about thirteen, blond and good-looking: one of the soldiers proved most anxious to see "her" home.'[10]

Years later Anthony Blunt wrote about the importance of his early days in France, describing the move to Paris as an event which 'undoubtedly coloured the whole of my later development'. France then, not England, or Russia for that matter, was Blunt's spiritual home. He could recall visiting the Louvre before the outbreak of war:

> I cannot remember any of the pictures, I can merely remember the fact. I developed a very strong French leaning which has coloured my whole attitude towards things ever since. I was brought up from a very early age, really almost unconsciously, to look at works of art and to regard them as of importance. This was partly due to my mother and father, but more particularly due to Wilfrid who was becoming a painter by the time I was growing up, and had far closer contacts, naturally, with the artistic world.[11]

Impressionist painters, the new patriarchs of the art world, were already on show at the Louvre. Yet when artists such as Cézanne, Monet, Degas and Renoir had exhibited their work in Paris in 1874, the public were appalled by the way these young men had turned the world into a haze of brilliant colour. The Impressionists starved in garrets until the 1890s when art-hungry American millionaires and a few perceptive French dealers began to buy their work. In England, however, the public remained unaware of dangerous avant-garde French painting until 1910, when Roger Fry opened a Post-Impressionist exhibition at the Grafton Galleries. Conventional taste in Britain at that time was epitomized by the exhibits in the Royal Academy's annual summer show. Sir Lawrence Alma-

Tadema was still painting topless Anglo-Grecian maidens, while the British Royal Family enjoyed Sir Edwin Landseer's studies of Highland stags. The artistic tastes of Stanley and Hilda were exemplified by a watercolour portrait of Wilfrid and Christopher painted by John Byam Shaw in 1906. Wilfrid described it thus:

> Dressed in purple velvet with a lace collar, and looking horribly like Little Lord Fauntleroy, I am seated on the ground under an immense chestnut tree and hold in my hands a splendid bunch of prize purple and white asters – flowers that I especially dislike. Christopher, aged two and in a white pinafore, stands at my side languidly presenting arms with a brace of moon daisies.[12]

Paris was the artistic capital of Europe and Wilfrid immersed himself in studying the city's many artistic factions. He made sure, too, that he passed on the knowledge he acquired to Anthony, who was an enthusiastic and able pupil. According to Herbert Read:

> From every direction young artists made their way to Paris. In the first ten years practically every artist who was to become a leader of new movements in the new century visited Paris, and many of them came to stay. Some of them were born in or near Paris – Rouault, Picabia, Delaunay, Utrillo, Derain, and Vlaminck; other French artists moved in from the provinces – Braque and Léger in 1900, Arp and Marcel Duchamp in 1904 . . . Picasso came to Paris in 1900 and soon returned to stay. Brancusi came via Munich in 1904, Archipenko in 1908, Chagall in 1910. Kandinsky visited Paris in 1902 . . . Klee in 1905 . . . Juan Gris settled there in 1906 . . . Modigliani in 1906.[13]

Science, too, was helping to change conventional perceptions of reality by demolishing formerly sacrosanct definitions of time, space and matter, but it also created the weapons that were responsible for millions of deaths in the First World War. Reactions to this carnage, of course, differed widely. Anthony's father watched soldiers die in agony in France and after the war lectured to the boys of Marlborough College (including his elder sons), on why the Versailles Treaty would prevent a similar tragedy. Anthony was still in Paris, and with remarkable detachment noted that the end of the war would mean the resumption of normal artistic life.

. . . during the war everything was shut; there were no pictures to look at at all; only very occasional exhibitions, and therefore if one wanted to look at works of art one was automatically compelled to look at architecture and it was perhaps for that reason that I developed an interest in architecture which I have never lost. At that time my taste was extremely conventional.[14]

The avant-garde was far less detached than young Anthony. It was in uproar over the war. Anarchic 'anti-art' followers of the Dada movement, like Hans Arp, who had been in the French capital when war broke out, were, said Arp:

Revolted by the butchery of the 1914 World War . . . While the guns rumbled in the distance, we sang, painted, made collages and wrote poems with all our might. We were seeking an art based on fundamentals, to cure the madness of the age, and a new order of things that would restore the balance between heaven and hell. We had a dim premonition that power-mad gangsters would one day use art itself as a way of deadening men's minds.[15]

Dadaists believed that if society was worthless and corrupt then so, too, was its art, along with leaders and philosophers. Marcel Duchamp, an accomplished modern painter, began exhibiting works which proclaimed the group's anti-bourgeois philosophy. In left-bank cafés and galleries in Paris the Dada group started to issue poems and manifestos. On 5 February 1920 one anti-art demonstration ended in riot with the audience hurling all kinds of missiles at the Dadaists. Also in Paris were refugees from the Russian Revolution, including white Russian *émigrés* who wanted the West to declare war on the Soviet Union.

Anthony, however, simply went on examining paintings and buildings. At first he collected coloured postcards from the Louvre, favouring religious pictures: 'Botticelli madonnas and that kind of thing,' said Wilfrid later. Anthony and Wilfrid 'went off to see everything together,' said Christopher Blunt, 'while I collected coins, a pastime in which they were not in the least interested.'[16] Their father had allowed Wilfrid to take art lessons at the *atelier* of an academic painter named M. Renard. Stanley thought that the Frenchman's art was really just like one of the English Pre-Raphaelite painters whom he so much admired. It was here that Wilfrid saw his first nude woman, posing for the students. He noted dryly that 'what I saw did not excite me, it merely surprised me'.

Even at this age Anthony was showing an unusual appetite for scholarly argument. Wilfrid said: 'He looked at pictures intellectually. He was deeply excited when he succeeded in attributing a picture which was thought to be by someone I hadn't heard of.' Anthony also told his brother what he should read. But Wilfrid did not seem to mind this precociousness: 'And it was then in a sense that he became almost the elder brother and I the younger one. I was getting directions from him. He was very keen on architecture, we'd study buildings and go to picture exhibitions.'[17]

The Blunts' nine-year sojourn in Paris was drawing to a close. During the exceptionally hot summer of 1921, in temperatures reaching over 100 degrees Fahrenheit, Stanley Blunt announced that he had decided to give up his living at the British Embassy Church. He had accepted the living of St John's, Paddington, in west London. As they prepared to leave Paris Wilfrid decided to hold an exhibition of his paintings at his parents' home. He was gratified, if a little surprised, when family friends bought most of them. Anthony, meanwhile, had departed in January that year for Marlborough, having won a scholarship to the school which he had heard so much about from his brothers. He was already the academic star of the family, a brilliant and independent-minded boy, who knew more about art and architecture than many adult critics. He was as sure as his parents that he would enjoy a glittering school career. And he was not wrong.

CHAPTER 2
Marlborough Youth

Anthony Blunt arrived at Marlborough College in January 1921, following, with mixed feelings of dread and excitement, his elder brothers Wilfrid and Christopher. Teenage years are always crucial in the formation of character, but even so, it would be hard to exaggerate the importance of Marlborough in the development of the youngest of the Blunt brothers – though anyone looking for easy clues to explain why the brilliant scholarship boy became a Soviet spy will be disappointed. During his time there his enthusiasm for art matured into a precocious expertise. He became increasingly disdainful of 'the Establishment' – a term used to denote people, ideas or conventions that were boring or trite or which merely irritated Blunt or his friends. It did not signify any reasoned objection to capitalism. It was based partly on the arrogance of youth, the natural and healthy rebelliousness of teenagers living in a closed, hierarchical society. It was, too, the reaction of an extremely bright boy who felt that he and his gifted contemporaries, and perhaps a handful of enlightened masters, knew more and understood better than anyone else.

Blunt forged important and lasting friendships at Marlborough: with John Betjeman, the future poet laureate; Ellis Waterhouse, knighted after a distinguished career as an art historian; John Hilton, who became a diplomat and man of letters and, in retirement, a crusader for justice for victims of schizophrenia; and, most significantly, Louis MacNeice, also the son of a clergyman, though his father worked in the slums of Belfast.

Anthony grew into a gangling, physically awkward young man, who was as uninterested in girls after puberty as he was before. He was iconoclastic, arrogant and homosexual in inclination if not in practice. His friends complained that he could be narrow-minded and bigoted. Psychiatrists or social historians might argue that Blunt's later treachery was a symptom of alienation; that, as a homosexual, he felt that society had rejected him and that he, in turn, was right to reject it. (It was even argued in America during the 1950s that homosexuals were more likely to become spies than heterosexuals because they were already practised in pretending to be what they were not.) But there is no such pat explanation for Blunt's actions.

In 1972 Blunt wrote a lengthy essay entitled 'From Bloomsbury to Marxism' for the art magazine *Studio International*. It is an account of his intellectual growth and is relaxed, informal and occasionally jokey, in contrast to most of his published works which were dry and scholarly. It was based on talks to students that he had given in his last years as Director of the Courtauld Institute of Art in which he tried to explain the complex forces that had played on the emotions of young intellectuals in the 1920s and '30s. For all its merits the essay betrays traces of the smugness that his critics always found so irritating; it is also, inevitably, dishonest, since Blunt could hardly describe accurately the consequences of his Marxism. He wrote that he wanted to talk in detail about Marlborough, 'because the intellectual influences I underwent there coloured the whole of my later development and because we lived in such a peculiar atmosphere'. Marlborough, he wrote, was 'a notoriously tough school'[1] though he claimed it was not quite as hideous as John Betjeman had claimed in his autobiographical poem, *Summoned by Bells*:

> John was in fact, though he might not like me to say it, rather happy at Marlborough. He had a brilliant way of dealing with the toughs. He pulled their legs and laughed at them and had a far more enjoyable time, apart from physical discomfort, than you would gather from his autobiography. However, it was very unpleasant.[2]

Marlborough had been founded in 1843 by clerics and devout laymen anxious that there should be a good school for the sons of clergy and for middle-class families who had neither the money nor the desire to send their sons to one of the older public schools. By the 1920s boys came from what John Hilton called 'a hotch-potch of roughly upper middle-class families, small landed folk, army, entrepreneurial and professional'.[3] The school's comparative youth did not mean that it lacked tradition. Indeed, Marlborough seemed to have over-compensated for not having had a glorious past by spawning many curious rituals, described in a mystic language that was incomprehensible to outsiders and which reinforced the boys' sense that they were privileged members of a unique society. Marlborough had always been spartan, emphasizing what masters called 'character'. This implied that Marlburians did not lie or cheat, they worked and played hard and relished tests of physical hardship. They were loyal to King and Country and God – it was precisely the kind of muscular Christianity that had sustained the British Empire. But the school was also proud of its academic record, pointing out that half the pupils went on to Oxford or Cambridge.

Marlborough school stands at the western edge of the town, which has an unusually wide, handsome high street (full of cake shops), astride the road to Bath. Town and school nestle in a hollow, surrounded by chalk hills topped by clumps of trees. To the south-east is the Savernake Forest and the Kennet and Avon canal. To the north-east lie the Marlborough Downs. It was, and to some extent still is, classic English countryside; hills and streams and winding lanes where boys could safely race their bicycles even after the coming of the motor car. Nearby is the mysterious Silbury Hill, a 130-foot-high artificial mound dating from around 2660 B.C., which historians calculate would have taken 700 men ten years to build.[4]

In the school grounds, so legend suggests, is a mound marking the burial site of King Arthur's magician, Merlin. In the eighteenth century, Frances, Countess of Hertford, had added a couple of grottoes, later used by the school to store swedes. There was a castle moat, overhung by laburnums, which boys used as a swimming pool. There were well-tended lawns and magnificent yew trees. All the dormitories were cold and noisy but a few had a redeeming architectural splendour. Louis MacNeice noted with satisfaction that one was 'a long high room with lime green panelling, egg and dart moulding around the cornice and a series of majestic windows that looked out on an elegant velvet lawn'.[5]

When Blunt arrived at Marlborough the headmaster was Cyril (later Sir Cyril) Norwood, a cultured reformer who thought that the school had concentrated too much on the building of 'character' through hardship. He was worried that individualism was being stifled, especially among the more sensitive, academic pupils. He wanted to encourage the study of science so that the boys could contribute to a changing world. But he was no revolutionary: he believed in the same values as the school founders. He wrote of Marlburians: 'Their homes and families have implanted standards to which they will not lightly prove false and they have known very well that their future in the world depends on what they prove themselves to be.'[6]

Not everyone found the Marlborough ethos attractive. Whereas boys from wealthy families at schools such as Eton could afford to be lazy, Marlburians tended to be pushy and ambitious. They came from homes where the father or grandfather had worked hard to achieve social status and, like the modern upwardly mobile middle class, they were keen to defend and improve their position. Louis Mac-Neice wrote:

Conversation was infected with the social snobbery they brought from home. During term we wore uniform black but at the end of term we were allowed to wear ordinary suits to go home in. At the end of term accordingly everyone was jealously competitive and those boys were despised whose clothes were not well-cut. As for the boys who went home in their school clothes – of whom I was one, for I was ashamed to ask my family for a decent suit – they were almost pariahs.[7]

Before the First World War most Marlburians had made their careers in the army, the Church, the colonial services or teaching. But the war had detonated social changes which ensured that assumptions and attitudes could never be the same, however much headmasters such as Norwood liked to pretend that the notion of King and Country, buttressed by Christian faith, stood unchallenged. Norwood was popular with the boys, who nicknamed him 'Boots' because weak insteps forced him to wear supports. He hired bright young masters to teach science and broaden the classics-based arts curriculum. He introduced daily PT to try and cure the notoriously poor posture of the boys. He encouraged them to set up chess, arts and debating societies – developments that did not please the older masters who thought boys would become soft if they spent too much time talking in the relative warmth of the school.

Anthony Blunt went straight into 'A House' in January 1921, by which time Norwood's reforms were well under way. 'A House' was where most new boys spent their first two or three terms before being transferred to other junior houses or into the upper, senior school. Houses were supposed to instil in boys a sense of loyalty to a smaller entity than the school, while they made their way at their own pace into senior classes specializing in the arts or sciences. Wilfrid Blunt described 'A House' as 'a cubical red-brick prison with a central well and two presiding gaolers' which would have made 'any modern gaol seem like a paradise'.[8] MacNeice, too, used a penal analogy when he wrote:

> You could look up from the basement and see the prisoners listlessly parading on every floor, their shrill voices echoing metallic, the air sombre and stale, steaming in the bathrooms and dense in the afternoons with frying fat. There were often one or two little boys trudging down and up the stairs from the ground floor to the basement, turning automatically at the bottom step or the top, just down and up, down and up; these boys were doing 'Basements' – a punishment inflicted on them by boys one term or more their seniors.[9]

The constant threat of punishment, sometimes for breaking rules that new boys did not know existed, hung like a cloud over Anthony in those first few months, though he had the advantage of having had survival tactics outlined to him by Wilfrid and Christopher. But he could not do much about the cold, which made boys think Marlborough must be 'the coldest place in England'. Boys 'lived in constant fear of infringing petty regulations laid down by an oligar-

chy of tyrants, a desk not quite shut, a late arrival for prep,
a word thoughtlessly whispered in a neighbour's ear could –
and often did – lead to a savage and sadistic public
beating.'[10] The only way to cope, Wilfrid told Anthony,
was to be very, very careful. Yet when Wilfrid had come
home during the holidays he could not wait for term to
begin; Anthony concluded from this that Marlborough
could, despite everything, be enjoyed.

Added to the physical discomfort and the futile rituals
was a sense of isolation from the rest of the world. Terms
were long and parents rarely visited their children apart
from perhaps attending the speech day in June. The road to
Bath was usually deserted, and at night the only sounds
were the occasional clunking of goods wagons on a nearby
old railway line.

The school day began at 6.30 A.M. with compulsory cold
baths, unless boys could escape the checks of the prefects.
One Old Marlburian, John Parker, later wrote:

> There was little privacy. Relieving oneself was commu-
> nal with two long troughs with rows of seats separated by
> partitions. After breakfast queues three or four long
> awaited a doorless vacant place. Every ten minutes a
> flush cleared the whole trough beneath one. Meals, eaten
> in a huge hall with distempered red walls and decorated
> with crumbling plaster busts, were loathed by every-
> one.[11]

The food was so bad that two local firms, Duck and
Bernard, used to sell bread and other provisions in the
school yard every morning. The school diet consisted
mainly of stodge: suet pudding, rice, semolina and huge
potatoes. Some boys alleged that in 1924 the school was still
serving margarine made in the First World War. As a result
of this diet, in which roughage, vegetables and salad were

usually missing, many boys suffered from constipation. John Hilton could recall details of the terrible Marlborough menu sixty years later: 'The meat was iridescent. The cabbage was full of blackfly. The water was so heavily impregnated, I suppose with chlorine, that I found it distressing.'[12] Louis MacNeice complained that he ate virtually nothing in his first few days because no one had told him about the tradition of 'rushing' whereby a boy had to stake his claim on his food or risk having a neighbour whip it away from beneath him. Then there was the ritual of 'condescending' ('could you send'), which allowed senior boys to demand that younger pupils pass down the table whatever they were themselves hoping to eat.

After breakfast came chapel. This was an occasion for the seniors to compete with each other to see who could be the last to stroll to his place, while the juniors watched in admiration and envy. Blunt knew more than most boys about chapels but had never believed either in God or Christianity. Marlborough did nothing to change that.

The morning was divided into three lessons, interrupted by a session of PT. Blunt disliked most sport; perhaps the only activity at school he hated more was the Officer Training Corps (OTC). This required him to dress up in army uniform, march and parade and sometimes take part in field exercises, which often disintegrated into farce, to the fury of the masters. Christopher Lloyd, a contemporary of Blunt's, recalled that Blunt and Betjeman were the jokes of the platoon, forever dropping their rifles and behaving in a most unsoldierly manner. In 1966 Blunt told two boys preparing an article for the school magazine, *The Marlburian*:

The only athletic ability I had was being able to run rather slowly over long distances and we used to love running over the Downs – not on sweats [compulsory runs] because there was always a time limit on those, although in my last year I was let off them. We used to go out on Saturday nights and also for night walks. My housemaster was a Wiltshireman and he let me do this, which was the only thing we had in common.[13]

After lunch, which was as inedible as breakfast, boys were allowed into town, usually to stock up with food. On winter afternoons, there were cross-country runs for those boys not taking part in team sports. Summers were better. If boys were not required for cricket they could often get permission to go on long cycle rides. Blunt soon made it clear that he had no interest in (and no aptitude for) cricket and, as he moved up the school hierarchy, he became self-consciously eccentric when he took to the cricket field. Christopher Lloyd recalled:

I remember Blunt was reading a book on Picasso when we were all supposed to be playing cricket. We were on one of the outlying fields and so we all forged the score book and then retired under the hedge to read our books. Unfortunately, a prefect turned up and we all had three strokes of the stumps.[14]

Tea-time was a major event for the whole school. One Old Marlburian recalled that for all boys, ranging from tiny juniors with just one bent fork to the seniors who owned grand china tea-sets, tea was a chance to consume vast quantities of sausages, eggs and cakes.[15]

As Blunt moved up the school the petty privileges that his seniority brought made life more tolerable. He could cross this or that lawn or leave his jacket buttons undone. He had less reason to fear other boys and could ignore announcements which he had previously dreaded.

Blunt was soon marked out as a high-flier. E. G. H.

Kempson, then a young master at Marlborough, recalled that he was moved up the school as quickly as possible.[16] During his first two years Blunt regularly came top of his class in mathematics as well as winning a succession of school prizes.

Stanley Blunt, meanwhile, had settled into his new parish. One side of St John's was bordered by bustling Praed Street and the Edgware Road, on the other lay Hyde Park. Wilfrid was living at home after an unhappy term at Worcester College, Oxford, which he had found horribly hearty and barbaric, and a spell studying art in Paris. He enrolled at the Royal College of Art before taking a job in 1923 as an art master at Haileybury, a public school north of London. He relished the challenge; nothing could be better, he thought, than being paid to teach art to boys (Wilfrid never behaved improperly with any of his pupils though he adored their company).

But neither Wilfrid nor Anthony grew any closer to their father. Stanley Blunt was becoming more difficult with age, and as they developed their own interests, his views on art and literature seemed absurdly old-fashioned. Friends such as Ellis Waterhouse thought that the Blunts were an hospitable and relaxed family. 'Anthony was devoted to his mother but his father was, I would have said, rather a silly ass.'[17] However, all three sons adored Hilda Blunt and she, in return, was proud of them, especially Anthony.

Hilda was inflexibly honest and incapable of flattery, a virtue that her sons found led to embarrassing conversations with house guests who did not expect their hostess to be quite so frank. She enjoyed playing cards but abhorred betting. She knew her sons had long outstripped her intellectually but did her best to stay in touch with their work, reading, no doubt without much understanding, one of Christopher's learned essays on Anglo-Saxon coinage. If anything, she became more puritanical as she grew older, monitoring her husband's intake of wine and tobacco and reprimanding him if his waistline seemed to be thickening. But she knew her duty; and that was to support and encourage her husband, whatever his faults. Hilda was an anachronism who clung to a set of Victorian moral values. But the lack of any common ground did not affect her relationship with Anthony. She doted on him and he on her.

If Anthony's relationship with his mother was a vital emotional prop, his development as an intellectual owed much to Wilfrid. While at the Royal College of Art in London, Wilfrid had met Roger Fry, the renowned critic who dominated the London art world for nearly half a century. Fry had been the director of the Metropolitan Museum in New York from 1905 until 1910 when he returned to London to edit the influential *Burlington* magazine. He had organized exhibitions of the Post-Impressionist French painters in 1910 and 1912 and had founded the London group of avant-garde artists. Wilfrid patiently explained the latest trends in art to the eager Anthony, but the shift in their relationship that had begun in France was now unmistakable. Wilfrid later said: 'He soon outstripped me and for all that he introduced me to I am deeply grateful.' Wilfrid acknowledged that they had similar interests; it was their approach that differed so much:

Mine was of the emotional, undisciplined romantic; his was classical and scholarly. He cast his net deep; I cast mine wide. My urge was to create; his to study and analyse. Politics – Marxist or any other brand – meant nothing to me. Persian miniatures and Japanese prints left him unmoved, and my idol, Wagner, was both to him and my more orthodox brother, Christopher, anathema.[18]

From late in 1922 until he left school in the summer of 1926, Anthony specialized in pure mathematics though he also studied some physics, Latin and Greek, as well as modern languages at which he excelled (his French was so good that he taught some classes). The school records show that he was in the top half of his form during 1923, when most of the boys were a good deal older than him; in 1924 he had climbed to the top third; by his final year he was top. He continued to pick up prizes, not just for his specialist subject, pure maths, but also in the arts. For example, he was awarded the Cotton English Essay Prize for his study on 'the place of drama in modern life'.[19]

Despite his well-known contempt for school tradition Blunt was made a prefect in his final two terms, serving under a senior prefect called Henry Brooke. In 1964 Brooke was the Home Secretary who agreed to MI5's request to guarantee Blunt immunity if he was prepared to tell the full story of his work for the Soviet Union. (E. G. H. Kempson, a lifelong friend of Brooke, insisted that he, Brooke, would never have allowed a personal friendship to affect his judgement.)[20] Marlborough's records are vague about the exact chronology of Blunt's progress towards coveted senior status. He certainly would have passed through Upper School, where boys of varying ages spent most of their waking hours after they had moved into a senior house. It was the most feared institution at Marlborough, but it is impossible to say how many terms he endured there. 'Upper School' was a great, barn-like building dating from around 1850, where the hearties could easily ridicule and torment the aesthetes. E. G. H. Kempson could understand the views of both camps. He was cultured, well-read and liberal but he was also an athlete

(his proudest achievement was to found a school moun-
taineering club whose members included John Hunt, later
conqueror of Everest). Kempson thought: 'You could
enjoy school if you were not an athlete but there certainly
was antagonism between the two sides.'[21] Some boys, too,
were respected by both hearties and aesthetes. James
Mason, later a distinguished actor, was quite capable of
seeing off a group of bullying hearties and often did so. One
Old Marlburian, Sir Peter Tennant, recalled: 'James
Mason was tough and also an aesthete. I remember one day
the hearties threw someone into the swimming pool.
James, who was very senior then, quietly picked up the
hearties, one by one, and threw them all in. Then he walked
away. It really was a most splendid gesture.'[22]

Blunt slept in a house called 'C3', in the west wing of the
former Castle Inn, a fine brick edifice built in the first half of
the eighteenth century and once the main resting place for
travellers between London and Bath – until a railway
extension wrecked trade in 1841. For the first few months of
Blunt's time there the housemaster was Clifford Canning,
one of the school's most respected and popular masters.
Canning, a 'funny and remarkable man',[23] married Norwood's daughter, became a clergyman and then left to
become headmaster of Canford public school. John Hilton
described him as 'a great friend to many of us'.[24] Canning
moved to take charge of another house outside the school
grounds but 'C3' remained, by the standards of other
houses, reasonably civilized. However, there were unpleasant elements in 'C3'. For example, boys could be 'bum
shaved' by prefects. This involved two boys standing back
to back and being made to bend over with their bottoms
touching. Then the prefect made a vertical cut with his
cane. The trick, as Anthony learnt from Wilfrid, was to
relax the pressure at the last moment so that your unfortunate partner caught the sting. It was no good moving out of

the way, as common sense dictated; the prefect wanted to hit something and if he missed first time the punishment would only become tougher. Then there was the humiliation called 'hot-potting' where a pottery toothmug containing a piece of flaming paper was stuck on a boy's bare bottom. With two mugs so attached he was forced to parade naked in front of the rest of the dormitory. But the real horror was 'Upper School' itself, an institution that old Marlburians recalled with mixed emotions – disbelief that it ever existed and pride that they survived it. Louis Mac-Neice said that it hardly seemed like a building at all; it was just a great tract of empty air, cold as the air outside but smelling strongly of stables and enclosed by four thin walls and a distant roof.[25] One half of the hall was packed with desks; the other half was empty apart from two fires radiating precious warmth. One was called Big Fire and the other Little Fire. Big Fire was reserved for twenty or so older boys renowned for their toughness. The rest of the pupils, 100 or so, had to huddle around the other, smaller blaze. After the evening meal, while the humble juniors sat at their desks awaiting the arrival of four sixteen-year-old 'captains', the members of Big Fire barricaded the doors of the hall to try and prevent the inspecting 'captains' from entering. Sometimes the Big Fire clan ran around the hall, whooping and shouting. Anyone caught out of their seat when the captains forced their way in was caned; the challenge for the members of Big Fire was to remain out of their desks until the last possible moment. Sometimes, however, they miscalculated and the juniors were treated to the spectacle of seeing the bullies themselves being beaten. Then there was fagging, which most public schools of the period practised in some form or other. At Marlborough, fagging meant that juniors had to run and fetch anything that the seniors wanted – sometimes milk or coal or hot water. Beatings were common, but the worst fear was of being singled out by Big Fire for a savage humiliation. MacNeice wrote:

They would seize a boy, tear off most of his clothes and cover him with house paint, then put him in a wastepaper basket filled with rubbish and push him around the hall. Meanwhile Little Fire, dutifully sitting at their desks, would howl with delight – a perfect exhibition of mass sadism. The masters considered this a fine tradition, and any boy who had been basketed was under a cloud for the future. Because boys have an innate sense of justice, anyone they basket must be really undesirable. Government of the mob, by the mob, and for the mob.[26]

Blunt thought Upper School was 'a bestial place'. His life was made miserable, he said, by the bullying of one boy and the perpetual fear that he might one day be basketed. John Betjeman felt sick in later life whenever he remembered it. He was haunted by the memory of a victim in the wastepaper basket, peering through the slats like a frightened animal as he was hoisted into the air.[27] On the other hand, John Hilton and Ellis Waterhouse argued that no one was actually beaten up and that it was possible to outwit the system.

According to Kempson, Blunt would probably have spent no more than a couple of terms in Upper School and would then have been given his own study. A few boys who were senior to Blunt, such as Waterhouse and John Bowle, later an historian, had already launched a campaign against the philistine hearties. Bowle's life had been made almost unbearable by the bullies. Blunt recalled that Bowle used to come and shelter in his study, 'absolutely terrified, saying they're threatening to throw me into the swimming pool. And they probably were'. Betjeman fared rather better. Blunt said: 'He did not make a single concession. In his last year he had them eating out of his hand. His tastes were very unconventional. He used to bicycle over to Swindon to see a tram or attend a dissenting religious meeting. These eccentricities and even his poetry were considered a joke.'[28] Blunt added that it was the Betjeman-Bowle generation which had fought 'the absolute dominance of games' and who 'fought for the affirmation of the liberty of the individual'. They were brave, he thought, but just a little precious.

Blunt, too, threw himself into the resistance movement. In the spring of 1924 he and a fellow-pupil, Philip Harding, founded a magazine called *The Heretick*. Blunt said:

> We planned to express our disapproval of the Establishment generally, of the more out of date and pedantic masters, of all the forms of organized school sport, of the Officer Training Corps and of all the other features that we hated in school life. I wrote for it my first defence of modern art. It wasn't a very good or original article, but I was only sixteen. The motto on the outside of the Heretick was 'Upon Philistia will I triumph'. And that really was our great battle.[29]

There was a major problem, however, over the next edition in June 1924. Blunt admitted that he was to blame:

> The Heretick was suppressed after the second number, owing, I am sorry to say, to an article which I wrote on the theme that all art is amoral. This was provoked by a row with my housemaster [H. L. Guillebaud] who thought that the reproductions of Matisse and Rouault which I had in my study were indecent. The article was apparently regarded as so shocking that one parent threatened to remove his boy from school. But the second issue was already duller than the first and it did

not sell nearly so well. I remember that we were almost scraping together our pocket money to pay our debts for the thing. After that it folded up, which was the fitting end for such a production.[30]

The offending article was remarkable only because it was written by a sixteen-year-old. Blunt thought that 'to call a work of art immoral is like calling an ink pot sympathetic; it is applying an adjective applicable to one class of objects to an entirely different class. An ink pot may be heavy or dirty but it cannot under any circumstances be sympathetic. Similarly, a painting may be good or bad but not moral or immoral.' Art, Blunt argued, tried to create a new reality; it was an expression of an artist's personality and no more. If the artist was sincere then he would produce a 'great painting whatever his subject or his lack of technical skill'. But if the artist set out to shock his audience he became a social reformer. All art, Blunt concluded, was both moral and above morality. Some of Anthony's schoolmates found all this tiresome. John Bowle thought Blunt was pompous and conceited:

We had had the whole thing very well-arranged. Norwood, who was a very great headmaster, had shown the utmost tolerance. He arranged it so that all the boys who could get the agreement of their parents had the subscription charge for the Heretick put on their school bill. The only condition he imposed was that we wrote about things that were reasonable. Then we invited Blunt to write an article and he made the ridiculous claim that art superseded morality. And of course that upset a lot of Old Marlburians. I am not impartial about Blunt. He was a man I very much disliked. I can't tell you any good of him. To be quite candid I can only remember him as a colossal bore. Spelt B.O.R.E.[31]

One master, at least, was willing to be patient with the young rebel author. In July 1924 Clifford Canning wrote a lengthy and flattering review of Blunt's article, saying that the author of the piece on art and morality had lived up to his name; the spirit of *The Heretick*, Canning continued, was the spirit of youth. Blunt described Canning as 'an encourager of rebels', who protected boys from a reactionary art master called Christopher Hughes. Blunt was scathing about Hughes, a retired colonel who commanded the school OTC and whom other boys, including the aesthetes, liked enormously. But Blunt had no time, either at school or afterwards, for the colonel. Blunt said that Hughes believed that all art ended with the Pre-Raphaelites and that anything after that was 'wrong and wicked'. Christopher Lloyd had a totally different memory. 'Hughes was a very good art master and he encouraged Blunt although I have to say that he was a rather dim person.'[32] Betjeman also noted that Hughes was definitely provincial in his artistic tastes, but recalled that he took great trouble to arrange painting expeditions into the countryside.

No one could now dispute that Blunt was an influential character at Marlborough. Self-consciously he began publicly to defy school convention with the adoption of what he called 'the child cult'. He said:

We went out of our way to be irritatingly provocative. We used to walk down the aisle of chapel flaunting our silk handkerchiefs – I used to wear mine from the strap of my wrist watch and they could not stop me because there was no rule preventing it. And on Saturday evenings we used to go upfield to where other boys were playing rounders and infuriate them by playing catch with a large, brightly coloured ball right across their game.[33]

He was helped by having powerful allies, notably Canning and George Turner, headmaster after Norwood went to Harrow school in 1926. Most of the masters, Blunt thought, were just competent teachers who knew nothing about the arts and who were not interested in doing anything outside the classroom. There were exceptions: G. M. Sargeaunt, master of the Classical Upper Sixth, had founded his own, private religion based on ancient Greek Stoicism and had resigned from his housemastership, refusing to teach his boys religious instruction. He was tall, slim and had grey hair that he swept back dramatically from his forehead. MacNeice concluded that he was a genuine romantic, homesick for fifth-century Greece, who hated the modern world. His refuge was his little home in the town which he shared with his Dutch wife and piles of rare first editions.

Other masters among the fifty or so staff were just as colourful. There was the housemaster who flogged his boys before matches against rival teams to ensure they gave their all for the house. He also had a habit of throwing books at pupils if he thought they were not paying attention in class. There was an elderly master who found that caning was too exhausting; he punished miscreants by making them grind his coffee. And there was the alcoholic whom boys taunted by regularly bringing a dog into the classroom – on the assumption that he would think he was hallucinating. But he ignored the dog and took his favourite boys out to expensive dinners in town.

In the autumn of 1924 Blunt again decided to confront the school establishment:

In counter-attack I founded what I wanted to call an Art Society. I was championing the cause of Cézanne and the Impressionists. So I went to Canning and asked if he would be the president of the art society. One afternoon he met me on the touchline of a bitterly cold rugby game and told me that Hughes had been to him and said that if there was going to be an art society at Marlborough then he, Hughes, was going to be the president of it, which I suppose was not unreasonable. That idea had to be dropped but we wanted to have our society all the same. We could not think of a name; I suggested that we called it the Anonymous Society – well, nobody could object to that![34]

The formation of the society consolidated Blunt's reputation as one of the most interesting aesthetes in the school. MacNeice wrote later that Blunt had been the dominant intellectual in his house; a tall, very thin figure with deadly sharp elbows and the ribs of a famished saint:

He had cold blue eyes, a cutaway mouth and a wave of soft brown hair which fell over his forehead. When he was annoyed he had a tendency to pout and stick out his lip and then he looked simply sulky rather than handsome. He had a precocious knowledge of art and was contemptuous of what he called conservative authorities. He told everyone who would listen that he preferred Things to People and considered it very low to talk about politics.[35]

Blunt was just as intrigued by MacNeice. He wrote: 'By far my closest friend and the strongest and most important figure in the school at that time was Louis, who was already a person of extraordinary vivacity, imaginative force and charm. I shared a study with him in my last year and we formed the centre of a group of slightly bloody-minded rebels.'[36] The two made an unlikely couple. Blunt was austere and delicate; MacNeice, as well as being the aesthetes' literary consultant, enjoyed rugby, cricket and tennis, which he played with gusto. (He used to speculate over the likely result of a cricket match between a team of classical authors and a squad of Norse gods.) His idea of tennis was to volley and smash continually.

Others were soon drawn into the newly formed Anonymous Society. John Hilton, who was as tough as most hearties, was one recruit. At first Hilton had disliked Blunt, noting of one party in 1923: 'A nice select little party only, just as we were beginning tea, that terrible boy Blunt came to ask for the key to the classroom and of course had to stay to tea and monopolize the conversation.' Hilton had been equally dismissive about *The Heretick*: 'It is a very high-brow sort of thing I believe. Blunt's got a lot to do with it. He says it is meant to form a literary focus for the school.' When Hilton attended his first meeting of the Anonymous Society he mused: 'It isn't really eccentric. Its members include a member of the school cricket eleven.' But he soon threw himself into the spirit of rebellion and the so-called child cult, writing nonsense rhymes about oranges and wine and carmine crinolines. Hilton later wrote of Blunt:

Anthony pursued his scholarly study of the arts with the same, dedicated, unswerving intensity that he has given it ever since and with the most infectious enthusiasm. Old for his years in knowledge of the world and knowledge of where he was going he was a dominating figure both in his assurance and incandescent spirit and in his imposing height and large, handsome, long-haired head. We traipsed along eagerly with him as well in his more special domains of passion for Blake, Bruegel, El Greco . . . He was an austere hedonist living for disciplined gratification of the senses, with an eye for social esteem and seeking anchorage in system and scholarly detail. Louis was a ribald seer, an anarchic and mocking seeker after the deep springs of action and faith or at least a mythology which would keep hope alive in a world always transient and mostly trivial, sordid or brutal.[37]

The society used to meet at Canning's home in the town, after he had been persuaded by its members that he might properly become their president. They read papers, including one by MacNeice – which was described by Hilton as an 'astounding and magnificent conglomeration of dreams, fables, parables and theories, which made you want to howl with laughter' – and then ate large quantities of egg sandwiches. Blunt recalled:

> We used to have wonderful meetings. I remember reading a paper proving that art went underground at the end of the Renaissance, re-emerged at El Greco and then submerged again until Cézanne and the Impressionists. Hughes read a reply to this and in the middle I'm afraid that I got the giggles. With tears in his eyes he said: 'You've hurt me many times and now I'm hurting you.'[38]

The society, Blunt said, was a great success. True, they went from the serious to the frivolous and in doing so became philosophically disorientated. Blunt favoured the early Gothic revival while Betjeman had a passion for high Victorian Gothic and for Methodist chapel architecture. At the time Blunt thought that this was a joke but concluded later that Betjeman's continuing passion for such matters meant that the schoolboy joke had got the better of the adult poet. As early as 1922, Ellis Waterhouse could recall arguing with Blunt about whether Ingres was 'better' than Giorgione. Waterhouse recalled, too, that even then the shadow of Nicolas Poussin, the seventeenth-century French master who became one of Blunt's lifelong passions, had touched his friend.[39]

Helped by Wilfrid, Blunt was able to stay in touch with

developments in the art world. He was intrigued by
Baroque art, which had never been fashionable in England.
(In the summer of 1925, on a family holiday to Belgium,
Wilfrid and Anthony were reprimanded for showing an
unhealthy interest in northern Baroque architecture by
their parents who thought it vulgar and decadent.) He
discovered William Blake, the late-eighteenth-century
poet, philosopher and romantic visionary. Blunt later con-
gratulated himself for supporting Blake at a time when
'everyone else' dismissed Blake as a madman. But his most
significant 'discovery' was modern art.

In the early 1920s in Britain Cézanne and the other
Post-Impressionists were, thought Blunt, still regarded as
dangerous revolutionaries. He admired les Fauves (the
'Wild Beasts'), a group of French painters including
Matisse and Marquet, whose works were full of distortions,
flat patterns and violent colour. Blunt was a devotee of the
Cubists, who by now had moved well beyond impression-
ism to a more intellectual conception of form and colour.
Under the influence of the Cubists and inspired by English
critics such as Roger Fry and Clive Bell, Blunt believed in
Pure Form, art unsullied by decoration, fantasy or indi-
viduality; painting should have no literary content. He
carried this to absurd levels. Gauguin, the Post-
Impressionist French artist who had rejected Western civilization and sought Truth through the art of primitive
peoples, was considered 'too romantic and a bad thing';
Van Gogh caused the Marlburians major difficulties because he had shown 'religious urges and literary qualities'
and because he had admired people whom Blunt had
dismissed as worthless.

Blunt later admitted that much of what he had believed
about art at school was rubbish. He wrote:

> We were totally unaware of the degree to which we
> totally misunderstood these artists [El Greco and
> Bruegel] . . . we argued that the symbolical side of
> Bruegel was irrelevant – in fact we tried to deny its
> existence; in El Greco, the religious elements, which
> were very distasteful, couldn't be ignored, but they
> had, of course, no bearing on his qualities as an
> artist.[40]

All in all, Blunt conceded, they picked up a 'good many of
their wrong ideas of artists from the wrong ideas of artists
whom we rightly very much admired'. Art had to be
'obvious and geometrical, like Cubism'. Negro art was
acceptable because Picasso and Braque had been inspired
by it, but the Blunt aesthetes simply ignored what he later
called 'the elements of magic' intrinsic to it. English art,
though, was not even worth discussing: 'We were extremely snooty about English art which we thought was
either literary, as indeed a great deal of it was, or deriva-
tive.'[41] Occasionally, the Marlborough aesthetes decided
that something worth their attention was happening in the
English art world. When the American-born sculptor Jacob
Epstein was attacked for his relief of Rima, unveiled in
Hyde Park in 1923, they defended it 'because it was
Modern Art', though deep down they thought it was 'a sissy
little relief' and not worth the effort.

At this point Blunt knew nothing about Italian Futurism
or German Expressionism. The only art that mattered
came from France – or so he thought. He later defended
himself by emphasizing that there were few books covering
modern art, apart from the works of Roger Fry and Clive
Bell. He would visit specialist bookshops in London
whenever possible, but the choice was limited, and the only
effective way to keep in touch was to visit Paris and tour the
dealers in the rue de la Boétie.

Literature and art were vehicles for expressing the aesthetes' disgust with the Establishment. Blunt said they loathed everything about Victorian England. MacNeice dictated the circle's reading: Tolstoy, Thomas Hardy and Lucretius, late Latin and medieval poetry, Norse mythology and the Elizabethan poets. Shakespeare, however, was part of the hated Establishment, so Marlowe and Webster were designated more worthy of study. From the eighteenth century there was Voltaire, and Edward Lear provided inspiration for the aesthetes' child cultism. Blunt knew little about music but still drew up a list of artists who were 'acceptable': Bach, Handel and Mozart were good; Wagner, who was a romantic, was bad. The leading members of the Anonymous Society believed that they were destined to go out and change the world, at least in art and literature. They knew they were intelligent, though they hoped they were not 'clever' because that would be 'vulgar'.

The final few months at Marlborough allowed Blunt and MacNeice, who had won scholarships at Christmas 1925 to Cambridge and Oxford respectively, to enjoy themselves thoroughly. MacNeice confessed that they had nothing to do 'except amuse ourselves and infuriate everyone else'. They shared a study which they decorated with photographs of works by Picasso, and argued late into the night, using the then-fashionable language of the London intellectual world. They delighted in outraging what they called 'The Boy in the Street', and spent much of their time nurturing their reputation as *enfants terribles*. But they were young and believed that they were 'the cream of the world and that life was one big party.' As for politics and religion – moral values were a delusion and politics and religion a waste of time.[42]

Others were not so sure. John Hilton was less prone to self-conscious posturing, as befitted an applied mathemati-

cian. But he understood why they had all been so determined to escape into fantasy:

> We were growing up in the dregs of a beastly war. On
> Sunday afternoons the sixth form sat at the feet of the
> Master, Dr Norwood. We were supposed to discuss
> serious matters but I can't think what these were; except
> at one point Norwood asked the audience for their ideas
> on the supreme value. The only response, I think, was
> Anthony's offer of 'goodness, truth and beauty'. Nor-
> wood's face momentarily softened. We were being con-
> ditioned to be useful to King and Country and Empire
> though one of Norwood's sermons was about Wider
> Fellowship. If communism is counted as a religion then
> Anthony's later life could be said to conform to the
> pattern of our schooldays, of putting ideas above pat-
> riotism.
>
> When you mentioned that he [Blunt] might be narrow-
> minded in a tactful manner, you found that he was
> perfectly aware of it and indeed that he was proud of it.
> Perhaps this tendency to adopt blinkers, together with an
> inclination to defy authority, helped in his plunge into
> communist conspiracy.[43]

MacNeice, too, thought that Anthony had 'a flair for
bigotry', although this did not prevent the two friends
enjoying an idyllic summer in 1926. They would run over
the Downs, silk handkerchiefs floating in the breeze, and
return to school with their arms filled with azaleas. They
would then eat an iced walnut cake or bananas and cream in
their study, the white walls golden with the reflected sun-
light. In the afternoons they would lie naked on the banks
of the school bathing pool, eating strawberries and cream
while Anthony recited nonsense rhymes. One day Blunt

took an easel and canvas down to the pool to compose a
picture of a corrugated iron shed:

> The Bathing Master, who did not know about Pure
> Form, rushed up, scandalized, told us that it was strictly
> forbidden to take photos or paint pictures of the bathing
> place. When Anthony explained that he was only in-
> terested in the shed the master grudgingly gave him
> permission to continue; provided, he said, you don't put
> in any figures.[44]

The younger boys were in awe of the MacNeice–Blunt
set. Sir Peter Tennant, who later worked in banking,
diplomacy, business and academia, was four years younger
than Blunt. He said: 'One was full of awe as far as Blunt was
concerned. He was fearfully intellectual. He once talked to
an art class that I was in. He introduced me to modern art.
He was very kindly and extraordinarily nice to those who
wanted to know.'[45]

Politics held no interest for Blunt. The General Strike of
1926 seemed irrelevant, despite the fact that it was probably the most important crisis in Britain since the First
World War. The strike lasted for just nine days, from 4 to
12 May, although the miners, disgusted by the decision of
the Trades Union Congress to call off the fight, held out
until August. Blunt admitted that he found the whole thing
very silly. He was particularly irritated by the way that the
middle classes and Oxbridge undergraduates helped to
maintain vital services:

> Even a thing like the General Strike was treated very
> largely as a sort of joke when one's elder brothers and
> one's parents went and did curious things. It did not
> impinge on us as a real event at all. The most striking
> thing about the whole period at Marlborough was its

complete unreality and the fact that we lived in this little, self-contained world of art and literature, with no awareness of what was taking place in the outside world. Politics was simply a subject never discussed at all and what was going on in Europe at that time was no concern of ours. Inflation in Germany merely meant that one could get an incredibly cheap holiday. Fascism in Italy was something remote which we really did not take in. We lived in this protected existence, very contented but absolutely unreal. You might think that this was because we were terribly rich or something; not at all, we were not any of us well-off but our own family system and the school system provided a sort of shell into which we could retreat and where we were extremely happy.[46]

Blunt was eighteen when he left school and must have had some sort of homosexual experience – though no one can be sure how far he had gone in these romantic encounters. Sir Peter Tennant said:

Marlborough was riddled with homosexuality. I suppose all public schools are full of buggery. Masters were deeply involved in it. I won't name names but as far as I can make out they were practising homosexuals and did it with some boys. Some of the boys were ambidextrous. One chap was sent down for buggery and for producing a bastard with a servant girl. He was a very lusty fellow. I remember the headmaster, George Turner, giving a speech, saying, we will have no more buggery.[47]

E. G. H. Kempson admitted that while homosexuality was not discussed, it was recognized as a fact of life that some boys would 'be interested in' younger boys, but if 'this' kept on happening then boys would be expelled. There is no record of Blunt ever having been warned about approaches to other boys. John Hilton, who was never attracted to other boys, thought that most Marlburians only went as far as sending each other notes. MacNeice, however, recalled seeing older boys prowling around the toilets, an area masters did not bother with, after breakfast looking for their favourites. Although sex was being talked about more openly in the 1920s, sex education was almost non-existent. Parents of boys at public schools hoped that their children's ignorance would mean that relationships never went beyond the exchange of harmless love letters. But many boys, such as Wilfrid and Anthony Blunt, did not grow out of this supposedly temporary phase. At Marlborough the boys had the facts of life outlined to them by embarrassed masters. Louis MacNeice recalled that in the weeks before boys were confirmed, at fifteen or sixteen, they were told that when they met a woman they should think of her as their sister or mother. Masturbation, they were warned, would destroy the body and send the sinner into the madhouse. Wilfrid recalled his talk with Clifford Canning when the master brushed aside the question of sex by saying that Wilfrid's father must have outlined the key points. Wilfrid lied and said that this was correct, leaving Canning's room as ignorant as he had been when he had gone in. Other housemasters began discussions with boys by suggesting that they might have noticed a little tube between their legs. Of course, boys gossiped and information on the various functions of the little tube circulated from the initiated to the uninitiated, but such information was not always accurate and there was no one available for boys who were confused by the swirling emotions of puberty to confide in. Since there were no girls the boys flirted with each other. MacNeice said that most of the older boys had 'mild homosexual romances – an occasion for billets and elaborately engineered rendezvous'. He selected a sixteen-year-old with large, grey, feminine eyes and invited him to tea. He then wrote a poem and was warned by Anthony to be careful of being influenced by Tennyson. But MacNeice was resolutely heterosexual and soon forgot the sixteen-year-old. Wilfrid was twenty-eight before he accepted that he would never be attracted to a woman. He wrote: 'So ignorant were most of us, in those days, of the very existence of homosexuality that I think that till then I had been clinging – though only just – to the hope that one day "Miss Right" would come along.'[48] But it was not Miss Right who swept Wilfrid off his feet. It was an eighteen-year-old boy. Still a virgin, panic-stricken, horrified at the discovery that he was sexually attracted to another man, Wilfrid sought the help of a Harley Street specialist. It was possible, he was told, that he could be helped, but it would be a long and expensive treatment without any guarantee of success. Much better, said the doctor, for Wilfrid to accept his 'affliction', rather like a disabled person. It was not until he was in his thirties that Wilfrid came to terms with his sexuality. He realized gradually that, while homosexuality was still illegal, there were ways to enjoy a reasonable sex life. A colleague at Haileybury told him that he had an entirely separate life outside the school; he had an Irish boyfriend in London 'for emergencies' whom he could see when he was feeling lonely, and several resorts to which he retreated during the school holidays. It was not ideal but it was better than nothing. Despite a protective shell of sarcasm, Wilfrid was a more modest and sensitive character than his younger brother. Where Anthony was confident, Wilfrid was self-deprecating. Wilfrid seems not to have heard Freud preach that it was sexual repression that was immoral. Anthony had no such problems. He may have left Marlborough a virgin but it was clear from his private life at Cambridge and then in London that his agonies over being homosexual in a heterosexual world were mercifully short.

CHAPTER 3
Cambridge Romantics

Anthony Blunt, now a gangling six feet two inches tall, arrived at Trinity College, Cambridge, in October 1926 knowing that while he might not be able to match the elegance of many of the other freshmen he would eclipse most of them academically. He had a limited income and few clothes, though he was proud of his Oxford bags, the trousers that every fashionable student wore. He collected his dark blue Trinity gown from Arthur Shepherds, the tailors, and moved into lodgings, popularly known as the Ritz, not far from Trinity Great Gate. Already he felt at home; indeed Cambridge, he said later, was no more than 'an extension of life at Marlborough'.[1]

Blunt was one of 700 undergraduates at Trinity, the biggest and wealthiest Cambridge college, which lived off endowments dating from the Middle Ages. Like every freshman he spent his first few days wading through invitations to join numerous university and college clubs and societies. He was inundated with letters from the town's booksellers, grocers, tailors, shirt-makers and shoe-makers. Since he had just enough money to live on he had little use for most of these establishments, but other students were determined to spend a fortune developing their own self-conscious style. Cecil Beaton, for example, an Old Harrovian who became a photographer and designer, had begun his Cambridge life as he intended to continue it:

wearing an evening jacket, red shoes, black-and-white trousers, and a huge blue cravat. He started busily planning to buy for his room green curtains, green cushions, green china and tall, twisted wooden candlesticks. As the weather got chillier, he brightened the Cambridge scene with an outfit comprising fur gauntlet gloves, a cloth-of-gold tie, a scarlet jersey and Oxford bags.[2]

Blunt, on the other hand, looked what he was: a scholarship boy living on a limited income. 'He wasn't exactly shabbily dressed but he certainly didn't exude money,' said George Pinney, who went up to Caius College in 1927. 'I think he was pretty hard up . . . But then he had quite grand connections. His father was a friend of Queen Mary. I knew that then so I suppose Blunt must have told me.'[3] Steven Runciman, younger son of the Liberal statesman Viscount Runciman, who as an undergraduate carried a parakeet on his heavily-ringed fingers and who later became an historian, had little time for Blunt:

> To be perfectly honest I never frightfully liked Anthony. He was always very supercilious and I rather disliked being patronized when I was a young don. He was tall; unkind people might say he was an old-fashioned type of aesthete. He was always, I think, rather pleased with himself. But he could be very good company. I never felt terribly at ease with him in all the years I knew him, right up to the end.[4]

Pinney's circle of undergraduate friends included Trinity students like Prince Chula Chakrabongse, a member of the Thai royal family and an Old Harrovian man-about-town who would have been heir to the Thai throne had his mother not been Russian. He was rich, intelligent and handsome. He had an allowance of £500 a year which he topped up by borrowing from his cousin, Prince Damras, a diplomat in the Thai embassy in London. He was one of the most glamorous figures in Cambridge, yet he became close friends with Blunt, the badly dressed son of an unknown churchman. They had one thing in common: both could boast friendship with the British Royal Family, though Chula actually lunched occasionally with the King and Queen at Buckingham Palace, while all Blunt could do was explain that his family were 'awfully close' to the Palace. Chula described Blunt as 'one of the bright stars of the intellectual firmament', but that did not mean that the prince felt he had to copy Blunt and spend his evenings in earnest, erudite discussions. The prince had no compunction about enjoying himself; he had money and had no qualms about spending £600 a year on cars alone (about three times the average annual wage). A young man such as Chula was rarely short of company. But Cambridge, he noted, was full of students who always seemed to be alone, even when they were eating in the imposing, high-ceilinged hall, watched over by a portrait of the college's founder, Henry VIII. Sometimes these students might be asked to join the Master of Trinity, Sir Joseph John Thompson, a scientist who was always seen decked out in a bowler hat and ancient overcoat, and whose favourite topic of conversation at meals was sport (this made him, thought Blunt, a person to be avoided at all costs). Chula felt sorry for college contemporaries who seemed to know no one. 'One soon sorted oneself out and went to Hall with one's friends and generally sat in the same places. I have known men who, although they dined in Hall . . . for three years, never got to know anybody in their own colleges.'[5]

Chula was fascinated by English débutantes (and eventually married one) but he admitted, too, that he found other men attractive. This did not mean that he was a

practising homosexual. Exaggerated shows of affection for
friends of the same sex were perfectly normal; most students had only ever had male friends and it did not mean
that every public schoolboy was a homosexual. Nonetheless, there was a strong undercurrent of homosexuality at
the university, which undergraduates who did not come
from public schools found unsettling. Malcolm Muggeridge, the journalist and author, had come up to Selwyn
College from Selhurst Grammar School. He thought that
being homosexual was simply 'an accepted practice that
was caught up with the ethos of having been to a boarding-
school'. Muggeridge viewed most of his fellow-students
with contempt; not because so many had affairs with each
other, but because they were such ignorant snobs:

> Public schoolboys, whatever their particular school –
> from the most famous like Eton, to the most obscure –
> had a language of their own which I scarcely understood,
> games they played which I could neither play nor interest
> myself in, ways and attitudes which they took for granted
> but which were foreign to me – for instance, their accept-
> ance of sodomy as more or less normal behaviour . . .
> The University, when I was there, was very largely a
> projection of public school life and mores, and a similar
> atmosphere of homosexuality tended to prevail. There
> was also a hangover from Wildean decadence, with
> aesthetes who dressed in velvet, painted their rooms in
> strange colours, hung Aubrey Beardsley prints on their
> walls and read *Les Fleurs du Mal*. The nearest I came to
> being personally involved with these was when a High
> Church ordinand after dinner read to me from Swin-
> burne's *Songs Before Sunrise* in a darkened room faintly
> smelling of incense. I emerged unscathed.[6]

Blunt's first love affair at Cambridge was probably with another Trinity College student, Peter Montgomery, a talented musician and the second son of Major-General Hugh Maude de Fellenberg Montgomery. Peter's uncle later became Chief of the Imperial General Staff, Field-Marshal Sir Archibald Montgomery-Massingberd; his second cousin was Bernard Montgomery, the legendary Second World War commander. His father had an estate at Blessingbourne, Fivemiletown, in Northern Ireland though he had been educated at an English public school, Wellington College. The friendship between Peter Montgomery and Blunt lasted throughout their lives. Most of their mutual gay friends assumed that they had begun as lovers and then, in the parlance of the homosexual world, become sisters. One of Blunt's wartime lovers, Jack Hewit, recalled: 'Peter Montgomery was particularly timid and shy . . . What was Peter like? Well, he was tall, slightly stooping with fair rather wavy hair and a broad forehead. He had quite a sensual mouth, a cleft chin and blue eyes.'[7] Another friend, the Irish writer, Robert Harbinson, who became a keen observer of the Blunt circle after the war, thought: 'Anthony had an uncanny hold over Peter. They were in love, at least for a time. Hugh, who was one of Peter's brothers, said that Blunt was an evil influence. He put it down to Anthony's atheism.'[8]

Peter Montgomery was always terrified that his family would discover his homosexuality. He knew very well that his relatives in Ulster, many of whom were members of the Protestant Orange Order, would be outraged if the Montgomery family name were ever publicly associated with homosexuality. Of course, Blunt and Montgomery had much more in common than sex. For example, they both enjoyed the arts (Montgomery became an accomplished conductor). Most of their friends were astonished when the delicate and gentle Montgomery joined the Intelligence

Corps at the outbreak of war. Unlike Blunt, he stayed
in the army, ending as the ADC to the Viceroy of India,
Field Marshal Lord Wavell. 'It was difficult to believe that
Peter could do much else in life than occasionally conduct
an orchestra for the BBC,' said Robert Harbinson.[9]
Montgomery's wartime career haunted Blunt. He always
insisted that 'dear Peter' had never been involved in
espionage and took enormous trouble to deny allegations
that his friend had been implicated. Montgomery admitted
that he 'had never had secrets from Anthony' – though
that did not mean that the habitually secretive Blunt told
Montgomery about his work for the Russians. Montgomery said, too, that since the war he had always feared
'that it was all going to come out and then I would get the
chop'.[10]

   Although homosexuality was a tolerated fact of life at the
university it was as illegal there as anywhere else, and gay
students knew that they risked a humiliating court appearance if they were ever caught. Blunt and his new boyfriend,
therefore, like all homosexuals, had to be careful, pretending that they were just close, platonic friends. This tactic
was surprisingly successful, especially with students who
were not gay and who did not understand the nuances of the
gay world. For example, George Pinney, who thought he
knew Montgomery fairly well, had no idea that the two
were lovers. But others did notice. Steven Runciman, for
one, knew that Montgomery was devoted to Blunt. Many
homosexuals, including Anthony Blunt, went out of their
way to take risks; but there were many others who found
the constant deceiving of friends and family an intolerable
strain. It may have reassured the latter group to know that
so many respected dons were homosexual. There was the
Trinity poet A. E. Housman who, Auden had said,
'seemed so perfectly to express the sensibilities of the male
adolescent'; there was the novelist, E. M. Forster; and

there was Andrew Gow, a classics don who was a Fellow of Trinity and Housman's biographer.

Gow and Blunt soon became close friends; indeed, Gow remained one of the main guiding forces in Blunt's life, a mentor and confidant until his death in 1978, aged ninety-one. Noel Annan, a Fellow of King's who became one of the country's most influential academics, said of Gow:

> He belonged very much to the high and dry Trinity don set who took as their paragon A. E. Housman. Like Housman, of course, Gow was unmarried. I didn't like him. He was a tremendous man for not admiring anything very much. He was a rock-ribbed conservative and wasn't interested in politics. He was clearly crypto-homosexual but never laid a finger on anybody. Like all that generation they were perfectly open about what they liked: bright young men, preferably good-looking ones, and launching them into life.[11]

The Times obituary on 4 February 1978 could not avoid criticism:

> To many Gow appeared as a rather grim, censorious person, gifted with a tartness of language that lost nothing in its delivery. Fastidious, with a high sense of duty, he was scornful of what he reckoned as slipshod, pretentious, ill-considered. His prejudices were strong and he did not conceal them, though in matters of moment they seldom betrayed him into decisions hasty or unfair . . .

But Gow had a wide circle of friends, who, said *The Times*, knew him to be 'wise, warm-hearted and possessed of a rich sense of humour'. Blunt clearly felt that *The Times* had been too harsh and on 11 February he sent this tribute to the newspaper:

During the years after his return to Cambridge in 1924 he was almost the only don to take a positive interest in the art of the past and his rooms were the one place where one could find a good library of books about the Italian Renaissance, a fine collection of photographs, of paintings and above all, stimulating conversation about the arts in general. Though his influence in this field only spread to a relatively small circle of undergraduates it had a vitally important effect on them and through them on others in Cambridge and eventually elsewhere. Though he had clear ideas on what was good and what was bad he was willing to discuss the ideas of even the most heterodox student and often helped to clarify his thought.

Gow built up a magnificent collection of late-nineteenth-century French paintings and drawings which he bequeathed to the Fitzwilliam Museum in Cambridge. Blunt prepared the catalogue for that bequest, and prefaced it with a fulsome tribute to Gow.

Most Cambridge students who knew Gow had mixed feelings about him; he was brilliant and, if he liked undergraduates, was capable of great kindness. He had been George Orwell's tutor at Eton and had won the writer's lifelong gratitude for his support and encouragement. But he could also be extraordinarily rude and unforgiving. Martin Robertson, a Trinity classicist in the 1930s, recalled:

Gow was a typical bachelor don in the old mode (and a very good classical scholar). He was homosexual, at least in inclination, and a fine connoisseur and collector. He was devoted to Anthony, who in turn was very fond of him and who was exceedingly good about coming to see

Gow when he was old and ill. Gow would, I am sure (for what my opinion's worth) have been very upset and horrified by the revelations.[12]

Peter Montgomery was just one of many well-connected, potentially influential undergraduates who were close to Blunt. There was nothing sinister about this; John Hilton thought that Blunt just had a natural flair for cultivating the unusually talented. There were future writers, poets and artists as well as some of the cleverest young dons in the university. Blunt kept in regular contact with his friends at Oxford, including Hilton and Louis MacNeice. They would eat at The Trout, a pub on the Isis, mulling over the days at Marlborough and comparing experiences from their two universities. Blunt seemed as intellectually vigorous as ever, as Hilton remarked when he wrote to his own parents after a weekend in Cambridge in March 1927: 'I had tea with Blunt and Co. and lunch the next day. His chief asset is an extraordinary vivacity; he is the perfect conductor for the life force.'[13] Once Blunt captained Cambridge in a scratch hockey match against an Oxford side led by the poet Stephen Spender: the only recorded case of Blunt volunteering for a sporting event. It was supposed to be a leisurely encounter between gentlemen aesthetes, said Hilton, but Cambridge, rather unfairly, had recruited a rugby blue. Blunt's performance was, he added, enthusiastic but ungainly.

Anthony Blunt seemed to be even more intolerant than he had been at school. That narrow-mindedness which had always been so irritating was now more noticeable than ever; he was loudly critical of a wide range of people, including the celebrated philosopher Ludwig Wittgenstein, who had rooms above his own. Blunt himself confessed that 'Our sheltered existence went on through the late twenties . . . and we continued to live in this kind of dream world, spinning our intellectual webs.'[14]

In the Easter vacation of 1928, Hilton and Blunt
travelled to Vienna together, intent on improving their
German. Hilton remembered:

> It was bitterly cold – Vienna streets were lined with banks
> of frozen slush. And I was wound round with an excess-
> ively dark muffler of my mother's; I must have looked a
> caricature anarchist. Plain-clothes police followed us
> back to the train and demanded papers. We broke the
> journey to walk, through the brilliant sun and deep
> shade, to the Baroque monastery of St Florian – dazzling
> white and ochre without; explosive gold and colour in the
> church. This was of course the era before aesthetics were
> overlaid by politics. Our Viennese families lived far
> apart, but we met often enough to spend many hours
> attending to pictures, palaces, operas. Breughels in par-
> ticular. Anthony left before me, but we spent a couple of
> days with rucksacks looking at the monasteries on or
> near the stretch of Danube called the Wachau. The
> fitting climax was the fabulous Melk, whose photographs
> we had pored over in the close confines of our studies
> at Marlborough. From our hotel window Anthony
> preached a sermon to the empty moonlit street.[15]

Blunt returned to Cambridge to resume his course in
modern languages, having dropped mathematics to the
surprise of his parents, who thought that that had guaranteed him a solid career. He had concluded that he was really
just interested in art. He wanted to become an art historian
– though art history was recognized as an independent
academic discipline only on the Continent – and thought
that languages would be more relevant than the mental
gymnastics of pure mathematics.

Many of Oxbridge's self-appointed intellectual élite were
obsessed with the rivalry between aesthetes and hearties.

The majority of students, of course, belonged, consciously anyway, to neither camp. They studied, played sport, had affairs and then vanished into the obscurity of the colonial service, the Church, the army, teaching or the civil service. But the writers of memoirs and diaries had no doubt that this clash – between the cultured, self-aware aesthetes and the philistine sportsmen – was one of the vital elements in university life during the late 1920s. When MacNeice arrived in Oxford in October 1926 he observed:

Oxford in 1926 was just at the end of its period of postwar deliberate decadence – the careful matching of would-be putrescent colours. At the first party I went to there was no drink but champagne, a young man played by himself with a spotted stuffed dog on a string and the air was full of the pansy phrase 'my dear'. I discovered that in Oxford homosexuality and 'intelligence', hetero-sexuality and brawn, were almost inexorably paired. This left me out in the cold and I took to drink.[16]

Prince Chula thought:

Oxford then was clearly divided between the 'Aesthetes' and the 'Hearties', but the division was less clearly defined at Cambridge. One aesthete I knew had his sitting-room painted black and the ceiling red with the heavy silver curtains permanently drawn so that no daylight penetrated the room, and he often wore a black polo-neck sweater with a pearl necklace and drank vodka even on a warm afternoon. Strangely enough he be-longed to Jesus College, the accepted citadel of the 'hearties' but living outside, and after some talk about smashing up his rooms, it was finally decided that he was a sportsman really to have dared put up such a show. There were also many other aesthetes who were not quite so odd; they discussed art and recited modern poetry, but I also knew men who really enjoyed art without finding it necessary to behave so strangely, such as Anthony Blunt.[17]

Goronwy Rees, a brilliant young Welsh student, whose life was to become inextricably and disastrously linked with Blunt's, went up to Oxford in 1926. He said that there was a clear social divide between the hearties and the aesthetes:

The Hearty saw himself as representing virility as opposed to decadence, the Aesthete was the self-conscious champion of culture against barbarism. Hearties went in for beer and games, club scarves and blazers, fast cars and motor cycles, picking up girls on Saturday night . . . and throwing Quintin Hogg into Mercury, the pool that adorns Tom Quad at Christchurch. Aesthetes were dedicated to poetry and the arts, they were, or affected to be, homosexual, spent their holidays in Germany and came back with stories of the wonderful decadence of the Weimar Republic . . . Between these two camps there raged an undeclared war; they represented as it were the two poles towards which undergraduate life gravitated. They were divided by a kind of plain or marsh, neutral ground in which the majority of undergraduates had their being, uncommitted to either side but each responding in his particular way to the pull exerted by the one or the other.[18]

A. J. P. Taylor, the historian, was then an undergraduate at Oriel College, Oxford. He watched the antics of the aesthetes, led by Harold Acton, with amazement:

At the George restaurant, their great gathering place, waitresses – being safe by their sex from the attentions of undergraduates – served the food, and painted boys, themselves undergraduates, walked up and down the aisles until they got a free meal in return for their services . . . I never signalled to any of the painted boys, many of them now elderly clergymen.[19]

MacNeice was not just fighting the hearties; he felt that he was waving what he called 'the banner of intelligence'. He despised most of the grammar-school boys, such as Goronwy Rees, who had battled their way by sheer brain power to Oxbridge. MacNeice was at Merton College which, to his disgust, had an unusually large number of grammar-school entrants:

The climate was muggy and there was none of the geniuses around that there ought to be . . . I hated my tutorials – the endless interpolation into Greek composi- tions . . . I thought that was a game for the 'monsters', i.e. the grammar-school boys, those distorted little crea- tures with black teeth who held their forks by the middle and were set on making a career. I used to sit wedged between these monsters at dinner, listening supercili- ously as they discussed Noël Coward and Bernard Shaw; in my opinion no one intelligent would mention such writers.[20]

During the 1920s few Oxbridge students had much sym- pathy for communism. Cambridge, like Oxford, had rallied behind the government during the General Strike of 1926. About 2600 Cambridge undergraduates – half the student population – registered for emergency duty and many were allocated vital strike-breaking duties. Many dons also ral- lied to the defence of the forces of law and order. Joseph Needham, the brilliant biochemist who became a commu- nist in the 1930s, drove a steam engine from Cambridge to London. Those students and dons who could not be bothered to become involved regarded the strike as a useful opportunity to catch up on their reading. Steven Runciman, for example, said that he managed to read every volume of the Cambridge Modern History series. Most students had never thought about politics; they had been brought up to believe that their lives would be a smooth progression from school to Oxbridge and thence to a solid, respectable career. The empire offered enough jobs for even the dullest boy, providing that he wore the right school tie and spoke with the correct accent. And there was no reason why that should not go on for ever.

Naturally, the trades unions, the Labour Party and the Communist Party of Great Britain (CPGB) did not see it in quite those terms. The Left in Britain was slow to forgive the students for their performance during the strike. The government, however, was delighted. 'You have to be proud of your young chaps; healthy, strong, keen and entirely the right stuff,' Admiral Sir Charles Royds told the Cambridge university vice-chancellor when the strike had been smashed.

Some students simply could not afford to be involved in politics. Without private incomes to fall back on or relatives to pull strings for them they knew that everything depended on a good degree. Dick White had gone up to Christ Church, Oxford, perhaps the most snobbish of any Oxbridge college, in 1926. (White went on to become head of both MI5 and MI6 and became arguably the most influential figure in the history of British Intelligence.) White's parents were separated and it was only because he had won an exhibition (a college award) that he was able to go to Oxford. He was a superb athlete, which meant that he was immediately welcomed by the college. During his time at Oxford he ran the mile in a creditable four minutes twenty-one seconds, which, as he said later, was rather respectable since athletes then tended to train on chocolate biscuits and beer – always assuming that they could be bothered to train at all. White said:

> It was pretty entirely a college for ambitious well-to-do young men who were going places. There were several contemporaries of mine who were cabinet ministers later. That was the atmosphere. At that time you were an obedient scholar; you took your work seriously and didn't kick everything to the wind. I can't recollect any political discussions at the time . . . In my day you either went into the diplomatic service or politics . . . that was what Christ Church was there to produce . . . young men of the ruling class. I wanted to get a good job . . . and that wasn't altogether easy.[21]

Nevertheless, a few students risked the abuse of their contemporaries and sided with the strikers. Maurice Dobb, the son of a prosperous Gloucestershire landowner, first became interested in Marxism while he was a schoolboy at Charterhouse, and by the time he became a student at Cambridge after the First World War he was a fervent Marxist. He had fair hair, a bright red face and an infectious, warm nature, but he soon found that personal popularity would not save him. When he tried to convert his fellow-students at Pembroke College he was thrown, fully dressed, into the river Cam by a group of hearties, who knew from the newspapers that 'Reds' were a Bad Thing. Dobb, however, was undeterred by this setback. He became a Fellow of Trinity and by the 1920s was one of the country's few Marxist economists. He was a driving force behind the foundation of the Communist Party of Great Britain in the summer of 1920 and became a member of its central committee that year. Dobb remained largely isolated. He argued for the dictatorship of the proletariat in Britain but he insisted that the subsequent nationalization of the country's resources did not have to mean greater bureaucracy. Like all communists, he believed in the miracle that had taken place in the Soviet Union. And like all communists he saw in Britain only injustice: the exploitation of the weak by the rich. He was always scrupulously polite to his students, who mostly came from the ruling class which would have to be crushed by the revolution. But that revolution seemed a long time coming in Britain. In the critical days before the General Strike, twelve leading activists of the CPGB had been jailed for sedition under the Mutiny Act of 1797. In raids on the party's headquarters in King Street, London, the police had found documents which apparently proved that Moscow wanted to wrest control of the working-class movement from the Labour Party, which believed that socialism could be achieved peacefully. Some communists argued perversely that 1926 had actually been a glorious victory – an argument which showed how a well-trained communist theoretician could see success where others could see only defeat – but Dobb knew that the party had failed to take advantage of the opportunity provided by the 1926 strike to reverse the disheartening decline in support.

The CPGB had had trouble locating the revolutionary potential of the working class, which distrusted a party that had men like Rajani Palme Dutt, a part Indian, part Scandinavian academic, as its main theoretician. The party was altogether too foreign for conservative workers. True, it was led by a man with an unmistakably English name – Albert Inkpen – but that was not enough. The communists also had the problem of how to present the Comintern – the organization which the Soviets insisted all communist parties had to join. Lenin said that 'all decisions of the congresses of the Communist International [Comintern] are binding on all parties belonging to the Communist International.' The British communists had no choice but to accept Lenin's 'invitation' to join the Comintern, although some of them must have realized that being overtly controlled by the Soviets would only further damage their public image. Lenin decided that he did not trust the British communists to run their own affairs, even on this limited basis. He sent Michael Borodin, travelling under the alias George Brown, to London as the Comintern's representative in London. Borodin was soon picked up by Scotland Yard's Special Branch, after promptings by MI5, Britain's counter-intelligence service. The hapless Borodin was given a short prison sentence and deported.

The few students who did try and rally to the communist cause in 1926 found that the party seemed to have gone on holiday. A. J. P. Taylor was both a communist and a member of the Labour Club. With his friend Tom Driberg, the future Labour MP, Taylor set off to find out which barricade they would be manning. They were disappointed. Taylor wrote:

> Tom Driberg and I, expecting to lead the coming revolution in Oxford, decided to seek instructions from Communist headquarters. We . . . sought the headquarters in King Street and found them bolted and barred. After much banging by us, there was a rattling of chains and an elderly Scotch communist called Bob Steward appeared. He said, 'There's no one here. I am only the caretaker. Get along home with ye.' These were the only instructions I ever received from the Communist Party of Great Britain. I developed a great admiration for the British working class . . . the General Strike destroyed my faith, such as it was, in the Communist Party. The Party that was supposed to lead the working class had played no part in the strike except to be a nuisance . . . I lapsed from the Communist Party . . . thus escaping the soul torments which troubled so many intellectuals during the 1930s.[22]

CHAPTER 4
The Secret Apostles

In May 1928 Anthony Blunt returned to Cambridge from his invigorating holiday in Austria with John Hilton. Shortly after term began Blunt was invited to join the Apostles, otherwise known as the Cambridge Conversazione Society, sometimes simply as the Society. The invitation delighted him; to be asked to join the Apostles was, and still is, the ultimate accolade for any undergraduate with intellectual pretensions. Apostles had become eminent academics, writers, artists, civil servants and scientists. And, like freemasons, they knew that their duty was to help other members of their society. Founded in 1820 by George Tomlinson, an Anglican bishop, it had included among its early members the poet Alfred, Lord Tennyson, and by the 1920s was recognized as the forum for the intellectual super-élite of the university. It was far more than just another debating club. There were only two, perhaps three, new members each year. The membership list was secret and Apostles swore never to discuss the society's rituals. Guy Burgess after his defection talked happily about his work for MI5 and the Foreign Office, but refused ever to discuss his time as an Apostle.

Students could not *apply* to join the society; potential recruits, called 'embryos', were spotted first by an Apostle and then, if they were considered suitably 'Apostolic', were sponsored for membership at a society meeting. Like freemasons, too, the Apostles had evolved their own private language to describe their affairs. The first meeting for a new member was his 'birth'; his sponsor was called his 'father'. After he had been welcomed into the society he addressed his fellow-Apostles as 'brother'. The King's College classics don, John Sheppard, who became Provost of the college in 1933, thought that an Apostle needed to be 'very brilliant and extremely nice'. The society met on Saturday evenings in Cambridge and held annual dinners in London, attended by both Apostles and by Angels, the term used to describe members who had 'taken wings' and moved from Cambridge. Michael Straight, who became an Apostle in 1936, described fifty years later how he had been initiated:

> We met in [Maynard] Keynes's rooms. I held up my right hand and repeated a fearful oath, praying that my soul would writhe in unendurable pain for the rest of eternity if I so much as breathed a word about the society to anyone who was not a member. It seemed a bit harsh, but Sheppard, who carried a cushion with him wherever he went, patted me with his free hand and told me not to be alarmed.[1]

It was a Trinity–King's dominated society, and Apostles' meetings were always held in rooms in one of the two colleges. They opened with a 'brother' standing on the 'hearthrug' (it was not necessary actually to have a rug) and reading out a paper on a philosophical subject agreed the previous week. Once the speaker, known as the 'moderator', had finished his essay, the other Apostles drew lots to decide the speaking order; then, one by one, they moved to the hearthrug. The debates were supposed to be abstract but they did not have to be serious. Bertrand Russell, for example, once wrote an elegant paper setting out the advantages and disadvantages of electing God to the society. At the end of the debate sardines on toast, known as 'whales', were served. Apostles (and Angels) included some of the greatest minds in the country. There was Maynard Keynes, the economist; the historian, G. M. Trevelyan; the art critic and champion of the Impressionists, Roger Fry, an honorary Fellow of King's; the novelist, E. M. Forster; the biographer and essayist, Lytton Strachey; and the philosophers G. E. Moore and Ludwig Wittgenstein. It was, in fact, the Cambridge branch of the London-based Bloomsbury group.

Apostles believed that they were striking out bravely into uncharted intellectual and moral territory. They were proponents of a new world order in which the intellect and love would matter more than anything. Keynes described his own days as a student Apostle:

> We were the forerunners of a new dispensation; we were not afraid of anything . . . Nothing mattered except states of mind . . . timeless, passionate states of contemplation and communion . . . The appropriate subjects of passionate contemplation and communion were a beloved person, beauty and truth, and one's prime objects in life were love, the creation and enjoyment of aesthetic experience and the pursuit of knowledge. Of these, love came a long way first.[2]

Apostles had a very high opinion of themselves. When John Sheppard was once asked if anyone had ever resigned, he said: 'There was a horrid man long ago who was thought to be Apostolic and who, indeed, was elected to the society. He said then that his only interest was in being elected and that he could not afford to waste his time by attending meetings. His name is never mentioned in the society.'[3]

Wittgenstein, who had become Apostle number 252 in

1912, left Cambridge at the outbreak of the First World War. He enlisted in the Austrian army and was captured on the Italian front in 1918. In 1919 he decided to abandon philosophy; he gave his money to relatives and announced that he intended to lead a simple, ascetic life. He worked as a schoolteacher, then tried to make his living as an architect and finally became a gardener in a convent. His admirers insisted that he was wasting his unique talents and, in 1929, he returned to Cambridge. But the Apostles made their displeasure clear. He had abandoned the life of the mind and in doing that had rejected everything the society held precious. At their meeting in Keynes's rooms on 20 April 1929 the Apostles generously decided to forgive him. The meeting decided to 'absolve him from his excommunication'.

By the late 1920s the society was overwhelmingly gay; its members argued adroitly that homosexuality was purer than heterosexuality. John Sheppard told his 'brothers' that sex between men was the most exalted love in the world.

Many of the Apostles were also part of the Bloomsbury group during the 1920s. The Bloomsberries, as they called themselves, had grown up around Thoby Stephen and his two sisters, Virginia (Woolf) and Vanessa (Bell), after they had left Cambridge in 1905 and moved to London. They were mainly Cambridge-educated writers, philosophers, economists and artists united in their 'scepticism towards politics and tolerance in sex'. Bloomsbury believed in the importance of the arts and championed something called 'liberal humanism'. But the group had no true corporate identity; it could have existed only in a society whose intellectual élite was drawn from the tight circle of the public schools and Oxbridge. It was based on shared experiences and personal friendships more than on any precise philosophy. If it had a central ethos then it was drawn from G. E. Moore's book, *Principia Ethica*, which had been published in 1903. In that Moore concluded that 'affectionate personal relations and the contemplation of beauty were the only supremely good states of mind.' If Bloomsbury can be said to have had a guiding philosophy then that is as good a summary as any. Lytton Strachey (Apostle number 239) wrote to Moore (Apostle number 229):

> I am carried away. I think your book has not only wrecked and shattered all writers on Ethics from Aristotle and Christ to Herbert Spencer and Mr Bradley, it has not only laid the true foundations of Ethics . . . It is the scientific method, deliberately applied, for the first time, to Reasoning. Is that true? You perhaps shake your head, but henceforth who will be able to tell lies one thousand times as easily as before? The truth, there can be no doubt, is really now upon the march. I date from Oct. 1903 the beginning of the Age of Reason.[4]

Bloomsbury had set itself firmly against the First World War. In 1916 Lytton Strachey told the Conscientious Objectors' Tribunal:

> I have a conscientious objection to assisting, by any deliberate action of mine, in carrying on the war. This objection is not based on religious belief, but upon moral considerations, at which I arrived after long and careful thought. I do not wish to assert the extremely general proposition that I should never in any circumstances, be absolute upon a point so abstract . . . would appear to me to be unreasonable. At the same time, my feeling is directed not simply against the present war: I am convinced that the whole system by which it is sought to settle international disputes by force is profoundly evil; and that, so far as I am concerned, I should be doing

wrong to take any active part in it . . . I shall not act against those convictions, whatever the consequences may be.[5]

Frances Marshall (later Frances Partridge), who went up to Girton College, Cambridge in 1918, had been brought up by her parents to believe that anything the men and women of Bloomsbury said must be right. After graduating she moved back to London and worked in the group's bookshop that had been opened in the ground floor of a communal house in Taviton Street, Bloomsbury, used by the London literati – Virginia and Leonard Woolf, the Bells, Maynard Keynes and Lytton Strachey. Frances concluded:

To begin with, they were not a group, but a number of very different individuals, who shared certain attitudes to life, and happened to be friends or lovers. To say they were 'unconventional' suggests deliberate flouting of rules; it was rather that they were quite uninterested in conventions, but passionately in ideas. Generally speaking they were left-wing, atheists, pacifists in the First War (but fewer of them also in the Second), lovers of the arts and travel, avid readers, Francophiles. Apart from the various occupations such as writing, painting, economics, which they pursued with dedication, what they enjoyed most was talk – talk of every description, from the most abstract to the most hilariously ribald and profane . . . Comfort didn't rank high in Bloomsbury houses (though beauty did), but there would be good French cooking, and wine at most meals . . . They valued friendship extremely highly . . . And since they believed marriage to be a convention and convenience and never celebrated it in church, love, whether heterosexual or homosexual, took precedence over it and its precepts.[6]

Maynard Keynes had joined the Apostles in 1903. By the late 1920s he had established a reputation as one of the world's most daring and original economists. His book *A Tract on Monetary Reform*, published in 1923, had argued that governments could and should 'manage money' to help regulate the economy. But his greatest, most influential work, *The General Theory of Employment, Interest and Money*, which argued that capitalism would suffer permanent high levels of unemployment unless governments assumed hitherto undreamed-of responsibilities in economic management, was not published until 1936. In 1925, aged forty-two, he had unexpectedly married a Russian ballerina, Lydia Lopokova, and they departed for a fortnight's honeymoon in Moscow. This puzzled many of his fellow-Apostles/Angels, who had never thought that a bisexual like him would settle down to a conventional marriage. He had been happy enough as a member of a ménage-à-trois with the Bloomsbury painters, Duncan Grant and Vanessa Bell. To homosexual Apostles the marriage was heresy, but Keynes thought that if Bloomsbury meant anything it was that every individual had a right to live by his (or her) own standards. He wrote:

We entirely repudiated a personal liability on us to obey general rules. We claimed the right to judge every individual case on its merits, and the wisdom, experience and self-control to do so successfully. This was a very important part of our faith, violently and aggressively held, and for the outer world it was our most obvious and dangerous characteristic. We repudiated entirely customary morals, conventions and traditional wisdom. We were . . . in the strict sense of the term, immoralists. The consequences of being found out had, of course, to be considered for what they were worth. But we recognized no moral obligation on us, no inner sanction, to conform or obey.[7]

Like many Apostles, Blunt could never decide whether or not Keynes was really one of them. He was brilliant but he displayed a disturbing interest in areas of life (politics, the economy) which the Society had turned its back on. Blunt speculated:

> Keynes was a very great puzzle to us. He was deeply involved in worldly matters, even in finance, and he was a practical man. This was regarded as a very useful thing by his college, of which he was Senior Bursar, but it was regarded by the strict Bloomsbury figures as being somewhat eccentric.[8]

Despite this confusion over the Apostolic integrity of Keynes, Blunt was delighted to be mixing regularly with some of the best, most creative minds in Britain, although he preferred the Cambridge wing of Bloomsbury since he found London 'rather oppressive'. He thought, however, that his generation had a healthier view of the Apostles: 'If one heard people like E. M. Forster and Strachey talking about it it was clear that the Saturday evening meeting of the Apostles was the centre of their life, and that everything was regulated to it, and everything that was non-Apostolic was in some way inferior.'[9] But these were minor criticisms.

Blunt should have been blissfully happy. He was an academic and a social success. His tutors told him that he was destined for a brilliant degree. He was a member of the most talented clique in the university. Better brains than his could prove that homosexuality was one of the greatest glories in the world. This did not mean that Anthony was actually happy – that would have been too simple. His Marlborough friend, John Hilton, said: 'He always seemed to be going through a crisis for his friends, I don't know what kind of crises they were but he was always going through one.'[10]

The Apostles and the Angels had a weekend retreat at Clive Bell's house at Charleston in Sussex where they would read aloud essays to each other. There was also Lytton Strachey's Regency house, Ham Spray, in Wiltshire, which Strachey had bought with the royalties from his popular biographies, *Queen Victoria*, published in 1918, and *Elizabeth and Essex*, published in 1928. Strachey, who died in 1932, has been dismissed as a facile popularizer, but during the 1920s he was a cult figure for the Bloomsberries. At Ham Spray he enjoyed entertaining distinguished Angels such as Roger Fry as well as fine young Apostles like Anthony Blunt and George Rylands (known to his friends as 'Dadie'), a fair-haired Old Etonian who was five years older than Blunt and who was considered one of the university's most promising English Literature scholars.

Visitors to Ham Spray, conscious that they were members of a glittering group, liked to commemorate the occasion by taking photographs of each other. There is one study, for example, of Vanessa Bell cutting Strachey's shoulder-length hair, watched by Roger Fry, Clive Bell and other Bloomsberries. But Blunt was not content to sit and admire his elders. In 1928, with Michael Redgrave (later Sir Michael, the actor), he had set up an avant-garde literary magazine called the *Venture*, in opposition to another magazine, *Experiment*. *Venture* limped along until 1930, carrying articles by Blunt on the Gothic revival, poems by MacNeice, John Lehmann and Julian Bell, son of Clive and Vanessa Bell and one of the university's bright new talents. In retrospect, Blunt did not think much of the magazine:

It would not commit itself on anything. It was safe and Georgian and respectable on the literary side, and it contained articles by me on the art side, on German Baroque architecture, on Bruegel and on Cubism. I did go as far as to make an attack on what I thought was the over-sophistication of certain kinds of modern art but in a very timid way.[11]

He was studying and socializing hard but his central interest remained art. His brother Wilfrid recalled that Anthony's knowledge was constantly expanding; he would talk excitedly about the merits of new continental artists of whom Wilfrid had never even heard. Increasingly, Blunt found that his views on art were not shared by the elder statesmen of Bloomsbury. They could appreciate Picasso but they had no understanding, he thought, of the new 'socialist realists'. For example, Blunt had been much impressed by the work of the Parisian, Fernand Léger, who had become fascinated by the relationship between workers and technology during the First World War. Léger's work, thought Blunt, made all the talk about non-representational art and Pure Form, which had seemed so stimulating, appear slightly old-fashioned. Léger created impressive, sweeping visions of the noble worker, set against the awesome backcloth of modern industry. It was a more stylish version of the new Soviet art; which was hardly surprising since Léger had joined the French Communist Party after the War. It was ironic that Blunt, who had always been so contemptuous of politics, should have sought to champion the cause of a painter who was so committed to communism.

Blunt soon had more immediate problems than the new social realists of art; in November 1929 his father fell seriously ill. Doctors diagnosed inoperable cancer and within a few weeks he was dead. He was fifty-nine years old. At the end of November a letter arrived from their old friend Queen Mary: 'What a loss he will be. Why should he have been taken, who was doing such good work on earth, when such useless, evil people are allowed to live? However, this we shall never understand.'[12]

In April 1930, four months after her husband's death, Hilda Blunt, now fifty years old, moved back to Ham, where she had spent the first six years of her married life. She bought a small Edwardian house, the Pond House, which overlooked the common. She was, she assured her sons, perfectly happy. She busied herself with charity work and renewed old friendships. She had her faithful maid, Daisy, to look after the house. She took great pride in her garden, which she mowed assiduously with a machine that her sons suspected was as old as she was. She was not poor but had an aversion to spending money, especially on labour-saving gadgets that might have made her life a little easier or on new-fangled inventions such as the wireless. Basic comforts were regarded as sinful; she did not even own a refrigerator or an electric fire. She bought low-wattage light bulbs to save a few pennies a year on her electricity bill and even these tiny flickers of light had to be switched off in the corridors. Age and widowhood had not mellowed her. When Wilfrid visited her on Sundays she insisted that he attend the local church where she kept her prayer-book safely locked up in a wood box-hassock. She was as intolerant as ever, reserving a special contempt for Protestant 'perverts' who had converted to Catholicism, and could not imagine anyone of good taste and breeding voting for any party other than the Conservatives. When Wilfrid held a modest sherry party for some friends from the village, Hilda was so incensed by the sight of people enjoying themselves and drinking alcohol that she banned future social gatherings. She was terrified of being burgled and insisted that every door in the house was bolted. The three brothers found that they were constantly locking each other in as they faithfully followed their mother's instructions to secure the home against intruders. Wilfrid recalled:

There was the acute discomfort of the house: the cold of it in winter; the hard chairs; the prehistoric, concave mattresses; the quite unnecessary draughts and the ancient gas fires, hardly glowing. Comfort was self-indulgence: 'You mustn't get soft dear boy.' She, herself, being still very active, did not yet feel, and had never felt, the cold.[13]

Anthony saw her less than did either Wilfrid or Christopher, who had joined a merchant bank in the City. But it was Anthony's visits that she most looked forward to, even if he was showing an unhealthy interest in artists such as Picasso who was, thought Hilda, a 'charlatan'.

One afternoon in late June 1930, Hilda was more excited than usual at the prospect of seeing her brilliant youngest son. Anthony was at the centre court, Wimbledon, watching Helen Moody outplaying the smaller, weaker Elizabeth Ryan in the Ladies' Final. With him was Lady Mary St Claire-Erskine, the eighteen-year-old daughter of the third wife of James Francis Harry St Claire-Erskine, fifth Earl of Rosslyn. Anthony had told his mother that he would be bringing Lady Mary to tea after the tennis. She was a pretty, vivacious girl who had met Anthony through his friend Victor Rothschild, a brilliant and dashing member of the famous banking dynasty. Rothschild was reading history at Trinity College and was later considered one of the cleverest British polymaths of the twentieth century. He was a political radical but did not let that interfere with his enjoyment of fast cars, parties and attractive women. Mary was not, and did not pretend to be, an intellectual. She was being groomed to make her formal entry into London society in 1931 as a débutante. Her parents intended to ensure that their daughter had a magnificent launch at their home in Eaton Square which would, they hoped, be the first step towards ensuring a good marriage for her.

By Hilda's unrelenting standards, Lady Mary's father was a debauched rogue. His obituary in *The Times* caught the flavour of his life, which ended shortly after making a trip up the Amazon at the age of seventy:

> He was known for his good looks and his indifference to convention. He was an outstandingly handsome man – dashing would best describe him . . . As a young man he had been high-spirited and reckless, characteristics which involved him in several escapades. After the briefest of spells at Magdalen College, Oxford, he took his place in London society and his good looks, charm and interest in the Turf made him a close friend of the Prince of Wales . . . he took up racing with great enthusiasm and gambled heavily, which resulted in bankruptcy in 1897. He then became a professional actor.[14]

All this was bad enough, but there was another problem. Lady Mary was a Catholic. On the other hand, Hilda would have been gratified if Anthony had married a member of the aristocracy. She felt he deserved no less.

Mary was under the impression that Anthony Blunt was a serious suitor. She had not known him long but she thought she knew enough about men to be able to tell the difference between a polite flirtation and real emotion. She recalled:

> I was deeply fond of him. He had indicated that he wanted to marry me and I felt that afternoon, when I met his mother, that I was being vetted. He was great fun and terribly interested in people. After indicating that we might make a happy life together it wasn't a question of him saying, 'Will you marry me?' It was just that he had had more fun with me than with any other girl.[15]

They made an unlikely couple: the fun-loving girl whose father was a gambling earl and the earnest young academic. Nonetheless they enjoyed each other's company. Mary liked art and listened with admiration, if not complete understanding, as Anthony explained the merits of various artists. He kissed her just once, but this showed, she thought, a normal and quite proper reserve. She had no idea that he was homosexual; indeed, she did not know that such people existed: 'I had never heard of that side of life. Very few people of my generation had, I suppose. He seemed completely normal. He was shy and romantic. But he was very attractive.'[16]

By her own standards, Hilda seems to have been remarkably civil that afternoon. Even so, Mary felt that her hostess was definitely not pleased that she was a Catholic. But Hilda must have been reassured to see Anthony with a girl at last; Christopher planned to marry a young woman called Elizabeth Bazley but Wilfrid showed no interest in the opposite sex, and until that June day neither had Anthony.

There is no way of knowing whether Anthony Blunt was really considering marriage in 1930. It was common for homosexuals to marry, because they wanted social respectability or because it might help their careers. These marriages were not necessarily charades; some homosexuals discovered that they could love women, sometimes emotionally, sometimes physically. However, in the autumn of 1930, while he was still seeing Mary, Blunt was conducting a passionate affair with Julian Bell, who had gone up to King's College in 1927 to read history. He was unsettled at first; he missed his parents, Clive and Vanessa, and the cosiness of the Bloomsbury group. He neglected his work and spent his time beagling, writing poems and preparing speeches for debates at the Cambridge Union. He also grew a beard, which he hoped added gravitas. He was anxious to establish his cultural credentials and in his first speech at the Cambridge Union proposed the motion that 'England thinks too much of her athletes and their doings'. In his second year he was elected to the Apostles, along with Anthony Blunt. The two students found that they had much in common. Anthony admired Clive Bell's art criticism, and Julian reciprocated by devoting his own poems to Anthony. In the early summer of 1929 Bell wrote to his mother and admitted that he was having an affair with Blunt. He asked her not to be shocked and implored her not to mention it to Virginia Woolf, which would, he said, be the same as telling the press. But Bloomsberries prided themselves on their open-mindedness and Vanessa noted at the time that she was pleased that Julian had been so frank with her. But not everyone approved. Maynard Keynes wrote to Vanessa in May 1929 saying that her son was doing splendidly at King's. He was one of the most promising young men at the university, but it was unfortunate that he so admired Anthony Blunt: 'The magazines are plastered with his poems – some not at all bad; whether Anthony Blunt (with whom he's completely and hopelessly infatuated) is quite all that Julian thinks may be found doubtful in the future – but that doesn't matter at present.'[17]

Bell remained deeply unhappy. He once told an Old Etonian friend that he was tired of love affairs. 'Only hardness, strength, tragedy are endurable. In fact, I've had an overdose of romance and beauty. Cure: Beethoven and ten mile walks in big boots and the slaughter of innocent birds.'[18] He tried to find peace by moving in with Lattice Ramsey, widow of Frank Ramsey, a mathematical genius who had been a Fellow of King's and who had died tragically young in 1930. (Bell, too, died young: he was killed in 1937 during the Spanish Civil War.)

Blunt had graduated in the summer with a first in Modern

Languages and had now started research for a Fellowship at Trinity, working on Nicolas Poussin, the French seventeenth-century painter. Blunt's rooms were decorated with reproductions of some of Poussin's better-known works: 'Narcissus', 'Venus and Adonis', and 'Apollo and Daphne'. He was still seeing Mary St Claire-Erskine, though she was, by now, more interested in Victor Rothschild, who occasionally let her drive his Bugatti sports car. When Steven Runciman announced that he was holding a party in his suite at Trinity College, Blunt and Rothschild decided that, since women were not allowed into college rooms, they would have to smuggle Mary in. She said:

> I cut my hair and borrowed a dinner jacket. We played hunt the slipper at the party. It was quite a rough evening and they had to push me out by the back stairs at the end. I don't think Steven Runciman was very pleased with me. The next time I saw him he cut me dead.[19]

Throughout the 1920s most Oxbridge students had been staunch supporters of the Conservatives. When the Tory Prime Minister, Stanley Baldwin, had been entertained at the Lion restaurant, Cambridge, in 1927 the students had repeatedly sung 'For he's a jolly good fellow'. That year the university's Conservative Association had boasted a record 700 members, almost double the figure for 1923. At the Cambridge Union rebellious motions might be passed but that owed more to the oratorical skills of the speakers than to any widespread student radicalism. Enjoyment was far more important to most undergraduates than worrying about the fate of the world. Yet there were signs, albeit faint ones, that the cult of hedonism was being questioned. When the Marshall Society was founded by student economists in 1927 they tried to attract members by asking: 'Have you ever thought of taking an interest in the lives of other people? In all of us as a community? Of the boons of some and of the sorrows and difficulties of others? Oh, no, not a political society; nor a religious society – but a society unmoved by such prejudices.' Within a year the society had 150 members, who started to show a strange concern for the world outside the university. They visited factories and invited East End dockers and their families to Cambridge. Even sportsmen seemed to be affected by this new spirit. In November 1928, Carl Aarvold, captain of the Caius College Rugby XV and a future Recorder of London, told his fellow-students: 'The approaching winter will mean starvation and misery to many thousands in this country . . . unemployment insurance benefits are totally inadequate to cope with a catastrophe of such dimensions.' That same year the economist, Maynard Keynes, attacked the Tories' stubborn faith in the free market system and their refusal to accept that government should try and regulate the economy. He told the Cambridge Union that Conservatives' 'one definite idea, that of insisting on economy at all costs, has become with them an obsession so disproportionate as to exclude all others . . . all schemes which would cause more employment are indiscriminately turned down by the government on the grounds of expense.'

In the general election of May 1929, the Labour Party, led by Ramsay MacDonald, had defeated the Conservatives. But Labour appeared to be as bereft of new ideas as the Tories. And, as the world economy lurched towards the Depression, Labour seemed just as bewildered as its political opponents. Capitalism, which had always been seen as self-regulating, appeared to be on the point of collapse; a view that was reinforced when the motor of the world economy, the American stock exchange on Wall Street, crashed.

The CPGB had fought the 1929 election with the slogan: 'Class against Class. The Labour Party has chosen the capitalist class. The Communist Party is the party of the working class. The Labour Party is the third capitalist party.' The communists had also rejected the idea that they might cooperate with the trades unions, which were tools and props of the capitalists. With this programme it was hardly surprising that the CPGB polled a miserable 50,000 votes nationally. From the date of that election, which brought Labour's Ramsay MacDonald to Downing Street, the communists lost tens of thousands of members: it boasted a membership of 80,000 in 1925 (which was probably an exaggeration) and by 1930 admitted to having just 2500 members (which was probably also an overestimate).

The collapse of MacDonald's administration in August 1931 indicated that the Labour Party, too, was in poor shape. The communists believed that Labour would split into two camps: the true socialists who were, at heart, communists and the rest who were no more than lapdogs of the capitalists. During the October election MacDonald urged former Labour voters to reject the manifesto of the Labour Party ('Bolshevism gone mad') and argued for a national coalition. The Labour Party, led by George Lansbury, gained just fifty-two seats in the House of Commons against MacDonald's national coalition, which had 554 seats.

At Cambridge the new generation of students was markedly less respectful than its predecessors. The politicians who had sacrificed millions of men for no obvious reason in the First World War seemed little more than incompetent buffoons, who would talk about the country's great imperial heritage but were incapable of dealing with the present. When MacDonald arrived in Downing Street 10 per cent of the British workforce was unemployed; in the eighteen months after the Wall Street crash that figure had more than doubled. Cambridge students now shouted and hooted when patriotic films were shown at the Vic cinema in Market Square. War films that would have brought applause a few years before provoked discussions about the immoral profits of arms manufacturers. The Labour Club, the only radical political society at the university, which had always had about 150 members, started to grow. By 1931 it claimed to have over 1000 members.

The shift in student opinion was unmistakable. On 7 March 1930 the Reverend F. Homes Dudden, Master of Pembroke College, Oxford, told his congregation: 'There is a widespread dissatisfaction with the conditions of life . . . all seem more or less unhappy . . . we have been woefully let down . . . our hopes have not been realized.' Even the giants of Bloomsbury began to seem irrelevant. When Lytton Strachey's book, *Portraits in Miniature*, was published in 1931, one academic wrote: 'Mr Strachey's values seem bland and banal. It is less easy these days to do without a conscience.' Tutors at Cambridge were struck by the militancy of new students. Herbert Butterfield, who later became Master of Pembroke College and then university vice-chancellor, commented:

I noticed that one particular Grammar school at Lytham in Lancashire almost invariably sent us scholarship boys who arrived already full of communist teaching. It proved difficult for some of them later on when they applied for jobs outside, especially in the public services . . . I can recall the bubbling, communistic enthusiasm of an undergraduate who seemed to regard the Soviet Union as more perfect than paradise.[20]

But it wasn't just the grammar schools which were producing political rebels: the public schools were also breeding troublemakers. From Gresham's, an Elizabethan foundation in Norfolk, came Donald Maclean, the son of Sir Donald Maclean, a Liberal MP who became a Cabinet minister in 1931 in Ramsay MacDonald's emergency National Government. His son was tall, strikingly good-looking and already regarded himself as a socialist by the time he arrived at Trinity Hall in the autumn of 1929, aged eighteen, to take up his scholarship in modern languages. He was shy and physically awkward. There was an effeminate quality about him which led many people to conclude that he was a sublimated homosexual. For the rest of his life Maclean fought to convince others (and himself) that this was not true. Another Greshamite, James Klugmann, who went up to Trinity College as a modern languages scholar a year later, had no such personality problems. He was the son of Jewish immigrants who had made a prosperous new life in Hampstead, and called himself a communist at school. He did not join the Communist Party until 1933, the year he took a first in French and German, but that was a technicality. Klugmann was one of the most influential Marxists at the university almost from the day he arrived there. He described his conversion:

> When I was at Gresham's I felt so much out of things as the clever oddity who got most of the prizes, but not even the humblest office, that I cast around for a title to bestow on myself. I hit on an ingenious one in my last year and I surmised at once that the authorities wouldn't like it. For I called myself a communist, advertising myself as the only specimen for miles around. I hadn't any clear idea, to begin with, what a good communist really stood for; but having a very inquisitive mind, I soon remedied that.[21]

Harold Adrian Russell Philby, known to everyone as Kim, after the hero of Rudyard Kipling's novel, was the son of the adventurer Harry St John Philby. A former civil servant in India, St John Philby identified with T. E.

Lawrence and spent much of the time while his son was growing up wandering around the Arabian deserts. He was a tough, authoritarian father. Perhaps as a result of this, Kim Philby was always careful, calculating and introverted; he had a stammer which he never fully conquered. He went to Westminster School in London before going up to Trinity College, Cambridge, in October 1929 to read history. He was not considered an outstanding student, unlike the other undergraduates who were fated to have their lives linked to his for ever by their dedication to communism. Nor, unlike many of these fellow-Marxists, was Philby homosexual.

The same could not be said of Guy Francis de Moncy Burgess, who went up to Trinity College in the autumn of 1930 on an open scholarship in history. He was by far the most extravagant and unlikely of all the Cambridge spies. His father, Malcolm, had been a naval commander and died in 1924 when Guy was thirteen. Burgess told friends that he had heard his mother Evelyn scream out during the night and that he had discovered his father lying across her, having died of a heart attack while making love. The story may have been true or partly true, but Guy's friends knew him well enough to suspect that whatever had happened that night it had been considerably embellished. They were also sure that Guy was not as badly shaken by the manner of his father's passing as he claimed. He had been sent first to Eton and then to the Royal Naval College at Dartmouth from where, it was hoped, he would follow his father into the Royal Navy. But poor eyesight ended his hopes of a naval career and he returned to Eton. He was an extrovert who employed his considerable charm and cherubic good looks to ensure that he always got what he wanted. He read widely and showed a particular interest in books which exposed conditions in London's East End. He argued that socialism was the only solution to the country's problems.

In 1929 he had cheered wildly, to the irritation of the other boys, when a dockers' trade union organizer had visited Eton and attacked the injustices of capitalism. Eton's headmaster, Robert Birley, wrote to Francis Dobbs, Guy's housemaster:

> At the moment his ideas are running away from him, and he is finding in verbal quibbles and Chestertonian comparisons a rather unhealthy delight, but he is such a sane person and so modest essentially that I do not feel this really matters. The great thing is that he really thinks for himself . . . It is refreshing to find one who is really well-read and who can become enthusiastic or have something to say about most things from Vermcer to Meredith. He is also a lively and amusing person, generous, I think, and very good-natured.[22]

There was always something disreputable about Guy, even when he was a teenager, before drinking, smoking and general dissoluteness wrecked his good looks. When Michael Berry (later Lord Hartwell, proprietor of the *Daily Telegraph*) campaigned to have Guy elected to Pop, the élite sixth-form Eton society, he was told that Guy was not welcome. Guy was consoled by David Hedley, the school captain, who remained a close friend at Cambridge and, like Guy, became a communist. Their relationship, despite rumours, was asexual.

Guy Burgess enjoyed every minute of his Cambridge career. There were so many attractive young men to try and seduce; there were intelligent friends to gossip with and about; there were excellent libraries and the superb Pitt Club, modelled on a London gentleman's club, to relax in. Robert Birley noted after visiting Guy in the summer of 1931:

Of course Guy wasn't in when I arrived so I entered his rooms in New Court and waited. There were many books on his shelves, and I'm always drawn to other people's tastes in reading. As I expected, his taste was fairly wide and interesting. I noticed a number of Marxist tracts and textbooks, but that's not what shocked and depressed me. I realized that something must have gone terribly wrong when I came across an extraordinary array of explicit and extremely unpleasant pornographic literature. He bustled in finally, full of cheerful apologies for being late as usual and we talked happily enough over the tea-cups.[23]

Burgess would not have cared even if he had known that Birley had stumbled across his collection of pornography. Whatever people said about Burgess, no one could accuse him of trying to pretend he was anything other than a promiscuous homosexual. Indeed, he told anyone who wanted to listen, strangers as well as friends, about his sexual exploits. The following summer he visited his friend Maurice Bowra, then Dean of Wadham College, Oxford. It was there that he met Goronwy Rees, who had already heard that Burgess was one of the most brilliant undergraduates at Cambridge. Rees was then twenty-two and a Fellow of All Souls, the postgraduate college which traditionally admitted only the finest brains in the country. Rees was the grammar-school-educated son of a Welsh Methodist minister and, probably to his eternal regret, took an instant liking to Burgess:

. . . we drank whisky together for a long time. At first he made tentative amorous advances but quickly and cheerfully desisted when he discovered that I was as heterosexual as he was the opposite; he would have done the same to any young man, because sex to him was both a compulsion and a game which it was almost a duty to practise. He went on to talk about painting, and its relation to the Marxist interpretation of history . . . It was not that the matters he talked about were unusual; by 1932 they had become topics of almost incessant discussion by the intellectual-homosexual-aesthetic-communist young man who was establishing himself as the classical, and fashionable, type of progressive undergraduate. To such a young man, Marxism and communism were something to be argued about, debated, elucidated, defended; it was something which lay outside the bounds of his experience, and remained an opinion or a faith to be held with a greater or lesser degree of conviction. For Guy it was simply a way of looking at the world which seemed as natural to him as the way he breathed.[24]

There is no doubt that Anthony Blunt, Burgess's great friend, was affected by Guy's shift to the left. That is not to say that they spent much time talking about politics. Blunt, after all, was far more concerned about art than politics, especially if politics in Cambridge meant interminable discussions about unreadable Marxist texts. In November 1932 Blunt sponsored Burgess's entry into the Apostles – an acknowledgement of the genius that Burgess (and Blunt) knew he possessed.

It was not easy for an angry young man at Cambridge to find a focus for his disillusion. The socialist and pacifist societies did not go far enough for the new generation of students, and the handful of communists lacked leadership and direction. It was far easier for students to forget about politics and enjoy themselves, especially if they had money. This changed dramatically in April 1931, when a philosophy student called David Haden-Guest, the son of a former

Labour MP, returned from sabbatical leave in Germany. One evening he strode into dinner at Trinity sporting a hammer-and-sickle emblem on his jacket and started to describe how he had been imprisoned by pro-Nazi police after taking part in an anti-Hitler demonstration. He talked about the horrors of Nazism: the anti-Semitism and the violence against opponents. Haden-Guest then joined the Communist Party of Great Britain, believing that only the communists understood the real threat posed by the Nazis.

Rajani Palme Dutt, the CPGB's leading theoretician, and his brother Clemens watched the developments in Cambridge with increasing interest. Their father was a doctor in the town and they were well aware that more and more students seemed dissatisfied with the existing political groups. True, Maurice Dobb, the economist, had bravely kept the Marxist cause alive but he had soldiered on more or less alone. Perhaps, the Palme Dutts concluded, it was time to organize the future leaders of the nation. Rajani was well equipped to handle this tricky task. He was a persuasive thinker, as the journalist Claud Cockburn discovered: 'Rajani Palme Dutt was one of the most brilliant thinkers I have ever encountered. He had that kind of luminous intelligence which enables a man to follow the exact minutiae of dogma while retaining the fullest flexibility in relation to reality – a mind in fact similar to Karl Marx himself.'[25]

In June 1931 Clemens Palme Dutt visited Dobb at his home in Chesterton Lane, Cambridge, to discuss forming a communist group at the university. Dobb was delighted at the prospect of having the chance to share his Marxist wisdom, accumulated over many years, with new comrades. Everyone knew him as a communist. He had been one of the key members of the British branch of the League Against Imperialism which was controlled by Moscow-backed Comintern activists in Europe and which in 1930 was proscribed by the Labour Party, by then alert to the Soviets' use of apparently harmless groups to infiltrate the European parliamentary Left.

The meeting at Dobb's home – popularly known in the town as the 'Red Household' – was crucial in laying the foundation for the communist fervour that gripped Cambridge during the 1930s. It was a small meeting of dons and undergraduates, including Haden-Guest and Maurice Cornforth, who was studying for a doctorate in philosophy and who later married Klugmann's sister, Kitty. There was Roy Pascal, a Fellow of Pembroke College, and his wife Barbara, who shared the house with Dobb; an ex-miner, Jim Lees, who had won a scholarship from the Workers' Educational Association, and Jack 'Bugsy' Wolfe, a working-class boy from London's East End. There was John Desmond Bernal, the physicist and crystallographer, regarded as one of Cambridge's most promising scientists. The meeting agreed that students were ripe for recruitment to Marxism. Dobb later wrote: 'War, inflation, deflation, with their devastating effect on the value of investments, have weakened the whole idea of property in people's minds . . . The Russian experiment has aroused very great interest inside the university. It is felt to be bold and constructive.'[26]

At first the newly formed communist cell, with dons tending to remain discreetly in the background, found it hard to attract recruits. Haden-Guest used to summon the comrades to his rooms at Trinity, empty apart from a portrait of Lenin, some books and a piano, and lead morale-boosting renditions of party battle anthems. There was much angry talk about the petty-mindedness and class treachery of the 'social fascist reptiles' in the Labour Party who still believed that socialism could be won through the ballot box. The communists tried to recruit in the town but found that most of the working class had no time for talk about revolution. The communist zealots had more luck with their fellow-students; by 1932 the cell had grown to twenty-five members which was, at least, a start. There were cells, too, at Oxford and London universities. The students, for so long the enemies of the workers, might not, after all, thought the King Street bureaucrats, be irredeemable.

CHAPTER 5
Radical Young Gentlemen

In the autumn of 1933 hundreds of freshmen (and a few freshwomen) poured into Cambridge for the start of their university careers. Among them was a young man called John Cornford, educated at Stowe, the son of a Cambridge classics professor and already marked out by his tutors at Trinity College as a young man of great promise. Cornford had won a major open scholarship in history a year earlier at the age of sixteen – a considerable achievement even for a boy from an academic family. His mother was a poet and the granddaughter of Charles Darwin. She had insisted that her son, born in December 1915, should be named Rupert John, after their close friend the poet Rupert Brooke who had died in April that year. John was a committed Marxist by the time he arrived at Trinity. He had become one at Stowe, and in the year before coming up to Cambridge he had immersed himself in left-wing politics at the London School of Economics. Unlike other student communists at Cambridge, who had little experience of (or interest in) cooperating with the working class or with trades unions, Cornford was already an experienced agitator with a shrewd grasp of how to organize and manipulate the workers. He was tall, well-built and handsome, with a tendency to stoop. His eyes were set in a high-cheeked face, topped by a mass of curly black hair. At school he had shown a precocious talent for impassioned poetry. He was a

committed anti-militarist and atheist and had absorbed
Marx's *Das Kapital*, the three-volume work which Marx
hoped would 'lay bare the laws of motion of capitalist
society' and which was so densely argued that most communists never managed to get beyond the first 100 pages.
Cornford began reading it when he was seventeen, feeling
as if he was being initiated into a marvellous new religion. It
had been 'slow going but not too difficult'. It was, he told
friends, a 'very great book', though Marx had not followed
up properly some of the 'really exciting ideas that his facts
and theories might lead to'.[1]

Cornford had huge will power and seemed able to shape
events to his personal whim. Despite his communism he
was highly competitive. His brother Christopher recalled
that, although he was the better athlete, John would always
win whatever game they played simply by refusing to be
beaten. It did not matter whether it was an impromptu
game of ping-pong at home or a race between two lamp-
posts, the result was always the same: John won.[2] By the
time he reached Trinity, John had decided that communism
wasn't inevitable, like wars or catching measles during
childhood; communism was *necessary*. Nor did he think
that it would be achieved by selling the *Daily Worker* to
factory workers or drinking sherry with fellow-comrades in
Cambridge sitting-rooms. He was a *bona fide* revolutionary
who believed in the almost certain need for violence. He
once wrote to his parents of the 'need for a revolution with
fighting':

I think all that is needed is enough force to hold up
communications and get wireless stations and newspaper
offices. Army must be managed with fairly clever propaganda. After that fighting would simply be a function of
the enemy resistance . . . But the more I read of party
politics, the more I despair of a constitutional success; an

election organized party could never do it. I think English moderateness and compromising is largely a result of
many years' prosperity . . . I think anyone will fight when
they have been hungry long enough – as we will certainly
have to do sooner or later while capitalism continues.
And I think the longer they [the workers] are kept down
the nastier the actual outbreak will be; better to control
and organize it from the start. There really needn't be
much fighting as (if people are sensible) there are so very
few people to fight against.[3]

Within a few weeks Cornford was rivalling James
Klugmann for the title of Cambridge's best-known revolutionary, although Anthony Blunt thought that they com-
plemented each other well. Klugmann had taken a
first-class degree in French and German and by that time
was a research student. Blunt wrote in 1972 that he was 'the
pure intellectual, a good scholar and political theorist who
ran the administration of the party with great skill.' It was
Klugmann who decided which organizations and societies
the communists should try to infiltrate. Cornford played a
more symbolic role. They were both mega-stars of the Left
but Cornford was 'much more imaginative than the cold,
clear-minded Klugmann'. He was able to carry an audience
with his 'vehement oratory'.[4] Cornford was glamorous too
– now the word would be charismatic – and both men and
women frequently fell in love with him. Klugmann had a
brilliantly incisive mind and was able to summarize world
events, albeit from a partisan standpoint, in a crisp and
convincing way. Like most communists he had an idealized
vision of the Soviet Union and was able to dismiss reports of
mass arrests, executions and starvation as the predictable
distortions of the capitalist press. He believed that the
system could not fail to bring prosperity, equality and
justice. Klugmann had toured a mining village in South

Wales early in 1933 and knew that the USSR would not have tolerated the sort of conditions that he saw there: 'empty houses furnished with bits of wood and orange boxes, children without shoes, rickets everywhere, small shopkeepers ruined because their customers couldn't afford to buy, tuberculosis and emigration.'[5]

If Klugmann was the driving force behind the communists' devious manoeuvres to dominate political life within the university, Cornford was the public symbol. He had become a legend even before he died in 1936 during the Spanish Civil War. Blunt thought that somehow martyrdom was a fitting end for him, a view that was definitely not shared by Cornford's many friends. Blunt thought:

> It may seem a callous thing to say but it was in a way appropriate, though tragic, that he should have gone to Spain and been killed; he was the stuff martyrs are made of and I do not know what would have happened to him if he had survived. He was a highly emotional character and I strongly suspect that he might have gone back on his Marxist doctrine and if so I think he would have suffered badly.[6]

Cornford's arrival in the autumn of 1933 coincided with a new phase in the communist movement both at Cambridge and nationally. From then until the Nazi–Soviet Pact of 1939 membership of the overall party rose steadily. There were around 2500 party members in 1930; by 1936 there were 11,500 and by 1939 the figure had soared to 17,500. Mostly this was due to growing fears that fascism would sweep through Europe. It was suspected, too, that the Western democracies, particularly Britain, were more interested in combating what they imagined was the threat of the Soviet Union than in countering Hitler and Mussolini.

The year 1933 had opened with a disastrous setback: the

election to power in Germany of Hitler's Nazi Party, an event which, according to Marxist theory, should not have happened. Klugmann recalled that this had been a 'bombshell for revolutionaries and progressive people' who had taken it for granted that Germany would follow the Soviet Union and become Europe's second communist state. As the nights lengthened and winter drew in at Cambridge the communists were still grappling with the implications of the German election. They needed inspiration to rekindle their belief. And they found it in the new firebrand at Trinity, John Cornford.

One Cambridge contemporary wrote: 'Conservative socialists were already shaking their heads. They felt that this new man was very young and wanted to go too fast. These were days of a new excitement in Cambridge politics.'[7]

Cornford began his student life at Trinity in fine rooms over a gateway between Bishops Hostel and New Court, but he made sure that he lived as frugally as possible. There was little furniture and only a bare light bulb to illuminate the comrades who came to his rooms for evening meetings, rather as if he was declaring to them that while he might be a member of a privileged community he was already preparing for the grim days of revolution. His friends found it difficult to keep him in one place for more than a few minutes. He would talk to them as he was moving towards some other vital discussion. He subsisted on mugs of disgustingly strong tea and large hunks of bread and jam. But underlying the breathless chaos there was method. He was an assiduous party worker and a conscientious student, who was determined to carry off all the academic honours available. This was not just personal ambition; he wanted to prove to non-communist students that he was better and stronger than them because of his faith. He hated fascism with what Klugmann called 'a physical loathing' and enjoyed taunting speakers at the rallies held by Oswald Mosley's Blackshirts (the British fascists). He swore often and could be insultingly chauvinistic towards women, though this seemed only to increase their adoration of him. He protested that he was unable to love more than one woman at a time which made him, he joked with friends, a monopoly capitalist in love if not in politics. He took the world very seriously and regarded the Communist International (Comintern) as the most important creation in history. But above all else he relished the sense that here, in Cambridge, he was in the vanguard of the revolution. And he fully intended to be the first to man the barricades.

There were some who could not understand the euphoria over Cornford. Steven Runciman taught mediaeval history to first-year Trinity historians and found that Cornford was not remotely interested either in the subject or his tutor:

He was an extremely clever and forceful boy. But he was merciless, rather inhuman. He thought he knew more than I did. He wasn't modest and I don't think he was frightfully nice. He may not have been the cleverest in his year but he was the most interesting. He thought that I was rather silly which did not endear him to me.[8]

But, as Runciman noticed, Cornford was exceptionally good-looking, a fact that did not escape the attention of Guy Burgess as he scoured the freshmen for possible conquests. Runciman thought that both Burgess and Blunt were 'totally glamourized' by the tall, dark-haired young communist. Runciman noted, too, that neither Burgess nor Blunt stood a chance with the heterosexual Cornford, though that did not stop them lusting after him from a distance and 'sighing in vain'.

There were hundreds of students in Cambridge willing to throw themselves into the communist cause. They came from all backgrounds: from wealthy, conservative families; from homes that were traditionally liberal; and from the working-class industrial cities and towns. But there were hundreds more who remember Cambridge in the 1930s for the countless hours spent in libraries or the afternoons spent playing rugby or rowing. Philip Allen (later Lord Allen of Abeydale), for example, who was at Queen's College, admitted that 'all the political ferment passed me by'. Allen was awarded a life peerage in 1976 after a distinguished career in the civil service. From 1973 he was a member of the Security Commission, a permanent group which investigates breaches of national security. He recalled:

> I was a humble grammar-school boy from Sheffield and I didn't know any of these people like Cornford or Burgess or Blunt. There was a social divide at the university. Boys like me tended to work. I was dependent on scholarships and worked hard to get my first. No, I wasn't involved in politics at all. I didn't lead a monastic life, I went rowing and played soccer. I knew the strength of feeling about fascism but I was never approached by anyone to become a communist or a spy. As it happens I would have been a very good catch.[9]

Fred Clayton came from Liverpool and was regarded as one of the cleverest students at King's. He was a classicist and, after graduating, stayed at King's as a Fellow until the outbreak of war. He took an instant dislike to Guy Burgess, mainly because he seemed to trade so effortlessly and effectively on the fact that he had attended England's most prestigious public school. He exuded confidence that he would be able to select his career, whether it was in the BBC, *The Times* or the Foreign Office. Clayton found it particularly irritating when Burgess exchanged jokes with the academic giants of the university. On one occasion

Burgess complimented Maynard Keynes on having written 'a jolly good article about Uncle Joe [Stalin]' in the *New Statesman*. Even worse, Keynes seemed to have been taken in by this unjustified familiarity; Clayton brooded that making progress in England seemed to depend on having the right style and being able to drop the right social codewords rather than on ability. Clayton came from a lower-middle-class background and although he was much, much cleverer than Burgess felt no such confidence. Certainly, he could not believe that a man like Burgess was a genuine socialist.

The brightest students were the main targets for the communist recruiters. It made more sense to target a student who was likely to win a first-class honours degree and then go into the Foreign Office than to waste time on a third-rate brain who would end up teaching in a secondary school. In the 1980s Clayton had vivid memories of the way in which the communists continually pestered him to join the party. In 1935, for example, he was unexpectedly invited to dinner by David Hedley, an old school friend of Burgess's:

Nothing was said during dinner. Suddenly they turned on me and started talking about politics. Yet the year before Hedley had been lying on the floor of his room saying that he didn't know why people bothered with politics. He said it was such a lovely world and there was no point in worrying. They set about recruiting me in the wrong way. I didn't like their tactics. I didn't like being encircled.[10]

Noel Annan, created a life peer in 1965 after a glittering academic career, was another who did not succumb to the communists. He had been educated at Stowe, as had John Cornford, and arrived at King's in 1935. Annan calculated that at that time, when the Left was claiming that most students were either members of the Communist Party or other, less extreme leftist groups, 'no more than one per cent of the undergraduates in any one lecture room would have called themselves left-wing'. Annan was a 'straight liberal' who found the dogmatism inherent in communism and the demands imposed by the omniscient party intolerable. He watched in amazement as communist friends tried to absorb the ever-changing instructions issuing from the party's headquarters in King Street. Annan was fond of telling friends that he felt he had missed the great experience of Cambridge in the 1930s, which was to join the party and then leave in confusion and disgust. One friend, who had enlisted, had spent hours and hours trying to convince non-communists of a particular point of doctrine, only to find, almost as he was talking, that the official communist line was changing. The friend quit the party saying he was 'fed up'. Annan said in 1985:

There were a lot of very clever young men who were never taken in by Marxism at all. I wouldn't want you to think that Cambridge was as white as snow and never a red in sight. There were a good many members of the Communist Party, certainly Marxisant, in Trinity, and the Left made a lot of noise as they did in the 1970s. But quite a few were starry-eyed improbables. 'I dislike Keats's *Ode to a Nightingale*, it's a status symbol,' was one prize comment. And when the man said to a working-class boy, Fred Clayton – aren't the working classes wonderful? Fred, who really knew what they were like, exploded.[11]

Charles Madge, whose varied career later included a stint on the *Daily Mirror*, Mass Observation surveys and development work overseas as well as the production of a string of poetry and non-fiction books, was another student who found the discipline of the party irritating. Madge had come up to Magdalene College to read natural sciences in the autumn of 1931 but had been forced to leave after one term after suffering a recurrence of intestinal TB. He returned in October 1932 and switched to moral sciences. He watched in horror as the hunger marchers from the impoverished north of England trudged through the city. Madge felt he ought to become involved and was advised by a fellow-student, who enjoyed near saintly status within the Left after serving a prison sentence for his part in a mass protest on a grouse moor, to join the Communist Party. Madge, whose brother John was also a communist, threw himself into the spirit of the cause. He founded a magazine, the *Cambridge Left*, and attended party meetings in London:

> The issue was how centralized the student party should be. The delegation from the LSE wanted to control the Cambridge and Oxford communists. We resisted that and I was the spokesman. I spent a couple of hours putting the case for letting us work out our own destinies and not being controlled by London. I didn't win out but I think I made a bit of an impact. I am not sure the decision made very much difference. I wanted a bit of internal democracy. I didn't realize how undemocratic the party was. It was a bit of an eye-opener. I was chosen to take over from David Guest as the secretary-organizer of the Cambridge University communist group but I had to leave Cambridge at the end of the summer term, 1933, because I went off with Kathleen Raine, who was married to Hugh Sykes Davies. I then felt that the best thing to do about the party was to be masterfully inactive. I think my card just lapsed.[12]

The first tangible sign of the new mood of Cambridge in late 1933 came during Armistice week in November. The week began with a demonstration by the Left (and a counter-demonstration by the Cambridge hearties) over a film, *Our Fighting Navy*, showing at the Tivoli cinema. The Left thought that the film was full of 'militaristic propaganda' and walked out halfway through. One contemporary account described what happened next:

A large crowd of 'patriotic' undergraduates collected outside the cinema to 'rag the cads' as they came out. It was the biggest anti-socialist and anti-pacifist turn-out that Cambridge had seen for years, complete with Union Jacks and a brass band. As the demonstrators came out they hardly knew whether they were being hooted or applauded. Then began a free-for-all fight; the situation might have been ugly for the demonstrators but once the scuffle began no one knew who was friend or foe. One demonstrator was debagged in traditional style and escaped on a lorry. Finally the band struck up and 'tough' Cambridge, having dealt with the cranks in the time-worn manner, marched back in mock procession.[13]

This setback only encouraged the Left to organize a bigger and better demonstration for the anti-war march on 11 November. Many students, who had not hitherto been especially interested in the communists or in the socialist groups, had been intensely annoyed by the boasts of the college hearties that they had given the 'reds' a good hiding. One of these was Sam Fisher, a first-year history scholar at Downing College. He knew more about the realities of unemployment than many of the communists. His father had been pensioned off from the navy and had tramped the streets of London for weeks looking for a job, any job, no matter how badly paid or menial. He found one as a bargeman on the Thames before becoming a messenger in the civil service, where he worked himself up to the grand post of office keeper. Sam Fisher had not been impressed by the public schoolboys at Cambridge and had been brooding on the injustices of life which meant that such people could enjoy the great quadrangles and magnificent libraries of Cambridge while cleverer friends of his were forced into dead-end jobs because they could not afford to go to university. He regarded himself as a pacifist when he was asked that November to go to the demonstration. 'There were two medical students on my staircase and they asked me to go. I said no. Then they said there might be a free fight with the Tories. I had been a boxer at school and so I went along.'[14] It was the start of a lifelong commitment to communism. Fisher joined the party in 1934 and became one of the university's most active communist campaigners.

Brian Simon was another student who watched the demonstrations of 1933 with fascination. He came from a classic liberal-intellectual background. His father, Lord Simon of Wythenshawe, was a wealthy industrialist and a Liberal MP. His mother had sat on Manchester Council's education committee. After going to Gresham's (the public school also attended by Donald Maclean), Simon was sent to study in Germany at the famous school at Salem run by Kurt Hahn, former secretary to Prince Max of Baden. The school was intended to promote international understanding, but there was precious little understanding being shown when Simon was a pupil there. Fifty years later he could still remember vividly Kurt Hahn being dragged away by Hitler's brownshirts: 'You could not help being political after seeing something like that. Many of us were deeply affected by the rise of Nazism. We had a clear view of what it meant for science, the arts, for culture and for peace.'[15] Brian Simon made his decision in 1935 and joined the Communist Party. As in the case of Sam Fisher it was a lifelong commitment, which endured the disappointments of the Nazi–Soviet pact, the Stalin show trials and mass arrests and the post-war occupation of Eastern Europe.

The march in Cambridge on 11 November was organized by the Socialist Society and the Student Christian Movement and was intended as a protest against the 'growing militarism of the Cenotaph celebrations in London and against the turning of the whole affair into a gigantic rag by poppy-sellers in Cambridge'. But the demonstration of solidarity by the forces of the Left and of pacifism was shown to be fragile. There were arguments over the message on the wreath that they planned to place on the war memorial. Some of the far Left, including John Cornford, demanded that some reference be made to 'the victims of the Great War from those who are determined to prevent similar crimes of imperialism'. But other demonstrators objected. They were supporters of the League of Nations, the organization which had the mandate of maintaining peace and preventing another major conflict. The League had a dismal record: America had refused to join, Germany had been a member for only seven years (1926 to 1933), and the Soviet Union, which joined in 1934, was expelled in 1939. The argument over the message, petty though it may have seemed at the time, presaged far greater disagreements among the Left and the anti-fascist forces that took place during the late 1930s.

From the start of the demonstration there was ill-tempered scuffling. As the march reached Peterhouse College, there was a full-scale fight. The police drew their batons; the hearties threw clouds of flour and feathers. At last, the Left felt that they had made an impact. One contemporary student account recorded: 'We felt like men who had won a battle and stopped feeling foolish. The event made us feel there was a need for protest and action on behalf of peace. A large number of demonstrators became from that time very active in the anti-war movement.'[16]

The national press was less impressed. In February that year the Oxford Union had debated and carried the motion that 'This House would in no circumstances fight for King and Country', and now the country was being treated to the disgraceful spectacle of students at Cambridge ridiculing the sacrifice of brave men in the First World War. They were denounced as 'young hooligans who had got what they deserved for desecrating a holy day'. The students, however, ignored the hostile publicity and continued to support unfashionably radical causes.

In February 1934 the hunger marchers again reached Cambridge on their way to London to protest against unemployment. The national press screamed that the bedraggled marchers were a 'mob of red dupes whose leaders were paid weekly in Moscow gold'. This sort of coverage confirmed to communists that they should never believe anything the capitalist press wrote, and it encouraged apolitical students to listen more carefully to the communist recruiters than they might otherwise have done. The communists had been active before the march reached Cambridge, explaining why students should be concerned with 'the militant working-class movement'. The Socialist Society, now dominated by Marxists, raised £120 for the men. A reception was organized at Girton, a women's college. An essay by a group of undergraduates noted:

Most of the demonstrators had little personal knowledge of the working class and of the militant working class almost none. It was a thrilling moment when they met the tired, cheerful, shabby column whose progress on the road they had followed day by day. Then the students and the unemployed formed up together and marched back down the long hill into Cambridge. At first some of the students were a bit shy and self-conscious, wondering whether they had a right to be there, wondering whether it would be a cheek to buy packets of cigarettes for the men. Gradually they began to enjoy it, singing 'Pie in the Sky' and 'Solidarity for Ever' and the rest of the marchers' songs.[17]

For many students the sight of victims of unemployment came as a huge shock. That evening there was an indoor meeting and the young Marxists and socialists listened spellbound to speakers from the march; rough men with broad regional accents who spoke with the same passion as the student communists, except that *they* spoke from experience. Some students, including Guy Burgess, decided they would link up with the march when it reached London in March. Others decided that they had no choice but to become communists. Brian Simon said it seemed that day as if the country could not go on much longer under the present system. He looked towards the Soviet Union, where the planned, centralized economy, he believed, would never allow so many men to fall so low as the hunger marchers.

Another student who was profoundly moved that day was Margot Heinemann, who was to become one of the British Communist Party's most loyal intellectuals. She had come up to Cambridge on an English scholarship in 1931:

I joined the party because this was the organization that was trying to do something about unemployment and fascism. We thought that everyone was winnable for the cause because capitalism was so obviously such a rotten system. Even Guy Burgess was on our side. I remember going on a march with him. He was wearing a Pitt Club yellow scarf singing, 'One, Two, Three, Four, Who are we for, We are for the Working Class.' The hunger marchers were older men and very fragile. Their faces had fallen in and they had ill-fitting boots. After seeing them it was only a matter of time before I joined the party.[18]

Heinemann was small and combative. Fifty years later she thought that the 1930s were 'the most effective period in my life' and that it was 'perhaps the only time the Communist Party got it right'. She came from a well-off German-Jewish *émigré* family who lived in Hampstead. Her parents were non-Orthodox and called themselves socialists, though this did not stop them sending Margot and her sister to Roedean, a public school for girls just outside Brighton. They told Margot that this was because they wanted her to have the best possible start in life, but they did not, of course, approve in principle of public schools. The Heinemanns had 'nannies and maids and girls to do the rough work' but prided themselves on having a social conscience and would have been horrified at the suggestion that they were actually living rather well. Mrs Heinemann had been a pacifist during the First World War and had become involved with the Women's International League. Margot came to the conclusion that society was unjust early in life when, on her way home from dancing classes, she considered the implications of a sign painted over a railway bridge in Kilburn: 'Orphanage for Female Orphans who have lost both their parents'. Her early attempts at Cambridge to come to grips with Marxism had not been successful – she tried to read Lenin's *Materialism and Empiro-Criticism* and gave up in despair – but it was inevitable that she would join the communist cause. Her home in Hampstead during the 1930s was filled with Jewish refugees from Germany; living proof of the consequences of fascism.

Heinemann's political life was complicated by the fact that she was a woman, a relatively rare breed in the

Cambridge student population. Women had been given degree-taking status in 1922. Most heterosexual male students regarded them as frumpy blue-stockings and preferred to hunt for girlfriends in London. There were logistic problems, too, if a student wanted to have an affair with a girl from the university. Women from Girton and Newnham needed chaperons if they had tea in a man's room. Girton had been built three miles out to ensure that contact with men was kept to a minimum. Girton students were bussed in to lectures and promptly bussed out again. For most male students, who had been educated at public schools, it did not seem odd that their day-to-day lives were spent almost exclusively in the company of other men. Margot Heinemann, however, managed to be both a success academically and with men. At first she was in love with David Hedley, Burgess's schoolfriend, but the relationship ended after she met John Cornford. She recalled: 'I had never met anyone like him. He was very good-looking and had hair that we always told him to cut. He was incredibly scruffy. He worked very hard at his studies and told me that he would have liked to have read English and not history because it would have given him more time for politics.'[19] The romance faltered because Cornford had had a child by another woman, but the attraction between him and Heinemann proved strong. They set up home together, becoming the perfect communist couple with an unimpeachable knowledge of Marx and Lenin and superb academic records – but then most of the leading communists, she pointed out proudly, had brilliant minds. Life as a revolutionary waiting for the big day was disappointingly mundane; they read reports to each other and talked endlessly about the tactics of the Communist International.

The growth in the student communist movement – not just at Cambridge but at universities around the country – surprised the apparatchiks at party headquarters in King

Street. Douglas Hyde, a former preacher and apprentice dental technician who later became news editor of the communist newspaper, the *Daily Worker*, and who was a veteran party campaigner, sometimes overtly, sometimes covertly, before resigning in 1948, recalled:

> The party was pleased, of course, about the students but it distrusted them and always had done. Don't forget that during the General Strike of 1926 the students had been strike-breakers. For a long time the party was the party of the unemployed and apart from a few people, like Palme Dutt, the intellectuals had dropped out. Even in 1931 the party was still concerned mainly with the unemployed. At no time, I think, did it make a beeline for the universities. But slowly the party realized that it had been a mistake to think that all students were just part of the reactionary petite-bourgeoisie.[20]

By late 1933 the party ideologues had relaxed their previously hostile stance towards anyone from the upper or middle classes and were only too glad to accept mandatory donations from members with a good income. But some theorists within the CPGB, such as Rajani Palme Dutt, stubbornly refused to accept that it needed to broaden its appeal. He said there was no point in trying to court the petite-bourgeoisie. The party's image had suffered, too, from the behaviour of its more active members. In 1929, thirty-one communists, including two Englishmen, Philip Spratt and Ben Bradley, were charged in India with 'conspiracy to deprive the King-Emperor of sovereignty over British India'. Four years later Spratt was sentenced to twelve years' transportation in Australia and Bradley to ten years. Then there was the unfortunate case of Arthur Eyles, an unemployed miner, and John Ryan, an unemployed labourer, who were found guilty in 1930 of distributing leaflets to British servicemen that were 'an incitement to mutiny'. Communists were also blamed for the mutiny by Royal Navy sailors at Invergordon in Scotland in 1931. Wherever people looked communists, probably acting on the orders of the Soviet Union, appeared to be actively trying to destroy the country. It was all very well to demand a fairer deal for the working class but why did that involve subverting the loyalty, for example, of the Royal Navy? The party theorists could see the justification but the workers could not.

Certainly the party could not have wished for a more propitious period. Even a Conservative politician such as Harold Macmillan, a future Prime Minister, thought in 1931 that the old order was crumbling. He said:

> After 1931 many of us felt that the disease was deep rooted. It had been evident that the structure of capitalist society in its old form had broken down, not only in Britain, but all over Europe and perhaps even the United States. The whole system had to be reassessed. Perhaps it could not survive at all; certainly not without radical change. Something like a revolutionary situation had developed, not only at home but overseas.[21]

Slowly King Street realized that the CPGB would never make any progress if it continued to show contempt for the rest of the Left in Britain. Harry Pollitt, a tough, no-nonsense member of the party executive, said in 1932 that communists had to convince trades unions that they did not want to destroy them. It was 'absolutely false', argued Pollitt, to argue that the unions were now 'schools of capitalism'. Of course, that was precisely what the party had claimed, but the British communist leaders, like politicians everywhere, had the ability to erase old policies from their minds as if they had never existed. Rajami Palme

Dutt, though, was still resisting and said that it was hopeless trying to work 'with corrupt union leaders'; much better to bypass them and appeal to the masses directly. Pollitt won the debate. There was one insurmountable problem for everyone at King Street, however: the workers showed no interest in taking to the barricades. In the absence of a spontaneous uprising the party would have to work through existing parliamentary institutions. But that was not much use either, since Lenin had declared that 'the capitalist class would never allow itself to be expropriated by successive acts of parliament'.

In 1977, as he surveyed the shattered dreams of the British communist movement, James Klugmann, the party's historian, tried to find an explanation for its failure to take advantage of a potentially revolutionary situation in the 1930s. The party had made democracy a 'dirty word' because it was part of the ideology of the bourgeoisie. That was a mistake, he conceded, in a country wedded to the notion that people had a right to decide their own fates. The communists showed contempt for British national pride, they were infatuated by the Soviet Union and were unable to accept that there were problems there, too. The historian Noreen Branson described the attitude then towards the Soviets:

It was clear that the foundations of an up-to-date economy had been established in record time and against overwhelming odds. It was not just the economic achievements which were impressive. To those on the Left it seemed a new kind of society was in the making. Unlike Britain, there were no unemployed in the Soviet Union and while workers in capitalist countries were struggling against wage cuts, in the Soviet Union wages were increasing.[22]

The victory of the Nazis in the 1933 German elections heightened the fears of the Soviets and their communist friends in Europe that fascism was not going to provoke the final revolution. Something had to be done to prevent other countries electing fascist governments. The Bulgarian, Georgi Dimitrov, told Stalin in Moscow in 1934 that communists would have to ally with other forces on the Left. Although the Communist International did not endorse this strategy until 1935 – which eventually led to Popular Front governments in France and Spain – the rank-and-file communists in Britain were already moving in this direction by 1934.

One stimulus to end the communists' sectarian isolation came from the popularity of Oswald Mosley's fascist Blackshirts. Mosley had started his political life as a Conservative, switched to the Labour Party and then, in MacDonald's government of 1929, in which he had served as Chancellor of the Duchy of Lancaster, veered off into extremism. He founded the British Union of Fascists (BUF) in 1932, to the approval of Lord Rothermere who owned the *Daily Mail*, the London *Evening News* and the *Sunday Dispatch*, and who wrote an article headlined, 'Hurrah for the Blackshirts'. The *Sunday Dispatch* even offered prizes to readers who could send in the best line on why they liked the Blackshirts. By 1934 the BUF had 40,000 members, many of whom came from the professions and the armed forces. But then Mosley, who had appeared to many to be simply bringing a radical but patriotic approach to politics, became openly anti-Semitic and Hitlerite. Many supporters dropped out, to be replaced by thugs who liked the idea of beating up Jews. There is no doubt that the rise of the Blackshirts helped the communists. It was thus more difficult for the Labour Party and the trades unions, still suspicious of the communists, to reject their advances to become allies in the fight against fascism.

While the CPGB was tentatively trying to link up with socialists and the unions (and trying to infiltrate them using covert communists) it had also begun to see if it could mobilize support in the universities. In the Easter of 1932 student communists from Cambridge, Oxford, the LSE and University College, London, had met at Klugmann's home in Hampstead. They were joined by Dave Springhall, the party's national organizer, who listened as the students argued about tactics and autonomy. By 1933 Harry Pollitt was saying that students, intellectuals, authors, doctors, scientists and professors – once the sworn enemies of the party – were valuable allies. The party had cells at Oxbridge and in London University as well as at the universities of Reading, Durham, Leeds and Manchester, although each cell had only a handful of members. At Cambridge the communists adopted the usual party ploy of infiltrating other leftist groups, such as the Cambridge University Socialist Society.

At Cambridge the early Marxists had been ashamed of their breeding and their intelligence; they wanted to show that they had renounced their past. Some gave up their private fortunes while others, such as John Cornford, found the idea of 'culture' repellent – he used to stroll around the university with Klugmann shouting: 'Keep Culture out of Cambridge.' But now the party wanted students to be successful, as students, not as would-be worker-revolutionaries. Klugmann recalled:

One of the dramatic moments was the visit of the Clydeside communist, Willie Gallacher. He was offended by the sort of language, clothing and attitude of the comrades who wanted to leave the university and who denigrated their own academic work. Out of this meeting came the slogan: every communist student a good student. He said: we want people who are capable, who are good scientists, historians and teachers. It doesn't follow at all you'll be good workers. We need you as you are. If you have a vocation it is pointless to run away to factories. One or two of you may become full-time revolutionaries but this is a thing only a few of you will be able to do. We want you to study and be good students.[23]

As a result of this speech, the proportion of communist students who were awarded first-class degrees rose from about 5 per cent to 60 per cent. But one thing did not alter: the attitude towards the Soviet Union remained as uncritical as ever. It was epitomized by a book called *Soviet Communism, A New Civilisation?* by the Fabians, Sidney and Beatrice Webb, published in 1935. They had visited Russia and reported that there was no oppression; there was 'widespread participation in government and near universal participation in multiform democracy'; and, the writers concluded, only under communism could intellectuals be free from the corrupting demands of the market economy.

Anthony Blunt later gave several, conflicting accounts of the way in which he had become a communist. In his article in 1972 for *Studio International* he said that he had spent the autumn term of 1933 away from Cambridge and returned in January 1934 to find 'almost all my younger friends had become Marxists overnight and joined the Communist Party'. But in 1979, at the press conference he gave after being named as a spy in the House of Commons, he dated it like this: 'I became a communist or more particularly a Marxist in 1935–36. The history is that I had a sabbatical year's leave from Cambridge in 1933–34 and when I came back all my friends and almost all the intelligent, bright undergraduates had suddenly become Marxists under the impact of Hitler coming to power.' Blunt was either genuinely confused when he gave this later version or he was lying, attempting to disguise the fact that by the beginning of 1934 at the latest he was, like his friend Guy Burgess, a communist. Blunt spent the academic year 1933–34 working on his thesis, 'The History and Theories of Painting in Italy and France from 1400 to 1700' and travelled to research this, spending some time in Rome with Ellis Waterhouse, who was librarian at the British School there. Waterhouse recalled:

> We took much trouble to explore the monuments of what we called the Passalacqua period which was as neglected then as it is fashionable now. And at meal times in the school the secretary would become exasperated at our language which she called Blunterhouse and which she was powerless to understand. Many of the less familiar buildings of Rome are enlivened in recollection by having been visited with him.[24]

Waterhouse also met Burgess for the first time in Rome, probably in the same year, although Waterhouse could not be certain of the date:

> We had a jolly interesting time. The trouble was that Burgess liked going to noisy places and I didn't. He was very funny and Anthony was devoted to him. He used to tell us stories about his adventures with politicians and young boys and Anthony and I used to decide they were probably untrue. He was the biggest liar in the western hemisphere, you know. But they were very funny. Anthony was politically naïve. I don't think he ever had the slightest idea about politics. We never talked politics at all. But that was all Guy wanted to discuss. He was exceedingly intelligent about politics and Anthony fol-

lowed what he did. As far as I was concerned I did not think Anthony was ever a serious communist. He wrote some silly articles but I thought always that he had given up after the Nazi–Soviet pact in 1939. I don't think he would have said he was one either.[25]

Most of their Cambridge friends knew that Burgess and Blunt claimed to be communists by late 1933 or early 1934. Burgess had been talking admiringly of the young Marxists for some time before this, although no one really believed that Guy was committed to anything except having a good time. Anthony's friends thought that his political sense was almost nil; if he was a communist it was because, first, Guy was one and, second, because it was fashionable. Brian Simon and Margot Heinemann thought of Blunt as just another dilettante leftist. Simon could not recall ever discussing politics with Blunt, who was, it seemed, interested only in art history. Heinemann recalled that Burgess was always attending party meetings, though no one could really take him that seriously. He would listen to Figaro's 'Aria' and ask her, can't you hear the bourgeois revolution in that? He was a handsome rogue who should not be taken too seriously. Blunt was a temporary fellow-traveller; one of many young dons who professed to be communists but who would never be seen selling the *Daily Worker*. In the 1980s Heinemann could not speak about Blunt without feeling angry. 'I don't regard what Blunt did as the proper way to bring revolution to this country. For people like myself who have been working to convince people this sort of thing, spying, sets things back. You have to convince the majority or settle for less. The Blunt affair was a disaster for the party.'[26]

Steven Runciman found Blunt 'supercilious and patronising':

There is no doubt in my mind that he was one of twenty people who were morally converted by John Cornford, who was relentless about recruiting people. I have no doubt that Cornford made an impact on Burgess first and then through Burgess on Blunt. I always had a soft spot for Guy. He was provocative but it was all done with a certain light-heartedness. Communism sat very strangely on him. But one didn't take it very seriously. But he was the only person who managed to explain Marxism to me in a way that made sense. When he was sober he was very good company but then he became so dirty one could hardly bear it. I didn't mind the drunkenness but I did mind the dirt.[27]

Many students could not believe that the gangling, aloof don who was always talking about obscure artists would stoop to active involvement in politics. The only reason someone like Blunt would be involved was if he found the men in the communist movement intellectually stimulating, socially acceptable and attractive. Charles Martin Robertson, a Trinity classicist, the son of a Trinity don and later Lincoln Professor of Archaeology and Art at Oxford, recalled:

I had been brought up to have a great interest in painting and the history of art and it was as an enthusiast for that, not as a political figure that I thought of Anthony Blunt. I think I did know that he was a communist, as a number of my friends were, including John Cornford and Kim Philby. John was a much more powerful figure, a dedicated communist in a way that I did not feel Anthony or Kim were. I disliked the idea of communism but fell for the idea of a Popular Front of all the left against the fascists. I wasn't at all politically minded and no one thought it worthwhile trying to recruit me. I thought of

Anthony in the context of intellectuals and aesthetes around the Apostles, who I thought were self-satisfied and precious. Perhaps that was sour grapes because I was never asked to join. The Apostles had a strong tendency then towards homosexuality and it was Guy Burgess who exhibited the least pleasant side of this. He was conspicuously dirty and drunk. He was repellent. But he was a great friend of Anthony's. I never knew what he saw in him.[28]

Neither Blunt nor Burgess made any attempt to disguise their communism but none of the key communist leaders, such as Brian Simon or Sam Fisher, could recall in the 1980s whether or not Blunt and Burgess had formally joined the party, although Burgess later claimed to have paid his dues and held a party card. In many ways this was irrelevant. Burgess had a large Marxist library and, to demonstrate his solidarity with the workers, had organized a strike of Trinity College's servants. He remained proud of this for the rest of his life. In Moscow he recounted the story to his biographer, Tom Driberg. The waiters, he said, had been employed on a casual basis and during the vacations had to find other work. Burgess helped organize a protest against these conditions, forcing the college authorities, or so he claimed, to give ground. On another occasion he boasted that he had bravely heckled the Chancellor of the Exchequer, Neville Chamberlain, attending a dinner at Trinity. No one, therefore, could pretend that Burgess or Blunt had been covert communists at Cambridge; they appeared to be just two more out of the hundreds who professed broad sympathy with the communists.

Many older dons found this extremely distressing. Maynard Keynes's biographer, Roy Harrod, noted:

Keynes could not but observe the tendency towards communism among the youth at Cambridge and most markedly among the choice spirits, those whom thirty years before he would have wished to consider for membership of the Society. He attributed it to a recrudescence of the strain of puritanism in our blood, the zest to adopt a painful solution because of its painfulness.[29]

But some Apostles could see why communism held such an appeal. One recalled:

There was a real sense of moral shock – above all, to those brought up more or less in the 'establishment' – as it became clear that nothing effective was to be done either about unemployment in this country or the rapid breakdown of peace . . . It was difficult for anyone to get jobs and the fate of those who had gone down a year before, simply to join the unemployed, pressed very realistically on those who were still up. We were all, moreover, of obviously military age and the war that we saw coming we did not want to fight. It was always clear to anyone with any sense that the main aim of British foreign policy was to send a rearmed Germany eastwards. We didn't think it would work or that it ought to work and we were damned well right. And it gave us, our consciousness of what was going on, a special kind of disgust for our elders, the politicians and so forth.[30]

Communists at Cambridge did not bother to found their own group. Instead they took control of the Socialist Society, driving moderates out to form their own organization in the summer of 1934. The communists adopted a new slogan: 'Socialist students the most active upholders of peace, democracy and civilization.' The unity of the Left – communists, socialists of varying shades of red, pacifists –

was brittle, but it held. The fear of war was a powerful bond at Cambridge, for students knew they would be high-risk cannon fodder in any conflict – just as they had been during the First World War.

The main forces responsible for recruiting young men at Cambridge into the party were James Klugmann and John Cornford, aided by their lieutenant, Sam Fisher. Fisher said that Klugmann was 'the arch recruiter, who roped them in by the score at Trinity.' At one time, Fisher said, there were fifty Communist Party members in that one college, although that was followed by mass resignations when there was 'a dispute over poetry' – the details of which have long been forgotten. Fisher proved so efficient that he was asked to join the party's organizing committee, the real heart of the student party. There he sat alongside Klugmann, Cornford and a fourth, unidentified student.

The tactics of the party were the usual, well-tried ploys used by communists throughout Europe. The most conscientious student activists would draw up lists, grading students as A, B or C, according to how likely they were to succumb to the arguments of the recruiters. But, to many, the not-very-efficient secrecy surrounding all this was more fun than the actual politics. Not all communists had to carry a party card; in some cases, where they might go on to become barristers or civil servants, this might prove a handicap so the party was understanding and waived the obligation of paying a membership fee. But this practice was common knowledge. Indeed, most party members could reel off the names of the so-called discreet communists. For the rank-and-file communists life consisted of trying to sell the *Daily Worker* to townspeople, most of whom ignored the students brandishing a publication that they had never heard of. There were dull meetings to discuss Marx. The 'fellow-travellers' who did not hold a party card were considered fortunate: they had the respectability of being left-wing without the drudgery.

Few Cambridge communists knew anything about the links between their leaders, the Klugmanns and Cornfords, and King Street. And even fewer could have had any idea that Soviet Intelligence planned to use selected students as future spies. It would have been regarded as a dreadful slander on the Soviet Union to have suggested that it would resort to such underhand tactics. The Soviets made sure that they never directly contacted students at Cambridge, a policy that was followed with communist organizations elsewhere in Britain. At the *Daily Worker* Douglas Hyde was instructed never to call the Soviet embassy; it was, he was told, essential to 'keep away and be separate'. Hyde had no doubt that the party was instructing members to go underground. After the Reichstag fire in 1933 he heard that the party would be expelling all homosexuals as security risks (there was a suggestion that van der Lubbe, who was homosexual, had been blackmailed into committing arson). But one of Hyde's party colleagues was told that his expulsion did not mean the end of his work for the cause. There were other ways to serve the party. Perhaps, Hyde speculated fifty years later, similar pressures were applied to others.[31] The surviving organizers of the student movement insist that they had no idea that the Soviets were talent-spotting. Sam Fisher, for instance, had no theories on who might have made the contact between the Cambridge Marxists and their Soviet case officers. But Fisher could see why the Soviets had reaped such a rich harvest; in the 1930s a request to help the Soviets would not really be treachery. After all, wasn't the British Establishment hoping to turn Hitler eastwards?

CHAPTER 6
Red Cells

It is not surprising that the spy-hunters of MI5, who later tried to unravel the left-wing movement at the universities during the 1930s, found it so hard to work out who had been a communist, never mind a spy. There were literally hundreds of elderly, distinguished old gentlemen and women in Britain in the 1970s who had been members, overtly or covertly, of the Communist Party and many more who had been regarded as 'fellow-travellers' by the party. Brian Simon, for example, estimated that there were 1000 members at any one time during the mid- and late 1930s of the Marxist-dominated Socialist Society. They included future judges, lawyers, academics, politicians, civil servants, writers and artists. There was even one case of a fully fledged Communist Party member, Andrew King, joining MI6 after leaving Cambridge.

King arrived in Cambridge in the autumn of 1933 to study economics at Magdalene College. He had spent the spring and summer of that year in Germany and had been horrified by what he had seen. Soon he was targeted by one of the college's most active recruiters, James Roualeyn Hovell-Thurlow-Cumming-Bruce, a future judge and Lord Justice of Appeal, who had rooms above his. Like most other proselytizing students, Cumming-Bruce did not know that student communists he was targeting were being singled out by the Soviets as future agents. King decided to become a socialist and joined the university's Socialist Society, but the communists continued to argue that only they were really determined to fight Hitler. It was suggested that should King agree to become a party member within the Socialist Society, he could stand for election as the society's treasurer, assured of the communists' votes. In 1934 King succumbed and joined the party. He said: 'I had a card which I lost. I had to pay about 20 per cent of my income to the party which was jolly high. Most students at Cambridge had private allowances from their families and we all had to donate money to the party. I certainly wasn't a covert member.'[1] King left the party a year later, disgusted that the communists had been so wrong about the result of the plebiscite in the Saar. (This was held in January 1935 to decide whether the area should return to German control. The communists argued that it would result in a rejection of Hitler; instead, there was a massive pro-German majority.)

Francis Edward Hovell-Thurlow-Cumming-Bruce (later Lord Thurlow) had a varied career in the civil service after leaving Trinity College. He was, among many other things, a deputy under-secretary at the Foreign Office and a governor of the Bahamas. Francis was naturally at home with the 'huntin', shootin' and fishin' set' before he was pressured into becoming a communist. He went up to Trinity in the early 1930s and became a communist after his brother James Roualeyn Hovell-Thurlow-Cumming-Bruce had convinced him it was the best thing to do. Lord Thurlow recalled:

I had two happy years before I became a Marxist in my third year. But my brother James became a very enthusiastic communist. He was converted, I think, by Charles Madge. I was dragged along psychologically. James was at Magdalene and became a sort of communist firebrand. We saw each other in the vacations. I couldn't answer all that terrible Marxist claptrap and if I couldn't answer I felt I had to accept it. We had the usual communist structure that they go in for all over the world. You know, cells and the like. We used to study Marx and Lenin and we used to talk about how to increase awareness amongst other undergraduates. Klugmann was in my cell. Remarkable chap. Very clever. And Donald Maclean was very much to the fore. The cell structure wasn't secret so much as confidential. I distributed the *Daily Worker* on the working-class council estates on Sunday mornings but they weren't the least bit interested in it. But I also belonged to the Pitt Club. It had nice premises and served a good lunch. It was just like a London club and I joined because my father had been a member. There was a £30 entrance fee which was a lot in those days, but my father paid. During the vacations I forgot all about Marxism because I didn't want to hurt the feelings of my parents. They didn't understand this Marxism thing so I forgot it and enjoyed hunting foxes.[2]

Lord Thurlow did not care much for Blunt. He thought that he was 'a pinkie, an aesthete who kept his fingers quite unsoiled by political matters'. It stood out a mile, said Thurlow, that Blunt was 'absolutely top notch intellectually', and that he looked down on people whose brains were not as fine as his. Burgess was altogether more likeable. Thurlow thought that he was 'incredibly clever and amusing but so devoid of wisdom and judgement that no one in their senses would ever employ him on anything practical'. When he heard that Burgess had joined the Foreign Office after the war he could not believe it and feared that it would end in calamity – which is, of course, exactly what happened. Thurlow could see that Guy and Anthony were extremely close, although it was curious, he thought, that Burgess clearly dominated the older man.

Michael Straight, a brilliant young American whose family was one of the East Coast's most influential dynasties, arrived at Trinity College in the autumn of 1934. He was already a socialist, though he had resisted making the final transition to fully fledged Marxism. He had spent the previous academic year at the London School of Economics, where political life was just as turbulent and perhaps more ruthless than at Cambridge. Straight had been educated at Dartington Hall, a liberal English public school in the West Country which had been founded by his mother and her second husband, Leonard Elmhirst. Straight's father, Willard, had been a career diplomat and his brother, Whitney, became a wartime pilot with the RAF, took British citizenship and later became chairman of Rolls-Royce and two airlines, BOAC and BEA.

Straight's ability to agonize, to debate endlessly with himself over his motives and emotions, was apparent even then. He felt guilty because he was independently wealthy, yet he could not bear to renounce his private income, treasuring the independence it gave. He adored surrounding himself with expensive pictures, such as the early Picasso he had bought in Paris, but to assuage his self-loathing he promised that he would give the painting to a museum – after he had 'clasped it to myself'. Neither British nor American, he debated with himself about the implications of not having a strong sense of nationality. 'Transplanted as I was, I lacked a sense of loyalty to British or American institutions; I was not held in place by a national tradition. I had been uprooted; I was waiting to be reclaimed. I believed in equality; I feared violence and war.'[3]

This agonizing continued at Trinity. He fretted about leaving expensive meat on his plate in case it offended the badly paid college waiters and he felt ashamed that he had his own personal servant – whom he fired despite the man's protests that he needed the job. He worked hard at economics, relishing Keynes's lectures.

Straight was a rebel waiting for a cause and soon after arriving at Trinity he found one. The talent-spotting team of John Cornford and James Klugmann, who had been given Straight's name by comrades at the LSE, persuaded him to join the Marxist-dominated Socialist Society. Straight calculated that it had 200 members then and 600 when he left in 1937; of that number, he reckoned one in four belonged to communist cells. From there it was only a small step for Straight to become a Marxist, joining the Trinity cell of twelve. After all, what did it matter whether one called oneself a socialist or a communist? By now the Communist Party had moved towards the strategy of a Popular Front to resist fascism. Straight insisted that he was only a casual member of the student movement, giving as much money as possible to the party's much-liked, down-to-earth Harry Pollitt, but remaining aloof from the intriguing that went on between leaders such as Klugmann and party headquarters in King Street. Straight reassured himself that he had not forfeited his intellectual freedom; he had not been asked to be a mole to penetrate non-communist student societies.

Straight was terrified that his communism might become known outside the closed student world of Cambridge. He enjoyed the status conferred by friendship with the giants of the Left, Cornford and Klugmann. It was, he thought later, not so much a question of believing in Marxism but rather of being given a 'sense of brotherhood', a feeling that, at last, he was accepted:

My role in the communist movement was in the [Cambridge] Union, where I discovered unknown qualities of being able to convert and persuade. John Cornford left me in charge and suddenly I was a person in my own right with a role to play among my contemporaries. I remember once making a speech against the blackshirts. I began: On behalf of the communist liberals. It was a crazy thing to say but it was precisely what others were saying. There is, of course, no connection between communism and liberalism but I meant by that someone who believes in freedom but who associated himself with the student communist movement because on everything that mattered – Hitler, stopping Japan defending Abyssinia, raising money for Spain, opposing Mosley – it was the most powerful and resolute movement that existed. The sense of belonging . . . was enormously exhilarating. I have no regrets about belonging to the communist movement. Keynes respected the student communists but neither he nor I nor anyone else understood what the movement's function was – a recruiting ground for a foreign arm of Stalin's foreign policy. So, in that sense, we were all betrayed.[4]

He tried to convey this to his mother in November 1935:

I'd lived in fear that I'd become incapable of loving. Now I've learned that I'm able to love the communist students, even if I don't love communism itself. I'm filled with a violent, uncontrollable love for them; an extraordinary sense of comradeship. It's unreasonable and inexplicable. It burns within me and I can't express it; I can't get it out.[5]

Straight insisted that he was never physically attracted to men, and that it had dawned on him only gradually that most of his friends were homosexuals.

Leo Long could not have been more different, in background and temperament, from the rich, self-obsessed Straight. Long arrived at Trinity on a modern languages scholarship in the autumn of 1935. His father was a carpenter in Holloway, north London. Long said:

> I called myself a communist about the time I went to Cambridge. I was a working-class boy from a secondary school. My father was often unemployed. It was a very poor background. Nowadays people talk about the numbers of people who are unemployed but there is really no comparison. The unemployed were not underpinned by social security. When I went to Cambridge I had a grant of £250 a year, which was wealth to me. My father's declared income was £110 a year. That is when he was in work. I had a deep sense of the inequity of society. We lived with some very harsh realities. I remember seeing the hunger marchers come through Cambridge. They couldn't eat the food we gave them, eggs and so on, because their stomachs had shrunk. It was a hunger march literally. If we thought about a future at all we wondered whether this country would face up to the Germans. You have to make a time jump and try to imagine what it was like. The Nazis were getting stronger and all the time there were concessions made [by the British and European democracies]. It looked like deliberate conniving.[6]

Within his first year Long had joined the Trinity communist cell. He was given texts to study to improve his knowledge of Marxism; he was instructed to work hard for a good degree, since communists had to be better than everyone else; he was asked to help recruit other students to the party; he was urged to try to become an officer of the supposedly broad left Socialist Society which the communists were determined to control. He did as he was told and became one of the joint secretaries. But then, Long said, there wasn't much harm in this type of infiltration; the

differences between socialists and Marxists were a minor
problem compared to tackling the threat of fascism. Long
recalled:

Cambridge was a strange world to me. Apart from a few
hard-working scholars it was an extension for most
people of life at public school. I had no natural brilliance.
I worked hard. I knew James Klugmann but I only knew
Blunt because he was my supervisor in French studies.
He was a very considerable scholar even then. He was an
aesthete. The world of politics meant nothing to him. It is
hard to know what his motivation was for being a communist. I think the conspiracy must have appealed to
him. He was quite a dry, humorous lecturer. His Marxist
views on art were well known. There was no reason to be
cautious. Burgess was fascinating just to look at. In a
sense he was revolting, a sort of Dylan Thomas figure,
who was larger than life, always drunk. He was a creature
from a different world. Loud and camp, though that
word didn't exist then. I have no idea how Blunt was
recruited to become a talent spotter for the Soviets. I am
sure that he was helped by James Klugmann who was a
brilliant and a very nice man. But he was never covert.
He was an open communist and a very valuable one.
Cornford was the other great figure. He was very close to
Klugmann. You have to remember that we were desperately committed. There was the Spanish Civil War and
we felt that we were the only people who took the threat
of fascism seriously. We did not trust the British government. It seemed to prefer links with the Nazis to having
ties with Russia. It wasn't that we were pro-Russian. A
lot of the stuff coming out of the Soviet Union was pretty
innocuous. It was all about the new education and the
new woman. I suppose it all came to a head with the
Spanish War. A lot of friends went to fight there. And

Cornford, who was a seminal figure, was killed there. What did we think would happen? I don't think there was much discussion about it. We just assumed there would be a war.[7]

Both Long and Straight became members of the Apostles. Straight was asked to join in the autumn of 1936 by David Champernowne, a student at King's College who went on to a distinguished career as an economist. Champernowne was never a communist though he knew both Blunt and Burgess well through the Apostles. He regarded Blunt as 'sherry red' – a reference to Blunt's habit of drinking large amounts of that beverage. Champernowne regarded Burgess, certainly before 1934, as a bright young man who was, probably temporarily, a communist. He often argued with Burgess, who used to recommend key Marxist texts in an effort to convert him. By 1935 Champernowne concluded that Burgess had 'gone over to the Conservatives' – a shift that seemed in keeping with Burgess's mercurial character.

As the newest and youngest Apostle Straight had to arrange the meetings. Helped by Keynes, he drew up invitation lists. Some of the most formidable brains in Cambridge were included: the historian G. M. Trevelyan, and G. E. Moore as well as the younger men such as Victor Rothschild, Anthony Blunt and Guy Burgess. There was Alister Watson, too, a quiet, brilliant science don at King's College. Watson was a communist, like many Apostles, though he was not a homosexual. Straight was intrigued by all the Apostles, but especially by Burgess:

He craved the companionship and the physical love of other men, which seemed to be a binding tie for many members of the society. With his curly hair, his sensual mouth, his bright blue eyes, his cherubic air, he seemed at first sight to embody in himself the ideal of male beauty that the Apostles revered. Then, on a closer look, you noticed the details: the black-rimmed fingernails; the stained forefinger in which he gripped his perpetual cigarette stub; the dark, uneven teeth; the slouch; the open fly. If he was angelic you sensed that he was a fallen angel. He smiled before he said anything but most of his comments had a cutting edge.[8]

Leo Long was unable to recall the exact date of his admission to the Apostles, though he thought he had been introduced by Michael Straight:

One has the idea now that it was a centre of espionage. That is not true. There was a great deal of silly, school-boyish jargon. A lot of us were Marxists because Marxists tended to be the brightest boys. Marxism was a dominant tone but we didn't think that strange. It is a self-recruiting body and if you were asked for the name of someone who might pass the test you thought of a friend. It wasn't sinister. Anyway, there was no point in communists trying to take over the Apostles. The Apostles weren't going to take over the world . . . It was all a bit of a racket really. They weren't the brightest people at all. It was a King's–Trinity monopoly and you got in because you happened to know someone.[9]

Cambridge science students were traditionally less politicized than their contemporaries in the arts. They spent their days in laboratories, talking about the mechanics of the atom rather than the meaning of life. But the economic crisis of the 1930s was so severe that many scientists, for the first time in their lives, began to wonder if there was not a better way of organizing the world. It was not logical or sensible to burn wheat, to dump oranges in the sea or to pour milk down the drain, just so that someone could maintain artificially high prices. It made no sense to cream off the best scientists to work on weapons research when the country needed to modernize its industries. Government grants for research had been cut, and unemployment, which rose to 3 million in 1933, meant that many science graduates had to take menial jobs when they left college.

Cambridge was the undisputed capital of British science. The university's excellence was best represented by the Cavendish laboratory, established in 1871, which was pioneering research in physics under its director Ernest Rutherford. Rutherford won the Nobel Prize for chemistry in 1908 and was now concentrating on finding ways to split the atom. He gathered round him some of the finest minds in the country and encouraged them to attack old, insoluble problems in new ways. In 1932 one of his protégés, James Chadwick, discovered the neutron – work which led to his Nobel Prize in 1935. The Cavendish had John Douglas Cockcroft and E. T. S. Walton, who produced the first laboratory nuclear reaction from accelerating particles to high energies. Cambridge also had John Desmond Bernal, the X-ray crystallographer and philosopher on the social role of science. Bernal was a brilliant source of original ideas but he was also an accessible teacher, with charm that captivated generations of students. He lived with Margot Heinemann for twenty years before his death in 1971 and although he regarded himself as a Marxist, and was regarded by others as one, he refused to hold a party card at first because he did not believe the party sufficiently appreciated intellectuals. Joseph Needham, the biochemist, was another scientific giant based at Cambridge. An expert on the history of science and civilization in China, he regarded himself as a 'Christian Marxist' – thus marrying two ideologies which less sophisticated minds found mutually exclusive.

In the summer of 1931 British scientists prepared for a meeting of the British Society for Social Responsibility in Science, due to be held in July at the Science Museum in London. It was expected that the conference would end without any answers on how science could change a world that was increasingly chaotic and without apparent purpose, apart from the manufacture of more efficient weapons. Only one Russian delegate had been expected to attend the conference, but late in June Stalin told the leader of the Comintern, Nikolai Bukharin, that he would head an eight-man delegation to London to swap ideas with the capitalists. Three days later the Soviet team left Moscow.

The Soviets did more than just exchange notes; they transformed the thinking of dozens of key British scientists.

J. G. Crowther recalled the excitement in his book *Fifty Years with Science*:

> The Soviet embassy became the headquarters of a unique publishing venture as their scientists frantically worked to produce a book. Embassy translators and proofreaders worked through the night. They missed the deadline and only managed to provide the delegates to the conference with unbound copies but when the book was published a week later it caused a sensation. It was called *Science at the Crossroads* and, in the minds of many left-wing scientists, provided a blueprint for the future role of science and scientists in the crumbling capitalist world . . . the Russians had crystallized the realization of the impossibility of using science fruitfully within the framework of capitalism. Bernal himself called the congress 'the most important meeting of ideas that has occurred since the Revolution'.[10]

Scientists who had previously not been sure how to translate their leftist ideas into action returned to their universities with a new confidence. Maurice Wilkins was a physics student at St John's College, Cambridge, who went on to win the Nobel Prize for medicine in 1962. The 1931 congress in London proved, he thought, that science could be used for the greater good of humanity; but it would not happen under capitalism. Marxism, however, emphasized the virtues of centralized planning in the interests of the people. Rid society of corrupting market forces, and science would be able to work for the benefit of humanity. That, at least, was how young men such as Wilkins saw the position. From 1931 onwards the number of scientists at Cambridge who were communists or communist sympathizers steadily increased. They united under the banner of the anti-war group, which used to meet in a basement beneath a café every lunchtime to discuss how to combat the 'militarism' of the government. The group concentrated for a time on the government's measures to protect the civilian population against air-raids. They pointed out that the shelters the government was building would not be strong enough to withstand the impact of modern bombs. And they proved that the low-cost gas-masks that would be issued during war were simply inadequate. The scientists were as blind as other communists to the realities of life in the Soviet Union. If there were imperfections there then this was because of 'the technical backwardness arising from Tsardom and the devastating wars of intervention backed by the allies'. Bernal argued that Soviet scientists had deliberately been isolated by the West; once there was peace and stability there they would outstrip their capitalist counterparts. But, like most left-wing scientists, he chose to ignore the mounting evidence that Soviet science was being suffocated by Stalin. Several members of the delegation to the 1931 congress died during the purges or were unable to work. Nikolai Vavilov, the biologist, died after being released from a prison camp in 1942. Bukharin, a veteran revolutionary who bravely if foolishly opposed Stalin's policy of 'super-industrialization', was executed in 1938.

Scientists at Cambridge valiantly tried to involve the workers in their work. At the Cavendish laboratory railway workers listened without comprehension as the nuances of atomic research were outlined to them. Medical students dressed the feet of the hunger marchers who passed through the town. Maurice Wilkins recalled: 'There were a lot of very sensible people who went along with Communist Party thinking. It is difficult to remember who held a party card and who didn't. In some ways that is academic. The point is that the party's policies were part of a broad stream. I can't remember if I held one or not.'[11]

In retrospect it is astonishing that the Soviet intelligence officers in London did not spend more time on the Cambridge scientists. There had been long-standing contacts, after all, between the British and Soviet scientific communities, despite Bernal's lament about Soviet isolation. The Soviets knew as well as anyone of Cambridge's lead in areas of research which had potential application for the military. In 1921 Peter Kapitza, a physicist who was lecturing at the Petrograd Polytechnical Institute, had arrived in Cambridge, intending to buy equipment for his own laboratory. But Rutherford had been so impressed by his visitor that he invited him to stay and become a research student. After producing stunning results in his chosen field, electromagnetism, Kapitza was elected a Fellow of the Royal Society in 1929 – the first foreigner in 200 years to be so honoured. In 1933 the Royal Society built a special laboratory to help him continue with his remarkable research. A year later, however, Kapitza decided to travel home on holiday. He had been back to the Soviet Union a dozen times since leaving in 1921. This time he was refused permission to return to Cambridge. A few months later the

Soviets bought Kapitza's entire laboratory; an indication that while politicians and the military in Britain might distrust the communists, the scientific community was more interested in exchanging information than worrying about political divisions.

Why then did Soviet intelligence officers in Britain not expend more energy trying to entice scientists to spy for them? Like most professional intelligence officers, the Soviets had an old-fashioned view of how they should operate. They had been brought up to believe that a spy was someone who worked in the enemy's defence ministry and was able to provide figures on regimental strengths or weapons supplies, or someone who was able to give the latest gossip from the inner councils of a government. Second, the Stalin purges affected the intelligence services as much as any other Soviet institution: men with flair and initiative were weeded out and the only way for officers to survive was to follow an orthodox line and avoid plans that could end in a recall to Moscow.

Klaus Fuchs was a German physicist and communist who had emigrated to Britain in 1933. He was naturalized during the Second World War so that he could work on the Manhattan project in the United States to produce the first atomic bomb. In 1946 he had returned to continue his top-secret investigations at the Harwell atomic research centre. In 1950 he was sentenced by an Old Bailey judge to fourteen years' imprisonment for passing secrets to the Soviets. Yet even Fuchs, one of the great post-war spying triumphs of the Soviet Union, had complained about the quality of Soviet case officers assigned to him. Fuchs told Sir Dick White, future head of MI5, that he was continually frustrated by the inability of his controller to understand theoretical physics. All the man could do, said Fuchs, was 'scribble equations on the backs of envelopes'.[12] There was only one other confirmed case of a British scientist passing secrets to the Soviets: the Cambridge-trained physicist Alan Nunn May. (The defence scientist Alister Watson, an Apostle who had been a Fellow of King's College and a member of the Communist Party, always denied that he had given information to the Soviets. MI5 did not believe him and had him moved from secret work in 1967.) Nunn May had been a communist as a student at Cambridge and appears to have been targeted by Soviet Intelligence when he travelled to Canada in 1943 to work on atom bomb research. He was arrested when he returned to Britain after the war and charged with passing secrets to the Russians. He was sentenced to ten years' imprisonment.

Maurice Wilkins thought that most scientists had just been too sensible to 'get mixed up in this spying business'. He had known Nunn May from school and considered that he had always been academically outstanding but hopelessly naïve. Wilkins thought that he had given material to the Soviets believing, foolishly perhaps, that it was wrong not to share the atomic secret:

> Spying is like terrorism. People only do it when they are frustrated. Most scientists think too clearly to become involved. When I worked on the Manhattan project no one asked me any questions about my political beliefs. In any event, it was only the politicians and the military people who kept saying what a great secret the atom bomb was. I am not saying that someone like Klaus Fuchs wasn't useful to the Soviets but not nearly as useful as people seem to think.[13]

Another friend of Nunn May, John Humphreys, recalled: 'He was a simple fellow. Brilliant but simple. He was a Communist Party member at Cambridge and when he went to Canada he was upset that the Russians were being kept out of atomic research. He felt there was a plot against the

Russian revolution. It was a very naïve thing to do.'[14]

Philip Gell, later a respected professor of pathology, had been educated at Stowe and was persuaded to become a communist by John Cornford. He was at Trinity, which had one of the strongest communist cells of any college. He spent his Sundays talking to railwaymen about cricket, since neither they nor he really wanted to discuss politics. He sold the *Daily Worker* and threw himself into local industrial disputes, though with little success. During one strike, involving the bus crews, the student communists managed to have their one friend at the bus garage sacked. Gell was just one of many decent, hard-working students who joined the party because they were terrified of fascism, not because they had any special love of the Soviet Union. He said:

Oh yes, I was an open communist. Burgess was an open communist too. He was very entertaining. I always thought that he was a very bitter person despite the outward charm and wit. Socially uneasy if you like. I thought Blunt was just another queen and an upper class intriguer, a remote, rather etiolated intellectual. We used to have lists of targets whom we would try and recruit. We used to have endless talks and read Lenin which bored me to tears. There was the usual communist technique of getting members elected on to committees and making them do things they didn't want to do. That was the tactic and I watched it. It was a lesson in how the minority can control the majority. And Cornford was central in planning it. It was party policy and happened everywhere. Both Cornford and Klugmann had contacts with headquarters in London and I know for certain that Cornford was aware that there were sleepers [the shorthand for communists who pretend to have renounced their faith] but personally I had no idea this was going on.

The Nazi–Soviet pact shook us rigid and that's what started my slide. I remember going to a party meeting in London when there were rumours of it and a party official said, no, no, there was no question of that happening. Then a week later that is what happened.[15]

Richard Synge, who won the Nobel Prize for chemistry in 1952, was another Trinity communist. He had been converted by John Madge and, like most scientists, was blissfully unaware of the depths of intrigue swirling within the student communist movement. He knew there were covert communists, but preferred to work in his laboratory rather than waste his time in idle talk. Few scientists then worried about their communism being made public, though many became more reticent after university, fearing that they would be blacklisted from sensitive work if their student membership of the CPGB were known.

John Humphrey was at Trinity from 1934 to 1937 and went on to become an eminent immunologist. He had been persuaded to join the party by James Klugmann, who had rooms above his. Years later Humphrey recited the familiar litany of reasons for his decision to join: unemployment, Hitler and the unwillingness of the British to stand up to fascism. But Humphrey, unlike many scientists, took time off from his studies to analyse the tactics of the movement that he had joined. He was, too, an Apostle, which gave him a valuable insight into how the intellectual élite viewed communism. 'Our relations with Anthony and Guy were social, aesthetic. We talked about big ideas. I didn't regard them as organized party members. Anthony was good company and Guy was a cynic but they were always together.'[16]

Meetings of the Apostles during this period were degenerating into arguments about politics rather than being, as they were intended, philosophical debates about the nature of reality. Many Apostles were communists only because so many of Cambridge's best and brightest were party members. Indeed, many of the student acolytes of Blunt's lifelong mentor, the classics tutor Andrew Gow, were communists, despite Gow's own conservatism. Gow, said Humphrey, simply found them livelier company than the average undergraduate. Humphrey spent countless hours with Klugmann and Cornford mulling over lists of possible recruits to the party. They aimed for the university's high-fliers. At Trinity College they managed to recruit all but three of one year's intake of scholars.

It was a sign of MI5's growing unease after the war – the feeling that something very odd had happened at Cambridge during the 1930s – that Humphrey was dogged by the security service's spy-hunters. He had lived in Highgate during the war and had taken as a lodger a Russian from the nearby Soviet trade legation. Two or three years later another Soviet visited Humphrey, saying that he was a friend of the former lodger. They talked about Shakespeare and then the Soviet asked a favour: could John obtain details of the US specifications for antibiotics? Humphrey saw no reason why he should not help:

> The British specifications were the same and I told him he might as well have them. Another time they said they wanted a catalogue of the radio chemical centre at Amersham. So I rang the boss there because I knew him quite well. I told him the Russians wanted a catalogue and he said, splendid. We might get some orders out of it. He sent me two copies . . . I sent them to the Russians but I imagine the envelopes were opened.[17]

MI5 did not seem to approve of Humphrey doing his bit for British exports. When he was working at the National Institute for Medical Research the director was warned that

Humphrey was 'in touch with a dangerous Russian spy'. Understandably, Humphrey was furious that MI5 did not have the courtesy to ask him about his contacts with Russians. He was refused a visa to visit the United States because he had once been a communist: 'No one ever accused me of being a spy because I am obviously not one. I have always taken the view that the right thing to do is to try and get understanding between countries. Neither capitalism nor communism has produced the right answers.'

At the outbreak of war in 1939 there were hundreds of Marxists who were, in theory at least, security risks. Most scientists ignored the Communist Party's instruction to have nothing to do with the war. When the Home Secretary, Sir John Anderson, was told that it might not be wise to recuit J. D. Bernal as a scientific adviser, Anderson said: 'I don't care if he's as red as the fires of hell. He's bright and he's committed to winning the war.'

CHAPTER 7
Sherry Pink

By 1934 Guy Burgess's potentially dazzling academic career was spluttering badly. He had begun his history course at Trinity marked out as one of those rare high-fliers who had the ability to become a Trinity don. His tutors believed in him, despite his drunkenness and promiscuity. Perhaps it was this appetite for 'experience', they speculated, which gave his work such freshness and originality.

Burgess was fascinated by the seventeenth century and regarded Thomas Macaulay and Winston Churchill as the only respectable chroniclers of British history. Everything went well when he sat part one of the history tripos; he was awarded first-class marks and a senior scholarship. Everything went according to plan, too, when he took part two; he sailed through with brilliant marks. The problem came when he sat his finals. Burgess collapsed and was unable to finish the examination. He later blamed this on the chronic insomnia that he had suffered from since the age of sixteen and the sedatives that he had been forced to take.[1] But friends were more cynical about his breakdown: they said that he had not prepared for the exams and that he had collapsed in frustration, not because of illness. Whatever the cause of his failure, he had to be satisfied with an aegrotat (an ungraded degree awarded to those too ill to take finals). It was not the glorious end to his undergraduate career that he had confidently expected. But it did not mean that he gave up all hope of finding a permanent niche in Cambridge. His many influential friends (and lovers) assured him that they would do everything to ensure that his temporary lapse was not held against him. He returned to Cambridge in the autumn of 1933 as a research student, doing a little gentle teaching (which he boasted he was superb at) while he hunted for a suitable subject on which to base a thesis. He thought first of writing about the background to 'the bourgeois revolution' of the seventeenth century, but, after he had set to work, a book by Professor Basil Willey appeared on this theme. Burgess was shattered. The book covered the area so exhaustively that all he could do was review it, generously, in *The Spectator*. Contemporaries thought that he was more deeply affected by this setback than he admitted. Lord Thurlow recalled:

> Burgess, we had been told, was going to make a very valuable and serious contribution to human knowledge. Then this book came out on the same theme as his and he was absolutely crushed. He had put all his eggs in one basket. And now he was left high and dry. From then on he went from bad to worse. He became more irresponsible and just drifted. I have no doubt that this disappointment changed his personality.[2]

Naturally, Burgess did not see it in quite those terms. He thought about examining the Indian Mutiny but then dropped the idea. When he reviewed his life from Moscow with his friend, Tom Driberg, he claimed that he had not really wanted to become a don. He said that he had decided to concentrate his many talents on politics; academia was too dry, too removed from real life. Few friends believed one word of this; they knew that Guy would have liked nothing more than to have been welcomed into the Trinity senior common room as a Master Historian. It was true, though, that he had been profoundly influenced by students who had come from the under-privileged, working-class areas of Britain. For example, he was close to Jim Lees – an ex-miner from Nottingham who had briefly been a communist before returning to the Labour Party, partly out of fear that he would be penalized for being a Marxist, partly because he objected to the dogmatism of the communists. Lees was older than Guy and once told him: 'You will get a first because your energies are not exhausted by life, because of the class prejudice of the examiners and because you got here easily and aren't frightened by it all. I shall do ten times as much work and get a good second.' Burgess said of Lees: 'He knew a great deal more than I did. He was interested in truth. I in brilliance. I made epigrams. He got the right answers.'[3]

Burgess threw himself into the exciting political tumult of Cambridge in the winter of 1933–34. He was a member of the anti-war movement as well as being a communist. He later reasoned that he had come to accept the validity of Marxism after a thorough study of what he portentously called 'the Modern State'. Lecturers in history did no more than expose each other's pettiness in endless bickering; they could not explain why the state had failed to meet the legitimate demands of the people. So, Burgess claimed, he had tried to find his own answers. The state had always been an instrument for the economically dominant groups within society. This was hardly an original thought, but Burgess claimed that it had shocked him. Then, after reading Lenin's *The State and Revolution*, he found that history made perfect sense. This explanation of his conversion to Marxism is far too pat. It ignores the evidence of friends who said that he was talking in admiring terms of communist students as early as 1932. Part of Burgess wanted to be convinced by Marxism – the part of him that wanted to believe in something beyond his own ambition. But he was, too, conscious that communism was fashionable; that no self-respecting intellectual could afford to be left out. He also enjoyed the prospect of upsetting the university establishment by organizing strikes and protests among college staff or by urging council house tenants not to pay their rents. He even told Indians in the town that they should rebel against British rule in their homeland. Observers of the new, committed Guy did not know quite what to make of it. He did his best to cut down on his drinking and was no longer seen downing his lunchtime bottle of wine at the Pitt Club; he was seen on marches and demonstrations and yawned through communist cell meetings.

Anthony Blunt had no such appetite for cold, wet street escapades. He was still concerned with his work and with finding new sexual partners. By 1934 he was a respected college don, basking in the warm approval of his colleagues in the Trinity senior common room. He admired Burgess enormously, placing him alongside James Klugmann and John Cornford as one of the town's three most influential Marxists. Blunt wrote of Burgess:

> So many things have been said against him as a result of his last disastrous years that it is, I think, important to repeat that he was not only one of the most intellectually stimulating people I have ever known but also had great charm and tremendous vivacity; and those people who now write saying that they felt physically sick in his presence are not speaking the truth. They are throwing back to his early years things that may have been true about Guy in his later years in this country. He was a terrific intellectual stimulus. He had a far wider range of interests than either Cornford or Klugmann. He was interested in everything and although he was perverse in

many ways there was no subject which one could discuss with him without his expressing some interesting and worthwhile view.[4]

Blunt was regarded as an armchair Marxist whose redness was only a skin-deep pink. Miriam Rothschild (later Mrs Miriam Lane), whom many considered cleverer than her brother Victor, and who achieved international celebrity with her investigations into the sex lives of fleas, recalled visiting art galleries with him: 'I was enormously impressed by his knowledge. We once went to an exhibition and he said that they had got the dates wrong for one picture. He told the manager and he agreed. That's how good Anthony was.'[5]

Patricia Parry (later Baroness Llewelyn-Davies of Hastoe) was at Girton College and had similarly fond memories of the young don:

Everyone knew Anthony at Cambridge. He was a tremendous figure there. He was clever, erudite and amusing but he was remote and deeply serious. We never discussed politics. It was well known that it bored him. I never thought he was interested. There was no question of his trying to influence people. What one liked about him was his intellectual side, although I would have said that he was a kind person. It was an interesting time at the universities. The Spanish war was very real and many people thought that it was a rehearsal for the bigger war that was coming. If you have a lot of men who know there's a war coming then of course they will be interested in politics because they know they will be the soldiers.[6]

Gavin Ewart, the poet, was at Christ's College from 1934 to 1937. He joined the Communist Party but allowed his membership to lapse after he went down because he 'didn't want to be involved in an organization'. Ewart said of Blunt:

> He was a very well read and cultured man. He was intelligent and entertaining but he always said that he couldn't understand my poems. He drank a lot but mainly because of Guy, who drank more. I would have thought that it was Burgess who persuaded him to become a communist. Burgess was a great arguer and persuader with a great grasp of history. He could say that what you were saying contradicted the lessons of history. He was also unscrupulous and full of vitality, a go-getting homosexual. I didn't know about the moles within the party. I was quite open about being a communist. I once initiated a debate in college that, This House would welcome the advent of communism in England.[7]

In the summer of 1934 Burgess made the trip that changed his life. He had been talking for some time about visiting the Soviet Union. Goronwy Rees, Burgess's first choice as a travelling companion, was unable to go. But the gregarious Guy had no intention of travelling alone; he managed to persuade an Oxford communist called Derek Blaikie to accompany him. Rees and Burgess later argued over who had suggested the holiday – Burgess insisted that Rees was the 'principal initiator and organizer', whereas Rees insisted that it had been Burgess who had been pressing him. In any event, the introductions that he carried with him, said Burgess, were provided by David Astor, later the proprietor of the *Observer* newspaper, whose mother, Nancy, Lady Astor, had visited Russia with George Bernard Shaw in 1931.

Burgess said that the trip gave him his 'first taste of international politics in the raw'. In Hamburg he had been drinking with a young German communist, a friend of Rees, who warned him that Hitler planned to liquidate all opposition, especially communists. The young man asked if Burgess could help him escape to Russia before it was too late, but then fighting broke out in the street. The German apologized and said that he would have to rejoin his comrades. That night, as Guy lay in his berth on board ship, he listened to the sound of gunfire echoing around the city. It was 30 June, the Night of the Long Knives, when Hitler eliminated rivals within the Nazi Party. Like other young men and women who visited Germany after 1933 Burgess was genuinely horrified by the reality of fascism. It was no longer just a term of abuse for people who did not share his views; fascism was terror and murder.

But Burgess did not let this spoil his holiday. He was determined to enjoy himself in Moscow, though he knew that he would have to be more restrained than at home. Penal restrictions on homosexual acts had been removed in 1918, but homosexuality again became a criminal offence in 1934 when it was described as 'a product of decadence in the bourgeois section of society and a fascist perversion'. The Russians could not believe that someone as young as Burgess could be a party member since that honour in the Soviet Union was awarded only after years of sacrifice and toil. But Burgess insisted to anyone who could understand English that he was, in fact, one of Britain's leading revolutionaries. He flitted around the city meeting English exiles and senior Russian officials. He saw an English professor called Alexander Wickstead who insisted that the Soviet Union was the freest country in the world; he told an official from the Ministry of Education that the government should be careful about some of the books they were planning to translate into Russian – Burgess could not, for example, understand why the Russians wanted to read John Galsworthy. Busy though Guy was in helping the Russians solve

their cultural difficulties, he had a niggling sense of anti-
climax. Moscow was drab and dour. There were even pigs
on the trams. Worst of all – and this was unforgivable – it
was boring. When he returned to Cambridge in the autumn
for the new academic year his friends realized that he had
changed. It was not just that he grumbled about Moscow;
he was disputing the fundamental principles of Marxism
and arguing that the fascist dictators were less reactionary
than Stalin. Then, to the astonishment of his comrades, he
announced that he was leaving the party.

Twenty years later Burgess explained why he had acted
like this.[8] He said that Donald Maclean and he had decided
that they could do more for the cause if they pretended that
they had forsaken Marxism. This would enable them to go
into 'public service' and serve the party from within the
Establishment. He confessed that from that moment until
his defection in 1951 he had 'cynically and consciously'
exploited the 'old boy network'. But he omitted crucial
details from this account of his trip to Moscow and his
subsequent 'disillusion' with communism. Goronwy Rees
claimed[9] that Burgess told him in great detail about a long,
private talk that he had had in Moscow with Nikolai
Bukharin, former secretary of the Comintern; he may also
have met Ossip Piatnitsky, who was in charge of the so-
called international liaison section of the Comintern and
responsible for building a worldwide network of Soviet
spies.

Somewhere within the vaults of the Kremlin there may
be a file setting out the precise chronology of Burgess's
recruitment as a Soviet agent. But if such a file does exist it
is probably just a jumble of names and dates of clandestine
meetings. There was, however, a philosophy of sorts behind the Soviets' recruitment of men like Guy Burgess.
Espionage is the world's second oldest profession. Every
country gathers information – economic, military, political;

some of it secret, most of it routine – about its enemies and friends. Insecure or ambitious regimes tend to lean heavily on their intelligence services and the Soviet government in the 1930s was both vulnerable and ambitious; it believed that it was still threatened by a conspiracy among the capitalist nations and it dreamed of controlling a wave of revolutions throughout Europe. Hence the Kremlin poured money into developing its intelligence agencies. The commitment to espionage and the subtle shifts in policy were described by a Soviet defector, General Walter Krivitsky, head of Soviet military intelligence in Europe. He fled to the United States in 1937 fearing that an order to return to Moscow meant that he would be purged, a fate already suffered by many of his agents. He told his American debriefers:

> For many years, while revolutionary prospects in Germany and Eastern Europe had seemed promising, the Comintern poured the greater part of its money into those countries. But when it became more decisively an appendage of the Soviet government and revolutionary objectives were sidetracked in favour of Stalinizing public opinion and capturing key positions in the democratic governments, Moscow's budgets for France, Great Britain and the United States were enormously increased.[10]

Guy Burgess returned from the Soviet Union to resume his uncertain academic career at Cambridge in the autumn of 1934. He was too old to take the examination for the civil service and was searching for an alternative. His Soviet controller had urged him to try and join one of the other great British institutions; perhaps the BBC or *The Times*. If he could not actually form policy he could at least try to influence it. Anthony Blunt, meanwhile, was not at all concerned by Burgess's change of political heart; he knew that Burgess had been told to distance himself from communism to give himself a better chance of making his way into the heart of the British Establishment. The Regius Professor of Modern History, G. M. Trevelyan, was an admirer of Burgess and did his best to find him an academic niche. Burgess, though, was happy in the meantime to exploit the kindness of friends like Victor Rothschild, a Fellow of Trinity from 1935 to 1939. Rothschild was also close to Anthony Blunt – an association which led to his being interrogated in the 1960s by MI5 in case he, too, had been a Soviet agent. In 1984 Rothschild recalled:

I was quite amused by Guy Burgess but he was fairly repulsive in spite of his charms. He was very drunk and very dirty but I wouldn't have trusted him in any circumstances. It seems to me to be quite fallacious to make a close correlation between the Apostles and the spy ring. When I first became an Apostle there was a great deal of talk about such matters as, Is the table really there. People like Keynes were still talking about, If I see a flower in a field, I shall pluck it. It is true that I was a scientist at the time and rarely attended meetings, but I do not remember any emphasis on Marxism. I think I first got to know Anthony Blunt a year after I went up as an undergraduate. Like many others I was immensely impressed by his outstanding intellectual abilities, both artistic and mathematical, and by what, for want of a better word, I must call his high moral or ethical principles. I knew or suspected he was homosexual, but I saw no reason why this characteristic should conflict with the others mentioned above. Blunt seemed to me a somewhat cold and ascetic figure but with a sense of humour. He was an excellent conversationalist and a habitual party-goer. I can't remember having seen him the worse for drink though in later years I heard that he drank a great deal. I was very ignorant about politics and ideologies in those days being, so I thought, too busy with my scientific work, sport and social life to have much time for anything else.[11]

Rothschild always insisted that, until he learnt of Blunt's confession in 1964, he had never suspected that Blunt had betrayed his country. The two men had remained friends during the war when they worked for MI5, although they were in different sections and saw each other infrequently. They had, Rothschild said, drifted apart during the 1950s but he still counted Blunt as a friend – at least he did until he learned the dreadful news in 1964:

> Many people, I suppose, suffer blows which seem devastating, crushing and beyond belief. I have had three such blows, the last nearly twenty years ago when I was told by the 'authorities' that a former close friend of mine, Anthony Blunt, had confessed to having been a Soviet agent for many years. I found it almost impossible to believe and childishly felt like telephoning Blunt to ask him if this appalling news was true. But there was no doubt, and why should 'they' wish to play a cruel and meaningless practical joke on me? What might I be stimulated to confess in return? The short answer was: nothing. As 'they' knew I was not a Soviet agent . . . You never get over a blow of this sort.[12]

Rothschild's mother, Mrs Charles Rothschild, came to the rescue of Burgess when he was hunting for a career early in 1935. Of course, nothing that Burgess ever said can be taken at face value. He was, by nature, an exaggerator; his claims often had a hard core of truth but the reality was often obscured by a dense fog of anecdote. But Burgess's account of how he convinced her to pay him a monthly retainer of £100 in return for his 'expertise' on how she should handle her investments seems uncharacteristically accurate.[13] Burgess recalled that he had been invited to the Rothschilds' country home at Tring by Victor. During dinner Burgess saw his chance to become an investment adviser, even though he knew nothing about the City. Mrs Rothschild seemed far from satisfied with the advice she had been receiving from men who had lost touch with the realities of financial life in the 1930s. As a result she had lost a great deal of money. Burgess leapt in and, according to his biographer Tom Driberg:

> She was much impressed by Guy's extemporaneous assessments of world affairs. For instance, the Rothschilds owned the railways in a Latin-American republic. Guy said that these railways were shortly going to be nationalized, and that the Rothschilds ought to liquidate this investment as quickly as possible. New Court [the headquarters of the British branch of the Rothschild empire] said this was mere propaganda; their information was that the investment was sound. Guy's prediction proved correct.[14]

This was the second time that Burgess had given good advice. A year earlier Victor had done well out of a Burgess tip to buy shares in Rolls-Royce. Mrs Rothschild concluded that Burgess, for all his boasting and wild stories, might actually know what he was talking about. She appointed him her financial adviser, gave him a list of her holdings and asked for a monthly report on what to buy and what to sell. In return Burgess was promised a monthly salary of £100. According to Burgess, he always did give her the best possible advice, even if that meant cutting across his own political beliefs. As war seemed increasingly likely he told his client that she should liquidate her investments in

Europe and Britain apart from shares in armaments companies. Mrs Rothschild refused, arguing that it would be unpatriotic to join other worried investors who were withdrawing their money from Europe and Britain. Burgess insisted, too, that he never allowed his philosophical objection to the Rothschilds, who were, after all, at the apex of the capitalist system, to influence him.

Miriam Rothschild's view of Burgess's role is rather different. As far as she could tell, her mother was not taken in by Burgess's spurious claims to being a financial wizard and had simply taken pity on him, a family friend who was extremely good value despite his obvious faults. He was still strikingly good-looking though heavy drinking and chain-smoking were beginning to take their toll. Miriam concluded that her mother knew that Burgess was 'out of his depth' when he talked about such arcane matters as the gold standard, but that she had created a job for Burgess, much as she had created minor jobs for other family friends who were financially embarrassed.

Whatever the reasons for the appointment, the Rothschild salary allowed Burgess to leave Cambridge and set up home in a flat in 28 Chester Square, near London's Victoria Station. For a time he had toyed with the idea of joining the research department of the Conservative Party. This would have been as good a starting point as any for a would-be Soviet agent, giving him access to useful gossip in Whitehall and Parliament as well as to hard if unsensational information. But Burgess's left-wing past was still a vivid memory, even though he protested that he had repudiated his old beliefs. His application, wisely as it turned out, was rejected.

In Britain the Soviets had had to regroup after the police raided the London offices of the All Russian Cooperative Society Ltd in 1927. The new director of Soviet Intelligence in the city was Samuel Borosovicj Cahan. He was under instructions from Moscow to exploit the great surge of communism among the country's students; although no one can know how much was left to his own initiative and to that of the middlemen from King Street whom he used to sound out likely recruits. This was Britain, not Europe, and Cahan had to edge forward gently. Arthur Koestler, who had been involved in the Comintern's European plotting, wrote:

> On the continent things were different. There conspiratorial cunning and underhand methods were in keeping with the political atmosphere created by Hitler, Mussolini, Franco and Metaxas. By force of contrast, England appeared an island of innocence, where plotting was confined to memories of Guy Fawkes and to Victorian melodrama, and where fair play was taken for granted even by members of the ridiculously small and provincial communist party. To be a communist in disguise in Shepperton, Middlesex, with a retired naval officer for a neighbour whose daughters came over for tennis and tea on the lawn, seemed as grotesquely out of place as the proverbial Yankee at the Court of King Arthur. Fortunately I was never asked whether I was a communist, under the circumstances a sign of almost extravagant discretion.[15]

Opposing Cahan was the small, understaffed British security service, MI5. When war broke out in 1939, Moscow insisted that communists had to oppose the war which was, like the First World War, an imperialist adventure. British Intelligence was ordered to prevent potential subversives from joining the forces. They blacklisted Douglas Hyde, the news editor of the *Daily Worker*, but he noted with satisfaction:

A surprising number of *Daily Worker* staff did, however, get into the Forces and the ease with which many well-known communists slipped through the MI5 net and were only caught up with, if ever, months or even years later reassured us as to the limited scope of the department's knowledge of the communist personnel and communist activities.[16]

MI5 was just as ill-equipped to handle the new Soviet tactic of targeting the future leaders of the Establishment. Maxwell Knight, MI5's most successful spy-catcher, had done his best with limited resources to track the contacts that he knew existed between Soviet Intelligence and British communists, but he was forced to concentrate on obvious suspects and not on the universities. He did, however, ask one student at Oxford to find out if radicals at the university were being backed by Moscow (or Berlin).

MI5 had had some successes. In 1925 twelve communists, including the future general secretary of the party, Harry Pollitt, were sentenced to short prison terms for seditious conspiracy. The conviction of Percy Glading in 1938 for trying to steal secrets on new anti-submarine weapons was a most spectacular coup for Knight. But MI5 did not have any idea of the real danger during the 1930s: the subversion of young, privileged intellectuals. To his credit, Knight seems to have had a gut instinct that something like this was happening. Soon after war broke out in 1939 he told a new member of MI5: 'The Russians are very patient. They will recruit a young man at university with communist views, tell him to disassociate himself from the party, watch him and keep him on ice for years. Then one day they will come to him and say: now we want you to do this.'[17] Knight was wrong on one key point: the Russians had already put this plan into action.

There was another dimension to Soviet espionage in

Britain.[18] In August 1933 Ernst Henri, a Soviet journalist based in London, had written an article for the *New Statesman*. It was headlined 'The Groups of Five' and described how German communists could resist fascism by forming cells of five, the members of each cell acting independently of other cells so that, should one cell be smashed, the others would survive. This was as much a blueprint for the British recruits to Soviet Intelligence as for the German communist resistance. There was no reason why a cell had to consist of five members. It was the principle – a small group whose names were known only to that group – which was important. At Cambridge the Henri principle was seriously applied only by those Cambridge Marxists who became agents/spies. Anthony Blunt said in the 1980s that as a talent-spotter for the Soviets he had passed names of possible recruits to Guy Burgess but that, with a few exceptions, he had not been told what had happened.[19]

Ernst Henri's real name was Semyon Nicolayevich Rostovski. He was charming, urbane and professed what appeared to be sincere contempt for the brutality of Stalin's Russia. He admired artists who were dismissed as decadent counter-revolutionaries in his own country. He wore well-tailored English suits and enjoyed the varied delights of London society. He was eventually recalled to Moscow in 1951 and was jailed for two years before being released. It seems likely that he was one of Guy Burgess's contacts; certainly he knew Burgess well enough to be invited to broadcast for the BBC during the war, when Burgess was a producer with the talks department. Henri's script seemed innocuous enough at the time; just another predictable piece of wartime propaganda in which he extolled the courage of the Red Army. But there was a phrase which, in retrospect, stands out: he said that the Soviet Union would never be defeated because it had one of the best intelligence services in the world. A suspicious mind might, of course, interpret this as a secret word of encouragement to Soviet agents in Britain such as Anthony Blunt.

Henri was living in honourable retirement in Moscow in 1985. He had not been surprised, he said, by the growth in the communist movement at the universities in the 1930s. The same thing had happened throughout Europe as the 'prosperous young' decided that fascism had to be fought. He had a high respect for many of these young Marxists, especially Donald Maclean, whom he knew well in Moscow. But, predictably, Henri said that he knew nothing about spies. 'These people have to sell their pamphlets and make money. I did not know anything about the spying activities of these people. And I didn't ask them about it. They acted according to their convictions.'[20]

MI5 never had the opportunity to question Guy Burgess. Anthony Blunt, it is true, was questioned for something like 200 hours after his confession in 1964, but his testimony was always suspect, especially when he was asked about Guy Burgess. Moreover, it is unlikely that Blunt knew in detail how Burgess the student communist became Burgess the Comintern agent. Guy Liddell, deputy director of MI5 from 1947 to 1952 and a close friend of Burgess and Blunt, believed that Dave Springhall, the CPGB's national organizer, had been the 'contact man' who had put students in touch with Soviet intelligence officers. But it is not known whether Burgess met his Soviet controller before or after he went to Moscow in the summer of 1934. It would, however, have been remarkable for an unknown student to have had a private audience with a senior Comintern official like Bukharin without an introduction from one of Bukharin's agents in London. The instruction publicly to renege on his communism seems to have been delivered in Moscow, but it is possible that the plan had been outlined already by the Soviets in London.

What did Burgess think that he would have to do as a Comintern agent? (The Soviets always emphasized to their moles and sleepers that they were working for world communism and not the Soviet Union.) He probably thought that being a spy would be amusing and that he might be able to draw in friends. He would have power, of a sort, and would travel. When the revolution came he would be given an honoured place in the Workers' State. If anyone had told Burgess in 1934 that it would end in a tedious Moscow suburb far from the London clubs, bars and his beloved gossip, he would have laughed in disbelief. Blunt always insisted that he had agreed to become a 'talent-spotter' for Burgess in late 1935 or early 1936 – almost certainly a lie since Burgess must have told his closest friend why he had renounced his Marxism in the autumn of 1934. Blunt said: 'In discussions with him I became convinced the Marxist interpretation of history was right and therefore this was where the logical break took place and one ought to be a communist. Guy put it to me that the best way I could help anti-fascism was to help him in his work for the Russians.'[21]

Dave Springhall was a regular visitor to Cambridge after 1933; the membership lists, nominally secret, were handed to him and the characters and potential of new recruits debated. That is not to say that student leaders such as John Cornford or James Klugmann knew why Springhall was asking so many questions about certain students; it would have been dangerous, in fact, to have confided in them. Springhall was well suited to the task. He had been thrown out of the navy in 1924 for 'causing dissension' and had been on the CPGB's central executive since 1932. He looked like an archetypal thug; he had small eyes, a pink face and what remained of his hair was closely cropped like a boxer's. In 1924 he had visited the Soviet Union as a delegate to the Comintern and during the Spanish Civil War was the first political commissar of the XI (British)

International Brigade. When he returned from Spain he was appointed the party's national organizer. Long before his arrest many communists had suspected that he was passing the material that came 'flooding into party head-quarters' during the war to the Soviet embassy. Douglas Hyde wrote:

> The information came from factories and the Forces, from civil servants and scientists. And the significant thing is that those who did it were not professional spies, they took big risks in most cases, received no payment whatosever and, this is doubly important, did not see themselves as spies and still less as traitors. As Party members they would have felt that they were being untrue to themselves and unworthy of the name of communist if they had not done it.[22]

The fears of the party faithful that Springhall would be picked up were justified. In 1943 he was sentenced to seven years' imprisonment for spying. The party was not pleased that Springhall had ignored warnings to give up before he was caught. Hyde again:

> He was expelled from the party. They were horrified that he had been so stupid. He was expelled for ignoring party discipline. Spies were not supposed to be party members. It wasn't that the party disapproved of what he had done but because we had no desire to get a reputation by then for spying. Second, it was a major indiscretion for the national organizer to do this.[23]

CHAPTER 8
Fascist Fears, Soviet Utopia

The new, Marxist Blunt looked much the same as the old, apolitical Anthony. It was his attitude to art that was obviously different. In his *Studio International* essay in 1972 he protested stiffly, and unconvincingly as far as many of his lifelong friends were concerned, that he had been 'deeply affected' by unemployment at home. He also said that he had been worried about the fascist threat in Europe; but then, so were many people. Blunt wrote that he had no longer been able to accept that Art was above Politics:

> The new ideas involved a complete reversal of everything that we had held before. Art for art's sake, Pure Form, went by the board completely. We believed, on the contrary, that art was a human activity, that works of art were created by men, that men were human beings, and that society was influenced by social conditions and ultimately by economic conditions. And this meant not just a reformulation of our theories but also our judgements on individual artists.[1]

While Blunt was indulging in this woolly theorizing, a stream of refugee art scholars poured into Britain. Among them was the Marxist Frederick Antal, a Hungarian who had studied under Max Dvorak in Vienna, and who landed in Britain in 1933. Antal argued that art had to be studied against a background of social, economic and political conditions, a statement which may not seem unusual today, but which was, said Blunt, a revolutionary concept in England at that time. Men such as Antal also brought with them a new, professional approach to the study of art. Blunt himself confessed that until the influx of the Europeans, British art scholarship had been hopelessly amateur. His interest in making a career in this new discipline was undoubtedly sincere. But it is undeniable, too, that by choosing a field where there were no native-born rivals, Blunt was assured of an eminence that would probably have been denied him if he had chosen a mainstream subject such as history, which was crowded with bright young scholars.

Blunt began to reassess the master artists according to the Marxist canon. The Spanish eighteenth-century master, Goya, was no longer just a brilliant technician; he was upgraded to the status of a revolutionary. This proved a little awkward, Blunt confessed, in view of Goya's 'slightly reactionary political opinions', but somehow he managed it. The real Goya was the savage satirist of the Church and not the conventional painter of frescos. Blunt claimed that Goya had always struggled against the limitations imposed by his patrons; after all, Goya had once said that as an official portrait artist his job was 'to make observations for which commissioned works generally give no room and in which fantasy and invention have no limit'. Goya's realistic depiction of the atrocities committed by French occupying troops between 1810 and 1813 was now viewed as social realism. His decision to leave Spain was a protest against a repressive regime. With other eager young Marxists, Blunt tried to find previously unsuspected revolutionary themes in art. He admired what he called 'semi-conscious social realists'; he applied this, for example, to Chardin, an eighteenth-century Frenchman who spent most of his life portraying kitchen utensils, vegetables, baskets of fruit, fish and objects which most non-Marxists saw as being apolitical. Blunt also admired Jean Baptiste Greuze, another eighteenth-century French painter, for 'his ideas on sensibility which were based on Rousseau and which led up to the Revolution'. But Blunt ignored Greuze's later work – titillating pictures of semi-nude girls under such titles as 'Sorrow' or 'Innocence' which the artist had churned out in a desperate attempt to earn money. The absolute certainties and arrogance of the Marxist are detectable in everything that Blunt wrote during the 1930s. He foraged through European art; his articles are a mass of clichés supported by the mind-numbing jargon of the far Left. There was a redeeming touch of self-mockery in Blunt's description of this process in 1972: 'According to the gospel of St Antal, we were allowed to see many of the great progressive artists of previous centuries as "all right".'[2] Thus Masaccio from the fifteenth century, Michelangelo and Raphael, Nicolas Poussin, Rembrandt – all represented, in the minds of Marxists, the 'progressive stages in the development of the bourgeoisie'. That word 'progressive', as Blunt admitted, was used an awful lot during the 1930s. Blunt also found hitherto undreamed-of qualities in the Mexican art of the 1920s and was particularly impressed by Diego Rivera and José Orozco. Rivera had lived in Paris in the early 1900s, the formative period of the Cubist movement, and had returned to Mexico and worked under the anti-clerical government of General Plutarcho Calles in the 1920s and then the reformist regime of General Lazaro Cardenas in the 1930s. Both Rivera and Orozco, Blunt thought, had moved away from 'the dead end of abstract art and surrealism towards a new realist, communal and monumental art'. As he looked back from the dignity of his position as the doyen of English art history, Blunt argued that this view was not altogether unreasonable. He wrote: 'I still personally have a great admiration for the early phase of those two artists although I should be more qualified in approval of what they did later. But that was all right because the revolution in Mexico failed and that ruined the movement in the arts.'[3]

In 1932 Blunt had started to write reviews for *The Spectator* and was given a regular art column. His writing was relaxed and the choice of subject catholic: one week a London art exhibition; the next a review of an exhibition at Harrods of British china. In 1935 he contributed to the magazine's series of letters from Oxbridge.[4] Blunt noted in his piece that the amateur dramatic society at Cambridge had returned to using all-male casts after a short flirtation with actresses. But this trivia did not mean that Anthony had given up his serious Marxism. Art had to reflect what Marxists knew to be 'reality'. (The word 'reality' occurred as often as 'progressive' in the work of the 1930s Marxists.) All art has to reflect 'social realities'; abstract art is worthless, self-indulgent, a symptom of bourgeois degeneracy. In *The Spectator* of 27 September 1935 Blunt turned to Soviet architecture, regretting the fact that Soviet architects were being seduced by Western influences. The projected Palace of the Soviets, he wrote, would end up 'looking more like a giant Selfridges wedding cake than a worthy monument to the October revolution'. The new metro in Moscow, which was simple and efficient, had a terrible 'chic'. At times, Blunt complained, one almost expected a top hat to emerge from its doors. But these were minor quibbles. Like most Marxists, Blunt regarded the Soviet Union as the nearest anyone had got to Utopia; at least, he did from the comfort of his Cambridge study. For Blunt, Soviet art under Stalin was quite correctly 'absorbing all that is useful in Western culture as a prelude to developing a real style appropriate to socialist conditions'. True, the results, for the time being, were not that attractive, but the Soviets were right to reject 'all experiments in abstraction'.

Blunt found other outlets for his polemical essays on art and architecture; essays which were described witheringly by Ellis Waterhouse fifty years later as 'rubbish'.[5] There was the *Left Review*, founded in 1934 to provide a forum for writers to discuss 'the threat to letters from fascism and the crisis in capitalism'. At first the *Review* concentrated on essays which expanded upon this theme. It had strong links with the European Left and its pages were filled with turgid attacks on capitalism and starry-eyed defences of communism. The Marxist art critic F. D. Klingender, one of Blunt's heroes, once ventured the view that it was naïve to assume that 'Soviet artists can do no wrong'. This was tantamount to heresy and in the next issue he was told that as a punishment he should be deprived of pen and ink for the duration of his natural life. There were countless essays extolling the Soviet Union, exploring how literature could expose the evils of capitalism. But even communists could see that the effort to influence a (non-existent) working-class readership was not producing any results. Hence, by 1936, when Blunt began writing for the *Left Review*, it had tried to broaden its appeal. His first article was on the exhibition of surrealist art in London which drew a crowd of 20,000. The surrealists were a problem for Blunt since he suspected that they had opted for 'purely optical effects'.

While he agreed that the surrealists were 'subversive of bourgeois values' – which was a good thing – they held out no hope of revolution – which was, of course, a bad thing. Art had to do more than merely appear to be revolutionary; it needed 'roots in the rising class'. The surrealists were helping to shake the foundations of capitalist culture but their contribution was destructive and they would wither and die in the socialist state. Blunt thought:

The real danger as we saw things was abstraction, towards an art which had lost all contact with humanity at large and was either concerned with playing about with pure shapes in abstract art or with the private images and feelings of the artist in the case of surrealism which, contrary to what would now be said, we regarded as purely private and not related to any general subconscious or anything of that sort. We launched a campaign against esoteric art and in favour of a realistic, appealing style.[6]

Blunt's most explicit piece of Marxist dogma was written in 1937. It is entitled 'Art Under Capitalism and Socialism' and was written for C. Day Lewis, a *Left Review* contributor who was organizing what he called a testament, *The Mind in Chains*, to show how the arts had to break the chains forged by the crumbling social system. Blunt's essay is seventeen pages long and is a classic piece of Marxist analysis. All art, he says, 'is a kind of propaganda' produced by two influences: 'the one composed of social influences, the other by the personality of the artist, the relation of the two being dialectical'. Art cannot be judged on whether it is good or bad, only whether it is effective. But, Blunt contends, since 'in the present state of capitalism the position of the artist is hopeless' there is little hope of any 'effective' art being produced. Why is this? In the Middle Ages the fact that artists depended on patronage did not stifle true creativity; but the rise of capitalism changed the position of the artist, forcing him to become more competitive as the old patrons, the Church and the aristocracy, were overwhelmed by the new merchant classes. At first there was a sense of freedom, but it was an illusion; artists became 'personalities' and were faced with the choice 'of either following the taste of the people who could afford to buy [his] painting or else starving'. Painters lost contact with their own class and with the proletariat and drifted into isolated, self-obsessed abstraction. Blunt continued:

> Now that the class struggle has grown more acute and has become the dominating factor in the world situation, any artist who cuts himself off from his class is automatically excluded from the possibility of taking part in the most important movement of his time and is therefore forced to take to some sort of escape, to find some consolation in his art for the reality with which he has lost touch in life.[7]

The modern artist is a prisoner of market forces, spurned by both the bourgeoisie, who hate his unsettlingly surreal view of the world, and by the People, who have no use for his work. Artists have to acknowledge that 'the culture of the revolution will be evolved by the proletariat and not imposed on it from above by the enlightened middle classes.' Thus, all an artist can do is help the people 'produce their own culture'. True, Blunt admits, the people are so steeped in 'the worst kinds of bourgeois culture' that their idea of art is appalling. But that will not always be the case; a new art will arise, which will be 'less sophisticated, but more vital than the old'. In the new socialist state the artist will be a public servant, working for the common good.

Anthony Blunt did not remain a Marxist art historian for long. In 1939 the first volume of his catalogue of the drawings of Poussin was published under the guidance of Walter Friedlander. Then his first solo work, *Artistic Theory in Italy, 1450–1600*, appeared in 1940, complete with a dedication to Guy Burgess for 'the stimulus of constant discussion and suggestions on all the more basic points at issue'. (This puzzled Anthony's art colleagues, who were not aware that Burgess had any special expertise in Italian art.) Had Blunt, like Guy Burgess, Donald Maclean and Kim Philby, been told to renounce publicly his Marxist beliefs as a preparation for trying to enter what Burgess called 'public service'? It is possible; though, it has to be said, Blunt's determination to become London's leading art historian meant that he would have quietly dropped opinions that might hold him back – whatever the instructions from the Soviets had been. It has to be remembered, too, that the techniques that he was picking up from Marxists such as Frederick Antal – studying an artist against his social and political background – could easily be incorporated into non-Marxist art history.

Not everyone liked the militant Cambridge of the mid-1930s. Louis MacNeice, then a lecturer in classics at Birmingham University, complained about the humourless Marxists who seemed to be everywhere. He recalled one house party where the word 'proletariat . . . hung in festoons from the ceiling'. He said: 'The gospel of Marx as sifted through Transport House seemed to be hardly more inspiring or broadminded than the gospels of Dr Arnold or Cecil Rhodes.'[8] Despite Blunt's Marxism, MacNeice and he were still able to enjoy days that reminded them both of Marlborough. On one occasion, MacNeice and his wife, Mariette, were entertained by a charade played by Blunt, dons, students and a handful of visiting intellectuals from Bloomsbury. A charade was considered a fine thing, recalled MacNeice, if it was risqué or blasphemous. It was just like being back at school: private gossip, tittering and a disregard for anyone who was not part of the charmed circle.

Blunt's expertise in art had been honed: he knew the location and provenance of any picture that MacNeice mentioned, but MacNeice disagreed violently with Blunt's Marxist interpretation of art. He ridiculed the idea that Goya could be seen as a great revolutionary. Goya's life was a colourful pageant; a tribute to Goya's sense of humour, pragmatism, even cynicism, rather than to his alleged revolutionary zeal. But then Marxists, thought MacNeice, should admire Goya's opportunism, since they were themselves masters in the art.

It is worth quoting MacNeice in full since the following passage, published posthumously in 1965, raises a fascinating possibility. Was it an accident that his scathing criticism of Marxists was followed immediately by a paragraph on Blunt's own, childlike faith in the cause? Or was MacNeice indicating, to Blunt and their tight network of friends, that he knew about Anthony's treachery:

The great danger of Marxism is that it allows and even encourages opportunism. After a bit the Marxist, who is only human, finds it such fun practising strategy – i.e. hypocrisy, lying, graft, political pimping, tergiversation, allegedly necessary murder – that he forgets the end in the means, the evil of the means drowns the good of the end, power corrupts, the living gospel withers, Siberia fills with ghosts . . . The Hammer and Sickle was scrawled over Spain that Easter. The walls were plastered with posters from recent elections, ingenious cartoons showing the top-hatted banker in rout or political prisoners peering out from behind a grill in the gaping mouth of the capitalist. If Spain goes communist, Anthony said, France is bound to follow. *And then Britain, and then there'll be jam for all.* Which incidentally will mean new blood in the arts – every parish a Diego Rivera. And easel-painting at last will admit it is dead and all the town halls and factories will bloom with murals and bas-reliefs in concrete. For concrete is the new medium, concrete is vital.[9]

So many good people, lamented MacNeice, had been infected by the Marxist virus. By early 1936, because of his new Marxism, Blunt was reluctant to perform a small favour for a hard-up friend of MacNeice's, a sculptor called Gordon Herrickx, who specialized in inoffensive studies of cyclamens and chestnut buds. MacNeice thought his work was excellent, but Herrickx had no idea of how to sell it. MacNeice suggested taking his 'Cyclamen', which had taken him the best part of a year to finish, to Blunt. With his connections, MacNeice told the delighted Herrickx, there would be no problem finding a buyer. MacNeice loaded the sculpture into the back of his car and drove to Cambridge, where he heaved it up to Blunt's rooms, 'coquettishly chaste with white panelling and Annunciation lilies'. But one of Anthony's friends, whom MacNeice had hoped might buy 'Cyclamen', had just had a baby and had no interest in buying anything, especially such an unfashionable sculpture. And Blunt, as a good Marxist, did not want to 'push a work that was primarily abstract or decorative' and hence ideologically flawed.

Since MacNeice's last visit to Cambridge the university had become even more obsessed with communism. MacNeice staged a small, private protest, becoming stupendously drunk before lunch in Blunt's rooms while his host was teaching students. It seemed an apt way to register disapproval of both the room and the continued arguments about Dialectical Materialism.

After lunch MacNeice drove back to Birmingham. He had offered a lift to three students. One was from Birmingham and dreamed of being an aesthete; the second was a Marxist who backed up his arguments with a string of statistics; the third was John Cornford. Cornford was also able to reel off a great many figures to support his theories about the decline of capitalism, but he had a different, special quality. MacNeice wrote:

For him the conception of career was completely drowned in the Cause; he was going to Birmingham to stand trial for causing an obstruction while distributing communist pamphlets in the Bull Ring (where the Chartist Movement had been launched in 1838). John Cornford was the first inspiring communist I had met; he was the first who combined an unselfish devotion to his faith with a first-class intelligence. He and the other Cambridge undergraduate sat in the back seat and talked about trade unions; the Birmingham aesthete sat beside me and talked about literary values. The Would-be Twenties and the Hard Facts Thirties cross-patterned in my mind as my forehead throbbed and the car swung wildly across the road; when we reached the Birmingham suburbs we found we had been driving for miles with a puncture. The Thirties at once jumped out, were cheerfully efficient; the Would-be Twenties stood listlessly by, composing his face to a deliberate disdain.[10]

MacNeice's impatience with the majority of communists did not apparently extend to Blunt. They still had much in common: a passion for literature and art, a mutual respect for each other's abilities and the shared experiences of having been at Marlborough.

During MacNeice's visit, the two men agreed to holiday in Spain in Easter that year. This would be Blunt's second foreign expedition within twelve months. The first was made in the summer of 1935 when Blunt visited the new Utopia – the Soviet Union.

By the mid-1930s many students, particularly young communists, were travelling there to inspect the revolution at first hand. Blunt had persuaded his elder brother Wilfrid, still teaching art at Haileybury, to accompany him. Wilfrid noted that while most of the young men on the boat that set sail from London to Leningrad were 'Left-wing pilgrims to the Promised Land', Anthony and he were 'making the journey in search of pictures and architecture'. And, Wilfrid sniffed, he was certainly not taken in by the communist propaganda that they were visiting Utopia. Also on the ship was a party of six undergraduates: John Madge, brother of the poet Charles Madge, was the organizer; there was Charles Fletcher-Cooke from Peterhouse College, who became president of the Union in 1936 and went on to a solid career as a Conservative Member of Parliament; Charles Rycroft, who became a distinguished psychiatrist; Michael Young, who had been educated at the liberal public school, Dartington Hall, in the West Country and who was at London University (he became a world-famous sociologist and was created a life peer in 1978, as Baron Young of Dartington); Brian Simon, who was one of Cambridge's most serious communists; Michael Straight, the perpetually perplexed American, was also a passenger. Also on board was Christopher Mayhew, a student at Christ Church, Oxford, who became a Labour MP before switching to the Liberals in the 1970s and becoming Baron Mayhew of Wimbledon in 1981. His travelling companion was an old friend from Haileybury, Derek Nenk.

Mayhew paid the Soviet state tour agency, Intourist, £15 for the trip to Leningrad and Moscow. As a good socialist, though not a Marxist, Mayhew hoped that he would discover the truth about the Soviet Union; that it was, in fact, a splendid new civilization, hitherto hidden under a blanket of capitalist propaganda. Joining the ship at London Bridge, Mayhew and Nenk had carefully chosen wardrobes of 'rather proletarian style which we judged would help us mix easily with the workers'. The young students and the Blunt brothers soon realized that the voyage might be a little more uncomfortable than they had hoped. This was the first test of their communist ideals. Mayhew, for example, was horrified at the state of the toilets. Why was this, Mayhew asked himself:

> Since the state of the lavatories was inconsistent with everything we had read about Socialism, it was obviously an accident, a hangover from the past age, a meaningless irrelevance, the kind of thing which would only be of interest to people from sheltered bourgeois homes such as ourselves. The ship's crew, dedicated to a high ideal, could not fairly be expected to waste their energies on such trivialities.[11]

Wilfrid was also less than delighted with the facilities. He was forced to sleep with seven others in a cabin that was designed for two. The frowst in the confined space was so unbearable that he decided he would be better off sleeping on deck. To add to his irritation there was a Chinaman on board who insisted on handing round what Wilfrid called 'dirty postcards'. There were also political discussions, led by John Madge, which Wilfrid had no time for. According to Michael Straight, Anthony Blunt, very pale, very slender and very tall, used to listen in silence during these talks. Straight found the prospect of setting foot in the Soviet Union immensely exciting. He was even overawed by the sight of a woman who worked as a deckhand; it was symbolic of the new equality between classless men and women. The voyage may have tested their faith but it was simply a foretaste of what was to come when they arrived in the Soviet Union. Straight recalled:

> We tried not to see the poverty, the squalor, the primitiveness that surrounded us wherever we went. It was not easy. We took an aged train from Moscow to Kiev. In its lavatory was a poster for those who could not read. It showed a stupid peasant squatting on top of the toilet

bowl and spraying his excrement around the floor. In an accompanying picture, an intelligent worker sat on the bowl with his trousers down and a beatific expression on his face. Judging by the state of the lavatory, most of our fellow passengers chose the first method. The Russians who shared our car smoked and talked and boiled their tea. We were aroused one night by gunfire. The train lurched to a halt; the gunfire continued. We made our way to the end of the coach. We saw, huddled against the iron steps, a dozen half-starved children. They had boarded the train in the darkness and the guards were firing their rifles to drive them away.[12]

The reactions of the young students to the Soviet Union now seem extraordinarily naïve. After all, what did they expect to find in a country that economically was still emerging from the feudalism of the Tsars and which had just undergone the trauma of revolution? Privileged and cosseted, they focused on physical squalor, apparently unaware that for many people in the capitalist West life was not much better.

Wilfrid and Anthony did their best to escape the tightly organized round of visits to factories. Landing in Leningrad, Wilfrid was scarcely able to believe the euphoria of his companions. One even shouted 'Freedom at last' as he fell headlong over a notice forbidding him to walk on the grass verge. But not everyone was disappointed. Brian Simon recalled: 'I think I was pretty impressed. We were very young and we were tourists. I wouldn't say that we were working all the time. We went to a trotting race and I won some money on it. We enjoyed ourselves. They seemed to be pushing ahead very fast. There was no unemployment. A planned economy seemed to be working.'

Charles Fletcher-Cooke had been given a grant to study

libel law under communism. He had been given 'all sorts of introductions to people who needless to say had almost all disappeared' in the Stalin purges by the time he arrived. It was hard for the young travellers, shepherded by guides and kept away from locals, to have any idea of what was happening. Mayhew, for example, often 'tried to engage the people of the Soviet Socialist fatherland in conversation' but noticed that once people realized that he was a foreigner they would scurry off. Mayhew reasoned that there must be something wrong with their approach; perhaps the Russians who seemed so reluctant to talk could not understand the halting Russian they spoke or perhaps they had better things to do than chat to ignorant capitalists? Mayhew later admitted that he felt ashamed at his obtuseness, his failure to realize the true nature of Stalin's dictatorship. But he added that he had assumed that because capitalism was so terrible its exact opposite had to be better. Wilfrid, though, was not fooled. He found the place dreary and humourless.

Sir Charles recalled that the trip was one of the most disillusioning experiences he had ever had:

> For some people, like Michael Straight, it was a political pilgrimage. It wasn't for me but I was very interested. We were on a train from Leningrad to Moscow, and apart from the dirt and filth, the crops looked so miserable. It was all very well to say that civil war had happened only fifteen years before but they ought to have better. I knew Anthony Blunt through Victor Rothschild and found him charming. He had a sense of humour which is unusual in a spy.[13]

The Blunt brothers slipped away as often as possible from the guides. In Leningrad they met Lady Muriel Paget who was, Wilfrid discovered, working on behalf of 'the

British-born who were marooned for one reason or another in the USSR'. Fifty years later Wilfrid still shuddered when he remembered the air of conspiracy in her flat, with its clandestine comings and goings and sinister figures half glimpsed through swiftly closed doors. In Moscow the Blunts were entertained by Noel Charles, the acting counsellor at the British embassy. It was not a successful dinner: the butler turned out to be a Soviet agent; the Blunts had not brought dinner suits; and there was the embarrassing fact that the hosts expected Wilfrid to be Wilfrid Scawen Blunt the writer, who would at that time have been almost one hundred. It was not easy, either, to enjoy sightseeing in Moscow. The party was staying at the huge National Hotel on the corner of Red Square. Christopher Mayhew found the restrictions on foreigners depressing: 'Tourists could do nothing. You weren't allowed to photograph the Kremlin walls so I got Anthony Blunt to hold my legs while I leant out of the hotel window so that I could take a picture.'[14] Mayhew, however, had convinced himself that this must be the shape of the future. Like most left-wing visitors he knew nothing about – or refused to believe – the mass arrests, the torture, the emergence of a police state that was every bit as ruthless as those being developed by the fascist dictators. Clearly the experience did not disillusion Anthony Blunt; unlike Wilfrid, who wrote an article for the Haileybury school magazine when he returned home, dismissing the Soviet Union as dirty, overcrowded, noisy and poor.

On the return voyage to London there was some light relief. Charles Fletcher-Cooke spotted Nancy Cunard, whose mother was a millionaire London hostess. He was intrigued by her and especially by her obvious interest in a black Russian dancer also on board. Another celebrity was Harry Pollitt, general secretary of the CPGB, who had been attending the Seventh World Congress of the Communist International (which had decided to cooperate with non-communist groups to try and defeat fascism). Mayhew recalled that Pollitt spent most of the journey scribbling notes and making plans for the new offensive against the fascists.

Donald Maclean had better luck than Guy Burgess in his search for a career that would satisfy his Soviet controller. Maclean had never made any secret of his communist beliefs at Cambridge. In one article for the *Cambridge Left* magazine he had argued that capitalist society was 'doomed to disappear'; there was, he noted gleefully, 'a rising tide of opinion which is going to sweep away the whole crack-brained criminal mess'. He was profiled in the student magazine *Granta* early in November 1933. The article is precious and stilted; the anonymous interviewer labori-ously satirizes Maclean by inventing various personalities for his subject. One is called, predictably enough, Maclean, the second is called Cecil, the third, Jack and the fourth, Fred. Maclean emerges from the interview as smug, ambi-tious and self-conscious, and left-wing in a muddled sort of way. He had been friendly with Burgess during his last year and it is possible, though unproven, that the two had a brief affair. Burgess always denied this, arguing that he could not have contemplated touching Maclean's 'large, flabby, white whale-like' body. Cyril Connolly once wrote: 'I think the simplest distinction between Maclean and Burgess was that if one had given Maclean a letter he would have posted it. Burgess would probably have forgotten or opened it and then returned to tell us what we should have said.'[15]

It is impossible to date precisely when Maclean was approached by the Soviet agents in London. Certainly, Maclean's family and friends noticed that he seemed to be moving back towards his late father's liberal attitudes. He had talked about becoming a teacher in the Soviet Union;

now, his mother noted with relief, he seemed more interested in working hard for his degree. He had shown great enthusiasm for John Strachey's books, *The Coming Struggle for Power* and *The Menace of Fascism*; both proclaimed that 'there is no force on earth which can long prevent the workers of the world from building a new and stable civilization for themselves on the basis of the common ownership of the means of production.' Now Donald had no time to waste on Strachey; studying for his French and German finals was all that mattered. Friends saw that he was more relaxed, less strident. He had always lacked willpower and guts, they thought, and his rejection of Marxism, which could have jeopardized his chances of a good career, was in character.

Maclean was awarded a first-class degree in the summer of 1934 and began cramming for the entrance examination to the Foreign Office; then (and still, even in the 1980s, when Britain had long been relegated to the second division of world powers) regarded as the élite department of the civil service. He passed the written test brilliantly though there was a brief problem when he was interviewed. He was asked about his communist background at Cambridge; had he shaken off these unfortunate views or did he still believe in the imminent revolution? Maclean paused, wondering whether to 'brazen it out'. He decided that disarming honesty was the best policy. He told the interviewing board that he hadn't quite shaken off his past radicalism. The chairman smiled and nodded with approval at the young man's laudable honesty. But then, as Sir Dick White pointed out, there was no reason for the FO to have disbarred Maclean:

Yes, Maclean did say that he had been a communist and that he hadn't quite got rid of it. That was the atmosphere at the time. A security service like ours, which was very small then, is just as much a part of the public attitude as any other government department. And the attitude then was relaxed. I suppose we were over-ready to get the best brains.[16]

It is likely that Maclean had been talent-spotted by Burgess and his name passed to the middleman – possibly Dave Springhall – being used by the Soviet agents in London. Whenever this had happened, the fact is that by the time he entered the FO in 1935, marked out as a man with great potential, he was prepared to risk everything as an agent of the Soviet Union.

Kim Philby had been rather more circumspect about his communism. He left Trinity in the summer of 1933 with a respectable second-class degree in economics and a college prize of £14, with which he bought the collected works of Karl Marx. In his autobiography, *My Silent War,* published in 1968, five years after he defected, Philby gives a cleverly blurred account of his political development:

How did it all begin? My decision to play an active part in the struggle against reaction was not the result of a sudden conversion. My earliest thoughts on politics turned me towards the labour movement; and one of my first acts on going up to Cambridge in 1929 was to join the Cambridge University Socialist Society (CUSS). For the first two years, I attended its meetings with regularity, but otherwise took little part in its proceedings. I became gradually aware that the Labour Party in Britain stood well apart from the mainstream of the Left as a political force. But the real turning point in my thinking came with the demoralization of the Labour Party in 1931. It seemed incredible that the party should be so helpless against the reserve strength which reaction could mobilize in times of crisis. More important still, the fact that a supposedly sophisticated electorate had been stampeded by the cynical propaganda of the day threw serious doubts on the validity of the assumptions underlying parliamentary democracy.[17]

Philby said that he had started to think of 'other alternatives' to democratic socialism. He was treasurer of the Socialist Society in 1932–33 and began to read the 'classics of European socialism'. It was, he said, a slow, brain-racking process. Not until his last term, in the summer of 1933, did he consider himself a communist. But he had never been widely known as a communist, which made him potentially a more useful recruit for Soviet Intelligence than the Blunts and Burgesses of Cambridge, all of whom had to convince the world that their Marxism had been a youthful aberration.

Philby has never explained how he became an agent for Soviet Intelligence; indeed, he has tried to give the impression that he was recruited after he left university. He gave a vital clue, however, when he admitted in his autobiography that he left Trinity in the summer of 1933 'with the conviction that my life must be devoted to communism'. It would have been more accurate to have said that he intended to devote his life to being a communist agent. Charles Martin Robertson recalled:

Kim's father was a very old friend of my father's so Kim and I knew each other all our lives, though we were not close friends. I liked him very much and always thought of him as a nice person. He was then a communist. I did write to him in Russia but the reply was artificial and I couldn't feel any real contact – too much had come between – and we didn't keep it up. Spying is of course a nasty activity but I can't feel the absolute horror of it as some people do. Secrecy seems to me the real enemy. On the whole the more people know the less likely they are to do silly things which might start wars and I can't help feeling that some such idea must have been in the minds of these spies, as well as other things: the trap of past actions, but also old loyalties, for though they were traitors to their country they surely felt (some of them at any rate at some stages) that they were not betraying something which to them was more important.[18]

Philby had switched from history to economics in October 1931. Like many politically active students, he felt that economics was the most important discipline any student could study. It provided the intellectual ammunition to fire at the conservatives and liberals who still defended capitalism. Moreover, it helped students find their way through the maze of Marxism. It was through his increasing commitment to communism and his switch to economics that he had met Harry Dawes and Jim Lees, both ex-miners on scholarships. Both men recounted harrowing stories of real hardship that gave the impressionable students a vivid insight into what exploitation under capitalism really meant. By mixing with men such as Dawes and Lees, Philby moved further from his former position as a democratic socialist. His friendship with Sir Dennis Robertson was also crucial. Robertson, like Maynard Keynes, believed that unemployment was not the inevitable, self-regulating mechanism of the market economy to force back wages when they had risen too high. Like Keynes, too, he argued that government could and should recognize its role in shaping and boosting the economy; if that did not happen, then there would always be high levels of unemployment. Robertson had written two seminal works in the 1920s – *Money and Banking Policy* and *The Price Level* – though it was not until Keynes's book, *The General Theory of Em-*

ployment, Interest and Money, was published in 1936 that this revolutionary view gained wide acceptance. Like many of the best brains at Cambridge Dennis Robertson was both an Apostle and a homosexual. Unlike many of his friends, he worried about his preference for men and, at one stage, travelled to Vienna to see Freud in an effort to find a 'cure'.

Philby also became friendly with Blunt. One of Blunt's friends recalled:

> Anthony was capable of long-term affection and to his dying day spoke of Kim Philby with great affection. And there was never the remotest suggestion of any sexual relationship between the two of them. The affection that Anthony had for Kim seemed to me at least as strong as any he expressed for Guy Burgess. Maclean was a different matter. Anthony thought that he was wet. Idiotic and unstable.[19]

In the Christmas holiday of 1932 Philby had seen for himself what life was like for the working class. He went to Nottingham and rented a flat from Sebastian Sprott, then lecturing in psychology and philosophy at the university there. Sprott, nicknamed the 'Queen of the North', still maintained his links with Cambridge by attending Apostles' meetings. But the Sprott flat was too removed from the realities of working-class life, so Philby had moved to the home of a miner.

By the time that he was preparing for his finals in the early summer of 1933 Philby had already been contacted by a Soviet intelligence officer. How was this done? Philby was, by 1932–33, a liked and respected member of the Cambridge Left. His name may not have been on a party list and he may not have proclaimed his faith in print, but no one doubted where his sympathies lay. It would, therefore, have been a simple matter for someone, such as Springhall or Klugmann, to suggest to the Soviets that young Philby might be worth talking to. It is possible that Guy Burgess was responsible for making the contact, though most Cambridge contemporaries argue that Burgess did not become a committed Marxist until 1933. His Soviet controller probably did no more than suggest to Philby that he mask his communism and hope that one day he might be in a position to help the cause of world revolution. Certainly, Philby thought about trying for the Foreign Office, but Sir Dennis Robertson told him frostily that he would refuse to act as a referee since he was far too left-wing for government service. Instead, Philby set off on his motorbike for Vienna. Any doubts about his new role as a Soviet mole were soon forgotten. Vienna was in turmoil as socialists fought with the private, fascist armies on the streets of Vienna. For Philby it was like watching the text of Marx come alive; the people versus fascism, the true, brutal face of capitalism. Philby watched the bloody defeat of the socialists in February 1934 when the new Chancellor, Engelbert Dollfuss, ordered an horrific attack by the army on the socialist-controlled housing estates on the outskirts of the city. As he watched the defeat of socialists who had believed in power by democracy, Philby became more sure than ever that force was the one language that the capitalists understood. He returned to London in May 1934, tougher and more resolved that communism was the only path. And he had a wife: a twenty-three-year-old Jewish girl, Alice Friedman, known as Litzi. She, too, was a dedicated communist and had married Philby partly from love and partly to escape the purges of the Austrian Left. (They parted in 1937.)

In his autobiography, Philby described the next two years thus:

During that period . . . I was a sort of intelligence probationer. I still look back with wonder at the infinite patience shown by my seniors in the service, a patience matched only by their intelligent understanding. Week after week, we would meet in one or other of the remoter spaces in London; week after week I would reach the rendezvous empty-handed and leave with a load of painstaking advice, admonition and encouragement. I was often despondent at my failure to achieve anything worthwhile, but the lessons went on and sank deep. When the time came for serious work, I found myself endowed with much of the required mental equipment . . . My reward came during the Spanish war, when I learnt that my probationary period was considered at an end; I emerged from the conflict as a fully-fledged officer of the Soviet service.[20]

In the autumn of 1934, after a difficult few months, Philby found a job in London as a humble sub-editor and writer on the *Review of Reviews*, a monthly magazine that provided him with a salary of £4 a week and precious little opportunity to collect anything of value for his Soviet controller. It did, however, equip him with the basic skills of journalism, which Philby put to good use when he reported the Spanish Civil War for *The Times* (and for the Soviets). From 1934 to 1936 Philby also did his best to convince the world that he had shaken off his left-wing past. He became a member of the Anglo-German Fellowship, an organization whose membership read like a social and political *Who's Who* and whose pro-Nazi stance served only to increase the fears of the British Left that the Establishment would never resist Hitler. Early in 1936 Philby was hired by the fellowship to edit a propaganda sheet which would show how the British press was misleading the public about Germany's intentions. Philby travelled to Germany;

he mixed with the wealthy and the powerful. After his hesitant start as an agent he was now able, in his own words, to start 'writing, or otherwise providing, information on an increasingly voluminous scale'. He wrote:

> In early manhood I became an accredited member of the Soviet intelligence service . . . 'Agent', of course, is a term susceptible of widely different interpretations. It can mean a simple courier carrying messages between two points; it can mean the writer of such messages; it can imply advisory or even executive functions. I passed through the first stage rapidly.[21]

CHAPTER 9
Burgess Pulls the Strings

Anthony Blunt and Guy Burgess saw each other as often as possible after Burgess left Cambridge early in 1935. And, it has to be assumed, Blunt was kept briefed about Burgess's complicated manoeuvrings in London and Paris. Blunt had, by now, his own good reasons for travelling frequently to London. In 1931 Samuel Courtauld, who headed the Courtaulds textile firm between the two world wars, was persuaded that Britain needed an institute which would develop the history of art as an independent academic discipline. On the continent, art history was already a respectable academic subject, but in England art was largely a hobby for scholars to enjoy in between 'serious' work. Painting and sculpture (even architecture) were simply appreciated visually; they were liked or not liked, but analysis of the works themselves was amateur and haphazard. Courtauld wanted to change that; he wanted British academics to be as expert in, say, the historical context of Rembrandt or Goya as any European. Urged on by Lord Lee, a trustee of the National Gallery, Courtauld provided a bequest that would support a new institute of art. He gave a fifty-year lease on a magnificent town house at 20 Portman Square, near Marble Arch. The institute was attached to the University of London to ensure academic respectability. One of the first members of staff was Miss Lillian Gurry. She had graduated in 1925 from King's College, London, with a degree in English and French. She had worked briefly as a teacher at a 'snob school' in north London before deciding that she would become a librarian. She recalled:

> We worked very hard to get all the books on the shelves for the first students in October 1932. We had a tiny library on the first floor. Most of the books were in a back room which used to be the ballroom. And we had Impressionist pictures on the walls from the Courtauld collection. There were only about twenty or thirty students at first. There were one or two débutantes. It was very difficult at first to attract postgraduates to do a degree in art history. I couldn't go to the lectures much in those days because I was so busy but I did listen to Roger Fry. The lecturers weren't attached to the staff and came from places like the Victoria and Albert Museum. Most of the students were fairly well off. There were examinations but there wasn't a syllabus. I first met Anthony Blunt in about 1934 when he started to lecture at the Courtauld. He was not what you would call upper class but he was – and this is what we called it in those days – a pansy. He was terrified of lecturing. He used to come along, chewing over what he would say, very frightened of his audience. But it didn't show. He gave well-made lectures with a beautiful speaking voice. He always wore, I remember, well-tailored suits with a red tie. He was well known as a Marxist in those days but then it was very common in those days for intellectuals to be communists.[1]

The house in Portman Square was the focal point of Blunt's life from the mid-1930s until his death. It was perhaps ironic that a Soviet agent should be so at ease in a mansion whose history was so aristocratic, and that the

Courtauld, which was the vehicle for Blunt's entire post-war career, should have been established by the sort of capitalist patron that he was attacking as late as 1937. The house had been built by Robert Adam in 1775 for Elizabeth, Dowager Countess of Home, widow of the 8th Earl of Home, who had amassed a considerable fortune by trading in the West Indies. Adam, who was paid £3500 for his work, created a house with a modest, unimposing exterior. But inside he aimed for grandeur. A magnificent, winding central staircase, topped by a huge glass dome, was the centre of his design. The house was designed for entertaining rather than for comfort; a fact that did not bother the elderly Dowager. In London society she had a reputation for raffishness (historians do not say that she had no children; only that she had no legitimate heirs) and was nicknamed the Queen of Hell. After her death in 1784 the house had a succession of owners. It was the French embassy throughout the revolution; from 1812 until 1819 it was owned by Earl Grey, who raised the top storey; and from 1820 until 1861 it was the town house of the Duke of Newcastle; Sir Francis Goldsmid lived there until 1919, installing a much-needed bathroom.

Samuel Courtauld bought the house in 1926, restored much of the original decor and, when his wife died in 1931, decided that it would make a suitably distinguished base for the first British institute dedicated to the study of art. He provided the Institute with the house, the library and his stunning collection of French Impressionist and Post-Impressionist paintings, including Manet's 'Bar aux Folies-Bergère', Cézanne's 'Card Players' and 'Lac d'Annecy', Van Gogh's 'Self-portrait with Bandaged Ear' and Gauguin's 'Nevermore'. The collection was enlarged when Roger Fry left his collection of Bloomsbury Group and Omega Workshop pictures to the Institute. It is now housed in a gallery in Woburn Square.

The first director was W. G. Constable, Courtauld's second choice after Kenneth Clark refused the post. In 1933 came an injection of continental expertise that transformed the British art historical scene. Aby Warburg had founded the Warburg Institute in Hamburg in the early 1920s. Michael Kitson, later deputy director at the Courtauld, said:

At that time anyone interested in the history of art had to go abroad to study. The Warburg was an admirable place of scholarship and when it was threatened by the Nazis a number of people here were very anxious to save it. London University academics were very keen to get it here and we did because we were faster and more generous than either the Americans or the Dutch, who also wanted it. London University agreed to pay the running costs and house it – accommodation was found near the Adelphi. It came over here in 1933 with a small staff and a remarkable library. The staff were more professional than anyone in England. They brought a new professionalism to art history. It is obvious that they enormously influenced the study of art here. Certainly there were very close ties in the early years between the Courtauld and the Warburg.[2]

Blunt's close friend John Hilton said that Blunt was a key figure in 'masterminding' the transfer of the Warburg to London.[3] Blunt was more than repaid by the European scholars he helped to rescue. Men like Johannes Wilde, later a deputy director of the Courtauld, had developed a structural framework for the study of art which Blunt eagerly adopted. His Marxism was, at first, easily merged with this technique and then quietly eliminated. What remained was the notion that all art had to be seen in an historical context; that all artists were creatures of their time; that science could be a useful tool in dating and analysing works of art. This was not so different, thought Blunt, from the Marxist philosophy; after 1938 he simply did not rely so much on the clichés of class war.

1936 was a watershed year in European history. In March Hitler showed his contempt for the Europe of the Versailles Treaty when he ordered German troops into the Rhineland, designated a demilitarized zone under Versailles and the Locarno treaties. The British and the French governments, which had little appetite, then or later, for a confrontation with Hitler, were, in any case, already agonizing over Mussolini's campaigns in the Abyssinian War. In November that year Hitler and Mussolini seemed to be moving still closer together; it was Mussolini who said in Milan that 'this Berlin–Rome line is not a diaphragm but rather an axis'. In response the Left in Europe was hastily regrouping. There was a Popular Front government in France from June 1936 until October 1938. This collapsed because of the Munich Agreement in September 1938, when the British and French governments allowed Hitler to occupy the Sudetenland, the industrialized region in northern Bohemia which had been part of Czechoslovakia. The British Prime Minister, Stanley Baldwin, also had to cope with the gravest constitutional crisis of the modern era. On 16 November King Edward VIII told Baldwin that he intended to marry Mrs Wallis Simpson, an American who had twice been divorced. The British press eventually broke their self-imposed censorship on the story in early December. The question was this: should the King, as the Supreme Governor of the Church of England, be allowed to marry a divorcee? Many members of the public, ranging from communists such as Harry Pollitt to fascists like Oswald Mosley, thought so, even if the King's new wife could not actually assume the title of queen. But Baldwin and the House of Commons (with the notable exception of Winston Churchill) did not. Faced with the choice of 'giving up the woman I love' or the throne, Edward, who had only succeeded his father George V in January that year, decided to abdicate. He was created Duke of Windsor and went into voluntary exile in France, marrying Mrs Simpson at the Château de Cande in June 1937. His departure was certainly mourned by the Nazis who regarded him, with some justification, as a reliable friend of Germany. As Prince of Wales he had made no secret of his admiration for the new Germany – an attitude that was shared by many of England's aristocratic families, some of them members of the now-infamous Cliveden Set. Historians still argue about exactly how sinister (or pro-Nazi) were the gatherings of the powerful, the rich and the famous at Cliveden, a country house by the Thames just outside Maidenhead owned by Lord and Lady Astor – but the Left was in no doubt. The communist journalist Claud Cockburn, who is credited with first breaking the story, wrote in his autobiography: 'Up and down the British Isles, across and across the United States, anti-Nazi orators shouted it from hundreds of platforms. No anti-fascist rally in Madison Square Gardens or Trafalgar Square was complete without a denunciation of the Cliveden Set.'[4] Astor himself, the owner of the *Observer*, wrote while on a visit to America:

There is complete ignorance in the public mind as to the reasons why some people desire to negotiate a settlement with Germany. This is largely due to the intensive and widespread anti-German propaganda being conducted by Jews and communists. Newspapers are influenced by those firms which advertise so largely in the press and are frequently under Jewish control.[5]

Astor had a useful ally in Geoffrey Dawson, editor of *The Times*, whose influence over opinion in Whitehall and Parliament was enormous. Dawson was determined to keep anything out of *The Times* which could possibly offend Herr Hitler.

But it was Spain which preoccupied Europe from 18 July 1936 onwards. The Popular Front government's socialist, anti-clerical policies were always likely to provoke conflict with the great forces of Spanish politics: the army, the landlords and the Church. Those forces found a champion in Francisco Franco, the forty-four-year-old general who was then governor of the Canary Islands. On 1 October he was declared generalissimo of the new nationalist government of Spain; a body that was recognized within a month by Hitler and Mussolini. So began the Spanish Civil War, a three-year-long confrontation that became an ideological battleground between the European Left and Right. For the British Left it was the supreme challenge; if Franco's forces, supported by the Nazis and the Italians, were not defeated, then what hope would there be for the rest of Europe? One historian put it like this:

To go and fight for Spanish democracy was a call that evoked a warm response in many young men thirsting for some such opportunity for action. It did much to turn the absolute tide of pacifism, and not only because it gave further proof of fascist intentions and ruthlessness. It broke the spell, so powerfully cast by Baldwinian politics, of inertia, helplessness and drift . . . it revived a sense of purpose in national politics. The Left became war-minded, militant. The Right became wedded to 'non-intervention', almost pacifism. The parliamentary parties were in some measure by-passed by the mass of new organizations – the Friends of Nationalist Spain who favoured Franco, the Friends of Spain and others, who opposed him. The press divided almost equally and hundreds of pamphlets and books appeared, expounding and passionately pleading. Such a commotion of opinion denoted something new.[6]

However, as the years passed, the unity of the Left began to crack. Left-wing intellectuals who had fought with the Republicans returned with harrowing stories about the brutality of their own side; they were also critical of the way that the communists, backed by the Soviet Union, were turning Republican Spain into a Stalinist state. George Orwell had been wounded fighting with the Catalonian workers' militia. In 1938 his *Homage to Catalonia* was published:

It sold badly at the time and was harshly reviewed by communist fellow-travellers and by sympathizers with the Popular Front, the alliance of the Left against fascism. But the book is now recognized as a classic of English prose, an extraordinarily honest description of war as seen through the eyes of the common soldier, and as one of the shrewdest and most biting polemics against the Stalinist and Communist attempt to use the civil war for their own ends, recklessly, fatally.[7]

Anthony Blunt was in a better position than many of his communist friends to understand the problems facing the Republican forces. In Easter 1936 he had toured Spain with his close friend, Louis MacNeice. Since MacNeice was short of cash Blunt offered to pay for the return boat ticket. On the trip they played piquet and debated the future of the Popular Front. They landed at Gibraltar and immediately met a 'perky Cambridge don who told us that Spain would soon have her spot of trouble – not just yet [it was March] but soon.' Blunt was determined to see as much architecture as possible and they spent most of their time, said MacNeice, 'walking and gaping'. They went to Toledo, Segovia and Aranjuez, Seville, Madrid – an endless round of churches, hotels and picture galleries. They went to Seville in Holy Week, expecting a high-spirited carnival; but all they saw was a depressing army parade of 'puny little creatures'. A few minutes later they watched young communists go off to a rally, red-shirted, defiant, fists clenched as if anticipating the coming civil war.[8]

Claud Cockburn was right when he wrote that people who had not lived through the Spanish Civil War could not hope to understand its significance in the 1930s. For the Left it was an exhilarating outburst by the People; a demonstration that ordinary workers could ally with intellectuals in the fight for a just world. Utopia seemed, albeit briefly, attainable. It was confirmation, too, that only the Soviet Union – the only non-fascist power not to pursue a policy of non-intervention – would resist the dictators. Britain and France banned the sale of arms to the 'Reds' while some newspapers argued that defeat for the Republicans would be a 'shattering and humiliating defeat of Moscow as the open partner of communist revolution in other countries'.

Thousands of Britons did not agree; 2200 fought in the Republican International Brigades during the war and roughly a half of these considered themselves communists. In all, just over 500 Britons died fighting the fascists of Franco, including John Cornford and Julian Bell (who died driving an ambulance) as well as hundreds of ordinary working men.

The death of Cornford sent shock waves through Cambridge, not just among the communists but throughout the university. He had gone to Spain soon after the outbreak of war and returned to England in mid-September to recruit a group to fight alongside the Spanish. In October he had returned to Spain with six Cambridge friends, including Bernard Knox, later a respected academic in the United States. They travelled by train through France and were soon involved in heavy fighting around Madrid. He was wounded once but refused to stay in hospital. In late December, one day after his twenty-first birthday, he was killed in action. According to contemporary reports he died 'magnificently', but later accounts suggested that Cornford had died because he had been careless. Walter Greenhaigh, one of the early British volunteers to the Republican cause, gave this account in the 1980s. If Greenhaigh is right, it does not mean that Cornford was any less brave than his contemporaries believed, only that he was more human. Greenhaigh recalled:

> We were told to advance under cover of darkness before dawn to within sight of the village of Lopera. We did this . . . we were all lying in a long straight line on the brow of the hill and there were three veterans who had fought in Madrid. John Cornford was one. John had a bandage round his head – he looked very like Lord Byron. The bandage was very white and he wouldn't wear a hat and he's up there and I'm on the other side . . . We wait and wait and finally John climbs up to the brow of the hill to look over and the early sun just catches his white bandage and that was it. He got one straight through the head.[9]

Knox heard of Cornford's death while he was recuperating from a wound. He wrote: 'John had always been so gloriously alive, so smiling and confident, that I, for one, had come to look on him as immortal. I didn't want to hear any details then. I got them later from an old Irish war veteran. It was an epitaph that John would have been proud of: "He was a lovely soldier." '[10]

There were lengthy tributes. The student *Cambridge Review* pointed out that Cornford had achieved more in twenty-one years than most people could hope for in a lifetime. His death was, it said, a bitter blow to English thought as well as to the working-class cause. Professor Ernest Barker said:

> He had a first-rate mind, but he also had something greater – very much greater. He was one of those willing to stake heart's blood upon their convictions, turning them into a faith and acting in the strength of their faith. One may disagree with the convictions; one can only bare the head before the testimony offered to them . . . He did what he believed to be his duty. He leaves a memory – dark hair, deep eyes, slow voice, steady thought and the ultimate testimony which a man can give to his conviction.[11]

The person who should have been most affected by Cornford's death was Margot Heinemann, the girlfriend to whom he had written a stream of passionate letters from Spain. But Heinemann was determined not to collapse; she said that 'the only way to get through it was to keep talking about the revolution'.[12] Michael Straight, however, had no such inhibitions. Heinemann watched his public display of grief with a mixture of pity and contempt – she had always thought that Straight was a weak character who had a 'schoolboy crush on John Cornford'. Straight busied himself organizing the letters and poems that Cornford had left in his rooms at Cambridge, believing, rightly as it happened, that here was a literary talent who would fascinate later generations.

In early February 1937, Anthony Blunt, in his role as Soviet talent-spotter, made his move to try and exploit Straight's grief. Several of Straight's contemporaries challenged key points in his autobiography when it was published in 1983. All that can be said for sure of this crucial episode is that Blunt did try to recruit him as an agent soon after news of Cornford's death reached Cambridge. Blunt asked him what he intended to do after he left Cambridge. Straight said that he had thought about becoming a British citizen like his brother Whitney; adding that perhaps he might try to become a Member of Parliament for the Labour Party. Blunt suggested that some 'friends' had other ideas. He confessed that he worked for the Communist International and that he had been instructed to inform Michael of his assignment as a Soviet agent. He should return to the States and become a banker, 'to provide appraisals of Wall Street's plans to dominate the world economy'. Blunt said that he had obviously been deeply affected by Cornford's death; now he had a chance to prove his own commitment to the cause. He had been selected, said Blunt, by a friend who knew and respected him but who could not, alas, identify himself (Straight later thought it must have been Guy Burgess). Straight returned to Blunt's rooms that evening. He pleaded 'to be released from the commitment that had been imposed on me in the name of my dead friend'. Blunt promised to talk again to the mysterious recruiter. A few days later Blunt told him that 'they' would compromise; Straight still had to break with the Communist Party, return to the States and 'go underground' but he did not have to become a banker. Once again, Straight said, he protested. Blunt listened patiently and said he would do his best; the whole affair would have to be considered 'in the highest levels of the Kremlin'. Straight insists that he had been so emotionally overwhelmed by Cornford's death that he somehow wanted to be a martyr himself. But, he claimed, his plea to Blunt was rejected by Stalin. 'I was trapped in a way that neither Anthony nor I could assess,' said Straight, not quite able to explain why he should feel trapped as a result of private conversation with a Cambridge don. Then came a far from satisfactory meeting with a Soviet controller:

When the time came for me to leave Cambridge he [Blunt] asked me to meet him in London. I picked him up in Oxford Street. He directed me to a roadhouse on the Great West Road. There, a stocky, dark-haired Russian met us. He barely smiled and very little was said. It was a sweltering day and the Russian spent most of his time in a large and crowded swimming pool. When he heaved himself out and dressed he ordered a beer. He said a few trivial things about telephoning from public booths to avoid detection. Then he departed. He was more like the agent of a small-time smuggling operation than the representative of a new international order. I drove back to London with Anthony. There was little more to say. He asked me as we parted for some highly personal document . . . he tore it into two ragged pieces. He handed one piece to me and kept the other, saying that it would be handed back to me by the man who some day in the future would approach me in New York. Blunt was carrying out Burgess's orders, I am convinced now. It was typical of his playful, immoral, amoral, imagination: we will put him into Morgan's Bank, where his father was a partner, as an undercover communist. Something like that, I am sure. Family ties meant nothing to Burgess. He hated his own father and had no sense of family. Anthony Blunt would never have thought that up. I don't think even a Russian would have thought that up. The predilection for martyrdom in me was a much greater force than my belief in communism. I wanted to be a martyr, I wanted to sacrifice myself. My closest friend had given his life. I wanted to give mine. It was very romantic . . . I couldn't repudiate relationships that were very deep, very compelling.[13]

Whatever was said at these various meetings (and in the 1980s Straight was trying to understand what had happened to him in 1937) one fact is indisputable. When Michael Straight returned to the States in the autumn of 1937 he had been earmarked as a potentially useful source by the Soviets. He should have been a good catch; he was clever, wealthy, well-connected and probably destined for public office. But he had neither the nerve nor the inclination to become a spy. Such was the influence of the Straight name that shortly after he returned from Cambridge he was able to petition President Roosevelt for a job – a privilege denied most job-seeking graduates. Eventually he became an unpaid volunteer in the State Department, drafting a report on how Hitler could find the money and materials to fight a war. In the spring of 1938 he was contacted by a Soviet agent calling himself Michael Green, a dark, stocky man with broad lips, a ready smile and a good command of English. One thing he did not have was the other half of Straight's document. But that did not matter. They continued to meet occasionally until the Nazi–Soviet pact of August 1939. In that time Straight moved from the State Department to the Department of the Interior to join the team that prepared speeches for Roosevelt, the Cabinet and Liberal members of Congress though he insisted that he only gave Green his personal and non-secret assessments of economic and political developments.

While Blunt was busily trying to persuade friends that they should publicly renounce their Marxist faith in preparation for lives as agents/spies of the Soviet Union, he was making no effort to disguise his belief in communism. On 6 August 1937 in *The Spectator* magazine he wrote a vitriolic review of Picasso's *Guernica*, the masterpiece which had been inspired by the fascist bombing of the Basque capital of Guernica. Blunt was outraged by the work, which had just been unveiled in Paris. The painting was 'a private brainstorm which gives no evidence that Picasso has realized the political significance of Guernica'. In October Blunt accused Picasso of refusing to recognize that the Spanish Civil War was 'only a tragic part of a great forward movement' which would end in the liberation of the common man. Picasso was interested only in reaching 'a limited coterie of aesthetes' with a grotesque surrealist vision that was irrelevant in a revolutionary age. Blunt acknowledged his error countless times after the war in lectures at the Courtauld and in articles published around the world:

> We had launched a campaign against esoteric art and in favour of a realistic, widely appealing style. From my own point of view the climax came in 1937 when Picasso exhibited *Guernica* in the Spanish Pavilion in the International Exhibition. I was very much moved by it but I was horrified by it from a theoretical point of view. I wrote an article in *The Spectator* saying that this was not the right way to commemorate a great human and revolutionary tragedy. Picasso of course at that time was not a communist, but he was a keen supporter of the government party and the left-wing movements in Spain, and I felt that *Guernica* was merely an expression of his private sensation of horror and was irrelevant to the revolutionary movement as a whole and to the basic problems of the Spanish Civil War. (The war was of course the main issue of the day and it is very hard now to realize just how personally and how intensely one was affected, even if one did not go to Spain and fight, by the atmosphere and the horrors of the war.)[14]

There was a celebrated row over Blunt's attack on *Guernica*, described by Blunt as a 'splendid set-to on the subject of naturalism'. The critic Herbert Read and Blunt argued fiercely, 'though in a friendly manner because we happened to be members of the same club'.

By late 1936 Blunt had begun to tire of the limited horizons of Cambridge. London offered a career in art history; a new discipline that he, as one of its British pioneers, would be able to dominate. Guy Burgess, too, was there, promising Blunt the opportunity for the high-risk promiscuity that Cambridge no longer tolerated as it had once done. In 1937 Blunt joined the staff of the Warburg Institute.

Burgess had found himself a job in 1935, as secretary, travelling companion and personal assistant to Captain 'Jack' Macnamara, an ex-professional soldier, aged thirty, who was Conservative MP for Chelmsford. Guy had been recommended by Major (later Sir) Joseph Ball, a former MI5 officer and the Conservative Party's director of research who had just rejected Burgess's application for a job. Ball found Burgess fascinating though quite unsuited to employment in his own office. The job with Macnamara may not have seemed much of an opening for a would-be spy, but it gave Burgess entry into the surreal world of international diplomacy which was inhabited by characters who were so bizarre that no self-respecting novelist would have dared invent them. Macnamara, for example, was a member of the Anglo-German Fellowship and was vigorously right-wing, offering a series of outlandish solutions to save Britain and 'white civilization'. Goronwy Rees was appalled by Burgess's choice, describing Macnamara as 'so far to the right of the Conservative Party that it was quite reasonable to call him a fascist'. Rees noted that the captain shared Guy's 'sexual tastes' and that part of his job as secretary was to ensure that Macnamara's 'emotional needs' were satisfied. Burgess worked, on and off, for the MP until he joined the BBC in October 1936. He used to regale friends with hilarious stories about his adventures with the captain. They travelled to Germany, ostensibly on fact-finding missions, though these usually ended up, according to Burgess, in wild homosexual adventures.

For example, there was the expedition in 1936. Apart from Burgess and the captain there was a churchman, the Venerable J. H. Sharp, a member of the Foreign Relations Council of the Church of England who also held the title of Archdeacon in South-Eastern Europe (though no one, including Burgess, seemed to know what responsibilities this job carried), and Tom Wylie, private secretary to the Permanent Under-Secretary at the War Office in London. After his defection, Burgess claimed that the trip was a serious attempt to discover the truth about Nazism; indeed, he said, Macnamara was appalled by what he saw. But Burgess had earlier given a far more colourful account to Goronwy Rees, describing with huge enjoyment a sub-culture of European homosexuality where English gentlemen such as Macnamara could indulge themselves with young, blond boys. Rees later recalled that Guy made the trip sound 'like an immense comic epic . . . interrupted by strange characters who popped up as if from nowhere, like the Anglican Archdeacon much interested in the affairs of the Orthodox Church whom Guy claimed to have rescued from a particularly scandalous predicament in Vienna.' The story was, thought Rees, 'like one of those eighteenth-century picaresque novels in which one is conducted scene by scene through the criminal world, only in this case that underworld was exclusively homosexual and thereby seemed to acquire a specifically modern flavour.'[15]

The Macnamara connection provided Burgess with useful gossip from the right-wing political world of the Anglo-German Fellowship as well as giving him an excuse to travel to Germany and pick up titbits for his Soviet masters. But Burgess had developed new and even better contacts in Paris. Édouard Pfeiffer was a thoroughly disreputable homosexual who had somehow become part of the team of Édouard Daladier, the radical politician who had been Prime Minister for ten months in 1933 and two months in 1934. Daladier returned to office from April 1938 until March 1940; he also ran the Ministry of War and Defence from June 1936 to May 1940. With the British Prime Minister Neville Chamberlain, Daladier desperately tried to appease Hitler. Burgess always fudged the circumstances of his first meeting with Pfeiffer, insisting that he had met him through contacts at the Anglo-German Fellowship. He did not, however, mind describing to friends his first impressions of the Frenchman. He said that he had gone to Pfeiffer's flat in Paris and found him playing ping-pong with a friend. Both men were dressed in tailcoats and were slashing the ball to and fro across the table. But there was no net; instead, a naked young man was stretched across the middle of the table, trying not to flinch when the ball ricocheted off him. Pfeiffer seemed to think this was unexceptional and, by way of explanation, told Guy that the young man was a professional cyclist. Burgess, of course, was more than capable of dealing with this sort of seedy eccentricity; he was astute enough to know that Pfeiffer would probably prove an invaluable source of high-grade French political gossip. He was right: Pfeiffer became Daladier's *chef de cabinet*, giving Burgess a steady flow of information which confirmed that Daladier wanted to avoid war with Germany at any cost.

Burgess made other invaluable contacts in Paris. Willi Muenzenberg had set up his headquarters there after fleeing from Germany in 1933. The Comintern's leading propagandist, Muenzenberg was short, squat, square-built, with powerful shoulders 'which gave the impression that bumping against him would be like colliding with a steamroller'.[16] He had been born in Thuringia, the son of working-class parents, and had worked in a shoe factory for six years. From that unpromising start he had become an international fixer, fund-raiser, propagandist and mischief-maker for the Kremlin. He had founded a trust in Berlin in 1921, the International Workers' Aid, known to communists as the Muenzenberg Trust, to raise money for the Soviet Union. From there he branched out into newspaper and magazine ownership; by 1926 in Germany he ran two daily newspapers and a mass-circulation weekly. He was also adept at exploiting liberals who could not bring themselves to join the Communist Party but who, nonetheless, wanted to help the cause. He had no time for the constant, sterile wranglings over policy that racked the communist movement; he was a meddler who enjoyed intrigue – as long as there were tangible results. He fled from Germany on the night of the Reichstag fire and set up a base in Paris where he resumed his activities, summed up by one contemporary as the production of committees faster than a conjuror could pull rabbits out of a hat. The purpose of all this frantic activity may not have been clear at the time. But Muenzenberg, whose title as head of the Comintern's West European Department for Agitation and Propaganda (Agitprop) made him sound misleadingly like a civil servant, knew exactly what he was doing. He was intent on causing as many problems for the capitalists as possible – by propaganda, by fostering local communist groups and by encouraging sympathizers to become agents of the Comintern. He set up a World Committee for the Relief of the Victims of German Fascism and proceeded to use its branches throughout the West as a cover for intelligence-gathering and propaganda. Arthur Koestler later wrote: 'The official Party bureaucracy hated Willi . . . this outward pressure moulded the people around him into an intimate clique; a kind of Party within the Party. The atmosphere . . . was a strange mixture of revolutionary camaraderie and of the jealousies of courtiers around a benevolent despot.'[17]

One of Muenzenberg's aides was Otto Katz, a small, plump man with a large head and abnormally wide shoulders who had an uncertain history and who changed his name with confusing regularity. Claud Cockburn first met Katz in 1932 at the anti-war congress in Amsterdam. Cockburn wrote:

Historians ought not to forget Otto Katz. No portrait gallery – rogues' gallery some would say – of this period would be quite complete without the putty-coloured visage of that most talented propagandist and intriguer. Pretty soon every schoolboy will think he knows all about that time, certified as having been full of starry-eyed do-gooders with pink illusions . . . Not much, probably, will be heard of the late Katz – a man, nevertheless, reeking of eighty-five per cent Zeitgeist, and producing some pervasive practical effects upon events.[18]

After fleeing Germany Katz, now using the pseudonym André Simone, had flitted from one European capital to another, trying to plant pro-communist stories in the press, scheming and plotting in a way that baffled even an experienced journalist such as Cockburn. He had ended up in Paris, from where he continued to try to further the interests of the Comintern. Arthur Koestler noted that Katz was 'smooth and slick' while Muenzenberg was 'rugged and earthy'. Katz was dark and handsome and spoke fluent French, English, Russian and Czech, in contrast to Muenzenberg who spoke only German. Katz was a skilful writer; his boss could barely write a literate sentence. Koestler had watched admiringly as Katz had toured

Europe over the years, setting up pro-communist newspapers and organizing dubious funds for charitable work. Koestler regarded him as 'the invisible Willi's roving ambassador'. He had superb political contacts throughout Europe, many of whom found him warm and entertaining. Koestler, himself a low-grade communist propagandist for much of the 1930s, both liked and despised Katz. He knew that Katz was the Kremlin's spy within Muenzenberg's extraordinary empire; an empire which many Kremlin bureaucrats argued had become too powerful, cavalier and independent. When Katz was executed in Prague in 1952 – accused of being a British and Zionist agent – no one raised the slightest protest.

Sir Dick White thought that knowing men such as Katz and Muenzenberg gave Burgess an excellent grounding in the arts of espionage:

> People like Muenzenberg were tremendously good operators. Burgess learnt a lot from them. It was the European intellectual world and Burgess probably shone in it. Then he would come back to England and use all the knowledge he had picked up. He would talk big and try to persuade people that they ought to be on the side of the Russians because no one else was going to resist fascism.[19]

By early 1936 Burgess had, therefore, found his way into a diplomatic sub-world inhabited by Comintern spies, agents of influence and many other assorted characters of uncertain loyalties. He had no right to be there; he held no job that gave him access to secrets. No one was sure exactly what he did or whom he met; but whatever it was, Guy's friends concluded, it sounded terrifically important. The writer Cyril Connolly was not as impressed. With Maclean, thought Connolly, one was always conscious of amiability and weakness, but Burgess was a different proposition. He was energetic, a great talker, a boaster who swam like an otter and drank 'like some Rabelaisian bottle-swiper whose thirst was unquenchable'. Connolly wrote:

> With all his toughness, moreover, Guy wanted intensely to be liked and was indeed likeable, a good conversationalist and an enthusiastic builder-up of friends. Beneath the 'terribilità' of his Marxist analyses one divined the affectionate moral cowardice of the public schoolboy . . . He was the type of debunking revolutionary who saw himself as Saint-Just, who enjoyed making the flesh of his bourgeois listeners creep by his picture of the justice which history would mete out to them. Grubby, intemperate and promiscuous he loved to moralize over his friends and to satirize their smug class-conscious behaviour, so reckless of the reckoning in store. But when bedtime came, very late, and it was the moment to put the analyses away, the word 'preposterous' dying on his lips, he would imply a dispensation under which this one house, at least, this family, these guests might be spared the worst consequences, thanks to the protection of their brilliant hunger-marching friend whose position would be so commanding in the workers' imminent Utopia.[20]

Goronwy Rees, having resigned his research fellowship at All Souls, Oxford, lost touch with Burgess for a time but in 1935 Rees moved into a flat in Ebury Street, by Victoria Station, a few minutes' walk from Burgess's home in Chester Square. The Marxist views that Burgess had shed were now back in evidence. If anything, he was now more haphazard in his personal habits. His flat had white walls, blue curtains and red carpet. He often spent weekends in bed, surrounded by his favourite books – *Middlemarch* by George Eliot, Dickens's *Martin Chuzzlewit*, the Life of

Lord Salisbury, Morley's study of Gladstone and John Dos Passos' *Manhattan Transfer*. The floor was always littered with books and the remnants of newspapers. When he decided to escape from the world for the weekend he stocked up with provisions, bottles of red wine and a large saucepan filled with a disgusting gruel of porridge, kippers, bacon, garlic and onion and any other vaguely edible substance that he could find. When Rees asked if this mess was nutritious enough to sustain a grown man for a weekend, Burgess smiled. What more could he want than wine, his books and the *News of the World*?[21]

During 1936 Burgess searched for a job that would satisfy both his own needs and those of his Soviet controller. His personal requirements could be summarized thus: the job had to be fun; it had to carry social cachet; it had to give him the chance to mingle (and exploit) the rich and powerful. The demands of his controller were, of course, vaguer; Burgess had only to keep moving up towards an as-yet-undefined position of responsibility. He had tried *The Times* on a month's trial as a sub-editor but was not regarded as suitable. He had better luck with the BBC. On 1 October he started a £500 a year job there as a producer in the talks department. He owed this welcome opening to two fellow-Apostles, the Regius Professor of Modern History, G. M. Trevelyan, and John Sheppard, Provost of King's. Trevelyan had telephoned Cecil Graves, a senior BBC executive, and fulsomely praised Burgess's extraordinary qualities. John Green, a former president of the Cambridge Union who had joined the talks department in 1934, recalled:

I was very clued up about what was happening in Cambridge politically. I was very right-wing then and knew what had been going on through my spies. I was older than Guy, a different generation. There was this dividing line between us, who were very ebullient, and students who were concerned about the dictators. I just had an instinct about Burgess. I said to George Barnes, who was my boss, I said: for God's sake, George, don't let this man into the BBC. But he told me not to be ridiculous, Burgess has got a marvellous recommendation from Sheppard. I said that I didn't need to say any more. It was a very good reason for not having Burgess. Sheppard was a notorious homosexual.[22]

Another BBC producer, Frank Gillard, who later became a senior executive, said:

Burgess was opinionated and conceited. But for a time he was regarded as the blue-eyed boy by the senior people in the department. He threw his weight around no end. I was in Bristol producing talks for the various networks and found him intolerable. But you have to recognize that he had a great deal of ability and a kind of charisma. Among the producers he stood out and he knew that. And he didn't hesitate to make use of it. But I never heard anyone criticize him for taking an extremist line. The BBC gave him the chance to meet people of power. They were always flattered to be asked to talk on the BBC and Burgess had the power to ask them.[23]

Burgess's first spell with the BBC lasted until December 1938. He soon established a reputation for having re-freshingly original ideas. One early success was turning what could have been a potentially dull programme on nutrition into a controversial debate about the poor diets of the unemployed and the meagre subsistence level thought adequate by the Ministry of Health. The Spanish Civil War also provided opportunities to ginger up the corporation. Understandably, Burgess felt 'restless and guilty' for not doing more, especially after the deaths of his friends, John Cornford and Julian Bell, but he took some consolation from the fact that he was able to persuade the BBC to run a series, 'Spain on both sides of the line', taking care, he said later, to ensure that the pro-Republicans were the more polished speakers. When he became producer of 'The Week in Westminster', a popular report on Parliament, he must have felt that, at last, he was making real progress, both professionally and as a spy. He was now responsible for inviting politicians into the studio to air their views; it was an influential job that gave him a foothold in the Westminster political world. He met dozens of MPs and picked up low-grade gossip about government policies that his Soviet controller relayed happily back to Moscow. Many years later Burgess's former colleagues at the BBC argued that Guy was an egotistical adventurer; he could not, they say, have been anything as simple as a spy. John Green recalled:

He taunted me for what I call my addiction to the Establishment. He loathed it because it was boring. There wasn't any deep philosophical conviction about that. He just thought they were a lot of bores. He had no time for patriotism. He would have laughed at it. I shouldn't have thought the Marxism went very deep. He would have thought it ridiculous. He would have thought that the Communist Party was very boring. I would have said that he was more against the Establishment. He had literally no principles at all. None at all. He was intellectually wicked. He was filthy dirty. He used to leave toffee papers and chocolate in his drawers and then we had a plague of mice. He chewed garlic all the time . . . But he was a very good producer. He wasn't at all like a spy. He was a snob. If I said that I had been talking to someone in the Carlton Club he knew who I was talking about and wanted to know more. But that was because he was a gossip. Guy always thought that one day there would be an English Tito and when that happened he would have a conversation role in Whitehall. As for his heroes, he admired Churchill far more than Marx.[24]

At the same time as Burgess was carving out a reputation for himself as a talented, if disreputable, BBC producer of political discussion programmes, he was shuttling to and fro across the Channel on a series of missions which he told friends were very important and very secret. He remained in touch with Otto Katz and Édouard Pfeiffer, but he had a new, valuable contact: a German diplomat called Baron Wolfgang zu Putlitz.

Zu Putlitz was a Prussian Junker – a military man with a highly developed sense of personal and national honour – who had become increasingly uneasy about the direction Germany was taking under Hitler. He had been secretary to Gustav Stresemann, the Chancellor for a few months in 1929 who had been joint winner of the Nobel Peace Prize in 1926 for his work to bring France and Germany closer together. Zu Putlitz, based at the German embassy in London, had first met Guy Burgess in 1932 at a party in Cambridge and had been surprised that a young Englishman from such a good family knew so much about Karl Marx. It was the Night of the Long Knives in June 1934 that finally convinced him that he had to fight Hitler. A German friend who had connections with British Intelligence suggested that zu Putlitz should see Sir Robert Vansittart, Permanent Under-Secretary at the Foreign Office. As a result, zu Putlitz became a genuine and valued agent of the British; moreover, one of his first contacts at MI6 was David Footman, a cultured, scholarly Old Marlburian who was then in charge of supplying political intelligence to the Foreign Office. It was Footman who first began employing

Burgess, more as a tipster paid on results than as an official agent of British Intelligence. Zu Putlitz claimed in his autobiography, written after his defection to East Germany in the 1950s, that he had never known about Burgess's role as a Soviet agent. The most he suspected, said zu Putlitz, was that Burgess was vigorously anti-Nazi and that he worked for British Intelligence.

One person certainly did know about Burgess's work for the Soviets: Goronwy Rees, the brilliant, but erratic Welsh scholar. In late 1936 Rees had written a sympathetic review of a long, emotional book about the depressed areas of Britain. As he drank whisky with Burgess in his flat, Rees listened with pleasure and then suspicion to his friend heaping exaggerated praise on the review:

> Slightly irritated, I said to him: 'I do think it was a good review, but all the same I don't quite think that it was everything you say it was.' Guy paused for a moment and said: 'It shows you have the heart of the matter in you.' . . . 'What on earth do you mean,' I said. A strangely detached expression came over his face, as if for the moment I did not exist and his eyes turned inwards upon some secret known only to himself . . . Then suddenly the life returned to Guy's eyes and he said: 'I want to tell you that I am a Comintern agent and have been ever since I came down from Cambridge.'[25]

At first Rees refused to believe the story; surely this was just Guy trying once again to convince his friends (and himself) that life was far more interesting and exciting than it really was. But as Burgess talked, Rees began to feel that perhaps he was telling the truth. After all, he had acted very oddly since leaving Cambridge; he had broken with his communist friends and had been mixed up with the Anglo-German Fellowship. Now it appeared this had all been a cover. But why, asked Rees, was Burgess telling him this? Burgess paused. He wanted Rees to join him; to become an agent. If he agreed then he, Guy, would tell Goronwy exactly what he had to do. But there had to be absolute secrecy. There were others, like Guy, who were working for the Comintern. He was prepared to give one other name, to reassure Goronwy that he would be in good company. The name was Anthony Blunt. However, in his autobiography published in 1972, Rees does not identify Blunt:

> I don't suppose he could have named a person who could have carried more weight with me. He was someone whom I both liked and respected greatly, and with whom I would gladly have joined in any enterprise. Nor was I alone in my admiration; there was no one I knew who did not praise his intelligence, his uprightness, his integrity. Indeed he quite conspicuously possessed all those virtues which Guy did not; all that they had in common was that both were homosexuals. But now it appeared that they were both also Comintern agents . . . 'But you must never speak to him about it,' said Guy. 'I shouldn't really have mentioned his name to you. It's essential, in this kind of work, that as few people as possible should know who is involved. You must promise never to mention the subject to him.' So I promised.[26]

Next day Rees grappled with the problem; was Guy serious or had it been an elaborate hoax, a convoluted test of friendship? Rees decided that if Burgess had told the truth then he could not, in conscience, disapprove. If anything, becoming a spy showed that Burgess was capable of real commitment, however painful that might be. Nor could he ask Blunt; that would be a betrayal of his promise to Burgess. Rees felt as if he was trying to solve a riddle.

Nothing with Guy was ever as it seemed; the whole thing was too preposterous and yet somehow there remained a nagging doubt that perhaps Burgess had not been fantasizing.

Despite his pledge to Burgess, Rees could not resist asking for advice. He turned to Rosamond Lehmann, sister of the left-wing writer John Lehmann. She was a graduate of Girton College, Cambridge and was beautiful and amusing as well as being a gifted novelist. Rosamond was married to Wogan Phillips, an old Etonian, Oxford graduate and the eldest son of a peer. Their home, Ibsden House near Wallingford in Oxfordshire, attracted a steady stream of visitors from Oxbridge and literary London. She knew and liked Wilfrid Blunt but found Anthony 'austere and not very forthcoming'. Of Burgess she thought: 'He was wildly homosexual, very indiscreet, brilliant. He was very affectionate and loved his friends.'

Rees was in love with Rosamond Lehmann and made no secret of it. She thought that Rees was as brilliant as Guy and that he, too, was just as unable to distinguish between the truth and what he hoped was true. She recalled:

Goronwy came to dinner in a state of tremendous agitation. My husband was in Spain driving an ambulance in the civil war. I had two children to look after so I had plenty to think about. Goronwy told me that Guy was a Comintern agent and that he had been asked to join him. I didn't think it was such a shocking announcement. All the young men were going off to fight for the International Brigades in Spain and I thought that this was just Guy's way of helping. It also explained his extraordinary behaviour when he joined the Anglo-German Fellowship. I had once asked Guy about this and he had laughed. He said, 'One has to know one's enemies.' Anyway, I asked Goronwy if he was going to help Guy. He just huffed and puffed.[27]

Many others in the Burgess–Blunt–Rees circle remain convinced that Rees's story is a concoction of half-truths and downright lies. Like MI5 they decided that Rees had been willing to help Burgess, passing on gossip from the conversations of politicians dining at Oxford college high tables and, during the war, when Rees worked for military intelligence, handing over genuine secrets. Sir Ellis Waterhouse recalled:

I disliked Rees very much. He was a rather irritating Welshman. Many years later, after the war, Anthony told me that Rees was one of Guy's sources. But then I think Guy had a lot of people like that. What I did know at the time was that Guy had got Rees out of a sticky situation. Apparently he had been distributing left-wing propaganda among the army in Wales and there was a possibility of his being arrested. Guy helped him then.[28]

Louis MacNeice was also wary of Rees. He recalled hearing him speak at an anti-fascist meeting, sounding like a revivalist, 'dogma on dogma, over and over-statement, washed in the blood of well, nobody asked of whom, but it certainly made you stop thinking'. Writers, said Rees, should take orders from the only progressive group in society, the proletariat; writers should make themselves the mouthpiece of the working class because only the workers knew the truth.[29]

No one, however, disputes that Burgess and Rees remained close friends. Rees was a frequent visitor to Guy's flat where Guy talked freely about his work as a Comintern agent; at one point even describing how he used to meet a Russian at a café in the East End to hand over whatever information he had picked up. Burgess's circle of friends was wider and odder than ever. Rees met Pfeiffer, whom he thought smelt of every imaginable kind of corruption; Otto Katz and Baron zu Putlitz. Kim Philby was also a regular visitor, though Rees could not quite understand why Burgess was so excessively enthusiastic about him. There was a new face, too: Jack Hewit, a nineteen-year-old working-class boy from the north-east of England. Hewit was good-looking and bright, without being an intellectual. He had met Burgess early in 1937. Apart from separations after their periodic rows they lived together continuously until Burgess's defection in 1951. He was Burgess's lover, his companion and his manservant. He was also a lover of Anthony Blunt during the war and was frequently 'given as gift' to people Burgess wanted to influence. Hewit was born in Gateshead in 1917:

My father met my mother during the First World War. He was working in the shipyard as a riveter and she was a riveter's mate. She had to throw the rivets up to him. They met and married within six weeks. After the war he became a tin-smith working for the Coke and Gas Company, making and repairing gas meters. My mother was very over-protective but she gave me the best of everything to her ability. I started off at a disadvantage because I was kept very clean and had shoes which other boys didn't. I wore glasses and was a bit plump. I was called porky suet and four eyes. So I was protected by older boys and in return . . . Well, I was steeped in sin by the time I was ten or eleven. Who with? With older boys and men. I have been gay as long as I can remember. You hear stories about masters interfering with boys but ninety per cent of the time it is the boys interfering with the masters. Of course I didn't mind. It's just that people like me were born against the law. In those days you went first to an elementary school and then took an exam when you were eleven or twelve to see if you went on to a secondary school, which was the equivalent of a grammar school, or to a central school. I passed but my father said I had to be a plumber. All I ever wanted to be was a dancer. It's extraordinary coming from a place like that but that is all I wanted. My mother committed suicide when I was twelve. I decided to leave and come to London at the first opportunity. I came to London in 1932 when I was fifteen. I slept out on the streets the first night then I went into a LCC [London County Council] shelter. Then I got a job as a page boy in a hotel, the Ilchester Chamber hotel in St Petersburg Place in Bayswater. Eventually I became a telephone operator there.[30]

Hewit spent the next four years in menial hotel jobs, with the occasional badly-paid job as a chorus boy on tours of provincial theatres. He was only five feet seven inches tall, a good four inches too short to make a living as a chorus-line dancer. It was while he was in London in between dancing jobs that he first saw Burgess:

I was going on tour with *No, No Nanette* and was waiting outside the stage door of the South London Palace. I saw this fantastic, rather gorgeous creature and thought, who the hell is he waiting for. He was waiting for someone else. Anyway, I went off on tour. Then I got sick of being on the road and thought I'd give London a try again.

One night I decided to go to a pub in the Strand called the Bunch of Grapes. I was in there having a tonic water with a slice of lemon. It looked like a gin and tonic, of course. It must have been about 6 o'clock. There was this character standing by the bar. He looked at me, looked at my drink and raised his eyebrows. I said, Yes? He

bought me a g and t. I thought, thank God, maybe I'll get
a meal out of this one. He said he was going to a party and
asked if I wanted to go. I thought there would be some
food there so I said, yes, I would love to go. We walked
down Whitehall to what I later found out was the War
Office. We rang on the door and someone came down to
let us in. The man I had come with was a Hungarian
diplomat. I met everyone there, Anthony Blunt, Guy
Burgess. It was a very BBC, art-intellectual party. It was
being held by someone called Tom Wylie, who was the
resident clerk at the War Office. The conversation was
fascinating but there was no food and that was the only
reason I was there. Then I was attacked by someone
called Otto Katz, a great fat slob of a man. Harold
Nicolson said, c'mon for God's sake. Then Guy rescued
me. He asked me if Katz was annoying me. I said I had
come with someone. But then Guy said oh he must be
with Tom now. I was pissed, stoned and weak from
hunger. I told Guy I had to go. He said, hang on and I will
give you a lift. He was utterly charming, wildly good-
looking and totally untidy. We went to his flat in Chester
Square. I spent the night with him. But then he had a
penchant for working-class boys. But that night we sort
of started a relationship. Oh yes, he was a good lover. I
just didn't leave. I became Guy's keeper. He was someone who needed looking after. You dressed Guy in a
clean shirt, brushed his suit and he would look immacu-
late. By the time he got to the door he looked as if he had
been through a bush. Cigarette ash would fall like snow-
flakes from him. His nails were filthy. He got them just by
scrabbling . . . always scrabbling around for everything.
I used to scrub them and make him take a bath twice a
week. But Anthony had baths twice a day. I wasn't a
manservant. That's wrong. I kept on my own place. I did
his washing and looked after him and slept with him.

He was the most promiscuous person who ever lived. He slept with anything that was going and he used to say anyone will do, from seventeen to seventy-five. He didn't have a type but I suppose they had to be attractive and come from a working-class background. People used to say when the whole thing broke in the fifties that Guy only became a homosexual because he found his father dead on top of his mother. That's nonsense. If anyone invented homosexuality it was Guy Burgess.[31]

Goronwy Rees did not take to Burgess's new boyfriend. Hewit recalled that he would always refer to him as 'Guy's bit of stuff'. The dislike was mutual. Hewit admitted that he was 'biased' against Rees, and he remains convinced that Rees knew about Burgess's work for the Russians. Sometimes Burgess made efforts to interest Hewit in politics:

Guy gave me Tom Paine's *Rights of Man*. I said that I couldn't afford to be a socialist. The only people who can afford to be are the rich. I had to earn a living. Oh yes, sometimes he used to talk about the Comintern. But I used to say, for Christ's sake, Guy, don't start on that again. Of course I knew they were all left-wing. I remember Guy once said to Anthony: the trouble with you, Anthony, is that you want to have your cake and eat it and you want it to look as if you are giving it to the poor.[32]

The London gay world was an illegal one. Burgess and Blunt were both intrigued by pretty, working-class boys like Hewit, known as 'rough trade'. There were certain well-known pubs, such as the Bunch of Grapes, where rough trade could be spotted. This was fairly safe. What was definitely not safe was 'cottaging' (hanging around in a public lavatory waiting for men willing to perform short, anonymous sexual acts in the cubicles); and both Burgess and Blunt found the excitement of this irresistible, though it could have led to an embarrassing appearance in a magistrates' court. It seems that Blunt managed to escape detection; Burgess did not. In 1938 he was accused of improperly soliciting another man in a public lavatory. The plaintiff said that a suggestive note had been pushed under the partition of the cubicle he was in. Burgess claimed that the note had come from the neighbouring cubicle while he was minding his own business reading *Middlemarch*. The charge was dismissed because of insufficient evidence but the experience persuaded Burgess and Blunt, albeit briefly, to take rather more care. Shortly afterwards Burgess went on holiday with his mother to the south of France. In Cannes he met a seventeen-year-old called Peter Pollock, described by Hewit as 'the most beautiful boy I have ever seen', and brought him back to London. Hewit did not mind this – he was used to Guy's promiscuity – but he did care if Guy ever became 'emotionally involved' with another man.

Hewit – Jackie to the circle – insisted that 'cottaging' was not his style; he preferred more elegant pick-ups:

> I was extremely lucky in the people I met through Guy. The majority of them took time with me. If I said something stupid they would say, no, no that's not right. E. M. Forster, for instance, was very kind to me. You have to understand that the gay world then had style which it doesn't now. There was a sort of gay intellectual freemasonry which you know nothing about. It was like the five concentric circles in the Olympic emblem. One person in one circle knew one in another and that's how people met. And people like me were passed around. I wasn't a trollop. Amoral perhaps but not a trollop.[33]

One member of the gay circle whom he did not relish meeting was Brian Howard. He was an old Etonian, like

Burgess, regarded by Evelyn Waugh as 'mad, bad and dangerous to know'. He was a snob and was contemptuous of Hewit. Hewit recalled that on one occasion in the bar of the Ritz hotel Howard lurched drunkenly across to him, screamed 'You are my enemy, my dear,' then collapsed. Astonishingly, Howard slipped into MI5 at the beginning of the war, though his career there was short-lived.

In 1938 Hewit went to Brussels to live with Christopher Isherwood, but it was a short liaison and he was soon back in London with Burgess. He did not mind obliging Burgess's friends, providing that they were attractive. When he was 'given' to Baron zu Putlitz, for example, he thought that he was performing a service for the nation. The baron, said Hewit, was providing the British government with vital secrets about Hitler's intentions and by having an affair with him he, Jack Hewit, the boy from Gateshead, was doing his bit for Britain by calming the diplomat's shaky nerves. What Hewit did not know was that Burgess was also feeding information from zu Putlitz to his Soviet controller. Hewit conceded that to the mostly heterosexual MI5 and MI6 officers who had the job during the post-war years of trying to investigate the Soviet infiltration of the British Establishment, the dynamics of the 1930s gay world must have seemed an incomprehensible web of interlocking relationships. But there was a logic to it. He knew for certain, he said, that Burgess and Blunt had never slept together. It was just not possible.

During 1938 Anthony Blunt was consolidating his position at the Warburg Institute and was preparing his first book, a study of Poussin. Burgess, however, was more active. The situation in Europe was becoming graver by the day. In Spain the Republican cause was now desperate. With German-Italian support, the pro-Franco forces broke through the Republican lines on the Catalan front. Barcelona fell on 26 January 1939; Valencia and Madrid soon followed. By late March the war had been lost. The British and French governments seemed as oblivious as ever to the growing threat posed by Hitler. In the spring of 1938 the German army marched into Austria and proclaimed that Germany and Austria were now united, despite the fact that this had been forbidden under the treaties of Versailles and St Germain. But there was worse to follow. On 29 September 1938 the British, French, German and Italian governments signed the infamous Munich Agreement which Chamberlain claimed would guarantee 'peace in our time'. The Left in Britain was outraged. It was confirmation, they thought, of long-standing fears that Britain would do anything to avoid war with the Nazis. Only a few MPs, led by Winston Churchill, seemed to acknowledge the terrible threat. Churchill told the Commons that Munich had been 'defeat without a war'.

Guy Burgess was in a better position than most to know just how strongly the spirit of appeasement ran through the British Establishment. His friendship with Pfeiffer was yielding a rich harvest. Chamberlain was anxious to bypass the Foreign Office and, in particular, the anti-appeasement Permanent Under-Secretary, Sir Robert Vansittart, in his communications with the French. Burgess would travel to Paris carrying letters from Chamberlain, receive Daladier's reply from Pfeiffer and then carry that back to London. He gave the package to the indomitable Sir Joseph Ball, who would in turn pass on the letters to Chamberlain. Burgess did not tell Ball, however, that he was also meeting British intelligence officers at the St Ermin's Hotel, Westminster, and showing them the French response. Finally, Burgess told none of these masters that he was also giving the material to the Russians. Burgess later said that the French replies to Chamberlain made depressing reading. Daladier was a 'confused and panic-stricken patriot' and Chamberlain was 'an ignorant provincial ironmonger'. Did any of this affect the policies of the interested powers? It certainly emphasized to Chamberlain that the French had no appetite for a confrontation with Germany over Czechoslovakia, despite the French pact with the Czechs that each would come to the other's aid if either was attacked. The Czechs had a similar pact with the Soviet Union in which each agreed to defend the other providing France also intervened. There was a Franco – Soviet mutual assistance pact, too, to deter Germany further from aggression. But Britain refused to be drawn into this net of treaties. On 17 March 1938 the Soviets proposed talks with the French, British and Americans but a few days later in the Commons Chamberlain said that his government would not guarantee to back France if it went to the aid of Czechoslovakia. If any further evidence of Chamberlain's attitude was needed it came in a radio broadcast on 27 September. He said: 'How horrible, fantastic, incredible it is that we should be digging trenches and trying on gasmasks here because of a quarrel in a faraway country between people of whom we know nothing.' On 18 March 1939 the Soviets pressed for talks with the French, British, Polish, Rumanian and Turkish governments – without success. In April the Soviets proposed a triple alliance with Britain and France. Britain's response was lukewarm and seemed to show, at least to the Left, that Britain was determined to resist any formal link-up with the Soviet Union. Margot Heinemann wrote of this period:

Our access now to information that was then secret, in Cabinet minutes and diplomatic dispatches, ministerial diaries and letters shows conclusively that the suspicions were fully justified. British government acquiescence in fascist aggression was not the result simply of military weakness or inefficiency or pressure of pacifist opinion in the country but represented a conscious, deliberate establishment and class policy. To quote one example, Foreign Secretary Halifax [we now know] visited Germany in 1937 and thought Hitler 'dangerous but sincere' and the regime 'absolutely fantastic'. He 'liked the Nazi leaders very much' and should not doubt they were 'genuine haters of communism'. It was 'essential for us to get along with them' and on his return to London he proposed to ask newspaper proprietors to stop drawing such cruel cartoons of Hitler and persuade English Christian leaders not to protest about the harassment of the German Church.[34]

If this was and is the view of the Left (and many historians), there is another interpretation of appeasement. After Munich, Britain increased arms production; 2827 planes for the RAF were produced in 1938 and 7940 in 1939. Appeasement may have bought valuable time. It was based on a laudable hatred of war, but it was based, too, on a fatal misunderstanding of Hitler and chronic suspicion of the Soviet Union.

Burgess's contribution to the decisions that led to war can only be guessed at; probably his information was just another tiny piece of a jigsaw. He was, though, determined to make the most of his links with British Intelligence. In May 1938, when the Czech quisling, Konrad Henlein, was staying at the Goring Hotel, Burgess told Hewit, who was working on the hotel switchboard, to log all the calls the Czech made. Hewit said: 'Guy asked me to meet David Footman and to tell David what Henlein was doing. We met in a pub near St James's Station. I think it was near the headquarters of MI6. Later I got an envelope with two £5 notes in it. That was marvellous. The first time I have ever been paid for services rendered.'[35]

During 1938 Burgess was also trying to convince the BBC that the government's policy towards Hitler was misguided.

By the end of the year he was organizing a series of talks on 'Aggression in the Mediterranean' which, he hoped, would expose the territorial ambitions of the fascist dictators. He had hoped that Churchill would appear, but he withdrew because of the Munich crisis. Burgess travelled to Chartwell to try and persuade him to change his mind. The two men had a long, gloomy talk about the gathering war clouds. At the end of their conversation Churchill handed Burgess a copy of his speeches, *Arms and the Covenant*. He wrote a short message on the inside cover: 'To Guy Burgess, from Winston S. Churchill, to confirm his admirable sentiments. September, 1938.' Burgess delighted in telling the story of that historic meeting. Unlike most of his self-glorifying anecdotes, he was able to silence doubters by producing the Churchill volume and the scribbled, signed message.

In December 1938 Burgess left the BBC for a job in a new department of the War Office. Burgess always claimed that he had resigned from the BBC on principle over the corporation's gutless approach to fascism; but the fact is that once he was offered an opening, even a junior one, in one of the intelligence world's rapidly spreading offshoots, he had no choice but to accept it. Sir Joseph Ball may have been instrumental in recommending Burgess; more likely he was taken on because he had become a familiar, if eccentric, face around Whitehall. He knew a great many important people – or claimed he did – and had done sterling work as a tipster for MI6. He might be dirty and outrageously homosexual but he had been to Eton. If anyone within Whitehall had known about his communist past, it would have made no difference; half of the Oxbridge graduate community would have been excluded from government service if that had been held against them. Burgess was in Section D (for Destruction), a unit which was supposed to train propagandists and saboteurs and which was under the command of an ex-military engineer, Colonel Laurence Douglas Grand. It wasn't the *real* secret service but it was nominally part of MI6. When Burgess visited Kim Philby in Paris in 1939 he broke the news that he had finally made the breakthrough. Just over a year later, in the summer of 1940, it was Burgess who persuaded his section head that they could do with a good man: Kim Philby, *The Times* journalist whose trip to the first months of the war in Spain had been financed by the Soviet intelligence service. (Donald Maclean was a high-flier in the Foreign Office and had been posted to Paris.) Anthony Blunt, too, was delighted. Now that Guy was in MI6, Blunt was sure that if war broke out he would also be able to slip into a position which would give him access to secrets that would help the Soviet Union. Jack Hewit believed, meanwhile, that Guy was just 'a middleman' who was indulging his appetite for intrigue and for 'playing the *éminence grise*'. The writer Cyril Connolly, meanwhile, thought the whole thing was absurd:

In January 1939 he [Burgess] had left the BBC and was doing highly confidential work for the War Office. Burgess is, of course, a power behind the scenes; a brigadier in mufti. Brigadier Brilliant, DSO, FRS, the famous historian, with boyish grin and cold blue eyes, seconded now for special duties. With long stride and hunched shoulders, untidy, chain-smoking, he talks – walks and talks – while the whole devilish simplicity of his plan unfolds and the men from MI this and MI that, SIS and SOE, listen dumbfounded. 'My God, Brilliant, I believe you're right – it could be done', said the quiet-voiced man with greying hair. The Brigadier looked at his watch and a chilled blue eye fixed the Chief of the Secret Service. 'At this moment, sir,' and there was pack-ice in his voice, 'my chaps are doing it.'[36]

CHAPTER 10
Blunt Joins the Colours

On 23 August 1939 the Soviet Foreign Minister, Vyacheslav Mikhailovich Molotov, and his German counterpart, Joachim von Ribbentrop, signed an agreement in Moscow which sent shock tremors through the British Left. It was a non-aggression pact which included pledges by both countries to remain neutral if the other was at war. There were secret clauses, too, which sliced up Eastern Europe between the two. For those many people in Britain who had grown increasingly wary of Stalin's repression of opposition, this agreement proved beyond doubt that Stalin was as unscrupulous as the fascists. Thousands left the Communist Party, but the hardcore of party faithful managed to find an explanation. Margot Heinemann said: 'I think the Russians were buying time. The British government had no intention of making an alliance with the Russians. The British thought that the Germans would go east. It wasn't difficult to see why the Russians had done it. It was the only way to dent the Western alliance.'[1] Brian Simon, on the other hand, confessed that he was 'shattered' by the news.[2] Claud Cockburn was saddened rather than angered. It may have been good strategy, he wrote, but it would mean that the Russians had 'effectively dynamited the Popular Fronts, the vague but comforting alliances between Reds and anti-Nazi Conservatives'. Communists, thought Cockburn, would now be 'out in a very, very cold cold'. But he did not lose faith. He had been a communist when it was socially acceptable; he couldn't quit now even if it meant that 'half one's friends were soon going to stop speaking to one'.[3] Leo Long also saw, he later said, why the pact was necessary. He recalled: 'Oh, you soon got over that sort of thing. After being initially shocked, trained communists were all right. Now we have had all sorts of things, like the invasion of Hungary, but then – well we said, if there was a pact, whose fault was it? It's the British government's.'[4] For Blunt it was simply 'a technical necessity for Russia to gain time and re-arm and get strong enough to resist what was clearly going to happen'.

Blunt and Burgess were on holiday in the south of France when they heard the news. Their first thought was to rush back to England to reassure sources such as Goronwy Rees. In his autobiography, Rees gives this account of his feelings:

He [Guy] left his car at Calais and crossed by night boat. His car was one of the possessions which he valued most in the world but on this occasion he appeared to have abandoned it without a thought. He was in a state of considerable excitement and exhaustion; but I also thought I noticed something about him which I had never seen before. He was frightened . . . when I denounced the treachery of the Soviet Union he merely shrugged his shoulders and said calmly that after Munich the Soviet Union was perfectly justified in putting its own security first.[5]

Rees claimed that they then agreed to forget their earlier conversations about spying for the Comintern. A few days later Rees enlisted in the army. But there are other accounts of what happened. Sir Ellis Waterhouse, for example:

Anthony told me that he and Guy were in the south of France and when they heard about the Nazi–Soviet pact Guy said instantly that various people like Goronwy would be upset and they would have to get back to reassure them. Guy was very acute about other people's psychology and he knew that he could lose Goronwy as a source.[6]

Rosamond Lehmann recalled:

After the Nazi–Soviet pact life went on. I asked Goronwy how would it affect Guy. He said that Guy had dropped his position as a Comintern agent. But they went on seeing each other a great deal. Guy got drunker and drunker as time went on. He and Goronwy used to argue all the time.[7]

The Communist Party of Great Britain also had its problems. The alliance between the Soviets and Berlin had been easy enough for good Marxists to justify but on 12 October, the *Daily Worker* announced that the previous party line over the war had been 'incorrect'. Dave Springhall had returned from Moscow with a handwritten note from the Comintern theoreticians which stated that the war against Hitler was 'unjust and imperialist'. British communists, who had been told to support the Allied cause since it was an anti-fascist fight, now had to accommodate this new policy. The British, French and Polish governments, said the *Daily Worker*, bore 'equal responsibility' for the war. Many British communists were disturbed by this declaration. Harry Pollitt, the party's general secretary, argued that it was no use waiting for the proletariat to rise. If Hitler was not beaten then Britain could fall, and if that happened the party would be wiped out. But he had no chance of convincing the rest of the central committee of this, since they were incapable of defying an instruction from Moscow. He was replaced as general secretary by Rajani Palme Dutt, a more reliable figure who would never oppose the Comintern. Having been forced to resign his post, Pollitt was then forced to write a craven apology in the *Daily Worker*, admitting that he had allowed his hatred of fascism to influence his judgement of the war. The war was now condemned in unequivocal terms: 'It is not a war for the liberties of small nations. It is not a war for the defence of peace against aggression . . . The British and French ruling class are seeking to use the anti-fascist sentiments of the people for their own imperialist aims,' said the party manifesto.

British communists were now legitimately regarded by the Establishment as potential saboteurs. And when the Red Army invaded Finland on 30 November 1939, it was clear evidence that Stalin was as unscrupulous and ambitious as Hitler.

Late in 1938, Anthony Blunt volunteered for military service. For someone who had hated the Officer Training Corps at school, it was an extraordinary decision. Only Guy Burgess knew what he was planning. Blunt had been told by his Soviet controller that he should manoeuvre himself into a position from where he would be able to infiltrate military or civilian intelligence if (or rather when) war came. The only realistic starting point was the Officers' Emergency Reserve, a branch of the Territorial Army which Christopher Blunt had already joined.

Anthony asked Christopher if he could help – that much is certain, although the details of the episode are unclear. Anthony was evidently embarrassed that he had used his family in this way while Christopher, who was in military intelligence during the war, refused to discuss his brother's action, saying only that he would not contradict the account that Anthony gave to Nigel West in the early 1980s. Blunt told West, author of several books on British Intelligence, that he had 'used or rather abused' Christopher's connections to persuade the War Office to offer him a commission in the reserve. According to West, Anthony 'was anxious not to upset his brother and did not want me to mention the story until after his death'.[8]

Blunt's application was rejected but Burgess told him not to be disheartened. It was essential, he said, that they kept trying to plant friends of the Soviet Union in sensitive posts within the Establishment. It was at times like these that Burgess proved so invaluable to the Soviets. West again: 'Anthony told me that Guy Burgess was the genius in the network, the key man. He was the person everybody had to go to for instruction, help and advice. Guy was always in touch with the Russians and could make decisions and could counsel other people.'[9]

Twelve months later and shortly before Britain declared war on 3 September 1939, Blunt again offered his services to his country. He received two, contradictory, replies from the War Office in the same post. One told him to report to Minley Manor and Mytchett, the depot of the Corps of Military Police, popularly known as the Red Caps, a few miles from Farnborough in Hampshire. The other letter, which Blunt tore up, was a rejection. The official records do not show how Blunt could simultaneously be accepted and rejected; even MI5 officers, such as Sir Dick White, were not sure how this happened. But is has to be remembered there was tremendous confusion and muddle in Whitehall. Government departments were trying to organize for war and MI5, which was charged with identifying potential subversives of the Right and the Left who might undermine the war effort, was badly stretched. The army had, for example, advertised for linguists to join a new unit, the Field Security Police, which would be responsible for hunting out fifth columnists behind the army lines and for interrogating suspected enemy agents. All these applicants had to be checked by the overworked spy-hunters of MI5. It is quite easy to imagine how an intelligence report on Blunt's Marxist past could be sent to one section of the War Office, while another government department, unaware that he had been blacklisted, approved his application.

When Blunt told Tom Boase, the Courtauld director, that he had volunteered, Boase, who had won the Military Cross in the First World War, was astonished. However, he assured Blunt that his job would remain open for as long as necessary.

Mytchett was a clearing-house for the army where men were given basic training before being transferred to other camps. There Blunt was joined by some of the best minds, and the most eccentric talents, in the country. For example, there was Enoch Powell, who had given up his job as Professor of Greek at Sydney University to join the Royal Warwickshire Regiment as a private. Even the army (famous for placing men in the wrong jobs) spotted that Private Powell was an exceptional character (he spoke thirteen languages) and sent him to Mytchett. He ended the war with the rank of brigadier. Another recruit to Mytchett was the middle-aged journalist Malcolm Muggeridge, who confessed that he really had no right to be there since he could speak French only with an 'atrocious accent'. He arrived there after a brief spell at the Ministry of Information in London, where he had worked alongside George Orwell and Graham Greene.[10]

Mytchett . . . stood out bleakly among pine trees, very much recalling the picture I had formed in my mind of a Soviet labour camp. I might even then, I thought, turn tail and run back to my typewriter. In the end, I just surrendered myself to the process of becoming a soldier;

filled in yet another prodigious form, stripped for the purpose of being medically examined, wandered about naked holding a phial of my urine; then swore on a dog-eared Bible to fight loyally for King and Country as and when required. Thus the matter was settled and the Ministry of Information knew me no more, and I became a private, acting unpaid lance-corporal, in the shortly-to-be-formed Intelligence Corps.[11]

At Mytchett Blunt (who, said his brother, Christopher, began the war as a second lieutenant) was kitted out at first in a uniform that made him look like a First World War cavalry officer: riding breeches, a tunic with an uncomfortably high collar, and a peaked cap. He was told that he would be given his battle-dress only when, and if, he completed training. Discipline was uncompromising. He was dumped in a hut with fourteen other recruits and told its floor had to shine like an ice-rink. Kit had to be laid out with mathematical precision. Caps had to be tilted at exactly the right angle. Even trouser creases had to conform to the military ideal. It was infinitely worse than anything he had experienced in the OTC; but Blunt knew that he could not afford to behave with the contemptuous disdain that he had shown towards the military at Marlborough. If he was thrown out of Mytchett his chances of finding a job in military or civilian intelligence would be wrecked. Therefore, Blunt polished his boots assiduously and marched up and down the parade ground with an aplomb that would have amazed Colonel Hughes, the art master and OTC commander from Marlborough whom Blunt had mocked and tormented.

Blunt did not fit easily into this strange world, but there was nothing he could do about it. He was a junior officer, much to the irritation of his mother, who thought that her brilliant youngest son should have started the war as a captain at the very least. The military police who ran the camp were not impressed by the volunteers. Muggeridge again:

An advertisement for linguists such as had brought us together there, was calculated to assemble as sorry a company in [the Red Caps'] eyes as could possibly be imagined; ranging between carpet-sellers from Baghdad and modern language teachers in grammar schools and colleges, with a stray expert on Bengali or Sanskrit, or a pimp from Marseilles or Beirut; as well as tourist agency men, unfrocked priests who had lived irregularly in Venice and Rome, and contraceptive salesmen who had roamed the world.[12]

In October, a few days after his thirty-second birthday, Blunt, as he had hoped, began a five-week course at Minley Manor designed to teach him the rudimentary skills of military intelligence. Brigadier John Shearer, the Minley commander, called it 'fairly routine material'. Recruits were told that they should never discuss their work, not even with wives or girlfriends; they were given guidelines on how to spot enemy agents operating behind British lines and they were warned about the likely treatment they would receive if they were captured by the Germans. But Shearer insisted: 'There was little sensitive material in the course. We told them what MI5 and MI6 stood for – that was all.'[13]

Muggeridge recalled:

The course in Security Intelligence . . . consisted of a series of lectures given by officers and NCO Instructors on how intelligence was collected, and how those collecting it on behalf of the enemy might be circumvented. The syllabus was based exclusively on 1914–18 War practice,

and even to our inexpert minds had an air of irrelevance
. . . [we were told] how an enemy agent was detected by
finding among his toilet accessories a tell-tale pen for
writing in invisible ink.[14]

On Blunt's third day, before the course had reached such
specifics, he was ordered to report to Shearer's office, where
he was told that there had been a 'rather adverse report'
about him to the War Office; he would have to leave Minley
immediately. Brigadier Thomas Robbins, one of the staff
officers there, recalled: 'I came down to breakfast and was
told that Blunt had been withdrawn. When I asked why I
was told that he had been a communist at Cambridge. It
was the only time anything like that happened at Minley.'[15]
Blunt was shaken and puzzled. He knew that he would be
able to justify his Cambridge Marxism: after all, many
students had been communists during the 1930s. But there
was a possibility that there had been a leak to MI5 about his
clandestine activities as a talent-spotter for the Soviets.

Blunt's interview at the War Office in London went far
better than he had hoped. He was questioned by Major
(later Major-General) Kevin Martin, the deputy director of
Military Intelligence. But Martin had no evidence against
Blunt and plainly knew nothing about the history of left-
wing politics at Cambridge. He waved two rejection slips
from a left-wing magazine to which Blunt had offered
articles and said that he knew that Blunt had once been to
the Soviet Union. Blunt was irritated that someone had
taken so much trouble to try to destroy his army career, but
he was grateful that the informant had made such a dreadful hash of the job; with a little more research in public
libraries he could have found dozens of published, pro-
Soviet articles that carried his byline. However, his articles,
published or rejected, were not a problem and by the end of
the interview Martin was convinced that these did not mean

that Blunt was a threat to national security. As for the trip to Moscow, Blunt dealt with that by listing some of the eminently respectable people who had travelled with him. Martin, who had better things to do than cross-examine a distinguished academic, had heard enough. He cleared Blunt and ordered his return to Minley.

As soon as he left the War Office Blunt rushed to Burgess's flat in Chester Square. It had not been a serious alarm but it was, nonetheless, a chastening experience. The stakes had risen since those heady days of plotting at Cambridge. The country was at war and the Soviet Union was, as far as non-Marxists were concerned, a treacherous ally of Hitler.

Blunt returned to Minley. When he had completed the course he was promoted to acting captain and dispatched to Boulogne, northern France, to take charge of Unit 18, Field Security Police. He was disappointed – first, because he had not managed to transfer to MI5 or MI6, both busily recruiting university dons, and second, because he had no wish to go anywhere near a battlefield.

The British Expeditionary Force, under the command of General Viscount Gort, had been in Europe for just over five weeks when Blunt arrived. (Kim Philby was already in France for *The Times*, though he had had little to report.)

The army proved to be hard, dull work. Blunt had to lead his men around the French countryside in fruitless hunts for German saboteurs. He tried his best but he was a hopeless soldier, as one of his men, George Curry, recalled: 'He was definitely not an army type. We all felt that he was a decent sort though he was less of a soldier than we were. None of us had any inkling of his political and sexual aberrations.'[16]

This was the period of the 'phoney war', and many within the British force began to wonder why they were there at all. The Maginot Line was surely impregnable; the Germans would not risk an offensive. The war would be over before it had begun.

Blunt spent his free time that winter trying to find a way out of the FSP. He wrote to friends in London, complaining that the work was unbearably tedious and that his talents would be better employed in MI5 or MI6. He hoped that his old Cambridge friend, Victor Rothschild, who had joined MI5, might be able to help.

In April 1940 Hitler occupied Denmark and attacked Norway. The German attack on the Low Countries began on 10 May, and within a few weeks the Wehrmacht had overrun Holland, Belgium and France and forced the British Army out of Europe for the next four years. By the third week of May, Blunt and half his unit had retreated to Boulogne (the rest of his group escaped via Dunkirk), but he seemed unable to decide what to do next. George Curry recalled:

> Blunt made no effort to get us out although all other support units had long since gone. Then one of us, a lance-corporal, quite illegally phoned Dover Castle Naval HQ and was ordered to get out as soon as possible. Blunt was informed and as the German troops were entering Boulogne (on 25 May) we went down to the docks and were able to get out. Why was Blunt so reluctant to leave? I don't think there was anything sinister about it; just ineffectiveness under tense conditions.[17]

According to his brother Christopher, who was an intelligence officer with another section of the BEF, Blunt remained cool throughout the evacuation. 'He was very relaxed about his predicament. He had an army car and I remember he said he drove it off the end of the pier at Boulogne. He talked about what had happened constantly.

We both did. Back in England we met and had a giggle about it.'[18]

Anthony had survived the ordeal but his future as a soldier, let alone as a Soviet spy, did not look promising. He had won no medals and was just one of hundreds of shaken, disappointed officers without a job. And, of course, there was no immediate demand for FSP officers. Blunt turned to Guy. Burgess was, as always, irrepressibly optimistic; he was sure that something would turn up.

Burgess was working for Section D, officially known as the Statistical Research Department of the War Office, when war was declared in September 1939. Section D had been set up in March 1938 by Admiral Hugh Sinclair, head of MI6, to investigate new forms of sabotage and was headed by Colonel Laurence Grand, an imaginative Cambridge graduate. The traditionalists within the War Office disapproved of this new unit which had plans to operate behind enemy lines in a disgracefully underhand manner.

Burgess worked conscientiously in his first six months with the section. Now that he was so close to the two British intelligence services he was determined to make the most of the opportunity. When war did break out, Section D would, he reasoned, be at the centre of clandestine operations against the Germans and he would be able to find his way into an even more interesting slot. This did not mean that he behaved less wildly. He drank as much as ever and was just as promiscuous, despite the unfortunate court case a few months earlier. He was remarkably careless, too, over his meetings with Soviet Intelligence. On one occasion he was having Sunday lunch with friends in a Chinese restaurant, called the Old Friends, in the East End:

Suddenly excusing himself from the table, he walked out, crossing the street, stood for a second in front of a seedy seaman's outfitters that was closed, removed an envelope from his jacket, slipped it through the letterbox, returned, and resumed the conversation without turning a hair. Some twelve years later, when the same friends pointed out the place to an official of the security services, they learned that the letterbox was one of several known for Soviet agents.[19]

Section D's vague brief meant that Burgess was able, in his words, to 'buzz around doing a lot of things', without anyone being sure who had authorized his schemes. He planned to establish a clandestine radio station in Lichtenstein to broadcast to Germany and went to the continent to arrange it, only to discover that an MI6 officer had ordered the wireless equipment from Germany – which was hardly the best start to what was supposed to be a secret operation. Section D abandoned the project amid furious recriminations from MI6.

Britain's propaganda effort in the first months of the war was handicapped by the competition between the various departments and sections responsible for undermining morale in Germany. There was also confusion over the demarcation lines between propaganda and sabotage – exemplified by Section D's own ill-defined mandate. The Ministry of Information dealt with straightforward, so-called 'white' propaganda, while a semi-clandestine body, known after its offices in Electra House on the Thames embankment, was manoeuvring for control of 'dirty-tricks' propaganda. This unit had been set up by Sir Stuart Campbell, a Canadian who during the First World War had been deputy director of a section called 'Propaganda in Enemy Countries'. Burgess was the liaison officer between Section D and Electra House, as well as representing Section D's interests on the Joint Broadcasting Committee (JBC), a Foreign Office-sponsored body which was supposed to produce more 'imaginative' propaganda programmes than the BBC. On one occasion, in March 1940, Burgess decided to dispatch himself to France. He invited Rosamond Lehmann, one of the few contemporary English writers who was well-known there, to travel with him. He told her that she was just the person to help Section D's propaganda effort in Europe, assuring her that the staff at the French radio station in Paris were expecting her. She recalled: 'Paris was a dead city. It gave me the creeps. Guy just left me. I was very puzzled. He said he had been too busy to come to the radio station. No one there had any idea that I was coming or why.'[20] When Burgess did turn up at Lehmann's hotel he muttered a few words of apology and launched into a tirade against the French who were, he said, more concerned with having the French Communist Party declared illegal than with fighting the Germans. Lehmann flew back to England, the latest (but by no means the last) of Burgess's friends to be ensnared by his charm. She soon forgave him, as all his friends always did.

Burgess did not dwell on the French mishap. He was determined to exploit Whitehall's burgeoning propaganda-espionage machine. His colleagues were both fascinated and appalled by him. Bickham Sweet-Escott, a banker who was the son of the first governor and commander-in-chief of the Seychelles, had joined Section D in March 1940 and watched disbelievingly as Burgess bustled from one committee to another during June and July of that year:

There were no minutes, there was no agenda and no chairman . . . there never seemed to be less than twenty-five people in the room. Besides the heads of 'D', innumerable other departments were represented . . . What generally happened was that somebody would throw a bright idea into the arena and let the others tear it to pieces, a process that was often amusing, but generally unprofitable . . . On the few occasions when it was agreed that action should be taken, it usually seemed to be obscure who was expected to do the job and I never discovered that any of the ideas really led to action . . . Perhaps I am doing these assemblies an injustice, and they may have sown seeds which bore fruit when we were all more closely organized.[21]

Burgess argued that Section D should set up a special school to train agents in sabotage (he suggested it might be called the Guy Fawkes college). Now that British troops had been evacuated from the continent it was vital, he said, that the government had the capacity to hit the Germans using unconventional methods.

Kim Philby, however, had still not found a job in the intelligence world. He had come infuriatingly close when he was interviewed by Francis Birch, an Old Etonian don on leave from King's College, Cambridge, who was based at the Government Code and Cipher School at Bletchley, responsible for breaking the codes of the enemy (and Allies). Birch told Philby that he would love to recruit him but that he wouldn't be able to offer him nearly enough money to tempt him away from journalism. Philby complained bitterly to Burgess that this was typical of the wretched luck he was having. Time was running out. If he was conscripted then he could easily end up in a routine military job. Burgess assured him that he would be offered a job in intelligence. And he was right.

British Intelligence could not afford the luxury of lengthy recruiting procedures. In peacetime it had always hired men on the basis of personal recommendation and it saw no reason to change. Robert Mackenzie, later knighted after a distinguished diplomatic career, recalled: 'I joined MI6 in 1940 after Dunkirk. Anyone who was not pro-German was all right for us. You can't say that we should have gone through the right vetting procedures. If you had just got out of France by the skin of your teeth you didn't go around being haughty about that sort of thing. You just felt you were bloody lucky not to be dead.'[22]

Once Burgess had fed Philby's name into the system, an interview was guaranteed. Within days Burgess's friend, Captain Leslie Sheridan of the War Office (the intelligence services never identified themselves), contacted Ralph Deakin, foreign editor of *The Times*, to ask if Philby was 'available for war work'. Deakin had no wish to lose one of *The Times*'s most promising correspondents but he could hardly defy the War Office. Philby was interviewed at St Ermin's Hotel, Victoria, by an elderly lady called Marjorie Maxse – a formidable character who became vice-chairman of the Conservative Party in 1945. The interview went better than Philby had hoped; he liked Maxse and she liked him. A desultory check was ordered on Philby but the answer came back 'NRA' (nothing recorded against). Burgess joined Maxse for the second interview. Philby recalled:

I was put through my paces again. Encouraged by Guy's presence, I began to show off, name-dropping shamelessly, as one does at interviews. From time to time, my interlocutors exchanged glances; Guy would nod gravely and approvingly. It turned out that I was wasting my time, since a decision had already been taken . . . So I left Printing House Square (and *The Times*) without fanfare, in a manner wholly appropriate to the new secret and important career for which I imagined myself heading. I decided that it was my duty to profit from the experience of the only secret service man of my acquaintance. So I spent the weekend drinking with Guy Burgess. On the following Monday, I reported to him formally. We both had slight headaches. The organiza- tion to which I became attached called itself the Secret

Intelligence Service (SIS). It was also widely known as MI6, while to the innocent public at large it was simply the secret service.[23]

Philby joined Section D just as Colonel Grand was setting up Burgess's Guy Fawkes college at Brickendonbury Hall, a secluded country house just outside Hertford, twenty-five miles north of London. It was essentially a school for saboteurs and attracted a suitably eclectic collection of freshmen including some Europeans who, Colonel Grand hoped, would one day return to their home countries to wreak revenge on the Nazis: Breton onion-sellers, Scandinavian seamen and a Flemish cavalry officer, Norwegians, Belgians and Spaniards. The instructors were an equally mixed bunch. One of the most extraordinary characters in this bizarre establishment was Tomas Harris, a thirty-two-year-old collector, art dealer and scholar and – to Guy's delight – a remarkably good cordon bleu cook. Blunt, too, was delighted that Harris had slipped into D Branch:

> He was one of the most complete human beings I have ever known. The first thing that struck one about Tomas Harris was the total and disinterested enthusiasm with which he threw himself into any enterprise on which he embarked . . . whether it was discovering an unknown painting by El Greco in an obscure Spanish collection, mastering a new painting technique or exploiting the possibilities of an intelligence scheme against the Nazis.[24]

Harris's mother was Spanish, and his father was the English art dealer Lionel Harris, owner of the Spanish Art Gallery in London which had become one of the main conduits for the sale of Spanish masterpieces in Britain. Tomas grew up in a wealthy, cultured home and at the age of fifteen won a scholarship to the Slade school of art – only to be told that he was too young to take up his place. He was not an intellectual but he did have great natural talents. Blunt's respect for Harris was so unqualified that it led many people to suspect that Harris too was a Soviet agent deliberately planted on the hapless Colonel Grand by Burgess. Yet Blunt always insisted that Harris had not known about the Soviet spy ring. This was certainly the view (as we shall see) of most of Harris's colleagues within the intelligence services, though a few, such as Malcolm Muggeridge, who joined MI6 in 1940, believed that it was possible that he had been implicated. Muggeridge speculated, for example, that Harris 'could have been the paymaster for Guy Burgess's Soviet network'.[25] It is probable that Harris was innocent, but since he died in a car crash in Majorca in January 1964 the nagging doubts persisted during the hunt in the 1960s for Blunt's accomplices.

Brickendonbury Hall came into its own after the British Army's scramble back to England in June 1940. D Branch's main concern now was the threatened invasion of the British Isles. Philby pressed on with his work, determined to make the most of this long-awaited opportunity. Guy, however, was so bored that he started to indulge in schoolboy jokes. Philby recalled:

Night had just fallen after a fine summer day. The Commander was in bed, nursing a sharp attack of eczema, to hide which he was growing a beard. A visiting instructor, masquerading under the name of Hazlitt, was at his bedside sipping a glass of port. There was a sudden shout from the garden, which was taken up by a babel in five languages. Trainees poured into the house, claiming to have seen one, three, ten, any number of parachutes falling in the vicinity. On hearing the news, the Commander ordered the Belgians to get into uniform and mount a machine-gun in the French windows . . .

He then made a disastrous mistake. He instructed Guy to ascertain the exact facts of the case, and telephone the result to the Duty Officer in London. Guy went about the business with wicked conscientiousness. I heard snatches of his subsequent telephone report. 'No, I cannot add to what I have said . . . You wouldn't want me to falsify evidence, would you? . . . Parachutes have been seen dropping in the neighbourhood of Hertford in numbers varying from eighty to none' . . . He went to report in triumph. 'I don't know what I shall do if I do get up,' said the Commander, 'but I shall certainly take command.'

Next morning, Guy . . . periodically spread gleeful tidings. The Duty Officer had alerted his Chief, who had communicated with the War Office. Eastern Command had been pulled out of bed, its armour grinding to action stations in the small hours. Guy made several happy guesses at the cost of the operation . . . One parachute had fallen. Attached to a landmine, it had draped itself harmlessly round a tree.[26]

Like many others within the secret world, Burgess had heard rumours that Churchill was planning radical reforms within the intelligence services. He feared that Section D and Brickendonbury Hall might not survive the new efficiency drive. Grand's unit had not been a conspicuous success, and Burgess decided that it was time to abandon Section D. His escape plan was a typical piece of cheek. He argued that Britain and the Soviet Union could and should work together. The Nazi–Soviet non-aggression treaty, he told incredulous friends, was merely an awkward not an insurmountable problem to a new era of British–Soviet cooperation. His biographer Tom Driberg wrote:

Guy . . . worked out a . . . plan for supplying the resistance forces in Europe more quickly and economically.
In France it was obvious that the communists, who had,
apart from ideology, the most rigidly disciplined organization, would become the most active and efficient
leaders of the resistance; in countries further east, such
as Greece and Yugoslavia, there were useful non-
communist forces. It would be sensible, Guy argued, . . .
if the British and the Russians worked out a reciprocal
supply scheme – the British agreeing to provide arms and
supplies to the communists in France if the Russians
would provide arms and supplies to non-communist
guerillas in Eastern Europe.[27]

Burgess also dreamed of travelling to Moscow and becoming a pivotal force in a new Anglo–Soviet alliance. He
lobbied energetically among his contacts and friends in
Whitehall, many of whom he had cultivated during his days
at the BBC. Anyone who scoffed at his scheme was told to
remember that he had connections at the very highest
levels. Doubters were shown the message that Winston
Churchill had scribbled on that memorable visit to Chartwell some eighteen months earlier. Then Churchill had
been an outcast; now he was Prime Minister. Guy reminded his colleagues that Churchill had promised to find
him a job if he was ever in a position to do so. Churchill's
appointment of Labour politician Sir Stafford Cripps as
ambassador in Moscow gave Burgess a perfect opening;
Cripps would surely need someone like Burgess to explain
why Britain had no intention of forging an alliance with the
Germans and turning them eastwards. Burgess asked for
backing from Harold Nicolson, recently appointed parliamentary secretary to Duff Cooper, the incoming Minister of Information. Nicolson, an occasional guest at Guy's
homosexual parties in Chester Square, was encouraging –

as were the mandarins at the Foreign Office. Guy proposed that the Oxford philosopher Isaiah Berlin should become press attaché in Moscow while he became a roving trouble-shooter. Berlin had filled in a Ministry of Labour form that had been circulated to Oxford dons a few months previous-ly, but as he had heard nothing subsequently, he had assumed that the country had no need of his services. Hence he was delighted, if a little puzzled, by the offer to join the embassy staff in Moscow. He remembered:

> I had no idea, of course, that Burgess had put up a scheme to Harold Nicolson about enlightening the Rus-sians about the truth in the West – I was not told this at all – only that there was no press attaché, that one was needed (all of which I believe was more or less false), and that I had the required qualifications. What seemed to me odd was that there was any work for a press attaché to do in Moscow – the idea of persuading the Soviet press to insert items favourable to Britain seemed an absurdly impossible task, even if this had not been the time of the Russo–German Pact. Nevertheless, Harold Nicolson and Burgess between them said that what with my knowledge of Russian and the need to know what was going on in the Soviet press, there was a job I could do.[28]

Whitehall finally appeared to wake up to the obvious risks of sending someone like Burgess to Moscow. When Cripps was told by Fitzroy Maclean of the Foreign Office Northern Department that he would shortly be joined in Moscow by Berlin and Burgess, he was furious and said that he was the only person who could authorize new appoint-ments to the embassy. Harold Nicolson was also having second thoughts, as he noted in his diary on 29 June: 'Guy Burgess comes to see me and I tell him there is no chance now of his being sent to Moscow.'[29] But Burgess refused to be disheartened. He told friends that he would shortly be leaving on a 'top-secret' mission to Moscow which, if successful, could change the course of the war. It may be that the plan was part of some elaborate Soviet conspiracy; it is more likely that Burgess had devised it as part of his romantic vision of himself as the pivotal force in European history. He gossiped about his new role to Goronwy Rees, then commanding an infantry platoon in the Royal Welch Fusiliers: 'I almost felt he was indulging his gift for fantasy again, and also had the momentary twinge of apprehension, as of an old toothache, that the fortunes of war should be taking him to Moscow. But in neither case was I seriously worried.'[30]

Despite understandable opposition from the Whitehall bureaucracy, Burgess and Berlin – the latter thinking that his appointment as press attaché had now been approved – set off in July from Liverpool for Montreal in the Cunard liner *Antonia*. They were due to land in Quebec, then travel to Washington and San Francisco before sailing for Vladivostok. In Washington Burgess found that his scheme, which he had bulldozed through Whitehall's red tape, had finally been blocked. He was told to return home immediately. Berlin, meanwhile, was offered a job in the British embassy in Washington. He turned it down and returned, confused and puzzled by the mysterious ways of diplomacy, to Oxford. (He took up a post in Washington in 1942.) Burgess was in no such hurry to return to London and the inevitable recriminations. He knew that he could protest that the trip had all been a terrible misunderstanding but, even so, there would be awkward questions. Much better, Guy reasoned, to delay his return, by which time the bureaucrats would have found new problems to fret over. He decided to look up his old Cambridge friend Michael Straight, now married to an American called Belinda and living in Alexandria, just outside Washington.

Straight's small house in Prince Street, Alexandria, had attracted a steady stream of visitors from Britain throughout 1940. Wystan Auden had arrived in February, claiming that America was the future, Europe the past. Esmond Romilly, Churchill's nephew, who had fought for the Republicans in Spain, had called, as had Stafford Cripps, then a War Cabinet representative, on his way back to London. Guy invited himself round to dinner and insisted on describing, in wholly unnecessary detail, some of his more interesting adventures. Straight wrote later:

He was, said Guy, a good friend of M. Édouard Pfeiffer, Chef du Cabinet to Premier of France M. Daladier. He and Pfeiffer and two members of the French Cabinet, he said, had spent an evening together at a male brothel in Paris. Singing and laughing, they had danced around a table, lashing a naked boy, who was strapped to it, with leather whips.

When supper was over, Guy slumped into an easy chair, gripping his fourth glass of whisky. We spoke for a time about the Apostles. I was anxious to hear about the friends whom I had sponsored for the Apostles. Guy in turn mentioned a scholarship student named Leo Long whom Anthony had brought into the society. Anthony had been enraged, so Guy said, when another Apostle had tried, unsuccessfully, to seduce Leo during a drunken party that had followed the annual dinner of the society in 1938. I remembered Leo as a quiet and resolute member of the Trinity College cell. I thought to myself, 'If Anthony has taken Leo under his wing, that can only mean one thing.' Guy glanced up at me in his sly way . . . 'I've been out of touch with our friends for several months,' he said. 'Can you put me back in touch with them?' So it was Guy who had been the invisible man behind Anthony. It was Guy who had drawn me out of my own world in Cambridge, and into this nether world. I had always suspected it; now I knew.[31]

There is no way of proving whether Straight's account of this conversation, given in his autobiography, is accurate. He had good reason to portray himself as the naïve dupe who had been emotionally blackmailed by Blunt into agreeing to help the Soviet cause, though it is possible that he really did not know that Burgess had been the driving force behind Blunt's talent-spotting at Cambridge. Straight's own work for the Soviets had been half-hearted. He had given them nothing that was classified, yet he was still meeting the agent of a foreign power; and that was enough to make the hyper-nervous Straight feel distinctly unwell.

Burgess eventually returned to England in late August to find that Section D had been disbanded and Colonel Grand had been shunted off to become director of the War Office's Fortifications and Works department. A new secret organization, the Special Operations Executive (SOE), responsible to Hugh Dalton, the Minister of Economic Warfare, had been set up by Cabinet directive on 22 July. Churchill charged SOE with setting 'Europe ablaze' and for the next five years it tried to do just that. Kim Philby was absorbed into SOE and within a year had moved to the heart of the secret world; he was given a job in Section V of MI6, then responsibility for penetrating Abwehr (German military intelligence) security in the Iberian peninsula. Guy, on the other hand, found himself out of a job again. When he was summoned to meet Colin Gubbins, SOE's Director of Operations, he was fired. Guy was not disheartened. He told Harold Nicolson that he still believed that, with Soviet help, he could help foment protests by the Left in Nazi-occupied Europe. Nicolson was unaware that Burgess had any links with the Comintern, as Nicolson's biographer noted: 'Like many other of Burgess's friends and acquaintances he was taken in by the mendacity and plausibility . . . There can be little doubt that Guy Burgess extracted from Harold inside information which he passed on to his masters in Moscow.'[32]

Burgess did not let this professional setback stop him enjoying London's nightlife. He went drinking and night-clubbing with friends such as Goronwy Rees and Brian Howard. Once he was at a Soho club with Howard when the police raided the premises for serving drinks after hours. Howard, then responsible for MI5's surveillance of fascist sympathizers in the capital, told the policeman questioning him: 'My name is Brian Howard and I live in Berkeley Square. I presume that you, Inspector, come from some dreary little suburb.' When Burgess, Howard and the poet Dylan Thomas visited the Gargoyle club, Guy showed that he was back on form. Sitting at their table was Mrs Marie-Jacqueline Lancaster:

> Mrs Lancaster was wearing leg-paint because stockings were in short supply. Thomas, gargantuanly drunk, in-sisted on licking the paint off 'in time to the music of the rather old fashioned band the Gargoyle affected'. When the band ended the evening with a limping version of the National Anthem, Burgess refused to stand up (not, as it happened, out of ideology but because he had lumbago and was very drunk). In an unexpected fit of patriotism Thomas, applauded by Howard, leant across the table and knocked Guy out.[33]

Burgess rarely fell out with his companions for long and he soon made his peace with Isaiah Berlin. Harold Nicolson invited both men to lunch to patch up their differences on 28 October and noted in his diary: 'Lunch with Guy Burgess and Isaiah Berlin who is just back from Washington. There is such a sense of suspense in the air that ordinary work seems hopeless.'[34]

Nor was Burgess unemployed for long. He rejoined the BBC, where he began working on a lonely-hearts programme called 'Can I Help You?' It wasn't much of a job for the linchpin of the Cambridge spy ring but, as Guy well knew, nothing was ever as hopeless as it might appear.

CHAPTER 11
Secret Manoeuvres

Anthony Blunt was called for an interview with MI5 in August 1940 after appealing to his old friend, Victor Rothschild, for help. Rothschild had duly provided the necessary reference, unaware, of course, of why Blunt was so anxious to join the security service. Blunt admitted in the 1980s that he was ashamed that he had abused a friend in this way, though he did not let these qualms unsettle him in his new wartime role as the Soviets' man in MI5. He was a commissioned officer who had performed ably, if unspectacularly, in France and had a brilliant academic background. In fact, he was just the sort of high-calibre recruit MI5 wanted. That was the conclusion of Brigadier 'Harry' Allen, a regular soldier who had responsibility for liaising between MI5, the War Office and the army. Allen chatted briefly with Blunt and then welcomed him to the service.

Half a century later it probably seems odd that Blunt should have been able to find a job so easily in the heart of British Intelligence. Yet, it has to be emphasized, the recruiters of MI5 and MI6 had no alternative other than to accept personal recommendations. Recruits were invariably drawn from that closed circle (the public schools –Oxbridge–the City–the Law), membership of which had always been a guarantee of a man's character and patriotism.

The basic pre-war structure of MI5 remained unchanged.

There were six divisions (known as branches after 1953): A, B, C, D, E and F. A Division dealt with the administration of the service. B was responsible for counter-espionage and was, arguably, the most important of the six. There was a bewildering number of sub-sections within B: groups dedicated to mail interception, counter-sabotage and analysis of enemy intentions. B1(a) and B1(b) were perhaps the most renowned of these sub-sections: they ran captured German agents who had been persuaded to send back information to Germany and analysed German intelligence intercepts. When Sir John Masterman, himself a former intelligence officer, was finally and grudgingly given government clearance in 1972 to publish *The Double Cross System*, which he had written in 1945, the men and women from other sections within MI5 felt that their work – vetting applicants for sensitive posts, keeping a watch on aliens, liaising with British territories overseas – had been made to look less crucial.

Whatever the merits of other sections there was no doubt that during (and after) the war B Division offered the most challenging jobs. As MI5 scoured the universities, the City and the legal profession for the most original minds, it was B Division which was able to pick the cream of the intake. Its remarkable talents included Herbert Hart, later a world-famous professor of jurisprudence at Oxford, responsible for analysing German intelligence radio intercepts; Victor Rothschild, who ended the war with a string of decorations, including the George Medal awarded for his courage in defusing a bomb concealed in a consignment of Spanish onions; and Helenus Milmo, known to everyone as 'Buster', a Trinity College-educated barrister and later a High Court Judge.

The organization which they joined had trundled gently along during the 1920s and 1930s. Its director-general, Major-General Vernon Kell, had run it since 1909, when two new intelligence services, which grew into MI5 and MI6, had been created. Kell was born in 1873, the son of an army major. A naturally talented linguist, by the time he went to Sandhurst in 1892 he was able to speak good German, Italian, French and Polish. He was a decent, honest man, though he had strong, obstinate prejudices. His officers had to be of good character – which ruled out men who had not been to public school, homosexuals and Catholics. Homosexuals, Kell thought, were disgusting and unreliable and Catholics were habitual intriguers with loyalties that extended beyond Britain. Kell's men were paid in cash and did not have to pay income tax, though they were paid very little in the first place since Kell assumed that all his officers had private means.

Kell was sacked by Churchill in 1940. There was a brief and unsuccessful interregnum by Brigadier A. W. A. Harker, who had been head of B Division, before he was replaced by Sir David Petrie, a former officer in the Indian police force. There were other reforms designed to make the British intelligence effort more efficient. In November 1939 Colonel Stewart Menzies, an Eton-educated Grenadier Guards officer, who had married into the aristocracy, was appointed head of MI6, the organization which was responsible, broadly speaking, for intelligence-gathering in countries that were not part of the empire. To ensure that MI5 and new organizations handling radio interception, cryptography and sabotage worked closely and smoothly together, Churchill established a security executive, chaired by Lord Swinton who, as Sir Philip Cunliffe-Lister, had been Chamberlain's Air Minister.

During the early 1930s MI5 was based in offices in the Cromwell Road, west London. In 1937 it moved to two floors in Thames House, Millbank, before spilling out to offices in Horseferry Road. In the autumn of 1939 it had taken over Wormwood Scrubs prison in west London and transferred its records and many of its staff to Winston Churchill's birthplace at Blenheim Palace, an eighteenth-century mansion a few miles north of Oxford. There were offices, too, in St James's Street, which connects Piccadilly and Pall Mall. MI5 even had its own interrogation centre – a grim Victorian building called Latchmere House, close to Ham Common where Blunt's mother lived.

The prison was hardly an ideal base for a secret service. Most of the cells that had been converted into offices had no telephones. Many of the doors had an infuriating habit of slamming shut, leaving the MI5 officers firmly locked in. One writer observed:

It was a great misapprehension to think that siting MI5 in the Scrubs meant good security. Four-foot-thick walls certainly failed to protect the Registry [where records were kept], and the stream of Mayfair types turning up each morning at the gates succeeded only in attracting attention. Several people claimed to have heard a bus conductor on the No. 72 Scrubs route announce 'All change for MI5' when he reached the prison . . . Most of the MI5 girls . . . were drawn from the same social backgrounds and inevitably the mixture of wartime conditions, beautiful girls and eligible young men lent something of a party atmosphere to the office.[1]

Sir Dick White, who joined MI5 in 1936, said of those early years of the war:

Remember the chaos of those days. Perhaps the security reservations about Blunt were available but didn't reach us. That was the order of the day. Everybody was all over the place. Before the war MI5 was really tiny, perhaps about twenty-five men. And then in a few months we had four to five hundred. The pace things had to be done was astonishing. I remember Guy Liddell (a senior MI5 officer) saying in 1939, You know anyone could come into the Scrubs and put up a sign saying he's starting a new section to cover this or that.[2]

Blunt was delighted that he had finally found his way into MI5. It meant that he would be able to feed his Soviet friends details about MI5's internal structure, the names of its officers, its tactics, especially towards British communists, as well as picking up whatever material he could on other intelligence organizations within the secret world. It meant, too, that he would have a thoroughly interesting, and safe, war. But there was one problem. He had been assigned to Brigadier Allen's D Division, which liaised with the War Office and with the three services. Blunt told friends that he loathed the work; it was dreary, routine administration and was as intellectually stimulating as the Field Security Police. He decided that only B Division offered the sort of challenges that he wanted (and it was B that most interested the Soviets).

For the time being at least, Blunt had to move slowly. If he pressed too hard for an immediate transfer he knew that there was a risk, albeit a small one, that someone might start checking the files. So he worked conscientiously for Allen. The Scrubs was bustling with old friends such as Brian Howard, who was soon fired for getting drunk in London pubs and bars and telling everyone that he worked for 'a very secret organization'. There was Constance Burgess, Guy's sister-in-law, who had been recruited on what her husband Nigel Burgess called the 'débutante belt'. A few months after she joined she suggested that Nigel might be a useful recruit for MI5.[3]

Nigel, Guy's younger brother, had started the war on an anti-aircraft battery. This was not wholly successful since he was so short-sighted that he was unable to tell the difference between British and German planes. Nigel was steady, heterosexual, apolitical and had little in common with his brother. He too had been educated at Eton and Trinity College, and had drifted into advertising before the war. During the war neither Nigel nor Constance was quite sure exactly what Guy was doing. They bumped into him occasionally at their mother's home at West Meon in Hampshire. Nigel recalled:

> Guy was riotously funny. He had tremendous charm when he wanted to use it. He may have brought the servants at Trinity College out on strike but my memory is that there was no one who was more demanding of my mother's servants than he was. Guy used to tease my stepfather [Colonel Jack Bassett] unmercifully. Jack really was Blimp's grandfather and as he was circulating the port Guy would suddenly propose a toast to Uncle Joe. You can imagine the effect that had. Guy always gave the impression that he was running the war single-handed. He said he could never stay long at the house because the war was waiting for him.[4]

Nigel went straight into an F2(a), a sub-section of F Division, whose duties included watching for any treasonable activities by the Communist Party of Great Britain. His boss was Roger Hollis, a professional intelligence officer who held the rank of assistant director. Hollis was knighted during a distinguished career with the service – he was deputy director-general from 1952 to 1956 and director-general from 1956 to 1965 – but his reputation was later savaged by former colleagues who argued, with catastrophic results for the morale of the service, that he may have been a Soviet agent.

Nigel worked hard, but was never certain that he was achieving much:

I wasn't altogether sure what was going on at the Office. I would spend my day reading dreary letters from one comrade to another and then go home in the evening. When Hitler and Stalin signed a pact together and the comrades were supporting Stalin they were therefore aiding Hitler as well. I think it was quite right we should take an interest. Actually I think I'm right in saying nobody knew what was going on. I think it must have been a policy of confusion. Perhaps deliberate, conscious muddle was a good form of security.

I liked Anthony. He was amusing and highly intelligent. I feel a lot of highly intelligent people make me feel stupid. He did not.[5]

Nigel was, however, not sorry to leave London for Cambridge where he became MI5's regional security liaison officer, charged with preventing the growth of a fifth column in East Anglia.

Blunt knew that there were two men he needed to impress if he was ever to escape the drudgery of Brigadier Allen's section: Guy Liddell, the director of B, and Dick White, his deputy. Both men were career intelligence officers, who lived their professional lives in carefully preserved anonymity. The post-war etiquette of Whitehall meant that two such important figures had to be listed in *Who's Who*, the guide to the British Establishment, but the job descriptions they gave (for example, civil assistant, War Office) were so unimpressive that only the cognoscenti knew that the two men were top-ranking intelligence officers. Both men, in different ways, played a vital part in the story of Anthony Blunt: Liddell because he was so trusting; White because he was so closely involved in the post-war hunt for Soviet spies and in trying to salvage something from the wreckage that followed the revelations of Maclean, Burgess, Philby and, finally, Blunt.

Liddell was born in 1892. His father, Captain Augustus Liddell, was a comptroller to the household of a member of Queen Victoria's family and could claim descent from Alice Liddell, the model for Lewis Carroll's *Alice in Wonderland*.[6] He had been educated at public school but had never been to university. He had won the Military Cross with the Royal Field Artillery during the First World War, as had his two brothers, Cecil and David, who were also members of MI5 during the Second World War. He joined Scotland Yard after the war and in 1919 had been given responsibility for Special Branch surveillance of extremist groups. In 1927 he had transferred to MI5's B Division. He was an expert on the CPGB and was convinced that it was a dangerous extension of the Comintern. He had striven to build up contacts with the American Federal Bureau of Investigation, and, say his friends, even won the respect of J. Edgar Hoover, the bureau's odious, misanthropic director. Liddell always seemed embarrassed by his appearance; he was balding, short and podgy. He had an unhappy personal life – his marriage to the Honourable Calypso Baring had collapsed before the war – which meant that he sought solace in his work and friends. He was a gifted cellist, reckoned by colleagues to be one of the finest amateur musicians in the country. He was a chain-smoker, a keen art collector and, like Blunt, was a member of the Travellers' Club. An old-fashioned man, he would have described himself as a Christian and a patriot. He was popular with younger colleagues who thought him decent, honest and unpretentious. Kim Philby had a high regard for him, describing him like this:

'I was born in an Irish fog,' he once told me, 'and sometimes I think I have never emerged from it.' No self-depreciation could have been more ludicrous. It is true that he did have a deceptively ruminative manner.

He would murmur his thoughts aloud, as if groping his way towards the facts of a case, his face creased in a comfortable, innocent smile. But behind the façade of laziness, his subtle and reflective mind played over a storehouse of photographic memories. He was an ideal senior officer for a young man to learn from, always ready to put aside his work to listen and worry at a new problem.[7]

Liddell was deputy director of the service from 1947 until 1952. He was working as a security expert with the Atomic Energy Authority when he died in 1958.

Dick White, knighted in 1955, was a few months older than Blunt, though they had little else in common. It is no exaggeration to describe White as the most influential and respected British intelligence officer of the post-war era, probably of this century. His entry in *Who's Who* was a mere seven lines long:

WHITE, Sir Dick (Goldsmith). KCMG 1960; KBE 1955 (CBE 1950; OBE 1942); formerly attached to Foreign and Commonwealth Office; retired 1972; born 20 December 1906; son of Percy Hall White and Gertrude White (née Farthing); married 1945, Kathleen Bellamy; two sons. Educated Bishops Stortford College; Christ Church, Oxford (Hon. Student 1981); Universities of Michigan and California, USA; US Legion of Merit, Croix de Guerre, France. Club: Garrick.

White was director-general of MI5 from 1953 to 1956, and from 1956 until 1969 he was head of MI6 – the only man ever to hold both posts. He then became the Cabinet Office's intelligence and security coordinator and, although he retired officially in 1972, he remained on call in moments of crisis. He was an elder statesman who knew the tricks of spying and spy-catching as well as anyone. He was trusted by both MI5 and MI6, and by politicians of the Right and Left. In his old age he was an elegant figure, ramrod straight, without an inch of spare flesh and with neat, clipped grey hair. He seemed more like a genial retired headmaster than a legendary spymaster whose memory was packed with enough secrets to keep teams of investigative reporters occupied for months. He tended to listen rather than contribute to a conversation, managing to give the impression that he regarded other people's views as far more interesting than his own. He always took a keen interest in life outside the closed world he inhabited, and in retirement was always accessible, listing his address and telephone number quite openly while other, lesser figures from the secret world hid from the press. Of course, there were critics. Philby, who had good reason to dislike White, said patronizingly that he was 'a nice modest character who would have been the first to admit that he lacked outstanding qualities'. Philby continued:

> His most obvious fault was a tendency to agree with the last person he spoke to. With his usual good sense, he was content to delegate a lot of work to his subordinates, and to exercise his gifts for chairmanship with a view to keeping harmony in the [B] division . . . his capacity for avoiding departmental fights paid off in the outcome. When Liddell became Deputy Director [of MI5] White was promoted to the top of B Division.[8]

White had drifted into intelligence by accident. He had gone up to Christ Church, Oxford, in 1926 to read history and, as we have seen, spent his time studying and playing sport. (He could have run in the British Olympic team but declined the invitation since he felt that he ought to devote himself to his finals.) After Oxford he went to America for two years as a Commonwealth Fellow, attending the University of Michigan in the Midwest and then Berkeley, California. It was a crucial experience. While many people in England, both of the Right and the Left, resented the post-war domination of Britain by the United States, White realized that American power and wealth made inevitable the erosion of British influence internationally. It was no use arguing about whether this was a good thing; it was simply a fact. Moreover, White liked America. It was a great mistake, White used to tell his colleagues, to imagine that just because Americans spoke a version of English they were the same as us. They were not, and the key to a successful Anglo–American relationship, in intelligence as much as any other field, was in accepting this and understanding the American mentality. White recalled:

> Going to America was very useful in career terms because it helped me understand the country. As an English student I was able to meet Senators and Congressmen and so on and that helped me get the hang of things. I became rather pro-American, which helped me when I became head of MI6 and had to deal with the Americans a great deal.[9]

After returning from the States he set off again on a tour of Europe. He lived on £2 a week as he travelled through France, Italy and Germany, picking up a working knowledge of Italian and German as he went. 'Although my interests were really cultural I made friends with a lot of people and that helped me understand what was happening in Europe. I suppose it helped get rid of my parochialism.'[10] Back in England he toyed with the idea of joining *The Times* but concluded that that would be 'a bit too stuffy', so he took a teaching job at Whitgift school in Croydon, Surrey, which he described as having 'extraordinarily high intellectual standards'. He was also a part-time journalist for the *Listener*, the BBC's weekly magazine of analysis and features, writing his unsigned pieces in the evening after he had finished marking homework. He enjoyed both teaching and writing and was unsure which career he would concentrate on when, by chance, he was offered a job with MI5. The school records show that he was an assistant master from 1933 until 1935 and note that he left to join the intelligence service at the War Office as the assistant to Guy Liddell. White had been taking a party of boys to Australia by boat when he met Malcolm Cumming, an MI5 staffer who was on his way to an army exercise in Australia. Months later, in 1936, when both men had returned to England, Cumming introduced White to Guy Liddell. White again:

> I had never heard of MI5 until then. But the job that Guy offered me sounded fascinating, even if it did mean that I earnt much less. I was offered £350 a year in cash, free of tax. I signed on with the idea that there would be a war eventually and that working for MI5 would be my war service. It seemed clear to me that fascism was a monumental threat and that something catastrophic was going to take place. Guy Liddell wanted me to go to Germany to study what was happening there. I was specifically instructed not to run any risks by getting close to defence establishments. I was intrigued by what was happening in Germany and, given the offer to go and study it for myself, I could hardly refuse.[11]

As he was introduced to his new colleagues, White realized that he was one of the youngest men in the office. There were retired army men, ex-colonial service administrators and former Indian Police officers – the only staff that Kell could attract. They used to gather, all twenty-five of them, every day at 5 P.M. for tea in their office overlooking the Thames to discuss the latest investigations. It was very dignified and low-key; rather like a fading London gentlemen's club.

White had never belonged to a political party but that did not mean that he had been unmoved by unemployment in Britain or by the alarming successes of the Nazis in Germany. If he did have party political views then he certainly never revealed them. He spent nine months in Germany. It was the year of the Berlin Olympics, when Hitler had hoped that German athletes would demonstrate their racial superiority. (Hitler could barely contain his fury when Jesse Owens, a black American, carried off three gold medals.) White was horrified by what he saw in Germany: 'What appalled me most was the way in which decent Germans were falling for Hitler, hook, line and sinker. They had suddenly been brought back from inflation and unemployment. Suddenly everyone had a job. There is no doubt that it was as great a con as any people has ever been subjected to.'[12]

When he returned to London he was given responsibility for studying European groups that had links with the Nazis and watching for any signs of German espionage in Britain. He monitored German businesses which had offices in London to make sure that they were not fronts for intelligence-gathering. When war was declared White was one of the bright young hopes of MI5 who was being groomed for high office; now there was no time to nurse him along gradually. He was one of the few professional intelligence officers in the country. Around him would have to be built a new organization that would be capable of meeting the challenges of a modern war. He was appointed deputy to Liddell in the key B Division. It was, said White, a happy working partnership. 'Guy was a very conservative, gentle soul. But he was very shrewd and well-informed. He was wise enough to know some of the tricks of the trade and I was young enough to carry all the detail in my head.'[13]

The two men realized that war meant that new tactics had to be devised. White, for example, argued that it would be stupid to execute German agents captured in Britain. He said:

I can remember writing a memorandum for law officers at the beginning of the war saying, look here, when we catch German spies we are obliged to shoot them. This seems uneconomical. Much better to make the best use of them. I argued that we should make them promise to work for us. The law officers agreed to this and this became a sort of strategy. Either you believe in retribution whatever the consequences or you decide that it's your job to make sure that you get the best information. We chose to do the latter.[14]

White argued that there was little anyone could have done to prevent men such as Blunt from joining MI5:

Remember the climate of the time. There was nothing resembling positive vetting. It was common for people to be very left-wing. If you talk about communists you have to ask yourself: could we have proved someone was actually a member of the party? Very few of them were card-carrying members of the party. Remember the size of the intake that came into MI5. We would have needed something positive to go on. And even if we had wanted to do that we would have been discouraged by the government. The feeling was that anyone who was against the Germans in the war was on the right side.[15]

Blunt soon became friendly with Guy Liddell, the man who could authorize his transfer to B Division. They used to go off in Liddell's battered Austin Seven to the West End art galleries, where Blunt would proffer expert advice on which paintings Liddell should buy.

Occasionally, Guy Burgess, now employed on mysterious errands for equally mysterious government departments, would pop into Blunt's office at Wormwood Scrubs and then in St James's, though White always maintained that Liddell did his best to keep Burgess out of MI5:

> Liddell thought that Burgess was a disgraceful figure. He did not approve of the goings-on that were associated with Burgess. He told everyone in MI5 that no one was to have anything to do with Burgess. It is always being alleged that he befriended Burgess and introduced him into our midst. That is just not true.[16]

Liddell became a member of the Blunt–Burgess social circle, and as proof of his confidence in Blunt he ordered his transfer from Allen's office to B Division. Many of Liddell's men thought that Blunt was working curiously hard to ingratiate himself with their chief. Christopher Harmer, one of B Division's wartime recruits (he had trained as a lawyer), always thought that Liddell was 'indiscreet and terribly susceptible to flattery',[17] and these were weaknesses that Blunt and Burgess could, and did, exploit. Dick White said: 'Guy Liddell was a very keen art collector and Blunt became his adviser. I think Blunt cultivated Liddell as a way of protecting himself.'[18]

Blunt's first job in B Division was to investigate the efficiency of MI5's 'watcher' service, the group which was responsible for following MI5 suspects. High-ranking regular army officers suspected of fascist leanings were being followed by police officers seconded to MI5. Blunt read the watchers' reports, which described in quite unnecessary detail the suspects' eating and drinking habits. Blunt concluded that the operation was a waste of men and money, and Liddell agreed. This decisive, well-argued report was a fine start to Blunt's career within B. It also proved a bonus for the Soviets, who learned the details of MI5's surveillance operations, including the monitoring of Soviet diplomats and their British contacts. But there were problems that Blunt had not anticipated. Liddell's secretary had taken a violent dislike to him and lobbied for Blunt to be shifted away from Liddell's immediate control. He was moved to B1(b) section, headed by Helenus 'Buster' Milmo, and became responsible for assessing Abwehr and Sicherheitsdienst (Nazi Security Service) sources. B1(b) also worked closely with B1(a), the unit which controlled captured German agents. Blunt was, thus, at the centre of MI5's most sensitive operations. He was charged with organizing surveillance of embassies in London, especially those, such as the Spanish, which were hostile to Britain. Together with a representative from MI6, Blunt ensured that the British were able to break open the neutrals' diplomatic bags. The transfer delighted both Blunt and his Soviet controllers, and he faithfully passed to them everything he learned. But, interesting though it was for the Soviets to have such a steady stream of diplomatic gossip, it was not vital material.

However, the camaraderie within MI5 meant that Blunt knew about virtually all MI5's operations, in general terms if not always in detail. His value to the Soviets was, therefore, incalculable. Before the German invasion of the Soviet Union on 22 June 1941 Blunt had no idea whether the information that he gave to the Soviets would be passed on to the Germans, but after June 1941 he would have argued that he was merely passing information to an ally. But this argument is flawed. Successful intelligence depends on maintaining secrecy; Blunt could not have known how the Soviets would use his material or whether their own intelligence network had been penetrated by the Germans. Dick White put it like this:

> I have to say that Blunt was the man I most resented in that group [of Cambridge spies]. I think he went further than any of them in trying to get us to accept him. He made a general assault on key people to see that they liked him. I was interested in art and he always used to sit down next to me in the canteen and chat. And he betrayed us all. He was a very nice and civilized man and I enjoyed talking to him. You cannot imagine how it feels to be betrayed by someone you have worked side by side with unless you have been through it yourself.[19]

Although MI5 officers were trained not to discuss their work with anyone who did not 'need to know' it, it is hardly surprising that this rule was not enforced effectively. They were working long hours in cramped conditions, dealing with a mass of information pouring in from the Bletchley cryptographers (see Chapter 12), from the double agents in Britain, from MI6 and from the military as well as dozens of other less regular sources. Many of the officers had sent their families to the country to avoid the terrible nightly pounding of German bombing (an average of 200 German bombers attacked London fifty-seven nights in succession during late 1940). MI5 staff had to trust each other – if they had not, then morale would have collapsed. Christopher Harmer said:

> We could have been at each other's throats. But we weren't. There was none of the backbiting that exists in big companies in peacetime. We didn't pry into each other's affairs but of course we talked amongst ourselves. I remember that after the German invasion of the Soviet Union there was genuine disagreement between a lot of

us on how much we should tell the Russians about our work. Some of us thought that we should tell them everything but others thought that we ought to look ahead and remember that the Russians were our potential enemies.[20]

Harmer was three years younger than Blunt and had been at Marlborough. However, he said that Blunt 'was never a friend of mine, either at school or in MI5. He was just doing a job like the rest of us. There was nothing special about him. He was a snob and a bit wet. But that was all.'

Other MI5 officers recalled that Blunt, normally reserved and quiet, would occasionally leap over chairs in the canteen with a colleague, Courtney Young, who, ironically, was one of the MI5 men who questioned Blunt after the defections of Burgess and Maclean in 1951.

The head of B1(a) was Lieutenant-Colonel Tom A. Robertson, known to everyone as 'Tar'. He was a professional intelligence officer who inspired enormous respect and affection for the way that he masterminded the 'Double Cross' operation. He had been a regular army officer until the 1930s:

In 1933 I went into the office [MI5] because I knew Johnny Kell, the son of the old man. I worked for Guy Liddell. We were very aware of the Communist Party which we thought the Russians were using. But it didn't occur to us to worry about the universities. My job was to work out the way that the Communist Party worked.

I'd met Burgess before the war in the St Ermin's Hotel when he brought back information from Paris. I thought he was a ghastly specimen. I sat on one end of the sofa and he sat on the other. He was smelly, dirty and slobbering at the mouth. Then he started to tell me how he was ambidextrous and how he had gone to bed with whoever the French foreign minister was. He was obviously trying to shock me.

Before the war MI5 was just a bunch of amateurs who used their common sense. Then we had all the new men. Some of them were pretty good brains. I used to see a bit of Blunt but I couldn't stick the man. One knew that he was queer and before the war one would not have countenanced letting him anywhere near the office. We knew he was a pretty rum fellow. Let's face it. He kept some strange company – people like Burgess and other odd sods. No question that Blunt was very damaging. He had access to top secret sources. He only had to see a paper on a desk and he could memorize it. Super chap to have as a spy.[21]

Tomas Harris joined B1(a) after the closure of Brickendonbury Hall and became one of Robertson's most effective officers, running the celebrated Spanish double agent Juan Pujol, whose codename was Garbo. Harris and his wife Hilda spent several hours each day inventing plausible reports to radio to the Abwehr. The Germans were so delighted with his work that he was awarded the Iron Cross (Second Class). Harris also found time to hold lavish parties for his colleagues from MI5 at his home in Chesterfield Street, Mayfair.

Tar Robertson recalled: 'Everyone went to Tommy's parties. Philby. Dick White. Liddell and Blunt, who used to see a lot of each other. I have no doubts about Liddell's or Harris' loyalty. But Harris was a strange fellow. I liked him enormously and he was a damned good operator. A brilliant man. But I think he may have been bi[sexual].'[22]

One of Robertson's case officers, William Luke – who ran the skilful double agent Tricycle (the Yugoslav Dusko Popov) – also had a high regard for Harris, though he knew that there had been 'unpleasant suggestions' about Harris's personal life. Luke, a successful industrialist after the war, said:

> I liked Tomas Harris. He was controversial but very clever. I can't say I liked Blunt. His office was two doors away from mine and I have no doubt that Blunt knew that we were running double agents although it would have been difficult for him to start fumbling around papers he had no business with. I wouldn't be surprised if Blunt did a lot of damage. I despise the man for what he did.[23]

Russell Lee, who joined MI5's B Division in October 1940, said he had 'no doubts' about Harris.[24] Blunt, too, was unequivocally loyal to Harris. When Harris held an exhibition of his paintings at a London gallery during the war Blunt was generous in his praise, even though many thought that the paintings were mediocre Post-Impressionist derivations. Blunt wrote a lengthy tribute to his friend in 1975 in which he said: 'This exhibition, in the constricted galleries of Reid and Lefevre, then in King Street, St James's, was impressive and even somewhat frightening through the sheer nervous intensity of the paintings, which reflected the strain under which Tomas was living and working.'[25] In that same tribute Blunt described Harris's brilliant work as a 'Double Cross' officer; indeed, by breaking the Official Secrets Act in this way, it seemed as if Blunt might well be taunting MI5:

> His greatest achievement was as one of the principal organizers of what has been described as the greatest double-cross operation of the war – 'operation Garbo' – which seriously misled the Germans about the Allied plans for the invasion of France . . . The success of the operation was mainly due to the extraordinary imagina-

tive power with which Tomas directed it. In fact, he 'lived' the deception, to the extent that, when he was talking in the small circle of people concerned, it was difficult to tell whether he was talking about real events or one of the fantastic stories which he had just put across to the Nazi-Intelligence Service.[26]

If any confirmation was needed that Blunt had known a great deal about 'Double Cross', then this was it.

For much of the war Blunt's home was a large flat, owned by Victor Rothschild, at 5, Bentinck Street, just off Oxford Street and a few minutes' walk from Broadcasting House. (Rothschild rarely visited the flat and was astonished when Rees published his account of life there when Burgess and Blunt were tenants.) Blunt had given up his own flat in west London to Ida Herz, a refugee from Europe who helped him prepare the manuscript for his book, *Artistic Theory in Italy*, published in 1940. Burgess soon joined Blunt there after his own flat had been bombed. Together they turned Bentinck Street into a cross between a high-class male brothel and a debating club for off-duty intelligence men, senior military figures, politicians and journalists. Goronwy Rees noted that the flat had:

> the air of a rather high-class disorderly house, in which one could not distinguish between the staff, the management and the clients . . . All appeared to be employed in jobs of varying importance, some of the highest, at various ministries; some were communists or ex-communists; all were a fount of gossip about the progress of the war, and the political machine responsible for conducting it, which sometimes amused me, sometimes startled me, and sometimes convinced me that I could not possibly be fighting in the same war as themselves.[27]

There were two new arrivals in September 1940: Patricia Parry and Teresa Mayor, whom Rothschild married after the war. The two girls had been bombed out of their flat in Gower Street and were grateful for Victor's offer to join Blunt in Bentinck Street. The flat was a maisonette on the three floors of a purpose-built office block, the ground floor of which was occupied by a medical magazine, the *Practitioner*. On the first level were the kitchen and sitting room. On the second floor were Blunt's bedroom and a dressing room-cum-bathroom. Guy's rooms – a bedroom and a bathroom – were on the same floor, down the corridor from Blunt's accommodation. The two girls lived on the top floor. There was a housekeeper, an Irish girl called Bridie, who came in every day to clean and cook for whoever happened to be in the flat. Patricia Parry, who had known Blunt well at Cambridge, recalled: 'Everyone who was there was working eighteen hours a day and we scarcely saw each other. I left at 8 A.M. and came back at night. I never socialized with Anthony. One came home and went to sleep. I know what people have said about the orgies but I never saw anything like that.'[28]

Malcolm Muggeridge saw Bentinck Street rather differently:

There, we found . . . John Strachey, J. D. Bernal, Anthony Blunt, Guy Burgess, a whole revolutionary *Who's Who*. It was the only time I ever met Burgess; and he gave me a feeling, such as I have never had from anyone else, of being morally afflicted in some way. His very physical presence was, to me, malodorous and sinister; as though he had some consuming illness . . . The impression fitted in well enough with his subsequent adventures; as did this millionaire's nest altogether, so well set up, providing, among other amenities, special rubber bones to bite on if the stress of the Blitz became too hard to bear. Sheltering so distinguished a company – Cabinet Minister-to-be, honoured Guru of the Extreme Left-to-be, Connoisseur Extraordinary-to-be, and other notabilities, all in a sense grouped round Burgess; Etonian mudlark and sick toast of a sick society, as beloved along Foreign Office corridors, in the quads and the clubs, as in the pubs among the pimps and ponces and street pick-ups, with their high voices and peroxide hair.[29]

Muggeridge had always disliked Blunt:

I could sense he didn't like me at all. A mutual hatred. Even when Goronwy Rees was talking about it all, all those years after the war I still couldn't believe that this rather aesthetic, snobbish character should really have wanted to promote the Soviet Union. The thing that he was most concerned about was art and yet the art of the Soviet Union is, to put it mildly, the most appalling that has ever existed. I still don't understand as a matter of fact. My own opinion is that the real motive is that he was madly, crazily in love with Burgess.[30]

There were other occasional residents in the flat. Patrick Day, an MI5 officer who was an expert on the German intelligence operations, lived there for a time, though it was not an experience that he cared to discuss. His only comment was, 'Ah, Burgess was Burgess!'[31]

Goronwy Rees was more forthcoming:

Guy brought home a series of boys, young men, soldiers, sailors, airmen, whom he had picked up among the thousands who thronged the streets of London at that time . . . The effect was that to spend an evening at Guy's flat was rather like watching a French farce which had

been injected with all the elements of a political drama
. . . civil servants, politicians, visitors to London, friends
and colleagues of Guy's, popped in and out of bed and
then continued some absorbing discussion.[32]

It was potentially disastrous for MI5 officers such as
Blunt or Guy Liddell to be associated with Burgess.
Homosexuality was illegal; there was always a chance that
one of Burgess's casual pick-ups would become violent or
resort to blackmail. Burgess, though, never dwelt on what
might happen; after all, when would London ever again be
packed with so many young working-class men in uniform?
Burgess was also lucky. After he was arrested for drunken
driving, his counsel told the court that his client had been
under great strain at the War Office. He was acquitted.

Blunt and Burgess were now closer than ever; they had
no secrets from each other and even shared boyfriends.
Jack Hewit, Guy Burgess's regular lover, recalled: 'I was
Anthony's lover at Bentinck Street as well as Guy's. When
Guy and I had one of our flaming rows . . . I said to
Anthony: "I can't stand this man any more." Anthony and
I were lovers for the whole of the war. I adored him.'[33]
Hewit, who was in the Royal Artillery, had been posted to
London in 1943. 'It was by special request of Anthony
Blunt,' he said. 'I was attached to the Directorate of Royal
Artillery, but my job was really with MI5.'

Hewit, as we have already seen, was used to being 'given'
to men whom Burgess wanted to use. He had had an affair
with Baron Wolfgang zu Putlitz, the German diplomat who
became a British agent. Hewit had an affair, too, with a
bisexual Swiss diplomat called Eric Kessler, who had been
recruited as an agent by MI5. Kessler's codename was
'Orange' and his job was to feed Blunt and Burgess with as
much high-level diplomatic gossip as possible. It is not clear
whether or not Kessler knew that his information was also

being fed to Moscow. Kessler, whom Hewit said was 'very bright and very nice', had a suite at the Dorchester Hotel, which was also a base for Peter Pollock, Guy's companion from his holiday in the south of France in 1938. Pollock, too, had been recruited by Burgess to help MI5; he was asked to keep foreigners, especially Hungarians, under surveillance, while Hewit ran errands for British Intelligence, such as checking out a suspect priest in north London. Hewit – amongst the most reliable witnesses in the Burgess–Blunt circle – vigorously disputed the account of Bentinck Street given by people such as Rees. Hewit, who slept in Hunt's dressing room when he was in London, said:

> There were no orgies while I lived there – more's the pity. I wish there had been. There was only one big party while I was there and that was on my birthday in May, 1944. Everyone worked very hard. As for Anthony being promiscuous and going cottaging – I'm very doubtful about that. The only other person I know he went to bed with was Peter Montgomery. He was always so fastidious. He didn't really like the gay scene. He thought it was superficial.

Like Hewit, Burgess had no right to be involved in intelligence work. He had been fired after the débâcle of his abortive 'mission' to Moscow but he was determined to claw his way back. Christopher Harmer recalled:

> Burgess was always in and out of the office. He was a great friend of Guy Liddell. I don't think Liddell consciously gave him information but he was very indiscreet. He did talk a lot out of school. Liddell was rather high and mighty by my standards. He had the aura of a fictional secret service officer. But Burgess was a spiv. He was very good company and had a very active brain. He

had some sort of BBC job that allowed him to go bulldozing into every government department. I don't think I knew that he was gay. We were all very naïve about things like that.[34]

As far as anyone has been able to discover, Burgess's only *official* wartime employment at this time was with the BBC. He remained there until the summer of 1944 when he wriggled into a temporary job with the Foreign Office's press department, a job which gave him legitimate access to Whitehall's propaganda departments. He spent three years with the BBC's talks department, helping to produce 'Can I Help You?' and 'The Week in Westminster'.

The BBC was, as it had been before the war, an excellent base for Burgess. Working for the BBC carried social kudos and it gave him access to politicians, civil servants and journalists. From June 1942 he was able openly to promote the Soviet Union by, for example, inviting Ernst Henri to broadcast on the invincibility of the Red Army.

John Green, who worked alongside Burgess at the BBC in the late 1930s, used to have coffee every morning with his eccentric but highly entertaining colleague. He recalled:

We were bored with our colleagues who were mostly older than us. There were very few what I would call able-bodied men or women. We used to talk endlessly about treachery and politics. I don't think Guy was very worried about the Nazi–Soviet pact. I don't think he ever said to me that he was even a member of the Communist Party. He would have found the party very boring. I would have said that he was just wicked and hated anything that was boring. The one thing you couldn't do with Guy was be boring. But he was a good talks producer. Politicians like Harold Nicolson were always in the office. Guy liked Establishment people who were bored by the Establishment.[35]

David Graham had been a junior member of the talks department when Burgess first worked there. Shortly before the outbreak of war he transferred to the German-language service which broadcast to Germany. Although they no longer worked in the same section, Graham occasionally found himself sharing bomb-watch duties with Burgess on the roof of Broadcasting House. Graham recalled:

He was always full of ideas. I remember that he had always said what a splendid thing it would be if Anthony Blunt did some broadcasts. Blunt had done some programmes and they were, in fact, rather good. Burgess was terribly interested in politics, particularly in diplomacy. I didn't think of him as being a communist. I knew that he had always urged the BBC to appoint a diplomatic correspondent. I think he saw himself as being just the person for the job. He used to flaunt his old Etonian tie but he wasn't conservative. He just liked to shock conservatives.[36]

The British obsession with secrecy has meant that both the BBC and the government have held back files relating to Burgess. It is possible, however, that, apart from details on the programmes that he produced for the BBC, there are no records of his work during the war. He had always been a superb bluffer and blusterer and his various claims – that he was employed by the Ministry of Information or MI5 – may have been fantasies. By talking so convincingly about secret missions his friends, many of whom did work in government or intelligence, might actually ask him to do odd jobs, assuming that there was no harm in this since Guy already worked for their department.

Burgess made sure that he cultivated friends within the fast-expanding Ministry of Information in Malet Street, Bloomsbury. He tried hard, too, to give the impression that he was a key figure in the ministry. He cultivated Tomas Harris's sister, Enriqueta, who headed the Spanish desk and who was already a close friend of Blunt's. She was a considerable art scholar, as was her husband Henri Frankfort, whom she married after the war and who became director of the Warburg Institute. Burgess even managed to persuade the ministry to give a job to his old friend, the Cambridge history don, Steven Runciman. Burgess told Runciman that he was the assistant to the ministry's director. He was not, but Runciman was nonetheless given a job. 'I owe my war career to Guy. He was working in the Ministry of Information and they needed someone who knew Bulgarian. Guy knew that and so it was on his suggestion that I was brought in,'[37] Runciman said.

Then there was Princess Dil de Rohan, who headed the Swiss desk. Born in India, she derived her title from her marriage to a German aristocrat who had died in the early 1930s. She had been one of Berlin's best-known hostesses and had set up home with the Russian ballerina Katusha. They had an impressive collection of Picasso drawings which Blunt studied keenly when the couple moved to London. The princess was also a lover of Mary Oliver, a London society hostess who worked for a short time at the ministry. Oliver claimed to be the illegitimate daughter of Gurdjieff, the Russian-born occult teacher who died in Paris in 1949, a visionary of genius to his followers and a charlatan to his critics. Mary was the widow of Jock Oliver, a former president of Pop (the exclusive Etonian sixth form society). They lived in a large house called Pembroke

Lodge in Richmond Park, near Hilda Blunt's home on Ham Common.

The circle that Burgess and Blunt inhabited seethed with complex rivalries, many of them sexual, which were unfathomable to outsiders. There were ideological rows, too. Enriqueta Harris, for example, detested Kim Philby because he had been so obviously pro-Franco in his reporting of the Spanish Civil War. One member of the Blunt circle recalled how Pembroke Lodge was a magnet for Blunt and Burgess until it was destroyed in a bombing raid in 1943:

> Anthony and Guy enjoyed taking their mothers to Pembroke Lodge, which the Oliver family had bought in the early 1920s and had once belonged to the Royal Family. Mary Oliver, the Queen of Richmond Park, gave tremendous society parties. There were always MOI people around. You see, Guy and Anthony were tremendous snobs and Pembroke Lodge was very fashionable. At the same time Pembroke Lodge had also become the Commandos' GHQ during the first part of the war and in the grounds was Sir Watson Watt's topsecret radar station. That is another reason for Guy and Anthony being there. They enjoyed mixing fashionable society and espionage under one roof. When the house was destroyed Princess Dil and Katusha, who had been living there, moved to Lansdowne Terrace, Bloomsbury, which happened to have a good view of the public toilets that Tom Driberg used to use to pick men up.[38]

What did the Russians make of the jumble of gossip that Blunt and Burgess picked up from their sources at the Ministry of Information or MI5? Perhaps it was of no use; perhaps it was of marginal help in gauging the mood of the British Establishment. It is possible, but unprovable, that

Blunt and Burgess provided real secrets, which even they did not recognize as such, that changed Soviet strategy.

At 4 A.M. on Sunday 22 June 1941, the Germans attacked the Soviet Union. Within a few days the Red Army had lost hundreds of tanks and aircraft. Thousands of Russians had been taken prisoner. Churchill fumed at Stalin's wilfulness in ignoring warnings from Britain and from Soviet agents in Europe that the attack was being planned. Intelligence analysts in Whitehall reckoned that the Soviets would be able to resist for a maximum of six weeks.

Many British communists had mixed feelings. There was relief that the unholy pact with the Germans had proved to be what they had always argued it was: a device by Stalin to ensure that the capitalists could not turn the Germans east, and a ploy to give the Red Army time to prepare for the inevitable battle. But many communists also feared that Britain would now sue for peace with Hitler. The historian Noreen Branson noted many years later:

> Anxiety on this score had been rising ever since Hitler's deputy, Rudolf Hess, had suddenly on 10 May landed by parachute in Scotland and asked to see the Duke of Hamilton. It was widely assumed that Hess had come to try to negotiate a German-British deal against the Soviet Union . . . the statement issued on behalf of the Central Committee [of the CPGB] on 22 June reflected these fears. Saying that Hitler's attack against the Soviet Union was fascism's supreme aggression against the people of the world it demanded 'solidarity' with the Soviet Union . . . but it also said: 'We warn the people against the upper class reactionaries and the United States who will seek by every means to reach an understanding with Hitler on the basis of the fight against the Soviet Union. We have no confidence in the present

government, dominated by Tory friends of fascism and coalition Labour leaders who have already shown their stand by their consistent anti-Soviet slander campaigns.'[39]

Margot Heinemann remembered waiting anxiously for Winston Churchill's statement on the BBC on the evening of 22 June: 'I wasn't sure even then that Britain would not make peace with Hitler. Britain had never had any intention of making an alliance with the Russians and the Russians knew this.'[40] These fears proved groundless. That night Churchill said that while he had been an opponent of communism for twenty-five years, he now regarded the Soviet Union as an ally in the battle against the most evil regime in history:

> I will unsay no word that I have spoken about it [communism] but all this fades away before the spectacle which is now unfolding . . . We have but one aim and one single irrevocable purpose. We are resolved to destroy Hitler and every vestige of the Nazi regime . . . Any man or state who fights against Nazism will have our aid . . . It follows, therefore, that we shall give whatever help we can to Russia and the Russian people. We shall appeal to our friends and allies in every part of the world to take the same course. The Russian danger is our danger . . . just as the cause of any Russian fighting for his hearth and home is the cause of free men and free people in every quarter of the globe.

The CPGB central committee hurriedly reconvened. Churchill's statement had been so unequivocal that the party had to respond. On 4 July the party issued a new manifesto headed 'People's Victory over Fascism', which pledged that communists would now back any government measure aimed at ensuring victory over the Nazis. Harry Pollitt, who had been ousted from his job as party general secretary because he had argued that anyone who wanted to fight Hitler deserved the party's support, was reinstated. In December, after the Japanese had attacked Pearl Harbor and forced the Americans into the conflict, Pollitt commented: 'The issue is now clear: victory over the fascist barbarians and social progress; or defeat and a return to slavery.'

From June 1941 Stalin, for so long reviled by the British press, became lovable 'Uncle Joe'. Douglas Hyde, the editor of the *Daily Worker*, watched with amazement and amusement as Establishment figures such as the Dean of Canterbury and Churchill's wife, Clementine, lent their names to Anglo-Soviet aid committees. Meanwhile the CPGB membership soared; official figures put the party strength at 20,000 in early 1941 and at over 50,000 two years later.

The Cambridge spies were greatly relieved by the attack on the Soviet Union. Now, they told themselves, there was no question of treachery; they were helping an ally of Britain. Blunt was now a 'double patriot', serving his country *and* the Soviet Union, although, like many people on the Left, he remained suspicious of the long-term intentions of the British Establishment.

There was one officer within MI5 who was an expert at infiltrating the extreme Right and Left, and who still believed, despite the popular regard for the brave Soviets, in the threat posed by the communists. Charles Henry Maxwell (Max) Knight was a former Royal Navy officer who had joined MI5 in 1924 and had established a reputation as the service's most formidable and mysterious spy-catcher. He was known as 'M' or 'Captain King' or 'Mr K'. He was an author of natural history books, a zoologist, fencer, cricketer and jazz drummer. He was also fascinated by the occult. He relished the mystique of working for MI5 and self-consciously developed an unsettling persona. He used to stuff his pockets with live insects and casually tell colleagues that he slept with grass snakes to keep them warm. He was based at a flat in Dolphin Square, Chelsea, from where he ran his own semi-independent empire of agents and sub-agents. He had taken an instant and instinctive dislike to Blunt. One of Knight's officers, John Bingham, later Lord Clanmorris, said: 'Max once said of Blunt: I'm not letting that bugger anywhere near the office. I think Max just had an instinct about him.'[41]

One of Knight's agents was the journalist Tom Driberg, codenamed 'M8', who had joined the Communist Party on Knight's instructions before becoming a Labour MP in 1942. Driberg, later Lord Bradwell, died in 1976, aged seventy-one, after one of the more bizarre careers in recent British political life. In his autobiography, *Ruling Passions*, he was disarmingly open about his homosexual liaisons in public toilets, relating, for example, how he had been taken to court in 1935 after taking to bed two unemployed miners. He explained, too, without any hint of embarrassment, how he had used his influence with Beaverbrook to prevent the story being given the publicity it might have merited. His obituary in *The Times* opened with this tribute:

> Tom Driberg . . . was a journalist, an intellectual, a drinking man, a gossip, a high churchman, a homosexual, a liturgist, a friend of Lord Beaverbrook, an enemy of Lord Beaverbrook, an employee and biographer of Lord Beaverbrook . . . a stylist, an unreliable man of undoubted distinction. He looked and talked like a bishop, not least in the bohemian clubs which he frequented. He was the admiration and despair of his friends.

The Russians were naturally anxious to know the identities of Knight's moles within the communist movement in Britain. Driberg used to send written reports to Knight who was, according to Knight's personal assistant Joan Miller, 'sexually besotted by Tom'.[42] Blunt managed to read Driberg's reports and, after he had applied his well-trained brain to the problem, concluded that Driberg had to be the anonymous mole who had penetrated the CPGB. Blunt told his Soviet case officer who in turn passed the news to Harry Pollitt. Driberg was promptly expelled from the party, much to his surprise. He wrote in his autobiography:

> This shattering news was conveyed to me in a curiously hole-and-corner manner. I was on my way to a branch meeting with the comrade whom I liked best in Fleet Street, a print worker named Harry Kennedy. He had called for me at the *Express* office . . . he was rather silent and seemed ill-at-ease. Then he said, in an unnaturally formal way: 'I have been instructed to inform you that you are no longer a member of the Party . . . You have been expelled.' I protested furiously and asked why. Harry didn't know . . . I went to see the most influential Party members I knew . . . Dave Springhall (who was later jailed for espionage). Why, I asked: was it because of sex? Or religion? Or something I had written in my column? They were acutely embarrassed but seemed genuinely as much at a loss as I.[43]

Blunt was furious with his Soviet case officer for using his information in this hamfisted way. What would happen if Knight worked out where the leak had come from? Surely Driberg could have been dealt with more subtly? But fortunately, Knight was more preoccupied with defending his own position within MI5 than with tracing the source of the Driberg leak. He had embarrassed the service when

Harald Kurtz, one of his agents, who claimed to be a nephew of Queen Mary, alleged, quite mistakenly, that Benjamin Greene, who had been Ramsay MacDonald's Private Secretary, was a Nazi sympathizer. Greene (cousin of the novelist Graham Greene) was imprisoned under the wartime Regulation 18b, along with genuine fascists like Oswald Mosley. Only the intervention of the powerful Greene family led to his release. Knight never recovered from the affair.

In 1943, after Stalin abandoned the Communist International, Knight submitted a report to Liddell and Hollis entitled 'The Comintern is not dead'. It was rejected, although it did find its way to Churchill, who did not need to be told that the Russians still believed in undermining the capitalists from within. By then Britain and the Soviet Union were allies. Knight continued his surveillance of the CPGB and suspected sympathizers but he was now an isolated force, out of step with the rest of the intelligence world, which had just one aim – the defeat of Hitler – and which had no time to waste trying to prove that there was a long-term communist plot to undermine British democracy.

CHAPTER 12
Treachery Within

Until the early 1970s very little was known about the role that Station X, Bletchley Park, had played in the defeat of Hitler. Then, as the British government reluctantly loosened the grip of secrecy and Bletchley staff hesitantly began to describe the work that they had sworn never to discuss, it became clear that this had been an extraordinary and quite brilliant operation. It is doubtful if the full story of Bletchley will ever be told. The British government may never release all the official papers, many documents have been lost or destroyed and time has taken its toll of key personnel who could have filled vital gaps in our knowledge. However, enough is now known about Bletchley to be able to assess its contribution to Allied victory; but it is far more difficult, despite the emotive accusations of the tabloid press after Blunt's exposure, to gauge precisely how much damage spies like him caused.

Bletchley Park, Buckinghamshire, was the home of the Government Communications Headquarters, the cover name for the top secret Government Code and Cipher School. It was an unattractive Victorian mansion, bought in 1938 by MI6's Admiral Sir Hugh Sinclair as a base for the service's controlled code- and cipher-breaking operation.

Before the war, the Germans had developed a new and, so they thought, secure system of radio communication. The prototype of the Enigma cipher machine had been built in 1923 by a private company and by the early 1930s had been adopted and modified by the armed forces. One of the Bletchley codebreakers, Peter Calvocoressi, later a journalist and publisher, put it like this:

> The Enigma machine had a keyboard like a typewriter. The keys were electronically connected with one another by a system of drums. The orientation of the drums could be quickly changed in many different ways so that one day by pressing, say, the g key you printed an x, on another day you printed a k and on another day you printed a completely different letter. The German sender of a message would first tap it out on the Enigma machine and turn it into gobbledygook before transmitting it in morse by radio. The recipient of the message also needed an Enigma machine which could reverse the process – before translating the gobbledygook back to its original German. But he could only do this if he knew what the couplings on the sender's machine had been when he originated the message. So, for the British cryptographers, learning the mechanical secrets of the Enigma machine was only half the battle. They also had the task of deducing for each new group of messages how the Germans had set their machines . . . it was a daunting problem of mathematics and perseverance . . . endlessly complicated by the regularity with which the Germans changed the couplings of their Enigma machines. If I remember right, the settings were changed fundamentally every twenty-four hours and also in minor ways every eight hours. Moreover, there were dozens of different ciphers or sets of couplings in operation at the same moment. The quartermaster's network of the German army would be using a totally different cipher from the one simultaneously in use by the German Air Corps in Norway.[1]

The British had been given an Enigma machine by Polish Intelligence and by the summer of 1940 were able to decode, albeit with difficulty, many of the radio transmissions of the German army, navy, air force, intelligence and security services. The Germans must have assumed that their low-grade, non-Enigma coded traffic was being broken by the Allies but they remained confident, as far as historians have been able to discover, that Enigma was secure. If the Germans *had* known, then the consequences would have been disastrous. The need for a suffocating blanket of secrecy over Bletchley was obvious. By the end of the war over 10,000 people were working there but very few had any idea of what was happening outside their immediate section or any notion of how wide-ranging the operation was.

German radio transmissions were monitored and thousands of messages poured into Bletchley every week. Many proved impossible to decipher, often because the original coded transmission had been imperfectly transcribed. If the code-breakers managed to make sense of the message, they carefully copied it, complete with sign-on and sign-off signals called 'top and tail'. These were complete, literal translations of what the Enigma operator had sent a few days, even a few hours, earlier. A number of copies were then made and dispatched to key organizations in London: to Colonel Stewart Menzies, head of MI6, the nominal controllers of Bletchley, to military, air and naval intelligence. The quality of the Ultra intercepts varied enormously. These messages were of such vital and immediate importance, Calvocoressi remembered, that 'our commanders in the field were able to make operational use of them.' These were marked 'Top Secret Ultra'.[2] For example, in the autumn of 1942 following the battle of Alamein, Bletchley had been able to warn Montgomery's 8th Army in North Africa of a dangerous new tactic by

Rommel; there were Ultra intercepts between U-boats and their supply ships in the Atlantic which gave the British the expected future positions of the U-boats; and in the winter of 1941–42 the British supplied information to the Red Army which gave them a vital edge over the Germans – though the British were careful not to reveal to the Soviets how they knew so much about German plans. In addition there was a mass of apparently trivial messages: routine service orders transferring German troops and specialist back-up units. All this material was scrupulously filed and indexed. It was analysed at Bletchley and by intelligence officers in London.

The circulation in London of the literal Ultra translations was, in theory at least, tightly controlled. At first even senior British commanders in the field were not aware of the source of the intelligence that they received from Bletchley. They were led to believe that the information came from agents but, early in 1941 after it seemed that some British officers were disregarding the intelligence, they were told that it was the product of code-breaking. British commanders were given summaries of the German messages that Bletchley had broken. Calvocoressi explained: 'What if the Germans intercepted our transmissions to our field commanders? If we had sent literal translations of Ultra then it would have been obvious to the Germans that we were reading Enigma. We could not risk that.'[3]

Urgent Bletchley intercepts were sent by teleprinter to London. The rest went by dispatch rider. There was no reason to send the literal translations to MI5 whose requirements were specialized; they needed only to know the response to the work of the 'Double Cross' team and they needed to know what the Abwehr was doing, and summaries of Bletchley intercepts were quite sufficient for this. Professor Harry Hinsley, author of the official history of

British Intelligence during the war, said: 'Anyone of any intelligence knew that MI5 were totally unreliable. They were counter-spies. Everyone knew that they were crazy. Spies are crazy people and you need crazy people to catch them. We did not let MI5 know about Bletchley. Or rather they shouldn't have known about it.'[4]

Hinsley argued, too, that MI5 received only low-grade Ultra, sent by the Abwehr. That was, he said, 'easier to read and less sophisticated' than the codes sent, for example, by the German navy. It has to be said that other experts disputed this analysis; any Enigma traffic, they contested, was highly classified by the Germans.

Forty years later the experts were still arguing over how secret Ultra had been, and why the secret survived for so long. Professor M. R. D. Foot, at Combined Operations Headquarters and then with the SAS Brigade, was in close touch with the Supreme Headquarters Allied Expeditionary Force (SHAEF). He said:

I got the results from Bletchley but I never thought how did they come by them. I had at my elbow the order of battle of the German army and I thought it must have come from people poring over German newspapers. Most of us came from that great swathe of English society which had been taught to accept that there were some subjects that one didn't discuss in front of the servants and the children. We were the little boys and the senior officers were the grown-ups.[5]

Sir Robin Brook, who was responsible for organizing SOE operations in France and the Low Countries and who liaised closely with MI5 and MI6, said: 'There was an intense clampdown on who knew about Bletchley. I knew that there was a field of intelligence at Bletchley outside my sphere. And it was important that I did know that. But it was not important that I knew the quantity of work being done at Bletchley. It was a very closely guarded secret.'[6] The fact that the secret of Bletchley Park lasted for so long after the war suggests that only a handful of people knew enough to piece together a comprehensive picture. Equally, common sense suggests that during five years of war many more people than the authorities acknowledged picked up a broad outline of Bletchley's work. Professor Hinsley, for example, thought that the security cover was probably 'not totally effective'. Peter Calvocoressi recalled:

There was a certain amount of deduction among the top people at MI5. After a year or so the penny dropped. It was rather a question of them reaching a conclusion than being formally briefed. The view about MI5 was that they had to have contacts with all sorts of funny people and people from Bletchley were kept very carefully away from MI5 and them from us. There was always the risk that someone would talk in their sleep. The list of people who were supposed to know about Bletchley was very small but when the Ultra messages were sent to London quite a few people had access. It is astonishing, you know, how well kept the secret was.[7]

Dick White was emphatic:

Bletchley was an extremely well-kept secret. I knew because I was senior enough and because I had contacts. At Bletchley everything was highly compartmentalized and in London the list of people who had access to information about it was very small. But I now think that the Russians were alerted by these chaps [Blunt and Philby] to the fact that we were on to the German codes.

But the Russians had good reason not to let the Germans know this.[8]

Many of White's officers believed that more people knew about Bletchley than anyone realized during the war. At MI5's offices in St James's, Herbert Hart was responsible for sifting through the summaries of the Abwehr traffic that had been decoded at Bletchley. Christopher Harmer recalled: 'Hart and Blunt were in the same office. Hart was analysing intelligence, everything from Bletchley that came to us. Hart then passed it around. He was the clearing house. Blunt was more senior than I was and if I realized what was happening then so must he.'[9] Russell Lee, too, believed that Blunt knew, in broad terms certainly, about Ultra. 'There is no doubt that Blunt knew. Quite clearly it was accepted in some circles that we did know. Hardly anyone who was under Guy Liddell did not know.'[10] Another MI5 officer, Ashton Roskill (later Sir Ashton), one of the many lawyers in the service during the war, recalled: 'Within the office there was a fairly open exchange of information. I had a very high opinion of Blunt's abilities. He had access to a lot of information and he saw fit to disclose some of that to the Soviets. I don't suppose anyone gave Blunt's political opinions a thought. It did not seem important at the time.'[11]

Hugh Astor, son of Baron Astor of Hever, worked in 'two or three sections' of MI5 and therefore had a better idea than most of his colleagues, who tended to stay in one job throughout the war, of how the office worked. Astor, who became a close friend of Christopher Blunt, said:

I knew about Bletchley and I knew how they were getting it. Blunt would have known about Enigma. He certainly knew it existed. He was rubbing shoulders with people who were regularly receiving the intercepts. Within their own sections people talked freely to their colleagues. I didn't get all of the intercepts, of course. It was a very wide-ranging thing. Blunt was a man of great intelligence and charm. It was quite well known that Blunt was left-wing and that he was gay. But as far as we were concerned everyone was concerned with winning the war and one assumed that people [in MI5] were beyond suspicion.[12]

It has to be remembered, too, that Guy Liddell, the head of B Division who spent so much time with Blunt and Burgess, was, like Dick White, aware of the Enigma secret.

Group Captain Frederick Winterbotham, author of *The Ultra Secret* (1974), was better placed than many post-war experts to comment on the Bletchley operation. He was effectively responsible for deciding who received Ultra. He was based at MI6 headquarters in London and worked to Menzies, head of MI6, and took charge of feeding Ultra to Churchill:

It wasn't until 1941 that we really started to get to grips with the German codes. Before then the list of people who received Ultra was very limited indeed. Guy Liddell would have been one of the people who received it. I knew him very well. He was a good egg. No doubt about that. I think he was one of our best people, very reticent and very wise. I would have trusted him implicitly.[13]

Kim Philby was also doing his best to discover how the British knew so much about the Germans. Philby was in Section V of MI6 which was headed by Colonel Felix Cowgill. An ex-Indian policeman, Cowgill was a solid but unimaginative officer who was ill suited to the labyrinthine internal politics of the wartime secret world. Section V was an anomaly in MI6, the organization which had dedicated itself to spying, rather than spy-catching. One half of MI6 was responsible for agents overseas; the other for assessing the results of this spying and passing them to the relevant government and military departments. Section V was charged with liaising with MI5, passing to the security service information about enemy efforts to undermine the war effort in Britain. But Section V soon found that it was actively involved in counter-sabotage; running agents abroad as well as assessing their work. Philby, who specialized in the Iberian peninsula, watched with disbelief as Cowgill feuded continually over how much information he should pass to MI5. Cowgill was jealous about the material that he received from Bletchley. In his autobiography Philby noted:

> He realized at once that he had been dealt a trump card, and from the beginning he guarded it jealously, even to the point of withholding information that might have been put to effective use. His foes held him guilty of seriously restrictive practices . . . after a hassle with Cowgill, Dick White claimed to have a nightmare in which the material concerned was on sale at the newsstands.[14]

Winterbotham, a close friend of Cowgill, recalled: 'Cowgill made a point that we should not let people like Philby receive raw Ultra. I think that is why Philby attacked Cowgill in his autobiography. But I think that Philby undoubtedly would have been able to tell the Russians that we were reading Enigma.'[15]

The historian Hugh Trevor-Roper (Lord Dacre), who worked for a time in Section V, thought:

> There is an element of farce about this. Here we were, taking great trouble to disguise the source of the material

that we gave to the Russians after June 1941, and all the time Blunt and Philby were giving them stuff. The point was that we were worried about a leak from the Russians to the Germans. Blunt would have received Ultra of a certain kind. It was sent to his section of MI5. He was not named on the distribution list but Liddell was and they worked so closely together that Blunt would have known that Enigma was being broken. He would have seen material from the Abwehr but would also have known that military and naval Enigma was also being broken.[16]

Philby himself casually remarked that he had been fully indoctrinated (i.e. briefed on a confidential matter) on Bletchley:

> The efforts of Section V were at first supplemented by the Radio Security Service (RSS) which intercepted enemy intelligence signals, and by GC and CS [Government Code and Cipher School] which read them. Before the war had gone on long, these roles were in fact reversed. Section V's investigations abroad were directed mostly to filling in the gaps in the extraordinarily comprehensive picture derived from signals intelligence.[17]

Naturally the Soviets wanted to study the intercepts that were pouring out of Bletchley. They knew (one has to assume) that MI5 received only summaries of Ultra; these would have confirmed that the British were able to read some German codes but by themselves would not have indicated how this was happening or on what scale. Nor would the MI5 summaries have helped the Russians break the Enigma code; they would have needed, just as the British had done, a full working model of an Enigma machine. Nonetheless, Soviet Intelligence badly wanted documentary evidence from Bletchley and told its London agents that this had to be their priority.

Blunt was usually careful to avoid taking any documents out of MI5. On the one occasion he did risk slipping a Bletchley summary into his briefcase he came unnervingly close to being caught when he was questioned by a policeman in Hyde Park and asked what he was carrying in his briefcase. Dick White thought that Blunt was probably telling the truth when he later insisted that he had had to memorize information: 'It would be nonsense to suggest that Blunt was able to send suitcases of information to the Soviets. The whole thing was limited by the fact the Soviets worked in a very conspiratorial way – dead letter boxes and the like.'[18] Blunt would scribble down notes for his Soviet controllers – sometimes based on documents he had seen that day in the office, sometimes general appreciations of staff changes within British Intelligence or shifts in strategy – and then drop these notes in pre-arranged spots (the so-called post-box system). Sometimes he would actually meet his controller Anatoli Gorski, also known as Anatoli Gromov, codenamed 'Henry'. Officially Gorski was the press attaché at the Soviet embassy; he was a bad-tempered, humourless man who was never satisfied with the information that Blunt was providing. Blunt was, therefore, delighted when Gorski was posted to Washington in 1943, to be replaced by Yuri Modin, codenamed 'Peter', who proved far more understanding of the dangers facing Blunt (codenamed 'Johnson' by the Russians).

A rare insight into how Soviet Intelligence ran its agents came from an American communist called Elizabeth Bentley when she described after the war how Gorski had demanded that Americans who had been working for her should now report to him. Bentley, a government employee, remembered:

'You will turn them over to us,' he said. 'We will look
into their backgrounds thoroughly and decide which
ones we will keep.' By the early part of January [1944] all
my contacts had been turned over and I found myself
completely tired, mentally and physically, from the
strains of leaving them . . . I regarded them as my
friends – an attitude that the Communist Party frowned
upon.[19]

Bentley, who was based in Washington, also described how
the Soviets had offered to buy her a fur coat and an
air-conditioning system for her apartment and on one
occasion offered her cash. The Soviets hoped, of course,
that Bentley would accept the gifts and, thus, be finally
trapped as an agent. But she found the offer insulting.
There is no conclusive evidence that the Soviets were ever
as clumsy as this with the intellectual British spies. But it is
likely, though unproven, that Burgess's extravagant lifestyle, which was one of the reasons that he knew so much
about so many people, was supported by Soviet cash.
Philby admitted in Moscow that the Soviets had helped
launch his career as a war reporter. Blunt, too, received
small sums to cover out-of-pocket expenses. But, unlike
some of the Soviet spies arrested during the 1970s and
1980s, the Cambridge spies were not driven by the promise
of cash.

The Soviets had one other source for discovering more
about Bletchley: Leo Long. (John Cairncross, who worked
at Bletchley on German air force intercepts, never publicly
admitted passing information to Blunt although MI5 remained sure that he was guilty.) Long was an officer with
MI14, the German section in the Directorate of Military
Intelligence. The section was mainly concerned with
assessing the strength and organization of the German
army but there were also sub-sections which monitored

enemy intelligence. Long insisted that, unlike his fellow wartime spies, he had not wanted a job in intelligence:

> After I left Trinity College I had gone to Frankfurt to do some language coaching. Then the war came. I went into the Oxford and Bucks Light Infantry and then one day this captain said that military intelligence desperately needed people with languages and we were told to put our names forward. I was commissioned into the intelligence. God, no, no one asked me about my politics. We were all against Hitler. I started off around December 1940 as a second lieutenant with MI14. I had no choice. It was sheer chance.[20]

Long remembered the grinding workload at MI14. The teleprinters chattered continually in the bomb-proof basement of the offices in central London, spewing out increasing amounts of information from the code-breakers at Bletchley. It had to be interpreted and summarized so that Britain's military chiefs knew the precise strength of German army units and the enemy's latest strategies. The strain threatened to break Long's health; at one point he was warned that he might have developed tuberculosis from working sixteen hours a day for six, sometimes seven, days a week. Then Blunt appeared. Long said:

> Blunt came into the office on business for MI5. That was the first time that I knew that he was in intelligence. But Blunt didn't say: 'Now, you've got to start giving me information.' He just started to go on at me. He said that we were all on the same side. That the Russians would win the war. We weren't sure that the British were giving the Russians as much information as they should. Blunt said that he had this friend . . . I was slightly nervous [about agreeing to help]. The thought crossed my mind

that Blunt was a genuine MI5 officer and that I was being led up the garden path.[21]

To his credit, Long never claimed that his agreement to help Blunt to pass top-secret intelligence to the Soviets came after the invasion of the Soviet Union. Long admitted that he did not know when he began to work for Blunt.

> I can't put a date on this and I honestly can't say whether it was before or after June 1941. In a way it's a meaningless question to ask me. I can't remember if the Soviet Union was an ally of Britain or not. I am not trying to whitewash myself but whether the Soviets were allies one day or the next did not matter all that much. Blunt knew my political sympathies. After all, my name had been given to him before he had even started supervising me at Trinity, probably by James Klugmann. I would not have done anything to impair the military power of this country. That's an objective statement, not a defence for what I did. I am not justifying people taking it upon themselves to override the rules of their country. I have to say that I didn't like the whole thing.[22]

The two men established a routine that lasted for three years. They would meet once a week if Long had been especially resourceful; once a fortnight if the MI14 teleprinters had not been that busy. Sometimes they met in snack bars – Rainers, on the corner of the Haymarket and Jermyn Street, was a favourite – sometimes in pubs. Long was always nervous, fearing that one day 'a hairy hand might come down and say, "I've got you."' The notes that Long had made were passed beneath the table, as both men watched for any signs that they were under surveillance. They had a cup of tea and a sandwich or a pint of beer and then parted – Blunt to deliver Long's material to Anatoli

Gorski, Long to return to MI14 wondering if he was still safe. Long said:

> Blunt never really commented on what I was giving him. He indicated once or twice that his masters did not think they were getting enough from me. At times he tried to get me to widen what I was giving him. He wanted details of personalities within the War Office. I just ignored him. All intelligence services, British, Soviet, it doesn't matter, have this obsession about getting the other side's order of battle [the internal structure of a military or intelligence unit]. I don't know why the Soviets were interested. After all, many of the people in the War Office were not professionals and would not be there after the war. And they were all moving around all the time. I never handed documents to him, just written notes. And there was never any question of money. I have no doubt that it was a breach of the Official Secrets Act. It was the arrogance of a young man who thought that he was doing something for a wider cause. We didn't discuss much. I was nervous but Blunt was always very controlled. He gave the impression that he was master of the situation, which he was. He looked gaunt, deadpan, as if he was working and playing very hard. He was certainly working bloody hard for his country like we all were, whatever he was doing for others. You have to remember that we did not have that much in common. And we never discussed politics. But there wasn't really any politics then. Surviving and fighting was pretty much a full-time occupation.[23]

Long insisted that he censored the information that he gave Blunt. This illogical, residual patriotism meant that he refused to pass 'raw Ultra', since that would have seemed 'uncommonly like treason'. One suspects, though, that

Long was also terrified of being caught with classified documents. But there was no doubt that Long was in a position to explain what was happening at Bletchley in far greater detail than many officers in other branches of the secret world. He said:

> I had never been to Bletchley but I knew what was happening there. I saw a lot of the material that came from there to our office. Yes, I knew about Ultra, though it had different names in different places. But I never passed that to the Russians. I gave them intelligence assessments based on it.[24]

For a time, Long was convinced that the British were not giving the Soviets as much information as they were morally obliged to; hence, he salved his conscience by telling himself that he was really only filling in the gaps left in the Soviets' knowledge by Whitehall. But that comforting thought was shattered when Long realized that the British were *not* holding back significant data. However, that did not mean that he refused to help Blunt. He was increasingly uneasy and reluctant, but he was still a communist and retained that blind loyalty to Moscow that non-Marxists find so incomprehensible. Meeting Blunt became a chore: 'I didn't have the nerve to go to Blunt and say, "Look, I'm finished." I used to think, "Christ, I've got to meet Blunt. I must cobble together something for him. I must write something up for him." '[25]

Long became an expert on what he called the German para-military units, such as the Gestapo and the SS. He was even asked to lunch at Claridges by an American film director who wanted his advice on SS uniforms. Long was naturally anxious to minimize his importance to the Soviets, but there is no way to assess whether the information which he handed to Blunt changed the course of the war or Soviet attitudes towards the Allies. Did he inadvertently betray anti-Nazi (and anti-communist) agents working in Europe? Some of MI14's intelligence came, as Long admitted, from agents. Did he fuel Soviet mistrust of the British by passing on information which the British had, for some reason, decided that the Soviets should not be given? Did he, at the very least, help confirm Soviet fears about the British by proving that they had a regular, reliable source which they would not share? Noel Annan, also a member of MI14 during the war, had strong views on Long:

> You were under instructions, an order, a military order, that all this material was secret. It was not the job of any intelligence officer to take it upon himself to communicate it to the Russians. Nor was there any reason to do this. There were ways in which material from Bletchley was passed to the Russians. But, of course, the Russians weren't told. No doubt they guessed but it was essential, the whole security for the invasion of Europe depended on it, that Ultra was kept secret. It could easily have been captured from the Russians in a German offensive. It was monstrous to communicate this material to the Russians. I have no sympathy with the argument that the Russians should have been told. None at all. That was the job of the British government. But then Long had the same sort of arrogance which Blunt had. The two were very alike in temperament. Long was very dismissive about anything which didn't coincide with his views.[26]

Long said that after three years as a Soviet spy he had had quite enough. He managed to engineer a transfer to Montgomery's 21st Army Group:

> I didn't tell Blunt that I had wanted this. He thought that this was either a normal posting or that I was under

suspicion. I had wanted to get away from the whole thing. Oh yes, I had been frightened. What I had done had been a treasonable offence. It all seems unreal and very remote now.[27]

By early 1944 Hitler's forces were in retreat, slowly yet inexorably, throughout Eastern Europe. In Britain there was feverish speculation over when and where, rather than if, the Allies would open a second front. Guy Burgess, who had slipped into a temporary job with the Foreign Office's news department, helping to ensure that British propaganda spoke with a united voice, was telling friends that the Allies should move as quickly as possible. At Bentinck Street the stream of friends all claimed to have special inside knowledge about the future of the war. Blunt's adoring friend Peter Montgomery was now with the Intelligence Corps and Goronwy Rees had moved from the Royal Welch Fusiliers to Montgomery's 21st Army Group.

In his autobiography Rees talked excitedly about those days in 1944:

I was at that time almost totally immersed in all the details of the invasion; I thought of nothing but beach gradients, underwater obstacles, tables of moon and tide and weather, figures of reinforcements, subversive activity, army-air support, and all the other factors which had to be fitted in precisely to the framework of that immense operation. The work of the planning staff, which for reasons of security was restricted to a minimum, was hard, the hours were long and an evening at Guy's flat was like some fantastic entertainment devised specifically to take one's mind off one's labours, though I doubt very much if Field-Marshal Montgomery would have greatly approved it. Watching, as if in a theatre, the extraordinary spectacle of life as lived by Guy, I felt rather like some tired business man who had taken an evening off to visit a strip-tease club.[28]

There is another, more interesting passage which emphasizes that Rees could be just as suspect a witness as Burgess. Rees wrote:

> Sometimes I used to remember that once . . . he had asked me to help him in his work as an agent, and it used to amuse me to think that at that moment I happened to be in possession of what I suppose was one of the most valuable, the most important and best kept secrets of the war; this is to say, the exact date, time and place of the invasion of Normandy, the precise naval, military and air force order of battle involved, and the fact that we had misled Stalin about the date at which we intended to launch the operation.[29]

If we are to believe Rees, he no longer thought that Burgess, despite still professing his communism, was a security risk. After all, argued Rees, Burgess shared a flat with Anthony Blunt, 'an extremely important member of the security services'. Clearly, Rees continued, all Guy's talk in the 1930s about him and Anthony working for the Soviets had been either exaggeration or fantasy. If Anthony Blunt was trusted by MI5, then that was good enough for him. Next Rees suggested that he was so trusted by the D-Day planners that he was involved in the most secret planning for the invasion. Both claims are dubious. The first claim – that he was unaware of Burgess's continuing flirtation with Soviet Intelligence – was never accepted by Burgess and Blunt, by many of their friends or by MI5. It is easy to accuse a dead man but, if nothing else, a very large question mark hangs over this claim. His second assertion brought this response from Sir Robin

Brook, the SOE officer who had become an adviser on special projects to General Eisenhower, the Supreme Allied Commander:

> Rees was quite capable of inventing knowledge of D-Day [in his autobiography]. Rees was a character with a query against him because of his contacts with the Russians. He was a truth twister. He was on the list of shady characters. I was aware that he was not trustworthy. Only a few people in central planning knew the details of D-Day. There was only one country that we were concerned to keep it from. And that was Germany. But we did not want to let the French know. They were quite capable of blowing it out of naïvety. But there was so much going on that it did become easier to interpret.[30]

Hugh Trevor-Roper also thought it possible that, as the number of people involved in the preparations for the invasion rose, men such as Blunt and Rees did pick up details of the plans:

> I was told about a month beforehand. Guy Liddell and Dick White would also have been told. If the plans had leaked then the whole thing could have been wrecked. If the Russians had thought that they could win the war on their own we would have been butchered on the beaches. I don't know if Blunt was told and I don't know if he would have dared to leak it. That would have been high treason. Harold Macmillan once said to me, 'Thank goodness, Blunt was so feeble.'[31]

According to Dick White, who moved to SHAEF to head the counter-intelligence team that would sweep into Europe with the 21st Army Group, Blunt was not involved in D-Day planning, although some historians have suggested that Blunt was a liaison officer between SHAEF and MI5, helping coordinate the Allies' efforts to deceive the Germans over the place and date of the landing. White recalled:

> I was a member of Eisenhower's staff and head of counter-intelligence. Blunt was not really at SHAEF. He was brought in by the fine arts people in London after the invasion to come over to Europe to try and find some of the works of art that had been stolen by the Nazis. I think he must have gone to Paris. He was brought over purely as an art historian. Goronwy Rees was, I imagine, an ordinary military intelligence officer with Montgomery's staff. You have to remember that even Eisenhower did not know the exact date of the landing. We sat and wondered what was happening because of the weather. I think it was all a fairly well-kept secret.[32]

In fact, according to other MI5 officers, Blunt went to Rome first before being posted to Paris.

As the war drew to a close in 1945, Anthony Blunt bumped into Tar Robertson, the former 'Double Cross' team chief. Robertson recalled that Blunt wanted to chat:

> It all seems very odd now, looking back on it. I think we were talking about what would happen after the war and talking about how we would react to the Russians. Then he said something like this: 'It has given me great pleasure to have been able to pass the names of every MI5 officer to the Russians.' Or whatever he called them. I was taken aback. I thought: why should he tell me this? It was an electrifying remark. I couldn't keep it under my hat. I suppose I must have told Guy Liddell.[33]

Only Blunt would have been able to explain why he made this extraordinary statement. Was he goading MI5, daring them to question him? Was it an aberration, the result of years of strain, of fearing that he could be caught and knowing that he had lied to colleagues who had trusted him? There is no evidence that Liddell did anything after Robertson told him what Blunt had said. Presumably Liddell dismissed it as a poor joke by his erudite friend who had made the war so much more bearable. But many years later, when MI5 (and the press) hunted for Blunt's accomplices, Liddell's failure to take Blunt's 'joke' seriously looked suspicious. Had Liddell, too, been a Soviet agent? But if that, surely, was too preposterous then perhaps he had allowed a friendship to influence his judgement; in other words, perhaps Liddell had been culpably naïve? By the time that Liddell's reputation was being savaged in this way he was no longer alive to defend himself; he had become, like many others, a victim because he had once been a friend of Anthony Blunt.

CHAPTER 13
The Palace Royal

On 28 April 1945, two days before Hitler committed suicide in the Berlin bunker, the *Daily Express* carried this news item:

Sir Kenneth Clark, Director of the National Gallery, has ended his search for a man to replace him as Surveyor of the King's Pictures. Major Anthony Blunt has been appointed. Like Sir Kenneth, Major Blunt has youth on his side; he is not a painter but in his thirty-seven years he has covered a wide field of art appreciation. Major Blunt now holds a hush-hush job at the War Office. This, he tells me, will claim his attention for some time. Meanwhile he will start the arrangement of the King's collection and continue as (deputy) Director of the Courtauld Institute of Art. Sir Kenneth tells me he has given up the surveyorship because he feels that the National Gallery is a full-time task now that the pictures, gone to earth during the war, are being brought back to the light.

On 30 April the London *Evening Standard* ran this background story:

You can look in vain in the usual reference books for mention of Mr Anthony Frederick Blunt, the new Surveyor of the King's Pictures, but this thin, lively-minded and scholarly person is well-known to modern artists. He is thirty-six, and a specialist in seventeenth-century art. With the rank of major he works at the War Office. He keeps an eye on the direction of the Courtauld Institute of Art during its Director's absence in the Middle East. He is also at work on a catalogue of the French drawings at Windsor Castle. He will have the task of looking after the pictures at Buckingham Palace, at Windsor and at Hampton Court. I expect he will also follow the practice of Sir Kenneth Clark, his predecessor, of acting as adviser to the King and Queen on buying pictures.

Sir Kenneth Clark had been Surveyor since July 1934. He had never enjoyed the job, which he hadn't wanted in the first place. (Clark could not see the point of working for a king such as George V who thought the royal collection was in excellent order.) The accession of George VI in December 1936 had made Clark's life easier, for the new king took an interest in the progress of the work that needed to be done. Clark persuaded the palace to allow him to appoint a deputy, Benedict Nicolson, son of Burgess's friend, Harold Nicolson, and together they arranged the evacuation of the royal treasures to Wales in 1939.

The royal collection had been built up over five centuries. Sir Oliver Millar, who was appointed Assistant Surveyor in 1947, Deputy Surveyor in 1949 and Surveyor when Blunt retired in 1972, wrote in 1977:

The great inventory of Queen Victoria's pictures, compiled by her Surveyor of Pictures, Richard Redgrave, in 1879 contained nearly five thousand items. He had made sheets for drawings, enamels, pictures on china and the like, which happened to be hanging on the walls as pictures; but, taking into account subsequent additions, the royal collection can, by now, hardly number less than five thousand pictures . . . This huge collection is the property of the Crown, held in trust for the nation by the Queen during her lifetime and administered, as it was when Redgrave's first recorded predecessor was appointed by Charles I in 1625, under the supervision of the Lord Chamberlain from whom the Surveyor of Pictures still receives his warrant to look after the pictures and help as far as possible those who enquire about them.[1]

The collection dated from the Tudors and had been built up by generations of English kings and queens, consorts and princes; it reflected their likes and dislikes, friendships, loves, hates, idiosyncrasies and obsessions and the network of dynastic associations that made up European royalty. It was Charles I, who came to the throne in 1625, who first saw the need for 'the services of a professional custodian' for the collection. Charles spent several fortunes buying pictures from around Europe, much to the fury of his critics who accused him of 'squandering away millions of pounds on old rotten pictures and broken-nosed marbles'. The master artist Rubens had no such objections. He noted 'the incredible quantity of pictures, statues and ancient inscriptions which are to be found in this Court'. In May 1625 Charles created a new appointment within the royal household: he made Abraham van der Doort, a Dutch craftsman, the Overseer or Surveyor of 'all our pictures of Us, Our Heires and Successors . . . at Whitehall or other our houses of resort'. The job was for life and was worth the then comfortable annual salary of £40. The duties of the surveyor were also outlined:

[T]o prevent and keepe them (soe much as in him lyeth) from being spoiled or defaced, to order marke and number them, and to keepe a Register of them, to receive and deliver them, and likewise to take order for the makeing and coppying of Pictures as Wee or the Lord Chamberlaine of Our Household shall directe. And to this End . . . hee shall have Accesse at convenient Times unto Our Galleries Chambers and other Roomes where Our Pictures are.

Much of the collection painstakingly built up by Charles was sold off by order of the Commons after his execution in 1649; the money raised, it was said, should go towards 'publick Uses of this Commonwealth'. It was ironic, thought Oliver Millar, that 'the great European royal collections, which with the passage of time and in the course of revolutionary change ultimately formed the nucleus of the permanent national collections in Paris, Vienna and Madrid, should have been enriched by plundering, with the active encouragement of a revolutionary regime [in England], a collection which had been honestly acquired.'

The accession of Charles II in 1660 led to a massive, only partially successful, effort to recover what remained in England of Charles's treasures. From that date until the present day, each monarch has, to varying degrees, relied on the Surveyor of Pictures to advise on the state of the collection – and on ways to improve it. The collection that Blunt took charge of in 1945 had been extensively enlarged by Queen Victoria and Prince Albert: 'Between them they acquired or commissioned many pictures: a few were good; hundreds were repetitive, indifferent or worse; and a handful were masterpieces of rare quality and great significance . . . Their patronage of contemporary painters was narrow and prejudiced.'[2] If Victoria's artistic tastes were questionable she had, at least, ordered a review of the organization of the royal collection; paintings were scattered without order around the palaces and, in many cases, were rotting away after years of neglect. Queen Mary, the Blunt family's friend, 'never managed to buy a good or important picture' although she did spend hours 'neatly labelling her acquisitions, carefully recording them in her own faultlessly compiled catalogues'. George VI and Queen Elizabeth II were both determined to inject freshness and originality into the sagging royal collection. The Queen wanted 'good, amusing or attractive pictures; a new purchase, ideas for a more effective display of existing works, suggestions for new frames could and did delight her'.

The appointment to the historic office of Surveyor delighted Blunt. The title was confirmation of his standing in the world of art history. It carried social clout, even if most people had no idea what the job involved; most mistakenly imagined that Blunt spent the evenings drinking port with King George VI. The title sat easily on Blunt, who was more conscious than anyone of his family's ties with the Royal Family. He must have found it reassuring too; it was not conceivable, surely, that anyone within British Intelligence would doubt his loyalty and, even if they had, no one would dare to suggest a royal appointee was a traitor. However, there is no evidence to suggest that his new job was part of some complicated plot by the Soviet intelligence service – there were no secrets among the libraries and art collections of the royal households. But some of his friends were not impressed. Sir Ellis Waterhouse, who had spent the war in intelligence in the Middle East, thought the job was a waste of time and effort:

I thought it was an insane thing for Anthony to do. So many silly duties. The collection is interesting but it takes up a lot of time. Maybe he was instructed by the Russians to take it, I don't know. After Anthony was exposed in 1979 he said to me, You know, Ellis, the only time I thought you might ever suspect me was when I became

Surveyor. Why did he do it? Well, he was very keen on doing anything that would help the prestige of the Courtauld and this did. I remember that when Oliver Millar became assistant surveyor (in 1947) his parents were very worried that he would be working alongside such a notorious queen as Blunt. You'll gather by that that everyone knew about Anthony's personal habits by then.[3]

To bring some semblance of order to the huge royal collection of paintings and drawings would have been a challenge for any art historian. Cataloguing is one of the supreme tests; it is the vehicle for demonstrating mastery of the subject. Faced with hundreds of works, the art historian has to analyse each work. When was it made? Was it the creation of a master artist or was it farmed out to the master's team of helpers? How should the work be dated and how does it fit into the known sequence of the master's career? In 1945 the technical aids that Blunt could draw on were limited, but as science developed more efficient methods of analysing paint pigments and canvas compositions, so he had to take greater note of the verdicts of his backroom laboratory staff, balancing their results against his own instinctive judgements. The cataloguer has to have a mental file on the changing composition of the paints and papers that have been used through the centuries, but technical data are not enough. George Steiner, the poly-math academic, thought that mastery of such 'intricate minutiae' was only the preliminary step. Other qualities were also vital: the ability to draw on a mental data bank of thousands of artists and the imagination to visualize the precise historical setting in which each painting or drawing was composed. But without total honesty all these qualities mean nothing:

Blunt's paternal grandparents, *c.* 1903. His grandfather was the Bishop of Hull

Blunt's maternal grandparents, friends of Queen Mary, at Montrose House, Petersham, Surrey

Blunt's father, the Reverend Stanley Blunt, then vicar of Ham, Surrey, 1902

In the vicarage garden, Holy Trinity, Bournemouth *c.* 1909. Left to right: Delling (Blunt's nurse), Anthony Blunt, and his brothers – Wilfrid and Christopher

ABOVE: The three Blunt brothers pose for the camera: (from left) Anthony, Wilfrid, Christopher

BELOW: Anthony Blunt, aged about ten, at St Peter's preparatory school, Seaford, Sussex, where he was a pupil for a short period

RIGHT: With his parents in Paris, 1921. They frequently visited the Parc Monceau, a public garden with mock ruins near the rue Jouffroy

ABOVE: Public school rebels. Anthony Blunt and the poet Louis MacNeice, with John Hilton, later a diplomat and writer. Photographed in 1926

LEFT: Guy Burgess, the Cambridge undergraduate and committed Marxist, taking the sun by the River Cam, 1932

BELOW: A snapshot taken by John Lehmann at Cambridge in 1929 or 1930 shows (from left to right) Anthony Blunt, Donald Lucas (also an Apostle), an unidentified companion, Julian Bell, and Jean Stewart (daughter of a Cambridge don)

Kim Philby, perhaps the most enigmatic of the Cambridge spies, at Cambridge in 1934. He kept in touch with Blunt for many years after he fled to Moscow

Andrew Gow, the Cambridge classics don and art enthusiast, who became Blunt's mentor

Michael Straight at Cambridge, 1936: the young American undergraduate whom Blunt tried to recruit as a spy

Victor Rothschild, a member of the well-known banking family, photographed while at Trinity College, Cambridge, where he became close friends with Blunt and Guy Burgess, c. 1932

Lytton Strachey's photograph shows (left to right): Anthony Blunt, Francis Warre-Cornish, Dickon Steel, George 'Dadie' Rylands, and Eddie Playfair, afterwards a distinguished Whitehall civil servant. After Blunt's confession in 1964 that he was a Soviet agent, Playfair was also interviewed (and cleared) by MI5 about his friendship with Blunt

A gathering of Apostles: (from left) Anthony Blunt, Alister Watson, Richard Llewelyn-Davies, Andrew Cohen, Hugh Sykes-Davies, Julian Bell. Apostles rarely posed for group photographs, partly through the Society's insistence on secrecy

ABOVE LEFT: George 'Dadie' Rylands, Cambridge don, poet and friend of Blunt

ABOVE RIGHT: Lady Mary Dunn, a former débutante whom Anthony Blunt thought of marrying, on her wedding day to Philip Dunn, son and heir of the industrialist Sir James Dunn

LEFT: Margot Heinemann, lifelong communist, pictured at Cambridge in 1932

BELOW: Left-wing writers Rosamond Lehmann and her brother John, with Bloomsbury celebrity Lytton Strachey, c. 1930

ABOVE LEFT: Professor Maurice Dobb, Cambridge economist and driving force behind the Marxist university movement

ABOVE RIGHT: Julian Bell, left-wing activist, who briefly fell in love with Blunt. He was later killed in the Spanish Civil War

RIGHT: Dick White, who later headed MI5 and MI6, at Oxford, *c.* 1926

John Cornford, idol of the student communist movement at Cambridge in the 1930s. He was later killed in the Spanish Civil War

Otto Katz, propagandist and Soviet agent of influence

Willi Muenzenberg, the most influential of the Comintern organizers. He was murdered in 1940 by Stalin's agents

Cambridge students heading for Leningrad and the promised Soviet utopia, 1935. Left to right: Michael Straight, Brian Simon (who never lost his Marxist faith), Charles Fletcher-Cooke (later a Conservative MP) and Anthony Blunt

Donald Maclean at Cambridge, 1934. Already a fervent Marxist, he kept his allegiance to communism until his death in Moscow almost half a century later

Lieutenant Anthony Blunt, photographed by his brother Christopher in September 1939, shortly before being posted to France with the field security police

Lord Thurlow, a former diplomat and Governor and Commander-in-Chief of the Bahamas, who was recruited to the Communist Party at Cambridge in the early 1930s. In term time he sold the *Daily Worker* while in the holidays he went fox-hunting and shooting

Rt Hon. Lord Justice Cumming-Bruce, a distinguished Lord Justice of Appeal, who as a Cambridge undergraduate in the early 1930s recruited students to the Communist Party. He is the twin brother of Lord Thurlow

Anthony Blunt on a military
intelligence course at Minley
Manor, October 1939

Tom Driberg, Labour MP, MI5
agent and promiscuous
homosexual

Jack Hewit, Burgess's faithful companion and Blunt's occasional lover,
photographed in 1946 and 1965

RIGHT: Baron Wolfgang zu Putlitz, German anti-Nazi and diplomat who worked for British intelligence before and during the war. Later he wrote a book which he dedicated to his close friend, Anthony Blunt. Photographed in 1958
BELOW: Anthony Blunt in the mid-1950s with Johannes Wilde and Wilde's wife, Judith. John Steer, later a professor at Birkbeck College, London, is in the foreground
FOOT: Anthony Blunt, wearing a white shirt and with his back to the camera, discussing art in the 1950s with students and staff from the Courtauld. His secretary, Elsa Scheerer, is sitting, hand over mouth, to Blunt's immediate left

Kim Philby at his mother's London flat, telling the press why he was not the 'third' man (1956)

Jim Skardon, the MI5 interrogator who tried to break Kim Philby

Guy Burgess relaxing in the sun in Russia in 1956, the year in which he and Donald Maclean appeared at a press conference to explain why they had defected to Moscow five years before

ABOVE: Anthony Blunt in his role as royal art adviser, 1959

RIGHT: With his brother Christopher in 1958, the year Anthony's friend Guy Burgess announced he wanted to visit Britain

BELOW: Blunt's beloved painting *Eliezer and Rebecca at the Well* by Poussin. Blunt left this picture to his longstanding companion John Gaskin; it is now in the Fitzwilliam Museum, Cambridge

Goronwy Rees, the Welsh academic who denied being a member of the Burgess-Blunt spy ring, 1971

A J P Taylor, Oxford historian, sitting in his Oxford garden. Taylor thought that Blunt's exposure in 1979 provoked an hysterical reaction

Sir Dennis Proctor, the Whitehall civil servant who was interrogated by MI5 about his friendship with Guy Burgess and Anthony Blunt

Captain Peter Montgomery, former intelligence officer during the war and ADC to Lord Wavell in India, who met Blunt at Cambridge and became a lifelong friend

Peter Wright, the MI5 officer who led the hunt for communist spies in the British establishment. Pictured in Australia, 1984

Alister Watson, a Cambridge Apostle and Admiralty scientist interrogated for weeks by MI5. Pictured in 1981

Leo Long, Cambridge Apostle and British intelligence officer, who admitted passing secrets to Blunt and the Russians during the war. Pictured in 1981

John Cairncross, pictured in Rome in December 1979. He always denied passing secrets to the Russians, although he admitted passing information to Guy Burgess

LEFT: Brian Sewell, art writer, who stood by his friend Anthony Blunt in 1979

BELOW: Anthony Blunt faces the press: November 1979

The business of attribution, description and dating demands complete integrity on the technical level. Margins must be measured to the millimetre; successive impressions from an original plate or woodblock must be almost microscopically differentiated if the sequence is to be numbered correctly. But in this area there are also pressures of a moral and economic kind. The outright value of a painting or drawing or engraving, the worth of a sculpture on the crazed art market depend immediately on expert attribution. The temptations are notorious.[4]

Oliver Millar, an old Marlburian and a former Courtauld student, thought any reasonable art historian could produce a good catalogue: 'I have come to the conclusion that it is a form of escapism. Once you have learned it you go slogging on.' Even after Blunt's exposure in 1979 most of Blunt's peers, whatever their views on the particular merits of cataloguing, remained faithful to his reputation as a scrupulously honest historian. True, they admitted, he had lied about politics but his art history was unaffected by prejudice. Throughout his life Blunt had emphasized to his students that they had to adopt the motto of Aby Warburg, founder of the Warburg Institute: God, said Warburg, lurks in the detail. It was this honesty, coupled with his prodigious energy and ability to research and write with what was, by the standards of the academic world, lightning speed, which Steiner thought enabled Blunt 'literally [to] put in order central rooms in the house of Western art'. His output was enormous: his catalogue of the drawings of Poussin began to appear in 1939; there was a succession of bulky volumes on the royal collection; there were books on general artistic trends and articles for learned journals. He masterminded the cataloguing of the James A. de Rothschild collection at Waddesdon Manor, near Amersham, one of the finest private art collections in the world. And

Blunt was involved for over twenty years as one of the editors in a series of books on architecture.

However, there were a few heretics who questioned Blunt's fidelity to the truth. The arrogance that offended so many people did, said some colleagues, show itself in a stubbornness about accepting other opinions – especially if they cut across his own theories. Professor Stephen Rees-Jones joined the Courtauld in 1935 after graduating from University College, Bangor, in Wales. He spent the war as a scientist working on aircraft production and then rejoined the Courtauld as its scientific expert. Sometimes he found that Blunt refused to accept unequivocal scientific evidence – though it has to be added in Blunt's defence that most art historians rely as much on instinct as on results obtained in a laboratory. Rees-Jones said:

> I used to examine pigments, oils, canvases. But Blunt was very selective when I presented scientific evidence to him. He would only accept my findings if it suited him. But as a man of science I was only concerned with the truth. He would ignore evidence. You can't do that with scientific evidence. After he became Director of the Courtauld in 1947 he ruled it like a mediaeval court. He was the prince and we were the court.[5]

The art historian Denis Mahon, a lifelong adversary of Blunt, went even further: 'Once you get away with lying on one subject, it spills over into the rest of your life and that is what happened with Blunt, he became a practised liar.'[6]

Blunt's critics, however, had to keep their doubts to themselves as he went from one triumph to another. The response to Blunt's first major catalogue had been enthusiastic. Entitled *The French Drawings in the Collection of His Majesty the King at Windsor Castle*, it was published in 1945 and was hailed as a major artistic triumph. It was over

150 pages of detailed, academic descriptions of more than 500 drawings which Blunt had researched in the last two years of the war. General readers would have found most of this dull and rather baffling. It was an academic exercise, intended to help other scholars in their assessment of the artists whose works were stored at Windsor. Each drawing is carefully summarized. For example, drawing number 345, 'Studies of men's heads, in Pen and Indian ink wash, attributed to Bernard Picart':

As far as can be ascertained at present no engravings exist exactly reproducing these drawings, but several of the heads in no. 344 and the middle head on the left-hand side of no. 345 appear in slightly different form in engravings by Picart, reproduced by M. Leloir, *Histoire du Costume*, c x pl. 34. (page 61)

Or of the drawing by Jean Michel Moreau the Younger, an Illustration to Ariosto, *Roger and Alcina*:

These two drawings are preparations for engravings in the Italian edition of the Orlando Furioso edited by P. and G. Molini and published by Baskerville in 1773. No. 331 is for the plate to Canto III, engraved by N. de Launay (Bocher, loc. cit., no. 278) and no. 332 for the plate Canto VII, engraved by B. L. Prevost (Bocher, loc. cit., no. 280). (page 60)

But there are also crisp descriptions of the artists, especially Blunt's beloved Nicholas Poussin. Windsor, said Blunt, had a remarkable series of 133 Poussin drawings, and he proceeded for several pages with his well-sourced thoughts on them. Was there any trace in this catalogue of the Anthony Blunt who had demanded that all art be interpreted according to Marxist principles? His assess-

ment of Poussin's drawings avoids the clichés of Marxist
theory that had peppered his work in the 1930s. He still
talks about the historical context in which Poussin was
working but in a carefully neutral way. Nor is there any hint
of criticism of patrons or commercial pressures; the Marxist
firebrand has been replaced by the well-balanced scholar.
Blunt's introduction is deferential:

> The debts which I have incurred in the preparation of this
> catalogue are many, partly owing to the nature of the
> task and partly because of the difficult circumstances in
> which it has been carried out. To His Majesty The King I
> owe the privilege of working in the Royal Library at
> Windsor, a privilege of peculiar value during the years of
> the War, when all other great collections of drawings
> were inaccessible for one reason or another. To the
> Royal Librarian, Sir Owen Morshead, I am indebted in
> both a general and peculiar way . . . without his enthu-
> siasm and energy this volume and the series of which it
> forms part would never have been prepared.

Blunt also thanked Dr Rudolf Wittkover of the Warburg
Institute and the Poussin specialist Dr Walter Friedlander;
just two of the European *émigrés* who had transformed art
history in Britain.

In the winter of 1946–47 Blunt had his first great public
moment as a royal employee when the Royal Academy
staged a lavish exhibition of the King's pictures. Among the
366,000 visitors was Queen Mary, who wrote of her visit on
23 October 1946:

> At 3. to the Royal Academy to see the wonderful colln.
> of pictures from Buck. Palace, Windsor, St. James's,
> Hampton Court & Holyrood which Bertie has lent for
> the winter exh. Met Bertie & all the family there, many

artists etc. – The pictures looked lovely and were well hung by Mr. Blunt and the Committee, all the rooms were filled – A most enjoyable afternoon.[7]

Blunt had selected the pictures and masterminded the production of an erudite catalogue. He farmed out some of the work to friends: for example, Ellis Waterhouse wrote on English portraits and Dutch pictures. It was the start, Oliver Millar thought approvingly, of a new, vigorously academic approach to the royal collection.

Shortly after his appointment as Surveyor of the King's Pictures, Blunt travelled secretly to Germany with Owen Morshead. The details of that trip are still officially classified though Blunt talked openly about the mission to friends such as Waterhouse. Blunt, still nominally an officer in MI5, was asked to recover a cache of papers stored at Schloss Kronberg, a castle near Frankfurt, the home of the Hesse family. The King was sure that among the papers there were letters written by Queen Victoria to her eldest daughter, the Empress Friedrich, wife of Frederick of Prussia, and correspondence from Queen Mary to her German relations. There was also a suspicion that boxes of letters and papers might contain potentially embarrassing evidence of the pro-Nazi sympathies of the King's brother, the Duke of Windsor. George VI had ample reason for fearing this. Prince Philip of Hesse had been an intermediary between the Duke of Windsor and Adolf Hitler before the war. In October 1937, the Duke and Duchess had inspected an honour guard of Hitler's élite Death's Head corps when they visited Germany. They had also spent two hours talking privately with Hitler. The prospect of any of this material being taken by the Americans and published by the disrespectful American press, which had no Official Secrets Act to keep it in check, was enough to make officials at Buckingham Palace feel distinctly uneasy.

One account suggests that when Blunt and Morshead arrived at the village they discovered that the castle was being used as an American army club.[8] They found the head of the Hesse family, Countess Margaret, in a local house and showed her the letter from the King asking if she would deliver the papers to his two emissaries. She wrote a note to the American officer in charge of the castle, authorizing the removal of the files. But the officer was unimpressed and refused to release anything without first being given permission by a superior. As he was telephoning, Blunt and Morshead sneaked into the attic where the papers were stored and smuggled the two boxes downstairs. They had disappeared en route to Windsor before the Americans knew what was happening. Ellis Waterhouse recalled:

> I saw Anthony when he came over. He talked to me about recovering some of Queen Victoria's letters from the Hesse family. I think it was a secret mission. He said he also brought back Queen Charlotte's crown and diamonds. When they got back to Windsor the safe was closed for the night so they put the valuables in a chamber pot.[9]

Hugh Trevor-Roper (Lord Dacre) said that he had wandered into MI5's offices in St James's one day in the summer of 1945 and found Blunt and Guy Liddell discussing this German trip, although Dacre's account contradicts this story about the American occupation of the Hesse home. Lord Dacre recalled:

> Blunt was saying how the Hesses had lived in great style. There were footmen serving behind every chair at

dinner. He said that he had been sent to collect some letters of Queen Victoria which the Palace feared might fall into American hands. Whether that was true I don't know. But I don't believe it was anything to do with the Duke of Windsor.[10]

A third source said that Blunt had another reason for travelling to Germany. Blunt, said the source, had been escorting home a German who had worked as a double agent for the British during the war and who thought the employment prospects were better in Germany than in England.

During his trip to Germany Blunt checked up on Leo Long, who was now working as a senior intelligence officer for the British Control Commission, the administration in the British zone. Long had left MI14 after 'two or three years' because, he claimed later, he found the strain of being a Soviet spy intolerable. He had gone to the 21st Army Group in Portsmouth, then planning for D-Day. Long was in what he called a 'real bullshit section', working on various hare-brained schemes to try and demoralize the German troops once the Allies had landed in France. Long was in the rearguard of the first wave of troops but soon tired of his job – dropping leaflets on the Germans – and decided to scout around to see if he could find real action. He was badly injured when his jeep overturned and repatriated to England. MI14 wanted him back, he said, when he had recovered, but he chose instead to go to Germany.

Noel Annan, Long's colleague from MI14, was in Germany from the end of the war until late 1946, serving as a colonel in the political division of the British Control Commission. He returned again during the Berlin airlift of March 1948 and the subsequent formal division of Germany in 1949. In his first tour he had two concerns: the first was to find a way which would ensure the future of a united

Germany; the second was the more immediate problem of dealing with millions of displaced people – not just native Germans but refugees from Russian-occupied Eastern Europe. The British assumed, said Annan, that the four powers – Britain, France, the Soviet Union and the United States – would rule Germany until 'in some distant future an acceptable German government could be elected'. But, as Annan saw, the war had created two superpowers who were already drawing up a new, divided Europe. 'Britain fondly imagined that she had won the war. She had not. America and Russia had won the war. Britain had merely in her finest hour not lost it.'

In the struggle to determine the shape of Germany, Annan recalled that Leo Long always appeared to support the Russians. Annan said:

> I was on the side of those who said that, look, we must realize trying to make a go of the four power thing was a façade and that we really must have a policy which recognizes that Germany must not be taken over by communism. Leo Long was opposed to anything which helped the Christian Democrats (led by Konrad Adenauer, who accepted the inevitable division of Germany). You could argue that Long was just trying to reach agreement with the Russians. But he certainly did not recognize early that the Cold War had begun and that it was essential to get Germany on its feet again because the Russians were never going to accept our Western interpretation of democracy.[11]

Long denied that he was a Soviet agent during his time in Germany and also rejected allegations that he had betrayed British agents working in the Soviet-controlled sector east of the Elbe:

All this stuff about me endangering British agents is a load of old codswallop. I didn't run any agents. I was studying political developments in Germany, writing reports and so on. I was just not in a position to know the names of British agents in the Soviet zone. When I went down to Düsseldorf as the regional intelligence officer I was also political adviser to the regional commissioner in the region. But it was all overt. I met Dick White in Germany and he was in favour of me. I ended up as a colonel though I was made a lieutenant-colonel retrospectively. I was flown back to London and sat before a board and then went straight back as a civilian to Germany with a contract with the commission. I was doing office work mainly, watching out for signs of any German underground movement, the Right or the Left. I had no dealings with the Russians at all. On paper at least I had authority in my field for the whole of the British zone.

When Blunt came over he was on some special mission which I didn't know about. It was all very hush-hush. I was the obvious man for him to contact as I was director of operations in intelligence. I drove him to some castle and that was it. I had got myself to Germany to get away from the spying business. Blunt didn't pressurize me. Nor did the Russians. It's remarkable but it didn't happen. I am thankful they didn't. I think Blunt sensed that I didn't want to know any more. We certainly didn't talk over old times.[12]

Perhaps Long was lying. Certainly, as a senior officer in British Intelligence, he had access to a steady stream of confidential reports on German morale and the emergence of new political forces. And it is undeniable that he would have found it hard to refuse a Russian approach. In 1946 Long tried for a job with British Intelligence in London; an application he claims he made simply because he wanted a new career:

> You mustn't have a picture of a man who is a spy 100 per cent of the time. I had been a part-time spy during the war. By 1946 I was naturally thinking of my future. Contracts at the commission were a maximum of seven years. It was perfectly natural for a man of my experience to be of some interest to the security services. I was seen by both MI5 and MI6. I saw Dick White, who had recruited one or two other people from Germany. Dick said that he didn't have anything for a person of my calibre and that they only took people in at the bottom. By that stage, of course, I was very much up the ladder. It was a very frustrating experience. I don't know whether this was a polite brush-off or not. Dick was a very nice man and he had depended on me a lot in Germany. I was not thinking about penetrating the security service. I suppose I was pretty naïve at the time. I was trying to draw a line down the middle of my life. I am very glad I didn't get in because if I had done then the Russians would probably have closed in and put pressure on me.[13]

Sir Dick White remembered Long well:

> Yes, Blunt tried to get Long in. Long struck me in Germany as an able man with a good grasp of things. The sort of chap one wanted to have on one's side. I advised him to get back to university. I didn't think that we wanted these chaps hanging around the service. I don't think I had any suspicions of Long at that stage. Indeed, when it was discovered that he had been helping Blunt I was rather appalled.[14]

Anthony Blunt later admitted that he had not been sure whether his Soviet masters would allow him to leave MI5 and return to the more relaxing world of art history. It would have made sense, Blunt knew in 1946, for the Soviets to have insisted that he remain in the secret world. He was respected, if not popular; there was no suggestion that he had been anything but loyal. Indeed, was there not ample proof of this in his appointment as Surveyor of the King's Pictures? Blunt turned to Burgess. The request, said Blunt, was then passed to the Soviets. To his relief, Blunt was told that he was free to leave MI5. After Blunt's confession in 1964, a faction within the MI5 team investigating the extent of what had come to be known as the Cambridge spy ring came to a terrible conclusion. The only explanation for the Soviet decision to release Blunt was that they had managed to infiltrate another spy into British Intelligence. This conclusion was certainly based on flawed premises but it generated a series of divisive inquiries within MI5 and MI6, the repercussions of which were still being felt in the 1980s. Blunt, meanwhile, was glad to escape to the Courtauld. Within a year he was made Director of the institute when Tom Boase left to become President of Magdalen College, Oxford. Blunt admitted that he found it hard to return to full-time scholarship. He wrote:

The Second World War caused a complete break. The break was particularly sharp for those whose primary interest was in the visual arts, because on the literary side one had some idea of what was taking place elsewhere, not much, but it leaked through a little bit, even from Italy and occupied France. From the point of view of painting one knew almost literally nothing and when, just before the end of the war, in the spring of 1945, there was a big exhibition of Picasso at the Victoria and Albert Museum, it came to us as a great shock. We were completely out of touch, we had no idea what Picasso had been doing and what he had been doing, partly under the stress of the war years, was pretty grim stuff and it took a lot of adjusting to grasp it. It caused a major scandal and the grand-daughter of Burne Jones stood on a chair in the middle of the exhibition and said this was the death of art etc., etc., etc. This was of course a familiar form – it had been said about the Cubists, it had been said about Cézanne, it had been said about Manet – but it was said with particular vehemence at this time. [15]

Blunt found it hard, too, to accept that Europe, and particularly Paris, no longer enjoyed an unquestioned hegemony in art. The New World was asserting its power. Not content with humiliating Britain in the realpolitik of the post-war, the Americans were now producing their own, brash art. Communists throughout Europe were finding it difficult enough to tolerate the influence of the States in the political arena; now it appeared that the Americans were convinced that they could start manufacturing Culture. Blunt made no attempt to disguise his distrust of them in art. He said:

We suddenly found to our great surprise – and to our slight horror – that Paris was no longer the centre of the art world, but that New York was. This took a great deal of getting used to and those of us whose links were with Paris felt an increasing disappointment, as what came out of Paris became more and more mediocre and less and less original. [16]

Since he was not able to 'get' the 'New Art' he gave up any attempt to understand contemporary developments. Blunt's art was rooted in the seventeenth and eighteenth centuries; Picasso was one of the few modern artists who interested him. But then Picasso was Blunt's conscience; a reminder of past ideals when art then had mattered and had been, so Blunt had imagined, a force for revolutionary change. With just a hint of regret beneath the smugness, he wrote:

> I had become more and more cut off from what was happening in art and more and more concerned with the art of the past, and since the war that has been my main preoccupation and I have very much lost touch with contemporary painting and indeed cannot altogether comprehend much of what has happened in the last twenty or thirty years. This is, I think, a quite normal process connected with age and the hardening of the arteries. But I know my place in history. It was defined to me with absolute precision by my friend Ernest Gimpel. I went to see one of his exhibitions of more or less abstract art and I could not make head or tail of it; and on the way out I said to Ernest, 'I am very sorry, I just can't get it.' And Ernest looked at me sadly and said: 'Pity, because you got as far as Picasso.'[17]

But this thoughtful, introspective passage was written in the 1970s when he was old and ill. In 1946 Blunt refused to accept that something had died in him during the war years. His natural arrogance, coupled with an impregnable conviction of superiority, meant that he felt no need to calculate the long-term cost of his wartime treachery to his personal and academic integrity. If there were any deep misgivings they were certainly not apparent to the students and teachers at the Courtauld; Blunt was a distinguished master craftsman with an encyclopaedic knowledge and a growing list of authoritative publications. True, he had once, long ago, been a Marxist, or so people said, but now he was one of art history's most eminent scholars.

Lillian Gurry, librarian at the Courtauld for fifty years, said that it was assumed by everyone there that Blunt would succeed Boase. He moved into the director's two-bedroom flat on the top floor of the institute and hired a housekeeper to cook and clean, though he dispensed with her services after colleagues joked that her cooking was giving him a pot belly. Like the rest of the Courtauld staff, Gurry knew that Blunt had been a communist in the 1930s and that he had worked in intelligence during the war; but there was nothing remarkable about that. Gurry liked and admired Blunt but she found him slightly frightening. He disapproved of her working late, since he made it clear to everyone that the eighty-room mansion was his private home after the official closing time:

> Anthony wasn't an Establishment figure in the 1940s. At least, he didn't behave like one. We all thought that it was a joke for a communist to get that royal appointment. But then I didn't think of him as being a red. He wore red ties but he was very English and very shy. So many Englishmen were then. I think he was persuaded by Tom Boase to accept. He said it would be very good for the Courtauld and very good for Anthony.[18]

Peter Lasko, Blunt's successor as Director in 1974, was a student at the Courtauld in the 1940s. Lasko remembered Blunt as a private, remote figure, but he was doing his best to make the Courtauld an internationally respected centre of art history. He was generous to students he liked – often finding them jobs in academia – but could be unforgiving, sometimes spiteful, if he took exception to one. Female students adored him; some fell hopelessly in love with him. Lasko insisted that those who knew about Blunt's homosexuality accepted him for what he was – an intellectual who happened to find men sexually attractive.[19] But there were others who thought that Blunt was a potential embarrassment to the Courtauld. Professor Stephen Rees-Jones recalled:

> There was anxiety among the teaching staff about his relationships with students. I don't think he had affairs with them. I remember that on one occasion there was talk of having life classes – nude male models being drawn by the students. But we didn't think it wise to have male models around the place. It would have been too tempting for Anthony. It would have been very bad for the reputation of the institute if anything had happened. I never discussed politics with him. One assumed that he was a sort of aristocrat. He was really a Whig, not a conservative. He was patrician, that's the word.[20]

George Zarnecki was another member of the Courtauld staff who sometimes felt uneasy about Blunt. Zarnecki, one of the most popular professors ever to have worked at the institute, had fought in the Polish army, winning the Polish Cross of Valour and the French Croix de Guerre before being captured by the Germans. He was a prisoner of war for two years before he managed to escape to Spain. He was interned there but managed to slip out to England in 1943. He was nominally with the Polish army in London, though he spent most of the time working on plans to recover works of art looted from Poland by the Nazis. For three years before the war he had been a junior assistant at the Institute of the History of Art at Cracow University. In late 1944 he was in the Courtauld borrowing some books and chatting in French (he spoke little English then) to Margaret Whinney, one of the institute's teachers, when she introduced him to Anthony Blunt. Zarnecki was desperate for a job after the war ended and, in one of those unpredictable acts of kindness of which he was capable,

Blunt found him a job translating texts. On another occasion Blunt tried to help when Zarnecki's sister wanted to leave Poland. Zarnecki was always confused about what Blunt really believed in:

He was a snob about the Royal Family and he hated the masses. I remember that he was thrilled when he was knighted [1956]. When Queen Mary came to the Courtauld in 1946 she was very friendly with him and the present Queen Mother and the Queen always called him Anthony. When Margaret Whinney was in charge of student admissions she was very keen to have what she thought were nice students. By that she meant someone who was well bred and well off. She was a snob. Anthony wasn't, not like that. When I took over as deputy director in 1961 I insisted Anthony take an interest in deciding on student admissions. He hated it and gave up after two years. But he wanted a cross-section of students. We even gave a place to one girl whose father was a gardener. On the other hand his political views were pretty appalling.[21]

Blunt's life during the late 1940s centred firmly on the Courtauld. He was establishing it as the most prestigious art historical institute in Europe, perhaps the world. Ellis Waterhouse wrote in 1967:

Before the war the Courtauld had something of the air of a curiosity in the London scene: by the end of the war, as a result of a change in our sense of values, it had almost insensibly become a force. The institution to which Anthony returned, and of which he became Director, was something which had never previously existed in London. Before the war the London art scene may be said to have consisted of Museum people, the art trade and a handful of 'amateurs' – and there was a very general distrust between these worlds . . . all this has changed and changed very much for the better. The Courtauld, under Anthony's directorship, trained recruits for the country's Museums, Universities and Art Schools, as well as for the art trade, and the various sides are now very much more concerned with the same standards than could have been said before.[22]

During the day Blunt prowled the Courtauld's elegant corridors, usually carrying a bundle of files and photographs. Students enjoyed his tutorials; unlike some academics, Blunt went out of his way to involve his pupils, to make them feel that their views were as interesting as his. But after the working day he treated the house as if it were his own; a grand town home in which he could entertain a ragbag assortment of young men he had picked up in pubs or public lavatories.

Blunt's survival owed much to his ability to divide his life into separate compartments. He tried to avoid letting friends from one area of his life mingle with those from another. It was not always possible, especially since the art and homosexual worlds often overlapped, but this policy meant that few people could ever claim to 'know' him. This deliberate compartmentalization stemmed partly from Blunt's need to feel in control of his professional and personal life; and partly it was based on fear – the less people understood his life the less chance they would have of drawing the right, damaging conclusions about his past. This was easy enough with most heterosexuals, but it was more difficult with close gay friends who understood his need for the excitement and danger of quick pick-ups. A few of these friends undoubtedly suspected that Blunt's wartime career was the key to his life.

Robert Harbinson Bryans (hereafter, Robert Harbinson), who had met Burgess in 1944, believed that he was one of the few people to ever understand Blunt's social world. Harbinson was then the teenage son of an Irish musician, and later became a prolific writer of travel books under the name Robin Bryans. At the time that he met Guy Burgess he was, unlikely though this seemed to people who knew him after the war, training to be a missionary at a Bible college in South Wales. He recalled:

> I met Guy at the home in Oxford of Ernest Bryans, the former warden of Radley College. Ernest was very wealthy and gay. I almost immediately had sex with Guy. Guy was like that. He wanted to see what you were like. He was working at the Foreign Office news department and was always going to bed with reporters.[23]

The young Harbinson may not have appeared much of a threat to anyone that summer in 1944, but he was a shrewd interpreter of the shifting sexual alliances of the circle and that, as we shall see, eventually proved disastrous for Anthony Blunt.

Harbinson relished the challenge of trying to make sense of Blunt's circle. He was helped by the fact that he was bisexual – which allowed him to understand and yet remain detached from Blunt's gay friends. Although he was an inveterate gossip, he did more than just talk; he would spend hours poring over reference books and newly published memoirs looking for clues of relationships which might have remained hidden from him.

Harbinson had a fund of entertaining stories about Blunt and Burgess. He was able, he said, to support these with what he called 'documentary evidence' in the form of letters, telegrams and photographs. Some of his claims and conclusions, particularly about sexual rivalries, were impossible ultimately to prove (or disprove). For example, in

the 1980s he claimed that he had first become suspicious of
Guy when, during the war, Guy had asked so many questions about a factory in Mitcham, south London, which
made aircraft parts for the RAF and in which Harbinson
worked for a time. Harbinson said, too, that he had been
sent to Ireland after the war on a 'spying expedition' by Guy
to investigate a 'right-wing figure'.

Some of Blunt's friends found Harbinson's assertions
difficult to believe. John Hilton recalled meeting Harbinson in the 1960s when he claimed, to Hilton's astonishment,
that he was a foster-brother of Louis MacNeice. Other
friends dismissed Harbinson as a gossip whose opinions
should be ignored. There is no doubt that Harbinson's
theories were Byzantine. But that does not mean he can be
discounted – whatever some of Blunt's friends may say.
Harbinson enjoyed explaining his various theories about
the mechanics of Blunt's life:

> Blunt never mixed people. Many of his oldest friends
> from the '20s and '30s did not meet each other until they
> came to my house in the 1960s. I didn't like Blunt and his
> double-dealing in friendships as well as politics. He was
> dangerous and heartless. If Anthony was with a young
> man he wouldn't be with him for more than ten minutes
> without trying to take the trousers off him . . . It was
> always said that he could talk the trousers off anyone
> when he was young.
>
> I knew all about cottaging. In 1961 I appeared in court
> myself, but I can talk myself out of anything and got off.
> It was dangerous but Blunt did it because he loved
> danger. Everyone knows the toilet he used at Hyde Park,
> the big one near Speakers' Corner. He used to go to the
> one at Russell Square as well but he didn't like that as
> much because Tom Driberg was there for two or three
> hours every day, holding his mac over his arm. Working-

class trade. That was what Anthony really enjoyed. Scruffy, dirty things. He liked sailors the best of all.

Anthony never got caught. Why? Well, he was a particular friend of a London magistrate at that time . . . The magistrate and Anthony used to drink all the time. But when Anthony was well-tanked up he could face the most dangerous cottages. As the ancients would put it, Anthony never got ape-drunk (when men make fools of themselves in their cups) but he did get goat-drunk (when men became amorous in their cups). Or perhaps it would be better to say that he could face cottaging better after a stiff drink.[24]

Harbinson mingled easily in London's gay society. Part of the fun was that it could, at the one and the same time, be both squalid and stylish. He particularly looked forward to so-called 'pyjama parties' hosted by a London theatre impresario who offered his guests delicacies that were difficult to buy in ration-book Britain. These parties were also renowned for the unrestrained sensual pleasures on offer – to suit every taste, including Anthony Blunt's passion for young men in uniform.

CHAPTER 14
Cold War Warriors

The National Government which had guided Britain through six years of war had been wound up on 23 May 1945 and a general election called for 5 July, though the result was delayed until 26 July to allow time for the votes from servicemen and women overseas to be registered. Winston Churchill confidently expected the Conservatives to be returned with a massive majority – not an unreasonable hope in view of his huge popularity. However, the Labour Party won a landslide victory. It had 393 seats, the Conservatives had 210, the Liberals a mere twelve, and the Communists a derisory two. The new Prime Minister was Clement Attlee, who had been educated at Haileybury and Oxford. He was a qualified barrister and had worked with the poor in the East End of London. During the Spanish Civil War he had been an outspoken supporter of the British who had fought with the Republican International Brigade. His left-wing credentials, as he posed for photographs on the steps of 10 Downing Street, were thus impeccable. The communists knew that he had always been suspicious of their efforts during the 1930s to work as a Popular Front; they also knew that he was committed to the sort of reforms that would provide the welcome beginnings of a truly socialist Britain.

Attlee's reforms began with nationalization: railways, coal, electricity, gas and steel. The Welfare State, which had been outlined in the Beveridge Report of 1942, began to take shape when Minister of Health Aneurin Bevan introduced the National Health Service Act in 1946, aimed at providing free medical care for everyone. The Butler Act of 1944, which had raised the school-leaving age to fifteen, was partly implemented. But these changes, significant though they were in expanding government responsibilities to its people, did not redistribute wealth, destroy capitalists or free the workers – all enduring dreams of the Left. To working-class people, life in Britain was just as hard as and less exciting than it had been during the war or in the grim 1930s. Britain, which had stood alone against Hitler, seemed to have exhausted its energy and strength. Everywhere there was decay, shabbiness, shortages and queues.

Guy Burgess, however, seemed pleased enough with the progress that the Attlee government was making. For the time being at least, arguments about whether or not a democratically elected government was capable of destroying capitalism seemed irrelevant. Guy was also enjoying himself. In January 1947 he had fulfilled a long-cherished ambition when he had persuaded the Foreign Office to take him on as a permanent member of staff, so ending his wearing and slightly humiliating existence as a freelance diplomat–propagandist–fixer who was always unsure if he would have an office or even a desk to go to. It was important for Burgess's self-esteem to be able to tell friends that his future was assured and that the mandarins of the FO had finally recognized his talents. It was comforting, too, to know that he would have a regular salary.

Labour's electoral victory threw up an unexpected opportunity to further his career. While working on 'The Week in Westminster' at the BBC, Burgess had met Hector McNeil, Labour MP for Greenock in Scotland. McNeil was a Glaswegian who had been a journalist before he decided on a career in politics; he was hardworking and conscientious but was a heavy drinker and smoker who enjoyed relaxing with the oddballs who inhabited wine bars such as El Vino's in Fleet Street. He had been impressed by Burgess and thought of him as a young man whose brilliant eccentricity would enliven any government department. When McNeil was made Minister of State at the Foreign Office, with Cabinet rank, he offered Burgess a job as his personal assistant. The offer was a twin triumph for Burgess: first, it confirmed his own view that he was destined for great things in the world of high diplomacy; second, it was a chance to meddle once more as a Soviet agent. This time he would not just be a middleman between friends who had access to confidential information and his Soviet controller, nor would he just be passing on tittle-tattle from the BBC or the House of Commons. Now he would have his own secrets to impress his friends with and leak to the Soviets. Even his own biographer, the partisan Tom Driberg, saw the humour in Burgess's sudden elevation:

> As an historian [Burgess] had always been fascinated by the idea and character of the *éminence grise*, the shadowy but influential figure lurking at the elbow of the public man. He liked the company of *éminences grises*; I have little doubt that, perhaps half-consciously, he saw himself, too, as McNeil's Personal Assistant, in this role. In the absences abroad or through illness of his chief, Ernest Bevin, McNeil often had to act as Foreign Secretary. At last, at the age of thirty-six, his steady inner purpose and his calculations assisted by a series of fortunate chances and coincidences, Guy Burgess was indeed near to the very centre of power.[1]

If Burgess had imagined that the new Labour administration would ally itself with the Soviet Union, he soon realized that Labour, just as much as the Conservatives, accepted the Cold War as a fact of post-war European life. Lingering hopes that Attlee would fulfil his pre-election pledges to work for better relations with the Soviets were shattered when he refused to repudiate Winston Churchill's speech at Fulton, Missouri, on 5 February 1946. Churchill was at his oratorical best as he described the 'Iron Curtain' which had descended across Europe and accused the Soviets of wanting 'the fruits of war and the indefinite expansion of their power and doctrines'. It was hopeless to try and appease this new imperialist power: 'I am convinced that there is nothing they admire so much as strength and there is nothing for which they have less respect than weakness.' It was up to the British Commonwealth and America, said Churchill, to work together to ensure that Soviet ambitions of world domination were thwarted. Many Labour MPs were outraged by Churchill's attack on the Soviet Union, though Hector McNeil was as hard-line an anti-communist as Churchill. Nevertheless, McNeil and Burgess still managed to get on well.

Burgess saw the speech as final proof that the war had turned Britain, economically and ideologically, into a satellite of the USA. His objections were not only based on his own haphazard Marxism; he was sentimentally patriotic and was possessed of a great sense of Britain's imperial past. He found it deeply depressing to see Britain tamely following the Americans.

Burgess began working for McNeil in April 1946. If anything, he became dirtier and more outrageous during his time in McNeil's office. Goronwy Rees thought Guy was now addicted to drugs as well as to alcohol. One minute he would be gulping down sedatives, the next he would be eating stimulants, apparently determined to 'modify whatever he happened to be feeling at any particular moment.' Rees could hardly believe that his friend could stand up, let alone work.[2] Burgess's desk at the Foreign Office was strewn with piles of paper and the ashtrays overflowed. He insisted on chewing garlic, to the irritation of his colleagues who demanded that the personnel department do something about Burgess's anti-social habits. Burgess enjoyed telling friends that he had received a formal note: 'Mr Burgess will in future refrain from eating garlic in office hours.' He took childish pride in his cruel, scribbled caricatures of Foreign Office colleagues and his political masters. On one occasion he doodled a cartoon of Ernest Bevin, showing Bevin racing back to shore in a boat because 'Hector Needs Me'. Burgess claimed, with his hand on his heart, that this had been shown to the Foreign Secretary, who thought it hilarious. Moreover, at a potentially tricky Cabinet meeting Bevin passed around Burgess's drawing, stamped as an official Cabinet document, hoping to create a more relaxed atmosphere – and succeeded. This story sounded too fantastic to bear any relation to the truth, but Burgess could produce the cartoon, complete with the Cabinet stamp, to prove it.

Fred Warner, an ex-naval officer later knighted after a distinguished diplomatic career culminating in his appointment as British ambassador to Japan, was McNeil's private secretary and shared an office with Burgess. He recalled: 'He was interesting and amusing but he could be an awkward customer. When I first met him he was extremely badly dressed. I didn't think his views were extreme at all. Hector McNeil was never a left-wing socialist and Burgess's views did not seem very different from McNeil's.'[3]

In the years after Burgess's defection, Warner insisted to friends that Burgess could not have smuggled confidential papers out of the office. That may be true, but Burgess did not need to remove files to know the details of British foreign policy. He was, as Tom Driberg rightly pointed out, at the heart of policy-making. McNeil trusted and liked

Burgess; he had hired him because he wanted someone who would not be frightened to express opinions which might run against current government thinking. Burgess was party to high-level discussions about the future of Europe, when he argued, he later claimed, that it was esssential to guard against a resurgence of German military power. The only way to ensure that was to 'remove from power the social and economic class that had caused two previous world wars'. Burgess realized it was no use; the Americans, backed by the British and the French, were determined to make the western sector of Germany a buffer zone between East and West. The American 'monopoly' capitalists, lamented Burgess, were determined to pump money into Europe. It was a gloomy prospect since he knew that prosperity was the enemy of revolution. But he consoled himself with the fact that he was helping to make history.

No one doubts that Burgess knew a great deal about efforts to form new Western European–American defence alliances. He travelled to Brussels with McNeil for secret talks on the Brussels Treaty Organization, which paved the way for the draft of the North Atlantic Treaty. He attended the meeting of the Council of Foreign Ministers in London in December 1947, but 'by this time', according to Driberg, 'his own mind was painfully schizophrenic – split as it was between duty to the nation's service and conviction that the nation was being led to disaster.'[4]

Throughout this period Burgess was briefing the Soviets on the shifts of British foreign policy. But, it has to be asked, did this matter greatly? Stalin knew perfectly well that the Western democracies were determined to prevent the spread of communism and that they were now effectively political and economic satellites of the United States. It was no more than the Soviets themselves were doing in Eastern Europe. The Soviet intelligence network needed only to read the British press to gather the drift of foreign policy. What Burgess *was* able to provide was a first-hand account of the way that decisions were made and the arguments that preceded them.

Stories about Guy Burgess became the conversational currency of the Foreign Office. There was the story about his urinating over a statue in front of Buckingham Palace, and the one about the time he handed around a photograph of his new boyfriend in an effort to brighten a dull meeting. But he looked and sounded like a man going nowhere, except perhaps to an early grave. His fingers were stained with nicotine from years of chain-smoking, his breath reeked of alcohol, tobacco and garlic; his stories became ever wilder and his opinions careered around the political spectrum with increasing unpredictability. Sir Dick White reflected:

It was very difficult to understand that this dirty, indiscreet chap could be playing this deep game and yet it was deeper than anyone else's. And his nerve was so strong and his arrogance was enormous. He didn't seem to mind what anyone thought of him. And this put him in a strong position. Imagine you are a spy and don't fear the outcome. Your self-confidence would be your best protection. Burgess was a chap who worshipped efficiency. He would have been a rather effective imperialist. That's what he should have been really.[5]

As a result of security problems during the war, the Foreign Office had decided to set up a new security unit headed by George Carey-Foster. Carey-Foster was a much-decorated former group captain in the Royal Air Force who had joined the Foreign Office in the autumn of 1946, but the FO establishment was less than enthusiastic about the presence of this new snooper; his presence implied there was something wrong with the chaps in the department. Carey-Foster had to struggle on by borrowing staff from MI6. He recalled: 'I was not always popular because of some of the things I had to do, and I did not get the full cooperation of the personnel department in the early days. It took the shock of the Burgess-Maclean defection [in 1951] for my department to be accepted as a real necessity.'[6]

When Carey-Foster first met Burgess in 1947 he was appalled by his appearance. Throughout the late 1940s he received a steady trickle of complaints about Burgess. Burgess was reprimanded for taking official papers home. Other FO staff also had to be warned about this, but it was not until Burgess's flat was searched by MI5 after he fled the country that Carey-Foster realized that Burgess had kept a cache of confidential files there. It certainly did not matter that Burgess was homosexual since, as Carey-Foster pointed out, homosexuality, although illegal, did not automatically make a man a security risk:

I had no reason to harbour doubts about Burgess's loyalty. But he was a headache to my department on disciplinary grounds and it was on this account that he was considered to be a security risk. We had no reason to suspect that he was a Soviet agent. I repeat, neither I nor MI5 had any idea that Guy Burgess was a Soviet spy.[7]

Burgess and Anthony Blunt saw each other regularly while Burgess was working for McNeil. Burgess had moved into a first-floor flat in Lower Bond Street, near the Royal Academy and handily placed for Soho's many drinking clubs. He was a devoted member of the respectable Reform Club, where he used to down immense beakers of port known to the waiters as 'double Burgesses'. He adored fast cars and often bored his drinking companions with his inexhaustible store of knowledge on the subject. His flat was a haven for diplomats, intelligence officers, politicians, intellectuals, many of whom, though by no means all, were homosexual. Every Monday evening he went to the Chelsea Palace in the King's Road with the same little group: Guy, two senior members of MI5 (one of whom was Guy Liddell) and MI6 and two women. Goronwy Rees later wrote:

During this period Guy's relations with the security services seemed to become increasingly intimate and confidential. Of course, the very existence of a secret service was for Guy a challenge, almost an affront, to his curiosity. He had always been possessed by a devouring interest in affairs that were none of his business . . . he liked to know, or pretend to know, what no one else knew, he liked to surprise one with information about matters that were no concern of his, derived from sources which he could not, or would not, reveal; the trouble was that one could never be sure whether the ultimate source was his own imagination . . .

Guy regarded sex as a useful machine for the manufacture of pleasure . . . and at one time or another he went to bed with most of his friends and in doing so released them from many of their inhibitions. He was a kind of public schoolboy's guide to the mysteries of sex and he fulfilled his function almost with a sense of public service. Such affairs did not last long; but Guy had the faculty of retaining the affection of those he went to bed with and also, in some curious way, of maintaining a kind of permanent domination over them . . . long after the affair was over he continued to assist friends in their sexual lives, which were often troubled and unsatisfactory, to listen to their emotional difficulties and when necessary find suitable partners for them. To such people he was a combination of father confessor and pimp and the number of people who were under an obligation to him must have been very large indeed.[8]

Burgess made no secret of his squalid personal life. He enjoyed shocking heterosexual outsiders, including his brother Nigel, with tales of his sexual exploits. He kept all his love letters, according to Jack Hewit, in an old guitar case and when that was full he put them in boxes or stuffed them into drawers. He was not hoarding this documentary evidence so that he could one day blackmail former lovers; rather, it was proof to himself of his own power to make men love him. Hewit and Burgess enjoyed the varied delights of Soho. They liked the Mandrake Club, in a basement off Dean Street, and frequented a bohemian collection of artists, writers and poets who seemed to spend most of their time drinking and playing chess. Burgess also favoured the Gargoyle Club, then owned by the Hon. David Tennant who was married to the actress Hermione Baddeley.

Burgess also stayed close to Wolfgang zu Putlitz, the German diplomat who had proved such a useful source for MI5 (and via Burgess for the Soviets). Zu Putlitz left England in January 1952 to live in East Germany because 'everything I abhorred was being restored' by the Allies in West Germany. He said in 1954 that he had decided he had no choice but to go over to the Russians. In 1956 his autobiography, *The Putlitz Dossier*, was published in East Germany. In the preface he said that he 'would never forget the kindness and understanding of Mr Anthony Blunt'.[9] Was this a coded signal to Blunt or even, for some reason known only to East German Intelligence, to MI5? But the hint, if that is what it was, went unnoticed. In fairness, it would have required an act of genius by someone in MI5 in the mid-1950s to have unscrambled the web of relation-ships protecting Blunt.

According to Burgess's account to Tom Driberg in 1956, his move from McNeil's office at the beginning of 1948 had been prompted by the minister's desire to have him up-graded from B Branch to the more senior A Branch. But before that could happen the personnel department in-sisted that he widen his experience. So Burgess was moved to the department dealing with Far Eastern affairs. Burgess did, indeed, end up there, but the rest of his account is a blend of half-truths, lies and significant omissions, includ-ing his account of his time at the Information Research Department of the FO.

Christopher Mayhew was parliamentary under-secretary at the Foreign Office in 1947. He was one of the Labour Party's bright young hopes; a fervent anti-communist who had already established a reputation within the party for his determination to weed out Labour MPs who owed their allegiance to Moscow and revolution rather than to West-minster and parliamentary democracy. Some MPs, thought Mayhew, were actually reporting to Soviet intelligence officers in London. In 1947 Mayhew had a brainwave. The Left in Britain still seemed to believe that Stalin was moulding a socialist Utopia. Mayhew felt that Britain and the other Western democracies were losing the Cold War propaganda battle. The world needed to be told the truth: Stalin was a dictator, killing thousands and imprisoning hundreds of thousands, perhaps more; Stalin and the Soviet Union were the new imperialists determined to colonize first Eastern Europe and then the rest of the continent. In 1947 Mayhew drafted his proposal to the Foreign Secretary Ernest Bevin. He wanted to set up a new department to launch a propaganda counter-offensive. Clement Attlee knew that many Labour MPs would be incensed if they heard that their own government was contemplating an attack of this magnitude on the world's first socialist country. But at a meeting at Chequers, the country retreat for British Prime Ministers, Attlee told Mayhew that he could go ahead, but that the new department had to remain secret. The plan was not debated in Cabinet, it would be funded by the secret vote – the device which allows governments to spend money on unspecified work of 'national importance'. Mayhew's brainchild was called the Information Research Department (IRD), a title which made it sound like an innocuous branch of the Foreign Office's press department. Mayhew remained convinced forty years later that IRD had been necessary:

> In those days many people on the left, even in the Labour Party, thought Stalin was a Socialist, just like us. The slave labour camps were just not known about. We wanted to broadcast the truth and destroy the Stalinist myth that the Soviet Union was a sort of paradise for working class people and that it was the champion of liberty and anti-colonialism. We invented the phrase Soviet imperialism, which made a colossal impact. IRD was highly secret and a grade more respectable than just dealing in black propaganda. We were dealing in the truth.[10]

Many of IRD's staff were *émigrés* from Eastern Europe and it had strong links with MI5 and MI6. It was not just dealing in external propaganda. IRD, thought Mayhew, should supply democratic socialists within the Labour Party and the trade unions with factual ammunition to fire at the covert communists. Mayhew recalled the moment that Guy Burgess was first suggested as a possible recruit to his new unit:

Hector McNeil came up to me and said that I was doing very well with IRD. I made appreciative noises. Then he said, I have got just the man for you. I said that I already had all the key people I needed. All I might consider were people with a thorough grounding in Marxism and the Soviet Union. He said he had just the fellow. Guy Burgess. Hector wished Guy on me. I interviewed Burgess and, by God, he did have all the qualifications that Hector said he had. It never occurred to me that he was a Marxist, never mind a spy. I am guessing, dammit, but I should think that Burgess had heard about IRD and told the Russians. And they told him to get a job with me.[11]

Burgess stayed with IRD for three months. This was long enough for him to provide the Russians with details of its staff and operations – with unpleasant consequences for close relations of IRD staff living in Eastern Europe. Mayhew was soon receiving uncomplimentary reports on his latest recruit. He had not liked Burgess from the start, finding him 'brazen and generally offensive'. Then Mayhew's private office suggested that he should examine Burgess's work. Mayhew found that the work was as unsatisfactory as his appearance. 'I threw him out. He was dirty, drunk and idle. I couldn't sack him. He was Hector's protégé. I just disposed of him. I sent him back to the pool with a very bad report. Hector was a splendid fellow. He was very patriotic. He was a good man. An able man. But he was taken for a ride by Burgess.'[12]

Burgess did not languish in the pool for long. He was still regarded by his colleagues as part of McNeil's inner cabinet; an impression that he carefully fostered. In 1948 he moved to the Far Eastern department. This was even better than IRD. The Far East was a key strategic area. There was civil war in China between Mao Zedong's communists and

General Chiang Kai-shek's nationalist army which, to the surprise of many military experts, looked by the winter of 1948 as if it would end in victory for Mao. Burgess was delighted with his new job. He knew a great deal about Chinese communism and was a special admirer of M. N. Roy, the Comintern representative there from 1926 to 1927. And for once he seemed in agreement with his colleagues. When Mao declared the founding of the Chinese People's Republic in October 1949, Burgess could not fault the FO's line. China was going to be governed by the communists and there was nothing anyone could do about it. It was, therefore, sensible to recognize Mao's regime – preferably sooner rather than later. Burgess saw a stream of classified reports despite his lowly status as a grade 4 officer. Documents released in Britain in 1981 under the thirty-year rule show that he was fully briefed on the deteriorating situation in Korea in 1949. He saw reports from military intelligence and from the Supreme Command Allied Powers Tokyo, General MacArthur's headquarters in the Far East. On 5 April Burgess commented on a secret report from the War Office which contained 'a summary of all information received concerning Russian assistance to the Chinese communist forces'. Burgess wrote a memo on 29 April in which he noted that the papers available to him 'contain the JIC [Joint Intelligence Committee; the committee which coordinated British intelligence operations] view on the nature of Russian air assistance'.[13] He also regularly ridiculed the American intelligence-gathering effort in the region.

In between drafting reports for his Foreign Office bosses and meeting his Soviet controller to pass on as much information as he could gather, Burgess took time to lecture MI5 and MI6 officers on China. Arthur Martin, a recent recruit to MI5 whose career later became inextricably tangled with Burgess and Blunt, recalled: 'I heard him talk about China. Burgess was clearly a clever boy. But it was more than that. He had a magnetic personality.'[14] But Burgess was soon in trouble. In the autumn of 1949 he blotted his already heavily stained record card yet again. He went on holiday to Tangier via Gibraltar with his mother Mrs Bassett, after suffering a nasty fall in yet another drunken incident, this time in a restaurant in Chelsea. The trip almost (and should have) wrecked Burgess's diplomatic career. The government White Paper published in 1955 'on the disappearance of two former Foreign Office officials' gave the impression that in North Africa Burgess had just been guilty of 'indiscreet talk about secret matters of which he had official knowledge'. Like most official pronouncements on Burgess, this was part understatement and part lie. The White Paper implied that his behaviour had been unusual whereas it was perfectly in character. Second, the information he yelled out around the bars of Tangier and Gibraltar had not been picked up in the Far Eastern department; it had been acquired through years of meddling and drinking with friends such as Guy Liddell. From the moment he left London he was rarely sober. In a Tangier bar he met an old school friend, David Herbert, the younger brother of the Earl of Pembroke. Burgess was horribly loud and indiscreet, screaming out his Marxist views to the increasing concern of Herbert. By noon each day Burgess had settled in at the bar of the Café de Paris, where he sung such gems as: 'Little boys are cheap today/Cheaper than yesterday.'

His behaviour in Gibraltar, where he met Princess Dil de Rohan and Mary Oliver, was just as bad. He told anyone who would listen that Britain would soon recognize Mao's regime. He pointed out the MI6 head of station on the Rock – this did not go down well with the gentleman in question who, like most spies, enjoyed the fiction that no one knew his real job. Burgess continued to fire off the names of every MI5 and MI6 officer that he could recall through the fog of drink. As he made his way back to London he left behind a trail of unpaid bills and a number of very angry British intelligence officers who were determined to have this man dealt with by the Foreign Office. Goronwy Rees wrote of the trip:

> He had left behind him a record of drinking bouts and brawls which would have done credit to a Dimitri Karamazov. He had also at each stage of his travels insisted on visiting the local representatives of MI6 and on discussing their characters, habits, opinions and professional inadequacies with anyone who chose to listen to him in any bar in which he happened to be drinking. In addition, he had personally applied himself to the task of trying to persuade MI6's slightly startled representatives of the errors of British foreign policy and the follies of MI6 in particular. His journey through the Maghreb became a wild Odyssey of indiscretions . . . which not unnaturally was reported to London.[15]

In London George Carey-Foster decided that enough was enough. He recommended that Burgess should be sacked. 'His loyalty was not in question. It was his behaviour on holiday. Against my advice it was decided to give him one more chance. One of the reasons, I suspect, was that he was a protégé of Hector McNeil.'[16] Burgess was as surprised as Carey-Foster that he was not fired. Goronwy Rees, too, could not understand why Guy had not been dismissed and assumed that he was being protected by men such as McNeil and 'friends in posts of great authority in the security services'. Burgess was not even shunted off in disgrace to some siding in the Foreign Office. Instead, astonishingly, he was posted to the embassy in Washington with the rank of Second Secretary. By any standards the decision was incomprehensible. Burgess was proud of his anti-Americanism. He was an acknowledged public relations liability for the FO. The thought of what he might do to Anglo–American relations when he became drunk at polite diplomatic cocktail parties, as everyone knew he would, made his friends blanch. And Guy claimed that he was as worried as they were. He talked about resigning and becoming a journalist. His brother, Nigel, confirmed that Guy had a pathological hatred and fear of America; so the anguish was probably genuine. He hated, too, the idea of leaving London, where he knew everyone and everyone knew him. But his Soviet controller must have been delighted. There was growing tension in the Far East – the Korean war began on 20 June 1950 – and there was no better place for a Soviet agent than inside the British embassy in Washington. George Carey-Foster said that the FO's Chief Clerk wrote to Sir Robert Mackenzie, the ex-MI6 officer who was head of regional security at the embassy, and told him 'that should Burgess misbehave in any way he should be sent straight back to London'. Burgess was told that he was on probation and that this was his last chance.[17]

The guest list at the farewell party Burgess threw at his flat in the early summer of 1950 showed just how wide, and bizarre, was his circle of friends. Jack Hewit said that it was 'a nice, quiet little affair',[18] in contrast to Goronwy Rees, who claimed that it had degenerated into a drunken brawl between 'two very tough working-class young men who had obviously been picked up off the streets either that very evening or not very long before'. Rees also claimed, though this was denied by Hewit, that James Pope-Hennessy spent the night with one of the 'rough trade' imported for the evening and that when he woke up in the morning his (Pope-Hennessy's) flat had been stripped of its valuables.[19] But Rees and Hewit did agree on the guests who came to Lower Bond Street to wish Burgess good luck on his American adventure. There was Hector McNeil, by then Secretary of State for Scotland; Guy Liddell, deputy director of MI5; David Footman of MI6; Wolfgang zu Putlitz and, of course, Anthony Blunt. There were three women: a German countess and the two women who had once shared Bentinck Street with Burgess and Blunt: Patricia Parry, who had married Richard Llewelyn-Davies, an Apostle, in 1943, and Teresa Mayor, who had become Victor Rothschild's second wife in 1946. Rees wrote:

> The only connection between us was Guy . . . the elaborate web of inter-relationships which had brought them together included strands which were political, social, personal, erotic, even criminal . . . I remember thinking that the oddest thing about the party was that no one seemed to think there was anything odd about it all.[20]

The party that night spawned one enduring legend. Someone – it could have been Footman, Liddell or even McNeil – was telling Burgess that he really would have to be careful in Washington and that he should avoid discussions about communism, homosexuality and the colour bar. Burgess is said to have replied: 'What you're trying to say in your nice, long-winded way is: "Guy, for God's sake, don't make a pass at Paul Robeson."'

CHAPTER 15
American Interlude

In September 1949, Kim Philby had become MI6's man in Washington. This triumph for Soviet Intelligence was reinforced a year later by Burgess's unexpected arrival at the embassy as a second secretary, responsible for explaining British policy on the Far East to the State Department. There were now two Soviet agents working in the heart of the British diplomatic–intelligence establishment in the United States. Philby, especially, was a vital source for the Soviets. He was working closely with the CIA and FBI at a time when the two agencies were fully stretched by demands at home and abroad. The Korean War imposed a huge workload on American Intelligence and Anglo-American efforts to undermine communist regimes abroad – in Albania and the Ukraine – ended in bloody failure, thanks to Philby's treachery. There were pressures, too, on the FBI to unearth communist traitors whom the American public believed were undermining national security. This was the infamous era of Joseph McCarthy, a junior Republican Senator from Wisconsin. In February 1950 McCarthy had shocked the American public by alleging that there were fifty-seven 'card-carrying communists' in the State Department. For four years McCarthy led a witchhunt for 'Reds'; he helped win the 1952 election for his party by smearing leading Democrats as communist sympathizers.

In 1953 he was made chairman of the Senate Sub-Committee on Investigations and for a year continued to wreck the lives of hundreds of American intellectuals whom he accused, often without a shred of evidence, of being secret communists. The roots of McCarthyism lay deep in the American subconscious but it owed much, too, to contemporary events. In 1950 Alger Hiss, the former US diplomat who had been accused by an ex-communist of betraying state secrets, was jailed for five years on perjury charges. The American public was bewildered by the country's apparent inability to do anything to stop the spread of communism in the Far East. Americans had been brought up to believe in the invincibility of the United States and the inevitable triumph of their way of life over godless communism. If that was not happening then, millions of ordinary men and women believed, it was due to a communist conspiracy within their country.

The arrival of Guy Burgess in Washington may have pleased the Kremlin; Kim Philby, however, had mixed feelings. Trouble trailed Burgess wherever he went. He had survived in London because of the loyalty of friends and lovers, because he had been to Eton and Cambridge, and because the English had a tradition of tolerating brilliant eccentrics. But Philby knew America was different. The Americans would react violently to Guy's blatant homosexuality, appalling manners and left-wing views. Philby had worked hard for the Washington job and he had no intention of allowing his career to be wrecked by Burgess. Even Guy realized that Philby might be a little worried. He wrote: 'I have a shock for you. I have been posted to Washington.'[1] In the same letter Burgess asked if he could stay with Kim and his wife Aileen. This was Philby's second marriage and had already produced four children; a fifth, Harry George, was on the way now. Philby calculated that Burgess was less liable to get into the sort of 'spectacular scrapes' which had marked his career if he was staying with a family. Philby wrote in his autobiography:

> In normal circumstances it would have been quite wrong for two secret operatives to occupy the same premises. But the circumstances were not normal. From the earliest days, our careers had intertwined . . . I had put forward his name as a possible recruit for the Soviet service, a debt which he later repaid by smoothing my entry into the British secret service. In between, he had acted as a courier for me in Spain. In 1940, we had worked closely together in SIS [Secret Intelligence Service; MI6], and he had paid me a professional visit in Turkey in 1948. Our association was therefore well-known . . . It seemed that there could be no real professional objection to him staying with me.
>
> There was another consideration which inclined me towards agreeing with Burgess's suggestion. I knew from his files that his record was quite clean . . . But, on reflection, I think that my decision to accommodate Burgess speeded by a few weeks at most the focusing of the spotlight on me.[2]

Philby was not the only person to be anxious about Burgess. Sir Robert Mackenzie, the British embassy's regional security officer for North and Central America, read Carey-Foster's letter describing Burgess's record with horror. Carey-Foster had warned Mackenzie that Burgess might get worse. 'What does he mean "worse"?' Mackenzie asked Philby, 'Goats?' Burgess was a draining house-guest; he was drinking and smoking heavily, though he endeared himself to Philby's children, Miranda, Josephine, John and Tommy, by continually buying them presents and always being available to repair John's train set which occupied a large portion of the floor in Burgess's basement room.

The one hope – that the British embassy was so large that no one would notice the new second secretary – was soon shattered. Within a few days Squadron-Leader 'Tommy' Thompson, a security official, had to warn Burgess for his 'carelessness with official papers'.

Burgess's degenerate lifestyle was not Philby's main problem. There was another crisis, one which threatened the entire Cambridge network. Before he had left London for the USA Philby had been told that the Americans had intercepted Soviet diplomatic radio traffic (codenamed 'Bride' by the Americans and 'Vinona' by the British) which pointed to two leaks during the mid-1940s – one from inside the British embassy in Washington, the other from the Los Alamos atomic research base in New Mexico. The second leak had been traced to Klaus Fuchs, a German-born physicist who had become a naturalized Briton before being allowed to work at Los Alamos in 1944. Fuchs had returned to England in 1946 to continue his atomic research and had been interrogated by MI5's William 'Jim' Skardon. Fuchs, jailed for fourteen years at the Old Bailey in March 1950, had also given leads to his contacts in the States. According to Kim Philby these 'led inexorably' to Julius and Ethel Rosenberg, who were executed at Sing Sing prison on 19 June 1953.[3]

By the late summer of 1950 neither American nor British Intelligence knew more about the other leak than that the spy at the British embassy in Washington was codenamed 'Homer' by the Soviets. But Kim Philby was sure that the spy was Donald Maclean – who had been based at the embassy from 1944 to October 1948, rising from the rank of First Secretary to Head of Chancery. A classified report, prepared for the US Attorney General after Maclean's defection, gave this description of Maclean's role, which shows his real value to the Soviets (unlike the anodyne pap that was issued by the British Foreign Office):

> During 1947 and 1948, he served as the United Kingdom Secretary to the Combined Policy Committee concerned with atomic energy matters. This committee was composed of representatives of the United States, England and Canada. During a portion of this period he possessed a non-escort pass to the Atomic Energy Commission, Washington, DC. In October 1947, Maclean attended a three-day declassification conference at which time discussions were limited to atomic energy information held in common . . . This conference included a discussion on atomic weapons.[4]

After discussions with his Soviet control in Washington, Philby was allowed to brief Burgess about the 'Homer' problem. Burgess immediately realized, as Philby had, that Maclean's days at the Foreign Office were numbered. Burgess knew, too, that they could not allow Maclean to be interrogated. One day, perhaps soon, Maclean would have to escape from England.

By November 1950 Donald Maclean had become the head of the American Department at the Foreign Office in London. Impressive though this sounded, insiders knew that his career, which had begun so promisingly, was going badly. He had a reputation as a heavy drinker prone to bouts of depression. Nevertheless, no one within the Foreign Office had any doubts about his loyalty. He may have been loudly and unashamedly anti-American during his four years in Washington, but many of his colleagues shared his hostility; the difference with Maclean was that he had been silly enough to risk his future by proclaiming it. Stories about Maclean had circulated freely around the embassy. Sir Isaiah Berlin, the Oxford philosopher who had been a specialist attaché in Washington from 1942 to 1946, recalled that Maclean complained that he was tired of meeting 'conventional and pompous officials' and that he wanted to meet radical Americans. Berlin remembered one dinner party at which Maclean surpassed himself:

> The evening was a disaster . . . some remark of mine set Maclean off. He said that persons who called themselves liberal had no business knowing reactionaries . . . All life was a battle and one should know which side one was on and stay faithful to it. One must be clear which side of the barricades one was on; relations with the enemy were not permissible – at this point he became exceedingly abusive . . . perhaps I should have realized from Maclean's speech that he was a sort of political extremist, e.g. a communist or very left-wing socialist, or something of that kind; but the thought never entered my head . . . The rest of the company thereupon took Maclean's side and attacked me passionately and unanimously.[5]

From Washington, Maclean had moved to Cairo to become counsellor and Head of Chancery at the embassy there. He started to drink even more heavily and on one occasion spent twenty-four hours in jail, protesting to the disbelieving Egyptian police that he was a senior British diplomat who had, by some inexplicable mischance, lost his shoes while out dining with friends. On another occasion, during what should have been a relaxing trip up the Nile, he became so violently drunk that an embassy colleague who tried to restrain him had his left leg broken. His recall to London seemed increasingly likely. And, in May 1950, after an extraordinary episode when he broke into the flat of the secretary to the US ambassador and ransacked it in an abortive search for whisky, that is precisely what happened. He returned to London with his wife Melinda.

George Carey-Foster recalled: 'Maclean was not under suspicion at this time. He was sent back to the UK by the ambassador in Cairo for what was considered to be a nervous breakdown culminating in a drunken orgy in which he broke up the American secretary's flat.'[6]

In London Maclean insisted that he wanted to see a psychiatrist of his own choice, a Russian-born woman with a practice in Wimpole Street, rather than a specialist chosen by the Foreign Office. Carey-Foster said:

> I was brought into this because the head of personnel thought that I ought to know what Maclean wanted to do. I advised caution and said that I would consult MI5 to see who this woman was. Maclean was in possession, after all, as a result of his work in Washington of very highly secret Anglo-American atomic matters. No adverse trace was found on her so Maclean was allowed to see her. I knew very little about the Maclean case. It was being handled purely as a disciplinary and medical matter and, although I later thought that I should have been brought into the deliberations, the personnel department in those days was not in the habit of consulting me on disciplinary affairs.[7]

At the beginning of November 1950, after six months on sick leave, Maclean returned to work at the Foreign Office as head of the American Department. Melinda, who had spent the summer in Spain, returned to try and make a go of their marriage. They bought a large house called Beaconshaw in the village of Tatsfield, in the North Downs northeast of Sevenoaks, Kent.

From Washington, Burgess wrote occasional, worrying letters to Goronwy Rees, who had become estates bursar of All Souls, Oxford. It was clear that Guy hated America and everything it stood for. Rees wrote in his autobiography:

Senator Joe McCarthy's anti-communist crusade was in full swing, and Guy had come to the conclusion that he was both the most powerful and the most representative politician in the United States and that the future of America was in his hands. What aroused Guy almost to hysteria was McCarthy's identification of communism with homosexuality in the United States, and especially in the State Department. 'Things have reached such a pitch,' he wrote 'that two members of the State Department daren't dine together in public for fear of being called homosexuals and therefore communists' . . . Somehow I had the feeling that Guy's stay in Washington would not be unduly prolonged . . . In England he was like some bizarre feature of the landscape, like the Needles or Stonehenge, which local inhabitants have long ceased to notice unless their attention is directed to them; strangers and foreigners did not find it so easy to overlook his eccentricities which, even for an Englishman, were outrageous.[8]

Early in 1951, while Rees was awaiting Burgess's inevitable return in disgrace, he met Maclean for the first time in fifteen years, at the Gargoyle Club in Soho. Maclean was extremely and offensively drunk. He lurched across to Rees's table and said: 'I know all about you. You used to be one of us, but you ratted.' Maclean crumpled to the floor, still screaming abuse. Then he heaved himself up and tottered off. Rees insisted that he was deeply disturbed by the incident; did it mean, he wrote twenty years later, that Maclean, too, like Burgess, had been a Comintern agent? Rees consoled himself with the thought that, even if that was the case, it was likely that both Burgess and Maclean had long since stopped passing information to the Soviets. After all, Burgess and Maclean were so openly left-wing and anti-American that it was not credible that they could be spies. Maclean's attack was, therefore, the anger of a communist against someone who had 'deserted to the forces of capitalism and reaction'. That is how Rees described his reaction to Maclean's outburst, though others suspected that this explanation was another carefully constructed package of half-truths and lies to conceal Rees's own role in the Cambridge spy network.

In America Michael Straight was a nervous spectator as the hysteria of McCarthyism swept the country. He had long since renounced his Marxism, though he remained a liberal, which he knew would not be much of a defence if the Red-hunters ever learned about his student Marxism or his subsequent meetings with a Soviet agent. Straight had had unwelcome reminders of his past when he visited London in 1949 and had attended the annual Apostles dinner chaired by Burgess at the Royal Automobile Club in Pall Mall. It had not been a happy evening. Straight had had a fierce argument with Eric Hobsbawm, the Marxist historian, over Czechoslovakia where the communists had recently seized power. Straight wrote:

> I remembered Hobsbawm as a member of the student communist movement at Cambridge. He made it plain that he, at least, had not given up his beliefs. I made some bitter comments about the Soviet occupation of Czechoslovakia. Hobsbawm countered . . . with a knowing smile: 'There are more political prisoners in the United States today than there are in Czechoslovakia.' 'That's a damned lie,' I cried. I continued to shout at Hobsbawm. I was aware that others were staring at me. I was not acting in a manner becoming to a member of the Society. Anthony [Blunt] was sitting at the far end of the room. I had managed to avoid him, but when the speeches were over and the dinner was breaking up, he came over to

me. 'Guy and I would like to talk to you,' he said. 'We'll meet you here tomorrow morning.'[9]

The next day the three men sat in deep, leather chairs in a dimly-lit corner of the RAC. Blunt explained that he had worked for MI5 during the war but that he was now a full-time art historian at the Courtauld. Burgess, on the other hand, was with the Foreign Office:

> Guy . . . had moved to the Far Eastern Department of the Foreign Office. It seemed to be probable that Guy was still engaged in espionage. I reminded him that when we had last met, in 1947 [in London], he had assured me that he was about to leave the government for good. 'I was about to leave,' Guy said, 'but then this offer came along.' He sensed my hostility. He added that he was about to go off on extended leave and that he did not intend to return to the Foreign Office. Where, then, did the three of us stand? We turned to the central issue of the day: the danger of a third world war . . . Anthony listened in moody silence. I sensed that he still deferred to Guy on political issues, although his interest in politics had diminished. The tension between us mounted. At last, Anthony broke in. 'The question is,' he said, 'are we capable of intellectual growth?' I said: 'Exactly!' Guy looked at me intently. 'Are you still with us?' he asked. 'You know that I'm not,' I said. [He said:] 'You're not totally unfriendly?' 'If I were,' I said, 'why would I be here?'[10]

Burgess and Blunt were thus reassured that Straight would not alert the authorities in the USA or Britain about their work for the Soviets. But Straight had omitted one crucial fact from his conversation with them:

I had reason to believe, from 1948 on, that the British government was fully aware of my story. I had recounted it to my wife on the evening when Burgess visited us in 1940. She recounted the story in turn to her analyst, Dr Jennie Welderhall. Dr Welderhall informed my wife in 1948 that, in violation of the traditional bond of confidentiality, she had passed the story on to her husband who was a British embassy official. I was greatly relieved, unwilling as I was then to act as an informer, and yet knowing as I did that the story should be told. I waited for the embassy to call me. I have been unable to find out why they did not call.[11]

Straight repeated this story in 1963 when he gave the FBI and hence, MI5, the necessary information finally to force a confession from Blunt. According to FBI files: 'Straight stated that in 1948 his wife . . . gave the names of Blunt and Burgess to an analyst whose husband was employed in the British embassy and requested that the names be passed on to the British authorities as two members of the Russian International working for the British government.'[12] Yet the embassy in Washington does not appear to have done anything about the tip-off. If Straight was telling the truth (and there is no reason to think that he was lying) then it seems that the information was simply forgotten; perhaps it was dismissed as a piece of irresponsible gossip, a symptom of the Red-bashing hysteria sweeping America.

Straight's next meeting with Burgess took place in Washington in March 1951. Straight recalled that he had been to a meeting with a British embassy economist to discuss an article that he, Straight, was writing for a magazine:

I saw Burgess as I was leaving the embassy. I was surprised and shocked to see him. I reminded him of the assurance he had given me in 1949. He replied: 'I believed at the time that I was about to leave the Foreign Office. I actually did go on an extended tour. I almost did leave when I returned, but they insisted on finding another job for me.' I feared that Burgess might have access to sensitive information. I swore that I would turn him in unless he left the Foreign Office within a month . . . [He said] 'Don't worry. I'm about to sail for England, and as soon as I return, I'm going to resign.'[13]

Straight also claimed that he was concerned that Burgess might have been in a position to leak plans to the Soviets of the American-South Korean push in October to the Yalu river. There they had been attacked by a massive Chinese force. Straight was furious. He asked Burgess if he had known about the US plans and Burgess, after admitting that he had, argued, with some accuracy, that 'everyone' had known. Indeed, the Americans, Burgess continued, had actually been warned by the Chinese that they would face annihilation if they pushed north.

Despite this conversation – and his fears that Burgess had cost American lives – Straight did nothing. He did not alert the FBI or the British embassy. He did what he was best at: nothing.

Burgess knew that he would have to return to England. He had been deputed by the Soviets to warn Maclean that the net was closing in on him. Philby explained:

Groping in partial darkness as we were, it seemed safest to get Maclean away by the middle of 1951 at the latest. The second complication arose from Burgess's position. He was emphatically not at home in the Foreign Office, for which he had neither the right temperament nor the right personality . . . As a result, his work for the Foreign

Office had suffered, so much so that it looked like a close thing between resignation and dismissal . . .

In somebody's mind – I do not know whose – the two ideas merged: Burgess's return to London and the rescue of Maclean. If Burgess returned to London from the British embassy in Washington, it seemed natural that he should call on the head of the American department. He would be well placed to set the ball rolling for the rescue operation.[14]

This plan suited Burgess perfectly. He wanted only to return to his beloved London where his brilliance was properly appreciated. He was confident that he would be able to find a job that was more suited to his talents. The bureaucratic world, he told friends, was too stuffy and unimaginative; it had outlived its usefulness. It proved easy for Burgess to accomplish the recall that he now wanted. He merely acted as he had always done. In March, shortly before his meeting with Straight, Burgess had been driving south in a car carrying diplomatic number plates. With him was one of his many Washington conquests. By the evening he had been stopped three times for speeding, and within a week the British ambassador, Sir Oliver Franks, informed Burgess that he was being recalled to London.

As Philby tried to calculate how long it would take the Americans and British to narrow the suspects down to Maclean, he mentally sifted through other evidence stored by MI5 and MI6, which might, he knew, suddenly take on new meaning if Maclean was ever interrogated.

There was the evidence of General Walter Krivitsky, the Soviet intelligence officer who had defected in 1940. Krivitsky had told the British that there were two spies within the Foreign Office: one was identified as a cipher clerk called John King; the other remained unknown. But, according to the general, he was 'an idealist, of good family, moved in artistic circles, wore a cape and had been educated at Oxford'. Although some of the details were wrong (Maclean had been at Cambridge) Philby knew that the description would lead to Maclean. For a time, though, snobbery and the belief that the Foreign Office was staffed by gentlemen beyond suspicion protected Maclean. The search for the spy was concentrated on non-diplomatic staff such as cleaners and drivers, even though it was patently ridiculous that 'Homer', who had been such a valued source for the Soviets, could have occupied such a humble position. Philby was shrewd enough – some would say ruthless enough – to remind London of the Krivitsky information. By doing this, he argued, he gave himself a chance to survive the inquiry that would undoubtedly follow the escape of Maclean. The reply came back that this was already 'very much in our minds'. Philby knew, too, that lying in the Krivitsky file was another damning piece of information: that the Soviets had recruited a young man who had worked as a journalist during the Spanish Civil War.

There was another skeleton in the Philby cupboard. In September 1945 Konstantin Volkov, an NKVD officer working as a diplomat in the Soviet embassy in Istanbul, had offered to supply the British with the names of three Soviet agents in London. One was a counter-intelligence specialist, he said; the other two were with the Foreign Office. Philby was detailed to negotiate asylum with Volkov but ensured that by the time he arrived in Istanbul Volkov had been bundled off to the Soviet Union. The episode had puzzled many British officials who dealt with the case and who had hoped that Volkov would prove to be a valuable source. John Reed, who was based at the British embassy in Istanbul, recalled:

At the time of Philby's visit I asked him the reason for the long delay in his coming to Istanbul. He replied in an off-hand way that it would have interfered with his office's leave arrangements. Treachery at that time was not in the air and I fear I did not suspect it. But I did suspect criminal incompetence. I was very much upset, because I suspected what had happened to Volkov, who had virtually placed his life in my hands. I spent an afternoon showing Philby round the sights of Istanbul. He was, as one might expect, an intelligent and charming companion. But, nevertheless, the doubt lingered.[15]

By the early spring of 1951, George Carey-Foster in London had a list of five Foreign Office men who could have been 'Homer' – simply because of their access to information at crucial moments. Carey-Foster said that within the Foreign Office only Sir Patrick Reilly, a career diplomat who was later ambassador in Moscow and then Paris, and Sir William Strang, the FO's Under-Secretary, knew how far the investigation had gone. The list included Paul Gore-Booth, later head of the Diplomatic Service; Michael Wright, a future ambassador to Norway; and Donald Maclean. It did not include the name of Roger Makins, later Lord Sherfield, ambassador in Washington from 1953 to 1956, despite persistent reports to the contrary during the 1970s. Makins had been ruled out, Carey-Foster said, because he had not been in Washington at the relevant time. Philby was even offered odds by Mackenzie that Gore-Booth was the guilty man. Philby did not find this very amusing.

But there was a remarkable lack of urgency about Burgess's departure. (One theory, based on the assumption that nothing in espionage is ever as it seems and too complex to explain in detail here, is that Burgess's return to London was an accident; Philby only said that it was part of a clever plan to cover blunders by the KGB.) On 30 April 1951, shortly before boarding the *Queen Mary* for Southampton, Burgess made a recording in a New York sound studio. A few minutes before sailing he rushed back in panic, as the technician later said: 'He [Burgess] wanted to hear what he had recorded – "in case there is anything incriminating in it". He sat down and listened to the playback. When it was finished Burgess said: "That's OK." '[16]

The plan that Philby outlined to Burgess was simple enough. In London Burgess would arrange to meet a contact from Soviet Intelligence. He would then visit Maclean, on the pretext of discussing American affairs, and use that as an opportunity to organize a clandestine meeting. Burgess would then brief Maclean on the danger facing him. From there it would be left to the KGB to organize Maclean's escape. Burgess was warned, finally and prophetically, by Philby: 'Don't you go too.' Burgess nodded and set off, determined to enjoy the voyage. He behaved relatively well, by his standards at least, though he did pick up a young American, Bernard Miller, the owner, so Burgess later told friends, of a fringe theatre off Broadway. The two talked about a trip together to St Malo and the Channel Islands.

As Philby waited anxiously in Washington for news from London he knew that, providing Burgess followed the plan, there would be no insoluble problems for the remaining members of the Cambridge spy circle. There were no suspicions and certainly there was no hard evidence against Burgess. Indeed, there was no evidence that would stand up in a court of law against Maclean. Only a confession by Maclean (or perhaps Michael Straight) could lead MI5 to Philby, Burgess or Blunt. But what if the unpredictable Guy somehow became entangled in Maclean's escape? The prospect filled Philby with horror. He knew that then even the clods of MI5 might start digging into the files, but he was still sure that he could outwit the opposition:

> A strong presumption of my guilt might be good enough for an intelligence officer. But it was not good enough for a lawyer. What he needed was evidence. The chain of circumstantial evidence that might be brought against me was uncomfortably long. But, as I examined each single link of the chain, I thought I could break it; and if every link was broken singly, what remained of the chain?[17]

By the end of March 1951 George Carey-Foster had further narrowed down his list of suspects. Thanks to British cryptoanalysts, a detailed picture had been built up of 'Homer's' movements and everything pointed to Maclean. Carey-Foster broke the news to Sir William Strang one afternoon as they were strolling in St James's Park. Carey-Foster recalled:

> You may know how in old-fashioned novels someone turns as white as a sheet. This is, in fact, what Strang did. I had never seen it before. He stopped, turned white and said: 'Carey, I don't believe you. You will have to go through all your facts again and submit your conclusions.' This delayed my official submission but did not alter my conclusion.[18]

Strang informed Ernest Bevin, the Foreign Secretary, of the growing weight of evidence against Maclean. The MI5 director-general, Sir Percy Sillitoe, was told and he notified Edgar Hoover, the FBI chief. The CIA also had to be told. Carey-Foster said: 'The American security authorities were kept informed of our progress in the case through Philby so he was in full possession of what was to happen. He engineered Burgess's return to the UK and then advised him of the date by which Maclean had to be got away.'[19]

Philby tried to keep calm when he heard that Maclean would be questioned, however reluctant the Foreign Office was to believe that one of its own men could even be suspected of treachery. Philby sent a coded note to Burgess in London, warning him that Burgess's car, which had been left in the embassy car park, would be soon towed away for scrap. Philby added that Burgess had 'to act at once or it would be too late'. Yet in London no one seemed to be hurrying. MI5 now had Maclean under surveillance, but manpower shortages meant that he was not followed beyond Charing Cross Station where he caught his train home to Kent. There was another reason for holding back from a full-scale interrogation. MI5 and Carey-Foster knew that the 'Homer' intercepts would be worthless in a British court. They now hoped to catch Maclean meeting his Soviet contact; perhaps, if they were lucky, even see Maclean hand over Foreign Office documents. However, by late May MI5 had concluded that they could not afford to wait any longer and decided that he should be pulled in for questioning on or soon after Monday 28 May 1951.

When the *Queen Mary* docked at Southampton early in May, Anthony Blunt, looking sallow and anxious, was waiting to see Burgess. As they travelled back to London the two men discussed how to ensure Maclean's escape. Burgess spent that night at Blunt's flat at the Courtauld Institute, and the next day he travelled to see Goronwy Rees at his country home at Sonning, a few miles outside Reading. Rees thought that Burgess looked healthier and cleaner than he had for many years, almost as if the Americans had forced Guy through 'a special dry-cleaning machine for diplomats'. Rees recalled:

So far as such improbable words could ever be applied to Guy, he was spick and span. He was gay and charming and delightful as I had not remembered him for many years . . . he gave us long, scurrilous and extremely amusing accounts of life in Washington. But it was evident that he was labouring under a tremendous sense of excitement, as if he were under fierce internal pressures.[20]

Burgess must have known that his Foreign Office career was over but clung to the hope that he would, at the last moment, salvage something from the mess. He showed Rees a note from Anthony Eden thanking Burgess for his help when Eden had visited Washington. Guy argued that Eden would shortly become Foreign Secretary (he did when Churchill took power in October 1951) and intimated that if he could hang on until then he would be saved. He complained that his analysis of the domestic American political scene, a *tour de force* which exposed the evils of McCarthyism and the dangers that this posed for world peace, had been blocked by the ambassador in Washington. If only, said Guy, the mandarins in London agreed to read it they would realize that they could not afford to lose him. But he was obviously delighted to be back in England and consoled himself with the thought that he could, or so he thought, walk into a job in journalism. He was sure that his friend Michael Berry, proprietor of the *Daily Telegraph*, would offer him something. Burgess fancied becoming the paper's diplomatic correspondent – a job which would help him reshape Britain's disastrous, slavishly pro-American foreign policy. He ignored the inconvenient fact that the *Telegraph*, a cautious, conservative newspaper, was unlikely to allow itself to be used as a platform for his far-Left, anti-American views. Many of Burgess's friends believe that Rees left out crucial elements from his account of Guy's visit. Jack Hewit said: 'I think that Rees was up to his neck in the whole business and that he was panicking. I think Guy went down to reassure him and tell him that everything was going to be all right.'[21]

Back in London Burgess went to great trouble to obtain Maclean's home telephone number. He called Lady Maclean and said that he had a message for Donald from Alan, Maclean's younger brother who was working at the United Nations in New York. It appears that Burgess was convinced that it would now be unsafe to call Maclean at the Foreign Office. But in 1956, in the Tom Driberg biography, Burgess claimed that he first met Maclean at the Foreign Office. Burgess said that he showed Maclean his memorandum on American policy:

> I'd put into it in strong terms, all the fear and disgust I felt about the trend of American policy in the far East; I'm pretty sure I also wrote about the threat that McCarthy represented . . . We talked about all this; and I can't tell you what a relief it was – to both of us, I think – to find that our views, the things we were afraid of, the things that made us angry, were identical . . . It was almost – well, almost uncanny. We sat talking on a sofa outside his room at the Foreign Office. I suppose he was afraid that his room was 'miked'.[22]

It may be that Burgess was telling the truth in 1956; perhaps he had not been able to contact Maclean at home and was forced to risk a face-to-face meeting at the Foreign Office. It is certain, however, that the two men lunched at the Royal Automobile Club in the middle of May. Maclean looked as if he was heading for another nervous collapse. On the way to lunch he had pointed out the two 'watchers' from MI5 or Special Branch who were trailing him around London. Maclean now knew that he was under suspicion; apart from the ever-present 'watchers', classified papers that he would normally have received were not reaching him. According to Burgess, they had lunch twice more. It was during the third lunch, said Burgess, that Maclean suggested that he was going to 'clear out and go to the Soviet Union'. Maclean then asked: 'Will you help me? The trouble is that I can't even buy a ticket. They'd be on to me at once – wouldn't even let me leave the country.' This account disguises Burgess's role as the intermediary between Maclean and the KGB, but he was probably not lying when he said that he had no intention until then of leaving the country with Maclean. Jack Hewit speculated: 'I think Maclean told Guy that he wouldn't go unless Guy went as well. He said that Guy was the only person he could trust.'[23]

Maclean and Burgess disappeared on Friday 25 May, Maclean's thirty-eighth birthday. It is not known whether the KGB ordered or even authorized Burgess's departure. Common sense (a commodity often in short supply in the world of espionage) suggests that Maclean's escape was being planned by the Soviets and that Burgess's role was supposed to be strictly limited; to help organize Maclean's travel out of England and, more important, to calm his nerves. But the plan went disastrously wrong.

Jack Hewit recalled:

Guy was vacillating all week. He was maudlin one minute and up the next. He was drinking an awful lot. He said that he was going on a cruise from Southampton to St Malo that coming weekend with Bernard Miller. I was furious. Then one night he said that Miller was leaving. I thought, marvellous, I will go instead. Then he said: 'A friend of mine is in a spot of bother. I'll use the tickets to get him away.' I thought that it was Donald Maclean. I knew that Guy had seen him. And Guy told me that Blunt had also seen Maclean. On the Thursday [24 May] I came back from dinner and heard a terrible row going

on. Guy and another man were arguing in French. Guy
said that it was OK. It was a friend of his who was drunk.
I think that must have been his [Soviet] control.[24]

That week, too, Burgess was more imaginative than
usual. He told Hewit that Blunt and he were having dinner
the following Tuesday at Michael Berry's home. The diplomatic job, Burgess said, was in the bag. He suggested that it
was time to settle down into a respectable marriage. Churchill's niece, Clarissa, whom Burgess had met through
James Pope-Hennessy, was, he thought, as good a candidate as any. However, it was nonsense to think that she
would even consider such a proposal: 'I hardly knew
Burgess. I met him, I suppose, about half a dozen times.
James Pope-Hennessy was a friend of mine and I met
Burgess with him.'[25]

On the morning of Friday 25 May Hewit left the flat at
around nine o'clock, believing that he would see Guy the
following Monday. Burgess pottered around, calling
friends, including the poet Stephen Spender. Did Spender,
by any chance, have W. H. Auden's address in Ischia?
According to one report Burgess then strolled round to the
Green Park Hotel, a few minutes' walk from Bond Street,
to tell Miller that their weekend break might have to be
cancelled. Burgess promised to let Miller know by 8.30 that
evening. Shortly before noon that day Burgess stopped off
at the Reform Club and telephoned Rees's home at
Sonning. Rees was in Oxford but Burgess did not seem to
mind. He rambled incoherently for twenty minutes to
Rees's wife, repeating again and again that he was 'about to
do something which would surprise and shock many people' but adding that he was sure that it was 'the right thing to
do'. Burgess said, too, that only Rees would understand
why he had been forced to act in this way.

Burgess hired a car – a cream Austin A40 – and returned

to Bond Street to pack. He did not seem to know where he was going: he took a tweed suit, which suggested a weekend in the country; a dinner jacket, which meant that he expected to be eating formally; and Hewit's overcoat, which indicated that he might be going east rather than south. He took, too, his beloved and very battered copy of the collected novels of Jane Austen and £300 in cash. Burgess recalled:

> [Miller] and I were thinking of going off to France for a jaunt, so I booked tickets for a weekend cruise to St Malo and the Channel Islands . . . and I got one of the tickets in his name. I'd arranged to go to Donald's house at Tatsfield, near Westerham – almost within sight of Churchill! – on the Friday evening. But until I got there I didn't know whether I was going to Moscow with Donald or to France with the American for a jolly jaunt. So I told the American to stay by the telephone at his hotel until eight thirty, and packed two lots of things, suitable for both purposes.[26]

Jack Hewit said: 'Guy just went. He said that he might go on to Paris and that if he did he would call me. That was the last time I saw him.'

On that same Friday, Donald Maclean seemed to be in far better spirits than he had been for some time. He had a birthday lunch with his old friend, Robin Campbell, who had been at the same crammer's seventeen years before, and Campbell's second wife Mary, formerly Lady Mary St Claire-Erskine (the girl whom Blunt had once half-heartedly courted). They had a relaxed meal of oysters and champagne at Wheeler's in Soho. Maclean, who had so often poured out his anguish – about his career, his inability *really* to believe in anything, his doubts about his own sexuality – now talked positively about the future. Melinda was pregnant and was due to give birth in early June. Mary Campbell (now Mary Dunn) recalled:

> We certainly had no suspicions that he was going to disappear. We were old friends and we were celebrating his birthday. We picked him up at the Foreign Office in our jeep. He had the brim of his hat turned up. This was our code if he was in a good mood. If it was turned down it meant that he was not feeling good.[27]

After lunch Maclean returned to the Foreign Office. He caught his usual train home – the 5.19 from Charing Cross to Sevenoaks. And, as usual, the 'watchers' who had followed him to the station stayed in London.

That night Burgess dined with the Macleans at their home in Kent. He told Melinda that his name was Mr Stiles and that he was a colleague of Donald's from the Foreign Office. He would, alas, have to take Donald away for a few days on 'urgent business'. What had happened that day to alter the plan to spirit Maclean quietly out of England? Clearly, Burgess had been warned that the net was closing in on Maclean. Although it is not entirely clear how this warning was delivered, the messenger could only have been Kim Philby. It is possible, but unlikely, that someone in Whitehall gossiped. In the MI5 inquiry that followed the disappearance of Maclean and Burgess, a series of names were mentioned. The suspects included MI5's own Guy Liddell who had, as many colleagues knew, been friendly with Burgess. But, according to George Carey-Foster, the explanation was really very simple: Kim Philby had told the Soviets that Maclean had to escape that weekend.

Why did Burgess become entangled, inextricably and disastrously, in Maclean's escape? Maclean could have bought his own boat ticket. There was no special watch at ports for him; Maclean did not know that he was about to be interrogated and, anyway, the FO was sure that Maclean, spy or not, was a decent chap who would not desert his wife, who was pregnant. Burgess's account of what happened – 'Donald dillied and dallied . . . we only just caught the boat'[28] – does not help us much. Perhaps the KGB in London did not think it mattered if Burgess defected; after all, while he had been immensely useful he had always been a potential liability. Perhaps, as some writers now suggest, the KGB did not realize that Burgess had shared Philby's home in Washington and that, by allowing Guy to defect, their star agent, Philby, would be fatally compromised.

After landing in St Malo Burgess and Maclean took a taxi to Rennes and then a train to Paris. They then moved on to Berne, Switzerland, where, Burgess said, Maclean went to the Czech embassy to apply for visas for them to go to Prague. On Tuesday 29 May they arrived in Prague. They hung around for over a week, with Burgess still hoping, quite forlornly, that somehow he would be able to return to England as if nothing had happened. Then the British press broke the news of their disappearance. There could be no turning back now. They flew to Moscow.

Twelve years later Donald Maclean described to Nigel Burgess the first forty-eight hours that Guy and he had spent in Moscow. Nigel recalled:

Donald showed me a great hotel balcony on the first floor overlooking the Kremlin. He told me that when they arrived they all had dinner on that balcony. They had got drunker and drunker on vodka until three in the morning. People were running about all over the place looking for them and there they were on the balcony boozing. The next day Donald was in bed with a hangover and Guy told him that he was going out. He had to find a bar, he said. Donald said that they were in Moscow now . . .

Guy said he could find a bar anywhere in the world. And after a long bar crawl he was hauled back to the hotel that night.[29]

Then came the interrogation from Soviet officials. Burgess and Maclean had to answer questions about British intentions over Korea. Then they were dispatched to the dreary provincial town of Kuybyshev for six months, well away from the Western correspondents in Moscow, who were frantically searching for them. Burgess told friends that it had been a terrible experience.

We were given a flat and servants and cars but it was a horrible place and things were made worse by the fact that Beria [head of Soviet Intelligence], in an effort to gain popularity after the death of Stalin, released 80 per cent of the criminals in Russia. Kuybyshev was invaded by gangsters and scoundrels. That's how I lost the teeth on one side of my face. I was walking along a street when a thug saw my watch and knocked me down.[30]

Maclean immediately began learning Russian. But Burgess, numbed that he had by a series of awful accidents ended up behind the Iron Curtain, never bothered to learn the language. He just could not believe that he would not soon be back with his friends in London.

CHAPTER 16
Runaway Friends

Anthony Blunt had a great deal on his mind in the last week of May 1951. He was organizing a surprise party at the Courtauld Institute for Johannes Wilde, his loyal deputy, who would be sixty on 2 June. Kerry Downes, then a student who later became a professor at Reading University, said:

> An enormous party was planned and Johannes was not to know anything about it. He was going to be presented with essays from colleagues. There was the catering to organize. It all worked wonderfully. Anthony had lunch with Wilde in his flat and then said, come downstairs. The room was filled with friends. There were tears. It worked perfectly.[1]

It seems certain that Blunt had no idea that Maclean would have to flee so hastily. Early that month Burgess had told him that Maclean was under suspicion, but that there was no need to panic. From Washington, Kim Philby would keep them briefed on the progress of the Foreign Office investigation. Blunt assumed that, if it was necessary, Donald and Melinda would travel abroad for a short break – and then vanish. He was sure that both Guy and he were safe. Even if there was a catastrophe, there would be no corroborative evidence to support a confession by

Maclean. There were no missing documents or photographs of meetings with Soviet contacts.

It is not clear, however, exactly when Blunt knew that Burgess's involvement in Maclean's escape had gone much further than anyone had anticipated. He may have been called by Burgess's KGB controller, but for much of the weekend he did not realize that Guy's plans to help Maclean had backfired. Ellis Waterhouse said: 'When Guy disappeared the first thing he [Anthony] did was telephone me and ask if Guy was staying with me. He seemed worried and puzzled. I am sure that he didn't know where Guy had gone.'[2]

Once he knew what had happened, Blunt realized that there would be a wider inquiry than if Maclean had fled on his own, an inquiry which would inevitably include Burgess's close friends. For the first time Blunt feared that his work for the Soviets might disturb his elegant, well-organized life. The KGB had destroyed Guy's life and were now trying to do the same to his. When the Soviets told him to follow Burgess, he refused; he had no intention of ending up in a cultural desert like Moscow. Blunt's most pressing problem, however, was not the KGB but Goronwy Rees. On Sunday evening, when he returned home from Oxford, Rees listened gloomily as his wife described Burgess's call on Friday. Rees wrote:

It was not easy for me to make out what Guy meant . . . the message was a warning of some kind, and also a farewell. I was not sure what the warning was, but at least it meant that Guy was going away and that this involved some action which might be regarded as sensationalist even for Guy. I did not by any means think quite so consecutively, but having got so far I suddenly had an absolutely sure and certain, if irrational, intuition, that Guy had gone to the Soviet Union . . . so much so that to my wife's utter bewilderment I said: 'He's gone to Moscow.'[3]

Rees telephoned David Footman of MI6 late on Sunday and told him that he feared their mutual friend, Guy Burgess, had defected to the Soviet Union. Footman had no idea what he was talking about, but Rees insisted that Footman alert MI5. Next he telephoned Blunt at his flat in the Courtauld. In *A Chapter of Accidents*, published in 1972, Rees coyly avoided naming Blunt:

> I also told another friend of Guy's, who had served in MI5 during the war and still preserved close connections with it, of what I had done. He was greatly distressed and said he would like to see me. On Monday he came down to my house in the country, and on an almost ideally beautiful English summer day, we sat beside the river and I gave him my reasons for thinking that Guy had gone to the Soviet Union; his violent anti-Americanism, his certainty that America was about to involve us all in a Third World War, most of all the fact that he may have been and perhaps still was a Soviet agent. He pointed out, convincingly as it seemed to me, that these were really not very good reasons for denouncing Guy to MI5.[4]

According to this account by Rees, Blunt argued that no friend would make such a damaging allegation without hard evidence. And there was none. Rees looked at Blunt and felt that this was 'the Cambridge liberal conscience at its very best, reasonable, sensible, and firm in the faith that personal relations are the highest of all human values'. Anthony reminded him of E. M. Forster's famous aphorism that if he had to choose between betraying his country or betraying his friend, he hoped he would have the guts to betray his country. Rees argued that this was an amoral over-simplification; what was a country if it was not a 'dense network of individual and social relationships in which loyalty to one particular person formed only a single strand?' He told Blunt that he was tired of Burgess's deceit. No matter how much he might disapprove, Rees said that he intended to 'get rid of all my doubts and suspicions and speculations and pass them on to those whose business it was to say what they were worth'.

Rees was not a consistent witness. He was always modifying his story of what happened in 1951. In his autobiography he said that he had travelled to London on Tuesday 29 May. There he met a senior MI5 officer, Guy Liddell. When he finished talking Liddell paused and said that it was much worse than Rees realized. Maclean had vanished as well. This was Rees's first story. But he gave a second, more elaborate version in the late 1970s. Then he said that he met Liddell for lunch at the end of the week. Liddell was not alone; he brought Blunt. Rees said that the two 'took up where Blunt had left off. They did their level best to convince me that I'd be wasting everyone's time if I went along and submitted the nebulous kind of evidence against Guy Burgess that I seemed determined to offer.' It wasn't until Wednesday, 6 June that Rees had a formal interview with Liddell and Dick White. Rees complained later that he was 'treated as if he were a spy and a traitor with lots to hide'. He told the story again; of how Burgess had once confessed to being a Comintern agent, how he had named Blunt as an accomplice and how he had asked Rees to join them. Dick White had a different memory:

I thought he was a four-letter man. If he had really known all these things why hadn't he come forward? Then he went into this explanation of how he thought we had known it all. So I said to Rees: 'You assumed we knew? Burgess was working for the Russians and we did nothing about it? What can you mean?' He was as slippery as an eel and had a violent antipathy to Blunt.

He said, why don't you ask Blunt about these things. But he did not say that Blunt was our man. No, he said nothing resembling that.[5]

Rees's family believe that he was doing his patriotic duty in 1951 and that it was unfair of British Intelligence to turn on him, as if he had been personally responsible for the misdeeds of Guy Burgess. One family member reflected the bitterness that they all felt that Goronwy had died with so many question marks against his name:

> Rees was a drinker and God knows what else. But he was a sound citizen. He didn't find Burgess likeable or attractive but he lived for the times when they would argue about politics. They used to row all the time. They would both be drunk and they would fight like crazy. With fury. Rees wasn't a climber on the backs of people. Not like all the others who were. It was a mafia of media and intelligence people who all had an idea to the main chance. We are all very angry. There's been a cover-up. We want to clear Rees's name.[6]

There is a less charitable interpretation: that Rees was so frightened that his own ties with Burgess would be discovered that he concocted a cover story which would save himself by leading MI5 to Anthony Blunt.

Meanwhile, Jack Hewit was desperately trying to locate his beloved Guy. Hewit knew that he had an important dinner planned for Tuesday 29 May when he hoped to persuade Michael Berry, owner of the *Daily Telegraph*, to take him on as a diplomatic correspondent. There was no sign of Burgess on Sunday evening; nor had he called, as he had promised he would if he was going to be delayed. Hewit thought that he might have decided to stay with Anthony on Sunday night. On Monday Hewit called Rees's home but he was not there, although there had been that strange call from the Reform Club on Friday. By now he feared that something awful had happened. He called Blunt:

> He told me he didn't know where Guy was. I said that I would call the Green Park Hotel to see if Bernard Miller was still staying there but Blunt told me not to do anything. I was used to taking orders from him so I didn't. I think that Anthony thought then that Guy was coming back. Anyway, he said there was no point in upsetting people. On Tuesday, the next day, Blunt came to see me. I said to him, He's gone, hasn't he? He said, yes. Then he asked me for the keys to the flat. He said that the office, which is what they called MI5, wanted them. Then I was bundled off for three days to stay with friends.[7]

Blunt was determined to search Burgess's flat before MI5 did. He knew that Guy had hoarded dozens of love letters from his many admirers; there were notebooks and piles of paper stuffed into shoeboxes and drawers. Blunt did not know for sure what leads, if any, might emerge from this paper hoard but he had no intention of letting MI5 find out. Since MI5 did not want to attract attention by applying for a search warrant, Blunt offered to try to persuade Hewit to lend them the keys for a few days. Hewit was sure that Blunt had a day, perhaps longer, to rummage through the flat before he gave the keys to MI5. There was a further twist. Blunt later claimed that he had had an accomplice. Shortly before his death he told Rosamond Lehmann that Rees had helped him search the flat.[8]

British governments of all political complexions tend to act in the same way when faced with an embarrassing failure in security: say nothing, admit nothing, the problem will go away. It is part of the Whitehall ethos for civil servants to act as if everything, from memos on paper clips to plans for new weapons, is secret unless someone in the upper reaches of the hierarchy decides otherwise. MI5 and MI6 did not officially exist and if any MP was naïve enough to ask a minister about them he would be stonewalled with this standard reply: 'It is not our policy to discuss security matters.' The heads of MI5 and MI6 were never identified and if newspapers did discover them, then Whitehall automatically issued a request not to publish the names. This was pointless since the Russians knew their identities soon after they were appointed, but British Intelligence saw nothing wrong with this arrangement; they believed that efficiency depended on absolute secrecy and they had contempt for their NATO colleagues, like the American CIA, who had stripped the profession of its mystique. The intrepid spies of MI6 and the spy-catchers of MI5 liked to live in the shadows; it was like that in novels and so it had to be like that in real life.

When Maclean and Burgess disappeared, British Intelligence was confident that it could manage the crisis without difficulty. It might not even be necessary to admit the entire truth to ministers since it was sometimes better if politicians' heads were not filled with the complex details of the great game of espionage. The intelligence mandarins were confident, too, that it would be impossible for the press to piece together the story. How could they? There were no records and no government would comment publicly on security matters. And, as a back-up, the Official Secrets Act could always be used to deter pressmen who refused to acknowledge that it was not in the national interest to write about Burgess and Maclean.

To be fair, no one in MI5 or MI6 had any grasp in the early summer of 1951 of the scale of the disaster. They knew only that Donald Maclean, a high-flier from the

Foreign Office who had worked on the top-secret nuclear programme, had vanished shortly before he was due to be questioned about alleged leaks from the British embassy in Washington. He had an impeccable family background, a fine academic record and had joined the FO freely admitting that he had once been a communist. He had behaved erratically and been under psychiatric treatment. Guy Burgess had never been suspected of anything, apart from being dirty, drunk and idle. He, too, had disappeared. It was feared that they had gone to Moscow. A few people within MI5, especially Guy Liddell, knew about Burgess's longstanding professional and personal links with the intelligence services, although the files showed nothing of this. Officially, Burgess was a comparatively low-grade Foreign Office employee. Viewed like this the crisis seemed manageable. There would be a stink in Washington with the CIA and FBI who would want to know why Maclean had been allowed to slip away, but that could be smoothed over. It would be regrettable if the missing diplomats surfaced in Moscow, but that could not be helped and the storm would soon pass.

It was soon apparent, however, that the wretched business was not going to die. No one in Whitehall had reckoned with the dogged persistence of the press. The days when newspapers were willing to respect unquestioningly appeals from the authorities not to discuss matters that might, in some unspoken way, affect 'national security' were over. Competition was intense between the mass-circulation popular newspapers. Here was a story that had everything – spies, high politics and sex – and while Whitehall huffed and puffed and said there was nothing in it, old boy, editors told their men to probe deeper. If Maclean had fled alone then Fleet Street might soon have tired of the chase, but the involvement of Burgess, whose eccentric lifestyle was soon being described to millions of disbelieving newspaper readers, guaranteed the promotion of the story into one of the most colourful scandals of post-war Britain.

The news of their disappearance broke in the press on 7 June when the *Daily Express*, closely followed by the *Daily Herald*, ran front-page stories about 'two British government employees who are believed to have left London with the intention of getting to Moscow'. There was a possibility, added the *Daily Express*, that they had 'important papers with them'. The Foreign Office tried to play down the story but the press demanded a statement. When it came it was a classic example of Whitehall damage limitation:

Two members of the Foreign Office have been missing from their homes since May 25. One is Mr D. D. Maclean, the other Mr G. F. de M. Burgess. All possible inquiries are being made. It is known that they went to France a few days ago. Mr Maclean had a breakdown a year ago owing to overwork but was believed to have fully recovered. Owing to their being absent without leave, both have been suspended with effect from June 1.

Reporters were dispatched around Europe to try and locate the missing men. But there were numerous leads to pursue in England, too. Melinda Maclean, who gave birth on 13 June, was besieged by reporters. She had received a telegram from her husband on 7 June explaining that he had had to leave 'unexpectedly' and asking her not to worry. Guy's mother, Mrs Bassett, had also received a message from her son, saying that he was 'embarking on a long Mediterranean holiday'. He asked her to forgive him. It did not take long for Fleet Street to discover Anthony Blunt. He had paid tribute to Guy in his book, *Artistic Theory in Italy*, and everyone who knew Guy insisted that the two had been inseparable since their time at Cambridge. Reporters camped outside the Courtauld trying to persuade the distinguished director to discuss the affair. Stephen Rees-Jones recalled: 'He was terribly upset after Burgess fled. The Courtauld was besieged by the press. He said that the press was a nuisance and told me, as if I hadn't read the papers, that a friend of his had disappeared. When he wanted to go to the dentist I had to help him escape through a back door.'[9]

Michael Kitson, later a deputy director of the Courtauld, was a student there in 1951. He said that Blunt's secretary, a German woman called Elsa Scheerer, did her best to shield her boss from the press:

> She was devoted to him and would have been upset beyond belief if she had known the truth. She held the press off. We all knew Anthony had worked for MI5 during the war and there was speculation that he had gone to MI5 and told them that Burgess had gone to Russia. But no one thought that he had been involved in working for the Soviets. By the 1950s he was in an extremely dominating position in the art world, partly because there was so little competition. We all knew that he had been left-wing in the 1930s and that he had been close to Burgess. But there was nothing Marxist about his art history and he never tried to influence people politically.[10]

George Zarnecki said that Blunt began drinking at 11 A.M. in his flat while Scheerer told journalists that the director was not available for comment. Most of the staff and students thought that Blunt was being unfairly hounded. What was his crime? He had been a Marxist in the 1930s and had been a loyal friend of Guy Burgess. But why should that be held against him?

The headlines of 7 June, however, sent shock waves through London society and Whitehall. Harold Nicolson, then working on the official biography of King George V, showed more perception than most when he made this entry in his diary:

> I come back to Neville Terrace and am horrified to read the headlines in the evening papers that Donald Maclean and Guy Burgess have absconded. If I thought that Guy was a brave man, I should imagine that he had gone to join the communists. As I know him to be a coward, I suppose that he was suspected of passing things to the Bolshies, and realizing his guilt, did a bunk. During my dreams, his absurd face stares at me with drunken, unseeing eyes.[11]

Rosamond Lehmann found the news unsettling. She recalled Goronwy Rees's bizarre claim that Guy was a Comintern agent. It had seemed ridiculous then but now she felt it was her duty to inform the authorities. This did not prove easy. She had once met Sir Stewart Menzies, the head of MI6, and decided to contact him:

> I thought it was the proper thing to do. But he said, my dear, it's Friday, I'm going away for the weekend. I asked if he would see me on Monday and he said that he was taking his little girl to Ascot. I felt that he was putting me off. He asked me if it was GB – he didn't use the name, just the initials. And I said, yes. Then he said is it about AB. I said I knew nothing about AB. He said is it about GR. And I said, yes, in a certain connection. He ought to have said come at once. But Menzies didn't call me back.[12]

Lehmann tried again. This time, via Harold Nicolson, she contacted MI5. To her relief they were anxious to listen. She met two officers, one of whom was William 'Jim' Skardon, in one of the security service's 'safe houses' in Mayfair. She said: 'I told them everything I knew. They asked me about Goronwy and obviously suspected him. Then they asked me about Blunt. They told me not to say anything about the meeting. Then they came to see me in the country about two months later and kept asking about Blunt and Rees.'[13]

Lehmann found that her efforts to help the security service were not appreciated by Goronwy Rees. She had imprudently mentioned her meeting with MI5 to her brother, John:

> I said that I was going to tell MI5 that Guy had been a Comintern agent for a long time. The poet Stephen Spender had been jabbering away that Guy wasn't a spy so my brother took the chance to snub him. He wrote to Spender in Italy, saying, keep your mouth shut, but someone we know well has told me that Guy is a communist agent.[14]

Spender then gave John Lehmann's letter to the *Daily Express*, which promptly splashed it over the front page. Goronwy Rees was furious with Rosamond, demanding to know why she had interfered in something that was none of her business. Not for the first time she had the impression that Rees knew far more about the Burgess-Maclean affair than he admitted.

By now MI5 and MI6 were as confused as Rosamond Lehmann. Their investigation was being hampered by the press. Reporters were tracking down potential sources before intelligence officers and, while their stories were sometimes inaccurate, the publicity ensured that the affair would not be forgotten. MI5 was also meeting resistance from friends of the two diplomats. Dick White realized that they would never unravel the mystery unless they first made sense of the homosexual subculture which Burgess had inhabited. White said:

> There was the feeling of the British public school that one ought not to be a sneak. A lot of it seemed to be based on homosexual friendships. I knew next to nothing about such things but it crossed my mind that Blunt was in love with Burgess. It was always evident to me that he was under the influence of Burgess, though I could not understand why that was.[15]

White went further than this. In his retirement he speculated: 'Burgess absolutely took over Blunt's soul. Blunt seemed to be a man of discrimination and civilized tastes. I don't understand how he could have been so besotted. I think Burgess sucked secrets out of people. It was a sexual and emotional hold over some people. He told people what they wanted to hear.'[16]

There was another problem for White: the traditional ill-feeling between the two secret services. MI5 thought that MI6 was slipshod and flashy, trading on a carefully cultivated image of its members as daring gatherers of intelligence. Yet what had MI6 achieved? Nothing. It was MI5 which had cracked Alan Nunn May and Klaus Fuchs, the two great successes of post-war British Intelligence. For its part, MI6 regarded the security service as a band of plodders, obsessed with their filing systems and card indexes, with nothing better to do than bitch about their more glamorous rivals. White had done his best during the war to heal this long-standing rift but one man could not break down such deep, institutionalized rivalry. When Kim Philby emerged as the most likely source of the tip-off to Maclean, relations between the two services plummeted to new depths. MI6 had always been contemptuous of MI5's meticulous internal security; MI6 officers were proud of the fact that their service was founded on trust. The attack on Kim Philby of MI6 was yet another ham-fisted effort to destroy MI6's good name. But MI5 was in jubilant mood: just look, it crowed, at the consequences of the Secret Service's smugness.

While the bureaucracies of the intelligence world were squaring up to each other, the hapless Jack Hewit was being turned into a scapegoat. He had agreed to let the *Daily Express* into Guy's flat. He insisted that he was not paid for this; he felt, naïvely, that by agreeing to talk to one newspaper the rest of Fleet Street would leave him alone. As a result of helping the newspaper that was doing the most to outrage the Burgess–Blunt circle, Hewit was frozen out. And yet, as far as he was concerned, he had done his best to protect both Guy and Anthony. When MI5 asked to see him he turned to Anthony. Hewit recalled:

> Anthony told me, for God's sake, say nothing. So I lied. Then I rejoined the army but that didn't last long. When Melinda disappeared in 1953 the newspaper published my picture on the front pages, saying, Have you seen this man? I was out of the army in a flash. My services were no longer required. Then I was interviewed by MI5 again. Mostly they were interested in Blunt. They wanted to know if I had been to bed with him. But I said that my private life was my business. Why should I get myself in trouble? I just kept saying, I don't chose to tell you. I signed statements but I don't think they were convinced.[17]

Anthony Blunt was questioned eleven times by MI5 between 1951 and 1964. During those early interviews he was just another of Burgess's homosexual friends. It has to be remembered, too, that at this stage the intelligence services did not realize that Burgess had been a key member, perhaps more important than Kim Philby, in the Cambridge spy ring, and that he was not just the bumbling messenger who had been dragged off in Maclean's wake. The first MI5 officer to interview Blunt was William 'Jim' Skardon, regarded by Kim Philby, among others, as the wiliest questioner in British Intelligence. Skardon, who had interrogated Klaus Fuchs, had been a detective in the CID before joining MI5. He had developed a bumbling approach to suspects, designed to put them at their ease; he pretended not to understand their replies and waited, hour after hour, time after time, for them to make a slip. But Anthony Blunt was not a suspect when Skardon visited the Courtauld. Skardon recalled:

I wanted to learn if he could tell me anything about Burgess and Maclean, especially Burgess as I didn't think he knew much about Maclean. I'd known him during the war and he always struck me as distant and aloof. Aloof, that's the word. As far as I knew he was a trusted member of the office and when I saw him in 1951 I expected him to be helpful and as far as I knew he was. I didn't make notes at the time necessarily. I would put it down afterwards. That was the Skardon method. I learned only one thing from him. While I was questioning him I noticed a Degas pastel drawing. I do a bit of painting myself and I'd copied this particular Degas. I told Blunt I thought I'd got the colours just about right but the only difference was that my drawing was on cardboard. 'So was Degas',' said Blunt.[18]

The most pressing problem for MI5, however, was not to discover how much Burgess's friends had known; he had led such a confused and promiscuous life that it could take months, perhaps years, to sort that out. The Americans, furious at the defections, needed to be reassured. But the mission in June to explain to the FBI and CIA how Maclean had managed to wriggle away seemed to be jinxed before it had begun. Once again, it was the *Daily Express* which embarrassed the harassed security service. Sir Percy Sillitoe, director-general of MI5, was pictured leaving Heathrow on 11 June. Sillitoe was furious; it seemed that his last months as head of MI5 were going to be as humiliating as the rest of his time there. An ex-policeman, he had joined the service in 1946 and always felt that his staff were laughing behind his back. He once complained to his son that some of his officers conversed in Latin in the canteen to ensure that he could not join them. The Americans were angrier than Sillitoe had feared. They wanted Kim Philby out of MI6, and if that did not happen then all deals, as they succinctly put it, with the British were off. Philby knew that his career would not bear close examination by the suspicious men of MI5, who were altogether rougher than his colleagues in MI6. He knew that there was no firm evidence against him but there was more than enough circumstantial evidence for his career, which he had hoped would end in his appointment as the head of the service, to be wrecked. He had never been a member of the Communist Party but his abrupt shift in the 1930s from being broadly left-wing to fascist now looked like a mistake. It had been too sudden, too obvious. He was worried about the defector Krivitsky, who had sworn that during the Spanish Civil War the Soviets had used a young Englishman who had posed as a journalist. His friendship with Burgess wasn't disastrous since Guy had known so many people in British Intelligence. But, overall, it did not look hopeful. If he did not clear his name then he knew that MI6 would have to sack him.

Philby was recalled to London in the summer of 1951 and was immediately interrogated by Dick White – though interrogation is probably the wrong word for what was a game of conversational hide-and-seek. White was convinced by the end of their talk that Philby was a Soviet agent, though he knew that he had no hope of proving it. Philby had made one crucial mistake: he admitted, quite gratuitously, that he had travelled to Spain without any financial backing from *The Times*. White pounced: how, then, had Kim managed to support himself? Philby wrote:

> It was a nasty little question because the enterprise had been suggested to me and financed by the Soviet secret service, just as Krivitsky had said, and a glance at my bank balance for the period would have shown that I had no means of gallivanting around Spain. Embedded in this episode was the dangerous little fact that Guy Burgess had been used to replenish my funds.[19]

Dick White reflected:

> I got an absolutely significant point out of him and he knew I had got it. From that point onwards I realized that I would have to work through a pretty alarming milieu in which I could be betrayed at any point. I had the whole weight of MI6 against me in pursuing the Philby theory. None of them believed that he could possibly be a traitor. That was one of the awful things about all this, having to accuse people of things like this. But it was just a professional judgement.[20]

Philby was sacked, with £4000 in lieu of a pension. But he was not given the lump sum. To his alarm he was paid just £2500 with the rest coming in half yearly instalments of £500. He thought that his friends might have done this to prevent him frittering away the money on drink. Another thought crossed his mind: that the money had been held back because someone thought that he might one day be sent to jail. Certainly Dick White had not given up. In the summer of 1952 Philby was summoned to what he called a secret trial, at MI5's headquarters in Leconfield House. His inquisitor was Helenus 'Buster' Milmo, a barrister who had worked for MI5 during the war. Philby wrote:

> Milmo . . . had a florid, round face, matching his name. On his left sat Arthur Martin, a quiet young man who had been one of the principal investigators of the Maclean case. He remained silent throughout, watching my movements. When I looked out of the window, he made a note; when I twiddled my thumbs, he made another note. After sketchy greetings, Milmo adopted a formal manner, asking me to refrain from smoking as this was a judicial inquiry.[21]

Milmo tried on three successive days to break him but he had no ammunition; he was firing blanks and Philby knew it. When he was asked, for example, about his friendship with Burgess he just shrugged. Dick White recalled that Philby had said: 'You can't believe this man is a Russian spy? You can't be serious about it?' White *did* find it hard to believe that Burgess could have made fools of British Intelligence for so many years. Then Skardon tried to find a chink in Philby's defences. Unlike Milmo he did not shout or accuse; he casually dropped in on Philby at home, probing for an opening. But he, too, failed.

There was, however, one casualty among Guy's tipsters and fellow-agents. John Cairncross's name was one of the few positive leads that had emerged from the search of Guy Burgess's flat in 1951. He was the author of a series of wartime assessments of the views of senior civil servants. He had not signed these reports but he had carelessly dated each one. He had been a communist at Cambridge before joining the Foreign Office in 1936 as their top-graded graduate entrant. Cairncross insisted that his tutor, not Soviet Intelligence, had urged him to try the FO. Nor, he claimed, had Anthony Blunt, one of the examiners for the Foreign Office, had anything to do with his decision to join. Cairncross said: 'Burgess was fascinating, charming and utterly ruthless. But he never told me he was a communist, let alone a communist agent. Like me he hated appeasement, fearing it was a disastrous strategy and, of course, it was every bit as disastrous as we had believed.'[22] He said that he had been a member of the Communist Party from only January 1935 until late in 1936. He had been so disgusted by the Foreign Office's policy of appeasement that he had asked to be transferred to the Treasury in 1939. He had worked at Bletchley and MI6 during the war and then returned to the Treasury after a spell in the Ministry of Supply. MI5 had John Colville, joint principal private secretary to the Prime Minister, Winston Churchill, to thank for leading them to Cairncross. Colville recalled:

They came to see me in Downing Street and handed me twenty-five sheets of paper they had found in Burgess's flat. One of the reports was about me. I didn't recognize the writing but I said I would go home and check that date with my diaries, which I had kept. I went home and saw that on that day, 15 March 1939, the day Hitler marched into Prague, I had had lunch with Cairncross. So I called the intelligence people and said, I think I've caught your spy. Cairncross was always asking people out to lunch. He was very brilliant but very boring. He ate very slowly, slower than anyone I've ever known. He asked me about Munich, that sort of thing [Colville was then assistant private secretary to Neville Chamberlain]. From the report he had written after the lunch it seemed he had been making mental notes all the time. But he

must have come to the conclusion that I was not a likely
candidate to help him. I asked to be kept informed of
what happened to him and I was told that he had been
forced to resign. I wrote to him saying that I was sorry his
name had come out. But I never got a reply.[23]

Cairncross left for the States, having refused to admit to
anything apart from writing those innocuous reports for
Burgess. It was wrong to say, he later protested, that he had
ever confessed to being a Soviet agent. MI5 had a different
impression. They could not prosecute him but the officers
involved in the case were convinced that he had been
spotted at Cambridge, either by Blunt or James Klugmann,
and then passed on to Burgess. It was through Burgess,
MI5 concluded, that Cairncross had met his Soviet controller. But it was still a murky picture. And, if this was roughly
what had happened, it made Burgess far more than just the
messenger who had warned Maclean. Cairncross saw himself as a victim of the post-defection witchhunt for Reds
under the Whitehall bed. All he had been guilty of was
giving Burgess his views on British foreign policy. He
argued: 'A lot of the allegations about me in the press came
from leaks from MI5. But the whole thing is very complicated. I am a victim of having been in the same college
at Cambridge as Blunt. But I didn't like him and he didn't
like me.'[24]

Other careers were also ruined in the hunt for spies that
followed the defections. George Carey-Foster, who had
been due to be posted abroad, had been vindicated and he
was now asked to help with the introduction of vetting for
civil servants with access to sensitive information. In 1948
Clement Attlee, the Labour Prime Minister, had decreed
that no communist or fascist would be allowed to work in
areas 'vital to the security of the state'. A committee of
three 'wise men' – veteran public servants with unimpeach-

able records – had been set up to hear appeals from anyone whose career was threatened by this new rule. But this did not seem nearly drastic enough in the wake of the Burgess-Maclean humiliation. *Positive* vetting was needed; this meant that from now on civil servants would have to prove their suitability to be entrusted with secrets by filling out a detailed questionnaire and giving the names of two referees. In 1956 a report by the Conference of Privy Councillors concluded that more safeguards were needed against Whitehall spies. The main threat, said the report, came from 'communists and by other persons who are subject to communist influence'. It was a tough report:

> It is right to continue tilting the balance in favour of offering greater protection to the security of the State rather than in safeguarding the rights of the individual . . . great importance must be paid to character defects as factors tending to make a man unreliable or expose him to blackmail or influence by foreign agents. There is a duty on departments to inform themselves of serious failings such as drunkenness, addiction to drugs, homosexuality or any loose living that may seriously affect a man's reliability.

There were echoes of McCarthyism here. But they were no more than echoes. George Carey-Foster said that a handful of civil servants were moved from key posts in the post-defection inquiry. But Whitehall was not going to be panicked into wholesale butchery of anyone with a left-wing past. If that had happened then dozens of senior officials would have had to be shifted. After all, this was not the United States – the British knew the difference between parliamentary socialism and communism.

CHAPTER 17
Moscow Nightmare

The search for Burgess and Maclean lasted until February 1956, when they gave a short press conference in Moscow in which they explained that they had decided they could best work for 'world peace' by living in the Soviet Union. The hunt for the two had taken up thousands of working hours in British and American Intelligence and in Fleet Street. From Fleet Street's point of view at least, it had not mattered when the two were found. The affair was good, knockabout stuff, always guaranteed to liven up a front page.

British and American Intelligence, however, did not find anything to smile about. The 'mystery' (the favourite word used by the media to describe the fate of Burgess and Maclean) was an embarrassment, drawing attention to the intelligence services in a most undesirable manner. From FBI files declassified under the Freedom of Information Act it is clear that an element of desperation soon crept in. For example, on 10 March 1952 the FBI director, J. Edgar Hoover, received a message about the two diplomats from the legal attaché at the United States embassy in London. Attached to the note was a four-day-old cutting from the *Daily Mail*: 'The hunt for Guy Burgess and Donald Maclean, the diplomats who disappeared last May, has been called off. Special Branch officers and Foreign Office agents have examined every conceivable clue in Britain and

Europe without success and the Foreign Office have decided to cease further inquiries.'[1] The *Mail* report was duly filed by Hoover, perhaps to reassure himself that the British had also failed to find the two men. Nine months later, though, the FBI was back on the trail. Hoover ordered the American embassy in Paris to contact a Yale graduate, Jimmy Robinson Smith, who lived in Nice and who had, said Hoover, located Burgess and Maclean. Hoover's information came from the November issue of the *Yale Alumni* magazine which carried this short item in the column, 'Class Notes':

Jimmy Robinson Smith writes from Nice, France, quite a letter. He is running the English–American library at 12 Rue de France. Besides this he has developed a new science, baptized, 'The Science of Comparative Frequency,' which will break the bank at any time. He also says he discovered the missing British members of the Foreign Office who had breakfast with him and left for Rome but are now in Prague. Good for Jimmy.[2]

In January 1953 the FBI decided to follow up a story by the *Washington Post* columnist Drew Pearson, who suggested that the Russians had lured Burgess and Maclean to Udine, Italy, through a 'combination of blackmail and bribery'. Pearson said that the two men had been flown to 'Red Austria' by a former Nazi agent who was now a Soviet intelligence 'mastermind' called Karl. The FBI recorded this unflattering description of him:

Age 50. Height 5' 9". Weight: 170 pounds. Hair: fair, balding, grey at temples. Complexion: yellowish. Eyes: blue-grey with tendency to squint. Peculiarities: slit-line mouth, thin lips, rounding chin, uses pince-nez or heavy tortoise-shell glasses to vary his appearance. Scars and marks: drooping underlip from scar which is partially obscured by a full blond grey moustache.[3]

All this was nonsense; Burgess and Maclean were in the Soviet Union throughout this period. After returning to Moscow from their six-month exile in Kuybyshev, Burgess had been given a job in the Foreign Literature Publishing House, where he bombarded the Soviet bureaucracy with ideas on which English-language books should be translated into Russian. His first success was persuading the Soviets that Graham Greene's *The Quiet American* was ideologically sound enough to be read by the proletariat, and he then launched a campaign on behalf of E. M. Forster. He attempted to re-create his London persona – the brilliant, lovable rogue who was at the centre of fashionable society – but the Soviets were not impressed by his eccentricities or by the little touches (the Old Etonian tie, the ribald jokes, the name-dropping) that had served him so well in England. He protested that he was 'very busy', portraying himself as a valued commentator on the Western democracies, with unlimited access to the Kremlin's most powerful figures. This was not true. He was lonely and bored. While Maclean was determined to build a new life in Moscow, Burgess's heart remained in London.

Maclean had one advantage over Guy – the comfort of family life. In September 1953 Maclean's American wife, Melinda, who had remained loyal throughout, and their three children, disappeared from their Geneva home. In October Melinda's mother received a letter from her postmarked Cairo, in which she said that the children were safe and well. By then she had been reunited with Donald in Moscow although she left him a decade later for his fellow-exile, Kim Philby. When the media discovered that she had vanished the Burgess-Maclean story was dusted down and given a fresh coat of speculation. Where had she gone? Had she, too, been a Soviet agent? But there was bitter dis-appointment in Whitehall, where officials wondered if this terrible business would ever end. Anthony Blunt was just as distressed. Every time that there was revived interest in the story he had to suffer the attentions of reporters, though his faithful secretary, Elsa Scheerer, did her best to protect him.

By the early 1950s Blunt's private life was more settled. This made it easier for him to cope with the strain of knowing that he could, at any moment, be publicly iden-tified as a suspect in the spy drama that obsessed Fleet Street. His new, permanent companion was John Gaskin, a good-looking but poorly-educated Ulsterman in his early thirties. One of Blunt's friends described Gaskin like this:

> John was deeply tanned, and very, very good-looking. The kind of man who was so good-looking that heads turned; everyone's heads turned, male and female. He had dark hair and was always immaculately dressed. He tended to wear dark blue suits, lightweight worsted suits. He was the most expensively dressed man to be seen at the Courtauld.[4]

Gaskin had been a member of the British Expeditionary Force to France in May 1940 and had been captured by the Germans near Louvain in Belgium. He spent the rest of the war as a POW. After he was freed he moved to London and became a travel courier, though friends insisted that John – known as 'Lady John' in Blunt's circle – was a cicerone. He then decided to try the jewellery business, taking a part-time job in a shop, Armour and Winston, in upmarket Burlington Arcade, Piccadilly. He was still working there when he moved into Blunt's flat at the Courtauld. He was not an intellectual. He had no interest in politics and knew little about art. But he tried to learn about the latter so that he would, at least, not make a fool of himself with Blunt's friends. But the harder he tried the more they resented him. If Anthony wanted to live with this attractive but coarse ex-soldier then that was his business, but he could not expect them to waste time making polite small-talk with him. Gaskin, in turn, tended to sulk in company, demanding Blunt's attention, feeling that Anthony's grand friends deliberately excluded him from conversations.

Gaskin's appearance at the Courtauld made little impact. Many of the students were homosexual and regarded him as just another of Blunt's boyfriends, albeit a more permanent one. The heterosexuals on the staff either did not understand the nature of the relationship or did not care. This was the 1950s, when homosexuality was still illegal and seldom discussed openly. Lillian Gurry said: 'It never occurred to me that they were a couple. John was just a good housekeeper and cook and that was just what Anthony needed. He was very nice and very friendly. He always cooked for Anthony when he had dinner parties.'[5]

Gaskin was rarely seen by the staff or the students. He was sometimes spotted carrying the shopping or going out with Anthony. When the institute had closed for the day – and it became Blunt's town house – he would become more confident. There were occasional parties, usually attended only by Blunt's homosexual friends, that the staff knew were happening but which they chose to ignore. But there were no public displays of affection between the two men. Robert Harbinson thought that it was a boost for Blunt's morale to be seen with the good-looking Gaskin. Gaskin could also ensure a steady supply of young male visitors to the flat.

Another of Blunt's art-world friends recalled:

John had the instincts and habits of a madame. He could not resist introducing people he thought would make beautiful sexual partners. I have no doubt that he introduced a few to Anthony. John was one of those people who would say: 'I know just the man for you.' He might then introduce you to the local dustman. He could not accept that other men operated differently from him.[6]

However, Gaskin had his allies. Michael Kitson took enormous trouble to make him feel welcome. Timothy Clifford, a future director of the National Gallery of Scotland, said that he was a 'delightful, retiring and very nice person'.[7] Whatever people's opinions of him, there was no doubt that Gaskin was a steadying influence, providing the emotional anchor which allowed Blunt to concentrate on his work. There were more books and more catalogues of the royal collection. In the late 1950s he took on a new responsibility, as general editor of a series of books on architecture published by Desmond Zwemmer, owner of a specialist art bookshop off the Charing Cross Road. The partnership with Zwemmer lasted until Blunt's death, by which time over fifty volumes had been produced. Zwemmer recalled:

Some of the books were pretty slow sellers. But you can't win them all. I liked Anthony very much indeed. He was charming and sensitive. A real gentleman. I became very fond of him though I had no homosexual leanings myself. He was a first class historian. And there were no politics in any of the books he edited for me.[8]

To the surprise of colleagues, Blunt also published a study of the contemporary French painter Georges Rouault. Apart from his long-standing fascination with Picasso, Blunt had shown no interest in modern art – which he always said baffled him – and there seemed no obvious explanation for this enthusiasm. Rouault, who died in

1958, was a devout Catholic whose work remained stubbornly realist while many artists retreated into abstraction. He focused repeatedly on the themes of sin and redemption, which seemed an anachronism in the post-war era. After Blunt's exposure in 1979, when colleagues and friends searched his art history for clues which might explain the contradictions of his life, the interest in Rouault seemed more comprehensible. Perhaps Rouault, like Poussin, had given Blunt a link with a more comforting age: when religion gave artists a sureness of touch that secularism had destroyed. This thesis, pretentious and elaborate though it was, had its supporters. For example, one of Blunt's protégés said: 'He found in Rouault a painter who was, like Poussin, inspired by the Christian ethic. Anthony could see a direct connection in a contemporary painter with things that were age old. That is why he could write about Rouault and not other modern painters.'[9]

Kim Philby had a wretched time during the early 1950s. While Anthony Blunt was consolidating his professional and social status (he was knighted in 1956) Philby was scratching out a living, first with an import-export company in the City and then as a freelance journalist. Throughout this time he appears to have been remarkably unconcerned about money, even though he had five children to support. True, he was helped by old friends from the secret world, many of whom felt that he had been sacrificed to satisfy the unholy alliance of MI5 and the Americans. It is possible that he also received financial support from the Soviets, though it is more likely that any contact would have been considered too dangerous in view of the suspicions held against Philby.

Tomas Harris was especially sympathetic. In 1954 he asked the publishers André Deutsch if they would be interested in a book by Philby, describing how his brilliant

Foreign Office career had been wrecked by his friendship with Guy Burgess. Deutsch paid a hefty advance but the book was never delivered. Philby said that he had had a 'writing block', leaving Harris to repay Deutsch. Harris was a frequent visitor to Philby's large, rundown house at Crowborough, Sussex, and took a keen interest in the children. He was godfather to the third, Dudley Tomas, and helped pay for the private education of one, possibly more, of the children. There is no evidence that Blunt saw Philby anything like as often during this period. There was, however, one incident which was an unsettling reminder to Blunt that he would never be entirely free of his past.

Sometime before 1956 – no one has been able to establish the exact date though some British intelligence officers thought that it was in the early summer of 1955 – the Soviets used Blunt to contact Philby. In his autobiography, *My Silent War*, Philby wrote:

> Several times during this period I revived the idea of escape . . . But each time I considered the project the emergency appeared to be less than extreme. Finally, an event occurred which put it right out of my head. I received, through the most ingenious of routes a message from my Soviet friends, conjuring me to be of good cheer and presaging an early resumption of relations. It changed drastically the whole complexion of my case. I was no longer alone.

Blunt had just finished a lecture at the Courtauld when Yuri Modin ('Peter'), the veteran KGB officer who had been one of the Cambridge ring's controllers during the war, appeared from the back of the hall and handed Blunt an art postcard. What, he asked, did Blunt think of the painting? Blunt turned the card over and recognized Burgess's spidery handwriting. The message instructed him to be at the Angel pub on the Caledonian Road, north London, at eight o'clock the following evening. Next day, nervous but intrigued, Blunt turned up at the Angel but there was no sign of Guy. Modin was on his own and he wasted no time explaining what he wanted. He wanted to meet Kim Philby but could not risk a direct contact. Anthony would, therefore, have to pass on the details of the rendezvous. Blunt agreed, partly because he had no choice, but partly, too, because of his loyalty to Philby.

Until the autumn of 1955 there was stalemate in the battle of nerves between Philby and MI5, which had still not given up hope of trapping him into a confession. By the end of the year, however, Philby was free, having been publicly cleared of suspicion by the government, thanks to a series of events that suggested that his guardian angel was a Marxist. The first piece of good luck was the publication on 18 September by the Sunday tabloid newspaper, *The People*, of claims made by a Soviet defector, Vladimir Petrov, about Burgess and Maclean. Petrov, who had defected in Australia in 1954, said that the two men had been recruited by the Soviets before they had graduated from Cambridge; that their escape from Britain had been organized by Soviet Intelligence and that Melinda Maclean's disappearance had also been engineered by the KGB. Philby was delighted. He had feared that Petrov had already named him as the 'third man'. If this was all he knew then Philby was certain that he could survive whatever MI5 threw at him. *The People*'s story naturally reawakened press interest in the Burgess-Maclean affair and, more important, in Kim Philby. Reporters pestered him for interviews but he sheltered behind the Official Secrets Act; he could not, he said, be expected to comment on matters of national security. MI5 watched, with increasing frustration, as the press dug deeper into the Philby case, threatening to ruin the years of patient work that should have led to the final, successful interrogation. All this was bad enough. But there was worse to follow.

On 23 September the government White Paper on Burgess and Maclean was published. It was glib and superficial and confirmed suspicions in Fleet Street that Whitehall was trying to hide the truth. News editors were sure that there was a major scandal waiting to be uncovered; and, in the absence of any new leads about the whereabouts of the two missing diplomats, the crucial break might come from Philby. He was now consulting regularly with his old friends in MI6. Should he make a statement? What should he do if a newspaper openly accused him of being a suspected traitor? He was advised that it might be best to surrender his passport and agree to more questioning, conducted this time by his chums in MI6 and not the louts from the security service. Philby was delighted by the obvious confusion in Whitehall as the two intelligence services battled over his fate. He later wrote: 'The interviews followed a familiar pattern which suggested that no new evidence had been turned up. Meanwhile, the fact that I had made no attempt to escape over a long period was beginning to tell heavily in my favour. With the passage of time, the trail had become stale and muddy.'[10]

On 25 October 1955, the first day of a new parliamentary session, Philby knew that he had won. He travelled from Sussex to London that day for a meeting with his Soviet contact, taking various B-movie-style precautions – nipping in and out of cinemas; buying a new hat and coat – to throw off anyone attempting to follow him. That evening, on route to catch his train home, he read the headline in the *Evening Standard*. A Labour MP had asked the Prime Minister, Sir Anthony Eden, how long the government would go on shielding the 'dubious Third Man activities of Mr Harold Philby who was First Secretary at the Washington embassy a little time ago'. The MP was Lieutenant-

Colonel Marcus Lipton, who had been the Labour member for Brixton since 1945, and his question was based on a tip-off from a reporter. There was nothing unusual about this ploy; reporters often used MPs (and still do) to raise issues that British libel laws prevented them from writing about. But Lipton had no idea just how disastrous his question was to prove for British Intelligence. That day in the Commons, Eden and his Foreign Secretary, Harold Macmillan, stalled. There would be ample time to reply, they said, on Monday 7 November, during a Commons debate on the Burgess-Maclean affair. Philby was delighted. He was disappointed that his name had been mentioned by an MP in the Commons – which meant he would not be able to sue for libel – but on the other hand, it would force the government to reveal its hand. He was now confident that there was no new evidence against him. He retreated to his mother's flat in Drayton Gardens, South Kensington, and waited for the Commons debate. That would be the moment of truth; either new facts would be produced or he would be cleared. The government could not go on fudging.

Philby was right. MI5 had not been able to provide the conclusive proof that British fair-play demanded. It was left to MI6 to assure Macmillan, the minister who, nominally at least, controlled them, that Philby was the victim of guilt by association. He had been a friend of Burgess but that was all. That Thursday Philby was cleared by the government, to the embarrassment of Lipton and the fury of MI5. Philby pressed home his advantage that Thursday when he held a press conference in Drayton Gardens. It was a measured performance which ensured that Fleet Street lost interest in the story. There was nothing more to be gained by pursuing Philby; it had been reasonable to assume that he was the third man but he had done the decent thing and faced the press. It was time to drop the story. It had been good for circulation but enough was enough. Readers did not want to see a man like Philby being unjustly hounded.

In the New Year Philby moved to the Irish Republic, where he started work on a literary project for William Allen, a retired Foreign Office colleague whom he had met in Turkey. Allen, a wealthy old Etonian who was married to a Russian and was the author of several books on the Soviet Union, wanted Philby to help with a history of his family's business in Cappagh, County Waterford. It was while he was in Ireland, considering his future, that Guy Burgess and Donald Maclean made their dramatic public appearance in Moscow.

Richard Hughes, the *Sunday Times*'s veteran Far East specialist, was in Moscow in February 1956 for a rare interview with a senior Kremlin figure, the Foreign Minister, Vyacheslav Molotov. At the end of their two-hour talk Hughes handed Molotov a note, headed, rather cheekily, 'For the Eyes of Marshal Bulganin and Mr Khrushchev'. The note requested an interview with Burgess and Maclean, whom the Soviets had never admitted were in Moscow. Hughes demanded that the talk should take place before 8 P.M. on Saturday so that he could meet the deadline for that weekend's *Sunday Times*. The note was, as Hughes admitted, a 'reckless long-shot'. Yet it worked.

At 7 P.M. that Saturday, 11 February, with one hour to go before his deadline ran out, Hughes was packing in his room at the National Hotel overlooking Red Square, feeling unwell and irritable. He had a painful tooth abscess. His note, which at the time had seemed the sort of brilliant ruse of which journalistic legends are made, had failed to elicit any response. Then there was a telephone call. A hoarse voice, speaking broken English, told him to go immediately to room 101. Hughes ambled along the corridor and from outside room 101 could hear voices. He knocked on the door and entered. Two elegant men, both in their forties, were sitting in antique armchairs. The taller of the two rose and introduced himself as Donald Maclean. The second man, younger, better-looking and sporting an Old Etonian tie, then shook Hughes's hand. It was Guy Burgess.

Hughes had been robbed of his exclusive, however. The Soviets had unsportingly invited a Reuters correspondent as well as journalists from Tass and *Pravda*. Nor were Burgess and Maclean very forthcoming. They read out a long, dull statement, which began by referring to 'doubts as to our whereabouts and speculation about our past actions . . . which may again be exploited by the opponents of Anglo-Soviet understanding'. They admitted that they had been communists at Cambridge but denied ever having been agents of the Soviet Union. They had decided to live in Moscow because it seemed that they could work more effectively for world peace from there. They complained about the anti-communism of the Foreign Office, so deep-rooted that it had become impossible to debate world affairs seriously. They added that 'as a result of living here we are convinced that we were right in doing what we did.'

Unsurprising though this was, the fact that Burgess and Maclean had declared themselves meant that the story appeared on newspaper front pages around the world. To the British public it was another chapter in an entertaining, if complicated, spy-sex saga. In Whitehall there was relief that the Soviets had shown their hand and fear that they might use the two defectors to embarrass the intelligence services. The unhappiest man in the country, though, was Anthony Blunt, who was sickened when he read Hughes's report in the *Sunday Times*. Now that Guy had surfaced, would he start gossiping to British correspondents in Moscow? He was notoriously indiscreet and, once he had been plied with drink by reporters, he might start dropping names. Would he try to return to England? Surely that could not happen, but the more Blunt brooded, the more worried he became. There was probably not enough evidence against Guy to prosecute him in a British court. What if Guy called the authorities' bluff and flew back? He might hold a press conference; that would be just the sort of theatrical gesture he was capable of making. Blunt reassured himself that the government would not allow him back; it would be too dangerous. Two months later Blunt uncharacteristically boycotted a reception at Buckingham Palace held in honour of the visiting Khrushchev and Bulganin. Robert Harbinson offered this explanation which, while it sounds melodramatic, might not be wholly inaccurate: 'Anthony would have believed that the Russians knew all about him and Guy. Perhaps he had been told to stay away from the reception. He was such a snob that there has to be some explanation for his absence at one of the most publicized social occasions of the year.'[11]

Tom Driberg, however, was delighted that his old friend Guy had turned up at last. Driberg thought that he could help him write a marvellous book about his adventures in the Foreign Office and in the Soviet Union. So, more in hope than the expectation that he would receive a reply, Driberg sent a letter to Moscow. In March he was delighted when Guy sent a long cable, followed by a letter. Yes, he would be pleased to see Tom. Driberg arrived in Moscow in August and spent the rest of the summer interviewing Guy for the book, *Guy Burgess, A Portrait with a Background*, published in December that year. Even though it was riddled with half-truths and lies, the book was – and remains – a fascinating insight into Burgess. He tried to convince readers that he regretted nothing:

I don't speak Russian very well – just enough to talk to my housekeeper at the dacha [country residence]. This is largely because the people I work with mostly speak

English so well that I haven't been forced to learn Russian. As a matter of fact, my inadequate Russian is the main thing holding me back from applying to join the Communist Party again – the Communist Party of the Soviet Union, of course, I mean. Of course, I miss London and my friends there, and New York, too. But I have become used to the ways of solitude and on the whole I like it. I read an enormous amount and I lead a very quiet life. In London my main expenditure was on drink and cigarettes. They're both very cheap here. I always smoke these very cheap cigarettes . . . The people at the office say I oughtn't to. I only drink wine . . . hardly ever vodka, unless I'm sick. Don't think I'm starry-eyed about this place. I criticize things and they take serious criticism seriously. But, despite all the things that are wrong, it is a Socialist country, and there is a real kind of democracy developing, different from ours but real . . . Sometimes I am lonely. I'd like to have a good gossip with friends. But here I'm lonely for the unimportant things. In London I was lonely for the important things – I was lonely for Socialism.

When Driberg returned to Moscow in the autumn with the page proofs of the book, Guy seemed more settled. He had moved into a new flat, brightened up by a few oddments of Scandinavian furniture that Driberg had shipped from London. They spent a weekend at his dacha an hour's drive from the city. They talked about Maclean, who thoroughly disapproved of their project, about the secret policemen who trailed him everywhere and about mutual friends in London. It was gossip that Guy most missed; the knowledge that all around him friends were busy with intrigues and love affairs. He admitted that he disliked most Russians though he insisted that he still had high regard for the political system. But it was clear to Driberg that, despite his usual bravado, he was living in enforced celibacy. This was not a state that Guy could survive for long:

> Because of his position he could not go in search of the sort of companionship that he used to find easily enough in London . . . Nor, indeed, if Guy had dared to look for the solace he lacked, would he have known where to go to find it. In fact, it was close at hand, in the middle of Moscow: a large, underground urinal, just behind the Metropole Hotel, open all night, frequented by hundreds of questing homosexuals – standing there in rigid exhibitionist rows, motionless save for the hasty grope and the anxious or beckoning glance over the shoulder – and tended only by an old woman cleaner who never seemed to notice what was going on. When I told Guy about this place he decided to risk one visit – and was lucky enough to pick up a decent and attractive young man, an electrician in a State factory, Tolya by name; they formed a strong mutual attachment and Tolya went to live with Guy.[12]

A restored sex life was not the only consolation. Now that the Soviets had allowed him to appear in public, Guy's beloved mother, Evelyn Bassett, was able to arrange a trip. It was not easy for her. After the February press conference her flat in Arlington Street, St James's, was once again besieged by reporters, but she was determined to see her errant son, even if it brought her more unpleasant publicity. She was a lifelong Conservative and had been ostracized by the genteel ladies of her local party association, who felt that they should demonstrate their patriotism by punishing the mother for the sins of the son. Despite these pressures she flew to Moscow and holidayed with Guy at the Black Sea resort of Sochi. When she returned to England she refused to admit how distressed she had been by the sight of her son, of whom so much had been expected, languishing in that dreary, godless state. She joked to Driberg: 'You know . . . I think that Soviet discipline is *good* for Guy.'

Anthony Blunt tried to concentrate on his work in the summer and autumn of 1956. Although there was no point, he kept telling himself, in worrying about the Driberg book he could not put it out of his mind. It was inconceivable that Guy would deliberately betray him, but what if he inadvertently gave British Intelligence a new lead? What if the KGB had decided that the Surveyor of the Queen's Pictures should be sacrificed as part of some mysterious global strategy? Blunt could not confide in anyone. Gaskin knew nothing about his involvement with the Soviets and was not, in any case, 'clever' enough to understand. Friends noticed that he was unusually tense. Rosamond Lehmann recalled how oddly he acted after they had both been at a party in Eaton Square, Belgravia: 'Anthony offered to drop me home afterwards in his taxi. He was very drunk. Suddenly he burst out crying and sobbed and sobbed. He cried as if his heart would burst. Then he said: "Rosamond, can you ever forgive me?" When I said: "For what?", he just shook his head.'[13]

Nevertheless, Blunt held firm, drawing on the same reserves of self-control that had helped him survive the crisis of the 1951 defections. Goronwy Rees, however, who had been appointed principal of the University College of Wales at Aberystwyth in 1952, was determined to pre-empt Guy and set to work on his own account of the affair. Rees protested in *his* autobiography, published in 1972, that people had misunderstood his motives in 1956. In 1972 he wrote about having felt the need then to 'pay' for not having realized that Guy had been serious when he said that he was a Soviet agent; he talked about the nature of truth and friendship. He concluded:

> The guilt I felt in regard to Guy and my dealings with him was exacerbated by a more general sense of guilt which was inspired by the support and approval which, in the 1930s and even later, I had given to the Communist Party of the Soviet Union . . . it seemed to me that there was something very simple which I could do . . . that was to tell the truth about my relations with Guy.[14]

His 1956 manuscript ran to 50,000 words. With a couple of extra chapters it would have been long enough to publish as a book, but it takes time to print books and Rees was anxious that his account should come out before Driberg's. So he told his literary agent to offer it to newspapers for serialization, which would bring the added bonus of a handsome payment. Rees did not mind who bought it and when he was told that *The People* was interested he raised no objection. Nor did he protest when the newspaper said that they wanted one of their staff writers to liven up his prose. His only condition was that he, the author, should be anonymous. When friends heard what he was planning they were horrified. It was bad enough that he had written anything about events that were best forgotten but it was unforgivable to sell out to the gutter press. The poet Stephen Spender pleaded with Rosamond Lehmann to persuade Rees to change his mind. She recalled: 'Spender said it would be an abominable series. Goronwy was very sheepish but would not change his mind.'[15]

The People series in November was as offensive as Spender feared. The opening burst set the tone:

> Now I will show how he was the greatest traitor of them all! GUY BURGESS. Stripped bare! . . . HIS

CLOSEST FRIEND SPEAKS AT LAST. This is the first in a series of profoundly disturbing articles. They reveal appalling facts about Guy Burgess, the missing diplomat, that the authorities HAVE NOT DARED TO LET THE PUBLIC KNOW. These disclosures come from the one man in a position to know the complete story. He was Burgess's friend for more than 20 years and now occupies a high academic post. Only he can reveal the depth of corruption that lay behind Guy Burgess's treachery.[16]

There was much more in this vein. Burgess was a 'strange and terrible man' who had been protected by 'friends in high places who practise the same terrible vices'. To illustrate the point *The People* reproduced a Burgess cartoon and captioned it: 'Two monsters that sprang from a monster's brain . . . when Burgess doodled, the nightmare fantasies of his monstrous life came to the surface. Was he drawing his own secret soul?' There was one immediate repercussion for Rees. Two officers from MI5 arrived at Aberystwyth and asked for a copy of his original manuscript. Next came the professional and social fall-out. He was forced to resign from the college. He was condemned as a Judas by friends. And then, at the age of forty-five with no job and no means of supporting his wife and five children, he was badly injured in a road accident. His family had always cursed the day that he met Guy; as they waited by the bedside, not knowing if he would recover, it seemed that Burgess was somehow still able to cast a malevolent shadow over Goronwy's life. There was, too, a tragic irony. Rees's pre-emptive strike had not, after all, been necessary. Driberg's book, which was published in December, contained little about him. Guy's most damning comment was this caustic aside to Driberg about the articles in *The People*: 'He [Rees] probably needed the money. He always did.'[17]

Now that they knew how to find Guy, some friends could not resist writing to find out how he was coping. Harold Nicolson was one of the first to make contact, having been told by Driberg that Guy did not want to embarrass anyone with unsolicited letters that might be leaked to the press. Nicolson's son Nigel, then Tory MP for Bournemouth East and Christchurch, said that this was a 'rather noble' gesture by his father. They wrote regularly to each other until Burgess's death in 1963, with Nicolson filing copies of his own letters in case of future allegations that there was something improper in the correspondence. He gave Burgess a running commentary on the changing London landscape; detailing the demolition of Guy's favourite landmarks and the construction of characterless sky-scrapers. There was social news, too; about the Reform Club and friends including Blunt, Fred Warner and James Pope-Hennessy. Burgess's letters were only ever dated by year. He was always affectionate and open. He said that he had given up promiscuity and that he was, more or less, faithful to his live-in lover, Tolya. Yes, he missed some things about England – his mother, the streets of London, the Reform, the countryside – but he maintained that he really was happy. Nicolson was not convinced.

Predictably, Blunt was uneasy about mutual friends having such frequent contact with Guy; as far as he was concerned the quicker they forgot him the better. In July 1958 Nicolson and Blunt were on their way to a party at the French embassy:

On the way Blunt told him that he had been informed by MI5 that if Guy Burgess returned to England he would be arrested. There would be a trial at which Blunt would be the chief witness, since he had lived with Guy for months. He would lose his job as Surveyor of the Queen's Pictures, and possibly his job at the Courtauld Institute. So he had conveyed to Burgess that he must not return.[18]

By February 1959 Burgess was again talking about returning to England, though he said now that he just wanted to see his mother who was dying of cancer. (She actually outlived him by a year.) The British Prime Minister, Harold Macmillan, was in Moscow that month to meet Khrushchev and was accompanied by a pack of Fleet Street reporters. This gave Burgess an opportunity to float the idea of a brief trip home. He sought out Randolph Churchill, Winston's son, who was covering the Macmillan story for the *Evening Standard*. Churchill wrote:

On Saturday evening I was sitting in my apartment minding my own business with my secretary Miss Lidiya Dubininskaya when the telephone rings. A chap introduces himself as Burgess and asks whether he can come and call on me. I think this is probably a practical joke . . . Well, he does and is wearing an Old Etonian tie. I know that it is not Mr Macmillan because neither he nor I would perpetuate the social solecism of wearing an old school tie in Moscow. Well, there we are in the National Hotel – and Burgess . . . says to me: 'I am still a communist and a homosexual.' Burgess further told me that he was thinking of coming back to England to see his aged mother to whom he speaks every week on the telephone. I warned him that the Attorney General, Sir Reginald Manningham-Butler, might have a word or two to say about that.[19]

Burgess asked if Churchill would find out whether it would be safe for him to travel to England. Churchill agreed. Other reporters soon heard about the meeting and one, George Hutchinson, had dinner with Burgess. Burgess told Hutchinson: 'I will not make embarrassments for HM Government if they don't make them for me. I will give no interviews without permission. I was grateful in the early days that HM Government said nothing hostile to me. I for my part have never said a lot of things that I could have said.'[20]

News of Burgess's extraordinary manoeuvrings reached Harold Nicolson, then in Colombo. On 25 February he noted in his diary:

The happiness of the day is clouded by a distressing episode. On entering the ship a Cingalese newspaper-man, whom I had just spoken to that morning before going ashore, rushes up to me. 'Oh, Sir Harold,' he said, 'I have been waiting for you for four hours. I have a cable to discuss with you.' I took him to my cabin and he undid his telegram. It ran something as follows: 'Our Moscow correspondent reports that at a press conference Guy Burgess stated that he asked Prime Minister for a safe conduct to England and back to Russia to see his mother who is seriously ill. Macmillan, when asked, said it was not for him to intervene: the Law must take its course. In subsequent conversation Burgess said that the only one of his friends who had kept in touch with him was Harold Nicolson, who had written regularly. Please get in touch with Nicolson, passenger Cambodge arriving Colombo February 25 and ask him to confirm.' I replied that certainly I had written to Guy since I had felt sorry for him, as he had acted on impulse, and that my principle was not to desert friends in distress. But that I had written not one word that could not be published in any paper. I made him repeat this since I do not trust the accuracy of Cingalese reporters when faced with a scoop. God knows what he will say.[21]

To the disappointment of Fleet Street, the prospect of Guy Burgess returning soon receded. He now said that he would not risk a trip home unless he was first assured of a safe conduct. And it was in no one's interest to pledge that. British Intelligence knew that they had no evidence against Burgess; and if he ever called their bluff that would have been obvious. The police would have needed witnesses, such as Anthony Blunt, to testify against him. And there was no possibility of Blunt – or any of the other, lesser members of the Cambridge spy ring – doing that. A few days later Burgess changed his mind. He told the *Daily Mail*'s man in Moscow that he would like to go home for a month's holiday but only if the British authorities publicly promised that he would be allowed to return to the Soviet Union.[22]

Unlike Maclean, who refused to talk to Western journalists, Burgess was always happy to meet for a drink but he had nothing new to say and correspondents rarely bothered to file his predictable quotes. When friends visited Moscow he usually made contact even though the Soviets felt uneasy about these meetings. For example, in 1960 Burgess insisted that Stephen Spender should have lunch at his Moscow flat. He kept apologizing for it but Spender was surprised at how tidy and comfortable it was: there were rows of books, a small piano, paintings and, taking pride of place, a fine headboard on his bed, which had, or so Burgess claimed, once belonged to Stendhal. He had lost his good looks and now seemed, thought Spender, rather like 'some ex-consular official you meet in a bar in Singapore and who puzzles you by his references to the days when he knew the great and helped determine policy'.

There were the usual protestations that he was happy ('I love living in this country. It's solid and expanding like England in 1860 and no one feels frightened') and the usual boasts about how important he was. He talked about his defection, which had been a terrible mistake since he had only intended to help Maclean reach Prague before himself going on to Italy for a short holiday. He argued that a great deal of nonsense had been talked about the damage that he had caused to Britain. What was he supposed to have done? Hadn't Churchill gossiped to the Soviet ambassador in London during the war when 'the rules of secrecy were considered to be suspended'. But he was starved of news about friends and that was what he really wanted to talk about. Spender asked if he had made new friends in Moscow. Yes, said Burgess. And then he added: 'No one has friends anywhere like they have in England. That's the thing about England.'[23]

Shortly after Spender returned to London he bumped into the Home Secretary, R. A. Butler, at a party. Butler said that he knew Spender had seen Burgess:

Please tell him that, as far as I'm concerned, he's perfectly free to come and go as he pleases. I know of absolutely nothing to prevent that. Of course, if he does come back and the Home Secretary takes no action then I'll be criticized, the press will be after me, but I'm prepared to face that. As far as I'm concerned there's nothing against him. Of course, the fellows at MI5 may take a different view of the matter. I know nothing about that. Tell him I'll stand by what I say.[24]

Butler might not have been worried by the prospect of Burgess appearing at the Reform, but that was not the feeling of Burgess's friends. Driberg told Spender that it would be a disaster for 'many people' and asked him to do everything possible to dissuade Guy. Spender recalled:

> I did not write to Burgess since it was clear to me that what Butler had said did not provide the slightest guarantee for his safety. MI5 would be sure to have the last word. Besides, Guy had not expressed any wish to come to London; only a faint regret that he would not be able to see his mother.[25]

There was one final alarm. In April 1962, Scotland Yard issued this dramatic statement, clearly designed to convince Burgess, still anxious to see his mother, that there was, whatever he might think, enough evidence to prosecute him:

> There are grounds for supposing Donald Maclean and Guy Burgess may be contemplating leaving, or may have left, the USSR for some other territory. In order that they may be arrested should they come, in transit or otherwise, within the jurisdiction of our courts warrants have been applied for and issued for their arrest for offences committed against Section One of the Official Secrets Act.

The warrant was granted by Sir Robert Blundell, Chief Metropolitan Magistrate, who was, coincidentally, a friend of Blunt. (There is no evidence that Blundell played any part in the decision to ask for the warrant although some people, such as Robert Harbinson, thought that Blunt had exerted pressure on Blundell to ensure that details of the warrant were leaked to the media.) Reporters were dispatched to Heathrow after reports that Burgess and Maclean were on board a flight from Moscow. Once again they were disappointed. In Moscow Maclean refused to answer questions about his rumoured travel plans. Burgess was more forthcoming. His 'many friends in high places' would be caused 'great pain and trouble' if he ever returned to England, he said. He continued: 'There would be an enormous scandal . . . The British Government are positively terrified of me going back to England. I have heard from my confidential sources and from my many friends in the Establishment and even in MI5. The British government is far more frightened of my going to England than I am of [their] warrant.'

On the evening of Wednesday 23 January 1963, Kim Philby failed to turn up at a dinner party at the home of Glen Balfour-Paul, the first secretary at the British embassy in Beirut. For the past seven years Philby had been based in the Lebanon, ostensibly working as a correspondent for the *Observer* and *The Economist* while continuing his secret life as a senior officer in the KGB. That Wednesday evening, however, knowing that British Intelligence were closing in on him – perhaps fearing for his life – he decided that it was time at last to declare his hand. He travelled to Moscow, to be hailed by the Kremlin and the KGB as a hero.

Philby had gone to Beirut in September 1956, after the *Observer* and *The Economist* had been assured by Whitehall that he no longer had any connections with MI6. This was untrue[26] and, indeed, Philby himself noted in *My Silent War* that 'it would have been odd if they had made no use of me at all'. What form this involvement actually took is still unclear. He was close to his old friend Nicholas Elliott, who became the MI6 representative in Beirut in 1959. The two men met regularly at Elliott's home to chew over developments in the region. Philby travelled extensively and must have fed titbits of information gathered during these trips. But his sole concern was to provide material – for example, assessments of British or American intentions in Lebanon – to the Soviets. After his defection, journalists working on the story, notably the *Sunday Times*'s trio of Bruce Page, David Leitch and Phillip Knightley, were assured by Whitehall 'intelligence sources' that for some time before he disappeared MI6 had known that Philby was working for the KGB and that, as a result, they had given him information designed to confuse the Soviets. Perhaps this is true – after all, nothing is impossible in the world of espionage – but no one in the 1980s was willing to confirm it. There is no doubt, however, about the sequence of events in the months before January 1963.

The evidence of Anatoli Golitsin, the KGB station head in Helsinki who had defected to America in 1961, had confirmed Sir Dick White's fears about Philby. But MI6's options were distinctly limited. They knew that Philby would not agree to another interrogation in London, especially in view of the fate of another Soviet spy, MI6 officer George Blake, who had been jailed for forty-two years in 1961. Why should Philby risk another session with British Intelligence? He had survived in the 1950s but he might be tripped up now; there was new evidence against him which, while it might not be conclusive, might be more difficult to dismiss. Early in January 1963 Elliott was sent to Beirut to question Philby. The meeting in a rented flat went better than MI6 could have hoped. Elliott, furious that Philby had abused their friendship, delivered this attack: 'You took me in for years. Now I'll get the truth out of you even if I have to drag it out . . . I once looked up to you, Kim. My God, how I despise you now. I hope you've enough decency to understand why.'[27]

Philby listened silently as Elliott went through the accumulated evidence. This time he did not bother denying it. Yes, it was true; he was a long-term Soviet spy. Elliott pressed home the attack. When and how had he been recruited? Who were his contacts? What had he told the Soviets? The answers were too general and Elliott had not been sent to Beirut to conduct a full-scale debriefing. That would take months, perhaps years. The experts in London would want to go through Philby's career in minute detail. The most important thing now was to persuade Philby to return to London. But Philby stalled. He wanted time, he said, to consider his position. Elliott had little choice. He could hardly arrest or kidnap Philby so next day, after dinner with Kim and his wife Eleanor, an American whom Philby had met in Beirut and married in 1959, Elliott flew back to England to report to his superiors. A few days later Philby vanished.

On 1 July 1963 the Lord Privy Seal, Edward Heath, rose in the Commons to make a statement on Mr Harold Philby, formerly of the Foreign Office, and the subject of much press speculation over the past months. There was as yet no confirmation, said Heath, that Philby was in the Soviet Union but he was now in a position to expand on the statement that Macmillan made in 1955:

> The Security Services have never closed their file on this case and now have further information. They are now aware, apparently as a result of an admission by Mr Philby himself, that he worked for the Soviet authorities before 1946 and that in 1951 he, in fact, warned Maclean, through Burgess, that the Security Services were about to take action against him . . . Since Mr Philby resigned from the Foreign Service in July 1951, he has not had access to any kind of official information. For the last seven years he has been living outside British legal jurisdiction.[28]

Heath's statement horrified MPs. When would this business end? How many more Macleans, Burgesses and Philbys were there? Was the government now telling the whole truth? Macmillan and the Labour leader, Harold Wilson, clashed ill-temperedly in the Commons. Newspapers, realizing that the Burgess-Maclean affair was not dead after all, launched new investigations into Philby's background. In Moscow Guy Burgess was, as always, ready to chat. He told the *Daily Mail* correspondent that he was baffled by the Heath statement:

[Kim] is one of my oldest friends, one of those good friends in bad times as well as good. I would have thought he would have got in touch with me but he has not. And that's straight. I am just as puzzled by his movements as the British government is. To my certain knowledge Kim was never a member of the Communist Party at Cambridge. He joined the Secret Service as an assistant of mine. Now let's deal with these third man stories . . . there was no third man, no unnamed MI5 man, no unnamed diplomat – no Philby who told me what was going on.[29]

A few months later Guy Burgess was dead. The years of hard living, heaving drinking and chain-smoking had wrecked his body. He died on 19 August 1963. He was cremated at Moscow's main crematorium on Monday 4 September after a short, unemotional ceremony. Maclean gave a brief oration, describing Burgess as 'a gifted and courageous man who devoted his life to the cause of making a better world'. Nigel Burgess was one of the handful of mourners. He chatted to Maclean about Guy. Guy had never adapted to life in the Soviet Union; he had nothing to look forward to and survived only on fading memories and sparse news from friends in London. Perhaps Guy's death had been for the best. Far better to go like this, with his mind as sharp as ever, than to sink into premature and muddled old age.

Anthony Blunt experienced conflicting emotions when he heard of Guy's death. He had fought to prevent his friend returning to England and his death was, in a sense, welcome; he would no longer have to worry about Guy blurting out the truth in a morose, drunken moment. On the other hand, Guy had been the most influential character in his life; it was unbearably tragic that Guy should have died, discredited and alone. But Blunt had survived too much to break now and start confiding in friends. He was sure that he was safe. Maclean and Philby were not going to gossip to anyone. The affair, Blunt believed, was finally over. He was, however, mistaken. He had forgotten Michael Straight.

In June 1963 Straight was offered the chairmanship of a new agency, the Advisory Council on the Arts, which was being set up by President Kennedy. Straight was horrified. He was told by friends at the White House that the appointment would have to be ratified by Congress and that there would be 'routine checks' on him by the FBI. Straight later wrote:

> Don't worry, I told myself, an FBI check would turn up nothing on you. Unless a Soviet defector had mentioned me by name. And if he did? I gave them [the Soviets] nothing save for reports of my own opinions. An FBI check would turn up nothing, I kept telling myself. Much later, as I lay in the darkness, I thought, That's not the point. If I become chairman of the arts council . . . I would be opening myself up to blackmail . . . At any moment, some former member of the Cambridge communist movement could say: 'Why . . . I knew him.'[30]

Straight decided that he had no choice. He had to confess. He went to the White House to see his friend, the president's special adviser, Arthur Schlesinger. There, Straight poured out his heart. When he had finished, Schlesinger agreed that Straight could not take up the arts job. Then he telephoned Robert Kennedy, the president's younger brother who was Attorney General. Next day Straight met the FBI and repeated his story to William Sullivan, the bureau's deputy director. The debriefing with Sullivan's men lasted for most of June 1963, but it was not until January 1964 that British Intelligence learned that an American had provided the long-awaited piece of evidence that they needed in order to force Sir Anthony Blunt into admitting that he had been a member of the Burgess spy ring. The MI5 officer whom Straight met was Arthur Martin, visiting the States to interview John Cairncross as part of the review into the Burgess-Maclean-Philby affair. The interview with Cairncross had gone much better than expected; he had not actually confessed but Martin was convinced that he had done much more than just write a few notes for Burgess after lunches with colleagues in Whitehall. Martin recalled:

When I got to Washington there was a message from Bill Sullivan to meet him outside the Mayflower Hotel that afternoon. When I saw him he said that he had someone in the hotel who I might like to meet. He said no more than that. He introduced me to Michael Straight and then left us to talk. Straight told me that he had been recruited by Blunt at Cambridge and he told me about Leo Long. He said he wanted to make amends and that he would be willing to come to England to confront Blunt. I can't explain why the FBI waited so long before letting us see Straight but I don't think it was anything sinister. It is natural for an intelligence organization to want to milk a source before sharing him.[31]

The two men could hardly have come from more different backgrounds. Michael Straight was handsome, privileged and self-consciously intellectual. Arthur Martin was unprepossessing, self-made and down-to-earth. He had been head of D1 – the élite section within MI5 with responsibility for Soviet counter-espionage – since January 1960. He was the son of an engineer and had been educated at a grammar school in Newcastle, in England's industrial north-east. He left school without taking his higher school certificate examination. He said:

> I knew I wasn't going to pass so I left school. If I had tried I suppose I could have had a scholarship to Oxbridge but it was the theatre that had got to me. I found a job in advertising and worked on a series of ads for the *Radio Times*. But I continued in the theatre in Islington. When the war came I tried to join the RAF – glamour I suppose – but they turned me down because I was colour blind.[32]

Martin spent the war in the Middle East with the Radio Security Service and ended his army career as a major. He joined MI5 in 1946 and after a spell in London was posted abroad, first to Singapore and then Kuala Lumpur. Martin favoured dark, baggy suits and, as he grew stouter, he began to seem more and more like a creation of John le Carré; a brooding spy-catcher, who used to sit with his hands clasped behind his head, listening patiently as suspects denied whatever allegation was being made against them. His mind was a constant blur of bluffs and double-bluffs and, although he never claimed to be an intellectual, he was quick-witted and open-minded. He was proud of his work and resented suggestions that in the post-war era MI5 consisted of a band of anti-left-wing bigots who blundered around wrecking innocent people's lives. He was always conscious of his responsibilities; to be fair, impartial and loyal, not to any political party but to British parliamentary democracy. In the 1980s, when he had retired from the Great Game, he would sit and ponder the unanswered questions of his career, wondering if perhaps he had missed a key point here or a clue there. But in January 1964, as he sat with Straight, he had only one thought. He wanted to get back to England to report that at last there was firm evidence against Blunt. Trained though he was to remain unemotional, Martin could not help himself. He was excited.

CHAPTER 18
Reluctant Confession

Arthur Martin returned from the USA a few days after his meeting with Michael Straight. The trip had gone better than Martin had dared hope. John Cairncross had, or so Martin believed, confessed to having passed information to the Soviets. Martin knew that 'it was not a matter for prosecution because the evidence was just not sufficient' but, nevertheless, it had been a valuable interview, another piece in the jigsaw picture of Soviet espionage in Britain. But that was a relatively insignificant triumph alongside the breakthrough provided by Michael Straight. Anthony Blunt had been questioned eleven times by MI5 since 1951. Some of these interviews had been conducted by Courtney Young, who had sat opposite Blunt for much of the war and who had irritated some of the office's more pompous staff by holding vaulting competitions with Anthony over chairs in the canteen. They had had polite and gentlemanly chats; conversations between friends and former colleagues. At no stage had Blunt come close to admitting that he had known about Burgess's or Maclean's spying – let alone confessing to having been involved himself. Yet within MI5 there had been a growing suspicion that Blunt had not just protected Burgess but that he, too, had been a member of the conspiracy. Now here was the confirmation that he had been a recruiter. Straight had mentioned one other name – Leo Long – but this was just the start. The implications,

Martin knew, were enormous. How many more spies had Burgess and Blunt between them planted inside the British Establishment?

There was no question of rushing round to the Courtauld to confront Blunt with the fresh evidence. The allegations from Straight were an intelligence coup but they could not, as Martin knew, be used in a British court. After all, what did they amount to? Before the war Anthony Blunt had asked Michael Straight if he was prepared to work for world peace by helping the Comintern, and as a result Straight had once met a foreigner in London who he thought, but could not prove, was a Soviet agent. And he had had a series of meetings with the mysterious Michael Green in the United States. It would not need a very clever lawyer to have the case against Blunt thrown out, and the security service would be made to look like blundering oafs. There was only one way to secure a conviction against Blunt – a signed confession. And Blunt had shown no signs of wanting to unburden himself so dramatically. There was another factor: MI5 did not want the Blunt case to be made public.

The intelligence world is pragmatic rather than moral. Faced with the choice between an unsatisfactory trial of a suspect and the opportunity to interrogate him privately, most intelligence officers would choose the latter. If intelligence really is 'the great game' then persuading an enemy agent to confess is rather like playing poker and being able to see your opponent's cards. The Soviets would never know that he had confessed; the British would be able to reassess old intelligence and plan new operations on the basis of the opposition's ignorance. Martin knew, too, that if legal action were taken against Blunt then he would lose most of his value as a source. MI5 would not be allowed to question him until after the trial; by that time the Soviets would have had ample opportunity to assess the damage that Blunt might have caused them.

There was a delay of several months between Martin's return from the States and his crucial meeting with Blunt when he presented Straight's evidence. There were several reasons for this. Martin's section, D1, which was responsible for monitoring Soviet covert activities in Britain, had just seven officers; all were continually stretched. The Blunt file, vital though it was, was just one of the many urgent cases. Then there was the problem of deciding exactly how to tackle Blunt. Should he be offered immunity from prosecution in return for his confession? Was there any other way of securing his cooperation? Whatever happened, MI5 had to be sure that it had the backing of the government's legal officers. Immunity had been held out as a bait only once before – to Kim Philby in Beirut – and that offer threatened to haunt British Intelligence for years to come.

MI5's director-general, Sir Roger Hollis, was only too aware of the ammunition a deal with Blunt would provide for the press. Secrecy was, therefore, vital. The immunity offer to Blunt, if it was approved by the Attorney General and the Home Secretary, would have to be seen to be the only possible course of action. Hollis had no wish for some high-minded, disapproving politician or civil servant, present or future, to leak the immunity deal. The thought of what the press would do with the story sent shudders through Hollis. There was another reason, too, for Hollis's caution: MI5 was still suffering from the fallout of the Profumo affair, the scandal that appalled (and intrigued) the British public during 1963.

The Profumo affair had rumbled for several years before its climax in the summer of 1963. Its main characters were John Profumo, Harold Macmillan's Secretary of State for War, Christine Keeler, an eighteen-year-old 'showgirl', Keeler's friend, the society osteopath Stephen Ward, and a Soviet intelligence officer, Eugene Ivanov, who was listed as an assistant naval attaché at the Soviet embassy in London. There was a rich cast of supporting players, including Keeler's friend Mandy Rice-Davies, and Lord Astor, who had been unfortunate enough to rent Ward the cottage in the grounds of his Cliveden estate where Profumo and Keeler first met. It had, therefore, all the ingredients necessary to titillate the nation: power, sex and spies.

Although millions of words were written about the scandal in the 1960s it remained a confused and contradictory blur of allegations and claims. Its tragic consequences, however, were not in dispute. Ward, aged fifty, committed suicide on 31 July 1963 as he was being tried at the Old Bailey on charges of running prostitutes, having been described by the prosecuting counsel, Mervyn Griffith-Jones, as 'a thoroughly filthy fellow' and a 'wicked, wicked creature'. Profumo, too, paid a heavy penalty; he gave up his seat in Parliament on 4 June. Griffith-Jones's condemnation of Ward was echoed in every newspaper in the country; Ward was publicly reviled as a treacherous, communist pimp who had tried to save himself by pretending that he had been working for MI5. By the early 1980s, however, the scandal was given a new dimension when it emerged that Ward had, in fact, been led to believe that he was helping MI5 by one of Martin's junior officers, Keith Wagstaffe, whom Ward had known only as Mr Woods. This did not make Ward a saint, but it did emphasize that, however 'degenerate' he had been, he had not deserved the public obloquy that had been heaped upon him. MI5 had blundered into the Profumo–Keeler–Ivanov triangle in the summer of 1961 when Ivanov was targeted as a possible subject for 'entrapment' – an intelligence-world euphemism for blackmail. It was hoped that the Russian, who had a taste for capitalist high-living, might be lured into a fatal indiscretion. And Stephen Ward, who already knew Ivanov, might be just the man to help with this tricky operation. Ward was a chronic name-dropper but he did surround himself with the sort of beautiful young women, such as Keeler, whom Ivanov might find irresistible. In June 1961 Ward met 'Mr Woods'. It was always thought that this was a low-key meeting during which Ward was supposed to have been warned to be careful of associating too closely with Ivanov. But in the 1980s it appeared that rather more was said. Ward was given the impression that MI5 was hoping for regular reports on Ivanov and that, far from discouraging Ward's girlfriends from having an affair with Ivanov, the national interest might be served if Keeler went to bed with the Russian. MI5 could not have chosen a more unsuitable tipster than Ward. He was a communist sympathizer and a fantasist; he soon saw himself as a key figure in a top-secret spying operation. He thought, too, that he could somehow become an intermediary between the British and Russian governments at a time of acute international tension. But MI5's plan went appallingly wrong. By the end of the summer Keeler was having an affair with Profumo *and* Ivanov. No one within MI5 realized, until it was too late, just how far Profumo was involved and by then the minister had ensnared himself with his own lies. As MI5 tried to distance itself from him, Ward was left to disappear under an avalanche of press condemnation. In September 1963 Lord Denning, the judge, submitted his lengthy report on the affair to the Prime Minister. It was a remarkable document which examined the inner workings of MI5 in unprecedented and, as far as Hollis was concerned, unwelcome detail. Denning cleared MI5 of major blame but Hollis and his officers knew that they had been let off lightly. At best, their perform-ance could be described as ineffectual. Martin himself, who had not been running the case, bitterly regretted what happened to the two men, especially Ward. But it was, alas, just one of the risks of intelligence.

In the 1980s Martin recalled that Anthony Blunt had been dragged into the Profumo affair. Blunt was asked by the Queen's private secretary, Michael Adeane, if he would perform a discreet favour. Ward, who was a keen portrait artist, had sketched members of the aristocracy and had, to the dismay of Buckingham Palace, actually persuaded the Duke of Edinburgh to sit for him. When the offending sketches were put on show at a Mayfair gallery, Blunt bought every one.

Martin and Hollis spent weeks debating how to handle the Straight material. Some retired MI5 officers, who became convinced that Hollis himself was a Soviet agent, have since argued that this delay was engineered by Hollis to give Blunt time to prepare his defence, perhaps even to escape. But there is no evidence to support this theory. Blunt gained nothing from the delay and, even if he had been warned about Straight's confession, certainly had no desire to flee to the cultural wastes of Moscow.

Martin was a member of the anti-Hollis faction, otherwise known as the Young Turks, though he always conceded that the case against the director-general was circumstantial. Martin added that there had been nothing sinister about Hollis's behaviour over Blunt: 'From the time I got back from Washington Hollis really took charge of the case. I never disliked him. He was a very kindly chap and I got on well with him. It is possible that we [the anti-Hollis group] were wrong about him.'

Martin agreed with Hollis that Blunt had to be 'recruited as a source'. Since 1951 Blunt had told a succession of MI5 officers, including Martin and Skardon, that he had been totally ignorant of Guy's work for the Soviets. Martin said:

He was able to fend us off with the story that, of course, he had been a communist at Cambridge but then, probably after the Nazi–Soviet pact, he had become disillusioned. He said that after that he was just pink and not red. He quite cold-bloodedly took that line and I am quite sure was guided to by the Russians. It was the sensible thing to do and he got away with it.[1]

Sir Dick White, who had moved to head MI6 in 1956, stayed in touch with his old office, fascinated to see how Blunt would react. At last, thought White, British Intelligence was coming to grips with the phenomenon of the Cambridge spy ring. It had, it now seemed obvious, owed much more to Burgess's almost hypnotic intellectual and sexual charms than anyone then had realized. Perhaps it had been as much about homosexual infatuation and a shared liking for working-class men as about ideology. No wonder that it had taken so long for MI5 to unravel the story. White recalled:

> It had always been evident to me that Blunt was under the influence of Burgess. I could not understand why he was besotted by Burgess. But I had no idea at the time about the gay scene and its incredible promiscuity. I think we had all felt that Blunt must have known about Burgess but had done everything in his power to protect him. I have to say that I wasn't startled when I heard about Blunt's confession.[2]

The only way to secure a detailed confession, Martin and Hollis agreed, was to offer Blunt immunity from prosecution and a guarantee that there would be no publicity. The moral implications of this were swept aside. Martin recalled:

> If you want a man to talk then you have to get him on your side. I am sure some people in the office would have been horrified and would have taken the line that this

chap should be punished. I honestly never felt that. The overriding need was to find out what he knew, what he had told the Russians about MI5 and why the Russians had allowed him to leave.[3]

Hollis needed clearance from the Attorney General, Sir John Hobson, and the Home Secretary, Henry Brooke, who had responsibility for MI5. Maurice Crump, the deputy Director of Public Prosecutions, recalled that Hobson was ill at the time and that he handled MI5's request to be allowed to offer immunity:

Sometimes the question of whether to give immunity is a difficult one. Sometimes it is not. In Blunt's case it was not. There was no evidence against him on which any criminal charge could be based and he obviously had valuable information to give, if he would talk. Without immunity he would not. The immunity which I gave him was therefore an empty shell, though he clearly thought otherwise. As a no-evidence case is, from the beginning open and shut, his case, like others such, doesn't provide much to remember save that Blunt was who he was. In future, as in the past, each immunity case must be dealt with on its merits, as Blunt's was. There is no other way.[4]

Next, MI5 had to inform Brooke. Hollis asked to see Sir Charles Cunningham, the Permanent Under-Secretary at the Home Office who had regular meetings with MI5 and who was already briefed on MI5's suspicions about Blunt. Brooke met Hollis in early March and agreed to authorize immunity. It was unfortunate that Blunt would escape punishment but the requirements of national security and the lack of evidence meant there was no alternative. One Home Office official recalled:

I understand that Hollis was convinced Blunt would not talk without the immunity offer. The allegations against Blunt related to the war, when for much of the time Russia had been our ally. Blunt had not been in a position where he had any access to secrets for many years. It has all assumed an importance that it just did not have at the time. The idea was for MI5 to get as much information from Blunt as possible.[5]

It was agreed, too, that the immunity deal would depend on Blunt not having spied for the Soviets after the war. But this rider, as everyone knew, was meaningless. It was there as a bureaucratic convenience; a safeguard for the government if news of the deal ever leaked. If that did happen then ministers could argue that they had only made a qualified deal with a traitor. But if MI5 needed Blunt's cooperation as badly as they argued they did, then it made no difference whether he had lost contact with the Soviets after the war or whether he had, for example, helped Burgess and Maclean defect. Indeed, it would be a bonus if he had continued to meet his Soviet controller after the war because his information would be that much more relevant to current operations.

Everyone who worked with Brooke ('the most conscientious minister you could hope to meet') insisted that he had not remembered that he had been at Marlborough with Blunt. Even if he had, said one former senior civil servant, it would have made no difference. There was, of course, one further problem: Blunt's job as Surveyor of the Queen's Pictures. Some Home Office officials found MI5's continuing obsession with the Burgess-Maclean affair baffling; it was, they thought, just another example of how the intelligence world fed on its own paranoia. Why didn't MI5 find something useful to do instead of trying to persuade elderly men to confess to having once, a long, long time ago, given a few titbits to the Soviets? But these civil servants knew that the Blunt case, whether they thought it worth pursuing or not, could have hideous consequences for the Palace.

In April, Cunningham, Hollis and Michael Adeane, the Queen's private secretary from 1953 to 1972, met at the Home Office. Adeane, educated at Eton and Cambridge, listened impassively as the case against Blunt was outlined. It was a quiet, informal meeting. There were no dramatic outbursts. Adeane, as one civil servant said, was 'not a man to be shocked' and after listening to Hollis he asked for advice. Should Blunt be asked to retire from his post? No, thought Hollis, that might alert the Soviets or, even worse, the media. Blunt's circle of friends might just guess what had happened and they were quite capable of leaking that to the press. Adeane knew that the press would take no notice of the fact that Blunt was rarely at the Palace, that he rarely saw the Queen, that he was really just a fringe member of the royal household. The press would sensationalize the story. Politicians would want to know why Her Majesty had been dragged into a squalid, private pact between MI5 and a traitor.

The Royal Family is the most well-shielded institution in the country. Whitehall never discusses its dealings with the monarch, especially on sensitive political issues. And the Palace never comments officially on the monarch's contacts with government. But there is no doubt that Adeane informed the Queen that Blunt was being interrogated, with the offer of immunity. One senior civil servant said: 'The Palace had no involvement, or veto, over the offer of immunity. I have no doubt that the Queen was told.'[6]

Martin now had to set a date for the interview with Blunt. He chose Wednesday 23 April.

*   *   *

By the spring of 1964 Anthony Blunt had accomplished more than he had thought possible when he decided in the 1930s to try and make his livelihood as an art historian. He had been knighted in 1956. He had transformed the Courtauld from a finishing school for wealthy young men and women into the powerhouse of British art history. His pupils were filling many of the newly created posts at universities around the country. Blunt had consolidated his position as a scholar by his steady flow of books and learned articles. He had produced several, acclaimed catalogues on the royal collection. His study of art and architecture in France, 1500 to 1700, published ten years earlier, had become a classic. He had been the Slade Professor of Fine Art at Oxford for the academic year 1962–63. He sat on numerous committees and was always dashing from one important conference to another. He was now, by the standards of the 1960s, a conservative art historian who had no time for the new wave, inter-disciplinary young academics. He remained, though, fascinated by Picasso and William Blake; two artists who represented a link with his youth, when he had believed that art was a weapon for social change. In 1962 he had written a study of Picasso's formative years and now he was preparing his adulatory work on *Guernica*, which appeared in 1969.

Oliver Millar, the deputy surveyor at the Palace, was responsible for the routine administration of the royal collection. Blunt, however, had no intention of being pushed into the background. There were occasional gratifying stories in the press, describing his sterling work in reorganizing the royal pictures. He chaired the Palace committee which was supposed to stimulate the purchase of works by British or Commonwealth artists, either to add to the royal collection or to give as presents to visiting heads of state. There were weekends at Windsor to discuss with the Queen how the collection might be improved. Certainly, the Queen had shown a welcome interest in art. She was anxious that more people should be able to enjoy the collection. In July 1962 there was the first exhibition at the new Queen's Gallery, built in one of the conservatories in the gardens of Buckingham Palace. On 22 July the *Sunday Times* reported respectfully:

> The opening to the public of the new art gallery at Buckingham Palace . . . is an exciting event. For years the Queen has wanted to have more of her pictures on general exhibition . . . The 4,500 royal paintings have never been catalogued but Sir Anthony Blunt, Surveyor of the Queen's Pictures, and his deputy, Mr Oliver Millar, are at present working on them and they hope eventually to produce a five-volume catalogue. The surveyor's duties are not extensive, except on special occasions, but the deputy is expected to spend an occasional weekend explaining pictures to the Queen's guests. Sir Anthony Blunt is better known as the Director of the Courtauld Institute and as Professor of the History of Art at London University. At Cambridge he read mathematics but wanted to become an art historian, even though at the time the profession hardly existed. An expert on Poussin he is now, in his spare time, typing out with two fingers three volumes on Poussin which he says he has been thinking about on and off for thirty years.

Blunt had survived the defections of Burgess and Maclean. He had, or so he thought, been unaffected by MI5's renewed interest in Cambridge that followed the disappearance of Philby from Beirut. But there had been scares. In 1961 Douglas Sutherland, once of the Foreign Office, now a journalist-author, met Blunt at the Travellers' Club. Sutherland was writing a book on the Burgess-Maclean affair and had gathered an impressive amount of circumstantial evidence which pointed to Blunt's involvement in their spying. Sutherland suspected, too, that Blunt had helped the two flee before Maclean could be interrogated. Sutherland described what happened:

> After a conversational preamble I confronted him with the question. I think he knew it was coming. 'There is much circumstantial evidence,' I said. 'Are you the Third Man?' His face was grim and direct, his mouth untypically set. 'If you print that I'll sue,' he said. There was nothing else I could say. I didn't pursue the matter . . . The news was obviously a terrible shock to him. I was probably the first person, apart from various MI5 officials, who had openly accused him of being part of the spy ring . . . Of course he denied it and claimed that Guy's defection had been as much of a shock to him as to anyone else.[7]

There had been another unpleasant false alarm just before Christmas 1963. The painter Peter Greenham, Keeper of the Royal Academy Schools, was working on a new portrait of the Queen for the Welsh Guards. At the end of one morning session he was invited to join the royal family for lunch. Burgess had died in Moscow earlier that year and the conversation turned to the subject of treachery. The Queen Mother was particularly indignant. She told Greenham that 'the one thing I cannot stand is a traitor'. Shortly after this Greenham casually mentioned the lunch to the writer, Robert Harbinson, who later told Blunt's old friend, Peter Montgomery. When Blunt heard about the Queen Mother's remarks his response was immediate. In retrospect it is clear that he feared that the Palace had been told about MI5's thirteen-year-long question mark over his name. Harbinson claimed that Blunt was panic-stricken and that he wanted to see Greenham as soon as possible. Harbinson said:

He got me to go round to the Courtauld with Greenham. I remember that he asked me not to bring Greenham's wife. By 1964 we were all pretty sure that Anthony had been involved with Guy. That's why I told him about Greenham. Greenham was invited around to Anthony's flat at the Courtauld, ostensibly to see Blunt's new Poussin picture. But he just wanted to hear first-hand the story about the Queen Mother. It was a remarkable evening. In one corner sat a sailor on a sofa. He had been picked up for Anthony. Then there was Peter Greenham, admiring the Poussin. The moment Greenham left Anthony disappeared into the bedroom with the sailor.[8]

Shortly before 11 A.M. on 23 April 1964 Arthur Martin walked into the Courtauld Institute in Portman Square. He had met Blunt before, in the 1950s, but then he had been firing blanks and Blunt had known it. Now he had an excellent chance of making the biggest intelligence catch since Klaus Fuchs. But it was not certain. Blunt might refuse to talk. Straight had offered to travel to Britain to confront Blunt, but that would be messy and there was no guarantee that Blunt would crack under the strain of meeting Straight. No, it had to be a confession. Martin recalled: 'Yes, it was exciting . . . one thought: At last . . . It would be an exaggeration to say that it is a game but it is, in a sense, I suppose just that, a fascinating game.'[9]

Blunt answered the door. Martin was ushered into the living room which overlooked the neat gardens of Portman Square. On one wall was Blunt's prized Poussin, 'Rebecca at the Well'. On another wall were several Italian seventeenth-century architectural drawings. On a small

table was a jumble of black and white photographs of paintings which Blunt had been studying with a jeweller's eye-
glass. There was a television, which Blunt, to the amazement
of his friends, used to watch regularly, irrespective of the
programme. There was a dining table and some scuffed
wooden chairs. There were two bedrooms. One had two
single beds and was shared by Blunt and Gaskin. The other
bedroom had one bed and was used by Peter Montgomery
when he was in London. There were hundreds of valuable
books, mainly on art and architecture, the fruit of years of
dedicated rummaging around market stalls and second-
hand bookshops. It was not, thought Martin, the home of
someone who was concerned with material comfort.

Martin sat down and asked if Blunt would mind if he used
a tape-recorder. Blunt, puzzled by Martin's formality,
nodded. Martin put the tape-recorder on the table. He
wasted no time. He told Blunt that he now had unequivocal
evidence that he had been a Soviet agent during the war.
Blunt, sitting opposite Martin, showed no emotion. He said
that there could not be any such proof, for the simple
reason that he had never been a Russian spy. Well, continued Martin, you may change your mind in a few minutes.
He then outlined the allegations made by Michael Straight.
'I think I said something like: I saw Mr Straight the other
day and he told me about his relations with you and the
Russians.'[10]

When Martin had finished Blunt was still staring at him,
expressionless. It was just as Martin had feared: Blunt
would not be panicked into a confession. He would have
to use the immunity card. Martin uttered the words
slowly, precisely, to ensure that the tape-recorder could
pick him up. He said: 'I have been authorized by the
Attorney General to give you a formal immunity from
prosecution.'[11]

Blunt got up, walked to the window and poured himself a

large drink. Martin waited. Then he turned to Martin and said: 'It is true.' With those words Blunt gave MI5 the opportunity it had been looking for since 1951, of understanding why (and how) talented and privileged Englishmen had betrayed their country. At that moment a weight seemed to have been lifted from Blunt. The two men talked for a few minutes more. Martin remembered:

> He said that he would find it very difficult when it came to betraying his friends. But then he said: 'I suppose most of my friends have drifted away now. It's going to be difficult for me.' I must have brought in the condition about him not having been a spy recently. He said that if you take the word 'spy' literally then he couldn't have been because there had been nothing for him to spy on.[12]

Martin then played back the key section of the tape so that Blunt could agree it was an accurate record of their conversation. Martin explained that this was just the start. MI5 would need to go over, again and again, in the minutest detail everything that had happened to Blunt from the moment he had gone to Cambridge. It would be a long, tiring business, but Blunt's total cooperation was the price of immunity. Blunt nodded as he showed Martin to the door. The entire meeting had lasted twenty-five minutes.

Martin returned to his office. While the tape was being transcribed by one of his secretaries Martin reported to Hollis that Blunt had finally broken. Next he wrote a memorandum to Michael Adeane at Buckingham Palace, explaining that the Surveyor of the Queen's Pictures was a self-confessed former agent of the Soviet Union. A few days later Martin returned to begin Blunt's debriefing. He explained that he was not primarily interested in Blunt's time at Cambridge. 'I told Blunt that the Cambridge side of things would be handled by another branch of MI5. I was interested in finding out what he had told the Russians about MI5 and what the Russians had said to him when he left. We had to know why they let him leave.'[13] That final point was crucial. Surely, thought Martin, the Russians would have pressured Blunt to remain in intelligence after the war. He was, after all, an established officer and in peacetime would probably have become one of the most senior officers in the service. Yet they had let Blunt quietly retire. Why? The question nagged at Martin. Did it mean that the Soviets did not need Blunt because there was another high-level mole already in place within MI5? There are other, more plausible explanations. For example, even if Blunt had applied to stay in MI5 it is almost certain that he would have been turned down. The service wanted to train its own career intelligence officers; not build for the challenges of peace by relying on men such as Blunt, a homosexual intellectual who had performed adequately, but not brilliantly, during the war. The Russians must have known this. After all, according to Blunt, hadn't Soviet Intelligence approved his decision to leave MI5? It is a long, long leap from that to the conclusion that there was another Soviet agent in MI5.

Blunt and Martin met about ten times between April and late November 1964. After two meetings at the Courtauld they switched for 'reasons of security and discretion', said Martin, to 'safe houses' dotted around London. Sometimes they met at Martin's own house in Lyall Mews, Belgravia. If that was not available they would meet at a flat in Chandos Court, Caxton Street, Westminster, owned by MI6's Maurice Oldfield who was based in Washington from 1960 until 1964, when he returned to London to become Dick White's deputy. When Oldfield came back to London Martin switched to flats owned by other members of MI5. It soon became obvious to Martin that Blunt had been deeply affected by the decline and death, in a lonely, miserable exile, of Guy Burgess. Martin said: 'It is quite conceivable that they had been friends without sleeping together. They clearly liked each other very much. As Burgess further deteriorated Blunt had become more and more sorry for him. Philby was embarrassed by Burgess. I don't think that Blunt was. He was sorry to see a friend disintegrate like that.'[14]

While Martin was not interested in the details of Blunt's sex life he knew that he had to understand the influence of homosexuality within the Cambridge spy ring. Martin recalled:

> We didn't sit down and discuss sex. I was pretty careful not to make moral judgements about it but we had to discuss it in the context of spying. I gave the impression that I knew about his homosexuality and that he should not be embarrassed by it. He knew that I knew and that was enough. Sometimes he would look ghastly when we met and would say that he had had a ghastly night. He had obviously been drinking a good deal. Yes, he talked about promiscuity and cottaging, but only in the context of the spy ring.[15]

It is a bizarre image: the Surveyor of the Queen's Pictures awaking at the Courtauld after a night with rough trade; then taking seminars with his students, emphasizing the need for art historians to be the champions of Truth and Beauty, before slipping away late in the afternoon for a session with Martin.

Martin was determined not to be overawed by Blunt's intellectual credentials:

> I would have felt out of my depth if we had started to discuss art but we never did. He was a very likeable man. But I never felt that he really came clean with me. When

we threw new information at him he would say that he had forgotten about it. The information didn't flow from him at all. I had the feeling that he felt that he had done the right thing by becoming a communist. I waited until the third meeting to see if he would mention Leo Long. He didn't so I threw the name at him. He said: 'That is one of my difficulties.'[16]

Martin knew that the immunity pact with Blunt meant that none of Blunt's conspirators, however damaging they might have been to the national security, could ever be prosecuted. If Blunt was safe then so were his conspirators. If they were ever charged then Blunt's name would inevitably be dragged into open court. So, Martin reasoned, Long would have to be tempted into a confession. He asked Blunt if he would talk to Long; to ask him if he was prepared to meet MI5. Yes, said Blunt, he would do that, though there was no guarantee that Long would agree.

Leo Long was living quietly in Hampstead. After leaving the Control Commission in Germany he had worked in the City and then in the film industry. He had always expected, he said, a 'knock on the door' from the security service but it had never come. Burgess, Maclean, Philby – they had all fled yet Leo had survived. He was a respectable and respected figure in the community, with a laudable commitment to local charities. His wife and family knew nothing about his involvement with the Soviets, they knew only that Leo had spent his war poring over teleprinters doing something important but rather boring. Then came the telephone call from Anthony Blunt. Blunt said: 'Something has come up. Can I see you?'

Twenty years later, Long was able to recall in vivid detail the meeting in Blunt's flat at the Courtauld:

When I went round there I didn't know what had happened. There was another man with Blunt. I don't know who. Maybe his solicitor. But I'm sure he wasn't from MI5. Blunt said: 'I'm terribly sorry but Michael has made a statement. I've told my story. It's up to you. Do you want to tell yours?' He said that the best thing for me to do would be to come clean. He was very sympathetic. It's difficult to say whether I was surprised by this. Not really, I suppose. I had thought for a long time that the heat must be on Blunt. He didn't say anything about being given immunity from prosecution. But I thought to myself . . . 'As long as Blunt walks around free I am going to do the same. They can't do anything to me. His title, his position. Just think of the embarrassment if it came out.'[17]

After half an hour Long left, having agreed to let Blunt fix a meeting with MI5. Two days later Blunt called. They met at the Courtauld and took a taxi to a flat in Kensington owned by a member of MI5. Blunt introduced Long to Martin and then left. They talked for an hour and a half. Long recalled:

He was a little, short chap. He had a tape-recorder and asked if I minded him turning it on. I didn't ask for immunity but he said – and I don't remember the exact words – that it was extremely unlikely that there would be a prosecution. No, he didn't say that Blunt had been given immunity. We had a very pleasant talk. There was no indication then or in subsequent interviews that MI5 was trying to uncover some vast conspiracy. I had the impression that they wanted to find out if any of these people were still in government service. But I didn't have any names to give them. I had no reason to believe or disbelieve that some of Blunt's friends had gone into government. But what could MI5 have done anyway? Take away their pensions? I told him [Martin] exactly what had happened. Without reservation. He agreed that I had not been in a position to pass on information of devastating value.[18]

Martin said:

I am bound to say that Long was someone I didn't really like. I don't know why; I can't tell you. With Blunt I really didn't feel that I disapproved, which sounds odd I know. But I probably did with Long. Long seemed shocked, craven. But then he realized that Blunt had confessed and that put him in a strong position. First there was fear and then a sort of cockiness.[19]

MI5's interest in Long was limited. He had been recruited by Blunt and was not a central figure in the Cambridge ring. The information that he had handed the Soviets may well have been extremely important at the time but it had been of transient value. MI5 was more concerned with finding out how many other spies had been planted in Whitehall. Long was questioned 'three or four times' more over the years. There was, he said, a change in the tenor of the conversations; the MI5 men seemed to become more aggressive. Long said:

They tried to give the impression that they were going to get tough on this sort of thing . . . But they weren't in a position to get tough with me, there was nothing else I could tell them. I never had the feeling during the war that I was betraying the country. We were young men and we had seen the might of the Nazis and the concessions that were being made to them. It had all seemed part of a deliberate plan. We made the mistake of the young. To see all the horrible things in the world as being part of a deliberate plan, when in fact it is all just sheer hopelessness. Sheer hopelessness.[20]

The battle of wits between Martin and Blunt continued until early December. Martin had hoped for a new lead; by now he was sure that MI5 had been 'penetrated' by Soviet Intelligence. Everything – especially the catastrophes of the Burgess, Maclean and Philby defections – pointed to an enemy mole in MI5. What other answer could there be? But the breakthrough did not come. Blunt was helpful enough on routine matters. Martin showed him pictures of former Soviet diplomats and from these Blunt identified his two case officers: Gromov/Gorski and Modin. He confirmed that he had given details of MI5's internal structure. He said that he had known about Philby and Maclean before the war. He argued, predictably, that before the German invasion of the Soviet Union he had only been able to pass, in his own words, 'routine information'. After that he had handed over whatever he could about German intelligence radio intercepts. He laughed when Martin suggested that he had tipped off Maclean in 1951. How, asked Blunt, would he have been able to discover when MI5 intended to question Maclean? He could hardly have called MI5, could he? He admitted, though, that Burgess had told him about the danger facing Maclean, though he also insisted that his role in arranging the defection had been peripheral. He explained, too, that Modin had appeared, quite unexpectedly, at the Courtauld in 1954 and asked Blunt to arrange a meeting for him with Philby.

Some of the names that Martin bounced off Blunt came from Michael Straight, who had been shown hundreds of photographs of Cambridge students from the 1930s and asked if he thought, just possibly, that they might have been secret communists. But Blunt usually shrugged noncommittally when Martin asked about old Cambridge friends. Straight had, for example, said that Alister Watson, a King's College scientist, had been a communist. However, this fact was of limited use, and Watson was not questioned by MI5 until 1967. When Martin mentioned Watson's name Blunt said: 'Watson is not relevant.' There were hundreds of ex-Cambridge communists, many of whom had become distinguished public servants. MI5 would just have to interview as many as possible but it would be a long, time-consuming haul. Had Tomas Harris, who had died in a car crash in Majorca in January 1964, known anything about Blunt's work for the Soviets? Hadn't Harris been very close to Philby and Burgess? asked Martin. Yes, said Blunt, but so had many other people and that didn't make them Soviet spies. No, added Blunt, Martin was wasting his time if he thought Harris had been involved in the spy ring. Martin recalled: 'There were grounds for suspicion against Harris but I don't know whether they were justified. Blunt said not. Blunt said that anyone who Burgess praised should be looked at . . . but he admitted to no one else apart from Leo Long. I never felt he came clean, but that is pure opinion.'

In September Michael Straight arrived in London to visit his mother, who had a flat in Upper Brook Street, near the American embassy in Grosvenor Square. Martin met him there and took Straight to one of MI5's 'safe' houses in South Audley Street. Martin explained that Blunt had confessed, but there were still gaps and worrying contradictions. Would Michael, asked Martin, be prepared to see Blunt? The two men might be able to 'jog' each other's memories and clear up the few remaining problems, he said, carefully giving the impression that he did not for one moment suspect anyone of telling lies. No, said Straight, he did not mind seeing Blunt. The meeting was fixed for the following day at the Courtauld Institute. There was one small point, added Martin. Anthony would like fifteen minutes on his own with Michael.

The next day Straight walked slowly to the Courtauld, feeling as if he was playing a crucial scene in some B-movie spy drama. Straight wrote:

> Anthony . . . looked pale and skeletal, as he always had; he did not appear to be broken in spirit. I had assumed that he would be bitterly hostile; I was surprised by his thin-lipped smile and the grip of his hand. We walked into his spacious living room. I glanced at the paintings on the walls. I was in no hurry to talk but was aware of his sense of urgency. 'I asked if I might see you alone for a few moments,' he said. 'I just wanted to tell you: thank God you did what you did! I was sure that it would all become known, sooner or later,' he added. 'I couldn't muster up the strength to go to the authorities myself. When they said that you had told them your story, it lifted a heavy burden from my shoulders. I was immensely relieved. We always wondered how long it would be before you turned us in.'[21]

Then Martin arrived. The three men talked for an hour, but, as Martin recalled, Blunt and Straight seemed to have little in common: 'I had hoped that their combined memories might throw up something new. But it was a total flop. The two men were completely incompatible. They must have had something in common when they were undergraduates. But that had gone by 1964.'[22] As the conversation faltered Martin warned Straight that it was possible that, one day, the story might become public. Blunt turned even paler. He said: 'If the story should be published that would be absolutely devastating for me.'

Straight met Blunt only once more; by then the latter had endured hundreds of hours of questioning by MI5 and told

Straight that the authorities had come to trust both of them. Straight, too, had a series of meetings with MI5 between 1964 and the mid-1970s, usually at his hotel in London when he was on business trips to England. The MI5 men always treated Straight respectfully. They would ask permission to tape-record the conversation before reviewing, yet again, his time at Cambridge. They showed him faded photographs of bright, hopeful undergraduates and yellowing lists of student communists. Could this man have become a spy? What about him; surely he was a mole? Mostly Straight could not help. He explained that, while it was true that there had been moles whom the party hoped would one day have access to secret information, there was no way of knowing whether these young men and women had stayed faithful to the cause. Straight felt uneasy; he agonized that by identifying these former friends he might be fuelling a McCarthyite purge by British Intelligence. But he found solace in this thought:

> For every 'mole' whom I felt that I had to identify, I was able, I believe, to help clear a score of men and women who had joined the student movement as I did but would not have embarked upon careers directed towards subversion and deceit . . . The last action I undertook for the British intelligence services was in the seventies . . . it was to clear my old friend Brian Simon of any role beyond the open and avowed one that he still carried on as a member of the Central Committee of the Communist Party of Great Britain. With that my role as an informer came to an end. It is a role that is despised in every country and in every context. It runs counter to a determination that we all share – not to inflict pain upon others.[23]

In the autumn of 1964, just as Martin felt he was starting to establish a working relationship with Blunt, he was told that he was being transferred to MI6. In the spring of that year, shortly after he had begun his interrogation of Blunt, he had had a furious argument with Hollis over a plan to transfer one of Martin's staff to another section. At least, that was the ostensible reason for the row. Hollis ended by accusing Martin of acting like the Gestapo – a reference to Martin's determination to weed out the Soviet spy (or spies) Martin seemed to think had been planted inside British Intelligence. Martin had been suspended for two weeks but had been allowed to return to the Blunt case. It was, though, a temporary reprieve.

This fear – that the Soviets had an agent undiscovered within MI5 and MI6 – had led to the extraordinary investigation in 1963 of MI5's own deputy director-general, Graham Mitchell. A fine chess player and keen yachtsman, Mitchell had been educated at Winchester and Magdalen College, Oxford, and had joined the service in 1939. Martin himself had been largely responsible for demanding that Mitchell should be treated as a suspect. Mitchell was followed by MI5 'watchers', his office was bugged and his files searched. He retired late in 1963, unaware that his loyalty had been questioned. When he was finally questioned in 1970 he was furious and hurt. He said:

I felt shocked. I had kept bundles of letters which people in the office had been kind enough to send me. But after I found out that I had been under suspicion, I spent the morning tearing them all up. I thought, well, if that's what the office thinks of me I don't set much store by them. Then, a few days later, I realized that these people had only been doing their duty towards me as they saw it.[24]

When it became clear that the surveillance of Mitchell had yielded little (though some MI5 officers still thought, despite the lack of evidence, that he might be a traitor) attention was again focused on Hollis. By now there was a committee of MI5 and MI6 officers – codenamed the Fluency committee – investigating the claims of Anatoli Golitsin. Golitsin had convinced some of the CIA's most senior officers, including Jim Angleton, the agency's director of counter-intelligence, that the West had been deceived by a massive Soviet misinformation campaign. In essence, Golitsin argued that *nothing* that the West believed about Soviet strategy was correct. After Martin had met Golitsin, codenamed Kago by the British, he argued that the claims, fantastic though they were, had to be thoroughly investigated. But Roger Hollis concluded that the pro-Golitsin camp within MI5 was doing more damage than good; its obsessive hunt for traitors within the service was wrecking morale and efficiency. The only solution was to fire Martin. In December Martin moved to MI6. The man who took over the Blunt interrogation was Peter Wright, but Hollis could not have made a worse choice.

CHAPTER 19
Maverick Inquisitor

Peter Wright became front-page news in the summer of 1984 when he decided, at the age of sixty-nine, publicly to accuse his former masters at MI5 and the government of wilfully ignoring his warnings about massive Soviet penetration of British Intelligence. Wright had retired in 1976 an angry, disillusioned man and had emigrated to Tasmania, Australia, where he hoped to start a new life breeding horses. But the anger festered and he started to leak information to selected journalists, in the hope that the authorities would be forced to reopen the files that had been gathering dust since the early 1970s. When he was interviewed on Granada Television's 'World in Action' programme in the summer of 1984, he repeated the claims that he had been whispering for years on what he used to call 'a strictly unattributable basis'. He pressed on; he gave interviews to the press and talked about sinister Soviet plans to undermine Britain. When all of this brought no response from the authorities whom Wright wanted to reopen the inquiry into Hollis, he announced that he would be publishing his own account of the great conspiracy. The British government, incensed by Wright's decision to break his vow never to discuss his work for MI5, and fearful that other retired officers might be tempted to publish their memoirs, launched a legal action aimed at stopping the book.

Wright had joined the service in 1955 from Marconi to provide what was officially described as 'technical and scientific support'. He thus became a member of MI5's overworked team of boffins, responsible for servicing all the paraphernalia of counter-espionage – the tape-recorders, bugs and radio transmitters – as well as having to develop ever-more ingenious devices to aid the defence of the realm. But Wright thought that his talents were wasted; he was determined to move into the élite of MI5, with the men who actually caught the spies. And he succeeded. His career culminated in his appointment to the personal staff of Sir Michael Hanley, director-general of MI5 from 1972 until 1979, as a 'consultant on counter-espionage with access to matters of the highest sensitivity'. Russell Lee, who retired from MI5 in 1978, recalled:

Peter Wright was not a chap I warmed to at all. It was always about number one with Peter Wright . . . things that could further the cause of Peter Wright. He came to us late in life and was always excused the chores that the rest of us had to do. None of us could understand how he got into the operations side of things. I think he impressed some of the senior people. They were mesmerized by this man, who seemed to be able to use a slide-rule. They thought that was marvellous. But I never liked him.[1]

Another former colleague, a senior man who wrote to *The Times* defending Hollis after Wright's appearance on television, said:

I was no great admirer of Peter Wright. To be honest, I thought there was something bogus about him. I had neither a high regard for his judgement nor his personality. But he was not the only person to believe in Golitsin, the guilt of Hollis and so on. The trouble with the sort of life we led is that people who didn't have their feet planted firmly on the ground were apt to get swept away by all sorts of theories of espionage which became more and more elaborate. Eventually they ceased to have anything to do with reality. There were others like Wright . . . people whose lives were centred on espionage and counter-espionage.[2]

Another ex-MI5 officer, a woman whose husband was a senior officer in the service, said of Wright:

Some people adored him, the ones who thought that he was correct about Golitsin and Hollis. But I know others who thought he was very strange. He was always going on about Soviet misinformation. That was his passion. Misinformation and what he called Soviet 'agents of influence' . . . That's why Wright became so odd in his retirement. He couldn't tell the difference between what was real and what was not.[3]

In 1963 Wright had helped with the bugging of the hapless Graham Mitchell; and in the autumn of 1964 had been present during one of the talks that Martin had had with Blunt, making himself useful when the MI5 tape-recorder broke down. Wright claimed to have spent hundreds of hours talking to Blunt between 1964 and 1976. They even started to exchange Christmas cards. For much of the time Wright seems to have believed that Blunt was being truthful; in retirement, however, he argued that Blunt had never been entirely honest: 'I know more about Blunt than anyone. I talked to him for 250 or 300 hours over the years. But, of course, I'm sure he didn't tell me anything.'[4]

Wright had several aims when he was debriefing Blunt.

First, he had to try and find out how many other spies or 'agents of influence' (intelligence shorthand for a person who agrees to work for the cause of a foreign power without actually passing secret information) had been recruited during the 1930s. He had to find out as much as possible about Blunt's own spying for the Soviets and why he had been allowed to leave MI5. He needed to know how the Soviets had managed to discover the date of Maclean's interrogation. He wanted to know why Philby had suddenly fled from Beirut. But Wright became increasingly certain that nothing that Blunt said could be properly understood unless MI5 believed in the Golitsin thesis. Wright, who was chairman of the Fluency committee, put it like this:

> Those of us intimately concerned with the Hollis investigation believed that Hollis had been a long-term Soviet penetration agent in MI5 . . . [In 1965] Hollis called me just before he retired into his office. He sat down beside me and said: 'Why do you think I'm a spy?' I thought very quickly because I felt I oughtn't to tell him a lie so I gave him a summary of the Fluency assessment and pointed out that he was by far the best suspect. His reply to that was: 'Peter, you have got the manacles on me. I can only tell you that I am not a spy.'[5]

Hollis, who died in 1973, would have been the prize catch for Wright and his allies in MI5 (and MI6). While they probed Hollis's past, Wright intensified his efforts to track down other, lesser traitors. An MI5 officer, Anthony Motion, was dispatched to Oxford to dig through files on the 1930s. Motion who, like Wright, chose Australia as his retirement home, said that his inquiries had only thrown up a few 'minor spies'. Wright, meanwhile, was pursuing friends and suspected friends of Blunt and Burgess with extraordinary enthusiasm and energy. Hundreds of people were questioned in the years following Blunt's confession; some for only a few minutes, others for weeks. Since this was Britain and not the United States, nothing was written at the time about this search for moles or spies. There were no public inquiries. There were no complaints to the newspapers from patriotic, respectable men and women who had to endure the indignity of being asked, in a roundabout way of course, if they were traitors. The majority were cleared, discreetly and promptly, by MI5. But a handful were not so lucky and Wright's men pencilled question marks against their names. Usually MI5 was powerless to do more since most of these suspects had long since left public service; a few, however, were within reach. They lost their security clearance and were transferred to lower-grade jobs. Wright claimed in 1984 that the Fluency probe had uncovered 'eight hitherto undisclosed members of MI5 and MI6 who were firm suspects and who left the service and . . . more than thirty other positive suspects were identified in other limbs of the government and in the universities.' But Wright was unwilling, or unable, to give details to support this assertion. Some MI5 officers, including Wright, even believed that the Labour Prime Minister, Harold Wilson, might be a Soviet agent. (This idea was, of course, nonsense.) Once again the source of the rumour was Anatoli Golitsin, who suggested that the Soviets had poisoned Wilson's predecessor, Hugh Gaitskell, who died suddenly in 1963. The inquiry by MI5 managed only to come up with the not-very-remarkable fact that Wilson had made twelve trips behind the Iron Curtain in the previous twelve years; MI5 could have discovered this by checking the press clippings.

Often, Wright's interpretation of what had been said (and admitted) during an interview with a 'suspect' was fundamentally different from that of the people he had been grilling. There are examples of Wright noting that a man had 'partially confessed' to helping Burgess or Blunt when the interviewee thought that Wright had been satisfied by his or her explanation. The MI5 spy-catchers carefully fudged the reason for the security service's renewed interest in the 1930s. They never revealed that Blunt had confessed and they peppered their interviews with false clues. The Philby affair was still smouldering and it was quite possible, some thought, that the MI5 inquiry had been provoked by that. Inevitably, when Blunt's friends compared notes of their talks with the intelligence service they agreed that Blunt might have been able to explain what was happening. Traditional British reserve and good manners meant that most did not dare to ask him.

Victor Rothschild was questioned 'four or five times'. He was cleared unequivocally but his friendship with Blunt continued to haunt him. (In 1980 Rothschild, irritated by rumours about his role in the Blunt affair, asked Peter Wright to come to London to confirm that he, Rothschild, had never been a Soviet spy.) Rothschild said:

I know quite a lot of people have asked the question: was Victor Rothschild a Soviet agent? I have survived that and I have occupied very, very senior positions in Whitehall. The probability of me being a Soviet agent wobbles around zero. But I was questioned very extensively. The authorities, as I call them, said that they wished to talk to me and they talked in quite a friendly way. I have a feeling that they believed me. I was quite happy to tell them everything I knew. We had a very long talk. I was quite happy to tell them how well I knew Burgess and Blunt. I have no recollection anyone ever asking me if I was a Soviet agent and it would have been naïve for a professional interrogator to do that. I think they were more interested in who were my friends. I know all sorts of people who were questioned in the same way. I know people of great distinction, greater distinction, who were also questioned. All sorts of people. There really was an investigation. It wasn't a witchhunt; it was a very serious investigation. And I don't object to that. You have to help your country and I think all the people concerned did that.[6]

The scientist Alister Watson, the former Cambridge don who had been both an Apostle and a communist, did not fare so well. Since 1953 he had worked at the top-secret Admiralty Research Laboratory at Teddington, Middlesex on classified anti-submarine research. According to Peter Wright, MI5 discovered from telephone taps and microphones planted in Watson's home that he was still a communist. He was then pulled in for questioning which lasted for six weeks. By then Wright was sure that Watson was a traitor, although he did not believe that the case would stand up in a British court. Wright recommended that Watson be moved immediately into non-classified work; a few weeks later he was transferred to the National Institute of Oceanography. Wright claimed that Watson had admitted meeting two KGB officers but that he insisted that he had never given the Soviets any secret information. Wright was unconvinced:

I fail to see why he was meeting KGB officers if he wasn't passing it over . . . [My conclusion was] that he had been a spy since 1938 and that he ceased being a spy when we moved him out of access. I think [he was very important] because he was right in the heart of the most secret part of defence, much more important than nuclear weapons because the Russians knew all about them. They don't know, or they didn't know all about anti-submarine warfare.[7]

Watson had a different version of what he had told MI5. In November 1981, aged seventy-three and living in retirement in Surrey, Watson decided to respond to stories that had been leaked to the press. Because of British libel laws these reports had not actually accused him of treachery but, even so, they implied that Watson knew more about Burgess and Blunt than he cared to admit. Watson used a well-known London solicitor, Geoffrey Bindman, who was used to handling the media, to issue a lengthy statement. He insisted that he had never given 'classified information to any unauthorized person' but said that during six gruelling weeks of questioning by the security service in 1967 he became so exhausted that he may have said things that he did not mean:

> I think that when MI5 started off they knew that I had had contacts with others who had confessed. They were justified in suspecting that I might be a spy but their technique was to press me to confess without specifying what they wanted me to confess to. Looking back on it I suppose that I became incoherent because of the pressure and my anxiety that related to the fact that my former friends had apparently been involved with spying. Because of my incoherence I might have failed to allay their suspicions or give an adequate account of myself.[8]

Bindman, who talked at length to Watson during the preparation of the press statement, recalled:

> Yes, he was pushed into a virtual confession. He was sleeping very badly. He would be questioned and then they would leave him alone for a while and then they would start again. In the course of the interrogation he discussed with his wife whether he should see a psy-

chiatrist because he was worried that he was saying things that were not true. MI5 said that they would choose the psychiatrist. The psychiatrist said that it was quite possible that under pressure he might be saying things he did not mean. As a result of the questioning by MI5 he lost his high security clearance and was moved to a mundane job.[9]

Sir Dennis Proctor, a distinguished civil servant who died in 1983, was another person whom Wright filed as having 'partially confessed'. Proctor's account of his experiences with MI5 is less harrowing than Alister Watson's, but it is more precise, partly because Proctor was a meticulous note-taker who regularly jotted down his thoughts on particularly interesting events in his personal life. As far as Wright was concerned, there was really little doubt about Proctor's guilt. He was an Apostle; he admitted having had 'Marxist leanings'; he was a close friend of Guy Burgess and of Anthony Blunt. In his retirement Wright told journalists how Blunt had confirmed MI5's suspicions of Proctor. For example, on 21 July 1983 Wright told Barrie Penrose in a long telephone conversation from his home in Australia:

> I'll tell you this much. Not to be quoted and I'll sue you if you do. But Proctor is one who annoys me intensely. He was a very close friend of Guy Burgess. Somebody, you can guess who, you have mentioned his name [Anthony Blunt], told me that Proctor was the best source Guy ever had for the Russians.

Sir Dennis Proctor was born on 1 September 1905, the son of Sir Philip Proctor, and was educated at Harrow and King's College, Cambridge. He was an Apostle and became close friends with Guy Burgess, though he was never homosexual. He was, he openly admitted throughout his life, sympathetic to Marxism but he always qualified this by adding he had never become a member of the Communist Party. His friends speculated that this was because he could never accept the discipline of communism; he had, they used to tell him, far too developed a sense of humour to endure endless, earnest discussions with committed Marxists. He joined the civil service in 1929 and, after a short spell in the Ministry of Health, moved to the Treasury. He soon emerged as one of the high-fliers within the home civil service. In 1934 he became assistant private secretary to the former Prime Minister Stanley Baldwin, then Lord President of the Council. During the war he was briefly principal private secretary to the Chancellor of the Exchequer, Sir Kingsley Wood. In 1950, believing that he had gone as far as he wanted in the civil service, he decided that he would try a career in business. He became the London representative for a Danish shipping company, but three years later he was back in Whitehall. The experiment in business had not gone as well as he had hoped, and his second wife, Barbara, a civil servant whom he married in September 1953, encouraged him to return to the job that he did best. He was delighted, therefore, when he was asked if he would be prepared to go back to Whitehall. He became Deputy Secretary at the Ministry of Transport and Aviation – a job he held until 1958 when he was promoted to Permanent Secretary at the Ministry of Power. He retired, a much admired and popular figure, on his sixtieth birthday in September 1965. He had always been passionately interested in the arts. He was particularly keen on paintings and was the chairman of the Tate Gallery Trustees from 1953 until 1959 and served for a time on the governing committee of the Courtauld. If his humour and sharp brain endeared him to Burgess, his interest in art ensured that he remained a friend of Blunt. He had been interviewed by MI5 twice in the 1950s. The first session was in the autumn of 1953 when he returned to Whitehall. The MI5 officer who interviewed him was, Proctor thought, Graham Mitchell. Lady Proctor recalled: 'MI5 wanted to know about Dennis's friendship with Guy Burgess. Dennis had never made any secret of it and had never thought for one moment that Guy was a Soviet spy. Dennis always thought that Guy had fled to Moscow in a fit of desperation.'[10] Mitchell flourished a copy of a letter that Proctor had written on 8 January 1950 to Burgess in Washington and which had been found when Burgess's flat had been searched. To a spy-catcher such as Mitchell, struggling to make sense of the web of friendships that Burgess had spun in order to feed him information and protect himself, the friendly tone of the letter suggested that Proctor may have known rather more than he cared to admit about Guy's extra-curricular activities. Proctor had opened the letter by apologizing for not having written earlier and continued with a point by point breakdown of his reasons for leaving Whitehall:

1. The economic spur. Impossible to reduce expenses. Necessary to increase income.
2. Tired of being told that a general purpose civil service has no scarcity value. Decided to test the market.
3. Not impervious to general climate of opinion about civil servants. Never liked officialdom anyway.
4. Hankering after shipping ever since I dealt with it during the war.
5. Disillusioned by five years of peacetime planning. Doubt the ability of any chosen few, however high-minded and intelligent, to order all the nation's affairs for the general good.
6. Wanted a change of life anyway after twenty years in the public service. Feel ten years younger as a result.

Now send me a p.c. to tell me how my Apostolic rating has fallen.
Love, Dennis.[11]

Proctor survived the Mitchell interview. In 1959 he was again questioned, though this was the routine positive vetting check to ensure that he could continue to receive classified information. Lady Proctor recalled:

It was very comic really. Dennis told me that he had got on very well with the chap, who was quite elderly. It turned out that they were both keen wicket-keepers. They started to show each other how they took a ball on the leg side. So you had these two men ducking down behind a chair pretending that they were playing cricket. Then, just as the interview was coming to an end, the man said 'I am sure you don't have any friends who are communists or anything like that?' Dennis said: 'Of course I do. Guy Burgess was one of my greatest friends. But I am sure you have already been told that.'[12]

Once again, though, Proctor convinced MI5 that his relationship with Burgess had been innocent. But Peter Wright thought the case needed a more thorough examination. In September 1965 the Proctors decided that they would spend the first year of Dennis's retirement at a tiny cottage they had bought in the Vaucluse, north-east of Avignon. They packed their bags and left for France with their three young adopted children for what should have been a peaceful, enjoyable year.

Soon after Christmas they received the following letter from Peter Wright. It was dated 22 December 1965 and was typed on paper headed 'Ministry of Defence, Room 056, Old War Office Building, Whitehall'. It said:

Dear Sir Dennis,

I am engaged in a considerable research into certain events that took place years ago and of which I believe you may have recollections. I wonder whether you would be willing to see me sometime and discuss your memories? I could come to France to see you at your convenience any time after the middle of January. On the other hand if you happen to be coming to this country within the next two or three months perhaps we could meet here? I hope you will be willing to see me because I think you may be able to help me. I hope you are having a pleasant retirement.

Yours sincerely,
Peter Wright.[13]

At first the Proctors thought that Wright must be an official historian researching into Stanley Baldwin. Proctor was due in London early in the new year and offered to see Wright there. But, no, Wright seemed keen on a trip to France. Perhaps, speculated the Proctors, he felt like a break from the dreariness of a London winter. Wright arrived in France on the evening of 8 February 1965, and Proctor picked him up at Carpentras, the nearest town to the cottage. Wright had dinner with the family and had to wait for three noisy, exuberant children to be sent to bed before he could begin his interview. Lady Proctor said:

I suppose by that stage my husband knew who Wright was. But I had been expecting a young man and here was this middle-aged civil-servant type. I was busy with the children at first. Then they went off to bed. Wright was asking the silliest questions . . . about people Dennis knew. I went to bed about midnight. I thought that Wright was a pompous bore. I think they sat up until about 3 A.M. I know that they were both drinking quite a lot.[14]

Wright emerged for a late breakfast, heavy-eyed after the previous night's exertions. He had left his briefcase invitingly open under the kitchen table, though the Proctors affected not to notice it. After some desultory conversation Proctor drove his guest to Avignon to catch a train back to London. Later that month Proctor scribbled a few notes on what had been said that night. Peter Wright and his allies might argue that these jottings were cleverly concocted Soviet misinformation; a mixture of fact and fiction aimed at discrediting, even ridiculing, British Intelligence. But it seems much more likely that Proctor was simply doing here what he had done thousands of times in Whitehall: making a note for future reference. Lady Proctor said that her husband's notes, written that February, showed that Wright had said that he was trying to find out who recruited Guy Burgess. He told her husband that Maclean and Burgess had been tipped off by Philby and that until 1961 there had been no firm evidence that Burgess had been a Soviet agent. It is obvious that Wright was trying to draw Proctor; by blending known facts, speculation and nonsense in an effort to elicit a damning comment. Wright eventually threw in Blunt's name. Lady Proctor said:

Anthony had never wanted to discuss Guy Burgess. We always assumed that it was because he had been in MI5 and it was for security reasons. Dennis told Wright that he would like to talk to Anthony. Wright said that he didn't mind but said he wanted to talk to Anthony first. Wright also told us that we shouldn't mention his name to anyone because his life would be in danger . . . Dennis said that Wright had said enough to make it clear that he was on the list of suspects and that the reason he had wanted to come to France, rather than meet in London, was that he had wanted to spy out the land as much as to find out about Guy Burgess's friends. Dennis thought that he had set a trap for him by leaving his briefcase conspicuously open. He was irritated by Wright but we soon forgot about him.[15]

It was a shame, Proctor thought, that the records of his previous interviews with MI5 appeared to have been lost. After all, he had always been open then about his relationship with Guy. Proctor later observed:

I certainly talked to Guy Burgess as a like-minded friend who was also in an official post engaged in the war effort about my job and about the way things in general seemed to be going. But I never, so far as I remember, disclosed any secret matters which were not already accessible to him in his own position. In point of fact, I was never in contact with operational matters in my own work and I had no real secrets to give him.[16]

After her husband's death Lady Proctor realized that Wright, by then talking publicly about his investigations, had concluded that that late-night talk in 1965 was supposed to have ended with a 'partial confession' by Sir Dennis. She said: 'My husband was a loyal friend of Anthony Blunt and Guy Burgess. And in some people's minds that means that he is tantamount to being a traitor.'[17]

Sir Edward Playfair, a senior civil servant, had considerable sympathy for his friend Proctor when he heard about the dreadful evening he had endured with Wright. Dennis, said Playfair, made no 'partial confession'; he had simply been fond of Burgess and had said so. Playfair had had his own brush with MI5 some years before, though the MI5 and MI6 men who were leaking to the media during the

1980s disagreed over whether or not he had ever been on the list of suspects. Playfair was educated at Eton and King's College, Cambridge. He joined the civil service in the early 1930s and rose to become Permanent Under-Secretary of State for War in 1956. In 1960 he was promoted to Permanent Secretary at the Ministry of Defence; a job he held for a year before leaving for a career in business. During the war he had warned Blunt, whom he knew from Cambridge, about an over-talkative girl who was about to be recruited into government:

> I was dining at the Café Royal with a most delightful girl who was a very overt communist. A friend of hers came up and said that she had a splendid new job at the centre of things at the Air Ministry. She said things she ought never have said to anybody. I went back and told Anthony that this girl, who still had to have her final interview for the job, should not be given it. I said she's not trustworthy. My communist friend later thought I was lousy. I even knew from Blunt that MI5 had a file on me. A German spy tried to get something out of me with no success during the war . . . I can't remember his name though I think he was later caught by the French. I reported all this to Blunt but he told me they already knew. They had the expense chit for lunch.[18]

Playfair forgot about these incidents. After the war he constantly asked if someone would like to 'positively vet' him. But no one saw any point in wasting the time of the Security Service in checking a patently loyal public servant like Playfair. He said: 'This ran against all the rules of security. I said: "I don't agree with this." They said they were too busy to do it. I took it up with the War Office and then the Ministry of Defence but they were all too busy.'[19] Then, shortly before he left Whitehall, MI5 visited him. He was, after all, an ex-Cambridge man; he knew Burgess and Blunt and there was that file lodged somewhere in MI5's registry. Playfair could remember only a 'dim face asking questions'. He said:

> I had always said of Guy Burgess, that I can't see him being a spy because who would hire anybody who was so grossly unreliable. The only thing in his favour, from the point of view of being a spy, was that his reputation was so bad that it was impossible to blackmail him. But Anthony was another matter. A cold, distant man. I always thought he was a political innocent.[20]

Wright insisted that he had seen Playfair twice, but another ex-MI5 man interviewed in 1984 insisted that *he* had seen Playfair. This source said that Playfair had used a 'very strange word . . . tangential'. But the significance of this in terms of assessing Playfair's loyalty was unclear. To confuse the issue further, Wright insisted that he never seriously suspected Playfair. The episode was unsatisfactory and simply emphasized the difficulty of unravelling exactly who said what and to whom during the post-Blunt investigations.

Andrew King, the former Cambridge communist who became a career intelligence officer with MI6, was twice questioned by MI5 and was probably one of the eight whom Wright alleged, without naming them, had been forced to quit the service. But King, who retired in 1967 after thirty years, many of them overseas, for British Intelligence, insisted that he was as patriotic as anyone:

> Oh yes, I was questioned by MI5. But they never tripped me up. I was interviewed twice. The first time was in 1951 a few months after Burgess and Maclean defected. I was head of the Vienna station and was called back to

London for consultations. Then I spent three days with
MI5. They were very nice but I don't think they understood what happened at Cambridge. I had told them
when I joined before the war that I had been a member of
the Communist Party and no one had minded. I told
them in 1951 that, of course, Guy Burgess had been a
communist at Cambridge. Lots of people knew that. But
the MI5 people said, yes, they are telling us that now but
no one ever told us and it wasn't on our records. They
were certainly never rude enough to suggest that I was a
Soviet spy or anything like that. Was I cleared? I don't
know. What could they do? Tap my phone? Open my
mail? They may have done that without my knowledge. I
saw MI5 again in 1967 just before I retired. I think that
they were happy. I am sure all this came from Peter
Wright. He had his own theories and he was right to
suspect me. He put forward the theory that I was pushed
underground [by the Soviets]. But you can construct
anything from the circumstantial evidence, just as he did
with Roger Hollis. But unless you get evidence, from
tapping phones or intercepting mail or from a defector,
you can't prove anything. That's the trouble with
intelligence.[21]

Many more were swept up in the MI5 inquiry. In 1968
John Hilton met an MI5 officer in a Whitehall pub. 'They
wanted to know about Anthony's friends. They were interested in someone with, I think, a Dutch name who'd
been at Marlborough.'[22]

Christopher Harmer, a wartime MI5 officer, was questioned in 1967: 'It was rather funny really. When they had
searched Burgess's flat in 1951 they found a note from
David Hedley [Harmer's cousin and a close friend of
Burgess] saying that he couldn't see Guy because he was

seeing me. It took them nearly twenty years to get round to me. But it was just a check.'[23]

Charles Madge, the ex-communist, poet and pioneer of Mass Observation, was contacted by MI5 in the early 1970s when he was living in France:

> They were building up an account of Cambridge. When I came to London I met them at the War Office. It was all very gentlemanly. But I thought it was vaguely inefficient. They knew quite a lot and had been working on it for some time. They were very interested in whether I had met Dave Springhall and people like that who were connected with the group who had been recruited [as spies]. Philby was of outstanding interest to them. When I was working in Birmingham in the 1960s [as Professor of Sociology at Birmingham University] I was convinced that my phone was tapped. I challenged the MI5 people about it and they said that they never tapped phones.[24]

Wright managed to establish that Soviet intelligence had been active during the 1930s among Oxford students. But the results of his inquiries in this area were disappointingly inconclusive. In 1967 Harold Wilson, then Labour Prime Minister, decided that he would offer a junior ministership to Bernard Floud, MP for Acton, London. Floud was the son of Sir Francis Floud, a former permanent secretary to the Ministry of Labour and a pre-war High Commissioner in Canada. Floud, MI5 believed, had been recruited as a Soviet agent, possibly by James Klugmann, when he was a student at Wadham College, Oxford. The appointment of a junior minister should have been routine. MI5 disagreed. Soon after becoming Prime Minister, Wilson had told MI5, which he had long believed was staffed by people who could not tell the difference between a democratic socialist and a communist, that they would need his personal authorization if they wanted to investigate an MP or a member of the House of Lords. MI5 now told Wilson that this was precisely what they wanted to do with Floud. There are conflicting accounts of how much Floud admitted during his session with MI5. Some reports, leaked by Wright and his friends in the late 1970s, suggested that he had confessed to having been a Soviet agent; but Floud's friends and family insisted that this was a cowardly calumny against a dead man. Soon after the interview – for reasons which were apparently unconnected with MI5 – he killed himself. Peter Wright, however, was sure that Floud had been implicated: 'Floud was definitely not offered immunity. He chose, rather than to talk, to knock himself off. Other things are said but that is the truth.'[25]

Equally unsatisfactory was Wright's interrogation of Jenifer Hart, an Oxford history don who in 1941 had married Herbert Hart, professor of jurisprudence and ex-MI5 officer. Jenifer, the daughter of the distinguished international lawyer Sir John Fischer Williams, had become a secret member of the CPGB in 1935, just as she was leaving Oxford. Hart said that Floud had been her first 'controller' and that she was then passed on to another British communist and, finally, to a 'rather sinister Central European' who never revealed his real name. She said: 'I joined the party like lots of people did because I was worried about social conditions and unemployment. I was called a secret member so I never saw a party card and was told not to communicate with members of the Communist Party.'[26] She had intended to go into the civil service, and her third controller encouraged her to press ahead with this, adding that it would be splendid if she could aim for a job in a major department of state. After taking the civil service entrance examination she was given a job – and marked down as a potential high-flier – in the Home Office. She ended up in the department handling telephone tapping and mail intercepts – work which involved her with MI5's surveillance of political extremists, including communists.

> They said that I ought to go into something where I would be useful to them. I saw a lot of the MI5 people and got on very well with them. One day the head or the deputy head of MI5 said – and I think that this was May 1940 – that they were desperately short of people and did I know any bright young men? I recommended someone who got in at once. They were very pleased with him. I could have easily recommended someone who either was or had been a communist.[27]

Her controller, whom she used to meet on Hampstead Heath, urged her to be patient. There was no point, he said, in risking her career by leaking low-grade material; much more sensible to wait until she rose in the hierarchy and had real secrets to hand over. She was, thus, a 'sleeper'. She said that she soon became disillusioned with the man she went for walks with on the heath; she found him 'creepy' as he launched into interminable lectures on the wisdom of Stalin's policies. Her motives, as she herself admitted, were confused; but she insisted that she never had any intention of becoming a spy. By 1938 she was so tired with her role as a 'sleeper' that she broke off contact with the man. She had not, she said, told him anything secret.[28] Peter Wright, however, was not convinced. Her controller, he said, had been Anatoli Gorski/Gromov, who had been flitting around London meeting Blunt, Burgess and Maclean. He disliked her heartily: 'I talked to her a lot and she kept shifting her ground. I am certain that Herbert wasn't involved. I think the truth is that she ceased being involved with the Russians when she married in 1941.'[29]

The Oxford philosopher, Sir Stuart Hampshire, was also

dragged into Wright's investigation. Hampshire's name surfaced in the summer of 1984, a few days after Wright had gone on national television. It seems likely that he leaked the story to the press as part of his campaign to force the government to reopen the Fluency investigation. The media reports exonerated Hampshire, but Wright seemed satisfied: the publicity about the case reinforced his argument that MI5 had been sloppy and ineffectual in its inquiries into the Burgess-Blunt affair. A front-page story on 29 July in the *Observer* newspaper, headlined 'MI5 blunder over top GCHQ probe', described MI5's questioning of Hampshire in 1969 and again in 1970. The investigation had, reported the *Observer*, been inspired by the testimony of Goronwy Rees who had told MI5 that Hampshire might have been recruited as a spy by Burgess. Rees's claim was given an unwelcome dimension because Hampshire, who had been with the Radio Security Service during the war, had been asked in 1965 by Downing Street to conduct a secret efficiency study of the GCHQ eavesdropping centre at Cheltenham. Yet, added the *Observer*, when Hampshire started his review at GCHQ no one at MI5 had checked the files, which would have shown that he had been named as a suspect by Rees. The Americans, who had little enough confidence in British Intelligence after the string of scandals in the 1950s and '60s, would be furious at this lapse in basic security. So, said the report in 1984, the British decided not to inform the Americans. Hampshire was cleared by MI5, having explained that, in retrospect, Guy Burgess may have tried to recruit him:

He may have said something about working for peace, but I'm pretty sure he didn't mention the Comintern. I thought it was just Guy going on. It was only in retrospect that I thought it might have been more sinister. At the time it was impossible to think that Guy might have been a spy; he was always drunk, I also took it that Anthony Blunt could not have been dangerous because he was an overt Marxist.[30]

What, therefore, did this all amount to? Peter Wright argued to his superiors that he had demonstrated a conspiracy by the Soviets to infiltrate the country's government and intelligence establishment; one that had been more effective than anyone had yet realized. In the summer of 1983 he said:

How many more names? Dozens. I think they will all be retired or dead now. There is another generation you must look at . . . because one of their most important functions was talent-spotting . . . I don't think they are recruited in the same way nowadays. It goes on. Have you ever asked yourself why Britain is in the mess it is in? Why fifty years ago it was a great country?[31]

Wright said publicly in the 1980s that men such as Proctor simply could not be believed. It was stretching credulity too far, he argued, to accept that all Burgess's Whitehall friends were just gossiping when they discussed official matters. Certainly, it was difficult for MI5 to distinguish between the normal, trusting gossip of close friends and the deliberate betrayal of state secrets. How could MI5 distinguish between someone who had merely been indiscreet with Burgess and someone who had talked to him knowing that whatever they said might be passed to the Soviets? In the absence of a confession from a suspect, MI5 had to rely on circumstantial evidence, intuition and common sense. If Goronwy Rees had known more than he ever admitted – a view held by Blunt and many of Blunt's friends as well as MI5 – then perhaps so had men like Proctor. Sir Dick White put the problem like this:

There is a great deal of difference between being a signed up member of the Russian intelligence service and being a fellow-traveller ready to give aid and comfort to such people. It is very difficult to assess how much help people like this were to Burgess or Blunt. Probably quite a lot. It would have been useful for Burgess to be able to talk things over with them.[32]

No one, however, could accuse Wright of erring on the side of charity. He described 'the suspects' who had confided in Burgess like this:

[Some] made partial admissions or admitted on some occasions that Burgess had approached them but of course they'd always turned it down. On other occasions they denied that Burgess had ever made an approach to them, and it was very difficult to believe them . . . there was a barrier against [me interviewing] MPs, politicians generally and people who were in high government [sic] departments . . . I was not allowed to talk to them until they retired.[33]

Senior civil servants watched, amused and fascinated, as MI5 continued the hunt for spies from the 1930s. One civil servant said:

We were aware of what was going on and from time to time we would scratch our heads and wonder what we would do if it all came out. I knew about Blunt and I knew about the people that MI5 were grilling but I didn't want to know too much. It was an operational matter. Every fortnight or so I was given the broad outline of what was happening and that was enough. I thought it was all a waste of time, but still . . . I knew a lot of the people [whom MI5 were questioning] and I didn't think they were clever enough to have done all the things they were supposed to have done. I suppose that's a cynical way of looking at things. A lot of names were bandied about but as far as I know they were all cleared. I knew about the inquiries into Graham Mitchell and Roger Hollis and, yes, I did wonder why MI5 didn't spend more time worrying about the Soviets . . . In that cloak and dagger world it is terribly difficult to know what MI5 are thinking. They like to be mysterious about it all. It's all a bit of a pose. But my main concern was what we should say if it all leaked out.[34]

Noel Annan, the academic who took a scholarly interest in the intrigues of the secret world, thought:

Intelligence is a curious thing. Some people who are brilliant, first-class officers can go off their heads. I don't mean mad but they get the wrong end of the stick and then they stick to it for dear life. They believe that all the evidence points in that direction. Sometimes these ideas come from defectors. When Golitsin started he was absolutely first class then he started to talk rubbish. For instance, all his claims that the whole conflict between Mao and Stalin was disinformation is just not credible. But it was believed by this gang [in MI5 and MI6].[35]

Wright, however, was not isolated. He was a senior, respected officer and had supporters in both MI5 and MI6. Arthur Martin, by now languishing in MI6, remained in touch with the investigations because he was on the Fluency committee. Martin thought that British Intelligence behaved totally responsibly:

If you take the case of Alister Watson you have to give the state the benefit of the doubt. Yes, he did lose his security clearance but that was a reasonable precaution. In the case of communist sympathizers that did happen on a number of occasions. But it was not just left to the security service to judge. There was a panel of three wise men [a committee which heard appeals from civil servants who had lost their security clearance] to judge these cases. An effort was made to ensure that people like Watson did not suffer financially. It was always very much in one's mind: the consequences of one's actions on people's lives. Yes, it did put a terrible burden on people in MI5.[36]

A colleague of Martin's in MI6, Stephen de Mowbray, was another supporter of the Golitsin thesis. He, too, said that none of his colleagues had lightly labelled a man a possible traitor:

A large number of people fell under suspicion. But they are only guilty if a court finds them guilty. There are many strange cases where it is hard to account for a man's actions but you can't go around saying that sort of thing in public. But you cannot study this sort of thing too carefully. New bits of information are always coming up to change one's interpretation.[37]

Men like Wright, Martin and de Mowbray were united on one point: the investigation into Soviet 'penetration' had to go on and if their masters in the intelligence services and in Whitehall tried to stop them they would have to fight. It was their duty as patriots.

CHAPTER 20
Disciplined Deceiver

It was testimony to Anthony Blunt's self-discipline that he never seemed to feel the need to discuss his confession or the hundreds of hours that he spent with Arthur Martin and Peter Wright. He did, of course, have the comfort of knowing that he had the protection of the immunity deal and that he, rather than MI5, was always in control of the interviews; if he chose not to answer certain questions or if he was found to be lying he knew that there was really nothing that the government could do. The confession that he had given Martin would not be admissible evidence in a British court. Moreover, as he well knew, MI5 was as anxious as he was that the affair should remain secret. Doubtless, as he sipped a large whisky late at night in his flat at the Courtauld after yet another session with Wright, Blunt would have permitted himself a smile at the thought of what a court case like that would do to the image of British Intelligence. It would not, he was sure, be allowed to happen. And, as a final safeguard, he could always frighten nosy investigative reporters with threats of a libel action if they dared impugn his patriotism. Having said all this, it was still extraordinary that he never confided in his lover John Gaskin, his family or his friends. His brother Wilfrid said:

I didn't have the faintest idea anything of this sort was going on. It is truly astonishing that John Gaskin, who lived with Anthony for years, did not know. Although Anthony and I were both busy with our own work I sometimes had a meal with him or spent a night at the Courtauld. But I never had the faintest idea what had happened. It is impossible to understand. This appalling thing was hanging over him like the sword of Damocles – with me it would have shown at once because I can never keep quiet – but Anthony had this ability to lead two separate lives. It is absolutely incomprehensible. I am sure he didn't tell our mother. It would have killed her.[1]

Gaskin was just as ignorant: 'I had no idea about the confession. None at all. I might not have even been in London. I think I was on holiday in Greece at the time.'[2]

One of Blunt's colleagues at the Courtauld said:

I can tell you that John did not know about the spying. That's what John told me and I believe him. That probably seems odd since it was a real love affair. They were very, very fond of each other. They were dependent on each other, emotionally and practically.[3]

True, after his exposure in 1979, newspapers reported that some people had, in fact, suspected that *something* very important had happened to Anthony in the 1960s. Take this letter written to the *Guardian* newspaper in April 1983 by Janet Kennish:

I was there [at the Courtauld] from 1961 to 1964 and we did not need to assess the Director's political ideals from attention to his lectures; it seems extraordinary now, but, as new students we were casually informed that the Director was also a Russian spy. It was even more specific than that — he was actually said to be 'the fourth man involved with Burgess and Maclean'. I have no idea who told us, but I believe it was the older students who were merely, and openly, passing on the folklore of the place to new arrivals. After I left, I thought no more of it for many years but when the Blunt scandal became public, my reaction was one of astonishment – but we all *knew*, why did no one else? Should we have told someone? I suppose we didn't take it seriously, and I was naïve enough to accept anything that I was told, so awed was I by the esoteric, socially élite atmosphere of the Courtauld in those years. Just another idiosyncrasy of the unfathomable upper classes – you might meet a spy on the Adam staircase . . . It wasn't even suggested that we were being told a secret and to keep quiet about it; it was common knowledge, and if the students knew, did the staff also know?[4]

Perhaps friends and colleagues did debate whether he had known more about Guy Burgess or Kim Philby (who was, after all, still front-page news in the mid-1960s) than he had admitted. But these were suspicions based on Blunt's admiration for Burgess, the fact that he had once been a Marxist and his continuing passion, curious in such a conservative figure, for the early, revolutionary Picasso. The rumours were certainly not based on anything Blunt said. Whatever the intellectual homosexuals with whom he shared ideas and boyfriends said over drinks at the Travellers' Club, they did not gossip to outsiders; there was not one press story during the 1960s that hinted at Sir Anthony Blunt's new role in life: as a self-confessed Soviet spy who had become an honorary consultant for MI5. If there had been a similar immunity deal in the United States then it would, inevitably, have been leaked; and that, in turn, would probably have led to a high-powered Senate inquiry under the glare of television lights. In France or Italy a similar story would probably have been an entertaining diversion from humdrum politics. But in Britain there was silence. Blunt went about his daily business, a respected art historian, loaded with academic honours, protected from unpleasant publicity by an habitually secretive Whitehall and an intelligence service which did not admit that it existed. Robert Harbinson claimed that Blunt had been protected by that amorphous entity known as 'the Establishment': 'When Blunt was exposed in 1979 there was much in the press about the Establishment that allowed Blunt to go free for so long . . . I know that there were many in the *gay establishment* who knew about the reds-in-the-beds, but I also know that to save the Establishment face many non-gays went along with the cover-up.'[5]

Harbinson maintained that Blunt did not sit down and admit that he had been a Russian spy for the simple reason that many of his gay friends already knew about what they used to call 'Anthony's troubles'. The incident with Peter Greenham in 1963 was only the most dramatic example of Blunt's sensitivity whenever the subject of treachery was mentioned.

Blunt had been extremely nervous when he realized that an unfinished manuscript of an autobiography by Louis MacNeice, who had died in September 1963, was being edited by one of MacNeice's friends, Professor E. R. Dodds. But when the book, *The Strings are False*, was published early in 1965 Blunt was delighted. There were scathing references to Blunt's Marxism during the 1930s but no mention of Guy Burgess, nothing about treachery and very little, apart from a few well-chosen adjectives that made it clear that Blunt was gay, to homosexuality. There was no mention, to the relief of his friends, of 'rough trade' or cottaging. Harbinson said: 'It was not until 1964 that I told Blunt about the existence of the manuscript of Mac-

Neice's book. He asked to see someone from the publishers [Faber and Faber] . . . he was naturally anxious that nothing about him and Guy should come out.'[6]

Peter Montgomery was staying at the Courtauld when the book was published. He wrote to Harbinson: 'I was waiting to finish Louis's book . . . but Anthony is delighted.'[7] Montgomery had been appointed to the BBC's General Advisory Council in 1963 and on his trips to London usually stayed with Blunt, much to the irritation of his brother, the Very Reverend Monsignor Hugh Montgomery, a Roman Catholic convert. He was worried that Peter, who at the age of fifty-seven had just been made the High Sheriff of County Tyrone, was spending too much time with a former Marxist. On 26 June 1965 he wrote to Harbinson: 'I feel in despair sometimes about Peter's apparent lack of religious feeling. I don't think that these Anthony Blunts and other atheistic friends of his probably have a very good influence. I suspect they hold other people's beliefs up to derision.'[8] But Peter Montgomery was still besotted with Blunt and he took no notice of his brother's warnings. Moreover, to borrow a phrase from the Blunt circle, Montgomery was 'housetrained'. Montgomery told the *Sunday Times* in 1980 that he had, in fact, known about Blunt's confession; but by 1980 he was an ill man and his memory could not be relied on. The interview was, therefore, never used. He said: 'I had no secrets from either Guy Burgess or Anthony but I did not like or trust Guy. I knew Anthony had been interrogated in 1964 by the security service and I feared that my name would come up. There were other occasions when I thought it would come out and I would get the chop.'[9]

Blunt had always taken great pride in his ability to spot and cultivate promising art historical talents. Although many of his protégés were homosexuals, his interest in most was strictly platonic; he wanted to fill universities in Britain and abroad with Courtauld graduates to prove that his institute was the dominant force in art history. One of his favourite young men was Brian Sewell. Slim and clean-cut, Sewell was sharp-witted, a talented writer and had a well-developed line in self-denigration. He had been a student at the Courtauld in the early 1950s and had immediately been marked out by Blunt as a potential academic. Sewell recalled:

> I was quite a bright boy at the Courtauld but I didn't think of myself as a scholar. I had no intention of going for a doctorate. Anthony said that I was mad. I had to go on and take a doctorate. He said that he would take me under his wing. So I worked under him at the royal library at Windsor in between 1957 and 1958. That was all very well but he forgot to pay me. It was all very well being under his wing but not much good if I had no money. At first the relationship was on the basis of scholarship but then it became a friendship.[10]

Sewell joined Christie's in 1958 as an Old Masters drawings expert. But his relationship with Blunt – which was never sexual – became steadily more intimate. Blunt enjoyed Sewell's refreshing irreverence towards some of the older members of the gay circle. Some of Sewell's elders, meanwhile, resented his growing intimacy with Blunt. In the years following Blunt's exposure in 1979 this developed into open warfare; veterans like Gaskin and Harbinson accused Sewell of courting publicity and making misleading statements to the media. But Sewell remained unabashed. He regarded Harbinson, for example, as an extremely unreliable witness.[11]

Sewell had met Guy Burgess, which helped him to understand why so many people including Blunt had remained so fascinated by him:

I met Burgess before he defected. He was always in and out of the Courtauld. The first time I had just left the institute and was walking to Baker Street underground station when he came out and started hurrying to catch me up. He insisted on taking me into a milk bar for a milk shake. I remember sitting on a high stool. He was an engaging but disturbing man. He was drinking raspberry milk shake and was utterly repellent. I remember finding his hand on my knee. I thought, shit, I'm not into this. I have to scoot. He was smelly and dirty. He drank and smoked and all people who smoke smell. On another occasion there was a party held by a girl from the institute. He was very drunk and disagreeable. He wanted to dance and I didn't. I was acutely embarrassed. But Anthony always had an undying affection for him.[12]

Sewell had enormous admiration for Blunt the art historian, but there was an 'ice-cold strand' in his nature which he found unsettling, even though Blunt had shown him, as he always did to young men he liked, great kindness. He knew, just as Harbinson did, that the Burgess–Maclean–Philby defections had caused Blunt personal anguish. But, throughout the 1950s and for much of the 1960s, that was all Sewell knew. 'In the summer of 1964 he was always inviting me round for drinks. It was as if he needed to talk, not about the confession, but about anything. Then there was a change of mood and he was back to the old Anthony.'[13]

There was another dimension to Blunt's life which Sewell could not avoid, though he did his best to ignore it:

There was a lot of gossip about Blunt's homosexuality but none of us knew for sure. I never knew him lay a finger on anyone. Of course it was different with people of his own generation. He was certainly not a screaming

queen. There was nothing in his behaviour or his vocab-
ulary which gave him away. You could have put him in a
roomful of army officers and they wouldn't have known
that he was homosexual. There are some people who are
one hundred per cent faggots. Whatever they do the
faggoting is there. But with Anthony this was something
you found out after you got to know him. I am convinced
that just as he was able to conceal his spying for Russia so
he learned to conceal his homosexuality. I know about
the working-class men. For men of Blunt's generation
that was the only way they were able to get satisfaction.
These were not love affairs. The window-cleaners, or the
painters, the soldiers and the sailors. Men like this would
agree to whatever was required because they were being
paid. They were paid liaisons.[14]

Sewell always regarded Peter Montgomery as a harmless
Blunt groupie; someone who both adored and needed
Anthony. John Gaskin felt neither threatened by nor
jealous of Peter; he was confident that he would never
breathe a word about the 'rough trade' who came to the flat
in the evening to perform hasty sexual acts with Anthony
for a few pounds. But Sewell added:

I do not believe that Montgomery was ever in a position
to receive or pass Anthony useful information [during
the war]. This does not mean that he did not tell Anthony
anything – but I ask you to picture Peter as permanently
in the state of a pre-pubertal crush on a prefect, present-
ing the object of his affection with unsolicited and largely
unwanted gifts . . . I know that Anthony was always
desperately worried that Peter's name would be dragged
out in connection with the spying business.[15]

After 1979 it was tempting for friends and colleagues to look back and say that they had thought at the time that Blunt had been under unusual pressure during the 1960s. There was, for example, the nervous tic, much discussed in the post-exposure era and regarded by some friends as a physical symptom of having to endure interminable interviews with MI5. Wilfrid Blunt recalled: 'He got something called Bell's Palsy, a facial paralysis which raised the left eye. Our mother was very worried about it. We thought that he might have been working too hard.'[16]

Blunt told colleagues at the Courtauld that the problem had begun when he was travelling back from a lecture in Ontario, Canada. The plane, he said, had been draughty, but some friends suspected that it was caused by the strain of his 'troubles' – a catch-all term used to describe anything associated with Guy Burgess. Blunt refused to let his lopsided appearance (according to friends he would occasionally try to correct the sag by using sticking plaster) interfere with his work. He had to lecture four or five times a week and hold seminars for his students. There were meetings to discuss Courtauld business, which were not as dull as they might have been since the committee of management included old friends such as Lord (Noel) Annan, Sir Edward Playfair and Sir Dennis Proctor. And there were his many commitments to external organizations.

In his handsome study overlooking the gardens in Portman Square, Blunt would expound the virtues of the French and Italian masters to his students and dismiss most British art, apart from his beloved William Blake, as gauche and third-rate; a view that was shared by many of his contemporaries who had been reared on art history written by Europeans in their native tongues. Timothy Clifford, director of the National Gallery of Scotland, was one of the small group who continued to see Blunt after

1979, despite risking being pilloried in the press for consorting with the media's favourite traitor. Clifford recalled:

> I knew Blunt terribly well. He was my tutor. The fact that he had made mistakes and had been a spy shouldn't take away from him that he was a very considerable art historian. He was absolutely charming in tutorials but, like others of his generation, his attitude was that Italian or French art was top. He had a good memory for facts but not a good visual memory. He reacted intellectually, rather than emotionally, to pictures. We would say that he did not have a 'good eye'. But many art historians are like that; they are people who work from books or photographs rather than by going into museums or galleries. But I thought that, despite this, he was a very distinguished academic. He was capable of great kindness. When my wife, who was at the Courtauld, was invited to the Royal Box at Wimbledon it clashed with an examination. She asked if she could sit the exam later and the Courtauld said that she couldn't. Then she went to Anthony and he said, of course, my dear, you must go. He said that she could take the paper later. But on your honour, he said, you mustn't look at the paper before.[17]

Many of his former students talked in similarly admiring terms. Blunt was a sensitive, encouraging tutor, who always went out of his way to give the impression that students were colleagues in the hunt for Truth and that their views were as valuable as his own. And no one has accused Blunt of stealing his postgraduates' ideas; a tactic that is, alas, only too often practised by professors. Neil MacGregor, later editor of the influential *Burlington* magazine, said:

He was difficult to get close to but that didn't stop one liking him. He had immense charm, which was his greatest gift. He was very generous, even if you had just written the dreariest essay. He was a kind, distinguished and honourable man. But I suppose that his homosexuality – which imposed on him the necessity to conceal part of his life – must have had an effect. Students just accepted that John Gaskin was there. He wasn't intellectual but he was always very kind if you were talking to Anthony in the flat. John would serve coffee or tea . . .[18]

Although he seemed remote and busy with his own important business during term, some students saw him in a totally different mood when they travelled to Europe for the annual summer schools; a chance for them to visit art galleries and museums with distinguished academics like Blunt. On these trips Blunt would take a small bag with a change of shirt, and swop his dark blue suit for a pair of slacks and an open-necked shirt. In the evening he would settle down with wine or whisky and chat about the art or architectural treasures they had seen that day.

In London he would welcome new students to the institute by saying that the teaching staff did not often say whether or not they actually liked a work of art; but that did not mean they had no emotions. It was just that professional art historians had to keep a firm grip on their feelings; otherwise their judgement might be affected. Towards the end of his term as director, George Zarnecki, the deputy director, suggested that it might help if Blunt talked to students a little more informally; it might, argued Zarnecki, persuade them that the director had not always shown such self-control. 'He would sit and talk about Marlborough, Louis MacNeice, Cambridge, Spain and communism. But then it would stop.'[19] These talks, the basis for Blunt's article in *Studio International*, were described like this in March 1983 by Caroline Tisdall, a former student at the institute:

> Contrary to the legend which now seems to be taking root, Anthony Blunt never made any secret about the passion of his opposition to fascism in the thirties. Every year . . . he used to give a devastatingly clear and fervent lecture on Picasso's painting *Guernica*. It was a polished and public statement, argued along the lines of Good and Evil – a classical theme in painting – and delivered with an intensity disturbing to those of us who as students were more accustomed to a manner which was both aloof and shy . . . To many of the élite of young art historians in search of the most refined kind of connoisseurship he was the great master, arming them with such affectations as the pronunciation of 'Milan' with the emphasis on the first syllable. He treated nervous interviewees and his own seminar groups with kindness but was only familiar to most students as a remote figure skirting round Portman Square like a nervous heron. But once a year he was transformed. With killing intensity he outlined the plunge into fascism, the 'Maenadic horror' as he called it. Each point was meticulously illustrated with slides. There was the 'obscenity of Franco' as portrayed in Picasso's cartoons, and the figure of Truth lying in a field, derived from Goya: 'Will she ever rise,' he asked . . . it made even the least perceptive student reflect on what its impact must have been on the young men of Cambridge . . . He outlined a tradition in which the artists he said felt obliged to depict not 'beauty or sweetness' but horror. Painting became 'a weapon of war for attack and not for defence against the enemy.'[20]

Despite worsening problems with his eyesight, Blunt showed no signs of flagging. He always seemed to be working; he would call colleagues early in the morning from his flat to discuss a new idea or to ask for their views on an article he was writing. He was the general editor of the catalogue on the magnificent collection at the Rothschilds' Waddesdon Manor. (No one appeared to see the irony in a former Marxist writing so approvingly of the world's most famous capitalist dynasty.) There were books on Poussin and Picasso's *Guernica*. His colleagues thought so highly of him that on his sixtieth birthday in 1967 they presented him with a collection of art historical essays, published as *Studies in Renaissance and Baroque Art*. There was a tribute by his old friend Ellis Waterhouse, who wrote:

> Teaching, together with the Institute and all its activities, has become one of the most important parts of his life. But it is teaching as much by example as precept, and the qualities of intellect and moral integrity which are the foundation of his books and lectures are conveyed to pupils willing to absorb them without pressure or parade of doctrine . . . the Surveyorship of the Queen's Pictures and the responsibility of being the leader of a sort of third estate in the art world has encouraged the imposition of further heavy burdens on one who has never had a great gift of saying 'No'. There are few government or official agencies seriously concerned with the promotion of the arts on which Anthony has not served or is not serving. The National Art Collections Fund, the National Trust, the Reviewing Committee on the Export of Works of Art and other bodies owe a great deal to his conciliatory rather than crusading contribution to their committees and have occupied a great deal of his time.[21]

It is, in fact, hard to find a really harsh criticism of Blunt during this period, apart from the usual sniping by rival experts on Poussin or Picasso – academic bitchiness which

Blunt was as capable as anyone of dishing out. There were occasional, reverential newspaper profiles. *The Times*, for example, ran a piece headlined 'His fine art is to advise the Queen on buying pictures'. The story opened by saying that if Blunt was ever stranded on a desert island the painting that he would most wish to be washed up on the shore would be 'The Kingdom of Flora' by Poussin. But sadly, added *The Times*, since the original was in a gallery in East Germany he had to make do with a reproduction, which hung in his kitchen at the Courtauld. The story continued:

> The day-to-day administration of the [royal] collection is seen to by his deputy, Mr Oliver Millar . . . Sir Anthony, however, takes a particular and expert interest in the restoration and cleaning of the paintings and has also catalogued many of the drawings at Windsor. Another of his responsibilities is to advise the Queen on what to buy for her collection – and it is her own and not the nation's – although the enormously high prices fetched today by works of similar quality to those she already owns makes this increasingly difficult.[22]

Blunt talked about wishing that he had more time to attend concerts and about his love of France and Italy; there was nothing to suggest to readers that he had once been a Marxist.

When colleagues and former students learned Blunt's secret in 1979 they reviewed some of his key works, searching for clues that might explain how he combined years of deceit with a dedication to truth in art. They found this passage on Poussin which suggested that Blunt had found Poussin's pursuit of reason somehow relevant to his own life:

His pursuit of a rational form of art was so passionate that it led him in his later years to a beauty beyond reason; his desire to contain emotion within its strictest limits caused him to express it in its most concentrated form; his desire to efface himself, and to seek nothing but the form perfectly appropriate to his theme, led him to create paintings which, though impersonal, are also deeply emotional and, though rational in their principles, are almost mystical in the impression they convey.[23]

Perhaps, too, Blunt's description of the suicide attempt of Francesco Borromini in 1667 contained some clue; perhaps Blunt was really talking about himself:

To have been under a strain so violent that it drove him to this act of violence – if not of madness – and yet immediately afterwards to be able to dictate such a lucid account of the event, reveals a combination of intense emotional power and rational detachment which are among the qualities which go to make him such a great architect.[24]

No one, however, goes through life without making enemies, and a sizeable minority of colleagues and students thought that Blunt was not the paragon of academic and personal integrity that his friends and protégés claimed. Blunt's status within the art world meant that most thought it wiser to keep their doubts to themselves. Some, however, could not restrain themselves. Patrick Mathieson, the son of a Bond Street art dealer, had left Oxford hoping to go into the army, but was rejected when it was discovered that his grandmother lived in East Germany. Mathieson decided to give art history a try and in 1965 he joined the institute as an external student, following his mother who

had been a student there in the 1950s. Soon he was 'bored
to tears' by the course and instead of attending lectures he
spent most of his time sailing. He took a hearty dislike to
Blunt – as Blunt did to him:

> Blunt was God at the Courtauld. He hated the art trade.
> Dealers were worse than lepers and my father had been a
> dealer, which didn't help. I wasn't frightened of him but I
> found him frightening . . . He only ever talked to people
> of the same intellectual stature as himself, though he was
> very sympathetic to the girls when they had romantic
> problems.[25]

In 1966 Mathieson decided that he would organize a group
of students to travel to Italy to help the government there
cope with the floods that had devastated Florence and
Venice. But Blunt said that anyone who went would be
rusticated, although there was nothing he could do about
Mathieson who was an external student and, in any event,
did not care if he never returned to the institute.
Mathieson, later a successful art dealer, explained:

> I went to the Italian Cultural Institute in London to
> collect the passes I needed to get to the flood areas. The
> documents weren't there. I was told that Anthony Blunt
> had rung the ambassador and asked that I should not be
> given the passes. It was a scandalous thing to do. But I
> went anyway. I never spoke to Blunt again.[26]

Mathieson was a restrained critic when compared with
Christopher Wright, who spent two years under Blunt
studying Poussin. Wright, regarded by Blunt's friends as
irresponsible and vindictive, came to the institute from
Leeds University; a pedigree which, he claimed, ensured
that Blunt dismissed him as third-rate. Wright argued that

Blunt was a charlatan whose academic work was as dishonest as his personal life:

> His method of teaching was to say, no, you are wrong. If
> he disagreed he would say that you don't read Greek and
> then just walk off. I am amazed that people say he was a
> good teacher. He used to throw out students he didn't
> like. It was a regular occurrence. He used to write things
> that were not true, but he was an autocrat and at the
> Courtauld he acted like royalty. No one dared criticize
> him. Intellectually he was on a shocking ego trip. He had
> to keep proving his own power. You wouldn't have
> thought that he was gay but he was petulant . . . what I
> would call a drama queen. He liked working-class men.
> But the ladies on the door at the Courtauld were too
> well-bred to notice the rough trade that used to appear to
> see Anthony. They used to think that they were plum-
> bers come to fix Anthony's pipes. But all I can say is that
> Queen Elizabeth couldn't have slept in so many beds as
> Anthony Blunt. He sometimes took a shine to unwashed
> students. Gaskin stayed loyal though.[27]

Blunt's allies dismissed Wright as an unreliable witness.
It was harder to do the same with colleagues such as
Professor Stephen Rees-Jones, the technical expert who
thought that Blunt showed a cavalier disregard for scientific
evidence when it conflicted with his own theories and who
admitted that there had been concern among the teaching
staff about Blunt's relationships with male students.
George Zarnecki was another powerful critic:

> I was always worried about Blunt's involvement with
> male students. I was afraid of a scandal. It was pretty
> obvious what was going on. He was indiscreet. There was
> usually a favourite who would go to the flat at odd times.

I won't name people he had affairs with; some of them are well known now in the art world. As for rough trade . . . I was shocked about that. He once had a painter here who seemed to be his friend and ate his sandwiches in Anthony's flat.[28]

Zarnecki was often baffled by Blunt. Here was a man who claimed to have been a Marxist and yet who revelled in his knighthood and professional links with Buckingham Palace:

His political views were pretty appalling. All top hats and royalty. It was well known that he had been a Marxist but when I knew him he wasn't concerned with the masses at all. He hated them and had no idea how to talk to working people. I once forced him to vote Labour [in the 1964 general election] and he insisted that I didn't tell anyone. He said that his mother wouldn't approve. He talked about her a lot.[29]

There were inexplicable incidents which made sense only after 1979. In 1968 the Courtauld summer school was due to be held in Poland but Blunt told Zarnecki that he would have to miss it because he was 'afraid that my friends who escaped [Burgess, Maclean and Philby] might try to contact me'. On an earlier occasion Blunt had insisted that it would be dangerous for Zarnecki to meet a Polish art historian who was visiting London. Had Blunt been worried that the KGB might try to meet him if he went to Poland? Did he suspect that the Polish academic had been sent to leak the story of his work for the Soviets? His anxiety probably was not that coherent; it was probably no more than a desire to avoid Eastern Europe and to ensure that as few of his colleagues as possible had contacts there.

There was another dimension to Blunt's life which disturbed his friends. Professional scholars in the art world who want to maintain their reputation for impartiality have to keep their distance – and be seen to do so – from the art trade. The value that the market puts on a painting can be increased or slashed by the verdict of a respected academic, especially if the provenance of the picture is doubtful. It is possible for an academic to make a mistake, but such an error has a distinctly sinister ring if it emerges that he has some financial stake in the painting. For example, the American scholar Bernard Berenson had been savaged in the 1930s for his ties with the art market. Blunt always emphasized how much he distrusted art dealers, but at the same time as he was warning students about the perils facing academics who became too friendly with dealers, he was becoming dangerously entangled himself. Ellis Waterhouse recalled: 'Anthony encouraged John Gaskin to go into art dealing. I told Anthony that it was a very bad idea for an art historian of his reputation to get involved with dealing.'[30] George Zarnecki, too, was concerned that the director of the Courtauld was risking his good name, and the institute's, by supporting Gaskin's new career: 'Gaskin started to deal in drawings and Blunt helped him. Brian Sewell used to bring piles of drawings to the flat.'[31]

There was no hint of this until March 1980 when the press reported that there were 'doubts about the authenticity' of twenty-five drawings sold in London during the 1960s and early 1970s by a painter and dealer called Eric Hebborn. The art world always provides a steady trickle of entertaining scandals, and the allegation that a minor character like Hebborn had sold some dud drawings, worth just a few hundred pounds each, would probably have been reported in a couple of sentences had it not been for the involvement of Anthony Blunt. Hebborn, it emerged, had been a friend of Blunt's and a business associate of John Gaskin. There was evidence, too, that Hebborn had used Blunt's name when he tried to sell drawings to dealers and that Blunt had authenticated two suspect drawings sold by Christie's. Blunt denied any such ties with Hebborn and the story died. However, it is now obvious that Blunt knew a great deal more about the Hebborn-Gaskin partnership than he dared admit in 1980. Hebborn had met Blunt in the 1950s when he was a student at the Royal Academy:

> I taught art for a while and dealt with paintings and antiques. I was very friendly with Anthony. He was a valued friend. I used to buy certain things from John Gaskin and John bought things from me. It was all fairly modest stuff. As far as I know it was all genuine. But experts change their opinions all the time and the general opinion was that some of the works were fakes. But I didn't draw them. Yes, of course, people said that I faked them but I think they said that to further blacken Anthony's name.[32]

Brian Sewell disputed this version of events. In the early 1960s Hebborn was a London-based dealer, selling works of art through the major auction houses, including Christie's. He was known to be friendly with Blunt and that association, thought Sewell, was extremely dangerous for the Surveyor of the Queen's Pictures who had always been careful to avoid having any links with the trade. By October 1964 Sewell was convinced that neither Christie's nor Anthony Blunt should have anything to do with Hebborn, who by now had moved to a villa near Rome. Hebborn had, said Sewell, exploited Blunt's name when he was selling drawings:

> As far as I was concerned the drawings that Hebborn was selling were suspect. You might be unhappy about one picture and you'll let it pass. You might start worrying by

the second picture and if it happens a third time then you have to do something. I went to Rome to find out what was going on. What I saw in Rome greatly disturbed me. I read Eric the riot act and told him that what he was doing could greatly damage Anthony. He was using Anthony's name to help his business. I came back to London and told Christie's and Anthony that they should have nothing more to do with Eric. My concern was for the reputation of Christie's. But I don't doubt that it would have damaged Anthony if it had come out.[33]

But that was not the end of the problem. Gaskin had pottered along quite happily as a small-time dealer in jewellery but by the mid-1960s he was struggling. He decided to try the art market. Sewell again:

For a time Gaskin occupied himself selling Anthony's own collection of drawings. Then, when they had all gone, Gaskin needed a new source. He found Eric Hebborn. I fear that the name of Anthony Blunt came up when Gaskin sold these drawings in London. I imagine that people assumed that whatever John was selling was either part of Anthony's collection or had been authenticated by him. Anthony should have been stricter. He should have told Gaskin that he couldn't go on; his own reputation was at stake. If it had become known what was happening then people would have put the wrong construction on it. But Anthony was the victim of his own generosity and affection. He wanted Gaskin to do well as a dealer.[34]

Hebborn always denied that he had, as newspapers suggested, actually manufactured the drawings. But he did not deny that Blunt had become involved in Gaskin's trading. Hebborn said:

I didn't show things to Anthony but of course John would have shown him what I was selling. I don't think that he would have attributed a drawing just to help John . . . I sent photographs of drawings that I wanted to sell to John not to Anthony. It's absolutely false to say I used Anthony's name. I once said to a dealer that Anthony had a similar drawing (to one the man had) in his house where I was staying. Brian Sewell said nothing to me in Rome about Anthony Blunt's reputation being damaged by his association with me. Anthony Blunt was never involved in dealing. A drawing is a drawing is a drawing. Like a chair is a chair is a chair. It's only when I sell it as a Chippendale when it's not that it becomes a forgery. There's no such thing as a faked drawing. I did not call any of these drawings Old Masters. I sold them at reasonable prices as attractive drawings.[35]

When Sewell left Christie's in 1967 to become a dealer and art critic Blunt persuaded him that he might be able to advise Gaskin:

Anthony said that since I was now dealing myself would I help and supply John . . . I did but I never gave John anything that wasn't absolutely identified. I had the same view as Ellis Waterhouse; that John's business had to be absolutely independent of Anthony. But I am afraid that when John was sent works by other dealers Anthony did say to John, this or that picture, might be this or that.[36]

It would have been disastrous if details of Gaskin's activities with Hebborn and then with Sewell had been made public. Inevitably, Blunt's famed impartiality would have been wrecked; his insistence that he had no time for the sordid world of dealing would have seemed a sham. Yet Gaskin shrugged off the suggestion that he had selfishly jeopardized his lover's reputation. He said: 'I can't remember buying anything from Hebborn except his own little bits and pieces . . . I had a book of modern etchings by him. The important [Old Master drawings] were, I think, all right. Who is to say? After all, a lot of people have put things in the salerooms and they've turned out not to be right, haven't they?'[37]

Hilda Blunt would have been devastated if she had lived to see her son's name savaged in the media. Despite failing health she had insisted on looking after herself in the house at Ham. She still managed to visit the Courtauld, though she was so scruffy that on one occasion a doorman mistook her for a tramp and asked her to leave, while she protested that she was the mother of Sir Anthony. In the summer of 1969, when she was ninety, she fell and broke her arm; in November she fell again and shattered her thigh. In hospital, said her son, Wilfrid, she talked deliriously about the Royal Family and, for no obvious reason, the Soviet Union. On 11 November she was operated on; the next morning she died. Wilfrid and Christopher were relieved that she had died peacefully, thinking that she was at home, surrounded by members of the Royal Family. Anthony must have felt similar relief, though for different reasons. Whatever happened now, at least his mother had died believing in the genius of her youngest and brightest son.

CHAPTER 21
Blunt's Legacy

In 1971 Blunt was told that he might only have a few months to live. He was operated on for stomach cancer and, though doctors were pleased with the results, the prognosis was not hopeful. At the headquarters of MI5 and in Whitehall news of Blunt's expected death provoked a flurry of activity. If he died then the legal obstacles which had prevented anyone from accusing him of being the fourth man in the by now infamous Cambridge conspiracy would be removed. There were disturbing reports that Goronwy Rees, now a professional writer, was planning to publish a more serious account of his relationship with Burgess than he had written for *The People* in 1956. No one knew whether Rees would be prepared to identify Blunt as the man whom Burgess had once named as a Comintern agent. If Rees, or indeed anybody, made that allegation then the government would be placed in an impossible position. To deny it would be to invite disaster; it would probably only be a matter of time before someone leaked details of the immunity deal and Blunt's subsequent confession. The government would have to admit that the late Sir Anthony had, indeed, been the much sought-after fourth man. It would be the only option, but that did not make it an attractive one.

But Blunt did not die. He threw himself back into his work at the Courtauld and began revising his classic study, *Art and Architecture in France, 1500–1700*. Goronwy

Rees's book, *A Chapter of Accidents*, appeared in February; it was thoughtful, well-written and packed with fascinating anecdotes. It did not, however, contain the revelations that Whitehall feared it might. There were ample clues to the identity of the fourth man and hints that British Intelligence had known much more about Guy Burgess's involvement with the Soviets than anyone had so far admitted. Rees was not prepared, though, to risk a repeat of the mauling that he suffered at the hands of his friends after the *People* articles; he was not going to be the person who openly accused Anthony Blunt of treachery. Rees was more interested in constructing his own defence against allegations – which he knew had circulated within Whitehall – that he had been a member of the Burgess spy network. For Blunt it was only a reprieve. A number of authors and journalists remained convinced that the full story of the Cambridge spies had yet to be told. Goronwy Rees's book might, they thought, lead to that elusive scoop. And they were right.

MI5, meanwhile, had reacted to the possibility of Blunt's death. First, there was a review of everything that he had told his interrogators. Peter Wright recalled: 'In 1972 an independent analysis of all the Blunt material was done and the conclusion of their analysis was that Blunt had never been truthful about his dealings with the Russians, that he did not tell me about any spies that were vulnerable, only those spies he thought we wouldn't prosecute.'[1]

The list of suspects that had been drawn up by MI5 was whittled down to twenty-one. Sir Dick White, now the Cabinet Office's intelligence coordinator, was called in by the Tory Home Secretary, Reginald Maudling, and asked for his opinion on MI5's continuing interest in events that to politicians concerned with the problems of Britain's decaying industrial society seemed of marginal importance. Shouldn't MI5 be more concerned with the new hard-Left groups, busy fomenting unrest in the factories and on the streets of the inner cities, than in ageing intellectuals who had once flirted with Marxism? White said: 'I said [to Maudling], well, one day it will be necessary to have a balance sheet on this subject. But it ought not to take precedence over contemporary inquiries. Yet we must know how at a particular moment in our history we were messed about and bewildered by all this.'[2]

Blunt's unexpected recovery meant that MI5 could continue to question him though, by now, they accepted that he would not provide them with any major new leads. It also meant that the moment when an enterprising writer or journalist would name him as a spy had been delayed. A live man can sue for libel; a dead man cannot. MI5 and Blunt knew that if a writer was sure enough of his evidence then the threat of a libel action would be exposed for what it was: a bluff. He would never be able to go into court to pursue an action. But no one outside Whitehall and British Intelligence knew that; and Blunt believed that it was in the interests of the Establishment, as much as his own, to remain silent.

Civil servants in Whitehall had to decide what to do about Blunt's approaching retirement as Surveyor of the Queen's Pictures. It was customary to offer the outgoing surveyor an honorary title; should the Palace be told that, in this case, it would be wiser to let Blunt sever his ties with the Royal Family? Blunt had no idea that this was being discussed and was just determined to make the most of his last few months as surveyor. For example, in May 1972 he travelled to West Berlin to deliver the seventh Queen's Lecture, held annually to commemorate the Queen's visit to the city in 1965. Blunt was as enthusiastic as ever about the value of royal art collections. *The Times* reported on 25 May:

Rejecting the criticism that the Queen's collection was closed to the average person, Sir Anthony pointed out the various opportunities for seeing many of the masterpieces. He said he was often asked whether the Queen was adding to the collection. The Queen, he said, had no special preference for the present young generation of British painters, and he confessed that he would find it difficult to advise her if she did.[3]

When Whitehall saw stories such as this they were given an unwelcome reminder of Fleet Street's fascination with anyone who worked at the Palace. Senior civil servants decided, therefore, that it would be best to offer Blunt the traditional honorary title; any other decision might alert the press that Blunt had offended the Palace. It would, too, have been difficult to block the appointment without widening the circle of people who knew about his confession. One senior civil servant recalled:

Blunt's appointment as Adviser for the Queen's Pictures was done automatically by people at the Palace and those people were not privy to the secret about him. And the people who were privy to the secret could not tell them. It was difficult. You could not treat Blunt exceptionally without having people gossip about why that might have happened.[4]

In November 1972 the Queen met Blunt at the Palace and thanked him for his hard work over the past twenty-seven years. She said that she hoped to see him just as often in his new role as adviser. It is not hard to imagine how the Queen, who had known since 1964 that Blunt was a self-confessed spy, felt as she went through this charade.

* * *

One question which had been perplexing British Intelligence for decades was, had there been an elder statesman at Cambridge who had helped to convert student Marxists into spies? The evidence suggested not, but it was, nonetheless, an intriguing thesis. Journalists, too, were convinced that the known facts about the recruitment of Messrs Burgess, Maclean and Philby were too pat; it could not, surely, have been as simple as that. In their enthusiasm to track down this mastermind mistakes were made. In June 1977, for example, Peter Hennessy, *The Times*'s expert on Whitehall, revealed that Donald Beves, a don at King's College, Cambridge, who had died in 1961, 'was suspected by security circles' of having 'played a critical role' in the transformation of student communists to Soviet agents. Hennessy, an astute and respected commentator, said that the allegation against Beves, a scholar of French sixteenth-century literature and a former Clerk of the House of Commons, would 'come as a severe shock to the Cambridge generations who knew him; the thought of him as possibly the man who guided Philby, Burgess and Maclean in the early years of their treachery will be hard to bear.' Beves had private money which enabled him to run expensive cars and indulge his passion for the finest wines. He was a large, jolly man, and threw excellent parties; he was considered 'mildly conservative' and although he never married he kept aloof from the homosexual scandals that were then a part of university life. By Cambridge standards his academic abilities were unexceptional. Hennessy wrote:

Cambridge was awash with young communists in 1932–33, providing a large, self-selected and obvious pool of Soviet sympathizers for the Comintern to recruit from. The crucial factor was the subsequent move underground by a handful of those people and the covers they assumed to explain away their earlier convictions . . . It was in assisting those who were chosen to take up a covert role that Mr Beves emerged as the main suspect . . . The evidence against him amounted to strong suspicion, but fell short, and still falls short of conclusive proof . . . MI5 recently decided that information concerning Beves and the Cambridge connection should not be made public as the time for its disclosure was not yet ripe.[5]

But *The Times*'s exclusive fell flat; it was dismissed as a clumsy, malevolent plant from retired intelligence officers. In fact, it was not as sinister as that. As Hennessy himself said: 'We made a mistake. It was a cock-up and the paper quite rightly backed down.'[6]

Five years before *The Times* published its story, Brian Sewell believed he had found the mastermind who had pushed Blunt into spying. The man was Andrew Gow, the classics don who was a mentor and friend of Blunt until his death, aged ninety-one, in 1978. Sewell did not name Gow until 1984, although he did write a letter to *The Times* after Blunt's exposure in 1979 saying that the fifth man was dead and that he had been 'an academic, who died full of honours'. Sewell's story was impossible to corroborate since Gow and Blunt were, by 1984, both dead. Peter Wright, however, thought that Sewell could be correct. Wright recalled: 'On occasion, when Blunt couldn't remember things he would say: "Next time I see Andrew I'll ask him." I often wondered exactly the part Andrew [Gow] had played.'[7] Sewell himself was adamant. No, he had not made a mistake; he was certain that Gow had been responsible for recruiting Blunt as an agent of the Soviet Union. It made no difference, said Sewell, that everyone who knew Gow regarded him as a crusty, apolitical old don, interested in communists only because communism in the

1930s attracted some of the brightest, most entertaining students. Sewell said:

I was working as an art dealer and had put on a small exhibition of drawings and sketches. There was a water-colour by an artist called Constant Troyon [a minor nineteenth-century French painter]. It was very beautiful and Anthony told Gow about it. He bought it unseen and I was asked to take it to Gow in Cambridge. I met Gow in his rooms at Trinity. We had supper there, just the two of us. I was frozen with a kind of fear and distaste. I wasn't sure whether Gow was asking me to do something which I didn't quite understand. We started by talking about Anthony and then the watercolour, which were the only two things we had in common. Of course, I had heard about him from Anthony, who was always popping up to Cambridge to see him. He was a permanent feature in Anthony's life. I was there for about three hours. I can't remember verbatim what he told me but it came down to this . . . He spoke a great deal about loyalty. Loyalty to this and loyalty to that. He went on and on about loyalty and out of that came the revelation. I suppose he had assured himself that it was safe to tell me. He said that he was responsible for recruiting Anthony and managing him. It was as direct as that. I found the whole thing alarming. He said that he had always controlled him. I can't remember us talking about motives. All I knew was that I wanted to get out of there as quickly as possible. I wondered if I could just get up in the middle of supper and leave. That is what I wanted to do. Here was this distinguished old man and I found him utterly cold, calculating and scheming. I thought then that he knew exactly what he was doing and exactly how far he could go. He seemed perfectly relaxed and in control. He was incredibly bright. Here was I, a tenth-rate art dealer,

talking to someone like Gow, who had a very distinguished art collection . . . He looked shrunken, as if he
had once been much bigger. I should have said that he
was a homosexual but he was impenetrable. You could
have talked to him until you were blue in the face and you
would never have known what he was thinking. There
was no mistaking what he was telling me. He had a
perfect command of language and all its nuances. He was
incapable of being vague. We didn't use the word 'spy'. I
think we used euphemisms, like 'working for' . . . But I
had no doubt that he was Anthony's controller. I am
quite certain that he would have enjoyed the emotional
predicament that Anthony had found himself in with
Guy Burgess. Gow's pleasure was that of a voyeur, of
watching other people. I don't know why he told me. But
it was quite clear what he had said.[8]

Sewell returned to London, puzzled and worried, unsure
if he should ask Blunt whether it was true. But he said
nothing and from that moment he thought that Blunt
assumed that he knew about his involvement with the
Soviets; in 1979, when Blunt was desperately worried that
he would be publicly accused of treachery, he behaved as if
Sewell had already been told what had happened at Cambridge.

Everyone who knew Gow dismissed Sewell's theory.
Noel Annan's comment was typical: 'Any conception of
Gow being the hidden power, the man who recruited
Blunt, is absolute fantasy. He was not a political person at
all. He was a rock-ribbed conservative.'[9] But Sewell had no
reason to lie about Gow. He was not trying to sell the story;
he had nothing to gain from alleging that a respected
Cambridge academic had been a traitor. Indeed, he had
everything to lose since he tried hard after Blunt's death to
rebuild a career as an art critic for newspapers and maga-

zines; the last thing he wanted to do, he always argued, was to remind people that he had been a confidant of the late Anthony Blunt. The file on Gow has, therefore, to remain open; with no prospect of anyone being able either to prove or disprove Sewell's claims.

In June 1973 the Courtauld announced that Peter Lasko, Professor of Visual Arts at the University of East Anglia at Norwich, one of the country's new universities, would be succeeding Blunt in autumn 1974. Lasko was cheerful, open and unpretentious; his father had been an actor/film director, and Blunt made no attempt to disguise his opposition to the appointment. When Lasko moved to a temporary office in the Courtauld to begin the handover, Blunt barely spoke to him. Lasko recalled: 'If I wanted to know something I went to see him but he certainly did not volunteer information. He made appointments until the last day. He made it plain that he was still in charge just as he had been for nearly thirty years.'[10]

In the summer of 1974 Blunt and Gaskin moved from the flat on the top floor of the institute to a seventh-floor flat in an imposing block called Portsea Hall, just off the Edgware Road. His retirement was noted in the Courtauld's annual report for the year 1973–74:

Professor Sir Anthony Blunt, Director of the Institute since 1947, retired on 30 September 1974 and the University has conferred on him the title Emeritus Professor of the History of Art. The Institute owes him a great debt of gratitude for his leadership in the post-war development and expansion and for the distinction that his teaching and research have conferred upon all aspects of its academic existence. He retires knowing how much he is appreciated, and we all wish him a long and happy retirement.

There were other, more fulsome tributes. In September 1974 the *Burlington* magazine ran a lengthy article that verged on sycophancy. The magazine was edited by Blunt's close friend Benedict Nicolson, son of Harold Nicolson and deputy surveyor at the Palace from 1939 until he joined the *Burlington* in 1947. Nicolson probably wrote the unsigned article himself; with its emphasis on Blunt's integrity and devotion to truth it seemed, after 1979, heavy with irony:

> It is difficult to assess the extent of his contribution to the Institute's destinies, but it has surely been greater than that of any other single person, in ways that are not always easy to define because he has never been a demonstrative man who laid down hard and fast rules but silently set an example to be followed . . . the tone of the Courtauld, its professionalism, the free exchange of ideas, the passionate addiction to the truth about the past that Blunt inculcated, is there for good.

There was much more in this vein. The *Burlington* talked about his brilliant lecturing technique, his clarity and precision of thought and the consideration he showed to colleagues and students. There was a brief mention of his early radicalism but the article insisted that he had always detested 'the exercise of dictatorial power'. Just look, it gushed, how he had mocked his youthful left-wing views in his *Studio International* article; only a man oblivious of his own status would have written such an article. As if to confirm that the adult Blunt had long forgotten his puerile militancy, the article noted that the Courtauld had been untouched by the student protests of the late 1960s (which was hardly surprising given the character of the institute's student population). The Anthony Blunt who emerged from this torrent of praise was unrecognizable to anyone who knew him well. No one, not even his dearest friends, would have described him as a self-effacing democrat; even they would have admitted that he had ruled the Courtauld absolutely, which was one of the reasons it had become such a force in the academic world. The *Burlington* tribute was perhaps testimony to Blunt's power within art history; he was a man whom very few dared to offend. There is another possibility: did Nicolson know more about Blunt's past than he admitted here? Was the article an elaborate joke written for that small circle of intellectuals who suspected that Blunt had been implicated in the Cambridge spy ring?

What was certainly not considered at all amusing was the bizarre behaviour of Robert Harbinson. He was pursuing a campaign against a publisher who, Harbinson alleged, had miscalculated the sales of the books he had written for the company. This dispute should have been a private matter but Harbinson wanted to enlist the help of his friends, especially Peter Montgomery. He was convinced that Montgomery's position as president of the Arts Council of Northern Ireland meant he would be able to testify to the popularity of his books in the province and so confirm that the publisher had not been frank with him. Moreover, he believed that Montgomery should help him, out of personal loyalty. Blunt, too, was dragged into the row and, like Montgomery, condemned for not backing Harbinson. That, in essence, was the argument but, while it might seem clear-cut, Harbinson managed to make it far more complicated. When Montgomery refused to become involved, Harbinson judged that it was out of fear that, under cross-examination, the full story of the Montgomery–Blunt gay circle would be dragged out. And that could not be allowed because it would be the beginning of the end for Sir Anthony Blunt; the press would start to dig for information and might come up with the story no one wanted to see in print, the story of Blunt's treachery. It does not matter whether Harbinson was right about the reasons for Montgomery's decision not to side with him; what is indisputable is that Harbinson, outraged at this 'betrayal' and convinced that what he called the Gay Establishment was conspiring against him, launched a campaign – not just against the publisher but against Montgomery and Blunt. At one point Harbinson was jailed for contempt of court after throwing a water carafe at a barrister. He wrote dozens of 'open letters' – to friends, enemies, politicians and government law officers – in which he made frequent, potentially explosive allegations about the gay circle, treachery, the Royal Family and Sir Anthony Blunt. These letters were a mass of accusations that were largely incomprehensible to anyone outside the circle; but Montgomery and Blunt knew precisely what Harbinson was talking about. For example, in one two-page letter to Montgomery he accused Montgomery of 'feudal arrogance' and 'brutality' while contriving to weave into this the anecdote about Peter Greenham's lunch at Buckingham Palace, when the Queen Mother had said how much she hated traitors. He wrote at length about Montgomery's homosexuality, a subject which would have been highly embarrassing if it had become public. Harbinson claimed that he was visited several times by officers from Special Branch, the police unit which is the public face of MI5, who warned him to stop the campaign. There were appeals, too, from members of the Blunt circle. In 1972 Sir Gilbert Laithwaite, a distinguished diplomat who, like Blunt, was a member of the Travellers' Club, wrote to Harbinson: 'Robert, I beseech you in the name of friendship not to send this to *Private Eye*. I cannot sleep in my bed at night unless I have your written assurance.'[11]

Harbinson waited until he was jailed in 1979 for attacking the barrister, before sending his bundle of letters to *Private Eye*, the satirical magazine which had a reputation for running stories that the mainstream press would not print, either because of libel fears or because of bias by proprietors and editors. But his unrelenting campaign took its toll; Montgomery had a stroke after he was questioned by Special Branch. Emotional, theatrical and indiscreet, Harbinson remained throughout the 1970s a time-bomb, ticking slowly and ignoring all efforts to defuse him, biding his time to wreak revenge on the man, Sir Anthony Blunt, who had encouraged Montgomery to defy him.

The Labour Party, under Harold Wilson, fought and won two elections in 1974. In June, Wilson's new Attorney General, Samuel Silkin, was shown the Blunt file. This should have been routine; a precaution in case the Blunt case ever became public and Silkin was asked for his comments on the immunity deal. But he was not satisfied with the way that the affair had been handled. All he could do, however, was let Wilson know this. Silkin said that it appeared as if the government in 1964 had simply offered immunity because MI5 had asked for it:

> It looked to me as if they [the 1964 Conservative government] had been advised by the Security Service that Blunt had been interrogated many times and that he would not say anything. It was something like: he knows we know and we have reached a point where the only hope of getting the information is to offer immunity. But I could not see any evidence that the law officers of the day had mounted a thorough investigation into this claim. I was surprised that a matter of such great importance had been dealt with in such a summary manner. But it would have been grossly unfair to have tried to go back on that offer. There was another factor. The only evidence against Blunt was a confession he had made after being given immunity. And that confession would not have been admissible evidence in court.[12]

Silkin was Attorney General until Labour's election defeat in May 1979 and made sure that he formally notified Downing Street of the Blunt case. When Wilson resigned in the spring of 1976, Silkin informed the new Prime Minister, James Callaghan, that the government might one day have to field some awkward questions about Sir Anthony. In 1978 Silkin again raised the case, warning Callaghan that several writers were thought to be preparing exposés of Blunt. If Blunt died then they would be free to publish and Downing Street would need a carefully prepared response. If these authors went ahead, irrespective of whether Blunt was still alive, then Downing Street would be in an impossible position. To confirm the allegation would be to renege on the immunity deal; to say nothing would provoke a storm of parliamentary and press outrage. After all, why should the Labour Party be pilloried for a case that had been handled by the Tories? Despite the fact that it threatened to drag his party into an unwelcome row, Silkin found that the Blunt file made compulsive reading: 'He had given a lot of names . . . people who had been left-wing or members of the Communist Party at Cambridge. A lot of it was just gossip. There was nobody who was accused of any crime. Some of the names were familiar to me. I raised my eyebrows because they were such respectable people, household names.'[13]

When Merlyn Rees, a canny Welshman with a refreshing attitude towards the Whitehall shibboleth of secrecy, became Home Secretary in 1976 he, too, was told about Blunt. Rees thought there was nothing to be gained by reopening the case; much better to accept that immunity had been granted and that, rightly or wrongly, Blunt would never be prosecuted. But Rees thought that the government should prepare a strategy. He concluded that it had a moral duty not to lie about Blunt if the issue were forced by a writer or an MP. Rees recalled:

It became apparent in my time at the Home Office that the story might come out. So, we began drafting a statement which we would have issued if that happened. We stuck to the facts although we had to consider whether there was anything which we had to keep quiet about to protect people. The statement that we drew up was substantially the one that Mrs Thatcher read out in 1979. It is rubbish to suggest that we tried to cover it up. My attitude was: say nothing unless someone gets on to it and if that happens tell the truth.[14]

Harold Wilson's controversial personal secretary, Marcia Williams (Lady Falkender), said in March 1977 that the Establishment would collapse if the Blunt story ever became known. It is not quite clear what she imagined would happen (the demolition of Marlborough school; the prosecution of all ex-Trinity students; the closure of the Travellers'?) but Wilson himself regarded the whole, messy affair as further evidence of MI5's ineptitude and of the ability of the upper-class, public-school-educated mafia to protect one of its own kind. However, even Wilson was astonished by the scale of the internal intrigues of the intelligence services. In the summer of 1974, Stephen de Mowbray, the MI6 officer who was convinced that Sir Roger Hollis had been a Soviet agent, strode into the Downing Street office of the Cabinet Secretary Sir John Hunt, and demanded a personal audience with the Prime Minister. De Mowbray said that he represented a group of senior officers from MI5 and MI6, including Arthur Martin and Peter Wright, who feared that the investigation into Hollis had been blocked to save the two services from embarrassment. Hunt assured de Mowbray that his views would be conveyed to Wilson.

Wilson's reaction was summed up by Falkender. When he told her about de Mowbray's allegation she said: 'Now

I've heard everything. The head of MI5 might have been a double agent for the Russians.' As a result of de Mowbray's visit, Wilson ordered an independent examination of the case against Hollis. This was carried out by Lord Trend, Hunt's predecessor and then Rector of Lincoln College, Oxford. Trend worked for a year; he had access to all the documents and conscientiously interviewed many of the dissidents within the two intelligence services. In 1975 de Mowbray was informed by Hunt that Trend had found no conclusive evidence against Hollis. It was, therefore, time to close the file and let British Intelligence concentrate on the contemporary challenges facing the country. The de Mowbray camp was furious. Martin returned to his retirement in the Cotswolds. De Mowbray quit MI6. Peter Wright was more bitter than anyone else. He felt that his life's work had been wasted; that his mission, to fight Soviet penetration of British Intelligence, had been thwarted by bureaucrats who had no understanding of the threat posed by the Kremlin. He retired to Australia within a year, still arguing with the MI5 management, this time over his pension rights. During his 1984 television interview he explained why he had objected to the Trend report:

Lord Trend was a very eminent civil servant and not an intelligence officer. I don't think he realized that in intelligence cases you very seldom got smoking-gun evidence. He, therefore, had to make what he called a value judgement and came down on the side that Hollis was innocent. All I can say is that I did not agree with that decision . . . It is no good clearing Hollis if you accept that there was high-level penetration without providing another candidate. I think the circumstantial evidence that has been set out for the high-level penetration of MI5 is irrefutable. And Hollis is the best candidate. And if it wasn't Hollis, who else was it?

Wright was not the only casualty of the battle within the intelligence community. The Oxford historian Martin Gilbert, official biographer of Winston Churchill and Anthony Eden who collaborated in the publication of Wilson's diaries, told the Prime Minister that elements within MI5 were spreading rumours that he ran a communist cell at Number 10. Understandably, Wilson demanded an explanation from Sir Michael Hanley, director-general of MI5, and Sir Maurice Oldfield, head of MI6. Both men confirmed that a handful of officers, the so-called Young Turks, incensed at the result of the Hollis inquiry, were responsible for the rumours. Wilson never forgave the intelligence community. After his resignation in the summer of 1976 Wilson asked to see two BBC television journalists, Barrie Penrose and Roger Courtiour. The two men were just beginning their lengthy investigation into allegations that Jeremy Thorpe, leader of the Liberal Party, had been implicated in a plot to murder Norman Scott, a homosexual male model who had had an affair with Thorpe. The Thorpe scandal, which ended in the summer of 1978 with his acquittal at the Old Bailey on a charge of conspiracy to murder, had many sub-plots, including dirty tricks by MI5 and BOSS, the South African secret police. When Wilson saw the two journalists he was extraordinarily frank. For example, he said: 'I am not certain that for the last eight months when I was Prime Minister I knew what was happening fully in security.'[15] He talked about a smear campaign against him by British Intelligence; he complained that MI5 and MI6 did not seem able to tell the difference between socialism and communism; he said that, according to these ignorant sources, even his secretary, Marcia Williams, was a dedicated communist.[16]

It was inevitable that sooner or later someone would amass enough evidence from enough sources to identify Blunt publicly as the fourth man. As the years drifted past, so more and more people in Whitehall and within British Intelligence were briefed about Blunt. Many of those connected with the case had retired and they wanted to gossip about their careers, particularly the more dramatic episodes. There were the MI5 and MI6 Young Turks, angry at having lost the fight over Hollis and determined to reopen the case – whatever the cost. In the summer of 1976 Andrew Boyle, a veteran BBC radio journalist who had been the founding editor of the highly regarded 'World at One' programme, was commissioned by the publishers, Hutchinson, to write a study of the Cambridge spies. Boyle was an accomplished author; he had written solid biographies of Brendan Bracken and the RAF hero Group Captain Leonard Cheshire, VC. Like other authors and journalists Boyle was aware of the rumours about Blunt; his job was to see if he could substantiate them. It was a daunting task. British libel laws had protected many guilty men and women in the past and, as Boyle knew, would protect many more in the future. The coherence of the British governing élite – that interconnected group which traditionally dominated the civil service, politics, the universities, the City, the arts and sciences – had been battered by the social changes of the post-war years. But it would still fight to stop muckrakers revealing unwelcome facts. The Official Secrets Act was another hurdle; the symbol of Whitehall's attitude that the less the public knew about what was really happening the better. Nonetheless, Boyle was sure that he could produce a worthwhile book:

Having grown up myself in the 1930s, but having studied at Paris rather than at Oxbridge or any less fashionable British university, I was fascinated by the strange distemper which had led so many of my contemporaries at home to find in the Gospel according to Marx a swift, painless panacea for all the ills then afflicting their country and the world. Anthony Blunt, as well as the better-known traitors, Kim Philby, Guy Burgess and Donald Maclean, happened to be products of Cambridge, though other seats of learning later provided in smaller measure their quotas of witting or unwitting accomplices.[17]

Boyle interviewed several hundred people, working out new perspectives on the known Cambridge spies. He had considerable help from retired American intelligence officers, including Jim Angleton, the ex-CIA chief, who helped to convince him that there had been a *fifth* man in the conspiracy; a British-born nuclear physicist called Wilfrid Mann who had worked for much of his career in the USA. Some of these American sources insisted to Boyle that Mann had been a Soviet spy in the 1940s working alongside Maclean and that he had been 'turned' – thus giving the Americans a double agent inside the Cambridge spy ring. Boyle did not name this agent when his book was published in 1979 – he codenamed him 'Basil' – but Mann himself had no doubt that Boyle believed he was the fifth man. Boyle's British sources, including some retired intelligence officers, tried to dissuade him from this theme. But Boyle ignored these sources and stuck stubbornly to his theory about Mann.

As he researched, Boyle also became convinced that Blunt had been a member of the Burgess network. He leaned heavily on Goronwy Rees's book, *A Chapter of Accidents*, and on Rees himself, who was terminally ill with cancer. This meant that Boyle had to accept Rees's account of his own involvement; this was unfortunate, but necessary if he wanted Rees's cooperation. Former MI5 and MI6 officers were unwilling actually to *volunteer* Blunt's name – that would have offended their lifelong passion for secrecy – but it was different when he asked for simple confirmation of facts that he had amassed elsewhere. Then it was just a question of nodding agreement and ensuring that Boyle's version of events was as accurate as possible. Even so, Boyle did not feel that it would be safe to confront Blunt. What if he denied the allegation? Boyle would either have to forget one of the book's central theses or plough on, risking an injunction stopping publication or, just as bad, a libel action. While Blunt must have known that a court action would be disastrous, Boyle was in an equally difficult position. His intelligence sources would never agree to appear as witnesses for the defence and a court would not accept as hard evidence the theories of people like Rees. So there was an unsatisfactory compromise. Boyle would give Blunt a codename – 'Maurice'. This was taken from the title of E. M. Forster's novel centring round a Cambridge homosexual academic who had, like Blunt, rejected his own privileged class's code of conduct. There were clues in the manuscript suggesting that Blunt and 'Maurice' might be one and the same; but Boyle managed cleverly to avoid stepping over the line that would have constituted a libel.

Late in 1978 Blunt seems to have discovered that Boyle had reached the conclusion that he had been a Soviet spy. Boyle himself was uncertain about the exact timing:

Writing books tends to be a lonely business. If no writer worth his salt should normally complain of that, I must say in my self-defence that my sense of loneliness was sometimes intense owing to the peculiarly fraught circumstances I created for myself, first by uncovering and then by identifying Blunt beyond all doubt as the 'Fourth Man' in the Cambridge spy conspiracy. That he knew I already knew far too much about him there could be no reasonable room for questioning. For he had some rich, powerful and influential friends; and those I was able to meet must have passed on to him my guarded suspicions, whether they already saw through him or not.[18]

In the autumn Blunt met the London libel lawyer Michael Rubinstein, a dapper individual who had long experience of dealing with the media and publishers. Rubinstein recalled: 'He said that he anticipated problems in the libel field. I had absolutely no idea at this time what it was.'[19]

The next move in the final act of the Blunt drama came in 1979. Lawyers began reading Boyle's manuscript for possible libels, checking to ensure that Blunt and the mythical 'Maurice' had not been too closely intertwined. Boyle showed the book to one of his intelligence sources, a former senior officer in MI5, hoping to ensure that there were no glaring errors. But Boyle refused to budge on his theory about Wilfrid Mann, alias 'Basil'. MI5, meanwhile, had finally realized that the book might detonate an explosion of renewed public interest in the Burgess–Maclean–Philby affair. Boyle said that his publishers were approached by a representative from MI5 who said that that mysterious entity, 'national interest', demanded that the authorities should be allowed to check the manuscript. Hutchinson refused. In September Blunt decided that he could wait no longer. The book was due to be published in November and he could feel the noose tightening around his neck. It was now that he made his fatal mistake; one which ensured that the book would not just appear but would attract huge media interest. He instructed Rubinstein to call Hutchinson. Rubinstein did not believe that Blunt, who was very keen to see the Boyle book, would be allowed to do so. And Rubinstein was right. Boyle wrote:

Rubinstein indicated that a distinguished but unnamed client of his had reason to believe that my book would defame him. My editor, Harold Harris, who was also deputy managing director of Hutchinson, asked which of his numerous clients this might be. 'Sir Anthony Blunt', said Michael Rubinstein. And Sir Anthony naturally wanted to see a copy of the book in advance, just as the smooth representatives of MI5 had done . . . Harris wrote a disarming reply, expressing mild surprise at the request and assuring Rubinstein that his valued client would find no cause for complaint when the book appeared.[20]

Brian Sewell had argued that it would be more sensible to let the book appear. Blunt had not been directly accused of treachery and if, or rather when, newspapers asked for a reaction, Blunt would be able to say that he had nothing to say. The government would, hoped Sewell, do the honourable thing and refuse to comment. There would be a stir for a few days then the whole affair would be forgotten. But news of the call to Hutchinson inevitably leaked to the press (the publishing world is not renowned for its ability to keep secrets, especially if there is a chance of promoting public interest in a book).

On 28 September *Private Eye* fired the first salvo. A story in the magazine's 'news' section, the launching pad for innumerable scandals and eagerly read by the main-stream press, described how Rubinstein had telephoned Hutchinson and explained that he feared that a forthcoming book might defame one of his clients, Sir Anthony Blunt. The *Eye* continued:

The reason for Sir Anthony's – and Mr Rubinstein's – concern about *The Climate of Treason* is not immediately clear. The book, which does indeed contain many references to Sir Anthony, traces in greater detail than hitherto the background to the Burgess–Philby–Maclean story. In so doing it introduces the so-called 'Fourth Man' – another senior official in the British Intelligence Service who was a long-serving Russian agent . . . He has never been exposed. What has this to do with Sir Anthony Blunt? Now 72 Blunt (Marlborough and Trinity College, Cambridge) had spent the late '30s as an academic at Cambridge and then London University [sic]. During the war, according to *Who's Who*, he was at the War Office. He was knighted in 1956.

Blunt was horrified by the story. Should he sue the magazine? Brian Sewell thought not; after all, said Sewell, who believed the *Eye*? Michael Rubinstein, too, urged caution. Blunt decided that he had no choice other than to wait and hope that the press would back off. He needed reassurance and sought it from his old Marlborough friend Sir Ellis Waterhouse, who lived in a splendid house on the outskirts of Oxford. Waterhouse said:

He stayed with me for four or five days before Boyle's book came out. I had not seen much of him for a long time. He had let me down badly over a personal matter and I realized then that I couldn't trust him. But in 1979 he was obviously very worried about the book. We didn't discuss it very much. We really talked about the Guy [Burgess] connection. I guessed that the book was to do with that. I assumed that Anthony didn't want to talk about that in detail. I think he told me that Guy had telephoned him several times in the two years before he died. He wanted to come back to England but Anthony told him that he would be arrested if he did. A couple of weeks later Anthony was exposed.[21]

The 8 November edition of the *Eye*, which appeared a few days after Boyle's book was published, accused Blunt of being the fourth man:

Ever since the *Eye* revealed the agitated interest of his lawyer Michael Rubinstein over the forthcoming publication of Andrew Boyle's book, *Climate of Treason*, squads of Fleet Street hacks have been pursuing an increasingly elusive Sir Anthony Blunt, adviser for the Queen's Pictures and Drawings . . . The reason for all this attention was the firm conviction on the part of the fearless newshounds that the fourth man, whom Boyle refers to by his code name of 'Maurice' and whose tip-off enabled Burgess and Maclean to escape was, in fact, this long-standing member of the Royal Household. One American correspondent even went so far as to say so in a story cabled from London, only to have his newspaper delete the name pending publication and/ or confirmation in Britain. Such publication seems unlikely at present, given our draconian libel laws and the cloaking of the whole story by the Official Secrets Act.

But why should it be that so many eager spy-hunters should have this idea about a prominent art historian honoured by his country? The answer can be found in the trail of clues left by Boyle's reference to 'Maurice' in his book. Consider the following:

'Maurice' was an intimate associate of Guy Burgess at Cambridge.

So was Blunt.

'Maurice' was, according to Goronwy Rees, a man of 'erudition' i.e. an academic.

Blunt was a Fellow of Trinity College, Cambridge 1932–1936.

'Maurice' was a homosexual.

So is Blunt.

'Maurice' enlisted in the army in 1939.

So did Blunt.

'"Maurice's" prosecution,' says Boyle, 'could have

embroiled many eminent people, perhaps even the Royal Family itself.'

Blunt is the only character in Boyle's story with royal connections.

Appearing on BBC Radio's 'The World at One' on 1 November, Boyle provided some further clues when pressed by Robin Day. He was asked whether 'Maurice' was 'a titled gentleman'.

Answer – yes.

He was asked whether he had been employed by the Royal Family.

Answer – Yes.

Finally, there is perhaps the biggest clue or red herring of all – the call from Michael Rubinstein to Boyle's publishers, indicating that Blunt understood he was about to be libelled. Putting all these factors together, it is clear that, as far as Andrew Boyle and Fleet Street are concerned, the Blunt truth is that 'Maurice' = Sir Anthony Blunt. And that would explain why, while lesser mortals received sentences of 10 to 20 years for handing over documents, and a key traitor such as George Blake was jailed for 42 years, 'Maurice' was able to confess and walk away. For at that time in the late fifties Blunt had recently been knighted (1956) and was employed as Surveyor of the Queen's Pictures. The scandal would have been even greater than that which had been caused by Burgess's and Maclean's flight to Russia or was later caused by Philby's escape there. Furthermore, the news would not have been taken lightly at Buckingham Palace. For as the Queen Mother once declared, a remark relayed back to Blunt, when talking about Burgess and Maclean: 'The one person I cannot stand is a traitor.'

As if this was not bad enough there was a second, shorter item in the *Eye*'s 'Grovel' section – devoted to scurrilous gossip – which explained how Sir Anthony Blunt shared his life with an ex-guardsman called John Gaskin, known to Blunt's friends as 'Lady John'. Blunt realized that someone who knew him well had briefed the magazine. How else could they have got so much right about his private life? They had somehow learned about that remark by the Queen Mother, legendary by now within the Blunt gay circle, but never before publicly mentioned. They knew about Gaskin. And they had been confident enough to accuse him of treachery – something that no other publication had dared do. Blunt concluded that he had been betrayed.

When rumours about Boyle's book and Blunt's possible involvement in the Cambridge spy network began to circulate around Fleet Street, someone at the *Eye* had remembered the Harbinson file – the 'open letters' he had amassed during his battle with Faber. These letters, with their interlocking arguments about personal treachery, homosexuality, the Royal Family and espionage, had been forgotten. Now the magazine sent Harbinson a telegram asking if he would contact them. Harbinson recalled:

I went into the *Eye* and went through all my letters with them. They hadn't understood what I had been saying until then. Then they began to see what I had been talking about. That is why the story was so accurate. They wouldn't have been able to say that Blunt was gay without my letters. And I was responsible for the items in 'Grovel' about Lady John. Blunt knew from that that the magazine was not bluffing . . . that they knew the truth.[22]

The *Eye* – renowned for taking libel risks – would probably have published *something* about Blunt without Harbinson's help. After all, most of Fleet Street had been chasing the Blunt story and the *Eye* could hardly fail to report that. But Harbinson ensured that the magazine was not just forthright but accurate. While journalists read and re-read the magazine, trying to find a way to flush out the truth, Blunt desperately sought advice from his solicitor and from friends. Rubinstein concluded that it would be madness to issue a writ for libel against the *Eye*. It would be expensive. It would take years to reach the courts, by which time Blunt's life would have been destroyed by publicity since anyone suing *Private Eye* always attracted special attention from the rest of Fleet Street. There were other considerations, too. Rubinstein said:

A possible plaintiff might say, OK, I will sue because they won't be able to prove it. But if you are vulnerable then I am against suing. Blunt would have been asked a lot of questions in the witness box. I can't remember exactly when I knew that he had been a spy. I am bound to say that by the time I met him he found it impossible to comment on how he had felt when it had all happened. He had set up a sort of wall, which sometimes happens with people who want to forget their past. They just won't think about it. I think that he must have been living in the expectation that one day it would come out. Perhaps it was a relief when it did. But he was not the type of man to show his feelings in that way. He didn't seem to react emotionally to what was going on.[23]

Blunt turned to Brian Sewell. Sewell recalled:

I had known from early September that a crisis was building up. I had been in Devon walking the dogs and when I came back to London there were endless messages to call Anthony. It was clear that the Boyle book was going to be dangerous. We didn't say very much. Anthony assumed I knew because of my meeting with Andrew Gow. After the second *Eye* story it seemed it was a question of *when* the crunch came, not *if* it came. I told him that he should say nothing . . . that he should say he was constrained by the Official Secrets Act, that people should leave him alone because he had nothing to say. I told him that on no account should he be provoked into saying anything.[24]

It was, however, too late for Blunt. Even now he could not bring himself to warn his family that they might soon be swamped by calls from the media. Wilfrid had seen the first *Private Eye* story about his brother:

Anthony never took me aside to tell me. I first saw it in *Private Eye*. It didn't actually make an accusation and I didn't believe it. It was inconceivable. I rang him up and he asked if he could come over to see me. I had the impression that he knew about the article but I didn't take it to mean that he was in any way guilty. I was absolutely dazed when the thing broke in Parliament.[25]

Blunt was now a prisoner in his own flat. Reporters from the Fleet Street tabloids, led by the ruthless news-gatherers of the *Daily Mail*, were camped permanently outside the main entrance of Portsea Hall, hoping to persuade Blunt to utter a few, preferably damning, words. But the pressure brought Gaskin and him closer together than for many years; indeed, Brian Sewell believed that the crisis saved the relationship. Sewell recalled:

If the events of 1979 had not occurred I don't believe that they would have lasted. Anthony was practically in tears, saying, 'I can't go on. After all these years there's nothing left.' I knew how he felt. If they came to my house for lunch I would invite a couple of young men for him to smile at. If Anthony and I talked about the history of art then John wouldn't be interested. In the end it became impossible. I once tried to get him to talk about politics and he said that he never voted. And that was the end of the conversation. In the days before the Thatcher statement the two of them were creeping around the flat like a couple of mice with the curtains closed, pretending that they weren't there. They were afraid even to pull the lavatory chain. I thought they were being very foolish. They were running out of food and it was obvious that they would have to be moved.[26]

By the middle of November Blunt, said Sewell, had told two friends, James Joll, Stevenson Professor of International History at London University, and John Golding, Reader in the History of Art at the Courtauld, that he was facing a crisis. The two men, who shared a house in Chiswick, west London, said that Blunt could stay with them – assuming that he could escape from his own flat without being spotted by the press. Meanwhile, Andrew Boyle was still refusing to confirm (or deny) that 'Maurice' was, in fact, Sir Anthony Blunt. His stock reply was to say that it was up to the government to identify 'Maurice'. Then Boyle's son Ed, a political journalist who worked in the lobby of the House of Commons, called his father. Two questions about security had, he said, been tabled by MPs for reply on Monday 18 November. And there was still better news. A third question, tabled by the Labour MP for Hartlepool, Edward Leadbitter, would be answered by the Prime Minister on Thursday 15 November. Neither Leadbitter, Boyle nor Blunt knew that Downing Street had already decided that they could not be associated with a cover-up. Sir Michael Havers, the Tory Attorney General, had told Mrs Thatcher that the administration would not be able to stand by and watch Blunt sue for libel if anyone repeated the *Eye* allegation. MPs now wanted a statement from the government – was Blunt the fourth man or was he the victim of a witchhunt? – and Havers advised the Prime Minister that she would have to answer truthfully.

Leadbitter had heard Blunt's name mentioned by newspaper reporters in early November and had even jotted it down on a piece of paper, which he put in his wallet and then forgot about. A few days later, as he was on his way to the Commons, he decided to have what he called 'a clear out'. Leadbitter recalled:

It was a very slack period at the Commons and I thought: I wonder . . . I called Downing Street and said that I was thinking of tabling a question about security. I had the impression that the question was creating interest. When I rang back Downing Street suggested that I table a question with Blunt's name in it. That is not my style. I do not like using parliamentary privilege to accuse people. I spent a bit of time formulating my own question, which eventually said something like, 'Will the Prime Minister in her role as minister responsible for national security make a statement on the name given to her by the Right Honourable member for Hartlepool?' The Table Office [which accepts MPs' questions] said they would have to consult before they accepted it. It didn't seem to me that they were just worried about the wording. It was more than that. Then I dashed round to Downing Street with a letter saying that the name I was referring to in my question was Sir Anthony Blunt. Then I went off to my constituency.[27]

While Thatcher studied the outline reply that had been drafted by her Labour predecessors there was one, final arrangement that needed to be made. Blunt had to be warned that the government was about to renege on the immunity pledge that he had been given in 1964, which carried with it the implicit promise that no government would ever discuss the case. It was, thought Downing Street, the least they could do. On Wednesday morning, 14 November, Michael Rubinstein was summoned to see Sir Robert Armstrong, the Cabinet Secretary. Armstrong said that the Prime Minister would be revealing to the Commons that Sir Anthony Blunt was a self-confessed traitor. Rubinstein remembered: 'There was nothing I could do to stop or change it. It was, I suppose, a warning to give Blunt time to hide from the press. He just said that Mrs Thatcher wanted you to know that she was going to make the statement.'[28]

CHAPTER 22
Unmasked

The Commons was hushed on the afternoon of Thursday 15 November when Mrs Thatcher rose to make her statement. Would she, speculated journalists, refuse to comment on security matters; the traditional response of all British governments when asked about the activities of MI5 or MI6? No, they immediately realized, she would not. The Prime Minister's statement astonished MPs and journalists accustomed to obfuscatory pronouncements in this field. Mrs Thatcher said:

The name which the Honourable Gentleman [Mr Leadbitter] has given me is that of Sir Anthony Blunt. In April 1964, Sir Anthony Blunt admitted to the security authorities that he had been recruited by, and had acted as a talent-spotter for, Russian Intelligence before the war, when he was a don at Cambridge, and had passed information regularly to the Russians while he was a member of the Security Service between 1940 and 1945. He made this admission after being given an undertaking that he would not be prosecuted if he confessed. Inquiries were, of course, made before Blunt joined the Security Service in 1940, and he was judged a fit person. He was known to have held Marxist views at Cambridge, but the security authorities had no reason either in 1940 or at any time during his service to doubt his loyalty to his country.

On leaving the security service in 1945, Blunt reverted to his profession as an art historian. He held a number of academic appointments. He was also appointed as Surveyor of the King's Pictures in 1945, and as Surveyor of the Queen's Pictures in 1952. He was given a KCVO [Knight Commander of the Victorian Order] in 1956. He was appointed as an Adviser to the Queen's Pictures and Drawings in 1972, and he retired from this appointment in 1978.

He first came under suspicion in the course of the inquiries which followed the defection of Burgess and Maclean in 1951 when the security service was told that Burgess had said in 1937 that he was working for a secret branch of the Comintern and that Blunt was one of his sources. There was no supporting evidence for this. When confronted with it Blunt denied it. Nevertheless the security service remained suspicious of him and began an intensive and prolonged investigation of his activities. During the course of this investigation he was interviewed on eleven occasions. He persisted in his denial and no evidence against him was obtained. The inquiries which preceded the exposure and defection of Philby in January 1963 produced nothing which implicated Blunt. Early in 1964 new information was received which directly implicated Blunt. It did not, however, provide a basis on which charges could be brought. The then Attorney General [Sir John Hobson] decided in April 1964, after consultation with the Director of Public Prosecutions, that the public interest lay in trying to secure a confession from Blunt, not only to arrive at a definite conclusion on his involvement but also to obtain information from him about any others who might still be in danger.

It was considered important to gain his cooperation in the continuing investigations by the security authorities, following the defections of Burgess, Maclean and Philby, into Soviet penetration of the security and intelligence services and other public services during and after the war. Accordingly the Attorney General authorized the offer of immunity to Blunt if he confessed. Blunt then admitted to the security authorities that, like his friends Burgess, Maclean and Philby, he had become an agent of Russian intelligence and had talent-spotted for them at Cambridge during the 1930s; that he had regularly passed information to the Russians while he was a member of the security service; and that, although after 1945 he was no longer in a position to supply the Russians with classified information, in 1951 he used his old contact with the Russians to assist in the arrangements for the defection of Burgess and Maclean. Both at the time of his confession and subsequently Blunt provided useful information about Russian intelligence activities and about his association with Burgess, Maclean and Philby.

The Queen's Private Secretary was informed in April 1964 both of Blunt's confession and of the immunity from prosecution, on the basis of which it had been made. Blunt was not required to resign his appointment in the Royal Household, which was unpaid. It carried with it no access to classified information and no risk to security, and the security authorities thought it desirable not to put at risk his cooperation. Successive Attorneys General in 1972, in June 1974, and in June 1979, have agreed that, having regard to the immunity granted in order to obtain the confession, which has always been and still is the only firm evidence against Blunt, there are no grounds on which criminal proceedings could be instituted.

Within minutes of Thatcher sitting down, Buckingham Palace announced that Blunt was being stripped of his knighthood; only the second time anyone had suffered such an indignity. Next morning the *London Gazette* carried this bulletin: 'The Queen has decided that the appointment of Professor Sir Anthony Frederick Blunt to be a Knight Commander of the Royal Victorian Order dated May 31st 1956 shall be cancelled and annulled and that his name shall be erased from the Register of the said Order.'

The statement from Thatcher raised many more questions than it answered. How had Blunt been recruited as a Soviet spy? What damage had he inflicted? Were there others who had been offered immunity from prosecution in return for a confession? Why, indeed, had immunity been offered to Blunt when other spies, who had not been educated at public school and Oxbridge and who did not hold positions at the Palace, had been sent to prison for several decades? How much had the Queen been told? It was obvious, even to those who thought that too much time had already been devoted to the Cambridge spies, that this was not an issue that would easily be forgotten. Certainly it was true that the Blunt scandal was a classic diversion from humdrum politics but it did, too, raise serious issues about the relationship between the intelligence services and government, and between government and the monarch. There were many fascinating sub-themes to be explored and newspapers ordered every available reporter to start digging. Friends and relatives of Blunt had to be found and forced to talk. The political correspondents bustled around the lobby in the Commons, scuttling from one senior politician to another, trying to obtain answers to the endless questions from their newsdesks. Leadbitter was by now sure that he had unwittingly done precisely what Downing Street had wanted: 'After the debate I met the Prime Minister outside the lobby and I took the opportunity of thanking her. And she said: "And it damn well serves him right."[1]

But Professor Anthony Blunt, the one man whom everyone wanted to inverview, had disappeared. At about 10 A.M. that Thursday Brian Sewell had driven to Portsea Hall in his Peugeot to collect Blunt and Gaskin. Sewell recalled:

Anthony had suggested that I come at 4 o'clock in the morning but I said that there was more chance of getting him out at a normal time of day. I went up to the flat and told Gaskin to get straight into the back seat of the car and not to faff around. I gave Anthony my old dog-walking hat and rammed it over his head. It worked perfectly. The *Daily Mail* reporters on the door didn't realize what was happening until we were on our way.[2]

Sewell realized that the *Mail* men would be able to trace him from his car registration (most newspapers 'know someone' who can help in this way). Sewell dropped off Blunt and Gaskin at Joll's home and then wasted several hours, calculating that reporters would be camped outside his own home in Kensington by the time he returned. Much better, thought Sewell, to let them think that he had driven Blunt out of London. 'When I got home in the middle of the afternoon I found two reporters from the *Daily Mail* waiting for me. I played innocent and said I didn't know what they were talking about. That's how I became known to the newspapers.'[3]

The headline writers had no difficulty in capturing the drama of the Thatcher statement. On Friday the *Daily Mail* screamed, 'TRAITOR AT THE QUEEN'S RIGHT HAND'. There was a logo above it – with the caption 'The Fourth Man', and a drawing of Blunt, Burgess, Philby and Maclean – of the type slung on to stories that newspapers think will have an unusually long life. Politicians who had

had any connection with security were quoted at length, even if many could remember nothing about Blunt. Yellowing press clippings on Burgess, Maclean and Philby were recycled into long, background features. Andrew Boyle was quoted; yes, of course, he was relieved that he had been vindicated and no, he was not going to name the fifth man, codenamed 'Basil'. Michael Rubinstein's office and home telephones rang constantly with calls from the press pleading for information. Where was Professor Blunt? Was it true that he had fled to Moscow? Would he grant an exclusive interview? If he did then he would be guaranteed 'a fair crack of the whip'. Throughout Fleet Street news editors dreamed of out-manoeuvring their rivals with the Big One: 'Royal Spy Speaks Out. Exclusive'.

Rubinstein and Sewell, thus, became the two spokesmen for the pro-Blunt camp. Sewell was pictured in his duffel-coat, walking his dogs, on front pages and on television. Both men were courteous and, more important, quotable. Sewell, for example, thought it was outrageous that the government had named Blunt. What was the point, Sewell asked, of giving someone immunity from prosecution if you then humiliated them in public in this manner? Blunt, said Sewell with unintentional irony, would never be able to trust anyone again.

That weekend Blunt spent much of his time sleeping; his habitual reaction when he was confronted with an awkward problem. Sewell kept in touch by telephone – not willing to visit Joll's home in case he was tailed by reporters. 'Anthony would telephone me and then I would have to go out and find a public callbox because he was convinced my phone was tapped, which I think it probably was. I remember that John was saying that none of this would have happened if they had gone away. That is how naïve he was.'[4] Blunt said little to Joll or Golding. He spent most of his time alone, reading or sleeping, and kept well away from the windows, terrified that he might be spotted. The newspapers, of course, ran thousands of words on the affair. In the absence of new facts some reporters grasped at very dubious leads. On 18 November the normally accurate *Sunday Telegraph* wrongly claimed that Blunt had been a lieutenant-colonel during the war commanding the Dutch section of the Special Operations Executive (SOE) and that, as a result of his treachery, hundreds of British and Dutch agents had been captured or killed by the Germans. The letters columns of the press were full of (mostly critical) contributions from readers. A few backed Blunt the academic and teacher. Brian Sewell loyally told *Times* readers on 17 November:

> The sound of Labour Members of Parliament baying for vengeance with cries of Privilege and Establishment is unedifying; they should recall that Blunt's experience of the thirties was clearer and sharper for him than is the mythology of that period for them and that views formed by him then were held with the same passion and for the same compassionate reasons as their own views now, and with many of the same changes in society as an aim. Heroism and treachery are obverse and reverse of the same coin . . . The 1964 bargain must have brought benefits in counter-espionage; these I cannot assess but the benefits to the history of art are well known to all who work in that field, for despite desperate illness, those fifteen years have produced more brilliant work than most plodders in a lifetime.

Former Courtauld students, such as Giles Waterfield, the amiable director of the Dulwich Picture Gallery in south London, wrote to *The Times* of Blunt's 'brilliant teaching and kindness'. It was a great shame, said the ex-pupils, that the Establishment should humiliate a distinguished old man in this way. But pleas like this, to let Blunt live out his remaining years in peace, were naturally ignored by the media. Michael Rubinstein realized that his client had no choice; sooner or later he would have to reply in person to the allegations. But how should the press conference be organized? Rubinstein was determined that Blunt would not have to endure the ignorant and rude questions from the 'gutter press'.

Rubinstein was under pressure from a former neighbour, Louis Heren, the deputy editor of *The Times*, to give that newspaper an exclusive interview with Blunt. But that, as Rubinstein knew, would enrage the rest of the press and would merely intensify, not reduce, the pressure on his client. On Monday 19 November, newspapers announced: 'BLUNT TO FACE THE WORLD.' Then Rubinstein said that his client was not prepared to face the massed ranks of the press. The *Sunday Telegraph*'s inaccurate story that weekend meant that the Telegraph group could not expect to be invited. The liberal *Guardian* had to be invited. The BBC and Independent Television News would have to be accommodated. But Rubinstein was determined to bar the tabloids:

I suppose I take a cynical view of the gutter press. They think that they're representing a public that would like to see all spies shot. They're not interested in the argument that it might be in the national interest not to do that. A spy turned is more valuable than a spy who is dead. Imagine what would have happened if we had allowed them in. They would just have insulted Blunt. And it would not have mattered what he said. A press conference was obviously not going to stop the harassment entirely but it was essential to have something to clear the air.[5]

This sort of apparent sanctimoniousness – from a lawyer who was representing a self-confessed traitor – incensed the media. What right had Rubinstein to decide which newspaper should be allowed to question Blunt? Rubinstein ignored all these criticisms and indeed fuelled media indignation with statements such as: 'Professor Blunt is still very much subject to the Official Secrets Act.' He told the *Guardian*: 'I recognize, and greatly regret, as does Mr Blunt, that many representatives of the media and the newspapers must be disappointed by the arrangements we have now made. But we hope that the reasons will be understood and respected.'[6]

Blunt was scheduled to appear on the morning of Tuesday 20 November. But the venue was to be kept secret. The main interview would be conducted by journalists from *The Times* and *Guardian*, and the transcript then given to the Press Association, Britain's national news agency. Their interview would be filmed by an independent producer and would be available to both television channels. The BBC and ITN news teams would have ten minutes each to question Blunt. This arrangement, which seemed eminently sensible to Rubinstein, smacked to the tabloids of a cosy deal between the posh traitor and the posh newspapers. Fleet Street tabloid newspapers are intensely competitive; the idea of taking a story verbatim from another newspaper, especially a posh one, is anathema. There was genuine fury among the excluded newspapers that their reporters would not be able to have a crack at Blunt. It had always been unlikely that Blunt would get any sympathy from the press; this decision made it certain that he would be given a drubbing by Fleet Street. The search for Blunt, meanwhile, had intensified and that Monday a BBC reporter tracked him down to Joll's house. In return for not identifying Joll or giving away his address, the BBC obtained a distinctly lacklustre scoop. Joll told the BBC that he had been a friend of Blunt for more than twenty years and continued:

> When the scandal broke he was in great trouble with reporters and the press and needed a little peace to sort out his ideas and think about the best way to present his case to the press. As I have a fairly quiet house in the suburbs I said that he would be very welcome to come and stay here until the press conference.

That Tuesday morning Blunt, escorted by a 'minder' from *The Times*, arrived at *The Times* building in Gray's Inn Road, half a mile or so north of Fleet Street. To their horror they realized that the 'gutter press' had discovered the location of the press conference. There was a phalanx of angry pressmen at the front entrance so Blunt, stooping slightly and dressed in a blue, houndstooth tweed jacket, grey trousers, a light blue checked shirt and a pullover, was bundled into *The Times* through a rear entrance. He was escorted into the lift and taken up to a wood-panelled boardroom on the seventh floor. Rubinstein, meanwhile, arrived separately. Blunt settled down in an armchair and was given a glass of whisky as television technicians tested lighting and voice levels. Meanwhile, the *Guardian*'s David Leigh found that no one at *The Times* wanted to direct him to the boardroom. Leigh, who had as much right to question Blunt as *The Times*'s Louis Heren and Stewart Tendler, did not intend to miss the story that was front-page news around the world.[6]

Blunt opened with a statement that had been prepared with Rubinstein (and which had been cleared by the intelligence services). He read slowly, deliberately, his sallow complexion lit by the television lights and his face set in that unfortunate lopsided expression which looked so much like a sneer. He explained that Guy Burgess had persuaded him in the 1930s that the best way to fight fascism was to join him in his work for the Soviet Union. This was a case, said Blunt, of 'political conscience against loyalty to country; I chose conscience'. He continued:

> When later I realized the true facts about Russia I was prevented from taking any action by personal loyalty; I could not denounce my friends. In 1964 an event took place which meant that I was no longer bound by this loyalty and being promised immunity I was relieved to give the authorities all the information in my possession. From 1945 I ceased to pass information to the Russians but in 1951 I was in contact with them on behalf of Burgess. I was myself pressed to go to Russia. I refused. Andrew Boyle has stated that I obtained from a colleague in MI5 the exact date on which Maclean was to be interviewed. There is no truth in this story . . . When I was told of the impending statement in Parliament by Mrs Thatcher I did not at any time contemplate leaving the country but I realized that there would be a barrage of inquiries from the Press while questions were being asked in Parliament and I knew that I could not give helpful answers to questions which might be put to me so long as I was unaware of exactly what the ministerial answers would say. I should add that I remained – as I still remain – under the constraint of the Official Secrets Act.

Blunt said, too, that he had not sought his position at the Palace, nor had he known about his knighthood until he had read the official announcement in *The Times*. It had been gratifying, he added, that so many friends, colleagues and former students had rallied to his support since the Thatcher statement.

Then came the questions from *The Times* and *Guardian*

journalists. Blunt chose his words carefully as if he had
been briefed on what he should and should not say. There
was regret, but it seemed to be regret that he was having to
go through this humiliating ordeal rather than contrition at
his treachery. If the press and the country wanted him to
beg forgiveness then they realized now that they were going
to be disappointed. He had been loyal, he insisted throughout, but to friends instead of country. He was asked first
about his recruitment as a Soviet agent and then moved on
to explain how he had joined MI5 – which he agreed had
been through the 'old boy network'. Once inside the intelligence service he had passed information to an English
contact and a Soviet controller, though he refused to name
either. At first the material was routine but it became 'much
more interesting' after his transfer to a new section which
dealt with 'German intelligence intercepts'. He gave as
much of this as possible to his controllers as well as outlin-
ing the structure and membership of MI5. He talked about
the power of Burgess's personality and about Dick White
and Guy Liddell. He again denied that he had been in a
position to know when Maclean was due to be questioned.
He said that he was now entirely 'reconciled' to the British
political system. His talks with MI5 before his confession
had been 'mainly comfortable conversations'. He had been
granted immunity, he thought, because his cooperation
could open up a valuable line of research. He clearly felt
that MI5 had betrayed that deal by allowing the Prime
Minister to name him in the Commons. No, he said, as far
as he was aware, the Queen had not been told in 1964 about
his confession; he thought she had first learnt about it in
1972, when he was seriously ill with cancer. Yes, he had
seen the Queen, but only occasionally, when there was a
particular problem over the art collection. It had been a
'tremendous relief' to get this 'off [his] chest' in 1964. Was it
possible, he was asked, that homosexuals were somehow

more likely to become spies because they feel rejected by society? Blunt thought not. Philby was not homosexual and Maclean was 'essentially normal'. He added: 'I think that obviously in certain other cases blackmail has been used but I think this has been grossly exaggerated. The connection is much slighter than has been suggested and, after all, there are other means of blackmail.'

Blunt became overtly evasive when the journalists pressed him for the names of his accomplices in the spy network. He was asked if it was correct that there had been twenty-five people in positions similar to his. He replied: 'My guess would be that there must have been a great many more people involved in this. I should think all of them have long since stopped.' The newsmen, sensing a scoop, tried again. Had these people been in public service? Blunt refused to be drawn: 'I imagine so and this is largely hearsay. I am partly talking about information I have officially, and I must shut up on this, but I think it is common knowledge that the network was considerable.'

Did he feel ashamed of what he had done? No, he did not. He had acted according to his conscience but he now realized, he said half-heartedly, that what he had done had been wrong. He repeated this sentiment to the television teams: 'I realize that I have made an appalling mistake. I acted according to my conscience in doing what I did in 1936 and that meant disloyalty to my country. As I said, I believed it was the right thing to do in the cause of anti-fascism, but now I realize bitterly this was totally wrong.'

Then, the ordeal over, Blunt retired for a lunch of smoked trout, veal, fruit salad and wine, with coffee and cigars to follow. He was reported later to have commented: 'I have always enjoyed smoked trout.' It was this lunch, as much as anything, which seemed to symbolize the attitude of the Establishment to Blunt the Traitor. Next morning the tabloid *Daily Express* raged:

Professor Blunt would not have been offered so much as a stale kipper in the *Express* offices. Not so much because there is room left for concern about his wartime role as a Soviet spy – assuming he is telling the truth – but rather because he is such a phoney old humbug. It would have been all too easy at yesterday's stage-managed press conference (decent chaps only) to have torn aside his veil of hypocrisy. In the event it failed to produce a satisfactory answer to the questions that matter.

The *Daily Mail* called Blunt 'the spy with no shame' and described his performance as one of 'supreme insolence'. The *Mail* ran a vitriolic front-page editorial:

When the 'gifted' and 'talented' Cambridge student Anthony Blunt decided to betray his country to the cause of Communism forty-three years ago the very act showed his indifference and contempt for the people of Britain. Yesterday, forced to explain his actions at last, he showed that, whatever else may have changed, the languid contempt he has for his fellow citizens remains untouched by time or treachery. What this traitor had to say told us very little. The manner of his saying it, however, revealed a great deal. Still cocooned by a protective Establishment, he sat in the offices of Times Newspapers and dismissed his betrayal as a 'matter of conscience'.

No one, in fact, seemed to think that Blunt had either been honest or that he really regretted anything. Hugh Trevor-Roper said: 'Be damned to his conscience.' George Young, a former deputy head of MI6, thought that 'there wasn't much of a thread of sincerity' running through what Blunt had said. Goronwy Rees, dying of cancer in the Charing Cross Hospital, said that Blunt was 'tough and unscrupulous . . . a classic agent . . . who has so thoroughly mastered the art of lying that nothing will shake or break him down.' In fact, Blunt had not told many obvious lies; rather he had fudged and blocked, blending truth with half truth. One falsehood was soon exposed. He had denied having had any contact with the Soviets after 1951 when he had, in fact, met Yuri Modin in 1954. Before the end of that week he was forced to admit that he had forgotten to mention that during the press conference.

Blunt was now trapped in his flat, refusing directly to answer any more questions from the press, leaving Rubinstein and Sewell once again to field the stream of inquiries. That week Mrs Thatcher opened a Commons debate on the affair with a lengthy statement. She emphasized to MPs: 'It is important not to be so obsessed with yesterday's danger that we fail to detect today's. We know what happened to a very few of that pre-war generation who had Marxist leanings and who betrayed their country. We find it deplorable and repugnant. Our task now is to guard against their counterparts of today.' Having made that point the Prime Minister summarized the main elements of the Blunt case, obviously determined to refute suggestions that there had been what the press had called 'an Establishment cover-up'. She was keen, too, to defend the intelligence services which had, she said, behaved properly throughout; the Cambridge spies had flourished many years ago and the contemporary secret guardians of democracy should not be blamed for the mistakes of their predecessors. It might seem extraordinary, said Mrs Thatcher, that an avowed Marxist should have been able to join the security service. But it was all very well to say that with hindsight; it had to be remembered that the intelligence services were under enormous pressure and had neither the time nor the manpower to vet every recruit. It was true that Blunt had 'very seriously damaged British interests' but there was no evidence that he had put at risk British military operations or British lives. (This was later taken to mean that he might have put Allied lives in jeopardy.) She outlined the dilemma facing MI5 in 1964. Blunt had been questioned eleven times since the defections of Burgess and Maclean and had never admitted anything. Then 'new information' – she did not disclose that this was the confession of Michael Straight – became available. She continued, explaining why he had been offered immunity:

> The security authorities were faced with a difficult choice. They could have decided to wait in the hope that further information which could be used as a basis for prosecuting Blunt would in due course be discovered. But the security authorities had already pursued their inquiries for thirteen years without obtaining firm evidence against Blunt. There was no reason to expect or hope that a further wait would be likely to yield evidence of a kind that had eluded them so far. If the security authorities had confronted him with the new information and he still persisted in his denial their investigation of him would have been no further forward and they might have prejudiced their own position by alerting him to information which he could have used to warn others.

A few Labour MPs tried to use the debate to attack the government but this floundered when James Callaghan, the ex-Labour Prime Minister, intervened. It had been a 'sorry affair' and one which had damaged the morale of the intelligence services. Yes, said Callaghan, there could well be other Blunts living in quiet retirement but they were by now almost certainly of no further use to the Russians. He concluded that the full truth of what happened during the 1930s would probably never be discovered. Only the spy-masters in the Kremlin knew that. But, as the debate wound up, no one believed that this would be the end of the Blunt affair. There were too many unanswered questions. And there were too many people determined to provide the answers.

CHAPTER 23
A Surfeit of Scandal

If Anthony Blunt had hoped that life would return to normal after his meeting with the gentlemen of the press then he soon realized that it had been the start, not the end, of the nightmare. Reporters were still picketing the entrance to Portsea Hall; the telephone in the flat rang continually as newspapers and television stations pleaded for interviews. And there were more humiliations. On 23 November Trinity College announced that 'Professor Blunt has placed his resignation as an honorary fellow in the hands of the Master. His resignation was accepted by the college council at its meeting and will take effect as from today.' Blunt, the first man to lose an honorary fellowship since the college's foundation in 1546, had been told that it was up to him: he could either resign or be forced out. While his remaining friends wrote supportive letters to the press his long-standing critics in the art world were increasingly vocal, impugning his integrity as an art historian as much as his patriotism. The well-known London art dealer Jean Gimpel, who had been briefly tutored by the young Blunt at the Gimpels' home on Lake Como, attacked him for the way that he had raised doubts about the authenticity of a Poussin owned by the family.

Yet to the few friends who were prepared to visit the flat – and risk having their names splashed over the newspapers – he seemed extraordinarily relaxed. Lillian Gurry, the

Courtauld librarian, said: 'Anthony slept marvellously during that period. Poor John Gaskin was the one who suffered. He had been terribly shocked by the whole thing. But Anthony was just determined to go on working.'[1] Sewell, who had nothing to lose, brought regular supplies of food, drink and sympathy.

Michael Kitson was another loyal ally, though even he was disappointed in Blunt:

There was an intellectual vanity about him . . . that he knew more than the rest of us. He never said that he was sorry for landing us all in the shit. That was the most unattractive aspect of his personality. It is quite fair to say that he showed contempt for ordinary people. John [Gaskin] once asked Anthony, 'Why did you do it?' Anthony replied: 'Cowboys and Indians . . . cowboys and Indians.'[2]

Kitson went on seeing Blunt, but many friends and colleagues were so appalled by what had happened that they could not bring themselves to visit him. A few were genuinely angered by his treachery but most had no interest in whether Anthony had, many years ago, been a Soviet agent; rather, it was the sense that they had themselves been betrayed. George Zarnecki, the Courtauld professor, said: 'I was very angry. He had deceived me . . . all those hours we had spent talking had meant nothing. Nothing at all. He had been playing a game with his friends. He even asked me if I would appear on television with him and with other friends so that he could prove that he had not been deserted.'[3]

Another lifelong friend, the art dealer Jim Byam Shaw, said: 'I am afraid that I am not prepared to talk about Anthony. I was a friend of his for forty years and knew nothing about his activities during the war. From the time that news of his disloyalty was published until his death I had no communication with him.'[4]

Timothy Clifford, the former Courtauld student, recalled: 'I felt terribly let down . . . I suppose a lot of us did. A lot of people dropped him. They were in an impossible position. I only saw him once or twice after 1979. I wanted to ask him about it but he didn't want to say anything. I remember that he was drinking whisky and shivering.'[5]

Blunt began writing his autobiography, but he soon gave up the project after writing 30,000 words. He told friends that it was hopeless because he had not kept his diaries; but they suspected that it was because he found the exercise too painful and depressing. Goronwy Rees, however, had no trouble justifying his role in the Cambridge spy controversy. Although he was terminally ill in the Charing Cross Hospital he insisted on dictating to Andrew Boyle what he called 'a last will and testament'; in effect, a revised summary of his book, *A Chapter of Accidents*. Apart from his family, Boyle was the only visitor Rees would talk to. After a scare that someone had tried to kill him he was given a police guard, which ended journalists' hopes of a deathbed scoop. Despite his illness he was as eloquent and credible as ever; he reserved most of his spleen for Blunt, who 'had cast a long shadow over my life'. He repeated and expanded many of the accusations that he had made to Boyle during the preparation of *The Climate of Treason*. He insisted that Burgess had had affairs with Blunt and Maclean; he also suggested that Philby had once been seduced by Burgess. Rees had hardened up his theory about Guy Liddell. He thought that Liddell had known much more about the Burgess–Blunt conspiracy than anyone had admitted. After Rees's death on Wednesday 12 December 1979, aged seventy, the *Observer* newspaper carried two prominently displayed articles by Andrew Boyle in which Rees was quoted extensively:

What I can and must say now is that, as a result of Guy's [Burgess] consuming inquisitiveness about matters that were strictly none of his business, he'd amassed considerable knowledge of the workings and methods of the Security Service as well as the names of and functions of its officials. His main source must have been Guy Liddell, with whom he and Anthony Blunt remained, of course, on very close terms. I was strongly convinced, though I had no direct proof, that Liddell was another of Burgess's predatory 'conquests'. I know that dead men cannot answer back, but there was to my mind something sinister about Liddell's protectiveness in regard to both Blunt and Burgess.

Rees then gave a lengthy account of Liddell's behaviour after Burgess's disappearance in 1951, though this was significantly different from the version in *A Chapter of Accidents*. There he had claimed that he had seen Liddell in London the day after Burgess and Maclean had vanished. Now he gave an entirely different story, claiming that there was a delay of ten days between first contacting Liddell by telephone and meeting him in London. He pressed home his attack, saying that Liddell had been transferred out of MI5 to the Atomic Energy Authority Establishment after the Americans had made it clear that they no longer trusted him. Rees said:

Liddell and Blunt were so close socially that I believe a single word would have been enough for a warning to be passed on to Burgess. In the last analysis Guy Liddell's close fairly lengthy association with Burgess and Blunt, which I've come to regard as sinister rather than careless, led to his partial undoing. He was probably let off too lightly.[6]

The *Observer* articles provoked normally taciturn ex-intelligence officers to emerge from anonymous retirement. In January 1980 Sir Dick White and William 'Jim' Skardon told the *Sunday Times* that Rees's allegations were 'grotesque and preposterous'. White said: 'I knew him very well. He was very industrious, a devoted servant of this country. Throughout the Second World War he hardly left his desk. To label him a Soviet spy is a grotesque charge. It is unforgivable that Guy Liddell's name should be blackened in this way.'[7]

Victor Rothschild, too, was outraged, though he blamed the press, hungry for new, shocking espionage revelations, for impugning Liddell's patriotism: 'G. M. Liddell . . . a brilliant sensitive and delightful man whose image, I am sorry to say, has become somewhat tarnished, with no justification, by what are nowadays called investigative reporters. If I am sure that anyone was loyal to his or her country, it was Guy Liddell.'[8]

Blunt read the *Observer* series with anger and astonishment. Even on his deathbed, Blunt told friends, Rees had lied to try and save what was left of his reputation. Despite advice from friends that he should say nothing, he wrote to *The Times* in January 1980, pointing out the discrepancy between the account in Rees's book and that given to Andrew Boyle. The novelist Rosamond Lehmann recalled that Blunt seemed determined not to allow Rees the final word:

Anthony rang me and said that he wanted to have lunch. I was very surprised to hear from him . . . I couldn't think why he wanted to see me. He drank an enormous amount of gin. Then he said: 'I simply think that you ought to know that Goronwy was up to his neck in it all. And I shall say so in the book that I'm writing.' I was dumbfounded. He said that Goronwy had helped him clear up

Burgess's flat in 1951 and that the truth usually sits on the lips of dying men, but not Goronwy's. Then he said that his book would not appear in his lifetime. That was all. He kissed me and left.[9]

Andrew Boyle had taken the credit for Blunt's exposure, but Fleet Street believed that there were more rich pickings for anyone who was prepared to dig. Surely, news editors speculated, there must be other Blunts waiting to be revealed? The fact that the government had insisted that there were no more self-confessed Soviet spies who had done private deals with MI5 convinced no one. In this search for spy scoops mistakes were made. For example, *The Times* suggested:

Did Anthony Blunt's Cambridge converts to Soviet-style communism include . . . Ludwig Wittgenstein? The question is prompted by the coincidence of the sale at Sotheby's yesterday of a postcard sent by Wittgenstein from Moscow on September 18, 1935 to the Cambridge philosopher G. E. Moore . . . Clearly Wittgenstein waxed enthusiastic about Marxism, because in July 1935 Keynes wrote to the Soviet ambassador, Ivan Maisky, saying Wittgenstein wanted to live 'more or less permanently' in Russia, and although not a Communist Party member, had strong sympathies with the way of life which he believed the new regime stood for.

The media set up teams to work on 'Blunt' – the shorthand for any story about spies. Journalists hoped to drag Victor Rothschild into the controversy but they gave up, unable to persuade him to say anything and knowing that his lawyers would act immediately if they tried to link his name suggestively to Blunt's. There were similar unsubstantiated rumours in Fleet Street about Peter Wilson, who had retired as chairman of Sotheby's and gone to live in the south of France only days before Blunt was exposed. Wilson, tall and urbane, Eton and Oxford-educated, worked for British Intelligence during the war and had once rented a house in Kensington from Tomas Harris. Although he had been married there were rumours that he was homosexual. All this made him eligible as a spy. Of course, no one dared print these allegations when Wilson was alive (he died, aged seventy-one, in June 1984) but he was certainly caused considerable distress by the knowledge that so many journalists were hunting his scalp. One friend, who stayed with him briefly in his French home, said that there was nothing to suggest that Wilson had been sucked into the Burgess spy ring, but she added:

> He told me that he had once been to bed with Guy Burgess. But it wasn't a proper affair . . . He had fallen out with Blunt some time before he left Sotheby's because Blunt had refused to authenticate a picture that Peter wanted to auction. Peter shared the house in France with a chauffeur, who was ex-army and very good-looking in a coarse sort of way. He was very muscular and tatooed and used to flaunt his looks. I don't know whether they were actually having an affair.[10]

The first genuine breakthrough came in November 1979 when Sir John Colville, the former private secretary to Winston Churchill, hinted to the *Sunday Times* that a former top civil servant, who had been 'one of the best brains in the Foreign Office', had passed information to Burgess. But, to the irritation of the newspaper, Colville refused to say more than that. A few weeks later Barrie Penrose, the ex-BBC reporter who had left the corporation after executives had tried to block his investigation into the Liberal leader Jeremy Thorpe, pursued the lead. Penrose called Colville and asked if he would name the man. He refused but he did provide some clues: the suspect had also worked at the Treasury and the Ministry of Supply. The stakes were high so Penrose decided it was worth investing time in research that would probably lead nowhere. For five days he plodded through the files at the Civil Service Library in the Mall, hoping to find a civil servant who had worked at the three ministries named by Colville. Then, on Friday 21 December, Penrose's laborious cross-checking threw up a name: John Cairncross. Penrose felt a surge of excitement, but he knew that the fact that Cairncross had worked at the Foreign Office, the Treasury and the Ministry of Supply proved nothing. Further checks, however, threw up details that lent weight to the theory. Cairncross had joined the Foreign Office in 1936, having come top of that year's entrance examination, and included among the list of the examiners was the name Anthony Blunt. It was now Friday lunchtime and Penrose had to make a quick decision if he was going to have a chance of 'turning the story round' in time for Sunday's newspaper. David Leitch, co-author of the classic book on Philby, dropped into the library just as Penrose was finishing his research. The two men agreed that they had to find and confront Cairncross as soon as possible. They could have waited until after Christmas but there was a risk, albeit a very slim one, that other journalists were working on the same story. They returned to the *Sunday Times*'s offices in Gray's Inn Road. Penrose called Colville: 'I said that I had the name. John Cairncross. Colville just said: "Oh dear." And from that I knew we had the right man.'

The next problem was to find Cairncross. The two reporters turned to *Who's Who* to see if Cairncross was included. He was not, but there was another Cairncross, Sir Alec, an economist who had had a string of high-powered government jobs and who had just retired as Master of St Peter's

College, Oxford. Penrose thought that it would be too dangerous to approach him since he might be tempted to warn his brother. So Penrose decided to backtrack. He flicked through the telephone directories for Lesmahagow in Scotland, where John had been born, and began calling the listed Cairncrosses. He was lucky. He found a relative who said that John had left Whitehall in 1952 and was now living in Rome. She had the address, but no phone number. It was now early evening and the last plane for Rome was leaving at 9 P.M. International directory inquiries gave Penrose Cairncross's number and, to ensure that he was at least there, a researcher rang Rome. A man answered and she hung up without saying anything.

At 1 A.M. on Saturday Penrose and Leitch were knocking on the door of Cairncross's fourth-floor flat in the Via Armando Spadini, in Rome's fashionable Parioli district. There was no reply. At 7.30 A.M. they were back and this time an elderly man, wearing sandals, grey flannels and an old cardigan, answered the door. Understandably Cairncross, sixty-six years old and separated from his wife Gabriella, was shaken by the allegation that he had been a Soviet spy but then he appeared to relax. He had just finished breakfast and his bed was still unmade. There were rows of books on France in the seventeenth and eighteenth centuries and many souvenirs from the time he had spent in South-east Asia. He said that he had provided Burgess with a '*tour d'horizon*' of Whitehall thinking on Hitler and of the appeasement posture being adopted by politicians and civil servants. It had been no surprise, he said, when MI5 had asked to interview him. They showed him the notes which had been found in Burgess's flat and which Colville had suggested had been written by him:

I had lived in terror ever since Burgess and Maclean fled to Russia – it put everything in an entirely new light. I knew that sooner or later they would get on to me. In the circumstances I was relieved that they believed what I told them, which was, in any case, the truth. In the end they suggested I resign, without a pension of course. We left England soon afterwards.[11]

Cairncross insisted that he had not *really* been a spy. True, he had been a communist at Trinity College but he had not known that Burgess was a Soviet agent and, when war broke out, he stopped meeting him. He talked about Blunt ('I knew him quite well at Cambridge and I knew he was working for intelligence during the war') and Maclean ('I never suspected he was still a communist, though I knew that he had been in the party as a young man, just as Anthony Blunt had'). He continued:

I never cared much for the Russian regime anyway. I left the Foreign Office and went into the Treasury at the beginning of the war because the FO appeasement line disgusted me. But there was nothing sinister about that . . . during the whole of my subsequent career as a civil servant I was never involved in SIS [MI6] or any other secret intelligence work.[12]

When other newspapers read the first edition of the *Sunday Times* early on Saturday evening they made frantic efforts to catch up. The Penrose–Leitch exclusive was headlined (perhaps over-dramatically), 'John Cairncross, ex-FO, confesses to *Sunday Times* – I was spy for Soviets', but did not, by agreement with Cairncross, disclose that he was living in Rome. The *Observer* dropped its first edition story, in which Andrew Boyle had said that there would be no more Blunt-related spy exclusives. The newspaper contacted Sir Alec but he would only confirm that his brother,

John, was living in Rome. Nonetheless by the final edition the *Observer* was running a new spy story claiming that Andrew Boyle had been responsible for the Cairncross scoop. That Sunday the Rome flat was besieged by reporters but Cairncross had already fled to escape them. Cairncross said later in a BBC radio interview that he had been 'fortunate not to be prosecuted' but he stuck firmly to his line that he had not known about Burgess's connections with Soviet Intelligence and that the material he had passed was, in any case, simply his personal assessment of the political mood in Whitehall. In London, Labour MPs were furious. Why, they asked, had Cairncross, yet another privileged Establishment figure, been allowed to slip away so quietly?

Blunt managed to survive the pressure of the Cairncross episode. Newspapers monitored his non-movements with renewed interest, discovering, for example, that he was due to lead a party of art-loving holidaymakers on a tour of Naples in spring 1980. Then, shortly after five o'clock on the morning of Tuesday 12 February, came disaster. Portsea Hall's caretaker, William Druce, heard a 'terrible thud' and, when he went out to investigate, found John Gaskin sprawled out on the iron fire-escape at the back of the building. Gaskin had clearly fallen over the three-foot-high balcony outside the sixth floor flat he shared with Blunt yet, miraculously, had not been killed. He gasped: 'I was looking for a breath of fresh air.' He was taken to St Mary's Hospital, Paddington, and operated on for internal injuries. That day Blunt was questioned by police, who immediately concluded that there were 'no suspicious circumstances'. Fleet Street, of course, did not believe this explanation. How could a man accidentally fall over a balcony in the middle of the night? Friends, however, who saw Gaskin in hospital, insisted that Blunt had been asleep when it had happened. Lillian Gurry said: 'He felt ill in the middle of the night and had got up to get some brandy. But he drank whisky instead and felt worse. So he went outside to get some air and went over the balcony. There is no truth at all in the suggestion that he had a fight with Anthony.'[13]

When Gaskin was discharged from hospital he went to his sister's to convalesce, leaving Blunt alone and, according to Michael Kitson, missing him desperately. That spring Blunt hesitantly ventured outside the flat. Brian Sewell escorted him to a local restaurant where, to Blunt's relief, he was given a warm welcome. In the absence of any fresh developments newspapers began to lose interest and, apart from the occasional story in the gossip columns (saying, for example, that Blunt had been booed when he visited a local cinema), he was ignored for months. He was again a regular visitor at the Courtauld where his former colleagues scrupulously avoided asking him about the controversy, though they all hoped that he would one day talk about it. He did not. Peter Lasko recalled: 'When he appeared he didn't seem at all put out by what had happened. He didn't refer to it. Not a word. It was quite extraordinary. I don't think he suffered very much really, not compared to people who were carted off to jail for twenty years.'[14]

In the summer there was a flurry of publicity when the academics of the British Academy squabbled over whether Blunt should be stripped of his fellowship. The Oxford historian A. J. P. Taylor told *The Times* on 24 June that he would have to resign from the academy if Blunt was forced out: 'I couldn't be a fellow of an academy which uses the late Senator McCarthy as its patron saint. It's not the duty of the academy to probe into the behaviour of fellows, except on grounds of scholarship.' At the academy's annual general meeting on 3 July there were impassioned speeches from both camps; those who demanded that Blunt should be told to resign and those, like Taylor, who argued that the academy was not a moral arbiter and that the only criterion for membership was academic distinction. The Taylor argument carried the day but that was not the end of the affair. The anti-Blunt faction threatened to resign *en masse*. Then, to the relief of the president Sir Kenneth Dover, Blunt said that it would be in everyone's interests if he left the academy. Dover said: 'Professor Blunt believes, and I think he is probably right, that if he resigns then a number of other people who are uncomfortable will not resign. Less damage will be done to the academy than by staying.'

A. J. P. Taylor was disgusted. He later wrote:

In my opinion the president should have told Blunt that the annual general meeting had confirmed his membership and that there was no reason for him to resign. At any rate it was clear to me that I could not remain a Fellow of a body which had hounded Blunt into resignation for reasons which had nothing to do with academic merit. So I resigned in my turn.[15]

At his bungalow home in Cygnet, just outside Hobart, Tasmania, Peter Wright had listened in horror to BBC World Service reports of Mrs Thatcher's statement in the Commons in November 1979. What point was there in offering a traitor immunity if you then named him publicly? Thatcher, argued Wright, had wrecked any hopes of progress in the Blunt inquiry and had probably jeopardized future operations. He said: 'I think exposing Blunt was disastrous. He should never have been blown and Thatcher committed a major crime by doing that.'[16] Wright was now more determined than ever to find a way to publicize his cause. He could not go to the press himself – that was a trump card he would play only if everything else failed – so he needed to find a capable journalist whom he could trust and who shared his world-view. There was one obvious candidate: Chapman Pincher, the former *Daily Express* star, by then living in squirarchical retirement in the Berkshire countryside. Pincher had been a pioneer in investigative journalism in the 1950s and 1960s, before anyone had coined that phrase to describe trouble-making reporters. Pincher had started life as a scientist and, indeed, wrote a number of books on such esoteric topics as the breeding of farm animals. But his passion was winkling out defence and intelligence secrets from Whitehall. However, he was certainly not left-wing. He was a radical conservative who firmly believed in the communist menace. In *Who's Who* he listed as his hobbies: 'Fishing, shooting, country life; ferreting in Whitehall and bolting politicians.'

Like any good reporter, Pincher would not discuss his sources, but the authors established that he was in touch with Wright in 1980. (Wright confirmed this in 1986.) Wright agreed to help Pincher with the preparation of Pincher's book, which would, so the two men hoped, prove beyond doubt that the Soviets had allowed Blunt to leave MI5 because they had had another, more valuable source already in place – Roger Hollis. In March 1981 Pincher's book, entitled *Their Trade is Treachery*, was published. It outlined the case against Hollis, the former director-general of MI5, and was an immediate, best-selling sensation. Pincher was happy to talk about Hollis but he refused to name other Soviet agents; he said that he had a 'list of twelve' but said that he could not identify them for legal reasons.

That spring, as the country was once again swept by spy-fever, a new espionage pundit emerged to compete with Pincher. His real name was Rupert Allason but he wrote under the pen name Nigel West. He was twenty-nine years old, the son of Lieutenant-Colonel James Allason, the wealthy former Tory MP for Hemel Hempstead, and liked to describe himself as a military historian rather than as a journalist. Allason/West had joined the BBC after reading English at London University. He worked on several espionage documentaries before being offered a contract to write a book on MI5. He was a little chubby, looked younger than his twenty-nine years and exuded enthusiasm. He hated newspapers using his real name or mentioning that he was a volunteer policeman, though he did not mind their saying that he had been the Tory candidate for Kettering in the 1979 election and that he would be contesting Battersea, south London, in the next election. He burst on to the national newspaper scene soon after the publication of Pincher's book, when he offered *The Times* his own, exclusive material on Blunt. West drove a Porsche, equipped with a radio telephone, and worked from his home in the countryside near Newbury, Berkshire, where he had built up a computer-based index on intelligence affairs in a burglar-proof office in the grounds of his house.

When West's book, *MI5, British Security Service Operations, 1909–1945*, was published by The Bodley Head in October 1981, it was obvious that he had been given assistance from MI5 officers. It was written in a low-key, impersonal style, but it was crammed with details that made it seem, at times, like an official history written by some diligent but apolitical member of the service. West later admitted that he had been surprised by the cooperation he received from former officers. He thought that he had just been asking the right questions at the right time:

I think some MI5 officers felt that so many disclosures had been made about MI5 that they were now free to put the record straight. I think they felt that not enough credit had been given to their service in books that had so far been published. I deliberately did not go in for phrases like 'senior intelligence sources told me', I did not quote anyone and I didn't try and expose anyone. That is not my style.[17]

West did not, for example, mention that he had had a series of meetings in 1981 with Anthony Blunt; whereas a journalist would have exploited those interviews as one of the book's main selling points, West absorbed Blunt's contribution without giving any hint that he had met him. There were suggestions from rival spy pundits that West was a creature of the Young Turks, but West, in fact, had never backed the theory that Hollis had been a Soviet agent, even though some members of the group did help with the MI5 book. West had no contact with Peter Wright until 1982, after the book had appeared and while he was preparing his follow-up, a history of MI5 from 1945 to 1972. West was always happy to chat to reporters. On Thursday 29 November Simon Freeman telephoned him. Were there, asked Freeman, any hidden leads in the book that other reporters might have missed? Yes, he said, there were. The clue was contained in a paragraph on page 334, in which he described how in 1964 Straight had given MI5 the names of two men who might have been Soviet spies. The first, not named in the book, was Alister Watson, the defence scientist. West had then written: 'The second, another Cambridge CPGB member who had "gone underground", admitted having once been a Soviet agent but assured MI5 that he had long since abandoned Marxism. He had held a sensitive post in Military Intelligence but had long since ceased to have access to secrets.'

How could these unsourced, vague allegations help to identify the 'new' spy? West suggested that Michael Straight might be able to help. Freeman then telephoned Straight at home in Washington and read out the paragraph. Did Straight have any idea what West was driving at? There was a pause. Since March that year, when he had talked publicly for the first time about his role in the Cambridge spy ring, Straight had been inundated with calls from the media but had always refused to discuss other, possible spies. But now, for no obvious reason, he decided to help. The clue, he said, was the repetition of the word 'long', and he suggested contacting a man called Leo Long, one of the two men whom he had told MI5 in 1964 might have been recruited by Blunt. To Freeman's surprise the London telephone directory had an entry for Leo Long. Freeman telephoned and said to Long: 'I would like to talk to you about the war and about your relationship with Anthony Blunt.'

There was silence. Freeman was bluffing. There was no evidence against Long and if he had decided to put the phone down, that would have been the end of the matter. Freeman decided to force the issue. 'I would like to see you tonight.' Long replied: 'No . . . not tonight . . . my wife is ill.' It was agreed they would meet the following morning.

The next day Freeman and a *Sunday Times* photographer, Duncan Baxter, met at 8 A.M. outside Long's terraced home in north London. A tall, balding, bespectacled man wearing a sweater and an old pair of trousers answered the door. He was neither friendly nor hostile as he shepherded Freeman into a room at the back of the house.

Immediately he admitted that, yes, he had 'helped' Anthony Blunt during the war:

Blunt took an interest in me from time to time. He indicated to me that it would be as well if I kept my head down. That is all there was to it. I don't agree with all this stuff about long-term recruitment of agents. I left Cambridge to spend a year in Frankfurt and when I came back to England in 1939 I was conscripted into the army. It was an accident that I ended up in intelligence work during the war.

He talked for several hours about the 1930s, about the threat posed by fascism and the complacency of the British Establishment. He made excuses and minimized his importance to the Soviets, but he was disarmingly frank and it was an undeniably brave performance. He agreed to allow Baxter into the house to take a portrait but at that point announced that his life would now be ruined. He would have no choice, he said, but to commit suicide. Freeman said that he was being melodramatic. The *Sunday Times* story would be accurate and factual; indeed, it would emphasize the historical background that had driven Long to becoming a spy. Long seemed reassured and went upstairs to change into a suit. As the minutes ticked by Freeman and Baxter had a dreadful thought; perhaps Long had killed himself? Then he came back. He posed for the photograph and agreed to come into the *Sunday Times* the next day to check the final version of the story before the paper's presses started to roll.

Long and his wife Vera spent Saturday afternoon at the *Sunday Times*. They then checked into the Waldorf Hotel nearby, courtesy of the newspaper, which had not wanted rival Sunday newspapers to be able to contact him after the first edition of the *Sunday Times* had appeared. The newspaper feared, too, that Long, already under considerable strain, might have found it intolerable if his home had been surrounded by reporters; far better to let him have a good rest before meeting the media on Sunday at a press conference at the Inn on the Park Hotel on Park Lane. Here Long once again acquitted himself with dignity. He said that he had only told Vera about his wartime spying that Friday, which gave the story a poignant twist that was seized on by the tabloid press. Long said: 'When I was aware that this story would come out I decided to end it all rather than face it. The only thing that persuaded me not to was that I could not leave my wife alone. I could not leave her to face the music.' He said that while he had not formally been offered immunity from prosecution by MI5 it had been obvious that there was no question of being charged with a criminal offence. He spoke of his 'deep regret and remorse':

I feel bloody awful. I have lived with it for so long. It's like a terribly aching toothache when you know you must go to the dentist. When you finally go it's like pulling out a tooth without an anaesthetic and leaving a gaping hole in your mouth. What is worse, toothache, or the cure? I still feel shattered although I do have a feeling of relief, I suppose, because at last I have been able to tell my wife.

Reaction was mixed. Some people felt sorry for Long and accused the *Sunday Times* of wrecking a man's life for the sake of a story that was irrelevant to contemporary Britain. Chapman Pincher claimed that he had known Long's name but had not used it for 'legal reasons'. Labour MPs accused the government of a cover-up and demanded an explanation from Mrs Thatcher. On 9 November she told the Commons that there was a risk that the press (and MPs) would go too far in their efforts to find more accomplices of Messrs Burgess, Philby, Maclean and Blunt. She said:

I believe we have to be very careful to avoid the risk of creating a climate of guilt by association. The contacts of those who are known to have acted as agents of the Russian Intelligence service have been extensively and exhaustively investigated and many people have been interviewed over the years . . . the fact that somebody

has been the subject of investigation or has been interviewed does not necessarily or even generally mean that
he has been positively suspected . . . Many people have
been investigated simply in order to eliminate them from
the inquiry. Others have been interviewed, not because
they themselves were suspected but for any information
they might be able to give about those who were.[18]

Once again, despite Thatcher's entreaty, Blunt was back
in the news. The following Sunday, 8 November, the
Sunday Times ran a front-page report headlined, 'Blunt's
secret visit to Philby in Beirut'. The story explained how
Blunt had met Philby in Beirut in 1961 and that there was
evidence, which was not conclusive, that there was a second
rendezvous, perhaps not in Beirut, shortly before Philby's
disappearance in January 1963. Blunt wrote to the newspaper on 22 November: 'My meeting with Philby was
entirely due to chance and occurred at a party at the British
embassy and we did not discuss the possibility of his going
to Russia. I should like further to state that I did not meet
Philby again in Beirut or anywhere else.' This denial was
puzzling since he had, through his intermediary Brian
Sewell, confirmed that the published story was accurate.
It now appeared that he had been laying a false trail;
cooperating because he wanted to draw attention away
from his dear friend, Peter Montgomery, whom the *Sunday
Times* was investigating. (Blunt also failed to mention that
in the 1970s he had sent a picture to Philby in Moscow via
the Soviet embassy in London.) Brian Sewell wrote to the
newspaper:

Anthony is convinced that the Montgomery story will be
made to seem discreditable. It is characteristic of him
that he would use that word, and care deeply about it, in
the matter of a personal relationship, while not caring at

all for what others might conceive as discreditable in a larger sense. Unlike ordinary mortals whose levels of response are either single or interwoven, Anthony has an ice-cold strand to his nature that is separate from his functions as an art historian and an affectionate and lively human being. His affairs are in order, his work as an art historian largely complete, he has discarded the promised book on his espionage role, and there is no reason why he should not make himself comfortable with a bottle of whisky and an overdose. I know how rationally he can balance the quality of life against the effort of living it.[19]

By now the public (and consequently the press) had had a surfeit of spy scandals. Ex-MI5 men like Arthur Martin and Peter Wright continued to hope that there would be new revelations that might, once and for all, solve the questions they had been puzzling over for so many years. Martin even asked Freeman and Penrose if they could arrange a 'chance' meeting between Blunt and himself to see if he could solve the unanswered riddles that he had puzzled over for so many years. There were bizarre, unpublished footnotes, such as the warning to the *Sunday Times* from a London solicitor that his client suspected that the newspaper intended to libel his client by alleging that he had been Michael Straight's Soviet controller in Washington. The newspaper assured the solicitor that they had never heard of his aggrieved client. But the incident was symptomatic of the unease felt by anyone who had been to Cambridge during the 1930s or who had been a communist or who had known Burgess, Philby, Maclean, Blunt.

While reporters were fielding complaints from people who feared that they might be libelled, Nigel West was researching his second book on MI5, having proved to his sources that he was trustworthy and discreet. They had given him the name of Long as a test – to see if he could successfully guide the press to Long. He had passed this examination with distinction. Long had been exposed and, to the delight of the retired intelligence officers, had told the *Sunday Times* more than he had ever confessed to MI5. The stakes were now increased. West was given detailed briefings on other classified matters – like the investigation against Graham Mitchell, the former deputy director of MI5 – which were designed to defend the battered reputation of MI5 and, paradoxically, also lead to a reorganization of British Intelligence. The authorities were not amused by the resulting book and began legal proceedings against West to prevent publication. In November 1982, after the *Sunday Times* approached some of West's sources, the Treasury solicitor wrote to the newspaper:

It is being emphasized again to all retired members of the Security Services that they are not at liberty to give any information whatsoever to the press or to authors wishing to write about security matters. It is also being pointed out to them that, if they do so, they may infringe section 2 of the Official Secrets Act of 1911 . . . I must also draw your attention to the fact that it is not only those who provide official information to unauthorized persons who may commit offences but also those who solicit or endeavour to persuade other persons to do so.[20]

On 6 March 1983 came news that Donald Maclean had died in Moscow, aged sixty-nine. The bulging library clippings on the Cambridge spies were once again recycled; there were long features and obituaries, analysing yet again the reasons for and the significance of the whole infamous affair. He died a convinced Marxist who had rebuilt his life by becoming a respected Moscow analyst of British affairs. Two weeks later his ashes were brought back to England by his son Fergus, and buried by torchlight alongside his parents in a churchyard in Penn, Buckinghamshire.

A few days later Anthony Blunt, too, was dead.

Epilogue

On the morning of Saturday 26 March, Blunt got up from the breakfast table at Portsea Hall and went into the study to look up a telephone number. Gaskin heard him fall and rushed into the study, to find Anthony, still wearing his pyjamas and dressing gown, lying face down on the floor. Panic-stricken, he called the porter in the front hall. Blunt's doctor, Adrian Whitehouse, was alerted. When the ambulance crew from the nearby Marylebone station arrived a few minutes later they realized there was nothing they could do. Blunt had died immediately of a massive heart attack. He was seventy-five. Two hours later, at 12.20 P.M., his body, covered by thick black linen, was wheeled out of the flats. A pack of pressmen looked on as it was placed in the back of an old white transit van which was then driven away at an undignified speed.

Throughout Fleet Street newspapers hurriedly prepared news stories. Wilfrid patiently dealt with dozens of calls to his home in the Watts Art Gallery, near Guildford, where he was curator. He refused to criticize his younger brother:

> I saw him on the Wednesday. He seemed perfectly all right. He never showed the stress which he must have been feeling. The family remained loyal to the Anthony we had always known. My brother's art pupils always admired him enormously. I spoke to him on the tele-

phone on Friday night and he seemed in very good form. I have always been totally devoted to him. He had made a remarkable recovery, you know. He had tremendous interests in art history and was working very hard. He had just finished a book on Roman Baroque churches and had been writing a book about the artist, Pietro da Cortona.[1]

Christopher Blunt, now a retired banker, said:

It is very difficult to know what to say at a time like this. I understand that it was a very quick and sudden death. I am very thankful for that. The events of recent years saddened us all but we are a very close family. I think my brother was misguided in doing what he did but I believe that he was absolutely sincere.[2]

Gaskin left the flat refusing to say anything. It was surprisingly difficult that morning to find anyone willing to deliver the instant condemnation of Blunt that the newspapers were expecting. Naturally, Brian Sewell was as accessible and as loyal as always. He said that he had seen Blunt that Friday and that he seemed to be in 'top form':

Anthony had thrown off a cold and seemed better than for many months. He had a brain which was of the highest calibre. Yet he also had extraordinary sensibility. He had a cataract operation shortly before the storm broke in 1979 and he had had a bout of cancer. But since then his health had held up well. Privately he found the publicity shattering but publicly he would not show anything. I think that he regretted that something which had started forty-four years earlier as a well-intentioned intellectual and emotional exercise had, within ten years, turned so sour. He worked just as hard after it all happened. He was in absolutely marvellous form, better than for many months. He had always been a glutton for work and sleep and those two things helped him survive. If he was depressed he would take to his bed for twelve hours and wake up completely refreshed. He travelled abroad a great deal but never told anyone about his plans. It is a great tragedy.[3]

Arthur Martin was at his cottage in the Cotswolds when he heard the news. One suspected that he felt cheated that Blunt had died before they had had one last sparring session: 'I am sorry for him. He had a ghastly life. I liked the man but I cannot excuse what he did though I dimly understand his motives. I have never felt indignation. I never despised him. I always had time for him. I have always thought . . . there but for the grace of God . . .'[4]

Other ageing spy-catchers from MI5 and MI6 were just as reluctant to provide the facile quotes which the headline writers wanted. In Australia even Peter Wright, embittered and obsessed, refused to condemn Blunt. He was just sorry that MI5 would never have the chance now to prise Blunt's remaining secrets from him.

Blunt would probably have been moved – though he would never have shown such a trite emotion – by the loyalty of friends and colleagues. In New York the art historian Sir John Pope-Hennessy, Professor of Fine Arts at New York University, said:

I am so sorry, a very remarkable man. He will be remembered, I hope, not only for his scholarship but for the scholarly work he sponsored, even financed and in which he was happy to let others take the credit. His achievements were wide and his work for the royal art collections will survive all the unpleasantness. He will be remembered in particular for his work on Poussin. I hope it is not as Shakespeare once said . . . 'the evil that men do lives after them,/The good is oft interred with their bones'.[5]

Sir Ellis Waterhouse, who had grown apart from Blunt, was obviously distressed; perhaps because the most vivid memories that he had of his old friend were so painful. He could only talk vaguely about Blunt's uncertain health and his 'marvellous library' and 'wonderful drawings'.[6]

Professor James Joll, the history professor who had sheltered Blunt for four days in 1979, said:

The revelations about him came as a great shock to me but I gave him sanctuary as a colleague whom I liked and trusted and as a fellow human being. He told me then that he bitterly regretted his idealism in the 1930s but I never went into detail with him. Maybe as a historian I should have done. He realized that his life was shattered and set out to pick up the pieces. He thought about writing an autobiography and wanted to set the record straight and began work. But every difficulty was put in his way. He was denied access to material. He realized, too, that it would be a best-seller and this worried him. He did not want to be accused of benefiting from the book and from what he had done.[7]

In Washington Michael Straight, who, since spring 1981, had made a new career by baring his soul in a welter of media interviews, justifying his own actions and theorizing about the nature of treachery, was ready with more complex analysis:

The mystery is why should this man of such great intellectual stature allow his life to be distorted by a young man like Guy Burgess, who was his inferior in all ways? Why would a man who would have been remembered as a remarkable art historian permit himself to be captured by Burgess, who was a vagabond, a gypsy and an adventurer? Blunt was a discreet homosexual whereas Burgess was a flamboyant, amoral and rootless character. How did he manage to rope and lasso Blunt? That remains the essential mystery.[8]

The Sunday newspapers ran thousands of words on his death. The *Sunday Telegraph*'s front-page story was headlined, 'Death of a Lonely Spy', and the *Observer*'s, 'Fourth Man Blunt Dies in Disgrace'. On Monday there was a fresh spate of allegations about the damage that Blunt had caused. The *Daily Telegraph* claimed that the 'traitor Blunt had put agents' lives at risk'. *The Times* was in a more reflective mood; it carried a leader article saying that 'this was not the moment to dance on the graves' of Maclean and Blunt who died 'sad, disillusioned men, plagued with ill-health'. In a sense, said *The Times*, they had been destroyed by the Nazi–Soviet pact of 1939, the moment when the young idealists of the British Communist Party were confronted with the true nature of Stalin's Russia. It took self-destructive cynicism or self-delusion to continue to believe in the cause after that. But there were lessons for the young in contemporary Britain. There was nothing wrong with fighting for a better world; in fact, that was the duty of the young. But the laudable anger of the Blunts and Macleans had become corrupted. It was not just that they had embraced the Soviet model; they had worked for the Kremlin, even if that meant endangering the interests of their own country. It was, said *The Times*, a 'chilling betrayal'. *The Times* concluded:

The lesson of the lives of Maclean and Blunt is not 'my country, right or wrong'. It is to illuminate in the starkest colours the frontier between the impulse to improve one's society through the mechanism of radical change legitimately and democratically pursued, and the washing of one's hands, the impermissible abandonment of hope about its future that can lead men into the service of their country's enemies, real or potential. To abandon Britain intellectually, spiritually and emotionally, would be wrong for us as it was for Stalin's English disciples.

Anthony Blunt was cremated on Wednesday 30 March 1983, at the Putney Vale Crematorium in west London. It was a cold, dark day, somehow in keeping with the occasion. The service was conducted by the Reverend Thaddeus Birchard, vicar of the same St John's church where the late Stanley Blunt had been based; a fact that the Reverend Birchard gratefully included in the sermon he was struggling to make. What, after all, could he, a humble vicar, say about a man who had betrayed his country and perhaps sent British agents to their death? There were few mourners. On the crematorium gates uniformed police stood guard to keep the press and television cameras at a respectable distance. 'No one amongst us does not merit love and consideration,' said the vicar. 'God's and ours. All have aimed and sinned and fallen short of God.' Eleven wreaths were laid, mostly without names. Outside, as the mourners made their way to their cars, the media again wanted explanations. Christopher Blunt, aged seventy-eight, said: 'He deeply regretted the whole episode. But he had no remorse because he believed that he had acted rightly. He was convinced that he had done the right thing at the time. He realized that it was wrong afterwards. He was very brave because he did have hell.' Wilfrid Blunt, half irritated, half amused by the hopelessly ignorant reporters, issued a few bland remarks that he knew would satisfy them. He had said it all before but newspapers had insatiable appetites for quotes, even ones that said nothing new. 'I was staggered you know, amazed. I thought I knew my brother well. But I did not have the slightest idea about all this. He never explained . . . you can imagine the difficulty and the tragedy.'

It was not much of an epitaph.

POSTSCRIPT TO THE
PAPERBACK EDITION

On a fine day in July, Christopher Blunt climbed Martin-sell, a hill near Marlborough which they had all loved, and scattered Anthony's ashes in 'a final act of brotherly affection'.[1] But Christopher and Wilfrid knew that it would not end there. Wilfrid wrote: 'I fear it will be many years before Anthony is allowed to rest in peace. Through probably there is little, other than wild surmise, that can be added until the release of State papers in thirty years' time, biographies are already on the stocks and at least two television documentaries are being prepared. All involved hasten to reassure the family, as they beg for interviews and titbits, that their approach will, of course, be completely free from muckraking. But will it be? In my opinion, all that can sensibly be written at this stage is a full and scholarly assessment of Anthony's contribution as an art historian – nothing more. However, there seems to be no eagerness to produce such a work; the public does not want to know about Poussin . . . it wants scandal and sex.'

It was self-evident that people like us would not have been interested in writing a biography of Blunt, The Art Historian, had he not also been Blunt, The Soviet Spy, and it would have been absurd to pretend otherwise. Our first approaches to Wilfrid and Christopher were, politely but firmly, rejected. The most they would do, they said, was to check our final manuscript for inaccuracies. We pressed, knowing that Wilfrid, in particular, would be able to offer unique memories and perspectives. We were trying to produce a fair, balanced book; was it not more sensible for them to help us? Finally, and a little reluctantly one suspected, Wilfrid (and Christopher) relented and agreed to talk to us. We spent a day with Wilfrid at the Watts Gallery, in the village of Compton, just outside Guildford in Surrey, where he was curator, responsible for looking after the collected works of the nineteenth-century English painter George Frederick Watts. This job was an old-fashioned sinecure which, as he readily acknowledged, was all that someone like him, an elderly man with more complaints than he cared to remember, was good for. But his mind was as sharp as ever. He spent his days in his dark, cluttered study, working on his autobiography (sadly, he only managed to complete two volumes before his death), answering letters and fending off journalists and authors. He had only agreed to see us out of curiosity and mischief – to see for himself how ill-informed we were – but when he realized that we were trying, however inadequately, to discover the truth about Anthony, he began to take the interview seriously. But it was clear that, like us, he was still puzzling over the central question: why had Anthony done it?

He was not content, however, to leave it to outsiders like us to try and solve this problem. He decided to write a postscript, entitled 'My Brother Anthony', for the second volume of his autobiography. He agonized over this chapter, showing successive rough drafts to Anthony, testing his brother's reaction, checking facts, perhaps hoping for a sign, a nod or a smile, that he had stumbled upon the answer. The care with which it was written is evident from the tone and style. Unlike Wilfrid's usual prose, all whimsy and anecdote, this is cautious, deliberate, like a piece of neutral reporting. Perhaps he was too close to his subject, as he conceded, though, against that, he was talking about Anthony, a piece of flesh and blood, not some abstract symbol of treachery or moral bankruptcy: 'I make absolutely no attempt to condone treachery, only to try to *understand* and very probably I am the worst person to attempt this because, inevitably, I am *parti pris*. But at least I was around at the time. For forty years Anthony had carried his dreadful secret ever with him, yet no member of the family had the faintest inkling that anything serious was amiss . . . Whatever he did, and however much I may deplore what he did, I remain devoted and deeply grateful to the Anthony whom I knew for more than seventy years. That other Anthony I never knew and may never understand . . . I very much regret that he did not leave behind, to two brothers whom he knew he could implicitly trust, a confidential letter which would have helped us to understand.'

The essay was littered with insights and low-key revelations. For example, there was evidence of Blunt's deep affection for Burgess when he pleaded with Wilfrid not to describe Guy as 'vile'. There was this sentence, which said much about Blunt's extraordinary ability to compartmentalize his life: 'Anthony, as is now public knowledge, had been for many years a practising homosexual: something that I did not know for certain, though of course I could have guessed it, until some time after the war, when we exchanged confidences at Windsor Castle.'

There was this gem, which the more enterprising newspapers might well have turned into a front-page exclusive (BLUNT FEARS ASSASSIN'S BULLET) during the spy hysteria which followed Thatcher's statement in 1979: 'When I went to see him in London, where he was virtually a prisoner, I would find him perfectly ready to talk on non-controversial subjects and showing no outward sign of his inner tensions. His study had a balcony that overlooked a derelict area with, about a hundred yards away, a number of big blocks of flats. As I had done so often in the past, I was about to step outside; but he put his hand on my arm and, without a word, drew me away from the French windows. It was only then that I realized that he feared the possibility of an assassination attempt.'

It was more likely, one has to say, that Blunt was merely concerned about photographers stationed opposite his flat. But this nugget would have caused more legitimate excitement in Fleet Street (BLUNT: I KILLED BRITISH AGENTS). Wilfrid again: 'Did his treachery lead, as some people allege, to the death of British soldiers or agents? Anthony sadly admitted to a friend that it *might* have been responsible for "some – not many".'

There was evidence of the pleasure which Blunt derived from the deception of spying. It was both a challenge and a game, rather like the 'artistic sleuthing' required to establish the provenance of a painting. He must, thought Wilfrid, have 'derived a certain intellectual satisfaction' from having established the 'perfect cover-up' as servant of the Royal Family. He was proud of his ability to play these various parts and once told Wilfrid, with childish delight: 'You must admit that I'm a very good actor.' This did not make Anthony wicked; Wilfrid thought it showed that he just lacked common sense, that he had no idea how ordinary folk would be appalled by 'the game' which he had played. He had always thrived on pressure. After the disaster of Thatcher's statement he said that he slept better and ate (and drank) more than ever. This did not mean that he was unaffected; he was obsessive about press reports about him and constantly wanted to reply to the more outrageous allegations. Family and friends usually managed to dissuade him, arguing that whatever he said would only make matters worse. But Blunt could not accept this. He fumed and sulked, apparently unable to take in the obvious point – he had no credit left; newspapers could say what they liked about him.

True, he had never been a political animal but, Wilfrid contested, his conversion to Marxism and his decision to work for the Soviets must have been based on more than love of Guy, of intrigue and role-playing. Wilfrid argued that Anthony had been genuinely concerned about the threat of fascism in the 1930s and that he calculated that he must do something to prevent a fascist takeover of Britain and Western Europe. He probably envisaged, Wilfrid thought, 'an independent, undominated Britain acting in partnership with Russia'. Of course, there must have been other, less noble motives. Perhaps he resented, subconsciously, living in a society which hounded homosexuals. Wilfrid was sure, however, that Anthony had been a kinder human being than anyone was now willing to believe. He was certainly not as arrogant or as cold as his enemies alleged: 'He has been accused by many people of arrogance but I believe that to make such a charge is to wholly misunderstand his nature . . . I cannot sufficiently stress his modesty, and his reluctance ever to push himself forward or use his distinguished position to his own advantage; but he was always ready to use it to help others, and then nothing was too much trouble. When the big Van Gogh exhibition was held at the Tate some years ago, a friend of his asked him whether he had seen it yet. "Yes," Anthony replied, "after waiting in the queue for an hour." The friend was amazed: "I went past the queue to the entrance and said, 'I am a friend of Sir Anthony Blunt' and they let me straight in!" '

Nor, insisted Wilfrid, was he a snob about his connections with Buckingham Palace although he did have a 'great personal regard for the Queen Mother'. He was 'a reluctant courtier' and always tried to wriggle out of royal occasions. He could make wry, self-denigrating jokes about his own homosexuality: 'I was dining with him one evening at the Courtauld, and he had just produced a delicious steak for me (he was a very competent cook). I noticed that he himself ate very little. "I imagine you had a good lunch," I said. "Where were you?" "At the Palace." Then came a throw-away line that surely nobody could have resisted: "It was rather a strain; I was put between two Queens."'

He was brusquely honest and was never able to disguise his impatience of amateurism. He despised people who wasted their talent, openly disapproving of his Marlborough friend, John Betjeman, the great popular poet, for squandering his potential as a scholar to write inconsequential verse. His manner could be off-putting. One Courtauld student talked enthusiastically about him being 'glamour personified', a man of 'effortless superiority' who had, and knew he had, charm and intellectual distinction. And while he wanted and sought academic acclaim he was so self-contained that there was always a part of him which could not be reached. After 1979 he wondered whether he should commit suicide – and decided against it since he wanted to finish two books which he was working on. By 1983 he had completed both books. Did he decide that his life was over and that to continue served no useful purpose? Wilfrid did not know for sure: 'There was no suggestion that anything other than natural causes was responsible for his death. It is, however, possible to die (and many Orientals do) by sheer will-power. I sometimes wonder whether Anthony, accepting that his life's work as an art historian was at an end, may not simply have elected to stop living.'

Wilfrid did not claim to have found a satisfactory *reason*. (In one aside he wrote: 'A split personality? Only a psychiatrist can hazard a guess.') Predictably, and understandably, he had been more charitable than us but, in essence, he had supported our view of Anthony: a jumble of conflicting impulses, an actor who changed characters effortlessly, a man who both hated and admired the Establishment. After he had read *Conspiracy of Silence*, and shortly before he died in January 1987, Wilfrid wrote to us. He thought that we were wrong about Blunt's snobbery – 'I know that many people say it but I think it derives from jealousy' – but he added: 'I think you have done a remarkable job, though naturally some of the book made painful reading.'[2]

John Hilton, meanwhile, was less pleased with our efforts. He protested that we had 'distorted and misattributed' what he had told us: 'Amid the whole phantasmagoria, willing suspension of disbelief is very necessary. I find it particularly hard to achieve when I am given an impression of an endless file of trades- and services-people streaming through the Courtauld in a cloud of public urine. Some there may well have been; but the picture I seem to be being given of an innumerable multitude does not appear to be substantiated by anything more than vague gossip or malicious innuendo.'[3]

Yes, we conceded, we had made small errors and they would be corrected. But we did not accept his main criticism: that we had been fundamentally, and culpably, wrong about Blunt. Of course, we said, Hilton had been shocked by the Blunt whom we described; like many friends, who thought they were close to him, he had only known one Blunt, not the whole man. Generously, Hilton replied that perhaps he had merely tried to convince himself that it could not be true: 'I was of course rather desperately trying to preserve something of the image of the debonair, fastidious Anthony that I thought I knew. As it turned out none of us knew him.'[4]

We were also criticized for including Brian Sewell's thesis that Andrew Gow, the Cambridge classics don, had been Blunt's 'controller'. In fact, we had not endorsed this theory; we had made it clear that there was no corroborative evidence (apart from Peter Wright's remark that Blunt often said he would 'check with Andrew') and that everyone who knew Gow thought the idea preposterous. But even this was too much. Dr Christopher Andrew, a Cambridge historian who was widely respected for his work on the intelligence world, said that Gow had been vitriolic about 'our advanced undergraduate thinkers' who had been so mesmerized by communism in the 1930s. Andrew wrote: 'When *The Times* claimed to unmask Donald Beves of King's as a probable Soviet recruiter in 1977 (an allegation which it later withdrew) many Cambridge observers believed that the phantom molehunt had reached its satirical limit. Gow, however, is a name which out-Beveses Beves in sheer improbability.'[5]

The evidence against Sewell was impressive. There was nothing to suggest that Gow had ever been remotely left-wing – and yet Sewell refused to admit that he might have made a mistake. There was no reason for him to mislead us; by 1986 his career as an art critic and travel writer was going well and he had no wish to remind the public of his association with Blunt. Had he misunderstood Gow? Had Gow been playing an elaborate joke? Or had Gow known about Blunt's work for Soviets because Blunt had told him? Whatever the critics say about Gow – and they are clearly right about Gow's distaste for communism – it is impossible to rule out this final possibility.

Other critics, who did not profess to know anything about espionage, were not concerned by side-issues such as this. They were more concerned with finding a solution to the riddles of Blunt. The satirist Auberon Waugh worried about the contradictions in Blunt – the apolitical student who became a Marxist; the snob who became a traitor; the dry academic who was fascinated by 'rough trade'. Waugh concluded: 'He was never a serious communist. His agreement to spy for Russia was partly, of course, inspired by his love and admiration for Burgess, but what had set him so violently against his fellow-countrymen was undoubtedly buried in his childhood. A weak, inconsiderate and foolish father, a mother who doted on him and on whom he doted – these may have provided the classic background to his homosexuality . . . But there were many homosexuals around then – and still are – who never feel the compulsion to treason. The fact that his father was a clergyman set him against Christianity and religion in general . . . His taste for the rough trade in homosexual encounters undoubtedly gave him the crook's mentality of someone who relishes a double existence. The essential key to his treason is to be found in the combination of all these things with the arrogance and conceit of the art historian. A double life between the Palace and the cottage was not enough for him. He had to have a third (in MI5) and a fourth (against everybody, spying for the Russians). What a mess!'[6]

Joseph Brodsky, the distinguished writer, thought that Blunt could not have cared less about Marxism and that it had all been 'done as a prank, as an indulgence of a proclivity for manipulating people, as a favour to a friend, or for want of anything else to do between his studies and carousing'.[7] He had become a spy because spying was fun and because the 'accompanying sense of danger' was exhilarating without being frightening. But by the outbreak of war Blunt was stuck; what had begun as a jolly escapade now carried with it the risk of real punishment. Brodsky concluded that it was impossible to find the real Blunt because he was a good example of what is known as 'negative reality'; nothing, not his books, his lecture notes, or anecdotes from family, friends, lovers or enemies, could ever give him substance.

Others sought an explanation by placing the Cambridge spies in a wider context. The historian John Keegan thought that Blunt and Burgess were uniquely English, the products of a class-obsessed, over-secretive society.[8] If they had been born in France they would have burnt out their radicalism in university politics. Keegan added: 'But, confronted as they were in this country by a culture of in-groups, each cherishing its own secrets, but conspiring automatically to defend the ethos of exclusivity, they opted for the one great contra-conspiracy that was in the market for recruits. The common thread . . . is the conspiratorial nature of communism. And it does seem that, just as the clubbability of the Foreign Office or the Brigade of Guards captured the loyalty of the natural belongers of their generation, communism exerted a complementary appeal on temperamental outsiders.'

This is the other dimension which helps explain Blunt and the Cambridge spies: the chronic secrecy which afflicts all levels of life in Britain, personal as well as official. John Keegan compared Britain with the United States: 'America is an open society in the largest sense. Its élites do not treat public life as an extension of the prefects' room or the club committee. And they do so because the nature of American democracy encourages a fullness of disclosure which still causes visible agony to their equivalents in Whitehall . . . Britain has never been a strong country in the way that America is today, and secrecy is one of its understandable defences . . . [But] a cultivation of greater openness [would] kill at the roots the weed of conspiratoriality which attracts the unstable to the life of government in the first place.'[9]

In the autumn of 1986, Whitehall showed how little had changed since the 1950s, when it had cheerfully tried to head off investigation into the defections of Burgess and Maclean and was then forced to watch, panic-stricken, as the truth dribbled out. The main course in this 1986 feast of bureaucratic paranoia, muddle, and hypocrisy was served up in November, in Sydney's Supreme Court of New South

Wales, when the British government, represented by Sir Robert Armstrong, the Secretary to the Cabinet, tried to stop Peter Wright, the ex-MI5 spy-catcher, publishing his memoirs. Whitehall, however, supplied an appetizer in London shortly before the opening of the Australian case. On Thursday 23 October, just a few weeks before *Conspiracy of Silence* was due to be published, the Treasury Solicitor, John Bailey, a civil servant who often finds himself in the middle of battles between secrecy-obsessed British governments and journalists, was telephoned by David Leigh of *The Observer* newspaper. Was Bailey aware that our book contained verbatim quotations from retired intelligence officers? Leigh, who had obtained a copy of the manuscript despite our publisher's security precautions, thought it odd that the government was doing nothing about our book when it was spending hundreds of thousands of pounds in Australia in an effort to block Wright. The British case there rested on the principle of confidentiality; that intelligence officers had a duty never to disclose anything, no matter how trivial, about their work. It was essential to maintain this rule, the British government argued, otherwise our allies would lose confidence in our ability to keep secrets. If Wright won then other intelligence officers would write their memoirs – with what Whitehall grimly described as 'disastrous' consequences for the country.

Leigh said that he could not see the difference between our book and Wright's; either the government wanted to ban intelligence officers from talking or it did not. Bailey said that he had not seen our book and promised to investigate. He moved quickly. He told Grafton Books that the book could not be released to the shops until the government had examined it. That Sunday, 26 October, *The Observer* ran a story, headlined 'MI5 Officers Break Silence on Blunt', which expanded Leigh's arguments to

Bailey: if the government did not injunct our book then it must, if it was consistent, drop the case against Wright. The newspaper asked several of our sources to comment. Sir Dick White, the distinguished former head of MI5 and MI6, said that he had no wish to 'embark on a confrontation with the government' and added that he had not told us anything which was 'security sensitive'. Another retired intelligence officer, Russell Lee, said that he could not understand what the fuss was about. Yes, he said, he might have talked to us about Peter Wright, but he could not see 'the security significance' of that.

It was evident from our sources in Whitehall that Leigh's intervention had not been welcome. If the government did nothing then it jeopardized its position in Australia. But if it tried to stop publication it risked embarrassment; perhaps even a court case which would involve some of the country's most respected intelligence officers. One Whitehall source reflected that it was all a damned nuisance; what a pity, said the source, that the book was not already in the shops because then it would have been too late to do anything. On Monday 3 November, we met John Bailey at his office in St James's. There was a second man in the office, MI5's senior legal adviser, whom Bailey asked us not to identify. (This was yet another example of secrecy for the sake of secrecy; the MI5 lawyer had already been named by journalists.) For three hours we argued with Bailey and the MI5 lawyer as they went through the book, picking out over 40 quotations which were 'causing problems' and arguing amongst themselves over what was potentially 'dangerous' and what was not. As they ploughed on, pointing to quotations about such security-sensitive matters as Blunt's character or Burgess's sexual habits, we kept asking whether they were joking. But they were not; the future of a book which had taken a great deal of time and effort really was at stake. So we defended ourselves as best we could, knowing that at the heart of this was Whitehall's determination to stop Peter Wright's book being published. We insisted that we were not threatening national security. We had written a responsible book. Other authors had quoted retired intelligence officers. We spent that Monday afternoon writing a lengthy memorandum for Bailey. Most writers are naturally anxious to hype their own books but we were in the odd position that Monday of having to argue that there was absolutely nothing new or interesting in *Conspiracy of Silence*. It was absurd but we had no choice. We could not fight the government on the basis that former intelligence officers should be allowed to talk to journalists; our only hope was to play down the information they had given us. So we wrote the memorandum and sent it to Bailey. Although we believed that Whitehall did not want to fight our publisher, we also knew that it had the resources to stall publication indefinitely. British judges tend to be sympathetic if 'national security' is invoked by eminent barristers representing Her Majesty's Government; we feared that our book would be 'frozen'; left in warehouse limbo while the Wright trial was heard in Australia.

We were mistaken. On 6 November, Bailey wrote to Grafton Books' lawyer: 'I should place on record that if ex-members of the Security Service who have been quoted in 'Conspiracy of Silence' did indeed speak to Mr Penrose and Mr Freeman as they are said to have done, and have communicated to them material acquired or derived from their employment, they have been guilty of a breach of their duty of confidentiality owed to the Crown of which a serious view is taken. Nevertheless, every such case is considered in the light of its particular facts and I am instructed to inform you that, having regard to considerations of public interest and national security, it is not proposed to make an application to the court to restrain the publication of the book based on breach of duty of confidentiality.'

Bailey followed this up by dispatching letters to our sources, warning them not to speak to other journalists or authors. Some intelligence 'experts' found it all very sinister. We had been critical of Peter Wright so we were, QED, part of a plot to discredit Wright. One 'intelligence expert' (there were many such 'experts' drifting around newspapers in the 1980s, trying to interest editors in theories so Byzantine that no one else understood them) suggested that our MI5 and MI6 sources had been told to talk to us: 'Given that these officers are still in close touch with the Office one can only surmise their participation has been approved at the highest levels, perhaps on the grounds that the Blunt book directly challenges the Young Turks' charges.'[10]

This was fantasy. There was no such plot; Whitehall had juggled clumsily, instinctively and without planning, to defend the shibboleth of secrecy, much as it had done throughout the Blunt affair. And it had decided to drop the case because it had more than enough problems in Australia without us. Whitehall believed that it could wriggle out of a messy confrontation with Grafton Books if it presented the Australian court with this 'bottom line' argument: of course, it was disgraceful if retired intelligence officers spoke to journalists but it was far worse if these officers put their own names to books. The former could be 'denied'; the latter category could not. To show that they meant business Whitehall's guardians of the secret society decided to stop publication in England of the biography of the late Joan Miller, who had worked for Maxwell Knight of MI5 during the war. Miller's book seemed harmless. She had no secrets to reveal; she was just a butterfly-minded old lady reminiscing about what it had been like to be a young, pretty little thing in MI5. It was not even the first time that she had spoken about her work with Knight. Her book was just an extended version, padded out by a ghost writer with background information, of an interview which she had given to Barrie Penrose in the early 1980s and which had been published in the *Sunday Times* Magazine. But the government was determined to stop the book; it had a point to make. No one who had worked for British Intelligence, even old ladies with nothing much to say, would be allowed to write their memoirs.

But this did not help the government. The campaign to silence Wright began as it continued – in a mixture of drama and farce – when Sir Robert Armstrong, the most powerful civil servant in the country, who had been chosen to put the government's case in Sydney, arrived at Heathrow to fly to Australia. As press photographers surrounded him, Armstrong decided that something had to be done about this intrusion into his privacy; so he lashed out with his briefcase. The newspapers and television news bulletins gleefully reported the incident but it was just the start of a horribly embarrassing ordeal for Armstrong. He was totally unsuited to his role as the Thatcher government's main witness against Wright. He was a career civil servant and thought and looked like one. His friends said that he was actually a decent chap but to most people, especially the Australians, he seemed pompous, arrogant, secretive and evasive. He was mugged verbally every day by Wright's lawyer, an abrasive young Australian called Malcolm Turnbull; every day, or so it seemed, he forced Armstrong to retract or apologize. The most remarkable admission came when poor Sir Robert, who was, after all, only doing as he was told by his political masters in London, admitted that he had been 'economical with the truth'. Turnbull translated this for the benefit of those people who did not understand Whitehall doublespeak; it meant that Armstrong had not told the whole truth. Daily, there were new revelations in court: of how the government had lied or struck secret deals. Despite these humiliations Armstrong plodded on. He was apparently unaware of how absurd he sounded when he first confirmed, and then denied, the very existence of MI6. (This was just another illustration of secrecy beyond reason: by some accident the British government had never admitted that it ran an organization called MI6 and Armstrong did not want to be the man to do so.)

None of this could have happened in Britain; a British court would have treated Sir Robert with the respect his office demanded. But this was not Britain. Even the judge, Justice Philip Powell, did not seem to appreciate the gravity of the case. Powell, who was, by Australian standards at least, a conservative, constantly delivered the sort of quotes which reporters dream about. At various times he said that the British government had been guilty of: 'non-sense/baloney/serpentine weavings/an exercise in futility/ a classic piece of fancy dancing/sophistry of the highest order/mumbo jumbo'. Powell clearly enjoyed the attention of the international press corps but his grasp of law was admirably quick and clear. Thatcher's ministers in London complained privately that he was an oaf, who was playing up to the international press. But most neutrals thought that he displayed good, old-fashioned common sense and that he was helping to expose cant and hypocrisy. It was not a good advertisement for Britain and even newspapers normally loyal to Thatcher said so. It was a fiasco and it should never have happened.

There is no need to detail here the mass of evidence from the Sydney hearings. (Judging by the number of 'instant' books being planned during the hearing it should be easy enough to find blow-by-blow reconstructions.) But much about this extraordinary contest was relevant to the story – and the puzzle – of Anthony Blunt. We were given a rare insight into the workings of the British intelligence services and their relationship with government. We saw how Wright, exposed for too long to the images of the looking-glass world of espionage, had become confused about what was real and what was not. First, though, there was Wright himself, a sickly 70-year-old man who limped into court every day insisting that he would never give in. 'They thought I'd be dead now,' he said at the beginning of the case. 'MI5 bullied my first publishers. They went to see them. MI5 spread all sorts of rumours about people they don't like, the bastards. But I'm not going to give in. Mrs Thatcher's frightened of me – I know that Parliament was lied to.' Everything that Wright said in Australia confirmed our impression of him: a zealot who believed that only he knew the Truth. He was fond of telling reporters that he had pinned this Latin quotation on the wall of his home in Tasmania: '*Dilexi justitiam et odi inquitatem propterea morior in ixilio*', translated as 'I have loved justice and hated iniquity, therefore I live in exile'. Newspapers probed his background, trying to find out more about this strange, obsessed man. Born in Essex, the son of an electronics engineer, he was educated first at a grammar school and then at a minor public school in the Home Counties. He studied agriculture but he was a natural scientist and joined the navy's scientific service. He then joined Marconi, where his father worked, and in 1955 moved to MI5. His family in England were tracked down by reporters and asked for their opinions. His sister, Elizabeth, and her husband, Robert Sutton, who was a retired Admiralty scientist, were not impressed by him.[11] He was, thought the Suttons, 'manipulative and devious'. He lived in a fantasy world. His word could not be trusted. Hadn't he once admitted to Robert Sutton that he could not help lying? But was this a smear campaign orchestrated by Downing Street to discredit Wright? Wright's son, Bevis, and his two daughters, Tessa and Jenny, insisted that their father was a patriot who was telling the truth because he believed it was in his country's interests to do so.[12]

It soon became clear to most people – including those who thought that it was in the public interest for Wright to be allowed to publish his book – that he was an anachronism from the Cold War, a man who had seen Britain slump from being a first- to a second-rate power and who blamed this on communists, liberals and immigrants. He really did believe, and he said so in court, that the post-war decline of Britain had been caused by the 'massive penetration' of the British Establishment by communist spies. It was a neat irony that a man such as this was being supported by liberal and left-wing newspapers, far more committed than the right-wing press to freedom of information and greater accountability of the intelligence services. Although only the lawyers and the judge were allowed to read the book, enough was said in open court or in interviews by Wright and his lawyer – reinforced by leaks from Sydney and from London – to establish its main themes. It was clear that Wright had effectively written two books. One was about Roger Hollis, the man whom Wright was certain had been a Soviet spy. This book gave a fascinating account of the rows and rivalries within British Intelligence which led Wright and his fellow Young Turks to leak stories to the press in the late 1970s and early 1980s. But there was a second book, and this was the one which seemed certain to have the lasting impact. Wright's theorizing about Hollis could be disregarded as the ravings of a senile old man, but this second book was not as easily dismissed. Wright described what he called 'lawbreaking' by British Intelligence, including plots to assassinate Colonel Nasser, the Egyptian leader, during the Suez crisis in 1956. But there was much more. Wright described in detail how British Intelligence had investigated the Labour Prime Minister, Harold

Wilson, and his aides during the 1970s because of fears that Wilson or members of his team were communist agents. He had written, too, or so it was reported, of plots to smear and discredit Wilson and perhaps to help organize a military coup to overthrow him. None of this was new – Wilson himself had complained many years before about British Intelligence's plots against him – but there was a difference. Now the allegations came from one of the men who had taken part in these operations. One Whitehall source, who had been allowed to read the manuscript, said that he went 'cross-eyed'; Wright, said the source, had shown how MI5 had 'bugged and burgled' their way around London during the investigation into Wilson. It would, said the source, be unbelievable if Wright had not also produced what appeared to be authentic evidence to support his allegations of illegal activities by MI5 against a democratically elected government.[13]

Wright himself, so closely involved with the campaign against Wilson, had turned against his former colleagues. He said: 'I have referred (in my book) to a great many acts by officers of MI5, including myself, which constituted breaches of the law. Our operations were officially authorized, illegal and deniable. I now believe this is the wrong way of doing things . . . intelligence services should not break the law . . . Practically every other intelligence service in the Western world today does not need to break the law to do its job and they are controlled by the law. And I don't think that the British intelligence service should break the law, which they do – I broke the law myself for them.'[14] He talked about his sense of public duty, saying that after leaving MI5 in January 1976 he had brooded about his work there during the 1960s and 1970s and had concluded that it had all been immoral. He now wanted, he said, an 'independent inquiry' into the methods of British Intelligence but, even in his new guise as a defender of civil liberties, he could not resist returning to his favourite theme – the 'penetration' of MI5 and MI6 by the Soviets. He said: 'Since 1950, let us say, there have only been 20 spies captured and prosecuted by MI5. It's pure chance that they have been caught by the efforts of MI5. Therefore something is very wrong . . .'

But that was not the whole story. Wright had more venal motives. During the trial it emerged that, bitter over his small pension from MI5, he had become involved in a financial deal with the journalist and seeker-after-Soviet-spies, Chapman Pincher. This was a tangled, complicated saga, the details of which were disputed by the protagonists. But the approximate sequence of events seemed to be something like this. In the summer of 1980 Lord Rothschild was increasingly worried by rumours that he, Rothschild, was a Soviet spy. He decided that Wright, who had interrogated him in the investigations that followed Blunt's confession, could help clear his name. In August 1980, Rothschild paid for Wright to fly to London to prepare a statement saying that he, Rothschild, was entirely innocent. In London, Wright, desperate to make some quick money, told Rothschild that he had decided to write a book about Hollis. But he needed expert help to finish the book and so Rothschild put him in touch with Pincher. Wright and Pincher agreed to share the royalties from the book, eventually published as *Their Trade is Treachery* in March 1981. Wright's version differed on a number of points but this was not important. The story, confirmed in outline by both Pincher and Wright, caused a sensation. It led to a series of newspaper revelations that the Thatcher government had lied about the Pincher book. The government had always given the impression that it was appalled by his book because the author had clearly been briefed by ex-intelligence officers. The government had claimed, both before and during the Sydney trial, that it would have injuncted *Their Trade is Treachery* if it had known what it contained. But all this was untrue. Whitehall had obtained a copy of the manuscript six weeks before publication and it had done nothing. There were several possible explanations for this. It could have been incompetence. It could have been that MI5 had illegally obtained its advance copy of the Pincher book and was, therefore, not able to ask government lawyers to seek an injunction (even British judges would frown on theft by MI5). Or perhaps MI5 thought that someone as right-wing as Pincher could be trusted to put across the 'correct' messages about British Intelligence. Pincher himself inclined to the third view. On 27 Janaury 1983, he had written to Wright: 'I can assure you that there is no intention whatever of [the British government] taking action against me which means you too. I lunched with Dickie Franks [Sir Arthur Franks, a former head of MI6] recently and he told me that they (the government) had my book weeks in advance and came to the conclusion that they would rather I did it than anyone else . . . I have been functioning for some months as a specialist adviser to the Parliamentary Defence Committee and have just been appointed chief adviser on an inquiry into positive vetting . . . So I do not think we are unpopular.'

And then there was Victor Rothschild. In late November 1986, he watched, helpless and shocked, as his name was splashed over the front pages of newspapers. He had fought for years to prevent this and now he could do nothing to stop it. On 27 November, the *Daily Express* screamed: 'Rothschild: Was He The Fifth Man? Labour MPs demand an answer'. On 4 December 1986 Rothschild made this extraordinary plea in the *Daily Telegraph*: 'Since at least 1980 up to the present time there have been innuendoes in the Press to the effect that I am the "Fifth Man", in other words a Soviet agent. The Director-General of MI5 should state publicly that it has unequivocal, repeat unequivocal, evidence that I am not, and never have been, a Soviet agent. If the regulations prevent him making such a statement, which in the present circumstances I doubt, let him do so through his legal adviser or through any other recognizably authoritative source.'

To journalists like us, who knew how successfully Rothschild had prevented anyone from linking his name to any of the Cambridge spies, this was quite unbelievable. He was, it has to be said, partly to blame for the continuing rumours about him; he had been so sensitive about the Cambridge spies that it was always assumed (wrongly) that he had something to hide. For example, in the late 1960s Phillip Knightley, then of the *Sunday Times*, was researching a book on Kim Philby. Knightley said: 'In those days a lot of people we approached said they could not talk to us because of the Official Secrets Act. When we contacted Rothschild he didn't even call back. His lawyer telephoned us and then confirmed in writing that if we mentioned Rothschild's name in connection with Philby or Burgess we would hear from him again. If you are writing about him my advice is to be careful. He is very litigious and has pots of money.'[15]

Nonetheless, one had to feel a little sorry for Rothschild, as he hid from the press, waiting for the Establishment, which he had embodied for so long, to rescue him. He was, like many others, a victim of past friendships. Everyone who had been close to either Burgess or Maclean at Cambridge had been a suspect, especially if they had ever been left-wing. Even if these suspects had not actually been fully fledged spies perhaps, wondered MI5, they had been accomplices? Perhaps they had known that Burgess and Maclean were traitors but had done nothing about it? This was, of course, unfair. It was guilt by association and was based on no more than the premise that friends of Burgess and Maclean *must* have known more than they had ever said. Rothschild, however, would have been better advised to have been more open with journalists investigating the Cambridge spies; to have told them that he was not a spy and never had been. The rumours would have died and he would not have become entangled with Pincher and Wright. But he did not and the result was that he was front-page news as he prepared to celebrate Christmas, 1986. It was not much of a present.

The rest of the world was astonished by these events, which confirmed that the British had nothing better to do than play out a black comic version of le Carré. In Sydney, a stuffy bureaucrat kept apologizing to the court for having 'forgotten' important facts and an embittered ex-spyhunter rambled about the Great Communist Conspiracy. Meanwhile, in London, the British government, so anxious to shut Wright up, wriggled and blustered as it emerged that it had connived in the publication of other books about the secret world, and an old man, who had served his country with such distinction, pleaded with MI5 to clear him.

Early in March 1987 Mr Justice Philip Powell delivered his judgement. It was 286 pages long and was even worse than the British government had feared. Powell, who had been dismissed during the trial by government ministers as a 'publicity-seeking cowboy', now proved that he was actually a highly skilled lawyer. His judgement was densely argued and supported with hundreds of legal precedents. He ruled that Wright could publish his book, provisionally entitled *Spycatcher*. The information in it, said Powell, had already been published and could not possibly jeopardize Britain's security. He accepted that MI5 officers had a general obligation not to reveal anything about their work, but Powell did not think that this applied here because most of Wright's material was so stale. The public, he continued, had a right to know if British intelligence officers had, as

Wright alleged, 'bugged and burgled' their way around London in the mid-1970s in their efforts to find out whether Harold Wilson was a Soviet agent. Powell also criticized the government for allowing many other intelligence officers to leak material to journalists and authors (*Conspiracy of Silence* was mentioned several dozen times in his judgement). If they had escaped unpunished why should Wright suffer? Again and again, Powell attacked the government for their inconsistencies and half-truths, reserving special scorn for poor Sir Robert Armstrong. He ranged over the great British post-war spy scandals of Philby, Blunt, Burgess and Maclean. He talked about Roger Hollis, and he speculated about the peculiar nature of the intelligence world. Indeed, the report is likely to prove an invaluable source document for the next generation of spy pundits. It contained, for example, fascinating evidence of the way that British intelligence officers could be sacked at will, without any chance of appeal. But Powell also showed that he had retained his sense of humour and of proportion. He peppered his massive document with jokes and frivolous asides (Wright's book was written in a '*Boys' Own* or Biggles style'). In London, the government's legal experts grudgingly conceded that Powell had done well, although they insisted that they had spotted 'crucial flaws' which would give their appeal in Australia a 'better than evens' chance of success. They could not accept that the farce had gone on long enough and that ministerial time would be better spent reviewing officialdom's attitude towards secrecy or investigating Wright's claims of lawbreaking by MI5.

It had taken an Australian judge, regarded as a conservative in his own country, to cut through the hypocrisies of Whitehall. Perhaps it was not so surprising, after all, that Britain had produced Anthony Blunt. Indeed, it might be said that Britain deserved Anthony Blunt.

REFERENCES

Chapter One: Royal Ties

1. Christopher Blunt, interviews with Barrie Penrose (BP), 1985.
2. Wilfrid Blunt, *Married to a Single Life*, Michael Russell, 1985.
3. Robert Harbinson Bryans, interviews with BP and Simon Freeman (SF), 1985. We have called Robert Harbinson Bryans by one of his pen-names, Robert Harbinson, throughout the book.
4. W. Blunt, op. cit.
5. Wilfrid Blunt, interviews with BP and SF, 1985.
6. W. Blunt, op. cit.
7. Ibid.
8. Christopher Blunt, interviews with BP, 1985.
9. W. Blunt, op. cit.
10. Ibid.
11. Anthony Blunt, essay in *Studio International*, 1972.
12. W. Blunt, op. cit.
13. Sir Herbert Read, *A Concise History of Modern Painting*, Thames and Hudson, 1959.
14. A. Blunt, op. cit.
15. Hans Richter, *Dada*, Thames and Hudson, 1965.
16. C. Blunt, interviews with BP, 1985.
17. W. Blunt, interviews with BP and SF, 1985.

Chapter Two: Marlborough Youth

1. Anthony Blunt, essay in *Studio International*, 1972.
2. Ibid.
3. Letter from John Hilton to BP and SF, 1985.
4. *Blue Guide to England*, Ernest Benn, 1980.
5. Louis MacNeice, *The Strings Are False*, Faber and Faber, 1965.
6. Cyril Norwood, in Brentnall and Kempson (eds), *Marlborough College: The First One Hundred Years. 1843–1943*, printed privately by W. A. Lewis at the Cambridge University Press.
7. MacNeice, op. cit.
8. Wilfrid Blunt, *Married to a Single Life*, Michael Russell, 1985.

9. MacNeice, op. cit.
10. W. Blunt, op. cit.
11. John Parker, *Father of the House*, Routledge and Kegan Paul, 1982.
12. Letter from John Hilton to BP and SF, 1985.
13. Anthony Blunt interviewed by *The Marlburian*, 1966.
14. Christopher Lloyd, interviews with BP, 1985.
15. Unsigned essay in Brentnall and Kempson, op. cit.
16. E. G. H. Kempson, interviews with BP and SF, 1985.
17. Sir Ellis Waterhouse, interview with SF, 1985.
18. W. Blunt, op. cit.
19. Letter from E. G. H. Kempson to BP and SF, 1985.
20. Ibid.
21. E. G. H. Kempson, interviews with BP and SF, 1985.
22. Sir Peter Tennant, interview with SF, 1985.
23. Sir Ellis Waterhouse, interview with SF, 1985.
24. Letter from John Hilton to BP and SF, 1985.
25. MacNeice, op. cit.
26. Ibid.
27. Patrick Taylor-Martin, *John Betjeman*, Penguin, 1984.
28. Anthony Blunt interviewed by *The Marlburian*, 1966.
29. Anthony Blunt, essay in *Studio International*, 1972.
30. *The Marlburian/Studio International.*
31. John Bowle, interview with BP, 1985.
32. Christopher Lloyd, interviews with BP, 1985.
33. Anthony Blunt interviewed by *The Marlburian*, 1966.
34. *Studio International/The Marlburian.*
35. MacNeice, op. cit.
36. Ibid.
37. Hilton, in Appendix in *The Strings Are False*.
38. Anthony Blunt interviewed by *The Marlburian*, 1966.
39. Sir Ellis Waterhouse, Personal Preface in *Studies in Renaissance and Baroque Art Presented to Anthony Blunt on His 60th Birthday*, Phaidon, 1967.
40. Anthony Blunt, essay in *Studio International*, 1972.
41. Ibid.
42. MacNeice, op. cit.
43. Letter from John Hilton to BP and SF, 1985.
44. MacNeice, op. cit.
45. Sir Peter Tennant, interview with SF, 1985.
46. Anthony Blunt, essay in *Studio International*, 1972.
47. Sir Peter Tennant, interview with SF, 1985.
48. W. Blunt, op. cit.

Chapter Three: Cambridge Romantics

1. Anthony Blunt, essay in *Studio International*, 1972.
2. T. E. B. Howarth, *Cambridge Between the Two Wars*, Collins, 1978.
3. George Pinney, interview with BP, 1985.
4. Sir Steven Runciman, interviews with BP and SF, 1985.

5. Prince Chula Chakrabongse, *Brought Up in England*, Foulis, 1942.
6. Malcolm Muggeridge, *The Infernal Grove*, Collins, 1973.
7. Jack Hewit, interviews with BP and SF, 1985.
8. Robert Harbinson, interviews with BP and SF, 1985.
9. Ibid.
10. Peter Montgomery, interview with BP and David Leitch, c.1980.
11. Lord Annan, interview with BP and SF, 1985.
12. Martin Robertson, interview with SF, 1985.
13. John Hilton quoted in Louis MacNeice, *The Strings Are False*, Faber and Faber, 1965.
14. Anthony Blunt, essay in *Studio International*, 1972.
15. Letter from John Hilton to BP and SF, 1985.
16. MacNeice, op. cit.
17. Prince Chula Chakrabongse, *The Twain Have Met*, Foulis, 1956.
18. Goronwy Rees, *A Chapter of Accidents*, Chatto and Windus, 1972.
19. A. J. P. Taylor, *A Personal History*, Hamish Hamilton, 1983.
20. MacNeice, op. cit.
21. Sir Dick White, interview with BP and SF, 1985.
22. Taylor, op. cit.

Chapter Four: The Secret Apostles

1. Michael Straight, *After Long Silence*, Collins, 1983.
2. Maynard Keynes, 'My Early Beliefs', essay quoted in Straight, op. cit.
3. Straight, op. cit.
4. Lytton Strachey, letter to G. E. Moore, 1903.
5. Lytton Strachey, testimony to Conscientious Objectors' Tribunal, London, 1916.
6. Frances Partridge, *Memories*, Gollancz, 1981.
7. D. E. Moggridge, *Keynes*, Macmillan, 1976.
8. Anthony Blunt, essay in *Studio International*, 1972.
9. Ibid.
10. Letter from John Hilton to BP and SF, 1985.
11. Anthony Blunt, essay in *Studio International*, 1972.
12. Wilfrid Blunt, *Married to a Single Life*, Michael Russell, 1985.
13. Ibid.
14. *The Times*.
15. Lady Mary Dunn, interviews with BP, 1985.
16. Ibid.
17. Frances Spalding, *Vanessa Bell*, Weidenfeld & Nicolson, 1983.
18. Ibid.
19. Lady Mary Dunn, interviews with BP, 1985.
20. Andrew Boyle, *The Climate of Treason*, Hutchinson, 1979.
21. James Klugmann quoted in Boyle, op. cit.
22. Robert Birley quoted in Tom Driberg, *Guy Burgess: A Portrait with a Background*, Weidenfeld & Nicolson, 1956.
23. Robert Birley quoted in Boyle, op. cit.
24. Goronwy Rees, *A Chapter of Accidents*, Chatto and Windus, 1972.
25. Claud Cockburn, *Cockburn*

Sums Up, Quartet, 1981.
26. Maurice Dobb, *Soviet Russia and the World*, Sidgwick & Jackson, 1932.

Chapter Five: Radical Young Gentlemen

1. Pat Sloan (ed.), *John Cornford: A Memoir*, Borderline Press, 1978.
2. Ibid.
3. Ibid.
4. Ibid.
5. James Klugmann in Jon Clark et al., *Culture and Crisis in Britain in the 1930s*, Lawrence and Wishart, 1979.
6. Anthony Blunt, essay in *Studio International*, 1972.
7. Sloan, op. cit.
8. Sir Steven Runciman, interviews with BP, 1985.
9. Lord Allen, interview with SF, 1985.
10. Professor Fred Clayton, interview with SF, 1985.
11. Lord Annan, interview with BP and SF, 1985.
12. Charles Madge, interviews with SF, 1985.
13. Sloan, op. cit.
14. Sam Fisher, interview with SF, 1985.
15. Brian Simon, interviews with SF, 1985.
16. Sloan, op. cit.
17. Ibid.
18. Margot Heinemann, interviews with SF, 1985.
19. Ibid.
20. Douglas Hyde, interview with SF, 1985.
21. Harold Macmillan, *Winds of Change*, Macmillan, 1966.
22. Noreen Branson, *History of the Communist Party of Great Britain, 1927–1941*, Lawrence and Wishart, 1985.
23. James Klugmann in Clark et al., op. cit.
24. Sir Ellis Waterhouse, interview with SF, 1985.
25. Ibid.
26. Margot Heinemann, interview with SF, 1985.
27. Sir Steven Runciman, interviews with BP, 1985.
28. Letter from Charles Martin Robertson to BP and SF.
29. Roy Harrod, *The Life of John Maynard Keynes*, Macmillan, 1951.
30. Unnamed source quoted by Bruce Page et al., *Philby: The Spy Who Betrayed A Generation*, André Deutsch, 1977.
31. Douglas Hyde, interview with SF, 1985.

Chapter Six: Red Cells

1. Andrew King, interviews with BP and SF, 1983–85.
2. Lord Thurlow, interviews with SF, 1985.
3. Michael Straight, *After Long Silence*, Collins, 1983.
4. Ibid.
5. Ibid.
6. Leo Long, interviews with BP and SF, 1981 and 1985.
7. Ibid.
8. Straight, op. cit.
9. Leo Long, interview with BP and SF, 1985.
10. Quoted in 'Science at the Crossroads; looking back on

50 years of radical science', based on November 1981 meeting at the British Society for Social Responsibility in Science.

11. Maurice Wilkins, interview with SF, 1985.

12. Sir Dick White, interview with BP and SF, 1985.

13. Maurice Wilkins, interview with SF, 1985.

14. John Humphrey, interview with SF, 1985.

15. Philip Gell, interview with SF, 1985.

16. John Humphrey, interview with SF, 1985.

17. Ibid.

Chapter Seven: Sherry Pink

1. Tom Driberg, *Guy Burgess: A Portrait with a Background*, Weidenfeld and Nicolson, 1956.

2. Lord Thurlow, interview with SF, 1985.

3. Driberg, op. cit.

4. Anthony Blunt, essay in *Studio International*, 1972.

5. Mrs Miriam Lane, interview with BP and SF, 1985.

6. Baroness Llewelyn-Davies of Hastoe, interview with SF, 1985.

7. Gavin Ewart, interview with SF, 1985.

8. Driberg, op. cit.

9. Goronwy Rees, *A Chapter of Accidents*, Chatto and Windus, 1972.

10. W. G. Krivitsky, *I Was Stalin's Agent*, Hamish Hamilton, 1939.

11. Victor Rothschild, *Random Variables*, Collins, 1984, and from interview with SF, 1984.

12. Ibid.

13. Driberg, op. cit.

14. Ibid.

15. Arthur Koestler, *The Invisible Writing*, Hutchinson, 1969.

16. Douglas Hyde, *I Believed*, Heinemann, 1952.

17. Anthony Masters, *The Man Who Was M*, Blackwell, 1984.

18. Christopher Andrew, 'There may never have been a Fifth Man', the *Listener*, 28 July 1983.

19. Based on interview of Nigel West by BP in 1985 after West's meetings with Blunt.

20. Ernst Henri, interviews with BP, 1985.

21. Anthony Blunt, press conference, November 1979.

22. Hyde, op. cit.

23. Ibid.

Chapter Eight: Fascist Fears, Soviet Utopia

1. Anthony Blunt, essay in *Studio International*, 1972.

2. Ibid.

3. Ibid.

4. Andrew Boyle, *The Climate of Treason*, Hutchinson, 1979.

5. Sir Ellis Waterhouse, interview with SF, 1985.

6. Anthony Blunt, essay in *Studio International*, 1972.

7. Anthony Blunt, 'Art under capitalism and socialism', 1937.

8. Louis MacNeice, *The Strings*

are False, Faber and Faber, 1965.
9. Ibid.
10. Ibid.
11. Christopher Mayhew, *Party Games*, Hutchinson, 1969.
12. Michael Straight, *After Long Silence*, Collins, 1983.
13. Sir Charles Fletcher-Cooke, interview with BP, 1985.
14. Lord Mayhew, interview with BP, 1985.
15. Cyril Connolly, *The Missing Diplomats*, Queen Anne Press, 1952.
16. Sir Dick White, interview with BP and SF, 1985.
17. Kim Philby, *My Silent War*, MacGibbon and Kee, 1968.
18. Letter from Charles Martin Robertson to BP and SF, 1985.
19. Brian Sewell, interviews with BP and SF, 1979–85.
20. Philby, op. cit.
21. Ibid.

Chapter Nine: Burgess Pulls the Strings

1. Lillian Gurry, interviews with SF, 1985.
2. Michael Kitson, interview with SF, 1985.
3. Letter from John Hilton to BP and SF, 1985.
4. Claud Cockburn, *Cockburn Sums Up*, Quartet, 1981.
5. Lord Astor quoted in Branson and Heinemann, *Britain in the Nineteen Thirties*, Weidenfeld and Nicolson, 1973.
6. David Thomson, *England in the Twentieth Century*, Penguin, 1979.
7. Audrey Coppard and Bernard Crick, *Orwell Remembered*, Ariel, 1984.
8. Louis MacNeice, *The Strings Are False*, Faber and Faber, 1965.
9. Judith Cook, *New Statesman*, 15 November 1985.
10. Pat Sloan (ed.), *John Cornford: a Memoir*, Borderline Press, 1978.
11. Ibid.
12. Margot Heinemann, interviews with SF, 1985.
13. Michael Straight, *After Long Silence*, Collins, 1983.
14. Anthony Blunt, essay in *Studio International*, 1972.
15. Goronwy Rees, *A Chapter of Accidents*, Chatto and Windus, 1972.
16. Arthur Koestler, *The Invisible Writing*, Hutchinson, 1969.
17. Ibid.
18. Cockburn, op. cit.
19. Sir Dick White, interview with BP and SF, 1985.
20. Cyril Connolly, *The Missing Diplomats*, Queen Anne Press, 1952.
21. Rees, op. cit.
22. John Green, interview with SF, 1985.
23. Frank Gillard, interview with SF, 1985.
24. John Green, interview with SF, 1985.
25. Rees, op. cit.
26. Ibid.
27. Rosamond Lehmann, interview with SF, 1985.
28. Sir Ellis Waterhouse, interview with SF, 1985.
29. MacNeice, op. cit.
30. Jack Hewit, interviews with BP and SF, 1985.
31. Ibid.

32. Ibid.
33. Ibid.
34. Margot Heinemann, 'Science at the Crossroads', op. cit.
35. Jack Hewit, interviews with BP and SF, 1985.
36. Connolly, op. cit.

Chapter Ten: Blunt Joins the Colours

1. Margot Heinemann, interview with SF, 1985.
2. Brian Simon, interview with SF, 1985.
3. Claud Cockburn, *Cockburn Sums Up*, Quartet, 1981.
4. Leo Long, interviews with BP and SF, 1985.
5. Goronwy Rees, *A Chapter of Accidents*, Chatto and Windus, 1972.
6. Sir Ellis Waterhouse, interview with SF, 1985.
7. Rosamond Lehmann, interview with SF, 1985.
8. Nigel West, interviews with BP, 1985.
9. Ibid.
10. Malcolm Muggeridge, interviews with BP, 1985, supplemented by material from *Chronicles of Wasted Time*, Collins, 1972.
11. Ibid.
12. Ibid.
13. Brigadier John Shearer interviewed by *Sunday Mirror* following the exposure of Anthony Blunt in November 1979.
14. Muggeridge, op. cit.
15. Brigadier Thomas Robbins, interviewed post-1979 by newspapers.
16. George Curry. Letter to authors, November 1986.
17. Ibid.
18. Christoper Blunt, interviews with BP, 1985.
19. Sutherland, op. cit. Confirmed by Jack Hewit, 1985.
20. Rosamond Lehmann, interview with SF, 1985.
21. Bickham Sweet-Escott, *Baker Street Irregular*, Methuen, 1965.
22. Sir Robert Mackenzie, interview with SF, 1985.
23. Kim Philby, *My Silent War*, MacGibbon and Kee, 1968.
24. Anthony Blunt. Introduction to Tomas Harris exhibition of paintings, dry points, lithographs, tapestries, stained glass and ceramics at the Courtauld Institute, February–March, 1975.
25. Malcolm Muggeridge, interview with BP, 1985.
26. Philby, op. cit.
27. Tom Driberg, *Guy Burgess: A Portrait with a Background*, Weidenfeld and Nicolson, 1956.
28. Sir Isaiah Berlin, information given to BP and SF, 1985.
29. Harold Nicolson, *Diaries and Letters, 1930–1964*, Penguin, 1984.
30. Rees, op. cit.
31. Michael Straight, *After Long Silence*, Collins, 1983.
32. James Lees-Milne, *Harold Nicolson: a Biography*, Chatto and Windus, 1985
33. Bruce Page et al., *Philby: the Spy Who Betrayed a Generation*, André Deutsch, 1977.
34. Nicolson, op. cit.

Chapter Eleven: Secret Manoeuvres

1. Nigel West, *MI5: British Security Service Operations, 1909–1945*, The Bodley Head, 1981.
2. Sir Dick White, interview with BP and SF, 1985.
3. Constance Burgess, interview with BP and SF, 1985.
4. Nigel Burgess, interview with BP and SF, 1985.
5. Ibid.
6. *The Times*, January 1980.
7. Kim Philby, *My Silent War*, MacGibbon and Kee, 1968.
8. Ibid.
9. Sir Dick White, interview with BP and SF, 1985.
10. Ibid.
11. Ibid.
12. Ibid.
13. Ibid.
14. Ibid.
15. Ibid.
16. Ibid.
17. Christopher Harmer, interview with SF, 1985.
18. Sir Dick White, interview with BP and SF, 1985.
19. Ibid.
20. Christopher Harmer, interviews with SF, 1985.
21. 'Tar' Robertson, interviews with SF, 1985.
22. Ibid.
23. William Luke, interview with SF, 1985.
24. Russell Lee, interviews with SF, 1985.
25. From Blunt's introduction to Tomas Harris exhibition, op. cit.
26. Ibid.
27. Goronwy Rees, *A Chapter of Accidents*, Chatto and Windus, 1972.
28. Baroness Llewelyn-Davies of Hastoe, interview with SF, 1985.
29. Malcolm Muggeridge, *Chronicles of Wasted Time*, Collins, 1972.
30. Ibid.
31. Patrick Day, interview with BP, 1985.
32. Rees, op. cit.
33. Jack Hewit, interviews with BP and SF, 1985.
34. Christopher Harmer, interview with SF, 1985.
35. John Green, interview with SF, 1985.
36. David Graham, interview with SF, 1985.
37. Sir Steven Runciman, interview with BP, 1985.
38. Robert Harbinson, interviews with BP and SF, 1980–86.
39. Noreen Branson, *History of the Communist Party of Great Britain, 1927–1941*, Lawrence and Wishart, 1985.
40. Margot Heinemann, interview with SF, 1985.
41. Lord Clanmorris, interview with BP, 1985.
42. Joan Miller, interview with BP, *c.*1980.
43. Tom Driberg, *Ruling Passions*, Cape, 1977.

Chapter Twelve: Treachery Within

1. Peter Calvocoressi, *Sunday Times*, 24 November 1974.
2. Ibid.
3. Ibid., supplemented by interview with SF, 1985.
4. Professor Harry Hinsley, interview with SF, 1985.
5. Professor M. R. D. Foot, interview with SF, 1985.
6. Sir Robin Brook, interview with SF, 1985.
7. Calvocoressi, op. cit.
8. Sir Dick White, interviews with BP and SF, 1985.
9. Christopher Harmer, interview with SF, 1985.
10. Russell Lee, interviews with SF, 1985.
11. Sir Ashton Roskill, interview with SF, 1985.
12. Hugh Astor, interview with SF, 1985.
13. Group Captain Frederick Winterbotham, interview with SF, 1985.
14. Kim Philby, *My Silent War*, MacGibbon and Kee, 1968.
15. Group Captain Winterbotham, interview with SF, 1985.
16. Professor Hugh Trevor-Roper, interviews with BP and SF, 1985.
17. Philby, op. cit.
18. Sir Dick White, interviews with BP and SF, 1985.
19. David J. Dallin, *Soviet Espionage*, Yale University Press, 1955.
20. Leo Long, interviews with BP and SF, 1981 and 1985.
21. Ibid.
22. Ibid.
23. Ibid.
24. Ibid.
25. Ibid.
26. Lord Annan, interview with BP and SF, 1985.
27. Leo Long, interviews with BP and SF, 1981 and 1985.
28. Goronwy Rees, *A Chapter of Accidents*, Chatto and Windus, 1972.
29. Ibid.
30. Sir Robin Brook, interview with SF, 1985.
31. Sir Hugh Trevor-Roper, interviews with BP and SF, 1985.
32. Sir Dick White, interviews with BP and SF, 1985.
33. 'Tar' Robertson, interviews with SF, 1985.

Chapter Thirteen: The Palace Royal

1. Oliver Millar, *The Queen's Pictures*, Weidenfeld and Nicolson, 1977, supplemented by interview with SF, 1985.
2. Millar, op. cit.
3. Sir Ellis Waterhouse, interview with SF, 1985.
4. George Steiner, *A Reader*, Penguin, 1984.
5. Professor Stephen Rees-Jones, interview with SF, 1985.
6. Denis Mahon, interview with BP and SF, 1985.
7. Millar, op. cit.
8. *Sunday Times*, 25 November 1979.
9. Sir Ellis Waterhouse,

interview with SF, 1985.
10. Sir Hugh Trevor-Roper, interviews with BP and SF, 1985.
11. Lord Annan, interview with BP and SF, 1985.
12. Leo Long, interviews with BP and SF, 1981 and 1985.
13. Ibid.
14. Sir Dick White, interview with BP and SF, 1985.
15. Anthony Blunt, essay in *Studio International*, 1972.
16. Ibid.
17. Ibid.
18. Lillian Gurry, interview with SF, 1985.
19. Peter Lasko, interview with BP and SF, 1985.
20. Professor Stephen Rees-Jones, interview with SF, 1985.
21. George Zarnecki, interview with SF, 1985.
22. From Waterhouse's introduction to 'Studies in Renaissance Art', op. cit.
23. Robert Harbinson, interviews with BP and SF, 1979–85 (supplemented by letters from him).
24. Ibid.

Chapter Fourteen: Cold War Warriors

1. Tom Driberg, *Guy Burgess: a Portrait with a Background*, Weidenfeld and Nicolson, 1956.
2. Goronwy Rees, *A Chapter of Accidents*, Chatto and Windus, 1972.
3. Sir Fred Warner, interview with SF, 1985.
4. Driberg, op. cit.
5. Sir Dick White, interview with BP and SF, 1985.
6. Letter from George Carey-Foster to BP and SF, 1985.
7. Ibid.
8. Rees, op. cit.
9. Wolfgang zu Putlitz, *The Putlitz Dossier*, Allan Wingate, 1957.
10. Lord Mayhew, interviews with BP and SF, 1985.
11. Ibid.
12. Ibid.
13. *The Times*, 2 February 1981.
14. Arthur Martin, interviews with BP and SF, 1980–85.
15. Rees, op. cit.
16. Letter from George Carey-Foster to BP and SF, 1985.
17. Ibid.
18. Jack Hewit, interviews with BP and SF, 1985.
19. Rees, op. cit.
20. Ibid.

Chapter Fifteen: American Interlude

1. Kim Philby, *My Silent War*, MacGibbon and Kee, 1968.
2. Ibid.
3. Ibid.
4. From files released in Washington under the Freedom of Information Act.
5. Sir Isaiah Berlin, interviews with BP and SF, 1985.
6. Letter from George Carey-Foster to BP and SF, 1985.
7. Ibid.
8. Goronwy Rees, *A Chapter of*

Accidents, Chatto and
Windus, 1972.
9. Michael Straight, *After Long
Silence*, Collins, 1983.
10. Ibid.
11. Michael Straight, interviews
with BP and SF, 1981–85.
12. FBI files, dated 1951.
13. Straight, op. cit.
14. Philby, op. cit.
15. Letter from John Reed to
Andrew Boyle, November,
1979.
16. FBI files, dated 1951.
17. Philby, op. cit.
18. Letter from George Carey-
Foster to BP and SF, 1985.
19. Ibid.
20. Rees, op. cit.

21. Jack Hewit, interviews with
BP and SF, 1985.
22. Tom Driberg, *Guy Burgess: a
Portrait with a Background*,
Weidenfeld and Nicolson, 1956.
23. Jack Hewit, interviews with
BP and SF, 1985.
24. Ibid.
25. Clarissa Churchill, interview
with BP, 1985.
26. Driberg, op. cit.
27. Lady Mary Dunn, interviews
with BP, 1985–86.
28. Driberg, op. cit.
29. Nigel Burgess, interview with
BP and SF, 1985.
30. Stephen Spender, *Journals,
1939–83*, Faber and Faber,
1985.

Chapter Sixteen: Runaway Friends

1. Professor Kerry Downes,
interview with SF, 1985.
2. Sir Ellis Waterhouse,
interview with SF, 1985.
3. Goronwy Rees, *A Chapter of
Accidents*, Chatto and
Windus, 1972.
4. Ibid.
5. Sir Dick White, interview with
BP and SF, 1985.
6. Member of Goronwy Rees's
family who did not wish to be
named, interviewed by SF.
7. Jack Hewit, interviews with
BP and SF, 1985.
8. Rosamond Lehmann,
interview with SF, 1985.
9. Professor Stephen
Rees-Jones, interview with
SF, 1985.
10. Michael Kitson, interview
with SF, 1985.
11. Harold Nicolson, *Diaries and
Letters, 1920–1940*, Penguin,
1984.

12. Rosamond Lehmann,
interview with SF, 1985.
13. Ibid.
14. Ibid.
15. Sir Dick White, interview with
BP and SF, 1985.
16. Ibid.
17. Jack Hewit, interviews with
BP and SF, 1985.
18. Jim Skardon, interviews with
BP, 1980–81.
19. Kim Philby, *My Silent War*,
MacGibbon and Kee,
1968.
20. Sir Dick White, interview with
BP and SF, 1985.
21. Philby, op. cit.
22. John Cairncross, interviews
with BP, 1979 and 1985.
23. Sir John Colville, interview
with SF, 1985.
24. John Cairncross, interviews
with BP, 1979 and 1985.

Chapter Seventeen: Moscow Nightmare

1. FBI files, released under the Freedom of Information Act.
2. Ibid.
3. Ibid.
4. Brian Sewell, interviews with BP and SF, 1979–85.
5. Lillian Gurry, interview with SF, 1985.
6. Brian Sewell, interviews with BP and SF, 1979–85.
7. Timothy Clifford, interview with SF, 1985.
8. Desmond Zwemmer, interview with SF, 1985.
9. Brian Sewell, interviews with BP and SF, 1979–85.
10. Kim Philby, *My Silent War*, MacGibbon and Kee, 1968.
11. Robert Harbinson, interviews with BP and SF, 1979–85.
12. Tom Driberg, *Ruling Passions*, Cape, 1977.
13. Rosamond Lehmann, interview with SF, 1985.
14. Goronwy Rees, *A Chapter of Accidents*, Chatto and Windus, 1972.
15. Rosamond Lehmann,
16. *The People*, November 1956.
17. Driberg, op. cit.
18. Harold Nicolson, *Diaries and Letters, 1930–1964*, Penguin, 1984.
19. *Evening Standard*, 23 February 1959.
20. Newspaper reports, February 1959.
21. Nicolson, op. cit.
22. *Daily Mail*, 24 February 1959.
23. Stephen Spender, *Journals, 1939–83*, Faber and Faber, 1985.
24. Ibid.
25. Ibid.
26. Anthony Cavendish, interviews with BP, 1985.
27. Andrew Boyle, *The Climate of Treason*, Hutchinson, 1979.
28. *Hansard*, 1 July 1963.
29. *Daily Mail*, July 1963.
30. Michael Straight, *After Long Silence*, Collins, 1983.
31. Arthur Martin, interviews with BP and SF, 1985.
32. Ibid.

Chapter Eighteen: Reluctant Confession

1. Arthur Martin, interviews with BP and SF, 1985.
2. Sir Dick White, interview with BP and SF, 1985.
3. Arthur Martin, interviews with BP and SF, 1985.
4. Letter from Maurice Crump to BP, 1985.
5. Confidential source.
6. Confidential source.
7. Douglas Sutherland, *The Fourth Man*, Secker and Warburg, 1980.
8. Robert Harbinson, interview with BP, 1980.
9. Arthur Martin, interviews with BP and SF, 1985.
10. Ibid.
11. Ibid.
12. Ibid.
13. Ibid.
14. Ibid.
15. Ibid.
16. Ibid.
17. Leo Long, interviews with BP and SF, 1981 and 1985.
18. Ibid.

19. Arthur Martin, interviews with BP and SF, 1985.
20. Leo Long, interviews with BP and SF, 1981 and 1985.
21. Michael Straight, *After Long Silence*, Collins, 1983.
22. Arthur Martin, interviews with BP and SF, 1985.
23. Straight, op. cit.
24. Graham Mitchell, interview with BP, 1983.

Chapter Nineteen: Maverick Inquisitor

1. Russell Lee, interview with SF, 1985.
2. Confidential source.
3. Confidential source.
4. Peter Wright, interview with BP, July 1983.
5. 'World in Action', Granada Television, July 1984.
6. Lord Rothschild, op. cit.
7. 'World in Action', Granada Television, July 1984.
8. Geoffrey Bindman and Alister Watson, interviews with BP and SF, 1981.
9. Ibid.
10. Lady Proctor, interview with SF, 1985.
11. Ibid.
12. Ibid.
13. Ibid.
14. Ibid.
15. Ibid.
16. Ibid.
17. Ibid.
18. Sir Edward Playfair, interview with BP and SF, 1984.
19. Ibid.
20. Ibid.
21. Andrew King, interviews with BP and SF, 1984–85.
22. John Hilton, interviews with BP and SF, 1985.
23. Christopher Harmer, interview with SF, 1985.
24. Charles Madge, interview with SF, 1985.
25. Peter Wright, interview with BP, July 1983.
26. Jenifer Hart, interviews with BP and SF, and with Christopher Andrew, 1983.
27. Ibid.
28. Ibid.
29. Peter Wright, interview with BP, 1983.
30. *Observer*, July 1984.
31. Peter Wright, interview with BP, July 1983.
32. Sir Dick White, interview with BP and SF, 1985.
33. 'World in Action', Granada Television, July 1984.
34. Confidential source.
35. Lord Annan, interview with BP and SF, 1985.
36. Arthur Martin, interviews with BP and SF, 1985.
37. Stephen de Mowbray, interviews with BP and SF, 1981–85.

Chapter Twenty: Disciplined Deceiver

1. Wilfrid Blunt, interview with BP and SF, 1985.
2. John Gaskin, interview with BP, 1985.
3. Confidential source.
4. *Guardian*, April 1983.
5. Letter from Robert Harbinson to BP and SF, 1985.

6. Robert Harbinson, interviews with BP and SF, 1985.
7. Ibid.
8. Ibid.
9. Peter Montgomery, interview with BP and David Leitch, c.1980.
10. Brian Sewell, interviews with BP and SF, 1985.
11. Ibid.
12. Ibid.
13. Ibid.
14. Ibid.
15. Ibid.
16. Wilfrid Blunt, interview with BP and SF, 1985.
17. Timothy Clifford, interview with SF, 1985.
18. Neil McGregor, interview with SF, 1985.
19. George Zarnecki, interview with SF, 1985.
20. *Guardian*, March 1983.
21. From Sir Ellis Waterhouse's introduction to 'Renaissance Studies', op. cit.
22. *The Times*, May 1970.

23. Anthony Blunt, *Art and Architecture in France*, Pelican, 1953.
24. Ibid.
25. Patrick Mathieson, interview with SF, 1985.
26. Ibid.
27. Christopher Wright, interview with SF, 1985.
28. George Zarnecki, interview with SF, 1985.
29. Ibid.
30. Sir Ellis Waterhouse, interview with SF, 1985.
31. George Zarnecki, interview with SF, 1985.
32. Eric Hebborn, interviews with SF, 1985–86.
33. Brian Sewell, interviews with BP and SF, 1985.
34. Ibid.
35. Eric Hebborn, interviews with SF, 1985–86.
36. Brian Sewell, interviews with BP and SF, 1985.
37. John Gaskin, interviews with BP, 1985.

Chapter Twenty-one: Blunt's Legacy

1. 'World in Action', Granada Television, July 1984.
2. Sir Dick White, interview with BP and SF, 1985.
3. *The Times*, 25 May 1972.
4. Confidential source.
5. *The Times*, June 1977.
6. Peter Hennessy, interview with BP and SF, 1985.
7. Peter Wright, interview with BP, 1983.
8. Brian Sewell, interviews with BP and SF, 1985.
9. Lord Annan, interview with BP and SF, 1985.
10. Peter Lasko, interview with BP and SF, 1985.

11. Letter provided by Robert Harbinson. Sir Gilbert Laithwaite said in 1986 that he could not recall writing this letter.
12. Sam Silkin, interview with BP, 1985.
13. Ibid.
14. Merlyn Rees, interview with SF, 1985.
15. Barrie Penrose and Roger Courtiour, *The Pencourt File*, Secker and Warburg, 1978.
16. Ibid.
17. Andrew Boyle, *The Climate of Treason*, Hutchinson, 1979,

supplemented by interviews with BP.
18. Ibid.
19. Michael Rubinstein, interview with SF, 1985.
20. Boyle, op. cit.
21. Sir Ellis Waterhouse, interview with SF, 1985.
22. Robert Harbinson, interviews with BP and SF, 1985.
23. Michael Rubinstein,

interviews with SF, 1985.
24. Brian Sewell, interviews with BP and SF, 1985.
25. Wilfrid Blunt, interview with BP and SF, 1985.
26. Brian Sewell, interviews with BP and SF, 1985.
27. Edward Leadbitter, interviews with BP, 1985.
28. Michael Rubinstein, interviews with SF, 1985.

Chapter Twenty-two: Unmasked

1. Edward Leadbitter, interviews with BP, 1985.
2. Brian Sewell, interviews with BP and SF, 1985.
3. Ibid.
4. Ibid.
5. Michael Rubinstein, interviews with SF, 1985.
6. David Leigh, interview with BP, 1985.

Chapter Twenty-three: A Surfeit of Scandal

1. Lillian Gurry, interview with SF, 1985.
2. Michael Kitson, interview with SF, 1985.
3. George Zarnecki, interview with SF, 1985.
4. Letter from Jim Byam Shaw to BP and SF, 1985.
5. Timothy Clifford, interview with SF, 1985.
6. *Observer*, January 1980.
7. Sir Dick White, interview with BP, 1980.
8. Victor Rothschild, *Random Variables*, Collins, 1984.
9. Rosamond Lehmann, interview with SF, 1985.
10. Confidential source.
11. John Cairncross, interviews with BP, 1979 and 1985.

12. Ibid.
13. Lillian Gurry, interview with SF, 1985.
14. Peter Lasko, interview with BP and SF, 1985.
15. A. J. P. Taylor, *A Personal History*, Hamish Hamilton, 1983.
16. Peter Wright, interview with BP, 1983.
17. Nigel West, interviews with BP and SF, 1985.
18. *Hansard*, 9 November 1979.
19. Letter to the *Sunday Times* from Brian Sewell.
20. Letter to the *Sunday Times* from M. J. Kerry on behalf of John Bailey, Treasury solicitor, 24 November 1982.

Epilogue

1. Wilfrid Blunt, interview with SF, March 1983.
2. Christopher Blunt, interview with *Sunday Times*, March 1983.
3. Brian Sewell, interview with *Sunday Times*, March 1983.
4. Arthur Martin, interview with SF, March 1983.
5. Sir John Pope-Hennessy, interview with *Sunday Times*.
6. Sir Ellis Waterhouse, interview with *Sunday Times*.
7. Professor James Joll, interviews with *Sunday Times* and other newspapers.
8. Michael Straight, interviews with *Sunday Times* and other newspapers.

Postscript

1. Wilfrid Blunt, *Slow on the Feather*, Michael Russell, 1986. Further quotations from Wilfrid are taken from this book unless otherwise stated.
2. Extracted from Wilfrid Blunt's letters to the authors, 22 November and 1 December 1986.
3. John Hilton, letter to the authors, 28 December 1986.
4. John Hilton, letter to the authors, 18 January 1987.
5. Dr Christopher Andrew, *The London Review of Books*, 22 January 1987.
6. Auberon Waugh, the *Independent*, November 1986.
7. Joseph Brodsky, *The Times Literary Supplement*, 30 January 1987.
8. John Keegan, the *Daily Telegraph*, November 1986.
9. Ibid.
10. Andrew Lownie, 'MI5 Protects its Rotten Apples', the *Spectator*, November 1986. Lownie described himself as 'the London representative of the National Intelligence Study Centre'.
11. *Daily Mail*, 18 December 1986.
12. *The Times*, 22 December 1986.
13. Confidential source to Penrose/Freeman, the *Sunday Times*, 23 November 1986.
14. Peter Wright, quoted in *City Limits* magazine, 29 January 1987.
15. Phillip Knightley, interviewed by Freeman, the *Sunday Times*, 30 November 1986.

BIBLIOGRAPHY

Andrew, Christopher, *Secret Service*, Heinemann, 1985.

Attfield, John and Stephen Williams (eds), *1939, the Communist Party and the War*, Lawrence and Wishart, 1984.

Berger, John, *Picasso*, Penguin, 1965.

Bethell, Nicholas, *The Great Betrayal: the Untold Story of Kim Philby's Biggest Coup*, Hodder and Stoughton, 1984.

Blue Guide to England, Ernest Benn, 1980.

Blunt, Anthony, *Artistic Theory in Italy 1450–1600*, OUP, 1940.

Blunt, Wilfrid, *Married to a Single Life*, Michael Russell, 1983.

—, *Slow on the Feather*, Michael Russell, 1986.

Boyle, Andrew, *The Climate of Treason*, Hutchinson, 1979.

Branson, Noreen, *History of the Communist Party of Great Britain, 1927–1941*, Lawrence and Wishart, 1985.

Branson, Noreen and Margot Heinemann, *Britain in the Nineteen Thirties*, Weidenfeld and Nicolson, 1973.

Brentnall, H. C. and E. G. H. Kempson (eds), *Marlborough College: The First One Hundred Years. 1843–1943*, printed privately, 1943.

Bullock, Alan, *Ernest Bevin: Foreign Secretary*, Heinemann/OUP, 1985.

Bullock, Alan and Oliver Stallybrass, *The Fontana Dictionary of Modern Thought*, Collins, 1983.

Bullock, Alan and R. B. Woodings, *The Fontana Dictionary of Modern Thinkers*, Collins, 1983.

Carpenter, Humphrey, *W. H. Auden, a Biography*, Allen and Unwin, 1981.

Carritt, Michael, *A Mole in the Crown*, Carritt, 1985.

Clark, Jon, Margot Heinemann, David Margolies and Carole Snee, *Culture and Crisis in Britain in the 1930s*, Lawrence and Wishart, 1979.

Clark, Ronald, *J.B.S.: the Life and Work of J. B. S. Haldane*, OUP, 1984.

Cockburn, Claud, *Cockburn Sums Up*, Quartet, 1981.

Connolly, Cyril, *The Missing Diplomats*, Queen Anne Press, 1952.

Cookridge, E. H., *George Blake*, Hodder, 1970.

—, *The Third Man*, Puttnam, 1958.

Coppard, Audrey and Bernard Crick, *Orwell Remembered*, Ariel, 1984.

Daix, Pierre, *Picasso*, Thames and Hudson, 1965.

Dallin, David J., *Soviet Espionage*, Yale University Press, 1955.

Deacon, Richard, *'C': a Biography of Sir Maurice Oldfield*, Macdonald, 1984.

—, *The Cambridge Apostles*, Robert Royce, 1985.

Dobb, Maurice, *Soviet Russia and the World*, Sidgwick and Jackson, 1932.

Driberg, Tom, *Guy Burgess: a Portrait with a Background*, Weidenfeld and Nicolson, 1956.

—, *Ruling Passions*, Cape, 1977.

Farago, Ladislas, *The Game of the Foxes*, Hodder and Stoughton, 1972.

Forster, E. M., *Maurice*, Edward Arnold, 1971.

Graves, Richard Perceval, *A. E. Housman*, OUP, 1981.

Harbinson, Robert (Bryans), *Ulster*, Faber and Faber, 1964.

Hinsley, F. H., *British Intelligence in the Second World War*, HMSO, 1979.

Hodges, Andrew, *Alan Turing: the Enigma of Intelligence*, Unwin, 1985.

Howarth, T. E. B., *Cambridge Between the Two Wars*, Collins, 1978.

Hyde, Douglas, *I Believed*, Heinemann, 1952.

Jones, R. V., *Most Secret War*, Hamish Hamilton, 1978.

Knightley, Phillip, *The Second Oldest Profession*, André Deutsch, 1986.

Koestler, Arthur, *The Invisible Writing*, Hutchinson, 1969.

Krivitsky, W. G., *I Was Stalin's Agent*, Hamish Hamilton, 1939.

Lees-Milne, James, *Harold Nicolson: a Biography* (vol. II, 1930–68), Chatto and Windus.

Lockhart, R. H. Bruce, *Memoirs of a British Agent*, Macmillan, 1974.

Lucie-Smith, Edward, *A Concise History of French Painting*, Thames and Hudson, 1971.

Maclean, Donald, *British Foreign Policy Since Suez*, Hodder and Stoughton, 1970.

MacNeice, Louis, *The Strings Are False*, Faber and Faber, 1965.

Mann, Wilfrid Basil, *Was There a Fifth Man?*, Pergamon, 1982.

Marwick, Arthur, *British Society Since 1945*, Penguin, 1984.

Masterman, J. C., *The Double Cross System, 1939–1945*, Granada, 1979.

—, *On the Chariot Wheel*, OUP, 1975.

Masters, Anthony, *The Man who was M*, Blackwell, 1984.

Mayhew, Christopher, *Party Games*, Hutchinson, 1969.

Millar, Oliver, *The Queen's Pictures*, Weidenfeld and Nicolson, 1977.

Moggridge, D. E., *Keynes*, Macmillan, 1976.

Muggeridge, Malcolm, *Chronicles of Wasted Time*, Collins, 1972.

—, *The Thirties*, Collins, 1967.

Murray, Peter and Linda Murray, *The Penguin Dictionary of Art and Artists*, Penguin, 1985.

Nicolson, Harold, *Diaries and Letters, 1930–1964*, Penguin, 1984.

Orwell, George, *Essays, Journalism and Letters,*

1920–1940, Penguin, 1982.

Page, Bruce, David Leitch and Phillip Knightley, *Philby: the Spy who Betrayed a Generation*, André Deutsch, 1977.

Palmer, Alan, *The Penguin Dictionary of Modern History*, Penguin, 1983.

Parker, John, *Father of the House*, Routledge and Kegan Paul, 1982.

Partridge, Frances, *Memories*, Gollancz, 1981.

Pelling, Henry, *The British Communist Party*, A. and C. Black, 1958.

Penrose, Barrie and Roger Courtiour, *The Pencourt File*, Secker and Warburg, 1978.

Philby, Kim, *My Silent War*, MacGibbon and Kee, 1968.

Pincher, Chapman, *Inside Story*, Sidgwick and Jackson, 1978.

—, *Their Trade is Treachery*, Sidgwick and Jackson, 1981.

—, *Too Secret Too Long*, Sidgwick and Jackson, 1984.

Piratin, Phil, *Our Flag Stays Red*, Lawrence and Wishart, 1948.

Putlitz, Wolfgang zu, *The Putlitz Dossier*, Allan Wingate, 1957.

Read, Herbert, *A Concise History of Modern Painting*, Thames and Hudson, 1959.

Rees, Goronwy, *A Chapter of Accidents*, Chatto and Windus, 1972.

Richter, Hans, *Dada*, Thames and Hudson, 1965.

Robertson, Bryan, John Russell and Lord Snowdon, *Private View*, Nelson, 1965.

Rothschild, Victor, *Random Variables*, Collins, 1984.

Seale, Patrick and Maureen McConville, *Philby: the Long Road to Moscow*, Hamish Hamilton, 1973.

Sloan, Pat (ed.), *John Cornford: a Memoir*, Borderline Press, 1978.

Spalding, Frances, *Vanessa Bell*, Weidenfeld and Nicolson, 1983.

Steiner, George, *A Reader*, Penguin, 1984.

Stevenson, John, *British Society 1914–45*, Penguin, 1984.

Straight, Michael, *After Long Silence*, Collins, 1983.

Sutherland, Douglas, *The Fourth Man*, Secker and Warburg, 1980.

Sweet-Escott, Bickham, *Baker Street Irregular*, Methuen, 1965.

Taylor, A. J. P., *A Personal History*, Hamish Hamilton, 1983.

Taylor-Martin, Patrick, *John Betjeman*, Penguin, 1984.

Thomas, Hugh, *The Spanish Civil War*, Hamish Hamilton, 1977.

Thomson, David, *England in the Twentieth Century*, Penguin, 1981.

Trevor-Roper, Hugh, *The Philby Affair*, William Kimber, 1968.

Wadia, J. B. H., *M. N. Roy, the Man*, Sangam Books, 1982.

West, Nigel, *A Matter of Trust: MI5 1945–1972*, Weidenfeld and Nicolson, 1982.

—, *MI5: British Security Service Operations 1909–1945*, The Bodley Head, 1981.

—, *MI6: British Secret Intelligence Service Operations 1909–1945*, Weidenfeld and Nicolson, 1983.

Wilson, Edmund, *The Thirties*, Macmillan, 1980.

Wright, Christopher, *The Art of the Forger*, Gordon Fraser, 1984.

Young, Michael, *The Elmhirsts of Dartington*, Routledge and Kegan Paul, 1982.

INDEX